I HEAR AMERICA TALKING

I HEAR
AMERICA
TALKING

AN ILLUSTRATED TREASURY
OF AMERICAN WORDS AND PHRASES

By Stuart Berg Flexner

A HUDSON GROUP BOOK

 VAN NOSTRAND REINHOLD COMPANY
NEW YORK   CINCINNATI   ATLANTA   DALLAS   SAN FRANCISCO
LONDON   TORONTO   MELBOURNE

Van Nostrand Reinhold Company Regional Offices:
New York   Cincinnati   Atlanta   Dallas   San Francisco

Van Nostrand Reinhold Company International Offices:
London   Toronto   Melbourne

Library of Congress Catalog Card Number: 76-42454
ISBN 0-442-22413-3

Manufactured in the United States of America

Published by Van Nostrand Reinhold Company
450 West 33rd Street, New York, N.Y. 10001

Published simultaneously in Canada by Van Nostrand Reinhold Ltd.

15 14 13 12 11 10 9 8 7 6 5 4 3

Library of Congress Cataloging in Publication Data

Flexner, Stuart Berg.
I hear America talking.

"A Hudson group book."
Includes index.
1. Americanisms.   2. English language—Slang.
I. Title.
PE2846.F5   427'.9'73   76-42454
ISBN 0-442-22413-3

To my mother and father,
with love and gratitude.

I Hear America singing, the varied
carols I hear. . . .
  Walt Whitman, "I Hear America
  Singing," 1860, from *Leaves of*
  Grass

Contents

Preface

As a dictionary writer I have often wished I had a recording of everything everyone had ever said in America. Then I would know what words were used when, and why: I would know what words were the most common and heartfelt. Such a recording would also be the best history of America we could have—it would tell us not only what people said but what they thought and felt. Since there is no such recording we can hear, I have tried to make this book the next best thing, an historic presentation and discussion of some of the most common, revealing, and interesting words and phrases Americans have used. This book is not exhaustive. I have had to pick and choose and have tried to emphasize typical and common American terms that best reveal our history and social history, the words and expressions used in the march of history and in the stroll of everyday life.

What this book attempts to do, then, is present the American language through American history and, of course, to present America and American history through our language. This is not a history of the American language but an attempt to present and reveal the language itself against the broad background of our history, to display the language in its historical and human context. I hope that some will read this work as a book about our language and that others will read it as history, and that both will find something of interest about America and its people. If nothing else, I hope that all who read it will come to realize that our language is an integral part of our history, that it can help us understand history and ourselves, and that history resides in the legacy of our language long after the battles and the events, great and small, are over, the fads and fashions spent.

Since that recording of everything everyone said in America is not available, I have tried to chronicle our words and phrases from such sources as: books, newspapers, magazines, official documents, letters, diaries, songs, radio programs, movies, and television shows. This book is a selection of what I consider to be the most revealing, interesting, and typical words and phrases from the American language and American history. Most of the sections or entries fall into one of three general categories: entries containing words that are basic to or typical of our language, showing where our language came from, how it was created and grew (such as THE AMERICAN LANGUAGE; BLIZZARDS, TORNADOES, AND HURRICANES; CANOES AND CANNIBALS; GRIZZLY BEARS, RATTLE SNAKES, AND BALD EAGLES; OK; and THE JEWS); entries basic to American history, its events, periods, and movements (such as TAXATION WITHOUT REPRESENTATION; RECONSTRUCTION—CARPETBAGGERS AND THE KKK; WORLD WAR I; THE NEW DEAL; and WATERGATE); and entries mainly concerned with social history or which are just interesting to and revealing of Americans as human beings, showing something of note about the American experience and personality (such as WHERE'S THE BATHROOM?; CAKES, PIES, PUDDINGS, AND DOUGHNUTS; THE CIRCUS IS COMING TO TOWN; GOIN' COURTIN'; MAD!—MAD!—MAD!—; CALL THE POLICE!; and TITS, BELLIES, RUMPS, GAMS, AND MEATHOOKS).

I ask the reader to be patient if he doesn't find everything he would like in this volume. All books are slim compared to the vast bulk of the American language and it would be impossible to treat everything of importance and interest in one volume, or one lifetime. To keep this present volume to size I have, in general, not included terms from American party politics and government, the Cold War and the Space Age, from sports, the field of entertainment, or fads, from the professions, business, and labor, or from such areas of our social history as child rearing, clothing, the American home, etc. I have begun research and writing for a supplementary book emphasizing these facets of our language and history and hope the present book will be successful enough so that I can complete it.

Following most of the words and phrases discussed in this book are the dates when they were first recorded or were first in common use (these dates follow the words and phrases either in parentheses or separated from them by commas); unless otherwise indicated the words and phrases are Americanisms. Treat these exact year dates with a grain of salt: history and lexicography are not exact sciences. The exact year dates are of the first substantiated recorded use and are thus conservative—many words are in use for several years before they are ever written down and some are even used by specialists and insiders for decades before they become known to the general public. Thus it's possible that you may have some old family letters or diaries in your attic which prove a word was in use before I say it was. At times I've not given exact year dates for when a word or phrase first came into common use but only note that it was in use by a specific decade, as in the "1890s," or in the "early 1890s," "mid 1890s," or "late 1890s." By early or late I mean during the first or last five years of the decade and by mid I mean the middle four years, thus "mid 1890s" means between 1893 and 1896. I have used the word *America* to mean many things, the continent, the land area that was to become the continental United States, the English colonies in what is now the United States, and the United States itself (context always makes clear which is meant).

It's unusual for a book about language to have illustrations. I wanted them because when we see or hear words they often conjure up a visual image in our mind; having these images in drawings and photographs can help show what the words meant, what they evoked in the minds of those who used and heard them. I chose the marginal quotes to illustrate how words are used, what people were saying, writing, and singing, or to give a few lines

Language is the archives of history.
  Ralph Waldo Emerson, *Essays: Second Series,* 1844.

from some speeches, letters, books, etc., in which well-known phrases were coined.

Obviously, a book such as this couldn't have been written without H. L. Mencken's *The American Language* to pave the way or without Mitford M. Mathews' *Dictionary of Americanisms*, on which I relied for the dating of many words. I also owe much to John Russell Bartlett's *Dictionary of Americanisms*, *A Dictionary of American English on Historical Principles* (edited by Sir William Craigie), John Farmer's *Americanisms*, George Matsell's *Vocabulum*, *The Oxford English Dictionary*, Eric Partridge's *Dictionary of the Underworld*, R. H. Thornton's *American Glossary*, and Harold Wentworth's and my own *Dictionary of American Slang*. I also used many of the more specialized books, such as Ramon Adams' *Western Words: A Dictionary of the American West*, J. L. Dillard's *Black English*, Leo Rosten's *The Joys of Yiddish*, William Safire's *The New Language of Politics*, and others dealing with everything from circuses, cooking, and steamboats to the Civil War, Darwinism, and American foreign policy. I used a great many articles from scholarly journals in language and history, a great many clippings from popular magazines and newspapers and, of course, relied heavily on published letters and diaries, official documents and archives, and on popular songs, movies, and radio and television programs as sources for words.

I would like to thank Gorton Carruth of The Hudson Group for his help in putting this book into final form and to thank the supplementary researchers provided by The Hudson Group, including Roberta J. Buland, Judith and Thomas Cuddihy, Barbara Italie, and Ada Morduchowitz, our picture editor Marion Urban Bodine, who found many fine illustrations, our typographer and book designer Martin Connell, our indexer Martine Roland Matzke, our typist Emma K. Clark, and our xerographer Christopher Carruth. I would like to thank David H. Scott, also a member of The Hudson Group, for his special interest in this book. Last but not least I would like to thank my wife, Doris, for reading the galleys.

Stuart Flexner

I HEAR
AMERICA
TALKING

Fugitive slaves arrive at a "station" in Newport, Indiana. They were smuggled from house to house along the underground railroad, a secret network of abolitionist groups that helped them reach northern free states or Canada.

Abolition—The Underground Railroad and Uncle Tom

Abolition! (a 16th century English word) was the shout of the colonists in 1765—by which they meant the repeal of the hated British Stamp Act. After the act was repealed in 1766, some colonists liked the word so much they began to apply it widely to the abolition of slavery. In 1775 the Pennsylvania Society for Promoting the Abolition of Slavery was formed in Philadelphia (the Quakers had started the fight against slavery in 1696), then a similar group was formed in New York. Soon many northerners were joining the *abolition societies;* by 1840 there were 2,000 such groups with over 2 million members. Until the 1830s, however, *abolition* didn't necessarily mean abolishing slavery; to many abolitionists it merely meant abolishing the slave trade, then perhaps buying the freedom of the existing slaves and sending them back to Africa.

The slave trade did end, on January 1, 1808 (the Constitution had said Congress couldn't ban it before that date), but this ban on importing slaves was poorly enforced and, of course, thousands of slaves were still being bred and born every year in America, many of them on special *slave rearing plantations* (see THE BLACKS). In 1817 abolitionists and humanitarians founded the *American Colonization Society* to purchase and free slaves and colonize them in Africa, *Liberia* from Latin *liber*, free) being founded in 1822 for this purpose. From about 1819 until the mid 1850s all America seemed to be arguing whether or not slavery should be allowed to spread into the territories and the new states made from them. Antislavery and proslavery politicians debated and worked out various compromises which we still talk about, including:

Famous abolitionist William Lloyd Garrison (1805-79) published the radical antislavery journal The Liberator *until 1865 when the 13th Amendment ended slavery.*

The Missouri Compromise, 1820, in which Maine (formerly part of Massachusetts) entered the Union as a free state and Missouri as a slave state. This kept the number of slave states and free states equal. Slavery was also prohibited in the rest of the Louisiana Territory above Missouri's southern boundary of 36° 30′.

The Texas Compromise, 1845 (see 54-40 OR FIGHT—MANIFEST DESTINY for details).

The Compromise of 1850, actually a collection of five laws called the *Omnibus Bill*, offered by Henry Clay, "the Great Compromiser." This compromise admitted California to the Union as a free state and ended the slave trade in the District of Columbia, but said that states formed from the rest of the land acquired in the Mexican War could choose for themselves whether to have slavery or not and included a strong *Fugitive Slave Act* (see below).

Harriet Beecher Stowe (1811–96) lived for many years in Cincinnati, Ohio, where she gathered much material for Uncle Tom's Cabin, *which was actually written at Brunswick, Maine.*

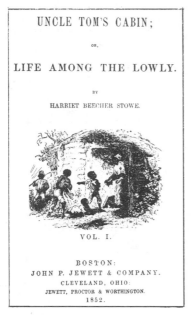

Title page of the first edition of Uncle Tom's Cabin.

The Kansas-Nebraska Act, 1854, repealed the Missouri Compromise by permitting the territories of Kansas and Nebraska to decide for themselves whether to permit slavery or not. Such local option on slavery was called *popular sovereignty* (1848), a term Stephen Douglas popularized in his famous debates with Lincoln during the 1858 election campaign for the senate. Antislavery groups called popular sovereignty *squatter sovereignty* and southerners called it *States Rights*. It led to the bloody fighting between proslavery and antislavery groups in Kansas, which was soon called *Bleeding Kansas* (see THE CIVIL WAR for more about these and similar terms).

By 1830 the talk among many abolitionists was that merely stopping the slave trade, buying the freedom of some slaves, and compromising on slavery in new states and territories would never abolish slavery—in fact ever since Eli Whitney had invented the *cotton gin* in 1793 (*gin* had been used to mean "engine, machine" in America since 1640) slaves had become more valuable to the South and the number of slaves had greatly increased. Thus some more radical abolitionists, such as journalist William Lloyd Garrison and his followers, attacked moderate abolitionists, refused all compromises, and demanded immediate freeing of all slaves, forming the American Anti-Slavery Society in 1833. Now *abolition* became a militant word, polarizing the country and becoming anathema in the South, which was to call Union troops in the Civil War *abolition soldiers*.

Some individuals and abolitionist groups had been helping runaway slaves escape northward since around 1815. Around 1832 they grew into the *underground railroad*, a secret cooperating network which smuggled fugitive slaves from house to house to eventual freedom in the northern free states or in Canada. The *underground railroad* got its name because railroads were just being introduced in the early 1830s (see THE IRON HORSE) and had caught the public's imagination. By the 1840s the network was often simply called the *underground*, a word which was to be used in World War II to refer to European patriotic groups fighting the occupying Nazis and then used in the 1960s to refer to radical student groups fighting the American establishment. The abolitionists delighted in the railroad image of their network: the houses and barns where the slaves were hidden by day were called *stations*, those who took the fugitives on to the next station by night were called *conductors*, and established routes to freedom were called *lines*. Though the underground railroad probably took no more than a thousand slaves to freedom a year, abolitionists talked of it with excitement and pride while southern slave owners talked about it with hatred from the 1830s until the Civil War.

The abolitionists also organized or supported new political parties and factions, giving us further new words and names.

They formed the *Liberty Party*, whose presidential candidate drew few votes in the 1840 and 1844 elections, then merged it with the more successful *Free Soil Party*, which was formed by antislavery Whigs, called *Conscience Whigs*, and antislavery Democrats, including the New York faction called *Barnburners* (because its enemies accused it of being willing to "burn down" the Democratic "barn" to get rid of the proslavery "rats"). The Free Soil Party existed from 1848 to 1853 and was dedicated to free land for settlers and to barring slavery from the territories and any new states: its slogan was "Free Soil, Free Speech, Free Labor, and Free Men." Now *free soil* (1848) meant states or territories where slavery was not permitted (*free state* is an 1809 term) and *free soiler* meant a person opposed to slavery. The country was also talking about the more radical antislavery *Free Democratic Party*, which existed from 1852 to 1854, and especially about the formation of the modern *Republican Party*. This Republican Party had been formed in 1854 after the bitter abolitionist opposition to the Kansas-Nebraska Act had split both the Democrats and Whigs, and it soon absorbed the other abolition parties.

The Fugitive Slave Act of 1850 not only provided a stiff fine and imprisonment for those helping slaves escape but allowed slave owners to pursue and claim runaway slaves in any state, including free states. This so angered the abolitionists that many changed their cry from *Abolition!* to *Emancipation!* Thus after 1850 many who were against slavery no longer called themselves *abolitionists* but *emancipators* (it and the 17th century English political word *emancipation* come from Latin *ēmancipāre*, to release from bondage).

One of those the Fugitive Slave Act angered was Harriet Beecher Stowe, who then wrote her 1852 *Uncle Tom's Cabin*. It became one of the most talked-about and influential books ever written in America, selling 300,000 copies in its first year (over 7 million have now been sold) and stirring up tremendous antislavery feelings in the North. The names and phrases used in *Uncle Tom's Cabin* immediately began to enter the general language. The names of the hero of the book, *Uncle Tom*, *Black Tom*, and *Tom* were used by abolitionists as early as 1853 to refer to any poor, patiently suffering slave, while proslavery people sneeringly used *Uncle Tomism* to mean sanctimonious, sentimental love of Blacks. Many traveling troupes performed the enormously popular melodrama based on the book, the performances being called *Tom Shows* and their performers *Toms* (after the Civil War these terms were applied to any melodrama or Black touring troupe). In 1943, some 90 years after the book was written, an *Uncle Tom* came to mean a subservient or sycophantic Black, currying the white man's favor instead of

3

fighting for his own rights. In addition, the name of the book's villain, the cruel slave dealer *Simon Legree*, came to refer to any harsh taskmaster or cruel person (Legree is the Americanized respelling of the common French Huguenot name Legarés), and little Topsy's expressions "I 'spect I [jist] growed" and "I's wicked,—I is. I's mighty wicked..." became popular expressions.

But it wasn't to be the abolition societies, the underground railroad, political debates, or books that finally ended slavery. When the Civil War began there were still 4 million slaves in the U.S. During the war slavery was abolished in the District of Columbia and all the territories, then on September 22, 1862, on the strength of McClellan's September 17 victory at Antietam, Lincoln issued his preliminary *Emancipation Proclamation*. It took effect January 1, 1863, freeing "all slaves in areas still in rebellion." Since the Confederacy still controlled the areas in rebellion, no slaves were physically freed on that date; but January 1, 1863, became the official date for the ending of slavery in the U.S. After the proclamation Lincoln gained the sobriquet *The Liberator* and *The Emancipator*, with the name *The Great Emancipator* not being popular until the 1890s. For decades after the war, Blacks talked about and celebrated *Emancipation Day*, but its exact date varied from place to place, often being celebrated on the anniversary a Confederate city or state had fallen to Union forces.

The final triumphant use of the word *abolition* occurred in 1865, in the 13th Amendment to the Constitution:

Abolition of Slavery
Neither slavery nor involuntary servitude, except as a punishment for crime whereof the party shall have been duly convicted, shall exist within the United States, or any place subject to their jurisdiction.

"Uncle Tom."

Ain't It the Truth?

It's a pity schoolteachers and critics won't sanction our use of *ain't*, which is a perfectly good and very useful word. It started out as *an't*, a contraction of "am not" first recorded in England in 1706, and this form was used in America by 1723. By 1778–79 *an't* had become *ain't* on both sides of the Atlantic (though many Englishmen and some New Englanders still pronounced it with a broad *a* like *an't*). It was completely acceptable and used by "gentlemen and scholars"; in fact, it's still used as a contraction for "am not" by the English landed gentry and aristocrats in the Carolinas and Georgia.

Ain't got into serious trouble in the 1830s: then it was still acceptable as a contraction for "am not," but many people had come to use it to mean "is not," "are not" (whose contraction *aren't* was often pronounced "*airn't*" in the early days and sometimes sounded like and influenced *ain't*), "has not," and "have not," as in *He ain't going, They ain't going, She ain't got any,* and *They ain't got any.* It was these later uses of *ain't* that were criticized—*ain't* was the obvious contraction of "am not" and should be used only to mean "am not." Now so many people began to criticize or disdain the other uses of *ain't* that it became socially unacceptable in all its uses, including its legitimate use as the contraction of "am not."

Despite the fact that we aren't supposed to use *ain't* anymore, when we hear America talking we do hear *ain't*. Educated people use it with a self-conscious smirk or grin, uneducated people use it naturally. Our American expression *Ain't it the limit?* was first recorded in 1908, *Ain't it the truth?* in 1915, *Ain't we got fun?* was a popular catch phrase from the end of World War I through the 1920s, and *Ain't that a laugh?* was first heard around 1930. I don't know whether or not it will ever become socially acceptable again but you can bet that America hasn't heard the last of *ain't*.

Alibi Ike

Alibi (Latin for "elsewhere") has meant any excuse in the U.S. since about 1915 (legally it is an accused person's defense that he couldn't have committed a crime because he was elsewhere at the time). In the 1930s and 40s *Alibi Ike* was a popular term applied to any person who was always making excuses, the term coming from the main character and the title of a 1924 Ring Lardner short story and later a popular comic strip.

Ring [gold Wilmer] Lardner, the well-known sports reporter, columnist, and writer of humorous short stories, was a recognized expert of the nuances of American speech. He had a remarkably keen ear for the way American English was actually spoken by ordinary people, and was a master at writing it down; H. L. Mencken acknowledged his debt to Lardner in his classic *The American Language* (1936).

Ring Lardner (1885–1933).

America and the United States

Amerigo Vespucci
(1451–1512).

America, the continent, was named for the Italian navigator Amerigo Vespucci (Latin form *Americus Vespucius*) by German mapmaker and geographer Martin Waldseemüller in 1507. The Florence-born Vespucci definitely sailed to the New World four times between 1497 and 1503 and also claimed to have been a member of Alonso de Ojeda's 1499–1500 expedition which first discovered and explored the American mainland (the northern coast of South America). Vespucci's accounts were published in Waldseemüller's book *Cosmographiae Introductio* (containing a map of the world in 12 sheets) in 1507, and there Waldseemüller suggested the new land be named *America*. Amerigo Vespucci himself had coined a term for the continent he had sighted in 1499, he called it *Mundus Novus*—the *New World*. By 1650, British colonists were using *America* to mean only the British colonies in North America; then in 1781 *America* was first recorded as meaning the United States.

Since *America* originally meant the continent, *American* was originally used (1578) to mean a native of it, an Indian. Many British writers, including essayist Joseph Addison, used *American* to mean Indian well into the 18th century, calling the colonists not Americans but transplanted Englishmen. Beginning in 1697, however, our own Cotton Mather popularized the word *American* to mean an English colonist in America. Our language was called *American* by 1780; a citizen of the United States was called an *American* by 1782; and Thomas Jefferson used *Americanism* to mean United States patriotism in 1797.

My country, 'tis of thee,
Sweet land of liberty,
* Of thee I sing;*
Land where my fathers died,
Land of the pilgrims' pride,
From every mountain side
* Let freedom ring.*
"America," better known as "My Country 'Tis of Thee,' by Baptist clergyman and poet Samuel Francis Smith, sung to the British tune "God Save the King." The piece was first printed on a broadside for an Independence Day celebration of the Boston Sabbath School Union, July 4, 1831.

The name *the United States of America* is said to have been created by Tom Paine; it was first used officially in the Declaration of Independence, whose subtitle is "The Unanimous Declaration of the Thirteen United States of America." Its last paragraph begins:

We, therefore, the representatives of the United States of America, in General Congress assembled . . . do, in the name and by authority of the good people of these colonies, solemnly publish and declare, That these united colonies are, and of right ought to be, free and independent states. . . .

This distinction between colonies and states confused many people and throughout the Revolutionary War many called the new country *the United Colonies.* In 1776, too, the name *the United States of America* was already shortened to *the United States* (in the proceedings of the Continental Congress) and even to the shorter *the States.* George Washington wrote the abbreviation *U.S.* in 1791, and the abbreviation *U.S.A.* was recorded in 1795. Even though *the United States of America* appeared in the Declaration of Independence, the new government used the official title *the United States of North America* until 1778, when the "North" was dropped from the name by act of the Continental Congress.

The American Language

Noah Webster (1758–1843) published his first dictionary in 1806. His magnum opus, An American Dictionary of the English Language, *appeared in 1828. Its direct heir is* Webster's Third New International Dictionary *which was published in 1971.*

When this new nation took its first census in 1790 there were four million Americans, 90% of them descendants of English colonists. Thus there was no question that English was the mother tongue and native language of the United States. By 1720, however, some English colonists in America had already begun to notice that their language differed seriously from that spoken back home in England. Almost without being aware of it, they had:

(1) coined some new words for themselves;
(2) borrowed other words from the Indians, Dutch, French, and Spanish;
(3) been using English dialect words in their general speech;
(4) continued to use some English words that had now become obsolete in England;
(5) evolved some peculiar uses, pronunciations, grammar, and syntax.

Doing these things was very natural. Many of the coinages and borrowings were for plants, animals, landscapes, living conditions, institutions, and attitudes which were seldom if ever encountered in England, so the English had no words for them. The widespread use of English dialect words was also natural: most of the Puritans came from England's southern and southeastern counties and spoke the East Anglia dialect, most of the Quakers spoke the midland dialect, and after 1720 many new colonists were Scots-Irish, speaking the Ulster dialect. The continuing use of words that had become obsolete in England, and of unusual usage, pronunciations, grammar, and syntax, was also natural for colonists isolated from the niceties of current English speech and English education. Thus, naturally, a hundred years after the Pilgrims landed, English as spoken in America differed from that spoken in England.

In 1756, a year after he published his *Dictionary of the English Language*, "Doctor" Samuel Johnson was the first to refer to an *American dialect*. In 1780, soon after the American Revolution began, the word *American* was first used to refer to our language; in 1802 the term *the American Language* was first recorded, in the U.S. Congress; and in 1806 Noah Webster coined the more precise term *American English*.

Was American English good or bad? By 1735 the English began calling it "barbarous" and our native words *barbarisms*. When the anti-American Dr. Johnson used the term *American dialect* he meant it as an insult. Such English sneering at our language continued unabated for a hundred years after the Revolutionary War. The English found merely colorful or quaint such American terms as *ground hog* and *lightning rod* and such borrowings as *oppossum*, *tomahawk*, and *wampum* (from the Indians), *boss* (Dutch), *levee* (French), and *ranch* (Spanish). But they laughed at and condemned as unnecessary or illiterate hundreds of American terms and usages, such as:

allow, guess, reckon, meaning to think, which had all become obsolete in England.

bark up the wrong tree, a vivid American term since 1832.

belittle, coined by Thomas Jefferson in 1787.

bluff, used in the South since 1687, instead of the British river "bank." This has the distinction of being the first word attacked as being a "barbarous" American term.

bureau, meaning chest of drawers, which was obsolete in England.

card, meaning a person who likes to joke, an American use since 1835.

clever, meaning sharp witted, an East Anglia dialect use common to all Americans.

fall, obsolete in England where "autumn" was now the preferred word.

fork, which the British ate with but which we also drove or paddled on, using it since 1645 to mean the branch of a road or river.

gotten, obsolete in England where "got" was being used as the past participle of *get*.

help, meaning servants, an American use since 1630.

how?, which only Americans used as an interrogation, since 1815.

loan, which only Americans used as a verb meaning "to lend."

seaboard, an American coinage for "shore," used since 1788.

spell, which we have used to mean a period of time, a while, since 1705.

wilt, which was obsolete in England.

It wasn't only our words that the English disliked, but our pronunciation and grammar as well. They jeered when we said "missionary" instead of "mission'ry," "shew" for "show," and "whare" and "bhar" for "where" and "bear." In 1822 visitor Charles Dickens said that outside of New York and Boston all Americans had a nasal drawl and used "doubtful" grammar. In 1832 Mrs. Trollop said that during her visit in America she seldom

John Witherspoon (1723–94).

heard a correctly pronounced sentence. And in 1839 visitor Captain Frederick Marryat said it was remarkable how debased the English language had become in such a short time in America.

On the other hand, during and after the Revolutionary War we became proud of our American language. It was a badge of independence. In 1778 the Continental Congress recommended that when the French minister visited "all replies or answers" to him should be made "in the language of the United States" (not only as opposed to French but also as opposed to English English). In his 1789 *Dissertations on the English Language* Noah Webster wrote that

> The reasons for American English being different than English English are simple: As an independent nation, our honor requires us to have a system of our own, in language as well as government.

Such men as Thomas Jefferson and Benjamin Rush agreed—it was good politics. And it was sensible: being a different people in a different country and having different experiences, we Americans were bound to continue to develop our own brand of English. What the English called barbarisms we proudly called *Americanisms*. John Witherspoon coined this word in 1781, in a series of papers he wrote for the *Pennsylvania Journal and Weekly Advertiser*, and defined it as any word or usage peculiar to English as used in America. A Scot who came to the colonies as president of the College of New Jersey (later Princeton University), Witherspoon was a signer of the Declaration of Independence and a member of the Congress. In this series of papers he presented his observations on the state of the English language in America, giving the first good list of American words, pronunciations, usages, and blunders. He noted our use of *mad* for "angry" (since the 1770s); our cant use of *to take in* (since the 1770s) and *to bamboozle* (since 1703) for "to swindle"; our heavy use of such contractions as *ain't, can't, don't,* and *couldn't;* common mistakes as "lay" for "lie" and "knowed" for "knew"; and such pronunciations as "winder" for "window."

Later, of course, we were to add more Indian and Spanish words to our language in our westward movement, borrow words and intonations from such immigrant groups as the Germans and Italians, and—like the English themselves—continue to coin new words and change the meanings of old ones, develop our own dialects and pronunciations, and evolve more of our own grammatical and syntactical uses and misuses. Since World War II, however, best-selling books, movies, TV shows, popular songs, and jet-propelled tourists have spread American English to England and English English to the U.S. Modern politics, pop culture, jet planes, and electronics seem to be bringing the two "languages" closer together again.

Some Apples!—and Some Cider

Until the 20th century citrus boom, apples—raw, in cider, and cooked in many dishes—were the most popular and talked about fruit in America. The trees withstood our harsh New England winters and the fruit was stored fresh in barrels to last most of the winter, or was dried for long keeping in colonial *dry houses* (1776). By 1800 Americans were talking about such native-bred apples as *Baldwins, Johnathans, Winesaps, William's,* and almost a hundred others.

If you had gone into an early American inn, tavern, or home the drink you would have heard mentioned most would have been *cider* (Hebrew *shēkār*, intoxicating drink). Cider was to early Americans what drinking water, milk, orange juice, soft drinks, and martinis are to us. Cider meant *apple cider,* though *cherry cider; peach cider,* sometimes called *peachy* (1781); and *pear cider,* sometimes called *perry,* were also well liked. Hard cider was called *apple jack* by 1816 and *apple john* by 1856. *Boiled cider* was a 1700s term for cider that had been boiled to remove the alcohol and preserve it, and in the 1820s and 30s *apple water* was cider diluted with water. Cider was also made into a brandy called *apple brandy* (1780), *cider brandy* (1800), or *apple whiskey* (1837).

Cider pap, a mixture of cider and hominy, was a dish of the 1700s; cider was often used in making *apple butter* in the 1730s; and *cider cake* was a specialty of the 1820s. Until after the Civil War cider was sold on street corners from *cider carts* (cider barrels on wheels).

A legendary American name should also be associated with cider—*Johnny Appleseed.* Kind, eccentric John Chapman (1774–1847) gained fame as Johnny Appleseed in his wanderings of 40 years from the Alleghenies to Indiana, distributing Swedenborgian tracts, scattering apple seeds, and distributing bags of dried apple seeds to westward-bound travelers in advance of the settlers. Where did he get all those apple seeds?—from the ever-present American cider mills.

Besides eating raw apples and drinking cider, Americans have eaten and talked about cooked apples in many dishes. In the 1740s and 50s we talked about the popular *house pie,* made of whole crushed apples, including peeling and core; in the 1760s such terms as *apple pie, apple fritter, apple brown Betty* (baked bread, butter, and apple slices), and the similar but grander *apple Charlotte* became common; in the 1770s common native American terms included *apple butter, apple sauce,* and *apple preserves,* which were served several times a week in most homes. *Apple cobbler, apple duff* (a pudding, sometimes with a bottom crust), and *apple slump* (a raised dough with apple filling) were common in the 1840s and 50s. *Marlborough pie* or *Marlborough pudding* (an apple or applesauce cream pie) was popular in the 1860s–80s, while New England's

Johnny Appleseed was a legend in his own lifetime along the Ohio Valley frontier of the early 1880s.

apple pandowdy (sliced apples baked in sugar and spices in a deep dish and with a thick top crust) became nationally known in the 1920s, said to have gotten its name because it is a simple, homey, or dowdy dish.

Meanwhile there have been dozens of farm and kitchen terms for the implements used in handling apples, from *apple parers* (1833) to *apple poles* (1910), and people were talking about the vendors who sold apples at *apple stands* by the 1830s, a hundred years before *Apple Annies* were "selling apples from street corners" during the Great Depression.

Apples have been so common and popular in the United States it's no wonder they figure large in our speech. We had said that things are *in apple pie order* since 1813, said that any remarkable person or thing was *some apples!* since the 1840s, humorously called pocket knives *apple peelers* in the 1850s, and referred to red-cheeked Victorian girls as *apple cheeked*. We were *upsetting the apple cart* as early as 1796 and our grandparents were telling people to *go climb a sour apple tree* (go to hell) in the 1900s, saying that something was *as sure as God made little green apples* by 1909, and calling exaggerations and lies *applesauce* by 1910. By 1915 *apple knocker* was a disparaging way to refer to a farmer or rustic (though no apple grower has ever been able to harvest his fruit by merely knocking it off the trees), and by 1928 we were calling sycophants *apple polishers*, referring to the toadying student who brought "an apple for the teacher" to school.

In the mid 1920s, too, a guy could be an *apple* and a smart one a *smart apple* (which soon meant smart alec), and *apple* was then also slang for a baseball, with some sporty types referring to ballparks as the old *apple orchard* and to an eager player or sticky-fingered fielder as an *apple hawk*. In the 1930s New York City became *the Big Apple*, full of opportunity, ripe for plucking, while another *the big apple* was the biggest dance craze of the swing era. New York, a dance craze, baseball, or cider, the apple itself is even more American than apple pie and Americans have used the word often.

Apples were selling for 1¢ and 2¢ in the 1840s.

The prettiest gal that ever I saw,
Was suckin' cider through a straw.
I told that gal I didn't see how,
She sucked the cider through a straw.
   Carey Morgan and Lee David, "Suckin' Cider Through a Straw"; all *s*'s and *c*'s in the song were sung with a pronounced lisp to represent a sipping sound.

The Atomic Bomb

The first atomic bomb exploded in the desert at the Alamogordo, New Mexico, air base, 34 miles north of Santa Fe, at 5:29:45 A.M., July 16, 1945. It was the beginning of the *atomic age*. Three weeks later, on August 6, 1945, 66,000 people died in Hiroshima when the B-29 Superfortress, the *Enola Gay*, dropped the first atomic bomb ever used in war, wiping 4½ square miles of the city off the face of the earth. Three days later the B-29 Superfortress, the *Great Artiste*, dropped the second atomic bomb used in war on Nagasaki, Japan, killing 36,000 and destroying 40% of the city.

Japan surrendered five days later, on August 14, 1945. World War II was over.

In the 30 days from July 16 through August 14, a new way of life and a new vocabulary began. *Atomic bomb* was first heard and

FIRST ATOMIC BOMB DROPPED ON JAPAN; MISSILE IS EQUAL TO 20,000 TONS OF TNT; TRUMAN WARNS FOE OF A 'RAIN OF RUIN'

NEW AGE USHERED

Day of Atomic Energy Hailed by President, Revealing Weapon

HIROSHIMA IS TARGET

The *"mushroom"* cloud at Hiroshima, August 6, 1945.

Sixteen hours ago an American plane dropped one bomb on Hiroshima, an important Japanese Army base. That bomb had more power than 20,000 tons of TNT.

With that simple announcement on August 6, 1945, President Harry S. Truman changed our life and language forever.

was immediately shortened to *atom bomb*, then became *A-bomb* or simply *the bomb* before the year's end. In those 30 days *fireball* took on a new meaning and *mushroom cloud* was first heard. In the last months of 1945 we read the spectacular accounts of the events and research leading up to the bomb, absorbing the terms its developers had used since 1942, such as *atomic pile, chain reaction, reactor, fission, U-235, U-238,* and *radioisotope* (immediately shortened to *isotope*—heavy words seem to have a "half-life" too, breaking down into simpler ones quickly). Names that had been almost unknown became household words: *Oak Ridge,* Tennessee, and *Los Alamos,* New Mexico, where the bomb was made, and *the Manhattan Project,* code name for the bomb's development.

In 1946, as work on and tests of the atomic bomb continued, we heard the terms *atomic testing, underwater testing, proving ground, nuclear test site,* and *Geiger counter* (first made by Hans Geiger and Walther Mueller in 1928 from Geiger's prototype of 1908). Atomic-bomb tests were conducted at *Bikini* and *Eniwetok,* Pacific atolls, and in Nevada, and millions of Americans who could get to a television set (all homes did not yet have them) watched the broadcasts of them. These put the word *countdown* into the language and made the dramatic "10 . . . 9 . . . 8 . . . 7 . . . 6 . . . 5 . . . 4 . . . ." widely known (in 1961 with the televised launching of man into space, *countdown* became completely associated with the space program and most of us forgot its earlier use).

In 1946 we first heard of the *AEC,* Atomic Energy Commission, formed to promote "the peacetime use of atomic energy"; but we also heard *SAC* for the first time, the newly created Strategic Air Command of the Air Force's long-range bombers and missiles (soon to have 2,700 planes and "1,000 missiles always on the ready, each equal to all the bombs dropped in World War II"). *Nuclear weapons,* shortened to *nukes* that year, were in the news; we were warned that the atomic bomb would not be our exclusive property forever; and we realized that war was, perhaps, not a thing of the past after all. In 1949 we heard the term *nuclear club,* those nations having nuclear weapons. The Soviet Union joined that year by exploding its first A-bomb; by the late 1960s Britain, France, and Communist China were all members.

The 1952 H-bomb shown two minutes after detonation and from 50 miles away. Its destructive effect was the greatest yet for a single bomb.

Things grew even more ominous in 1950 with talk about something under development called an *H-bomb*—few ever used the full term *hydrogen bomb*—which we also referred to as the *superbomb, thermonuclear bomb,* and *fusion bomb* (*thermonuclear* and *atomic fusion* were also new words to nonscientists that year). In 1952 the U.S. tested the first H-bomb, 250 times more powerful than the A-bomb dropped on Hiroshima, and the term *radioactive fallout,* immediately shortened to *fallout,* frightened us all.

The period 1953–58 was a time of government concern and public fear over fallout from the Pacific H-bomb tests and the *strontium-90* scare (radioactive strontium-90 was reported to be found in increasing quantities in milk). Such fears and concern led to some people joining organizations like *SANE* (the National Committee for a Sane Nuclear Policy) and marching in "ban the bomb" protest rallies. They also led to the development of a U.S. H-bomb without widespread deadly fallout, called a *clean bomb* in 1957, and to discussions of a *nuclear test ban* and a *nuclear test ban treaty,* such a treaty being signed by the U.S. and Russia in 1963. By that time we had all heard *underground testing,* which would not release radioactive material into the atmosphere, and *fail-safe,* a reassuring 1962 term seeming to guarantee that nuclear bombs, warheads, reactors, etc., could not explode spontaneously.

Since 1945 we have used the adjectives *nuclear* and *atomic* interchangeably, speaking of *nuclear fallout, nuclear fission, nuclear energy, nuclear generators* (since 1951), *nuclear submarines* (1948), etc., and of *atomic fallout, atomic fission, atomic energy, atomic generators, atomic submarines,* etc., almost equally. Neither adjective has won out over the other in nonscientific use.

All these terms cannot begin to suggest the importance the atomic bomb, and the knowledge that an atomic holocaust is possible, have had on our life and language since 1945. The bomb has changed not only our ideas and vocabulary abour war, peace, science, and politics, but it has changed our philosophies, morals, and life styles, and the words that go with them. The bomb has given rise to a permanent wartime psychology and vocabulary, both in the government and in civilian life; it has given youth a "live for today because tomorrow may be canceled" attitude. Thus "the bomb" has helped create, or at least been a subconscious force in shaping, many new concepts, beliefs, social groups, and words, ranging from the obvious *cold war* (1947) and *brinkmanship* (1956) through *moral rearmament, rebellious youth, dropouts, drug culture,* and *swingers* of the 1960s to new positive ways of looking at things (*open marriages* and *ecology*) of the late 1960s and early 1970s. As our talk of the atomic age progressed from exhilaration in 1945 to fear in the 1950s to a more-or-less passive awareness in the 1960s, we Americans learned to live with the atomic bomb by talking about it—and so perhaps in some small measure, we exorcised our fears of it.

Atomic bomb damage at Hiroshima.

Babbitts, Joiners, Boosters, & Boobs

were talked about a lot in America in the 1920s and 30s, with patriotic pride by those who were and with intellectual scorn by those who weren't. *Babbitt* has been a popular word for an American philistine ever since Sinclair Lewis's hero and novel of that name appeared in 1922, to instant acclaim. George F. Babbitt was the biggest joiner and booster, the smuggest conformist, the most extroverted but dissatisfied character that the fictitious Zenith, "the zip city," or American literature had ever known. He probably got his name from the author's early memories of advertisements for the B. T. Babbitt Company, manufacturers of household cleansers, and, according to Sinclair Lewis himself, Babbitt got much of his personality from H. L. Mencken's description of *the great American boob.* By 1923, writers in *The Nation* were already referring to "A group of American businessmen! . . . A circle of Babbitts" and to "Busy, boasting, and Babbitt-ful Kansas City."

Boob was one of Mencken's favorite words, and he also popularized *booboisie* in attacking the complacent American bourgeois. *Boob* has been around since 1909 in America, as a short form of the 18th century *booby* (Henry Fielding has a satirical character named Lady Booby in his 1742 novel *Joseph Andrews*). *Booby prizes* were an American invention, talked about as early as 1893; we called insane asylums *booby hatches* by 1897; and *booby trap*

Famous American author Sinclair Lewis (1885–1951), whose satirical novel Main Street *(1920) was called "the most sensational event" in 20th century American literature.*

The Sphinx Motor Patrol, part of a parade in New York City (1964) of "joiners," or members of the Ancient Order of the Nobles of the Mystic Shrine of North America, a group sometimes called the "playground of Masonry."

appeared during the First World War. However, *booby* in America first referred to a small, clumsy carriage, especially a carriage body on sleigh runners (a device known in England since the 1760s). Our word *boob* may come from this clumsy device, or simply and directly from *bobo*, a Spanish word for fool.

Joiner was first recorded in 1890, in the *Ann Arbor Record:* "Ypsilanti is a good place for 'jiners.' There are over 100 societies and organizations that a person can join." *Booster* seems to have first appeared around 1910 in the Southwest, referring to a booster of Texas stock deals, boosters of Oklahoma towns, and boosters of Nevada vacations. As always, language follows life: talk, novels, and articles about the all-American Babbitt, joiner, booster, or boob flourished, as did the type, from the 1890s to the late 1930s. What happened to this type of American? He seems to have been a casualty of the Second World War; few rampant Babbitts, joiners, boosters, or boobs have been heard from since.

Badmen

The early colonists brought such words as *bandit, robber, highway robber, cutthroat,* and *outlaw* with them from England. Mounted men who robbed travelers, and later banks and trains, soon appeared on American roads—especially on western roads from about 1850 to 1900—and became a much talked about part of American life. We still use many expressions associated with them, such as:

gang, first used in America to mean a herd of animals in 1657, then used by 1823 to mean a pack of dishonest politicians, and finally around 1870 to mean a group of criminals.

horse thief, as an armed robber who took horses, 1760s.

bank robber, 1799 (see BANK ROB-BERS AND THE FBI).

quick on the trigger, 1808; *to have trigger itch,* 1903, which became *to have an itchy trigger finger* by 1940.

road agent, early 1850s.

desperado, a western badman, 1850s.

badman, 1855.

mail robber, of stages and trains, 1855.

cattle thief, a western-style rustler, 1862.

holdup, 1878, but until the late 1890s used only to refer to stopping and robbing stages and trains (*hold up* meant stop, delay, by the 1830s).

hideout, 1870s.

robber's roost, a robber's rendez-vous or hideout, 1879.

train robber, 1870s.

gunman, any outlaw, 1880s.

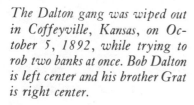

The Dalton gang was wiped out in Coffeyville, Kansas, on October 5, 1892, while trying to rob two banks at once. Bob Dalton is left center and his brother Grat is right center.

15

A few badmen were admired as Robin Hoods or unrepentant Confederate army veterans, but most were talked of with fear and loathing in their own time. *Dime novels* (1864, the Dime Book Series began publication in 1860) began to romanticize badmen in the 1860s and ever since we have been talking about such men as: Sam Bass (1851-78), the steal-from-the-rich-give-to-the-poor Dakota and Texas train and bank robber, called "the Robin Hood of Texas" and "the good badman"; "Cole" (Thomas Coleman) Younger (1844-1916), who with his brothers James and Robert formed "the Younger Brothers" who sometimes rode with Jesse James' gang; the Dalton Gang, which was wiped out in Coffeyville, Kansas, in 1892; Butch Cassidy (real name Le Roy Parker) who, with the Sundance Kid, was a cowboy between bank robberies and who from 1896 led "the Wild Bunch," a name first given them by a saloon keeper; and, of course, the two who play the biggest part in American badman mythology, BILLY THE KID and JESSE JAMES.

The Younger Brothers, Bob (top) and Cole, captured while on a raid with JESSE JAMES, were sentenced to life imprisonment at the Minnesota State Penitentiary.

Ballyhoo, Pitch, Spiel, and Flack

mean a sales talk, exaggerated praise, or advertising. *Ballyhoo* (perhaps from the boisterous village of Ballyhooly in County Cork) was a traveling show and carnival term by the 1890s and meant the pitchman's or barker's spiel and free "sample" of the show given on the *bally stand*, or platform, in front of the tent (a tent show or carnival staying in one place long enough to build such a platform was called a *bally show*). *Ballyhoo* was used to refer to advertising as early as 1901.

Pitch was common in the early 1900s, originally being the spiel of a *pitchman*, a seller of wares from a temporary stand, as a sidewalk vendor. His *pitch* was originally his stand, since the old meaning of the word was one's property, originally land selected by or apportioned to a settler, as in a 1699 colonial record referring to "the laying out of John Pringle's pitch upon the good hill." *To make one's pitch* originally meant not to give a sales talk but to settle down on one's land, establish a farm or home, as in James Fenimore Cooper's first Leatherstocking novel, *The Pioneers* (1823): "Elizabeth saw many large openings [clearings] . . . where . . . settlers had, in the language of the country 'made their pitch.'"

Spiel (German *spielen*, to play a musical instrument) has meant a sales talk, line, or any colorful noisy speech, be it of a barker, huckster, or preacher, since the 1880s and used in advertising since the 1940s. *Flack*, originally *flak*, may come from the World War II *flak* (1940, from German *Flieger abwehr kanone*, "aircraft defense gun") antiaircraft fire, since exaggerated talk comes at one as thick and fast as rapid gunfire. It has meant both advertising copy or publicity, as well as the one who writes or promotes it, since the mid 1940s.

All of these terms have to do with one's *line, line of talk, line of gab, line of bull*, all of these *line* terms being in use since the early 1900s and very popular since the 1920s.

Bank Robbers and the FBI

Although the 1799 term *bank robber* is sometimes used to refer to western-style BADMEN, we have used it most for their car-driving counterparts of the Depression-era 1930s. These highly publicized bank robbers popularized such older terms as:

Bonnie Parker and Clyde Barrow were killed on May 23, 1934, in a roadblock ambush near Giblaud, Louisiana. In this 1933 snapshot Bonnie and Clyde show a lighter moment; actually they were small-time, vicious killers.

> *stick up*, 1904; "stick 'em up" is a term from the 1930s.
> *get away*, 1907.
> *gun moll*, 1910, popularized by newspapers in the 1930s as the gun-toting, accomplice-mistress of a robber, this term originally meant a woman thief (from the 1830s *gun*, thief, from Yiddish *goniff*, thief, + the 1786 *moll*, woman).
> *on the lam*, 1920s.

Many of the car-driving bank robbers of the 1930s made bold headlines and were soon exploited in the movies, which kept their names and phrases on everyone's lips. Thus we still talk about "Machine-Gun" Kelly; John Dillinger (see PUBLIC ENEMY NUMBER ONE); "Baby Face" Nelson (real name Lester Gillis); "Pretty Boy" (Charles Arthur) Floyd, who hated his nickname; "Bonnie and Clyde" (Mr. and Mrs. Clyde Barrow), the subject of a landmark 1968 movie *Bonnie and Clyde;* and the Barker-Karpis gang. Such names also made another name famous, the FBI, which in 1934, the first year its agents carried guns, shot and killed three notorious fugitives who had resisted arrest: Dillinger, "Pretty Boy" Floyd, and "Baby Face" Nelson, and in the following year shot and killed Kate and Fred Barker and Russell Gibson of the Barker-Karpis gang.

Actually, the term *FBI* itself didn't become famous in 1934. It wasn't until 1935 that this bureau's name was changed to the *Federal Bureau of Investigation* and everyone began calling it the *FBI*. It had originally been established in 1908 under the Department of Justice as its *Bureau of Investigation*, to collect evidence against western "land thieves" and eastern trusts due for busting. By 1912 its unarmed, fact-finding agents were already called *the Feds* (which had meant Union soldiers during the Civil War and came to mean Treasury Department prohibition agents during Prohibition). These investigators were also called *DJs* or *Dee Jays* (from the initials for *Department of Justice*) and sometimes *Whiskers* (referring to Uncle Sam). By 1922 these investigators were also called *G-men* (Government *men*), though "Machine Gun" Kelly

J[ohn] Edgar Hoover (1895–1972), former Director of the Federal Bureau of Investigation (FBI).

17

popularized the term when he said when captured "OK, G-men, you got me." In 1924 "the Bureau" was reorganized and J. Edgar Hoover became its head, taking it out of politics, starting a centralized *fingerprint file* and, in 1932, setting up the bureau's *crime laboratory.* Then during the *crime wave* (a 1930 term) of the early Depression years Congress extended the bureau's jurisdiction to interstate kidnaping, bank robbing, white slavery, etc., authorizing agents to carry guns and make arrests in 1934.

Where's the Bathroom?

Many early pioneers and farmers used the great outdoors as the place to relieve themselves. When freezing weather, personal dignity, or increasing population demanded it they built what lower class and rural colonists called a *privy* (from Latin *prīvus*, private, hence a private place), *privy house*, or *outhouse*, all words brought over from England, or what more aristocratic and cosmopolitan colonists called a *house of office*, a *necessary house*, or simply *the necessary.* If behind a house, it might be called a *backhouse;* if earth were used to cover the excrement it might be called an *earth house.* If there were separate outhouses for women and men, a crescent on the door signified the one for women, a sun indicated the one for men.

The indoor *chamber pot* was used at night and by the sick and invalid, or for emergencies. It had been called a *piss pot* since the 15th century in England; a small one, as used by children, has been called a *potty* since the 19th century. The chamber pot was usually kept under the bed, but in the homes of the wealthy might be disguised as and called a *commode* or *chaise percé.* Some men also used terms such as *Cousin John* or *Jake* to refer to a privy or a chamber pot. Thus a Harvard College regulation of 1735 states that "no freshman shall go into the Fellows cus John," and Benjamin Franklin wrote that the English practice of

> Emptying their jails into our settlements ... [is] an insult ... [that] would not be equalled . . . by emptying their jakes on our tables.

Jake had meant a privy in England since 1530 and *John* was in use by the 1650s; it was also called a *Joe* in the 1840s and 50s in America.

When the privy first began to move indoors in some fine homes in the 1750s it was called the *water closet* (a term we still associate with British usage and which became the British *W.C.*) or sometimes the *closet stool* or *close stool.* This, of course, was just a closet-like room containing a chair with a hole in the seat and a chamber pot underneath, which had to be emptied. *Toilets* weren't really seen or talked about much until the 1820s and bathtubs until the 1830s—they had to wait for the first modern city waterworks and sewer systems to be built (Philadelphia completed the first such American waterworks in 1800 and Boston completed the first such sewer system in 1823). The first toilet was installed in the White House when John Quincy Adams became president in 1825, causing some debate and many jokes, and giving us the slang word *Quincy* for toilet. In 1838 the term *toilet cover* was added to the language; men began to use and talk about *urinals* around 1850; and finally in the 1880s *toilet paper* was a new term. *Toilet training* for children wasn't a common term until the 1920s, when parents began to discuss the new theory of American psychologists John Dollard and Neal Miller, that leniency in the matter would be healthier for the child.

Where's the word *bathroom* in all this? The concept and word are late arrivals—because baths are. Although some hardy men of the 17th and 18th centuries might swim or bathe in a creek or pond, bathing was in general considered unnecessary, uncomfortable, and immodest. Thus the English diarist Samuel Pepys (1633–1703) expressed surprise that his wife had taken one bath in her lifetime and was considering taking a second—and when Philadelphia's Elizabeth Drinker took a therapeutic *shower bath* in 1799 it was remarkable enough to be recorded in her diary as her first bath in 28 years! However, by the 1790s some wealthy, chronically ill, or eccentric people were building and talking about *bathing rooms* and in the 1830s *bathtub* and *bathroom* finally became generally known terms. Then a *bathtub* was a lead-and-wood or tin-plated lead affair and a *bathroom* was only a room for taking a bath (it still means only that in Britain, as many American tourists find when they reserve a room with a bath and discover that the toilet is down the hall). In the 1830s, too, *the Saturday night bath* began to be an American institution, in honor of the following Sabbath. Because the bathtub and bathroom were still uncommon this bath was usually taken in a big washtub or farm tub in front of the fireplace or kitchen stove, where boiling kettles provided the hot water.

A Saturday night bath in the 1800s.

It wasn't until the late 1850s that some fine houses had complete *bathrooms* as we know them, with both bathtub and toilet, one of the first being installed in George Vanderbilt's New York City mansion in 1855. By 1865 the new Vassar College required all girls to bathe twice a week, and by the 1880s it was estimated that 15% of all city dwellers in America had bathrooms of one sort or another. By 1890 *wash rag* was a common term and many called it a *wash cloth* by 1904; enough people were taking daily baths by 1935 that *bath towel* then became a common term, and people who could afford it were also asking that *showers* be installed in their homes.

Public bathrooms (toilets) were first called *washrooms* in 1878 (*roller towel* had been in the language since the 1840s), were referred to as *restrooms* by 1900, and were sometimes called *public comfort stations* after 1904. They were originally marked *for ladies only* and *for gentlemen only*, then *ladies* and *gentlemen* which by the 1920s became *women* and *men* or *gents*. In the 1920s also, speakeasy patrons began referring to the ladies' *powder room*, which term may come from the colonial "powder room" where men withdrew to powder their wigs, or may have come into use in the 1920s simply because now for the first time many women were using or admitting to using powder. Now the men's room became commonly known as *the John* and the women's was soon called *the Jane*.

Chic Sale became a term for outhouse in the 1920s, when that comedian published a humorous book about them, while the old rural term *shit house* became a common World War I soldiers' term for a latrine. *Can* for toilet and bathroom had been in use since 1900, *head* became U.S. Navy use around 1935 (a ship's toilet is often squeezed in near a ship's bulk*head*), and both *can* and *head* became very popular words with men during World War II.

Marilyn Monroe takes a luxurious bath in a scene from the 1955 movie The Seven Year Itch.

Bayous, Creoles, and Cajuns

Ever since La Salle claimed Louisiana for the French in 1682, Louisiana French customs and words have been among the most colorful in America. The first major Louisiana French word to enter American English was *bayou*, in 1766. The French got it from the Choctaw *bayuk*, creek, stream, and the word has been used since to mean a creek, channel, marshy inlet, and dry river bed. The Choctaws shortened their word *bayuk* to *bok*, which gave the Louisiana French *boque*, another word for bayou. This was used in American English by the 1820s, often spelled *bogue*, *boug*, or *bog*, and is found in such place names as *Bogalusa*, Louisiana, *Bogue Sound*, North Carolina, and *Bogue Chitto* and *Bogue Falaya*.

By 1792 *Creole* was used to mean a descendant of the early French and Spanish settlers in Louisiana, especially of the upper-class French who had retained their European customs and speech. The word comes from the French *creóle*, Spanish *criollo*, meaning

A Cajun bateau is a shallow craft ideally suited to navigate the bayous of Louisiana.

What would you give for the whole of Louisiana?

Napoleon I's minister of foreign affairs Charles Maurice de Talleyrand to Robert Livingston and James Monroe, whom President Jefferson had authorized in 1801 to attempt to buy New Orleans from France for $2 million. Jefferson's answer to Talleyrand was $15 million, Congress ratifying *the Louisiana Purchase* by treaty in 1803. This purchase of the old French province of Louisiana, lying between the Mississippi River and the Rocky Mountains, doubled the size of the U.S.; we called the area *the Louisiana Territory* by 1806; eventually it formed all or part of 13 states.

"a native." The slaves belonging to such people were often called *Creoles* too, and were considered superior to other slaves because they shared some of their masters' language and customs. By 1800 this last use of *Creole* had widened to mean any Black who had some French or Spanish blood. In the early 1800s all America seemed to talk about the New Orleans' *Creole balls* where wealthy White men danced with their Creole mistresses. By 1829 *Creole* also meant a native-born Black as opposed to one imported from Africa. In 1845 Creole was first used to mean any Louisianan, Louisiana was called *the Creole State* by 1871, and New Orleans *the Creole City* by 1880. The word was so popular it spread to Alaska in the late 1860s, where *Creole* meant a native of mixed Russian and Indian ancestry.

A *Cajun* or *Cajan* is a descendant of the French Acadians in Louisiana. After the British captured the French colony of Acadia (Nova Scotia and other Maritime Provinces in Canada) they demanded the French settlers pledge allegiance to Great Britain. Those who would not do so were deported in 1755, many to Louisiana (Longfellow's long 1847 poem *Evangeline* is about the separation, suffering, and final reunion of two lovers who were deported). Such a deportee was formally called a *French Neutral*, but *Acadian* was the usual word, soon shortened to *'Cadian* in Louisiana, and by 1868 *'Cadian* had become *Cajun*. The Cajun dialect is called *Bougalie*, which may mean "bogue talk," bayou talk.

Louisiana French has also given us:

French Quarter, the French-speaking section of New Orleans, 1865.
jambalaya, 1872. Though there is a French Provençal *jambalaia*, both the dish and its name were probably introduced into Louisiana by the Spaniards in the late 18th century (the word based on Spanish *jamon*, ham, with which the dish was originally made).

lagniappe entered American English in 1849. The French Creoles got it from the Spanish *la napa*, which comes from the Peruvian Quechuan Indian word *yapa*, addition—hence our use of it to mean a little extra given a customer with his purchase.

levee (French *levé*, an arising), 1766. It has also been used to mean a dock or quay along the Mississippi. A breach in a levee is called a *crevasse*, a French word used in American English along the Mississippi since 1813.

Mardi gras (French "fat Tuesday," which is Shrove Tuesday). Since the Middle Ages this Tuesday before Ash Wednesday and the fasting and penitence of Lent has been an occasion for wild merrymaking. The term first became associated in America with the specific New Orleans celebration around 1832.

parish was an English word used in all the colonies. In New England it meant an ecclesiastical unit or congregation; in the South it meant a subdivision of a county, being so used in Virginia by 1641, North Carolina by 1713, and Georgia in 1829. In Louisiana a parish meant a civil district corresponding to a county (from Old French *paroisse*). By the 1830s *parish* as a political unit was pretty well associated solely with Louisiana, which still has parishes in place of counties.

picayune (French *picaillon*, an old Piedmontese coin, a farthing) was used in Louisiana to refer to a small Spanish-American coin the half real or 6¢ piece, around 1800. By 1835 it meant any coin, of small value and by 1855 meant of little value, paltry.

An 1870s Mardi gras in New Orleans glorifying all the good things to eat and drink—just before Lent!

poontang, *poon tang*, some general southern use since the 1870s, meaning the vagina, coitus, or a woman considered as a sex object, usually applied to Black or mulatto women (via Louisiana French from French *putain*, prostitute).

Beaver!

was as enticing a word as *gold!* in the 1600s. The animals were then already extinct in Great Britain and scarce in Europe, thus American beaver skins were in great demand—for clothing, trimming, and especially for the high, sheared-fur felt hats worn by all gentlemen and called *beavers* (it wasn't until 1714 that *beaverette*, rabbit fur for making cheap substitutes, was in use). Thus the word *beaver!* was a major factor leading to the populating of the Eastern Seaboard, the forming of the Hudson Bay Company in 1670, the exploring of the American wilderness, and trading with the Indians. In parts of New England beaver skins were a medium of exchange, and a man's work or wealth might be reckoned in *beavers*, just as later in Pennsylvania they were reckoned in buckskins or *bucks* (a deerskin, 1748). *Beaver* was also an underlying cause of the French and Indian War (1754–63), in which England won control, from the French and their Indian allies, of the Iroquois trapping territories of central New York State and the upper Ohio. Later, *beaver* helped John Jacob Astor's American Fur Company amass over $20 million.

How times have changed. Today *beaver* is probably most often used in the phrases *to work like a beaver*, first in vogue around 1740, and *eager beaver*, a bit of army rhyming slang from the 1940s. The beaver's thick dark-brown fur (*beaver* comes from Old English *beofer*, the brown animal) is now acknowledged only in our use of *beaver* to mean a full beard or to refer to a well-haired pudendum or a picture showing it, which in pornography is called a *beaver shot.*

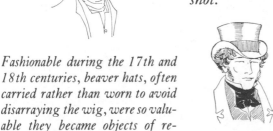

Fashionable during the 17th and 18th centuries, beaver hats, often carried rather than worn to avoid disarraying the wig, were so valuable they became objects of remembrance in wills.

French, 1822   *Child's beaver, 1848*   *American, 1850s*

Beer, Beergardens, and Saloons

For it's always fair weather
When good fellows get together
With a stein on the table and a good song ringing clear.
—Richard Hovey, "A Stein Song," 1898

The *Mayflower* Pilgrims landed in Plymouth Massachusetts, because they were running out of "victuals . . . [and] beer." Otherwise they would have sailed on to Virginia as originally planned. Early colonists talked about making *corn beer, potato beer, pumpkin beer,* and even *persimmon beer,* but they mainly talked about and

drank regular beer imported from England. By 1634 taverns charged a penny for a quart. Men, women, and children of all classes drank beer at meals and between meals as a *small drink* (cheap or common drink, with connotations of our "soft drink"). Only after it was found that native apples thrived in New England where grain did not, did cider (see SOME APPLES!—AND SOME CIDER) replace beer as the colonist's major drink.

George Washington limited himself to one "cup" of beer (*cup* was often used to mean a mug or tankard) and two glasses of wine at dinner, even though he owned interests in *brew houses* (breweries, the word *brewery* didn't enter the language until the 18th century). Early Americans drank their beer at home, but the men also drank it at inns, taverns, bars, alehouses, porterhouses, *beer cellars* (1732, from German *bierkeller*), and *beerhouses*, which around the 1830s were sometimes simply called *houses* or *homes*.

What did early Americans mean by the word *beer?* Until the 1840s beer was darker, stronger, and fuller bodied than the lager we have been used to since. Although some of it was *small beer* (weak, inferior beer, cheap beer, the term also meant an unimportant person by 1705), most of it was ale, porter, "stout beer," or malt liquor. All beers are basically made in the same way: malt (malted barley, barley that has been allowed to sprout), and regular barley or other grains are cooked in water, this liquid is boiled with hops to add flavor, then yeast is added and the liquid allowed to ferment. The differences in beers are only in the amount and type of malt, hops, yeast, water, etc. used. Here are the types of beers that Americans have talked about:

ale (Old English *ealu*) until the 17th century was simply made of malt, yeast, and water. Then brewers began adding barley and hops, making it identical to beer. Thus early Americans and their British counterparts often used the words *ale* and *beer* interchangeably: eventually the British came to prefer the word *ale* as the generic word and Americans to prefer the word *beer*. All this beer/ale was made by "top fermentation," the yeast floated to the top of the vat after it did its work. Today's American ale is still made this way.

beer (Old English *bèor*) was always made with malt, barley or other grains, hops, yeast and water. When barley and hops were added to ale in the 17th century, *ale* and *beer* became the same (see *ale* above). This remained generally true until the 1840s when Germans introduced new yeast that allowed "bottom fermentation," the yeast sank to the bottom after doing its work; this, combined with aging, gave us *lager beer* (see *lager* below). Since then in America *beer* has technically meant the kind produced by bottom fermentation, *ale* that produced by top fermentation. Thus since the 1840s in America there has again been a real difference between *beer* and *ale* and almost all American beer has been aged or "lagered." Since the 1840s when we have said *beer* we have meant bottom fermentation, aged *lager*. (British beer is still top fermented and unaged, hence less carbonated—when

the British say "beer" they still mean top fermentation "ale," and they call their cheapest type *bitters*.)

stout is from the 17th century expression "a stout beer" or "a stout ale," meaning a strong one. It did not become a specific kind of beer until the 19th century. It's a strong, dark, malty ale with more hop flavoring than any other beer/ale.

porter is short for *porter's ale*, so named in the 18th century because the porters who carried produce at London's Covent Gardens market favored it. It's a strong, dark ale with a medium hop flavor and higher alcoholic content than other beer/ale. Porter was popular in early America and alehouses were sometimes called *porterhouses* (about 1814 Martin Harrison, the proprietor of a New York City porterhouse, popularized the *porterhouse steak*).

Famous beergardens included the Atlantic Garden located in the Bowery, New York City, shown here in an 1870 wood engraving, and Pabst's Whitefish Resort (1889–1914) and Schlitz Park of the 1890s, both of Milwaukee and both with a more rural setting and decor.

These were the only beers early America knew. Then with the flood of German immigrants to America around the 1840s came the special yeast that permitted bottom fermentation, making a beer that when aged formed *lager*. The German immigrants and their lager changed American beer, beer-drinking habits, and our beer vocabulary forever. We were now to have:

lager beer or *lager* (from German *lager bier*, literally "storehouse beer," aged beer), 1840s, a pale, light-bodied, medium hopped, comparatively weak beer that is more carbonated than older beers. The several months of aging mellows it and clears it of sediment. Originally many American men mockingly called it a "woman's drink." From the 1840s to the Civil War it was usually ordered by its name "lager," after that it was just "beer"; it's what Americans have meant by "beer" ever since.

Pilsner or *pilsener* is a name that comes from the famous *Pilsner Urquell* beer from Pilsen, Czechoslovakia, where the water gives it a clean, fresh, light-bodied flavor. It is a term used by brewers all over the world to describe any light, lager beer, usually their lightest, smoothest brand.

25

Bock beer, *bock*, 1856, comes from German *bockbier*, originally *Einbecker* or *Einbocker bier*, a special beer from the town of Einbeck, Germany (Einbeck is pronounced "Einbock" in the Munich dialect). Since *ein bock* means "a goat" in German and sounds like "ein buck" in English, labels sometimes mistakenly picture a goat or a buck, and we sometimes call bock beer *buck beer* (1850s). It has also been called *double beer* (1867) because it can be twice as strong as lager. In Germany it is made in December and January for spring consumption; in the U.S. it is a heavy, sweet, hoppy beer made from the sediment of beer fermenting vats when they are cleaned out in the spring.

dark beer or *Munich beer*. Such beer, stout, etc., is usually dark because roasted malt is used.

light beer or *Vienna beer* uses nonroasted malt.

malt liquor is made in the U.S. like other beer, but it has a higher alcohol content, 4.08%–6.3%.

Thus in the 1840s *lager beer* changed everything. It was the beer that made Milwaukee, St. Louis, and Cincinnati famous, the beer that men drank in the new *saloons* (1841, from French *salon*, hall) while they ate their *free lunch* and made *saloon keepers* (1860) wealthy. It was the beer that all those *beer wagons* (1861) were carrying. Lager gave cities with a large German population a new industry. With a large brewery established by 1840, Milwaukee led the way and soon had people talking about its famous brands, such as *Blatz* (1851, owned by Valentine Blatz), *Miller's* (1855, owned by Frederick Miller), *Schlitz* (1874, owned by Joseph Schlitz), and *Pabst's* (1889, owned by Captain Fred Pabst). New York lagers included *Rupert's* (owned by Colonel Rupert, who at one time owned the New York Yankees) and *Rheingold* (established in 1855). St. Louis lagers included *Michelob* (produced by Busch, who at one time owned the St. Louis Cardinals). Thus between the 1840s and the 1880s lager took hold and gave us many brand names we have been talking about ever since.

At the same time that lager was becoming America's favorite beer, beer was becoming "the poor man's drink." During the Civil War, taxes made whiskey much more expensive than beer—whiskey was taxed $1 per gallon, beer was taxed $1 for each 31-gallon barrel! After the war, beer retained its popularity. Americans were soon talking about the *beer jerkers* (1863) or *beer slingers* (1875) who worked at the flourishing *beer mills* (1879), *beerhalls* (1882, German *bierhalle*), and the barreled beer dives called *barrel houses* (1882, soon the term came to mean a saloon where women were available, then a whore house, and finally a style of jazz played there). The German style *beergarden* (1868, German *biergarten*) also became popular. True to the German traditions, Americans were now drinking their beer out of earthenware *steins* (German *steingut*, stonegoods, stonewear) and *seidels* (a German word, from Latin *situla*, bucket). The large American *schooner* (1877, perhaps from the type of ship, *schooner*) was also common and held a pint or more.

In the 1880s mechanical refrigeration made possible the cheap mass production and aging (storage) of lager. Increased production led to giant breweries and these encouraged the establishment of more and more saloons. The saloons competed with each other and *lunch* (meaning "free lunch" since 1844) became a main attraction. It had all begun with the serving of salty thirst-arousing food: originally popcorn was the free bar snack, then *pretzels* (1824, German *Prezel* or *Brezel*) which were also called *Brezels* or even *Wunder*, and finally salted nuts. The serving of such salty snacks had grown into *free lunch* in the West and moved East in the 1840s. Before the Civil War most men drank expensive whiskey and fancier saloons could afford to put out platters of cracked crabs, oysters, clams, sausages, sliced chicken, tongue, veal croquettes, etc., as well as herring, cheeses, hard-boiled eggs, and bowls of beef and terrapin stews. Now in the 1880s and 90s, free lunch was again featured, this time for one or two 5¢ beers, and the fare was usually simpler, but ample: salty ham and other cold cuts, herring, cheese, headcheese, chili, baked beans, slaw, potato salad, pickled tomatoes, pickles, and several kinds of bread.

Now, too, the saloons seemed full of children sent to get dad's beer or apprentices sent to get it for a work gang. They brought in their buckets, cans, or pitchers and called them *growlers* (perhaps because they made a growling, grating noise when slid across the bar). Fetching beer from a saloon in a growler was called *rushing the growler*, *working the growler*, or *chasing the can* from the late 1880s until Prohibition. It seemed that many men couldn't eat or work without their *bucket of suds* (1904), and many a man had a fat *beer belly* (early 1900s).

So saloons and the saloon business proliferated. Their noise, beery smell, and drunkenness led to the formation of the *Anti-Saloon League* in 1893 (see THE TEMPERANCE MOVEMENT), which, with anti-German feelings against the German-named brewers during World War I, was beer's contribution to the passage of Prohibition. Prohibition had Americans talking about such beers as *homebrew*, *near beer*, *3.2 beer*, *needle beer*, and *wildcat beer* (see PROHIBITION for more details on these beers). Prohibition had its effects—it helped break the saloon habit. More American men began to drink their beer at home; more and more beer was sold in bottles and less "on draft." Until 1875 all beer had been *draft beer* (Old English *dragan*, to draw, as from a spigot on a cask). The British still spell it *draught* but we spell it *draft*, thanks to one of Noah Webster's spelling reforms, which he first suggested in 1789. Draft beer was also called *shenkbeer* in the 1870s and 80s (German *shenkbier*). *Bottled beer* was first produced by Schlitz in 1875, giving us such terms as "a bottle of beer" and *beer bottle*.

"Rushing the growler."

An empty beer bottle has been called a *dead soldier* or *dead marine* since about World War I. In 1935 Coor's Ale gave us *canned beer* and by the end of World War II "a can of beer" and *beer can* were becoming common terms. Unlike draft beer, most bottled beer and canned beer is pasteurized, so it can be shipped and stored without refrigeration.

Today many beer words are disappearing—the names of local brands. After Prohibition 700 companies were making beer; in 1976, after consolidations and mergers, only 54 breweries existed. How long will we talk about Rhode Island's *Narragansett* or New York's and New Jersey's *Ballantine* now that St. Louis' *Falstaff* has bought them? of Washington State's *Olympia*, now owned by St. Paul's *Hamms;* of *Schmidt's*, now owned by *Blatz?* Today five large breweries make up "the big five": Anheuser Busch (*Budweiser* and *Michelob*), Joseph Schlitz, Pabst, Coors, and Miller.

A workingman's bar, with fans clustered around the radio to hear the latest score. Ladies sat in the back room.

How often do Americans talk about beer? No one knows. But we drink over 107 million barrels of it a year, 14 billion quarts. Though Belgians and Germans drink more per capita, we are the biggest beer-producing country in the world. Unlike the *Mayflower* Pilgrims, we're not about to run out of it.

The King James Bible

is what most Americans have meant when we've said *the Bible, the Holy Bible, the Scriptures,* or *the Good Book* (all originally English terms). Prepared by 54 churchmen appointed by King James I of England, it was named the *King James Version* or *Authorized Version* even before it was published in 1611, nine years before the Pilgrims landed. It was revised in 1870, with some American scholars contributing to it, and the new edition is called the *Revised Edition.*

Many early Americans not only lived by this Bible but read aloud from it, quoted it, and referred to it in conversation more often than we can imagine. Its words and cadences permeated American speech, and it is impossible to overemphasize how often Americans referred not only to God but to the biblical Creation, Adam and Eve, Cain and Abel, the Flood, Jonah, Job, and hundreds of other biblical passages, stories, images, and phrases.

In America the word *Bible* has appeared in many combinations including:

Bible society (for printing and disseminating the Bible), a concept originating in Germany in 1710, the term was first used in England in 1780 and the First American Bible Society established in 1816.

Bible class, 1824.

Bible agent, a door-to-door seller of Bibles, 1847.

to kiss the Bible, literally or figuratively to swear on the Bible, 1884.

Bible school, originally for Bible instruction of students during regular school vacation, 1901.

Gideon Bible, a Bible purchased by the *Gideons* and placed in hotel rooms, pullman cars, and other convenient places for travelers, early 1900s. *Gideon International* was founded as "a Christian organization of American commercial travelers" in 1898–99 and named after Gideon, the judge of Israel who won a spectacular victory with only 300 men after an angel of the Lord called him to free Israel from the Midianite oppressors (Judges 6:2).

Bible belt, H. L. Mencken's term for the South, about 1925.

Title page of the famous "The Bay Psalm Book," the first bound book to be printed in the colonies. The translators, about 30 local ministers, based their work on the King James Version, and its cadences affected New England speech for generations. Eleven copies are known to exist today.

Bicycle

An 1813 celeripede (Latin celer, quick, fast + pēs, pedis, foot), an early type of bicycle that the rider had to push with his feet, like a kiddie car.

(*bi,* two + Greek *kuklos,* wheel) came to America via the French in the 1780s—but as the name of a two-wheeled bench, or "horse," pushed along by the rider's feet! In the next 30 years steering bars were added and this kiddie-car device was also called a *scooter, swift walker, dandy,* and *hobby horse.*

The first true bicycle—the machine that could be ridden with both feet off the ground—was developed in 1839, but with the seat over, and the pedals on, the rear wheel! Finally, by 1870, the pedals and seat were attached to the large front wheel, which had a diameter of 40 to 54 inches, about four times that of the rear wheel. This bicycle was also called a *high wheeler,* an *ordinary,* or a *penny farthing,* and by 1880, *bike* and *wheel* (then referring to

A high wheeler varied in size according to the length of the rider's legs and the extent of his skill—both of which had to be considerable, especially during the thrills of an elopement! But the modern bicycle (below), comfortable and easy to ride, allowed ladies as well as gentlemen to enjoy bicycling.

the large front wheel). The bigger the front wheel the more efficient was each pedal stroke.

Finally, in 1884 the modern bicycle came into use. It had wheels of the same size and pedals attached to that ingenious device, a *bicycle chain.* To distinguish it from the unstable high wheeler it was dubbed the *safety bicycle.* In the next ten years, as it swept its earlier rivals from the path, it became simply the *bicycle.* In these ten years, too, radical improvements, such as rubber tires, *coaster brakes, adjustable handlebars,* and cushioned *saddles,* made bicycling a craze all could enjoy.

The *tandem* bicycle, or the *bicycle built for two,* was perfected in the early 1890s. Greatly popularized by the highly publicized Sunday rides of Diamond Jim Brady and Lillian Russell in New York's Central Park, it quickly led to the popularity of *bloomers,* a bicycle garb for women, consisting of short, full pants fastened at the knee, a real eye-catcher in the days of long skirts. However, *bloomers,* or *bloomer costumes,* had actually been around since 1851, when the feminist and reformer Amelia Jenks Bloomer (1818–94) adopted them.

Harry Dacre's song "Daisy Bell," popularly known as "A Bicycle Built for Two," swept the country in 1892 and was soon followed by such songs as the militant "The March of the Bloomers," the facetious "When Trilby Rides a Wheel," the liberated lover's "I Love You, Bicycle and All," and the mournful tribute to a woman returned to the fold in "Her Bloomers Are Camphored Away."

By 1900 the bicycle craze had died down and bicycles were relegated to children. *Bicycle* then became a word all American children associated with Christmas or a major birthday, a word expressing new freedom and growing up. In the 1960s, however, *bicycle* again became an adult word, as ecology minded, health minded Americans rediscovered its nonpolluting, non-gas-gobbling fun.

Billy the Kid

An old tintype of Billy the Kid.

(William H. Bonney, 1859–81) was known in his day for his big grin and cold-blooded killing. Since then, he's been talked about, sung about, danced about (the 1938 ballet *Billy the Kid* has a score by Aaron Copeland) as one of our most romanticized western BADMEN. Born in New York City and raised by his widowed mother in New Mexico and Colorado, he is said to have killed the first of his 21 men at the age of 12. He went on to rob and murder Indians, hire himself out as a cattle-war mercenary, and become a quick-shooting cattle rustler. Sheriff Pat Garret captured him in 1880, and after Billy had killed two deputies and escaped, tracked him down and shot him dead in Fort Sumner, New Mexico, the following year.

The Blacks

Black slaves were first brought to the Spanish colonies in the New World in 1516, exactly 91 years before the first English colonist landed at Jamestown, Virginia. The first 20 Black slaves were brought to Jamestown in 1619, a year before the *Mayflower* Pilgrims landed in Plymouth. Since then, when we have heard America talking we have heard Blacks talking; today we hear over 20 million American Blacks, over 10% of the population—the "we" is Black and White.

Like the Spanish, Dutch, Irish, Germans, Yiddish-speaking Jews, Italians, Swedes, etc., the Blacks have influenced the American language in two major ways: (1) by using many of their native (Black African) words and speech patterns and introducing some of them into our general speech, and (2) by causing, doing, being, influencing things that have had all America talking, often using terms created or popularized by the Black presence and experience in America (many such terms are scattered throughout this book, for example all the terms having to do with ABOLITION, THE CIVIL WAR, and RECONSTRUCTION have in a very real sense to do with Blacks in America, as does *Buffalo soldier* at THE BUFFALO, etc.).

African words and names have played a diverse role in the American language. The slaves came from scores of different African tribes and subtribes, speaking scores of different languages from several distinct language families (Bantu alone includes over 500 languages and dialects, of which Swahili is but one, and, incidentally, one which very few slaves spoke). If we had heard slaves talking in 1650 or 1750 we would have heard many African languages, many African words—generations of American slaves were never taught English, because some masters considered them but human cattle who needed to know only a few commands, while others preferred they not know a common language in which they might plan rebellions or waste time talking. Once the legal importation of slaves was stopped in 1808, however, the large influx of African-speaking slaves slowed and African words rapidly began to disappear. Nevertheless, as late as 1949, in his book *Africanisms in the Gullah Dialect*, Lorenzo Turner identified over 6,000 African words in the speech of Blacks of coastal South Carolina, Georgia, and northern Florida and on the Sea Islands (the speech of these Blacks is called Gullah, most of the words were personal names and had never entered general American speech).

The slaves, of course, introduced some African words directly into American English, but other African words have come to us by way of England, from slaves on the Caribbean islands, from Spanish, Portuguese, and Dutch traders, and, since the late 1960s, from modern American Blacks rediscovering their African heritage. The words and names we have taken from African languages include:

banana, first recorded as a West African word from the Congo region in 1563, entered English in the 17th century via Spanish and Portuguese (it may have come into Black African use from Arabic *banāna*, finger, toe).

banjo, probably from Kimbundu *mbanya*, "stringed instrument," which may have come from the *bandore*, an ancient guitarlike instrument which the Portuguese had taken to Africa. The word was brought to America by slaves from the West Indies, and from the 1740s to the 1830s was often pronounced and spelled as *banjil* and *banjor*.

buckra (from Efik and Ibibio *mbakara*, master) was used by slaves to refer to and address their master; by the 1730s slaves and colonists used it to mean "White man" and it was often pronounced and spelled *buccara* and *boccra;* by 1775 it was also used to mean "gentleman;" and as late as the 1860s came to mean the color white.

chigger (via the Caribbean *chigo* from the African Wolof *jiga*, insect), 1743. Originally we pronounced and spelled it *chego* or *chiego* and it meant not only a chigger but also a flea.

cooter (from a West African word *kuta* or the Kongo *nkuda*) a box turtle, 1832. The word came into our Southern dialect through Gullah and is mainly heard in Georgia and Alabama.

Cuffy was recognized by the colonists as a common Black male name in America by 1713, was often shortened to *Cuff* by the 1750s, and before the Civil War was used by Whites to refer to any Black man. It's from *Kofi*, a name given on the African Gold Coast to a boy born on Friday.

cush, cushie appeared in American English in 1770 as a name for a sweet fried cornmeal cake. It comes from Gullah *kush* or *kushkush* and is related to Arabic *kusha* and the stewed meat and grated grain stew known today as *couscous*.

dashiki (from Yoruba *danshiki*), a loose, usually colorfully patterned, buttonless pull-on shirt. The garment and the word were introduced to America during the Civil Rights movement of the 1960s when some young Black men began to wear it to reassert and identify with Black African culture.

goober (from Bantu *nguba*), 1834. Another word for peanut is *pinder* or *pindal* (from Kongo *npinda*), which was first recorded in Jamaica in 1707 and in South Carolina in 1848.

Gullah (probably from *Gola*, a tribe and language of Liberia, or *Ngola*, a tribe of Angola), referring to Blacks living on the Sea Islands and the coastal regions of South Carolina, Georgia, and northern Florida, and also used to refer to their language.

gumbo (via American French from Bantu *kingombo* and akin to Umbundu *ochinggombo*, okra), 1805, a soup made of okra pods, shrimp, and powdered sassafras leaves. *Gumbo filé*, 1823, gumbo made with pulverized okra (from French *filer*, to twist, hence *gumbo filé* literally means ropey or stringy gumbo). This word *gumbo* also came to mean any thick goo or mud by 1881.

juba, 1834, a group dance with complex rhythmic clapping and slapping of the knees and thighs, as done by plantation slaves. Both the dance and the word are of African origin.

juke (via Gullah from Wolof *dzug*, to misbehave, lead a disorderly life, and akin to Bambara *dzugu*, wicked), 1936, a brothel, cheap tavern, or low dive, mainly Black use in the South; *to juke*, 1939, to make the rounds of taverns and low dives, go drinking, mainly southern use. By the early 1940s *to juke* came to mean to make the rounds drinking and dancing to *juke boxes* (1939) at *juke joints* (1942, taverns or roadhouses featuring juke boxes).

okra (from a West African word for it, *nkruma*), known to most Southerners by the 1780s.

poor jo, *poor Job* (from Americanizing a Vai dialect word of Liberia and Sierra Leone), 1736, the great blue heron, mainly heard in Georgia.

Sambo was known to most colonists as a common Black male name by 1700 and many Whites were using it to refer to any Black man or boy by 1806. It's a Hausan, north Nigerian, word and name meaning "second son."

tote (probably from an African word *tota* or *tuta*, to pick up, carry, as used in the western Congo and Angola), first recorded in Virginia in 1677 and still considered part of our Southern dialect today. *Totebag*, 1960s.

voodoo, *zombie*, *gris-gris*. See the article Voodoo, Zombie, and Gris-Gris for these and related words.

yam (via Gullah *njam* or Spanish *ñame* from Sengal *nyami* or Vai *djambi*, both meaning "to eat"), first recorded in America in 1676.

Not being taught formal English, the early slaves soon developed their own patois of English and African words, pronunciations, syntax, tones, and speech rhythms (with some Spanish and French mixed in from the West Indies, Florida, and Louisiana). This patois was first noted in 1702 and called *nigger English*, then simply *nigger* by 1825. It included such African words as *buckra* and *tote* (see above), such pidginlike English words as *sickey-sickey* and *workee* (for *sick* and *work*), and such pronunciations and forms as *berry* for "very," *de*, *dis*, and *dat* for "the," "this," and "that" (giving us *Who dat?*), and *gen'men* for "gentlemen." It also simplified or dropped the use of some verbs, especially such auxiliary verbs as *can*, *have*, *may*, *must*, and *will*. Thus it might use *do* for *does* and *get* for *have/has* ("Do she gots a green dress?"), *be* for *is* ("It be rainin'," "He be right"), or drop the *be* form altogether ("It rainin'," "He right"). This slave patois was influenced by the White Southern dialect—but it also had a strong influence on this White Southern dialect, especially through the many Black *mammies* (a term of around 1800) who brought up so many White southerners.

As succeeding generations of Blacks received more formal schooling, mingled more freely with Whites, and moved to northern cities, this patois of English and African elements weakened and became a dialect, a Black speech pattern. Many people thought it merely an ungrammatical and sloppy use of standard English, some Whites even thought it demonstrated an inferior intelligence or that Blacks' speech organs were vastly different from Whites'.

I ain't never been to heaven but Ah been told,
Comin' fuh to carry me home,
Dat de streets in heaben am paved with gold,
Comin' fuh to carry me home.
"Swing Low, Sweet Chariot," which lyrics are an example of Black English, including the treatment of the verb "to be."

All the world is sad and dreary
Ev'ry where I roam,
Oh! darkies, how my heart
    grows weary,
Far from the old folks at
    home.
"Old Folks at Home,"
Stephen Foster, 1851.

But the truth is that this Black speech pattern, its pronunciations, syntax, grammar, tones, and rhythms, goes back to African languages and the slave patois: it's a true dialect, a speaking of English with an African "accent." Like other American ethnic dialects it has been a source of disparagement, humor, and local color. Such Black speech, especially as heard in the Gullah region and on Virginia plantations, became popular as the "Negro dialect" used in early American plays, Harriet Beecher Stowe's *Uncle Tom's Cabin*, Joel Chandler Harris' *Uncle Remus Stories*, minstrel shows, vaudeville, radio, and movies. In a purer form it's still strong in many Black communities, especially in the rural South and big city ghettos.

Today the syntax, grammar, uses, and pronunciations of this Black speech pattern is called *Black English*, a term made common among educators by Joey Lee Dillard's 1972 book *Black English*, which analyzes and explains it. Black English has given generations of Black students difficulties in school, but now that it is recognized as a true dialect it is more widely accepted. In fact, this Black speech pattern (and the large number of Spanish-speaking children in our schools) has led to the realization that standard (White) English need not be demanded of all Americans in all situations and has led to the teaching of standard "English as a second language." Black English and the African words listed above are the major influences the Black African heritage has had on our language. The rest of this article concerns words and names coming from the Black experience in America.

The Black experience in America starts with 244 years of slavery: there were 20 slaves in 1619, 500,000 in 1776 (half of them in Virginia and South Carolina), and 4 million when the Civil War began (plus some 300,000 free Blacks). During these 244 years many freedom-loving Americans preferred to call the slaves *negroes* or *blacks*—some even used the euphemistic word *servants*—rather than use the blunt word *slave*. Thus in the list below the earliest terms referring to slaves and slavery often contain the word *negro* (never capitalized during the slavery period) rather than *slave*. It was the abolitionists who insisted on calling a slave a slave: thus as the abolitionist movement grew in the 1830s many of our terms containing the word *slave* itself were first recorded. Also, by the 1830s slavery had become a big business, the cotton gin, improved cotton mills, the steamboat, and the railroad had made large plantations and their slaves much more profitable than before: thus slavery was becoming even more impersonal and cruel, increasing the use of the blunt word *slave* and giving us such terms as *cotton slave*, *slave auction*, *slave breeder*, and *slave pen*. The following is a list of some of the common terms we used for slaves and various aspects of slavery; that there are so many of them shows how much America talked about slaves, how large a role slavery played in American life.

> *blackbirder*, a ship, ship owner, or sailor illegally engaged in the Pacific slave trade, capturing *Kanakas* (1838, meaning South Sea Islanders, from Hawaiian *kanaka*, person, man) and taking them to Australia. *Blackbird*, a Kanaka slave, 1820s.
>
> *cotton slave*, 1860; *cotton black*, 1862.
>
> *dower negro*, 1760, a slave given with a bride as part of her dowery or owned by her at the time of marriage.
>
> *field slave*, 1782; *hoe negro*, 1783; *field darky*, 1854.
>
> *free papers*, 1838, a document given a freed slave attesting to his status. Two of the best known free Blacks were the astronomer, mathematician, and natural scientist Benjamin Banneker (1731–1806), who published a popular almanac from 1790 to 1802 and who helped survey and lay out the city of Washington, D.C., and the freed slave Sojourner Truth (1797–1883, slave name Isabella Baumfree), who traveled widely in the North preaching emancipation and women's rights.
>
> *fugitive slave* was an increasingly common term after the 1830s when conditions on the large plantations got worse and abolitionists increased their efforts to help slaves escape. It's a much older term, however, Congress having passed its first Fugitive Slave Act in 1793. The most talked-about fugitive slaves were Frederick Douglass (1817–95) and Harriet Tubman (1820–1913). Douglass escaped from slavery in 1837, became a well-known lecturer for anti-slavery societies, founded the abolitionist newspaper the *North Star* in 1847, and helped recruit Black troops during the Civil War, then became the U.S. minister to Haiti in 1889. The iron-willed field hand Harriet Tubman escaped via the underground railroad in 1849, then during the next ten years became the most talked-about and successful conductor on that railroad, making 19 dangerous trips back into the South to help 300 slaves escape to safety, including her own parents, then during the Civil War served Union troops in South Carolina as cook, laundress, nurse, guide, and spy.

house negro, 1711, a slave who worked in the master's house, considered superior to a field slave and receiving better food, clothing and treatment; *house gang*, 1792. One of the best-known house negroes was the African-born Phillis Wheatley (1753–84), who became known as a slave prodigy and poet while "maidservant" to Mrs. John Wheatley of Boston; she made a widely acclaimed visit to England in 1773, the same year that she was freed and that her volume *Poems on Various Subjects, Religious and Moral* was published.

the middle passage was the middle leg of a triangular trade route of 19th century sailing ships. On the first passage or leg of the voyage the ships sailed from New England with rum for the African Gold Coast, where the rum was traded for slaves; on *the middle passage* or second leg of the trip, the ships took the slaves (usually shackled in a sitting position throughout the entire voyage) from Africa to the West Indies and traded them for molasses and sugar; on the final passage of the triangular trip the molasses and sugar were brought back to New England to make more rum—and the cycle began all over again.

negro overseer, 1748; *slave driver*, 1807, and by 1840 used figuratively to mean any demanding, unfeeling employer, teacher, etc. *Nigger breaker*, 1845, a harsh overseer.

negro quarters, 1734; *slave quarters*, 1837. *Negro house*, 1735; *negro hut*, 1787; *negro cabin*, 1790, all referring to slave quarters.

negro thief, 1827; *nigger thief*, 1853, one who helped a slave escape.

negro trader, 1732; *slave trader*, 1830. *Nigger monger*, 1741; *nigger dealer*, 1853.

plantation negro, 1771; *plantation slave*, 1853; *plantation darky*, 1865.

to sell down the river, 1830s, to punish a slave by selling him to a sugar-cane plantation owner on the lower Mississippi, where slave conditions were the worst. By the 1880s the term was in general use to mean to take advantage of another, to treat another badly out of greed or selfishness.

slave is a 13th century English word, *slavery* a 14th century one. It's from *Sclavus*, Slav (the Slavs of central Europe were enslaved by Germans in the Middle Ages, hence Slav came to be our word *slave*).

slave auction, 1839; *auction block*, 1846; *auction stand*, 1848.

slave breeder, 1846, one who bred and reared slaves on a *slave rearing plantation*. That slaves were considered as cattle is also shown by such terms for them as *black cattle*, 1819, and *black stock*, 1861.

slave car, 1859, a railroad car for transporting shipments of slaves, being more of a boxcar or cattle car than a passenger coach.

slave catcher, 1765; *negro catcher*, 1853, one who pursued runaway slaves for the reward. *Negro dog*, 1845, a dog used to track runaway slaves.

slave codes, 18th century, laws dealing with the restrictions, punishment, and treatment of slaves. Slaves were forbidden to own property, to enter certain areas or buildings, to marry without their master's consent, and were punished severely for a wide variety of crimes, etc. The codes also often forbade anyone to teach a slave to read or write, to help a runaway slave, etc. Some slave codes also had humanitarian aspects, as requiring owners to feed their slaves some minimum amount of food and providing penalties for the willful murder or torture of slaves.

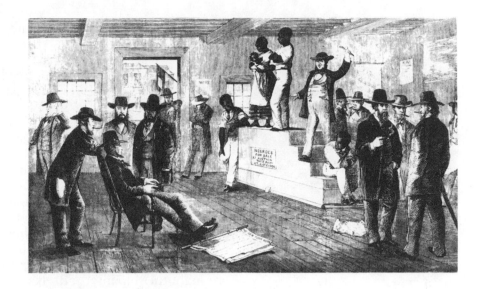

These codes were often called *black laws* or *black codes* by the 1840s, which led to the famous *Black Codes* of the Reconstruction period (see RECONSTRUCTION).

slave pen, 1835, an enclosure or shed for slaves awaiting sale; *slave warehouse*, *slave depot*, 1830s, where slaves were bought and sold.

slave property, 1810, land on which slaves were worked, as a large farm or plantation.

Slave insurrections (1619, the term was used the very first year slaves were brought to Jamestown) or *slave rebellions* (1777, when the British tried to incite them during the Revolutionary War) were widely feared and talked about in the South, and there were hundreds of such local rebellions. Slave ship owners and crews also feared them and there were several famous revolts aboard slave ships. The most talked-about such incidents were:

the Cato conspiracy, 1739, in which slaves at Stono, South Carolina, robbed a store for arms and set out for the Spanish territory of Florida, gathering recruits and killing Whites on the way until a hastily assembled White force stopped them. This "insurrection" took the lives of 44 Blacks and 30 Whites.

Gabriel's insurrection or *Gabriel's uprising*, 1801, in which the slave "General Gabriel" plotted with other slaves to attack Richmond, Virginia. Governor James Monroe was forewarned, called out the militia, and had the insurgents arrested, the leaders later being executed.

the Vesey Rebellion or *the Plot of Denmark Vesey*, 1822, in which Denmark Vesey, a "free negro," planned a slave insurrection in Charleston, South Carolina, but was betrayed and arrested along with 35 other Blacks, all of whom were tried and hanged.

Nat Turner's rebellion or *Nat Turner's revolt*, or *Nat Turner's Insurrection*, 1831. Nat Turner (1800–31) had been sold to a harsh master after having been instructed in reading, writing, and religion by his original owners, the Benjamin Turner family. He then had a vision of Black and White spirits in battle, became

37

Nat Turner was captured deep in the woods where he had hidden himself for six weeks.

a preacher among the slaves, and convinced many that he was divinely chosen to lead them from slavery. He received a "sign" that August 21, 1831, was the day of deliverance and, with seven other slaves, murdered his master's family, then with about 70 additional slaves marched toward Jerusalem (Virginia), killing 55 Whites on the way. The state militia and armed townsmen met and fought the "rebels," but Turner escaped and wasn't caught for six weeks, after which he and 16 of his companions were hanged. In all, some 100 Blacks were killed during the episode, some of whom had not even been among Turner's followers. This rebellion caused many southern states to pass laws further restricting slaves and efforts to educate them.

the Amistad case, 1839, in which a cargo of 54 slaves aboard the Spanish schooner *Amistad*, sailing from Cuba, staged a revolt under their leader Cinque, murdered the captain and three sailors and ordered the rest of the crew to sail to Africa. The sailors brought the ship into Long Island waters instead and the Blacks were imprisoned at New London, Connecticut. Abolitionists took up their cause and the Supreme Court freed these Blacks in 1841, on the grounds they had been kidnaped, and they were returned to Africa. This incident gave militant Blacks of the 1960s the cry of *Amistad!*, symbolic of revolt and freedom, and has provided several revolutionaries and urban guerrillas with the name *Cinque* (most notably Donald DeFreeze, leader of the Symbionese Liberation Army, the *SLA*, which kidnaped Patricia Hearst of the famous Hearst newspaper family in 1974).

the Creole Affair, 1841, in which the cargo of slaves aboard the American ship *Creole* overpowered the ship's officers, killed one crew member, and sailed to the Bahamas. The murderers were held for their crime but the British refused to return either the slaves or the ship to the United States, despite a loud uproar in the South (the British eventually paid a claim of over $110,000 to the U.S. for the slaves).

After the Civil War slavery was replaced by segregation and attempts to deny Blacks full civil rights. Thus slavery terms disappeared and such new terms as *White supremacy*, *Black Codes*, *the Ku Klux Klan*, and *night rider* appeared (see RECONSTRUCTION for these and other terms of the period). But in the 50 years between the Civil War and World War I Blacks made the transition from slaves to free men and began to fight for their full rights. In those first 50 years of attempts to suppress Blacks and of the Blacks' striving for full citizenship we used such terms and names as:

the Black Belt, 1875, the beltlike line through the South of the former slave states of Virginia, North Carolina, South Carolina, Georgia, Alabama, Arkansas, and Louisiana, heavily populated by Blacks.

civil rights, first used to mean the civil rights of Blacks in 1866, though many people called these *negro rights* until 1900. The term *civil rights*, and shortening it to *rights*, is old in English law, England having had a *Bill of Rights* since 1689, Virginia a state Bill of Rights since 1776, and the United States its Bill of Rights since 1791 (nine of these first ten amendments to the

Thomas D. Rice as "Jim Crow."

Constitution deal with civil rights). Congress passed the first *Civil Rights Bill* concerning Blacks in 1866 and other civil rights bills soon became the 14th and 15th amendments to the Constitution (in 1868 and 1870, respectively). See also *the Civil Rights Movement* in the list below.

Jim Crow became a very common term in the 1880s and 90s but goes back to the 1730s, which is when Blacks were first called *crows. Jim Crow* was first used to refer to any Black dances or jigs, and Blacks were said to "jump Jim Crow" when they performed them. Then in 1828 "the father of American minstrely," Thomas D. Rice, later known as "Jim Crow Rice," wrote the song "Jim Crow," which was widely sung and danced by Black performers and by White performers in blackface and contained the lines

> My name's Jim Crow,
> Walk about, and turn about,
> An' do jis so.

By the early 1830s this song had popularized the term *Jim Crow* so that it meant of, by, or for Blacks, as in "Jim Crow store" (a store catering to Blacks) or "Jim Crow pamphlet" (a religious or abolitionist pamphlet written by or for Blacks). By 1835 *Jim Crow* and *Jim Crowism* meant segregation of Blacks from Whites, giving us such later terms as *Jim Crow car* (1841, first used as a nickname for a "Black only" car on the Boston Railroad), *Jim Crow law* (1890s), and *Jim Crow school* (1903).

miscegenation (based on Latin *miscēre*, to mix, blend + *genus*, race) is said to have been coined by journalist David Goodman Croly, then managing editor of the *New York World*, in an anonymous pamphlet he wrote in 1863, *Miscegenation: The Theory of the Blending of the Races Applied to the American White Man and Negro.* By the 1870s Southerners were using the word in horror and calling any White who was even friendly to Blacks a *miscegenationist.*

mixed began to be used in 1863 to mean racially integrated (it's no coincidence that it and *miscegenation* both came into use the year Lincoln's Emancipation Proclamation went into effect). It was first used in the terms *mixed army units* and *mixed schools*, with the term *mixed marriage* appearing by the end of the 1860s.

the NAACP (the *N*ational *A*ssociation for the *A*dvancement of *C*olored *P*eople) has been called "the N-double-A C P" since its founding and often simply "the N-double-A" since the 1930s. It was founded in 1909 by Whites led by the crusader Mary White Overton, to obtain equal citizenship rights for Blacks through court actions and by arousing public opinion. Most Americans first began talking about it in 1915–16 when it led outraged Blacks in demonstrations against D. W. Griffith's movie *The Birth of a Nation*, which glorified the southern side in the Civil War and the Ku Klux Klan.

the National Urban League, better known simply as *the Urban League*, was founded in 1910 as a voluntary community service agency of civic, business, and religious leaders to eradicate racial discrimination, using research, negotiations, and conciliation to obtain equal opportunities and improved schooling and housing for Blacks.

W. E. B. Du Bois, 1918.

the Niagara Movement for racial equality was founded by Harvard Ph.D. and Atlanta University professor W. E. B. (William Edward Burghardt) du Bois in 1905 and merged with the NAACP in 1909. Du Bois then served as the NAACP's director of publicity and research until 1934, helping make the NAACP a predominantly Black and more militant organization. After World War II, W. E. B. Du Bois (1868–1963) became a Marxist and champion of the USSR, joining the Communist party in 1961, his communism leading to the naming of the Communist *Du Bois clubs.*

poll tax was first recorded in America in 1692. It refers not to voting polls but to the *poll* or head (Middle English *pol, polle*, head), hence is a *head tax*, a tax levied on persons rather than on property. In the late 1860s, to prevent the generally poor and uneducated Blacks from voting, southern states began making the paying of a poll tax or the passing of a complicated *literacy test* a requirement for all voters. By the 1890s all southern states had such discriminatory poll taxes. In 1964 the 24th Amendment to the Constitution finally forbade making the paying of a poll tax a requirement for voting in Federal elections, and in 1966 the Supreme Court ruled that the paying of such a tax could not be a requirement for voting in local elections.

grandfather clause, 1898. Since poll taxes and literacy tests also kept poor and uneducated Whites from voting, some southern states added clauses to their laws exempting from their poll-tax and literacy-test voting requirements those persons who themselves, or whose father or grandfather, had had the right to vote before the Civil War (naturally no Black slaves had had that right). The reference to "grandfather" in such clauses gave them the name *grandfather clauses.*

race had been used to refer to genetic groups since the 16th century, with the word *racial* not appearing in English until the 19th century. After the Civil War, Americans stopped talking about slaves and began talking about the *black race* or the *negro race*, and between the late 1860s and 1880 the terms *racism, race conflict, race issue, race prejudice, race problem*, and *race question* were first used.

Race riot entered our language in 1865, when almost 300 people were killed in various riots over the Blacks' right to vote, the most bitter riots taking place in New Orleans and Memphis. The term was first widely used, however, to refer to the week-long race riot in East St. Louis in 1917, and then became very widespread when there were race riots in 23 cities in 1919, the year after World War I ended, the major riot that year being the Chicago one in which 38 people were killed and 500 injured (many Blacks had first moved to large industrial cities during the war). See also *the long hot summer* in the list below.

segregation (a 16th century English word meaning separation from a group, from Latin *sēgregāre*, to separate from the flock, *sē*, apart + *grex/greg-*, flock) was first used in a racial sense in 1881 and *discrimination* (a 17th century English word meaning distinguishing, differentiation) was first used in a racial sense in 1883. They came into wide use after 1883, the year the Supreme Court considered a series of five Civil Rights cases and ruled that it was not against the Constitution to deprive another person

Nat Love, a Black cowboy, 1880s. His superior marksmanship earned him the sobriquet "Deadeye Dick."

of accommodations if an equal one existed for his use and that the government had no jurisdiction over social discrimination practiced by individuals—these rulings then leading to a vast increase in segregation and discrimination in the 1880s and 90s.

separate but equal. In the famous *Plessy v Ferguson* case in 1896 the Supreme Court upheld southern segregation practices by ruling that a Louisiana statute requiring railroads to provide "equal but separate accommodations for the white and colored races" did not violate the 14th Amendment (giving full citizenship rights to Blacks, in 1868). This decision plus the Court's five Civil Rights rulings in 1883 (see *segregation* above) led to the *separate but equal* phrase used to define and justify segregation until 1954 (see *with all deliberate speed* in the list below).

the Universal Negro Improvement Association (the *UNIA*), whose full name was the Universal Negro Improvement and Conservation Association and African Communities League, was founded by Marcus Garvey (1887–1940) in his native Jamaica in 1914. Garvey came to the U.S. in 1916, proclaiming the honor of being Black, the futility of seeking justice for Blacks in a White world, and the necessity for leading the Blacks back to Africa, enlarging on these themes in his UNIA newspaper, the *Negro World*, which he founded in 1919.

The *Back to Africa Movement*, to resettle Blacks in Liberia, was officially announced by Garvey in 1920, to the 25,000 delegates from 25 nations who attended his international UNIA convention at Harlem's Liberty Hall, where he also urged Blacks to accept a Black deity and expounded on Black history and rights. Garvey and his movement, by then called *Garveyism*, had 500,000 followers in 1923, but in 1924 the Liberian government rejected his plans for resettlement (fearing he and his followers would take over the country), and in 1925 he was convicted of mail fraud in the selling to his UNIA members stock in his bankrupt *Black Star Steamship Lines* (President Coolidge commuted his sentence in 1927 and he was deported back to Jamaica).

uppity, 1885, White southern use to describe Blacks who didn't "know their place" or acted as equals (most southern Whites then considered a Black "uppity" if he didn't step off the sidewalk to let a White pass).

Picking cotton in Alabama, 1930s.

In the years between World War I and World War II Whites saw Blacks mainly as stereotypes. Though we had heard of some Black cowboys, editors, soldiers, businessmen, educators, and scientists (mainly Booker T. Washington and George Washington Carver), they were the exceptions who proved the rule, the salve to White conscience showing that anyone could succeed in America if he really tried. Whites saw Blacks mainly as sharecroppers, maids, cooks, waiters, and porters—and they were stereotypes, often stemming from either the stereotypes of the woolly-headed Uncle Toms or of the mean Black fugitives of slavery days. Blacks were seen and talked about as slow-moving, watermelon-eating comic figures who rolled their eyes and said "Who dat?" and "Sho 'nuf"; as happy-go-lucky, superstitious children whom we let grow cotton, clean house, and carry our food and suitcases while they said "Yas sir, boss"; and as sullen "Black bucks" who came alive on Saturday night to live the sporting life, drink whiskey, shoot craps, fight with knives, and lust after White women. And overall was the White conviction that all Blacks "have rhythm." Ever since some slaves "jumped Jim Crow" jigs in the 1730s and performed the juba dance on plantations we had said Blacks had rhythm. Minstrel shows had begun in the 1840s and as time went on we associated Blacks with such new music and words as the *spiritual* (1866), *the blues* (1870), *ragtime* (1896), *jazz* (see THE ROARING 20s for details), *boogie woogie* (1920s, see *boogie* below), *jive* (1930s) and *soul music* (1950s, see *soul* in the following list).

Booker T. Washington (1856–1915) and (bottom) George Washington Carver (1864–1943) were the first two educated Blacks most Americans, White or Black, ever heard of. It was their work at Alabama's Tuskegee Institute that made them both famous. Washington was born a slave, Carver of slave parents; both worked their way through school. Washington opened the Tuskegee Institute in 1889 at first to prepare students for farm and factory jobs and for domestic service; later Tuskegee grew into a training center for the trades and professions. Carver's research at Tuskegee on peanuts, soybeans, and the sweet potato was so successful it helped end the South's dependence on a single crop—cotton.

Jitterbugging in Harlem, 1939

Rural life in the 30s was hard and unexciting; hundreds of thousands of Blacks left the South for northern cities where their presence made a deep impact on national life.

Bill "Bojangles" Robinson (1878–1949), dancer, 1935.

Louis "Satchmo" Armstrong (1900–71), jazz musician, singer, band leader.

All these stereotypes reached full flower in the 1920s and 30s. A half million southern rural Blacks had immigrated to northern industrial cities in search of wartime jobs during World War I, and many northern city people saw large numbers of Blacks for the first time (see *race riot* above). The Black neighborhoods known as *darktowns* (1884) mushroomed into ghettos, though some light-complected Blacks who came to the cities where they were unknown tried *to pass* (a 1920s term). These new Blacks in the northern cities after World War I made all Blacks, rural and urban, a topic of White conversation, a part of life and entertainment, a topic for plays and books. We saw and talked about Eugene O'Neill's *The Emperor Jones* in 1920 (Paul Robeson played the lead in 1923), Marc Connelly's *The Green Pastures* in 1930 (based on Roark Bradford's 1928 collection of stories *Ol' Man Adam an' His Chillun*), and George Gershwin's folk opera *Porgy and Bess* in 1935 (taken from DuBose Heyward's 1915 novel *Porgy* and his own 1927 play based on it). At the same time there were such all-Black Broadway productions as the 1921 *Shuffle Along*, the 1929 *Blackbirds*, and the 1931 *Rhapsody in Black*, featuring such performers as Josephine Baker, Ethel Waters, and Bill "Bojangles" Robinson.

Now too in the 1920s and 30s Harlem became the symbol of Black city life (a new concept and one which changed the Black image and language in America completely). Whites descended from *Sugar Hill* (the bluffs overlooking the west side of Harlem and where rich Whites with lots of "sugar" lived, *sugar* being a slang word for money since 1859) or went *uptown* to Harlem, to see and hear the *black and tan* shows. They went to such nightclubs as the Cotton Club to hear Cab Calloway, Count Basie, Duke Ellington, Louis Armstrong, etc. Such shows and such musicians were what the word "Black" meant to many Whites. And this image wasn't all bad, we did see some Blacks who weren't sharecroppers or porters, who weren't poor or comic parodies.

The famous Apollo Theater on West 125th Street, New York City, in Harlem. It was featuring the "4 Ink Spots."

Adam Clayton Powell, Jr. (1908–72), a flamboyant Black leader from Harlem, was first elected to Congress in 1945 and served for 25 years. Though barred from Congress for, in part, misuse of funds, he was overwhelmingly returned in special elections in 1967 and 68.

We also talked about the famous Hurtig and Seamon's burlesque house on Harlem's West 125th Street, which Frank Schiffman took over in 1934 and renamed *the Apollo Theater*, where only Blacks could perform and which featured Wednesday amateur nights, introducing the likes of Ella Fitzgerald. Also in the Black ghettos in the 1930s and 40s the stereotype of the grandiloquently chanting but slyly immoral rural southern preacher emerged in city garb and Whites talked with condescending amusement of the Black "folk religions." Mainly we talked of Father Devine (George Baker of Georgia) and his Kingdom of Peace Movement with its message "Peace, It's Wonderful." And finally in Harlem before the Civil Rights movement of the 1950s and 60s, we talked of the minister and long-time Congressman Adam Clayton Powell.

The Black stereotypes continued in vaudeville, radio, and the movies between the two world wars. We all talked about Pick and Pat, Step 'n Fetchit, *Amos 'n Andy* (a White radio show), and Eddie Anderson as Jack Benny's straight man and comic valet "Rochester." But as World War II approached, and especially during and after the war, some Blacks began to emerge as individuals—even though they were usually in the fields of music and sports. Jesse Owens was an individual when he drove Adolph Hitler and his theory of "the master race" out of the stadium by winning four gold medals in the 1936 Olympic games in Berlin. And even though we called Joe Louis "the Brown Bomber" and often spoke of him as "a credit to his race," he was known to us as an individual during his long reign as heavyweight champion (1937–49). In 1947 Jackie Robinson became the first Black in major league baseball, in 1948 Ralph Bunche became a United Nations hero, and in the late 1940s and 50s Black entertainers such as Lena Horne and Sammy Davis, Jr., were considered individuals, individual entertainers and not Black stereotypes.

But the stereotypes and the few Black individuals merely kept us from thinking about and talking about what was really the major truth between the wars. Blacks were being lynched, segregated, humiliated, given the lowest paying jobs and the worst housing and schooling—there were a few stereotypes and Black heroes and stars we all knew and talked about, but millions of Blacks were being segregated and humiliated every day. Then suddenly, or so it seemed to Whites, the Blacks seemed to demand their rights and to demand respect for being human beings and for being Black. "Sho 'nuf," "Who dat?," and "Yas sir, boss" were replaced by *Black Power!*, *sit-in*, and *Tell it like it is* (see below). The Civil Rights movement of the 1950s and 60s had begun. A large new group of names and terms burst upon us. As the news media covered Black protest demonstrations and as young White protestors adopted Black words as being antiestablishment, down-

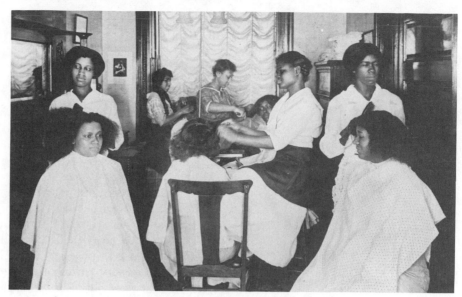

A Black beauty parlor, about 1919. Before the Afro many Black women copied White hair styles.

to-earth, and slangy it almost seemed as if the whole country was trying to assume the Black vocabulary, personality, and attitudes. Among some White groups, using the latest Black protest terms even became chic. But we all talked about the new Civil Rights movement and used some of its names, words, and slogans, including:

the Afro, also called *the Natural,* a forward-combed, sometimes very bushy, hair style for both men and women, was introduced during the Civil Rights movement in the late 1960s, when some young Blacks began to wear it as a badge of Black pride and African identity. It has been followed by a variety of African hair styles, including the *cornrow,* rows of small flat braids separated by half-inch parts.

Such styles were also a reaction against the years Blacks had copied White standards of beauty, especially in trying to straighten their hair. American Blacks had begun to talk about *hair straighteners* in the 1880s and the *permanent straight* in 1905 (invented by St. Louis laundress Mrs. Annie Malone and so popular it made her America's first self-made millionairess). Blacks also talked about *processed hair* (straightened with oil and a hot comb) and ways to *conk* their hair (treating it with lye preparations and a hot comb). One's *conk* (which had been slang for head since 1870) or processed hair was often covered with a protective *do-rag,* which is why Black militants of the 1960s called subservient Blacks *handkerchief heads.* Talk of special hair treatments and also of skin treatments and cosmetics to lighten the complexion subsided in the 1960s with the new "Black is Beautiful" pride in being Black and in the Black heritage.

Black took on a new connotation of self-respect and pride to American Blacks during the Civil Rights movement of the 1960s. Thus *Black* replaced *Negro* as the preferred noun and adjective (see the following list of names for Blacks) and we had such newly popular terms as *Black English, Black History, Black Studies* (a course or class in the history and culture of the Blacks), and *Black theater* (plays about Black life performed by and for Blacks).

45

Jack [John Arthur] Johnson (1878–1946), boxer, first Black heavyweight champion of the world, 1910–15.

Black is Beautiful, a slogan of the new Black pride and self-awareness of the 1960s. It probably comes from the Song of Solomon I, 1

I am black but beautiful

in the Douay version of the Old Testament (Solomon's Canticle of Canticles).

the Black Muslims. The Nation of Islam was founded by Wali Farad, who claimed to be the reincarnation of Allah, in Detroit in 1931. After his mysterious disappearance in 1934 his assistant Elijah Muhammad, formerly Robert Poole, was named "Messenger of Allah" and became head of the organization, spreading the belief that Christianity was but a tool of White oppression and that the Blacks would one day rule the world. Using some of the philosophy of Marcus Garvey (see *the United Negro Improvement Association* above), Elijah Muhammad developed the intricately structured, prosperous "Black Muslim" religious and political movement (it is not recognized by the Moslems). Now, with headquarters at *Mosque Number One* in Chicago, it asks members to contribute 10% of their income to the group, sponsors Muslim-owned businesses, runs highly disciplined schools teaching the Muslim religion and Black pride, and advocates complete separation of the races in America, wanting from one to four states set apart where Blacks can live in a "Black nation" free of the "White devils" or "slave masters."

> *the Fruit of Islam*, the Black Muslim paramilitary security guard, serving as a bodyguard for Muslim leaders and as police at Muslim gatherings. Some people also use the term to refer to all Black Muslims.

> *Islamic name.* In 1931 Robert Poole discarded his "slave name" and was given the "Islamic name" of Karriem, later being renamed Elijah Muhammad to indicate his position of leadership. Such name changes became a Black Muslim tradition, with heavyweight boxing champion Cassius Clay becoming Muhammad Ali, basketball player Lew Alcindor becoming Kareem Abdul-Jabbar, and playwright LeRoi Jones becoming Imamu Amiri Baraka. Other Muslims replace their last names with *X*, Malcolm Little becoming Malcolm X, other Malcolms in his group would then become Malcolm 2X, Malcolm 3X, etc.

> *Kwanza Festival* (*Kwanza* is from a Swahili word meaning "first fruits"), a festival, often featuring a parade, held in some Black communities annually to celebrate Black culture and the Black heritage, originally popularized by the Black Muslims.

> *the Organization of Afro-American Unity.* Most White Americans first began talking about the Black Muslims in 1964 when Elijah Muhammad suspended its "National Minister," the eloquent and charismatic Malcolm X, formerly Malcolm Little, who had become a convert while in prison. Malcolm X then formed his own Organization of Afro-American Unity, urging *black nationalism* for all oppressed non-White peoples in the world, before being assassinated in 1965, amid talk of a power struggle in the Black Muslim movement.

the Black Panthers. The Black Panther Party was founded as a revolutionary group by Huey P. Newton and Bobby Seale in Oakland, California, October 15, 1966, its members originally displaying guns in its policy of protecting Blacks and Black rights through "armed self-defense." Americans first started talking about the group in 1967 when the militant, often violent, speeches of its Minister of Information, Eldridge Cleaver, and its honorary Prime Minister, SNCC's 26-year-old Stokely Carmichael, made headlines.

Black power! James Meredith, the first Black to integrate the University of Mississippi (in 1962), was shot and wounded on June 6, 1966, during his Civil Rights walk from Tennessee to Jackson, Mississippi. A thousand SCLC, CORE, and SNCC members then continued his march, on which Stokely Carmichael's SNCC contingent first used the shout "Black power!" It immediately became a SNCC slogan and was adopted as a slogan and policy by CORE in July. Most Whites heard the phrase as a threat of violence, moderate Black groups such as the NAACP and the Urban League disavowed it, and others claimed it only meant the power of Blacks to change society and their own lives through political and economic means.

blood brother, late 1960s; *blood*, early 1970s, a fellow Black, especially one with Black pride and modern attitudes. *Brother* has been used for centuries to mean a fellow member of one's race, religious group, lodge, etc.

the Civil Rights movement, mid 1950s, refers to the movement to gain full citizenship rights and complete equality for Blacks in all phases of our national life, social, political, and economic, while giving Blacks full human dignity and pride in their race and African heritage. The term became most common in the 1960s, when it was associated with such groups as *CORE, SCLC,* and *SNCC* (see below) and with such leaders as Martin Luther King, James Farmer, Stokely Carmichael, and Eldridge Cleaver.

The movement had germinated after World War II when Black veterans who had risked their lives for America felt it owed them the same jobs, housing, and educational opportunities it did White veterans, and when postwar prosperity raised everyone's expectations, Black and White. It actually began with the 1954 *Brown v Board of Education* public-school desegregation ruling of the Supreme Court (see *with all deliberate speed* below) and made many of its legal and political gains while Chief Justice Earl Warren headed the Supreme Court (1953-69), during the administrations of Presidents Eisenhower, Kennedy, and Johnson. Thus in 1957 Congress passed its first Civil Rights legislation since Reconstruction and in the next eight years ordered desegregation of the armed forces (1957), outlawed segregation in public accommodations and facilities and prohibited racial discrimination by employers and unions (the Civil Rights Act of 1964), outlawed the paying of a poll tax as a requisite for voting in federal elections (the 24th Amendment to the Constitution, 1964), and provided for the suspension of unfair literacy tests as a requisite for registering to vote (the Voting Rights Act of 1965).

However, the most obvious advances were made on the local level as Blacks tried to obtain their rights and equality in schools, buses, lunch counters, local governments, etc. The major advance may well have been the change in long-held attitudes about Blacks by both Blacks and Whites.

CORE (an acronym for the *Congress of Racial Equality*) was founded in 1942 to carry out nonviolent "direct action" to end racial discrimination (in the early 1960s, when he was CORE's national director, James Farmer, one of its founders, defined "direct action" as "picketing, boycotts, demonstrations, and sit ins"). It was the first militant Civil Rights group, leading the way into the Civil Rights movement of the 1950s and 60s, and conducted the first *freedom rides* (see below).

the (dirty) dozens, joinin', sounding were all originally used to refer to a quasi-ritualized Black verbal insult game in which streams of insulting words and rhyming chants were used as weapons. In the 1960s the terms came to refer to any violent verbal attack against the White establishment or those who did not support the Civil Rights movement.

equal rights was used in 1867 to refer to woman's rights but not until the early 1940s was it widely used to refer to equal rights for Blacks.

freedom march and *Freedom now!* Early in March, 1965, segregationist governor George Wallace's state troopers used clubs, tear gas, whips, and electric *cattle prods* to disperse Civil Rights demonstrators marching to the state capital at Montgomery to protest voting restrictions against Blacks. In response, on March 21–25, the Reverend Dr. Martin Luther King, Jr., and many other Civil Rights leaders led some 3,000 people in a 50-mile march from Selma to Montgomery (where 25,000 more Civil Rights demonstrators were waiting) to present a petition to Governor Wallace. The petition began:

> We have come to you, the Governor of Alabama, to declare that we must have our freedom now. We must have the right to vote; we must have equal protection of the law, and an end to police brutality. . . .

Because of the wording of this petition this march was known as *the Freedom March*, subsequent marches for Civil Rights then becoming generally known as *freedom marches*. The wording of the petition also made *Freedom now!* a slogan of the Civil Rights movement.

freedom ride and *freedom rider*. In the summer of 1961 CORE broadened the efforts of local Black students who had been conducting *sit-ins* (see below) in the South by chartering buses and having its Black and White volunteers ride through Alabama and other southern states demanding the right to eat at any public eating place and to use any public facilities, concentrating on interstate bus terminals. CORE called these bus trips *freedom rides*, the volunteers on them *freedom riders*, and the buses *freedom buses*. Such demonstrations against and testing of local segregation laws caused the Interstate Commerce Commission, in September, 1961, to order desegregation of all bus terminals serving interstate routes and the Justice Department to order desegregation of public transportation.

Later in the 1960s *freedom ride* and *freedom rider* were used merely to refer to trips and riders on chartered buses to attend Civil Rights rallies and demonstrations in the South.

Signs pointing to segregated public facilities, Memphis, Tennessee, 1943.

the long hot summer was used in 1967 to refer to that summer and its riots in the Black ghettos (there were major riots in 18 cities that summer, including a week-long one in Detroit in which 38 people were killed and $200 million worth of property damage was done, and a six-day riot in Newark). The term comes from *The Long, Hot Summer*, a 1958 movie based on William Faulkner short stories (the title being one of his phrases), and it then became the title of a TV network show in 1965–66—thus it was well-known before the riots of 1967.

In 1964 *riot* came to mean a riot of Blacks attacking police and burning and looting in the ghettos; by 1965 such riots were sometimes euphemistically referred to as *racial violence*. The first of these riots of the 1960s occurred in New York's Harlem, July 18, 1964, following a CORE rally protesting the shooting of a Black youth by a White policeman, and was followed by riots in Brooklyn's Bedford-Stuyvesant, in Rochester, New York, and in Philadelphia and Chicago. The largest such riot occurred the following summer, in Los Angeles, August 12–17, 1965, this one being simply referred to as *Watts*, starting in that Black section of the city when White policemen arrested a drunken Black driver. The Watts burning and looting spilled over into nearby areas, 34 people were killed, over 1,000 injured, 3,000 arrested, and entire city blocks burned down, giving a few extremists the slogan "Burn, Baby, burn!" Thus the riots in the summers of 1964 and 65 set the stage for the long, hot summer of 1967—and what many Americans talked about in the summers was their fear of new riots.

nitty-gritty became a fad term in 1963, meaning the hard facts or essentials of a situation, a synonym for the 1900 *brass tacks*. It came from the Black militants' "let's get down to the nitty gritty," meaning let's get down to the hard facts or hard bargaining, let's face harsh reality. It may have originally referred to the gritlike nits (small lice) that are so hard to get out of one's hair and scalp, well-known to ghetto dwellers and poor southern rural people who seldom enjoyed hot running water and proper bathing facilities.

Oreo, late 1960s, a derogatory word for a Black who seems to share White attitudes and culture rather than Black ones. It comes from the Nabisco company's trademark *Oreo* for its cream-filled chocolate cookie, which is black on the outside and white on the inside. The term was too cute to be used widely in the Civil Rights movement but caught the fancy of White liberals and writers, who used it as a synonym for *Uncle Tom* (see Abolition).

rap has meant a rebuke or blame in English since 1733 and has been used as a verb in America, meaning to rebuke or criticize, since 1923 (to *take the rap*, take the blame, and *not give a rap*, not give a damn, date from the 1880s). During the 1960s *to rap* was first used by Blacks to mean to criticize Whites or to demand Black rights, then was widely used to mean "to talk," this use then quickly spreading to White youths (its popularity was aided by the nickname of H. "Rap" Brown, SNCC leader after 1966). The much older Black terms *to bad mouth*, insult, criticize, and *to sweet mouth*, flatter, compliment, may have originated in the American South but it has been suggested that they came to us

Rev. Dr. Martin Luther King making his famous "I have a dream. . . ." speech.

I say to you today . . . that in spite of the difficulties and frustrations of the moment I still have a dream. . . .

I have a dream that one day on the red hills of Georgia the sons of former slaves and the sons of former slave owners will be able to sit down together at the table of brotherhood. . . .

I have a dream that my four little children will one day live in a nation where they will not be judged by the color of their skin. . . .

I have a dream. . . .

The Reverend Dr. Martin Luther King, Jr., speaking in front of the Lincoln Memorial to Civil Rights demonstrators as the climax to the "March on Washington," August 28, 1963. Over 200,000 people attended this largest protest rally in the history of the U.S.

from the English-speaking Blacks of the British West Indies (who may also have given us our use of "man" as a form of direct address, both at the beginning of and sprinkled throughout sentences).

the SCLC (Southern Christian Leadership Conference) was founded by the Reverend Dr. Martin Luther King, Jr., in 1957 to seek "full citizenship rights, equality, and the integration of the Negro in all aspects of American life." It used his Ghandi-inspired *passive resistance* and *nonviolent mass protests* in its demonstrations—SCLC's and Dr. King's major influences on the Civil Rights movement of the 1950s and 60s may well have been to keep it nonviolent (such Civil Rights methods as the *sit-in* were obviously nonviolent mass protests) and to attract older, non-militant Blacks and Whites to the cause.

The Reverend Dr. Martin Luther King, Jr. (1929–68) had first gained national prominence in the Civil Rights movement when, as the newly installed pastor of the Dexter Avenue Baptist Church in Montgomery, Alabama, he was put in charge of the *Montgomery bus boycott* challenging the local bus segregation ordinance (the Black boycott began after Mrs. Rosa Parks was arrested on December 1, 1955 for refusing to give up her seat to a White man—235 days later the city was forced to desegregate its bus line, the Supreme Court having ruled that laws requiring the separation of the races on buses operating within a city were unconstitutional). Dr. King then formed the SCLC and built up the Civil Rights movement in the late 1950s and 60s, becoming its major figure, continuing his insistence on nonviolence despite being jailed, stoned, and beaten, and having his house bombed by segregationists, and contributed his leadership to the famous *Freedom March* (see above) and major protests and demonstrations from Birmingham to Washington, D.C., winning the Nobel Peace Prize in 1964. He was assassinated in Memphis, Tennessee, April 4, 1968, which date has been made an official holiday, *Martin Luther King Day*, in many states.

sit-in, CORE actually conducted the first sit-in at Stoner's restaurant in Chicago in the 1940s—but it wasn't called a sit-in at the time and gained no national attention. On February 1, 1960, four local Black college students in Greensboro, North Carolina refused to vacate their seats at Woolworth's "White only" lunch counter when they were refused service and asked to leave. The idea spread to other Black college students throughout the state, then was taken up elsewhere, with CORE's *freedom riders* (see above) popularizing the term *sit-in* during their 1961 freedom rides through the South, conducting sit-ins at eating places, bus stations, and other public facilities. The purpose of the sit-in was not only to disrupt the service at segregated places but to have the demonstrators arrested so laws and customs supporting segregation could be tested and fought in court.

Sit-ins were not limited to restaurant seats: Blacks and Whites could and did sit in "White only" and "Black" train- and bus-station waiting rooms and restrooms, beaches, segregated sections of theaters and movie houses, the lobbies of restricted hotels, etc. Sit-ins could be used to protest other things besides segregation, with students occupying college buildings and government offices to protest everything from college regulations to the Vietnam war. The popularity of *sit-in* in 1961 soon led to other types of "-ins," demonstrations on the premises, as *kneel-ins* and *pray-ins* for Civil Rights in churches, *play-ins* and *swim-ins* at segregated playgrounds and swimming pools, *teach-ins* to protest the Vietnam war in college classrooms, *fish-ins* on Indian reservations to protest infringement of Indian fishing rights, etc. There were so many "-ins" that by the late 1960s "-in" came to mean any rally or even a group activity or party, as the *love-in* rally in favor of peace and love and the *be-in* in which the participants provided or were their own entertainment. Incidentally, *to sit in* as a player in a card game was first recorded in English in 1599.

SNCC (pronounced as an acronym "snick," the *S*tudent *N*onviolent *C*o-ordinating *C*ommittee) was founded on college campuses in 1960 to fight to end racial segregation by nonviolent "direct action" (see *CORE* above for this phrase) and became the major student group in the Civil Rights movement. By 1964 it had 540 volunteers, including 150 lawyers and law students, working in Mississippi registering Black voters and operating *Freedom Schools*, which taught voter registration skills and Black history.

The summer of 1964 was in many ways the peak of the youthful Civil Rights effort in the South, with students from many groups working on voter registration drives, organizing Black groups and farmers' cooperatives, working against segregation and discrimination on all fronts. Southern segregationists resisted the "invasion" of the college students and all America talked of the three White Civil Rights workers, James Chaney, Andrew Goodman, and Michael Schwerner who were arrested, released, and killed on June 21 in Mississippi, and of the floggings, beatings, and shootings of others. In 1967, after H. "Rap" Brown had replaced Stokely Carmichael as the leader of SNCC, the group disavowed nonviolence.

soul, 1962, meaning of, by, or for Blacks and the basic, unique Black feelings and attitudes. It came from the 1950s term *soul music*, a synonym for the popular, soulful, Black *rhythm and blues* music, then became well known in King Curtis's 1962 song "Soul Twist."

> *soul brother*, a fellow Black, especially one displaying deep Black feelings and attitudes. The term first came to nationwide attention during the six-day Newark, New Jersey riot of 1967, when Black shopkeepers wrote "Soul Brother" on their windows, hoping the rioters would leave Black owned or operated stores unmolested. *Soul sister*, 1967.

> *soul food*, early 1960s, being the "down home" food associated with poor southern Blacks, Black ethnic dishes often stem from slavery days when slaves were given the cheapest southern staples and the food parts discarded by the plantation owners, to which they added greens they had grown themselves or picked wild—and a touch of African cooking. It includes *beet greens, collard greens, dandelion greens* (a term first recorded in 1887), *poke greens,* and *turnip greens; black-eyed peas* (1738, they were brought by

---

We shall end Jim Crow some day, some day;
Oh, deep in my heart, I know that I do believe
We shall end Jim Crow some day.
We shall overcome, we shall overcome,
We shall overcome some day, some day;
Oh, deep in my heart, I know that I do believe
We shall overcome some day.
"We Shall Overcome," set to an old Baptist hymn by folk singer Pete Seeger in 1955. It became the anthem of the Civil Rights movement of the 1950s and 60s.

Thurgood Marshall, the first Black U.S. Solicitor General and the first Black Justice of the Supreme Court, 1967.

slave traders from Africa to Jamaica in 1674 and from there to the American colonies); *hog maw* (stomach), *hog jowl* (an 1846 term, also called *jowl meat*), *trotters* (pigs' feet), and *ham hocks; sweet potato pie* (an 1829 term); and such ubiquitous southern favorites as corn bread, fried chicken, and watermelon. The new Black awareness and pride made soul food something of a fad by the late 1960s, and both Blacks and Whites were talking about the new *soul food restaurants.* Incidentally, the Black Muslims prohibit the eating of such food, calling it "slave food."

Tell it like it is!, 1965, a Civil Rights shout of encouragement and approval to speakers at demonstrations. It was replaced by *Right on!* in 1967, which then became a general term meaning "you're absolutely right, you tell 'em."

tokenism, 1963, employing or admitting a few Blacks to satisfy demands for total integration, as in offices, colleges, etc., hence a false show of integration.

white backlash, 1964, originally just as *backlash*, 1963, referring to the lashing back by some Whites against the Civil Rights movement. *White backlash* became a common term in the presidential election campaign of 1964, newspaper writers predicting that some White voters would vote against President Johnson because his administration had passed Civil Rights measures and would vote instead for the Republican candidate Barry Goldwater who, as a senator, had criticized special legislation for Blacks and had voted against the Civil Rights Act of 1964. There was little if any such White backlash; Johnson won by a landslide.

with all deliberate speed. The 1896 "separate but equal" doctrine (see the list above) was finally reversed by the May 17, 1954 *Brown v Board of Education* decision in which the Supreme Court unanimously ruled that state provisions requiring racial segregation in public schools were unconstitutional and ordered the integration of such schools "with all deliberate speed" (the phrase was that of Chief Justice Earl Warren who wrote the unanimous "majority opinion"). The case, which originated in Topeka, Kansas, had been argued by a battery of NAACP lawyers led by Thurgood Marshall, who later became the first Black Supreme Court Justice (in 1967).

It was mainly the southern states which had segregated public schools, and southern opponents of integration opposed the "with all deliberate speed" concept and phrase with "gradualism," which to many southerners really meant "never"—ten years after the Supreme Court's "with all deliberate speed" decision only 13,000 (less than ½ of 1%) of the 2¾ million Black students in the South were in integrated schools.

busing. A major reason many public schools in both the North and the South are not integrated is that neighborhoods are usually Black or White and children attend nearby neighborhood schools. To achieve school integration some courts began ordering the busing of some Black students to schools in White neighborhoods and of some White students to schools in Black neighborhoods—and *busing* children out of their own neighborhoods as a tool of integration and of improved schooling for Blacks has had many Americans arguing, and some Whites rioting and picketing, in the 1970s.

Ralph Bunche (1904–71) became a symbol of Black achievement in 1948 when he concluded a truce and armistice agreement in the Palestine War, for which he won the Nobel Peace Prize in 1950.

The most frequently used and revealing words from the Black experience in America are those referring to the Blacks as a race and as individuals. Some of these words are descriptive, many are derogatory. All ethnic groups in America have been given derogatory names, but the Blacks have been given the most—because they have been here longest, are the most obvious, and have been the lowest on the social scale (everyone could call Blacks derogatory names and seldom be criticized for doing so). Words we have used to describe and refer to Blacks include:

African, used in English to mean any Black since the 13th century. It was most common in America in the 18th century and many Blacks used the word to refer to themselves until well past the Civil War, hence *African* is found in the names of many of the older Black churches and organizations. *Africo-American*, 1835; *Afro-American*, *Afro*, 1830s; *African-American*, 1863, all these terms usually being used by northerners or to refer to free Blacks during the slavery period. *African dominoes*, 1901, dice, craps; one reason playing craps was associated with Blacks is that the French game of *coups*, *crabs*, or *craps* was introduced into America by the French in New Orleans and Creoles and Blacks then helped spread it northward (the English called the game *hazard*, with *crabs* being used in America since 1768 to mean the lowest throw, two ones).

black dates from the earliest days of slavery and was more common than *negro* until the Civil War. Since *black* was considered a slave term Blacks preferred to be called *colored* from after the war until the late 1880s; from the late 1880s until the 1930s they preferred to be called *negroes* (with a capital *N* after the late 1920s). Since the Civil Rights movement of the 1950s and 60s *Black* is the preferred word (though the Black Muslims prefer *Black man* or *Black woman* to the shorter *Black* when used as a noun). *Black face*, as a Black, 1704; as a minstrel, 1869. *Black fellow*, 1889. *Black gang* has meant a ship's stokers since the early days of steam, because so many Blacks were employed in this work.

blackamore, a 16th century English word (*black + Moor*, a North African of Berber and Arab descent). Originally this word had an exotic connotation but took on a menial one by the late 17th century.

blueskin, first recorded, and perhaps coined, in James Fenimore Cooper's 1821 novel *The Spy*, though he used it descriptively and with no derogatory connotation. Earlier, in 1787, a *blueskin* had meant a person of strict morals, especially a Presbyterian, and before that British Loyalists had used it to mean a supporter of the American Revolution. *Blue gum*, mainly Civil War use, especially for Black soldiers serving with the Union (the color here referred not only to "blueskin" but also to the blue uniforms these soldiers wore fighting for the Blue against the Gray).

boogie, *boogy*, 1923, and *spook*, 1940, are derogatory terms for a Black. Their connotation is that Blacks are strange and frightening creatures, the kind that appear suddenly out of the dark (thus the words stand as rather sad comments on White fear and ignorance). *Boogie* may come from the Northern England and Scotch word *boggle/bogey*, spook, goblin, which gave English *Old Bogey*, the Devil, and American English the 1866 *booger*, goblin, devil. *Boogie woogie*, late 1920s, a fast blues piece with a double-time eight-beats to the measure bass figure (the music was associated with Blacks, but both *boogie* and *boogie woogie* had meant syphilis, especially secondary syphilis, before they came to refer to either Blacks or music).

boy is a 13th century English word which originally meant a male servant or fellow of low estate (from Latin *boiae*, fetters), thus its meaning of a servant, menial, or slave is older than its meaning of a male child, which appeared in the 14th century. American colonists were calling male Indians, Black slaves, and White indentured servants *boy* by the 1630s. After the Civil War many Whites continued to call menials and ex-slaves *boy*, thus the term is still sometimes used to apply to all Black men and Black and White porters, shoeshine "boys," etc. *Girl*, 1740s as any female slave or servant under 40.

buck was used to refer to a young male Indian by 1630 (from its meaning of male deer and male goat) and was soon applied to young male slaves, with connotations of virility and breeding possibilities. *Buck nigger*, 1835.

colored dates from the earliest days of slavery but became very common among both Blacks and Whites in the South in the 1820s. By the 1840s the terms *man of color* and *woman of color* were widely used by abolitionists and free Blacks. Free Blacks then proudly used the initials *f.m.c.* and *f.w.c.* (*free man of color* and *free woman of color*) after their signatures, and these initials also appeared frequently in legal documents, laws, and newspapers. From the Civil War to the late 1880s Blacks preferred to be referred to as *colored*, considering *black* a slave word, and as late as 1909 the National Association for the Advancement of *Colored* People was formed. *Colored*, however, was used not only to refer to Blacks but also to Indians, Orientals, and Mexicans in the U.S., the U.S. Census Bureau classifying Mexicans as "colored" until 1940.

Colorphobia, 1841, as a fear or dislike of Blacks, especially that the rapidly multiplying Blacks might *Africanize* (1835) some states or territories. *Color line*, 1875, the social distinction between Blacks and Whites, a Reconstruction term; *to draw the color line*, 1875; *to cross the color line*, 1880s.

coon was originally a short form for raccoon in 1741 (see *raccoon* at THE INDIANS), then by 1832 meant a frontier rustic, and by 1840 a Whig. The 1834 song "Zip Coon" (better known today as "Turkey in the Straw") didn't refer specifically to either a White or a Black and the "coon songs" of the 1840s and 50s were Whig political songs. By 1862, however, *coon* had come to mean a Black and this use was made very common by the popular 1896 song "All Coons Look Alike to Me," written by Ernest Hogan, a Black who didn't consider the word derogatory at the time.

darky, darkey, 1775; it became a sentimental term for a Black in both the North and the South and after the Civil War southerners often used it to refer to a faithful, docile Black, one who didn't feel that his freedom should make much difference in the way he acted toward Whites. *Plantation darky*, 1865, originally meaning an uneducated, unsophisticated Black, as one who had been brought up as a slave on a plantation. *Darktown*, 1884, the Black section or district of a town, as used in the song "The Darktown Strutters' Ball," written by Shelton Brooks in 1915.

dinge, 1848; *dingy*, 1909, a derogatory term for a Black, perhaps from "dingy." *Dinge* was also used by our troops in the Vietnam war to mean a Vietnamese.

ebony, 1850s, but its poetic form *ebon* had been used to refer to Blacks since the 1820s (both forms entered English in the 16th century via Greek *ebenos* from Egyptian *hebni*, the ebony tree, which has a dark, almost black, heartwood).

eight ball, 1931, because in the game of pool the eight-ball is black. In World War II *eight ball* also came to mean a misfit, goof-off, or jerk, whether Black or White.

Ethiopian, a 13th century English word for a Black, having nothing to do, of course, with the modern country of Ethiopia (both this word for Black and the name *Ethiopia* come from the Greek *Aithiops*, referring to all the area and peoples of Africa south and east of Egypt). *Ethiopian* originally had an exotic connotation and was usually used in America to refer to a foreign, free, or educated Black, seldom being used to refer to a slave or a field hand. Thus the first minstrel troupe was billed as the *Ethiopian minstrelsy*, in 1843, and the troupe called *the Ethiopian Serenaders* commanded large audiences in 1845, with Americans calling minstrel shows *Ethiopian dramas* (1856) or *Ethiopian operas*, collections of minstrel show jokes *Ethiopian joke books*, and the upper balcony of a theater where Blacks were segregated *Ethiopian paradise* (which predates the 1875 term *nigger heaven*). Stephen Foster (1826-64) even called himself an "Ethiopian song writer," because he wrote so many songs for Black performers and about what he considered to be Black life.

Guinea (1789) originally meant a slave from the Guinea coast of Africa, then came to mean any large, strong, or mean slave; *Congo* (1760) originally meant a slave from the Congo region; and *Ibo* (1732) originally meant a slave from the Ibo tribe of the Niger Delta or any slave from the Niger—but they all eventually came to mean any slave and then any Black. In slavery days referring to a Black by the name of his tribe or the African region he came from meant that he was a first generation slave or a newly arrived *salt-water Negro*, such slaves being the most valuable as they hadn't yet been broken in health or spirit. *Zulu*, like *jungle bunny*, is a derogatory term of the 1920s, with connotations of uncivilized wildness and extreme Negroid features.

jigabo(o), 1910, and its short form *jig(g)*, 1923, are derogatory terms that could come from the minstrel show and vaudeville terms *jig band* (an all-Black band), *jig show* (an all-Black troupe or entertainment), and *Jiggs* (a Black performer), all of which may come from the 16th century English word *jig*, dance, sport, joke. However, *jigabo(o)* and *jig(g)* could also come from the 1830s terms *jigger boss* and *jigger*, both meaning a boy, often a Black one, who served out whiskey to canal-building laborers, perhaps because such boys sported and joked (*jigger* didn't mean a dram of whiskey until 1857).

moke had been a derogatory term for a Black since 1865 but became more common after the 1899 minstrel show song "Smoking Mokes." It's probably from *mocha*, the color, but could come from the 19th century English dialect word for donkey, *moka*, *mokus*, or even from the Icelandic *möckvi*, darkness (by way of some Icelanders who settled in Utah around 1855).

mulatto, a 1595 English word for a person born of one Black and one White parent (from Spanish and Portuguese *mulato*, diminutive of *mulo*, mule, mules being halfbreeds of a male ass and a female horse). By 1650 in America *mulatto* was also used to mean a person with mixed Black and White ancestry in any proportions. *Mulatress*, 1805. Our other major words designating percentages of Black ancestry include:

  quadroon, a 17th century word that didn't generally replace the 1707 Louisiana French word *quateron* until the 1830s (*quadroon* is from Spanish *cuarterón*, from *cuarta*, quarter). It, of course, means a person of one-quarter Black ancestry but, like all other terms in this category, is loosely used to refer to any person of mixed Black and White ancestry.

  octoroon (based on *octo-*, eight + *-roon*, by analogy with *quadroon*), a person having one-eighth Black ancestry. The first recorded use of the word is in the *Cleveland Plain Dealer* in 1860, in an article written by Artemus Ward, who may have coined the word.

  griff, griffe, griffane, griffone. Griffe first appeared in the West Indies around 1720, to mean a mulatto or quadroon, and by the 1840s was in fairly wide use in New Orleans and other parts of Louisiana, where the various forms and spellings evolved (and where *quadroon*, *griffe*, and *Creole* were often used as synonyms). In the U.S. it has often been used to mean a person lighter than an octoroon, one who has just *a touch of the tar pot/tar brush* (which terms may date from as early as the 1740s). *Griff(e)* probably comes from the Spanish *grifo*, frizzled, kinky, referring to the hair.

The terms *black* (for a 100% Black person), *mulatto*, *quadroon*, *octoroon*, and *griffe* were used by the U.S. Census Bureau until 1891, when Booker T. Washington persuaded the government that the single word *Negro* was quite sufficient and more dignified.

negro (via Spanish and Portuguese *negro*, black, from Latin *nigrum/niger*) was used in English by the 16th century, with *negress* appearing in the 18th. It was not as common as *black* in slavery days and from the Civil War until the late 1880s Blacks preferred the word *colored*. After the fight to get *negro* accepted as the preferred word after the 1880s came the drive to get it spelled with a capital *N*. The *New York Times* didn't begin spelling *Negro* with a capital *N* until 1930 and the U.S. Government Printing Office (hence all government publications) didn't capitalize it until 1933.

  White negro, 1775, to mean a mulatto or an albino Black; 1930s, to mean a "good Negro," one Whites liked and trusted; late 1950s and early 60s, a White hipster.

nigger originated as a northern England (and Irish) dialect pronunciation of Negro, first being recorded in English as *neger* in 1587. When the very first slaves were brought to the American colonies in 1619, John Rolfe of Jamestown, Virginia wrote in his *Journal:*

A Dutch ship sold us twenty Negars. . . .

This was the very first reference to Blacks in the American colonies—and John Rolfe and others pronounced that word "Negars" as "niggers" (at least he capitalized *Negar*). Noah Webster spelled Negro as *neger* all his life (he also spelled *zebra* as "zeber" until 1825). At any rate, *nigger* was a common word in both England and America by the 17th century; it was just considered a pronunciation of *Negro* until around 1825, when both abolitionists and Blacks began to object to it as disparaging. Then after the Civil War *nigger* became the most common contemptuous word for a Black. *Nigger* has given us such terms as:

nigger boy, 1825.

niggerhead, 1809, as a very dark, strong tobacco, especially home-grown tobacco as opposed to "store bought" (*Nigger Head* was a brand name of a tobacco from the 1840s until 1943). The word has also meant an exceptionally hard rock.

nigger heaven, 1875, the upper balcony in a theater, in which Blacks were segregated.

niggerish, 1825.

nigger lover, first applied to abolitionists, around the 1830s.

nigger luck, 1851, unexpected fortune, good luck, implying "fool's luck."

nigger killer, 1855.

nigger shooter, 1883, a southern term for a slingshot.

nigger show, 1879, a minstrel show.

niggertoe, 1880s, a Brazil nut, southern use.

We have also used *nigger* as the name of various devices that do hard physical labor as once done by Black laborers, thus *nigger* means a capstan. *To work like a nigger*, to work hard, dates from 1836 and *nigger in the woodpile*, a catch or hitch in a situation, a flaw, dates from 1852.

pickaninny, piccanniny is discussed at the entry SPANISH.

shine, 1902, a derogatory name referring to the highlights on Black skin, perhaps originally used by hobos.

smoke, early 1920s. This derogatory word for a Black seems to have originally been used to refer to Black soldiers and may thus have been a World War I term. *Smoked Yankee*, 1820, some southern "humorous" use to refer to a free Black.

snowball, 1780, as a "humorous" term for a light-complected Black.

spade, 1919. This originally seems to have been prison slang for a very dark-complected Black, who, of course, was "as black as the ace of spades."

Uncle (late 1820s) and *Aunt* or *Auntie* (both early 1830s), used to refer to or address an elderly Black. These uses stem from the fact that Whites had no terms of respect for, or terms of respectful address to, slaves—slaves were never called Mr., Mrs., or Miss, and their last names were seldom used (many slaves didn't even have last names). Thus when a slave was due respect because of age, service, or especially because a slave woman had served as one's "Mammy," Whites called him or her "uncle" or "aunt"

"Duke" [Edward Kennedy] El- lington (1899–1974), jazz mu- sician and composer.

(there was precedence for this, *uncle* has been used since at least the 16th century as a term of address to an old man). Thus we have such names as Uncle Tom in *Uncle Tom's Cabin* and Aunt Jemima in *Aunt Jemima's Pancake Mix* (see PANCAKES for more about her).

woolly head, 1827, a derogatory term for a Black, referring to the hair. The noun *kink* (from Low German *kinke*, a twist in a rope) has been in English since the 17th century, but the adjective *kinky* seems to have originally been coined and used to refer to the short, tightly curled hair of Blacks, first being recorded in the term *kinky-hair* in 1844. Incidentally, *kink* meant a mental quirk by 1803 and *kinky* came to mean full of mental quirks around 1915.

yellow, 1814, and *bright*, 1831, refer to a mulatto or any light-complected Black. *High yellow* was a common term by the 1920s, often pronounced "high yaller" and especially applied to a beautiful, sexually attractive young mulatto woman.

Other terms for mulattos in the 1920s included *head light* and *three-quarters Kelt*, both seeming to have originated as prison terms by White convicts.

Having given such a long list of terms for Blacks, it's only fair to give a list of some of the names Blacks (and Whites) have called Whites. Blacks call Whites *chalk*, a *gray*, *milk*, *paleface* and also:

honkey, 1950s, probably from the Whites' nasal tone, but some say it originated in Detroit and was first applied to the White men who picked up their Black girlfriends by sitting in their cars and honking the horn in front of the houses where the girls worked as maids.

lily white, originally used to refer to southern Republicans who wanted to exclude Blacks from the party after the Civil War, then applied to any "Whites only" organization (in the 1850s *lily white* was the name of a powdered cosmetic made of chalk, which may have given us this expression).

the Man, 1950s as meaning federal law enforcement officers. By the late 1950s Blacks were using it to mean any White or White group in authority, as policemen, landlords, etc., and by the 1960s to mean all Whites, the White world.

ofay, 1926, a derogatory word for a White, probably from the Pig Latin for "foe" (and not from French *au lait* as some claim).

peckerwood, 1930s, sometimes shortened to *pecker*, a poor rural White, a lazy, ignorant rustic (probably from inverting *wood-pecker*). Though originally White use, in Alabama, Blacks have used the word often in referring to poor southern Whites.

pink, before the 1920s, a White, from the pink complexion. Blacks also use *pink toes* to refer to a light-complected mulatto girl.

WASP (the acronym for *White Anglo Saxon Protestant*), early 1960s, originally used by intellectuals to refer to dominant middle-class Americans as opposed to Blacks, Irish, and Italian Catholic immigrants, Jews, Puerto Ricans, etc. The word is now used as a derogatory name by other ethnic minority groups.

white. Though early White Americans spoke of Blacks, Redskins, and the Yellow race, they didn't think or speak of themselves as White—they were people, citizens, men, and others were

Marian Anderson, 1930. All America talked about this famous contralto, the first Black to per- form at the White House. Because of her race, the Daughters of the American Revolution forbade her performance at Constitution Hall in 1939. In protest Eleanor Roosevelt sponsored her concert at the Lincoln Memorial. Miss Anderson first sang at the Metro- politan Opera House in 1955. She was appointed an alternate delegate to the U. N. in 1958.

slaves, savages, or heathen. Not until the 1830s did *white man* have much use in general conversation and it was not until the Civil War that *white*, meaning of, by, or for Whites was in wide use. Then we were to have: *white man's chance*, a decent chance, 1830s; *white country*, 1863, an area with no or few Blacks; *white (man's) hope*, 1911, any White prizefighter who Whites hoped would win a title from a Black, originally very common when "Jack" (John A.) Johnson was the first Black heavyweight champion, during 1908–15.

> *poor white*, 1819, an ignorant, shiftless southern White, considered as ranking below a gentleman's slave by White southern gentlemen. *Poor white trash*, 1833, said to have originally been a slave term for White servants, for Whites willing to do the work of slaves; *white trash*, 1855; *poor white folks*, 1864.

Since *Black*, *the Blacks*, etc., began to be used with pride and respect in the 1960s, the use of *White*, *the Whites*, etc., has also increased (the 19th century word *Caucasian* has never been popular). The most common derogatory word for Whites by Blacks since the early 1960s has been *Whitey*.

(top, left to right) Edward Brooke, U.S. Senator from Massachusetts since 1967; Carl B. Stokes, former mayor of Cleveland, TV commentator; Aretha Franklin, singer. (bottom, left to right) Muhammad Ali (Cassius Clay), world heavyweight boxing champion; General Benjamin O. Davis, Jr., pilot, first Black Air Force general (his father was the first Black Army general); Sidney Poitier, actor.

Blizzards, Tornadoes, & Hurricanes

The famous "Blizzard of '88," March 11–14, killed about 400 people and, in New York City, dumped 21 inches of snow.

Though well acquainted with rain, sleet, hail, and snow in England, the colonists were not forewarned of the severe American climate—the Pilgrims realized they were in for trouble with it only when they lowered boats from the *Mayflower* and rowed through freezing rain and snow looking for a place to land. Later colonists going to New England were purposely misled by being shown accounts of the mild climate in Virginia or the Caribbean or by being told that New England was, after all, in the same latitude as sunny Spain. Thus early Americans talked with despair and horror about the weather, and we've been talking about it ever since.

It was mainly the cold and heavy snows of New England that dismayed early Americans. We have coined such terms as:

snow shoes, 1664.
flurry, of hail, 1686; of wind and rain, 1772; of snow, 1883.
snowstorm, 1771.
cold snap, 1776. *Hot spell* was not coined until the late 1820s.

snow shower, 1779.
snow plow, 1792.
snow slide, 1841.
snowed in, 1859.
snow fence, 1872.

All that snow, of course, can be beneficial or even fun. Children have been talking about building *snow forts* since 1853; New England farmers hoped for *sugar snow* (1861, a late spring snow slowing the flow of sap and extending the time for gathering maple sugar); and we now enjoy not only skis but *snowmobiles* (1934, first used to refer to experimental vehicles used by Admiral Byrd in exploring the Antarctic). We named the *snow goose* by 1771 and the *snow egret* by 1895. People were said to be *snowed under* (overwhelmed) by 1880 and we overwhelmed people with exaggerations and lies called *snow jobs* by the 1940s.

But the main American snow word is *blizzard*. It may be from the German *blitz*, lightning, flash, but more probably is from an English dialect word *blisser*. By the late 1820s we were using *blizzard* to mean a violent blow, crushing remark, or any remarkable thing; by 1834 it meant a shot; and during the Civil War it meant a volley of musket fire. Not until 1870 did *blizzard* come to mean a snowstorm with gale winds and low temperatures. Then the Estherville, Iowa newspaper, whose editor loved new words, began referring to the town's "great blizzard" of that spring. The word then became common during the winter of 1880–81, still remembered for its severe snowstorms.

We Americans also talk about other unique storms. Besides *cloudbursts* (1817) we talk about:
  hurricanes (via Spanish *huracán* from the Carib Indian *huracan*, meaning "big wind" and also being the name of the evil spirit of storms), first used in England in 1589. The word was still so

The worst tornado in history swept through Missouri, Illinois, and Indiana on March 18, 1925, killing 689 people, 234 of them in one town, Murphysboro, Illinois. This photograph of a typical twister shows the deadly funnel.

I'm dreaming of a White Christmas,
Just like the ones I used to know.
"White Christmas," song by Irving Berlin for the 1954 movie of the same name. The expression "a white Christmas," a Christmas with snow, dates from the early 1900s.

The "eye" of a hurricane is its center, about 20 miles across, without much wind, and clear of clouds. The greatest fury of a hurricane lies along its inner edge.

new in Shakespeare's day that he used it around 1601 in *Troilus and Cressida* to mean waterspout.

tornadoes (Spanish *tronada*, thunderstorm, influenced by another Spanish word *tornar*, to twist), 1804. *Cyclone*, a meteorological term coined in England in 1856; *cyclone cellar*, 1887; *storm cellar*, 1900s. *Twister*, 1897.

New Englanders have called a gale wind from the northeast a *northeaster* since 1774, and we have referred to a strong, cold wind from the north as a *norther* since 1776 (probably influenced by the Spanish *norte*). People in the foothills of the Rockies have been talking about the *Chinook wind* since 1860, shortening it to *Chinook* by 1876 (after the Chinook Indian tribe that lived west of the Rockies, whence come these dry winds accompanied by rising temperature). The *Santa Anna* (1903) is a north wind of the southwest, said to be so named because it and its accompanying sandstorm kills and sweeps on, just as the Mexican general Santa Anna did.

The first widespread weather observations in America were made by a network of 600 telegraph stations under the direction of the Smithsonian Institution beginning in 1849, which allowed Ebenezer Merrian to publish the first *weather forecasts* in New York City newspapers in 1853. In 1859 the word *weatherman* appeared, *weather forecaster* not being recorded until 1909. A government *weather bureau* was widely discussed in 1857, but the *Weather Bureau* was not established by the Signal Corps until 1870, providing *weather maps* for the War Department by 1871. After being part of the Department of Agriculture from 1891 the Weather Bureau was moved to the Commerce Department in 1940, becoming the *National Weather Bureau* in 1970. Incidentally *smog* is not an American word, it's probably English (*smoke* + *fog*); our Weather Bureau adopting the term in 1926.

61

Blue Grass, Red Wood, and Poison Ivy

We have given many of our native trees, grasses, flowers, and shrubs descriptive names, often by combining two old words. Thus we have:

There are varieties of poison ivy growing in nearly all parts of the United States; but, since it is unknown in Europe, it was an unpleasant surprise to our first colonists. Here a branch has last year's berries and this year's leaves and flowers.

bluegrass, 1751, being any of several American grasses of the *Poa* genus and having a bluish cast, earlier called *Dutch grass* (1671). *Kentucky bluegrass*, 1849, a type of bluegrass, *Poa pratentis*, valuable as pasturage and hay; *Bluegrass region, Bluegrass country, the Blue Grass*, a region in Kentucky, 1860s; *the Bluegrass State*, Kentucky, 1886.

butternut, 1741, or *white walnut* (1743), called *butternut* from the oiliness of the nut. By 1810 *butternut* also meant the brownish dye obtained from the tree's bark, its color, and fabric dyed with it. During the Civil War *Butternut* (1862) meant a Confederate soldier, from the butternut dye used on some homemade uniforms. *The Butternut State*, Missouri, 1863.

buttonwood, 1674, because of its buttonlike burrs. This name was given the tree in New England; Southerners called it *sycamore* (1709), thinking it was that familiar English tree.

honey locust, 1743, because the pealike pods have a sweet taste.

Johnny-jump-up, 1842, from its quick growth. Also called *Johnny jumper, Johnny jump up and kiss me*, 1859; *Johnny jump*, 1894. The English call this the *viola tricolor* or *heartsease* (we use these names for any of the various American violets and wild pansies).

live oak, 1610, because, being an evergreen oak, it is "alive" all year.

poison ivy, 1784, earlier *poison weed*. It got its name because, as Captain John Smith wrote in 1624, "The Poysoned weed is much in shape like our English ivy." Colonists, who had never seen or heard of it until they landed in America, had to learn to recognize and avoid it, and care for its effects, by trial and error. It was particularly rampant in Virginia, all the more troublesome because it could be mistaken by uninitiates for the local climbing vine the *Virginia creeper* (1670s).

poison oak, 1743, so called because its lobelike leaves resemble those of an oak tree. This plant also was troublesome in early Virginia where it seems to have gotten its name.

poison sumac, 1820. It was originally called *poison wood*, 1721, and *poison tree*, 1756. It was also called *poison dogwood*, 1814.

redwood had been an English name for the red willow since 1634 and the colonists used it for the local red willow by 1770. The name was first recorded as being used for the large West Coast *Sequoia sempervirens* in 1832.

sugar maple, 1731, because its sap is used to make maple sugar.

Such descriptive combinations are not limited to America or to plants: the descriptive combinations *cattail*, *dogwood*, and *eggplant* are English, and our language also abounds in descriptive names for animals (see GRIZZLY BEARS, RATTLE SNAKES, AND BALD EAGLES).

The early settlers and frontiersmen also borrowed many plant names from the Indians, French, and Spanish. Other plants and trees are named after people, as the *Douglas fir* (1884, for the Scottish botanist David Douglas who discovered it while collecting and exploring in the Northwest in 1825) and the *poinsettia* (named in 1836 for Joel Poinsett, who collected and sent back many rare plants, including this one, while serving as the first U.S. minister to Mexico in 1825–29). Other native American plants were misnamed, merely because the settlers who first saw them thought they were identical to those back home in England when they weren't. Thus our *beech, hemlock, laurel,* and *walnut* are not the same as the English trees of the same names and our *bay trees* and *bay bushes* also differ from the English ones.

Lizzie Borden

Lizzie Andrew Borden (1860-1927) at age 29.

was the name on everyone's lips during June, 1893, when this 33-year old "spinster" was put on trial for the ax murder of her wealthy father and her stepmother in Fall River, Massachusetts. This not-so-gay double ax murder was the most discussed crime of the Gay 90s. We still talk about it when we recite the popular piece of doggerel from that summer of 1893.

> Lizzie Borden took an ax
> And gave her mother forty whacks;
> When she saw what she had done,
> She gave her father forty-one!

This rhyme distorts history; much to the public's shock, the verdict was "not guilty."

Breads—Rye 'n' Injun, Anadama, Sourdough, Sliced White, etc.

Baking powder had just been invented and there was much joking about the effects of eating the new aerated bread, as in this 1860 cartoon.

Colonists ate and talked about three types of bread. First, the Indian style bread, made only from cornmeal, water, and salt, and called *pone* (1612, from Algonquian *apan*, baked), *Indian bread* (1654), *pone bread* (1770s), and later *corn pone* (1880s). When made with milk and eggs this became the fancier *corn bread* (1750). Next, there was the dark brown New England staff of life made of rye flour, cornmeal, molasses, and yeast, and widely known as *rye 'n' Injun* (by the 1790s *Injun* or *Indian* stood for "Indian meal," which meant cornmeal). When baking soda was added and it was steamed, such bread was called *brown bread* (1831). When white flour was used instead of rye it was called *Anadama* bread, said to be from the phrase "Anna, damn her," mutterd by a New England fisherman so angry at his wife, Anna, for always serving cornmeal and molasses for dinner that he finally added flour

63

An 1860s label for the new self-rising flour, already mixed with baking powder and needing only cold water and milk.

Two modern flours, a bleached white flour suitable for both cakes and breads (top) and a ready-mix self-rising flour that requires no baking powder or yeast.

and yeast and baked the mixture while cursing her. These two general types of bread were for settled folks, the third type was *hardtack* (*tack* is an 18th century word for food), used by hunters, trappers, and others on the move.

The problem with making bread is producing the carbon dioxide bubbles that make it light. Colonial cooks talked of their *hop yeast*, then by the 1780s of *pearlash*, a refined form of potash. In the 1830s and 40s everyone was talking of the new, light *salt rising bread*, also called *salt bread*. Also in the 1830s *saleratus* (Latin *sal* + *aeratus*, "aerated salt") was a new miracle ingredient—at first it was potassium bicarbonate then later was sodium bicarbonate, which became known as *baking soda* in the late 1870s. Saleratus combines with the acid in buttermilk or sour milk to release carbon dioxide (if sweet milk is used, cream of tartar has to be added as the acid). Saleratus is why we still talk of how light grandma's bread was, of her *saleratus bread*, *saleratus biscuits*, *buttermilk biscuits*, *sour milk bread*, and *baking soda biscuits*.

In the 1850s the new *baking powder* had every cook talking. This combination of sodium bicarbonate (baking soda) and an acid salt produced *quick bread* or *lightin' bread*, sometimes called *aerated bread* at the time. When the baking powder was mixed with the flour by the packager it was called *self-rising flour* (1854).

Meantime wheat had long since come to America, one of the first famous products being George Washington's *Mount Vernon flour*. By 1821 yeast-leavened wheat bread was called *light bread* to distinguish it from the common, heavier cornmeal breads (see CORN). In the 1850s *grain elevator* was in the language and Minneapolis was becoming the center of the white flour industry. In the 1860s people were talking about the soft, white, bleached-flour *store-bought bread* or *bakery bread* and, even then, denouncing it for being tasteless, too soft, and not fit nourishment for hard-working men. By the 1880s it was cheaper to buy such bread than make other kinds (because fuel for the stove now cost more than the flour) and thus *white bread* became the American staple. Until the late 19th century 95% of the country's flour had been bought for home use; today only 15% is, the rest being used by commercial bakeries. By the late 1920s *grocery bread*, *sliced white*, or *sandwich bread* were what most Americans meant when they said "bread."

Sourdough bread became associated with Alaskan gold rush prospectors soon after 1896 and a *sourdough* came to mean such a prospector. Yet such bread and the idea of saving a lump of the yeasty dough from one batch of bread to start the next is a very old one: such *starters* were carried by Columbus on his trips, and evidence of them has been found at ancient Egyptian sites dating from 400 B.C.

Incidentally *breadbasket* has been a slang term for the stomach in America since 1821 and a thank-you note to a hostess has been called a *bread and butter note* since the 1890s.

Early Americans also ate some of their bread as *toast* (the English had eaten toast since the 14th century), made on *bread toasters*, long-handled forks to hold the bread over the fire. They usually ate it as *dipped toast* or *dip toast*, with milk or melted butter poured over it, which was commonly being called *milk toast* by the 1820s. Triangular pieces of bread were also fried in butter and were popular as *sippets* before the Revolutionary War. *French toast* was first a popular American dish and term in the 1870s. The last word in toast was the electric *toaster*, which everyone was talking about just before World War I.

Bromide and Blurb

are two words we owe to the humorist and illustrator Gelett Burgess (1866-1951). In 1906 he coined *bromide* to mean a boring, conventional person (from the use of bromide as a sedative) in his *Smart Set* essay "Are You a Bromide?" which became the title of a collection of his humorous essays the following year. By 1920 people were using the word to mean a conventional or trite remark as well. He coined *blurb* in 1907 when he facetiously called the enticing woman drawn on a comic book jacket "Miss Blinda Blurb," and within ten years any enticing recommendation for a book was known as a *blurb* (*squib*, a short, often witty, advertising paragraph or line appeared in the late 1940s).

Although *bromide* and *blurb* have been common terms, the words of Burgess' which we hear most often are these, written around 1896:

Gelett Burgess tinkers with his Nonsense Machine, which does nothing with 100% efficiency.

> I never saw a Purple Cow,
>   I never hope to see one;
> But I can tell you anyhow,
>   I'd rather see than be one.

The Buffalo

lived in America long before the Indians came. Small herds roamed the forested East (as shown by the name *Buffalo*, New York, founded 1803) while large herds roamed from the Appalachians to the Rocky Mountains. There were probably 60 million of them. Then the Indians came and called the buffalo *tatanka* and began killing it. When wild horses of Spanish descent strayed North from Mexico the Sioux captured and learned to ride them, then rode out onto the Great Plains to become *Plains Indians* (1852), living off the plains buffalo, eating buffalo meat, wearing and living in buffalo hides, and selling additional hides to canoe-traveling fur traders along the tributaries of the Missouri. In 1850 20 million buffalo roamed the Western Plains. Then the white men came with repeating rifles and hunted the buffalo relentlessly, finally supplying great quantities of buffalo meat to the growing cities and the crews building transcontinental railroads. Around 1895 there were about 800 buffalo left in the United States (today, living in protected preserves, there are about 10,000 buffalo).

Buffalo gals, woncha come out tonight,
Woncha come out tonight, woncha come out tonight?
Buffalo gals woncha come out tonight,
And dance by the light of the moon?
The most popular version of the song "Lubly Fan, woncha come out tonight," whose title and first word changed according to the locale, thus has been sung as "Kansas Gals," "Louisiana Gals," etc. It has been popular since 1844.

A stampede of buffalo in Yellowstone National Park.

Buffalo (Portuguese and Spanish *bufalo* from Greek *boufalos*, wild ox) is, of course, a misnomer, a word Europeans had used for the smaller, weaker Indian and African ox. Our buffalo is really the *American bison* (1796), but De Soto didn't know that when he first called it *bufalo* in 1544. The word appears in many American combinations, including:

buffalo beef, 1722, buffalo meat.
buffalo robe, 1723, also called *buffalo rug*, 1805. This Indian item was first described by Marquette and Joliet in 1681; it served many Indians and whites as robe, coat, blanket, and sleeping bag.
buffalo-headed duck, 1731, now known as the *bufflehead* (1858), a small, widely distributed duck with a large, squarish head.
buffalo road, 1750; *buffalo trace*, 1823; *buffalo trail*, 1834. These are all paths or trails worn by buffalo herds.

Oh, give me a home where the buffalo roam,
Where the deer and the antelope play,
Where seldom is heard a discouraging word
And the skies are not cloudy all day.
Dr. Brewster Higley, "Home on the Range," 1873.

A prosperous Buffalo Bill in 1909, 26 years after opening his famous Wild West Show.

buffalo fish, 1768, various fish of the sucker family, especially along the Mississippi and Ohio Rivers.

buffalo grass, 1784, a low-growing perennial grass common to the buffalo ranges.

buffalo dance, 1805, an Indian ritual dance, often performed in a buffalo skin and mask.

buffalo horse, 1827, a horse used in buffalo hunts.

buffalo wallow, 1834. These hollow places made by buffaloes rolling in the dirt sometimes filled with water, preventing many a horse and rider from suffering from thirst.

buffalo chips, 1840, dried buffalo dung, the common fuel of the prairie, also called *buffalo wood*, 1855.

buffalo boat, 1844, made by stretching buffalo skins over a wooden frame.

Buffalo Bill, William Frederick Cody (1846–1917), who had been a pony express rider and cavalry scout before earning this nickname as a buffalo hunter supplying large quantities of meat to Union Pacific Railroad construction crews in 1867–68. The name *Buffalo Bill* was given him by Ned Buntline (pen name of Edward Zane Carroll Judson, 1821–86), a writer of adventure fiction and one of the first dime novelists. Cody himself gave us the term *Wild West Show*, opening Buffalo Bill's Wild West Show in Omaha, May 17, 1883.

buffalo soldier, 1873, a Black soldier, so called by Indians because the soldiers' short, tightly curled hair resembled that of buffalo (there were two Black infantry and two Black cavalry regiments serving permanently in the West for 30 years following the Civil War). White soldiers called these Black soldiers *brunets*.

to buffalo someone, 1870s, to cheat or intimidate someone.

buffalo gun, 1907, a large-caliber rifle, as for shooting buffalo.

Such terms as *in the buff* (in the skin, naked), the brownish yellow color called *buff*, and *to buff* (to polish as with an animal skin) do not come from our word *buffalo* but entered English in the 16th century via *buffle*, the French word for that Asiatic and African ox.

Cakes, Pies, Puddings, and Doughnuts

Dessert (French *desservir*, to clear the table, as after the main course) had just become a popular English word when the Pilgrims sailed for America. *Pie*, however, was an old English word, used since the 14th century and going all the way back to Latin *pica*, magpie, a rather humorous reference to the bird's habit of filling its nest with miscellaneous objects, just as English meat pies might have rather miscellaneous fillings. For *pie* meant a meat pie to the English and the first colonists, with *tart* being their word for the pastry filled with fruit, berries, or jam—but colonists were soon calling both dishes *pies* and eating both for breakfast. The English *gooseberry fool* was also popular in colonial America, *fool* being a 16th century word for clotted cream but by the 18th century meaning a dish of crushed

Hasty pudding, traditionally eaten from large bowls, is a native American dish. It is a cornmeal mush and called "hasty" because it can be made in a few minutes.

or puréed fruit served with clotted or whipped cream, sometimes topped with macaroons.

Pumpkin pie was one of the first native New England dishes, being served at the Pilgrims' second Thanksgiving, in 1623. The dish, however, wasn't called *pumpkin pie* until 1654; before that, and for some time after, it was usually called *pumpkin pudding* because it was baked without a top crust (*pudding* came to mean food boiled with flour, originally in a bag, in the 16th century, and before that it had been an animal's stomach or intestines stuffed with meat, a sausage). *Apple pie* has been an American favorite since the 1760s (see SOME APPLES!—AND SOME CIDER for the various names and kinds of apple pies). *Huckleberry pie* became popular in the 1770s, the ten-seed American berry having originally been called a *hurtleberry* (1607) in confusion with that European blueberry, many colonists then corrupting "hurtleberry" into *huckleberry* by 1670. By the 1840s and 50s we were also talking about deep-dish *cobblers*, *duff* (a 19th century pronunciation of *dough* to rhyme with *rough*), which was fruit pudding, sometimes with a bottom crust, and *slump*, raised dough with a sweetened fruit filling. *Peach pie* and *peach cobbler* became very common in the 1850s, because *clingstone peaches* or *clings* then gave way to *freestone peaches* or *freestones* which had just been introduced from Shanghai.

Key lime pie appeared in the 1850s, inspired by the introduction of condensed milk, while in the 1860s-90s people were smacking their lips over the new *cream pies*, actually cake with a cream filling, and especially talking about *Boston cream pie*, which was also originally known as *Boston cream cake*. In the 1880s the most talked about pie was probably *vinegar pie*, which contained nutmeg, cinnamon, cloves, raisins, nuts, etc., as well as vinegar. *Blackberry cobbler* was most popular between 1870 and 1935; it wasn't popular earlier because until the 1830s blackberries had been considered a nuisance, good only for medicinal purposes, as in *blackberry syrup*, thus weren't cultivated or included in recipes. *Loganberry pies* were first eaten around 1881, after the *loganberry*, a cross between a western dewberry and the red raspberry, was developed by the California judge and horticulturist James H. Logan. *Boysenberry pie* appeared in the late 1930s, after the berry was developed by Rudolph Boysen from the loganberry and the blackberry. *Shoo fly pie*, said to be so named because flies have to be shooed away from the molasses filling, may have been a Pennsylvania Dutch favorite for generations, but wasn't well known until the 1930s—like a lot of "old traditions" it took a little advertising and car-driving tourists to popularize it. Incidentally, *pie à la mode* (French *à la mode*, "in the fashion," in the latest fashion) has been around since the 1880s, but became widely known only after the famous Del-

Icing *has gradually replaced the word* frosting *for the "coating" around cakes. Here a happy young lady celebrates her fifteenth birthday with fifteen candles on her birthday cake.*

monico's restaurant put it on its menu around the end of World War I.

As easy as pie has been a common expression since 1920, growing out of an 1880s term *to be pie*, to be easy. It replaced the older expressions *as easy as falling off a log* (1840s) and *as easy as old Tilly* (1900s) but came before three other phrases that sound much older but which weren't commonly used much before the 1930s, *as easy as taking candy from a baby*, *as easy as shooting fish in a barrel*, and *as easy as ABC*. Americans have also talked a lot about being *pie-eyed*, drunk, since 1880, a *pie card* meant a meal ticket by 1903, a *pie wagon* meant a police wagon by 1904, then came to mean a roadside diner in the 1930s.

When people talked about *cake* before the 1870s they meant something different from what we usually do today. Modern light cakes couldn't be baked in fireplaces, in primitive hard-to-control ovens, or without good artificial leaveners, such as baking powder (see BREADS for more about this). Thus to the colonists *cake* meant such dishes as *strawberry bread* and various *shortcakes*, with *strawberry shortcake* being a popular term by the 1830s (*strawberry* is an old English word, perhaps so named from the strawlike bristles). *Election cake* was a New England tradition, it was a spicy bread-dough fruitcake served on town meeting days after the men returned home from their deliberations and voting. *Gingerbread* was a popular American cake throughout the 19th century, differing from the older European variety which is thin and hard, like a cookie. It was rivaled by *pound cake*, so named because early recipes called for a pound each of flour, sugar, butter, and eggs, and popular because it was easy to make even before the days of measuring cups. Thus, in earlier times *cakes* meant what we now call *loaf cakes* (1828) or *bread-dough cakes* and certain boiled or steamed dishes such as *plum pudding*, a 17th century English pudding of flour, suet, raisins, currants, citron, and spices   but not plums, *plums* then meant raisins.

The cookstoves, baking powder, and commercial yeast of the second half of the 19th century changed baking and added many new breads, cakes, and words to American life. By the late 1870s and early 80s people were talking about *layer cake*, including *angel food cake*, with *devil's food cake* appearing around 1900. *Lady Baltimore cake* was first described in, and got its name from, Owen Wister's 1906 novel *Lady Baltimore:* in the novel one of the characters, Mrs. Mayberry Charleston, creates this white cake covered with almond syrup, and having a fruit and nut filling and white frosting. It wasn't until the 1920s that people were first talking about *upside-down cake*, and by then almost all our common cakes were known, be they flavored with bananas, applesauce, lemon, mocha, or anything else.

69

Originally *frosting* was what might be used to cover a cake and *icing* a somewhat thinner, fancier substance used to decorate it; but the word *icing* gradually came to replace *frosting* in our vocabulary, so that only knowledgeable cooks make the distinction between the two words today. The last word in cakes is *cake mix*, an American term common since World War II.

That takes the cake has been used to mean "that's outstanding, that's the ultimate," since 1846, referring to a cake given as a prize. Another common 1840s expression was *you can't hurry the cake*, you can't rush matters, be patient. Since Americans have always considered pies heartier than the newer cakes, *cake eater* came to mean an effeminate man in 1922 and then a person used to easy living. The *cakewalk* came in with the modern cake in the 1860s, originally as a parade or "walk around" by Blacks in which the prize for the fanciest steps was a cake. Soon it meant a contest in which participants paid to walk or dance on a numbered floor, hoping that when the music stopped they would be standing on a lucky number worth a prize. By the 1890s the *cakewalk* was a stage dance using the strutting walks of earlier days.

As seen from *pumpkin pudding* and *plum pudding* above, pudding has not been a precise word, sometimes meaning a dessert more like a pie and sometimes more like a cake. Basically, though, it refers to boiled or steamed dishes. One of the first widely talked about native American desserts was *hasty pudding* (1691), cornmeal boiled and served with milk or molasses over it. It was called "hasty" because it took only 15 or 20 minutes to boil the cornmeal until it was thick enough for a wooden spoon to stand up in it, indicating it was done. The dish was also called *Indian pudding* (1722), by the Indian name *sagamite* (1632), or simply *mush* (1671) or *cornmeal mush*. Joel Barlow (1754–1812) wrote in his poem "The Hasty Pudding":

> . . . how I blush
> To hear the Pennsylvanians call thee Mush.

Harvard's famous literary society, *the Hasty Pudding Club*, dates from 1795. There were a lot of other American puddings and by 1848 *pudding-head* meant a stupid or "soft-headed" person, as in Mark Twain's 1894 book *The Tragedy of Pudd'nhead Wilson*, in which lawyer David Wilson is called Pudd'nhead by townspeople who don't understand his eccentricity or wisdom.

Doughnuts are so called because they were originally small, solid balls or "nuts" of fried sweetened dough. The Pilgrims learned to make these solid doughnuts during their stay in Holland, 1607-20, and brought them to New England; the Dutch, who called them *olykoek* (oily cake) also soon brought them directly to New Amsterdam. The New Amsterdam Dutch also introduced *crullers* (Dutch *krullen*, to curl) to America. These pieces of sweet egg batter fried in fat were often shaped into love knots and called *love knots* or *matrimony knots* in the early 1800s. The Pennsylvania Dutch (Germans) also had doughnuts, called *fastnachts*, because they were served on Fastnacht Day (Shrove Tuesday) as the last sweet treat before Lent. To these Pennsylvania Dutch fastnachts we owe our round, hole-in-the-middle doughnuts: the Pennsylvania Dutch preferred the hole to a soft and soggy center. These doughnuts with the hole could easily be, and were, *dunked* (German *dunke*) by the Pennsylvania Dutch, and later by millions of other Americans. *Sinker* was a slang word for a silver dollar until the 1890s, then referred to a pancake and to a round breakfast biscuit or roll, but by 1925 had come to mean only a doughnut, especially a cheap, heavy one as served at lunch counters.

Calamity Jane

From the 1890s to the 1940s *Calamity Jane* was a common term for any vociferous female prophet of doom. It was originally the nickname of the notorious Mary Jane Canary (1852-1903) of Deadwood, South Dakota, who dressed, cursed, and shot like a man, claimed to have been an Indian scout and pony-express rider, and finally went into show business. History isn't sure whether she was a frustrated feminist or merely a foul-mouthed transvestite shrew; but in any event she was ahead of her time.

"*Calamity Jane.*"

Canoes and Cannibals

were two concepts Columbus and his men brought back to Europe from the West Indies (they also brought back syphilis, but that's another story). The first Indians Columbus encountered were the Taino tribe of the West Indies; from that tribe he and his crew carried the Taino *canoa* back to Europe. The Taino themselves had gotten the word from a South American tribe that lived near the mouth of the Amazon, a wide-ranging, aggressive tribe that used its big canoes to make warlike raids. Sad to say, Columbus and the canoe brought about the extinction of the Taino: they were wiped out by European ways and disease and by the onslaughts of that predatory South American tribe in its war canoes.

When later explorers saw American Indians paddling boats they used Columbus' word, *canoa* or *canoe*, to describe them, whether or not the boats resembled the Taino craft. For Indians, explorers, and settlers, the native "canoe" was a nearly perfect form of transportation. It could be made in almost any size to accommodate one man or a large party, was constructed from materials at hand—bark, animal skins, canvas—was easily handled on American rivers, and was light enough to be portaged around falls and rapids. Without the canoe the early exploration and settling of lands along the Ohio, Mississippi, Great Lakes, and other bodies of water would have been almost impossible.

Indians canoeing on the Hudson River.

It was not until the 1860s that canoeing became a sport. A popular 1866 book *A Thousand Miles in the Rob Roy Canoe*, by John MacGregor is credited with establishing canoeing as a summer pastime. Before that, in 1828, the expression *to paddle one's own canoe* became popular to mean to be self-sufficient or independent. Our other canoe expression *up the creek (without a paddle)* became popular in the 1930s, especially among students, to mean out of luck or in trouble. Many prim and proper Americans used this term not knowing its full form was originally "up shit creek without a paddle."

Columbus' crew also heard an Arawak tribe of the Lesser Antilles refer to a man-eating tribe of Haiti and Cuba as *cariba* or *caniba* (meaning "brave" or "strong man" in Arawak). Columbus himself was the first to record the word *caniba*, which became our word *cannibal*. In its *cariba* form this tribal word gave us our word *Caribbean*. Thus *cannibal* and *Caribbean* come from the same word and refer to the same tribe.

The earliest explorers of America were really exploring the West Indies. They saw many new things there, and the Caribbean Indians, especially the Taino and Carib tribes, contributed many new words to the explorers' vocabulary. These words were brought back to Europe, usually in Spanish forms, and then came into 16th century English. Later, many of these words became associated with American English, including:

A fanciful European depiction of Caribbean Indians eating human flesh. Notice how their head feathers have been arranged to look like the devil's horns.

A portage need not be all work!

barbecue, via Spanish *barbacoa* from the Taino, meaning "frame of sticks," on which meat was cooked, first recorded in the U.S. in 1709.

hammock, via Spanish *hamaca*, from the Taino.

hurricane, via Spanish *huracán* from the Carib. See BLIZZARDS, TORNADOES, AND HURRICANES.

maize, via Spanish *maíz* from Taino *mahiz*. See CORN.

manatee, via Spanish, probably from the Carib Indian *manati*, breast, 1672. This aquatic mammal is at least partially responsible for creating the mermaid legend.

papaw, *pawpaw*, via Spanish *papaya*, from a Carib word. Thus *papaw* and *papaya* come from the same Caribbean word. *Papaw* entered English in the 17th century; it was also called a *custard apple* in America by 1785.

piroque. We usually associate this dugout canoe with French trappers and explorers; English did get the word from the French in the 17th century, but the French got it from the Spanish *piragua* and the Spanish got it from the Carib *piraguas*.

potato, via Spanish *patata* from Taino *batata*, sweet potato. Not until around 1719 did the Irish bring the white potato to the colonies.

savanna, *savannah*, via Spanish from the Taino *zabana*, first recorded in America in 1671. This West Indian word gives us two place names, the *Savannah River* and *Savannah, Georgia*.

tobacco, via Spanish and Portuguese *tabaco* from a Carib name either for the pipe in which it was smoked or for a roll of it smoked like a cigar.

Al Capone

Al Capone, his face turned to hide the scar.

had everyone talking when he terrorized Chicago in the prohibition days of the 1920s and, as the father of organized crime, made popular several terms still in use. Naples-born, Brooklyn-raised Alfonso Capone (1899–1947) was called "Scarface Al" (movies usually shorten this to "Scarface") from a razor slash he received while a youthful member of Brooklyn's notorious "Five Points Gang," which also included Johnny Torrio. Soon after the 1919 Volstead Act, Torrio, who had moved to Chicago, had Capone join him as his *strong arm* (an 1828 term revived in 1903) to corner the Chicago bootleg market. Capone's men terrorized and murdered the competition, including killing rival gang leader Dion O'Banion in his flower shop in 1924. The newspapers began talking about Capone, his hiring of *torpedoes*, *trigger men*, *gorrillas*, and *rods* (meaning gunmen, *rod* had meant a handgun since 1904), their use of *pineapples* (hand grenades and bombs) and *Tommy guns* (the lightweight, 8½–10 pounds, Thompson submachine gun coinvented by General John Thompson, first manufactured in 1921 and first used by mobs in the 1925 Chicago "beer wars"), and the Chicago *gang wars* between the *mobs*. Capone took over from the shot and badly frightened Torrio in 1925, and the newspapers then began talking of Capone's *crime syndicate*, headquartered at the Four Deuces, Capone's combined saloon, whorehouse, and office.

Capone escaped a machine-gun raid on his Cicero, Illinois headquarters by O'Banion's old gang in 1926, continued vast bribes to police and civic officials, and in 1927 supported "Big Bill" Thompson for mayor (the election was called "the pineapple primary"). He now controlled bootlegging, gambling, prostitution, and even dance halls in the Chicago area, solidifying his position with the 1929 "St. Valentine's Day Massacre" in which seven of rival Bugs Moran's gang were lined up and machine-gunned in a garage. By 1931 when the Treasury Department indicted Capone for income-tax evasion, his income was $20 million a year (he was released from Alcatraz in 1939 as a helpless syphilitic paralytic, dying at his Miami Beach estate in 1947).

The Car

Thank Julius Caesar for the word *car*. He personally borrowed a Celtic word sounding something like "karra" to name his chariots, and from that and its Latinized *carrus/carra*, which came to mean wagon, cart, we get the English words *chariot*, *carriage*, and *car*. The colonists knew *car* only as a poetic word meaning chariot, as in the "Cars of the Gods." It wasn't until the 1820s and 30s that common people talked much about cars, by which they then meant *railroad cars*, *horsecars* and, by the 1860s, *streetcars*. Since about 1900, however, *car* has had one chief meaning to most Americans: an automobile.

The word *automobile* (Greek *auto-*, self + *mobile*, moving) arrived in the 1870s with the appearance of the *steam automobile*, also called a *steamer* (the British had called it a *steam carriage* since its beginnings in the 1830s). The *Stanley Steamer*, also known as *the flying teapot*, was manufactured from 1896 to 1925 by the Stanley twins, Francis and Freelan, and was the most talked-about automobile of the late 1890s. Various *electric automobiles*, going 25-40 miles at 15 mph on a battery charge, were also widely talked about at the time, but the *gasoline automobile*, first successfully built in the U.S. by the Duryea brothers in 1893, had few supporters—most people remembered that the famous *Electrobat* had beaten a Duryea gasoline automobile in a much-discussed 1895 race. But be it driven by electricity, steam, or gasoline, *automobile* was the word

Henry Ford (1863–1947) takes a drive.

74

There were women drivers right
from the beginning of automobiles. This is an early curved-
dash Oldsmobile.

generally used in the late 1890s, and was already shortened to *auto*.
Some of the over 50 inventors-designers-manufacturers of automobiles in 1898 were, however, using other terms, including
autopher, autovic, autobat, automotive, diamote, motorfly, self motor,
and *locomotive car.*

Francis E. and Freelan O. Stanley, twin brothers, manufactured the Stanley Steamer. To
heighten demand for it, they
entered races against gasoline-
powered cars and consistently
won. In 1907, the Stanley Special won the Daytona race at 197
mph. Another sensational victory was driving the car to the
top of the rutty and steep carriage
road up Mt. Washington (6,288
feet) in New Hampshire, 1899.
Sales were so good that the
company could not keep up with
the demand. In 1902, the two-
cylinder, 8 h.p. Stanley Steamer
without the folding top sold for
about $700.

The Baker Electric, manufactured from 1899 to 1916, was a "finely hand-built luxury ... car," costing $2,600 in 1910. The body was made of wood and the interior was usually red velvet.

The first definition of *motor-car* appeared in the 1890 edition of the *Century Dictionary:* "*Motor-car* . . . a car which carries its own propelling mechanism, as an electric motor. . . ." *Motor-car* was soon shortened to *car* and by 1910 *car* had replaced *automobile* as the more common word, though *automobile*, *motorcar*, and another early word for it, *machine*, were favored by some people well into the 1930s.

By 1900 the car was replacing the bicycle as a fad, and enthusiasts willingly donned *veils* and the clothes-protecting driving smocks called *dusters* (words used with a special meaning by auto-

mobile buffs since the 1870s) and *goggles* (which came in the 1890s). Since before 1890 *driver* had become the accepted word for one who could manipulate a car, although *chauffeur* was also in use (from French *chauffer*, to heat, originally meaning a stoker and then humorously applied to the driver of a steam automobile). By the end of the 1890s new names and words having to do with cars came thick and fast, and talking about cars became one of America's favorite pastimes—today new "car" words still appear every year and we still talk about cars avidly. It's been a long love affair. A sampling of some car names heard over and over in America includes:

Oldsmobile, introduced in 1897 by Ranson E. Olds (his initials also gave us the *Reo*).

Packard. In 1898 James Ward Packard was so disgusted when the new car he purchased from Alexander Winton, "bicycle and automobile manufacturer," broke down as he drove it home, that he decided to build his own. His 1899 car was a buggy-type, one-cylinder, 12-horsepower single-seater with a steering tiller.

Buick, famous since 1902 when bathtub maker David Dunbar Buick built the first car having a water-cooled, valve-in-head engine.

Cadillac, first built in 1902 by perfectionist Henry M. Leland and named after the French explorer.

The first Chevrolet, 1911.

The classic Duesenberg, late 1920s (above) and the Stutz, a famous sports car, are the two automobiles most often associated with the Roaring 20s. Increasingly expensive cars were built, some of them handcrafted and selling for as much as $40,000; but, after the stock market crash of 1929, they disappeared from the scene.

Studebaker, first appeared in 1904, when only one of the five famous Studebaker brothers was still living. They had built a blacksmith shop into one of the country's largest wagon and harness businesses, which had been a major supplier of the Union army during the Civil War.

General Motors, established by William C. Durant around 1909 from Oldsmobile, Buick, Cadillac, and many smaller companies.

The Model T, introduced as Henry Ford's ninth model in 1909 (the first *Ford* was built in 1903), it sold for $850 "In any color you choose as long as it's black." In 1914 Ford introduced the electric conveyor belt for the assembly of cars, and by 1926 mass production had lowered the price of a Model T to $350. Over 15 million Model Ts had been sold by 1927, when the *Model A* replaced it.

Chevrolet, introduced in 1911 as the first *six-cylinder* touring car, both the car and the Chevrolet Motor Company being named after and designed by former racing car driver Louis Chevrolet.

DeSoto, first built in Auburn, Indiana, in 1913, this expensive six-cylinder car then sold for $2,185.

Duesenberg, the brothers August and Frederick Duesenberg built their first cars in 1913, then introduced their *Roamer* in 1916, the *Revere* in 1917, and the famous *Model J* in 1928. The Duesenberg became the major American "classic car" of the 1920s, a type of fast (95–135 mph) expensive car which disappeared after the stock-market crash of 1929.

Dodge, the first model in 1914 introduced the "all-steel body" and had a widely discussed top speed of 44 mph; 45,000 were built in 1915, and in 1916 it became the first commercial car to have a hard top.

Stutz-Bearcat, the legendary sporty car after World War I and the car most of us associate with the Roaring 20s.

Nash, launched in 1918 by Charles Nash after he left General Motors and bought the *Rambler* automobile company, which had originally been a bicycle builder.

A "town car," about 1919, with a Model 36 Pierce Arrow chassis and an aluminum body. It often had two interchangeable bodies, one open and one closed, to accommodate the weather.

Cord. E. L. Cord produced his *L-29* in 1929 and the classic *Model 810* in 1937, introducing new designs, superchargers, and the disappearance of the running board.

Tucker. In 1947 the Tucker Corporation displayed pilot models of its rear-engine, three-headlight (the middle one turned with the steering wheel) *Tucker Torpedo,* later called the *Tucker 48.* Due to legal involvements, widely thought to have been initiated by "the big three" car manufacturers (Ford, GM, and Chrysler) supported by some government agencies, the car was never sold.

Henry J. Introduced after World War II, this, the first American "small car," and the larger *Kaiser-Frazer* were innovatively produced creations of Henry J. Kaiser. After building early West Coast highways, Kaiser became a major constructor in building the Boulder, Grand Coulee, and Shasta dams, then developed and built prefabricated Liberty Ships, and designed giant cargo planes with Howard Hughes in World War II, before using his experience and fame to build and sell his new line of cars in the mid 1940s.

Edsel, introduced with much fanfare by the Ford Motor Company in 1957, it was one of the most talked-about, joked-about flops in automobile history. Named after Edsel Ford, 1893–1943, son of Henry.

The Tucker, a 1947 pilot model (top); the Henry J Corsair, 1952 (middle); and the Edsel Citation, 1958 (bottom).

In addition to talking about specific cars, we Americans have constantly talked about parts of cars, types and styles of cars, and words for things associated with cars, using terms such as:

automobile tire, 1877 (wagon tires date from the 15th century); *jack,* 1877; *tread,* 1877, *retread,* 1890; *blowout,* 1915; *balloon tire,* early 1920s; *tubeless tire,* introduced by B. F. Goodrich, 1948; *radial ply tire,* 1967.

automobile accident, 1882; *car crash,* 1915; *hit-and-run,* 1920s.

fender, 1883; *hood,* 1906; *running board,* 1923; *rumble seat,* 1931.

crank, 1883; *self-starter,* 1894.

runabout, 1891; *touring car,* 1903; *station wagon,* 1904; *roadster,* 1908; *coupe,* 1918; *sedan,* 1920; *sports car,* 1925.

American Automobile Association, AAA, 1900.

license plate, 1901, when they were first issued by New York State.

garage, for housing an automobile, 1902.

road hog, early 1900s, had been applied first to bicyclists in the 1890s.

gas, 1905, from the 1865 word *gasoline,* which was originally considered merely a dangerous by-product in the making of kerosene.

spark plug, 1908, used to mean an energetic leader by the 1930s.

give her the gas, 1912; *step on the gas, tramp on the gas,* 1916; *step on it,* 1922; *give it the gas,* 1942. These replaced the older "don't spare the horses."

motorcade, 1912.

flivver, 1914 (the word originally meant a failure in the 1900s); *heap,* 1915; *tin lizzie,* 1915, originally meant only the Model T (*Lizzie* is from the common name for a Black maid who, like the car, worked hard all week and prettied up on Sundays); *crate,* 1920, following the World War I use for an airplane; *jalopy,* 1924; *gas buggy,* 1925; *rattletrap,* 1929.

traffic cop, 1915; *ticket,* 1930.

filling station, 1915; *service station,* 1922.

tourist camp, tourist court, 1916;

Surely one of the most stylish of our automobiles was this 1930 Packard, a two-passenger, convertible coupe.

motor court, 1936; *motor hotel*, mid 1940s; *motel* (from *motor* + *hotel*), late 1940s.

jaywalker, 1917 (from *jay* meaning a stupid or countrified person, 1889); *jaywalking*, 1919.

safety glass, 1922.

back seat driver, 1920s.

parking, parking space, parking lot, 1924; *parking meter*, 1935, the first ones installed in Oklahoma City.

used car, 1920s.

hitchhike, 1925; to *thumb a ride*, late 1930s.

trailer, 1926; *mobile home*, 1950s; *camper*, late 1960s.

drive-in, 1931 (referring to a filling station), first popularly applied to movies and restaurants in the mid 1940s.

streamlining, 1934, with the disappearance or covering of the square radiator.

automatic transmission, late 1940s (Buick introduced *Dynaflow* and Pontiac *Hydra-Matic* in 1948).

hot rod, drag race, mid 1940s.

The list goes on and on, for the car completely changed our life and our language. The car created the gasoline industry and all its words, reshaped the family vacation and resort industry and spawned many of our travel and recreational terms (*rent-a-car, fly-drive vacation, Hertz, Holiday Inn*, etc.); created fast-food chains (*McDonald's, Kentucky Fried Chicken*); and gave us hundreds of additional new words by creating new occupations (*car hop*), and new freedoms and lifestyles for youth (*joy ride*, 1915; *back seat necking*, 1922) and for adults alike (parents didn't drive away and need a *baby sitter* until 1945; *suburb* didn't mean a place where one lived while driving to work every day until the 1940s). We'll continue to use an ever-increasing number of words for cars and for our mobile life until the gas runs out—when we may again be talking about *steamers* or *electric automobiles*.

The Circus is Coming to Town

has been ringing in American ears ever since the first traveling circuses of the 1820s. The words *circus* (Latin "ring") and *arena* (Latin "sand," as used to cover the ring) go back to the days of the Roman amphitheaters, used for chariot racing, gladiator fighting, and throwing Christians to the lions. The modern circus was developed in England around the time of our Revolutionary War, mainly by trick riders. Philip Asley became the father of the modern circus by being the first man to ride a horse while standing on its back. This feat gave Asley enough fame to open his permanent Royal Grove Circus in London in 1769, and eventually helped him start 18 other "first" circuses across Europe from France to Russia.

A Ringling Brothers *circus poster of 1907 just before the* Ringling Brothers, Barnum and Bailey Circus *was formed.*

Mr. and Mrs. Tom Thumb with P. T. Barnum. The midget on the right is probably Commander Nutt. "General Tom Thumb" was really Charles Sherwood Stratton (1838–83), 2 feet 1 inch and only 15 pounds as a teenager—he later grew to 3 feet 4 inches and almost 70 pounds. He spent all but six years of his life with P. T. Barnum, marrying another Barnum midget, Lavinia Warren (1841–1919).

The Barnum and Bailey bearded lady of 1903, Grace Gilbert, the "female Essau."

In August, 1785 John Pool erected a small building in Philadelphia where he displayed animals, rode a running horse while standing on its back balancing a glass of wine, and also employed a singing, wisecracking clown to entertain his patrons. His success encouraged John Bill Ricketts to come from England and open his *Ricketts' Circus and Riding Academy* in Philadelphia, then the nation's capital, in 1793. This was the first American "circus" billed by that name. George Washington and his wife attended on April 22 of that year and *circus* almost immediately became a beloved American word. Originally, however, when people talked about circuses they meant a primarily equestrian show in a permanent building, with trick riding, dressage, and elaborate pageants on horseback. Soon, vaudeville-type acts were added to these and, meanwhile, some acrobats, jugglers, and exhibitors of a trained bear, trick monkey, etc., joined their roving acts into less pretentious "circuses," performing in taverns, on village greens, and street corners for whatever coins the spectators could spare. Here's a list of some circus terms and of some performers, acts, and events which people have talked about and which give the word *circus* the meaning and excitement it has today:

1826 Howe's and Turner's circus and Quick and Mead's circus (four wagons, nine horses, and one hurdy-gurdy) became the first two circuses to use tents, 50-foot ones. Now *circus tent*, *circus wagon*, and *circus horse* are in the language. (Incidentally, *hurdy-gurdy* is an 18th century English word and instrument, from the 15th century English dialect *hirdy-girdy* meaning an uproar, the word imitating the sound.)

1839 "The Apollo on Horseback," Levi North, is the first person to do a somersault on a running horse.

1846 *side show* is in the language.

late 1830s–50s Isaac Van Amburgh becomes the first famous American *wild animal trainer*, making the *wild animal act* a popular circus act. He was the first to put his head in a lion's mouth, as described by Nathaniel Hawthorne in his *American Notebook*, September 4, 1838.

1850s The famous circus performer and owner Dan Rice popularizes the *charity circus*, gaining local support for his circus performances by donating part of the proceeds to local charities, often to local firefighters to buy new equipment. During the Civil War Rice donated part of the proceeds from each performance to the Union Women's Relief Corps and the Sanitary Commission; when he played in Washington, D.C. in June, 1864 President Lincoln came to his tent to thank him personally.

1859 Charles Blondin has all America talking with his feat of crossing Niagara on a *tightrope*. Circuses begin to feature *rope dancers* (an old term for the wandering performers), *rope walkers*, and *tightrope acts*.

The same year, the French gymnast Jules Leotard (who

An ornate Barnum and Bailey bandwagon (1855), showing a gladiator scene (right). Used in circus parades, bandwagons had high decks so that musicians seated on them could be heard and seen by street crowds. A tightrope dancer or acrobat, here Con Colleano, is a standard circus performer (below).

He flies through the air with the greatest of ease,
This daring young man on the flying trapeze;
His figure is handsome, all girls he can please,
And my love he purloined her away!
"The Man on the Flying Trapeze," 1860, George Leybourne

designed the *leotard* that is named for him) invented the *flying trapeze*. In the next 30 years people were talking about seeing their first *aerial gymnast* or *aerobat*, later known as an *aerialist*.

1860–70s *Circus train* becomes an exciting term. "Doctor" Gilbert R. Spalding was the first to transport his circus by train (on flatcars); before that he had put circuses on Mississippi river steamboats (see *showboat* at Steamboat 'a Comin').

During the same period ornate *circus wagons* were introduced from England and people were talking excitedly about the *circus parades* to the *circus lot*. The last wagon in the parade was always a *musical steam engine*, or *steam piano*, otherwise known as a *(steam) calliope* (an 1858 word, from Greek *Kalliope*, "the beautiful voice," the name of the ninth muse, of eloquence and epic poetry). The first such instrument used by circuses had been Gilbert Spalding's 1849 "musical pipe organ on wheels," using air produced as the wheels revolved, the contraption being pulled by 40 horses (the first *forty-horse hitch*, which term is somewhat of a curiosity to horse lovers).

Now a *low grass show* became circus parlance for a big circus playing on a mowed lot, a *high grass show* was one too small or poor to mow the field before setting up.

1868 *Roustabout* is in the language, meaning a Mississippi river deckhand or longshoreman. Soon it will come to mean a circus laborer.

1870 "Daring Lulu," a man dressed as a woman, is "shot" from a springboard, eventually leading to *the man shot out of a cannon* act.

1871 *The Greatest Show on Earth* is what P. T. (Phineas Taylor) Barnum (1810–91) calls his circus that opens in Brooklyn. Barnum had already added such terms as *the Bearded Lady*, *the Thin Man*, *the Wild Man of Borneo*, *the Rubber Man*, *the Elephant Boy*, *Siamese twin*, and *bandwagon* (1855) to the language. He had coined these terms and become known for his saying, "There's a sucker born every minute," after he opened his American Museum of Curios in New York City in 1842, where he displayed both real freaks and fake ones, ranging from such real "curiosities" as the Bearded Lady and the Thin Man to *Feejee the Mermaid*, which was a monkey's head and torso sewn to a fish's body. There too he had made *General Tom Thumb* the most talked-about midget in history. He had also

Nearly FIVE MILLION PEOPLE in this Country have already Seen, with growing Awe and Wonder,

ALL-FAMOUS AND GIGANTIC
"JUMBO"

And of all that vast number, not a single one departs his tremendous existence as

THE MIGHTY LORD OF ALL BEASTS
AND
ALONE THE SHOW OF SHOWS.

All concede him to be, beyond all question,

The Largest Living Quadruped on Earth
And since his arrival in America,

HE HAS GROWN SEVERAL INCHES IN HEIGHT, and INCREASED OVER A TON IN WEIGHT.

THIS TOWERING MONSTER
AMONG ALL THE HUGEST ELEPHANTS,
IS REALLY A HISTORIC MAMMOTH

Barnum bought Jumbo, his largest and last major attraction, in 1881. It died in 1885 while trying to save the life of Barnum's smallest attraction, Tom Thumb, from a railroad train which hit them both, the giant being killed, the midget recovering—or so Barnum said! Jumbo's stuffed remains may still be seen in New York City's Museum of Natural History.

Emmett Kelly was a trapeze artist before becoming a clown. He has appeared in movies and on TV.

made the unrivaled Swedish coloratura, Jenny Lind, the beloved *Swedish nightingale* of all America when he brought her to America on a highly publicized concert tour, 1850–52.

1880s Ella Zuila walks the *high wire* on stilts; she also walks it while carrying her husband on her shoulders and while trundling her child in a wheelbarrow. Such *high wire acts* become a much talked-about circus attraction.

During the same decade *menagerie* becomes an American circus word and many circuses add them (it's a French word, from the French *ménage*, household).

1881 *The Barnum and Bailey Circus* is formed when P. T. Barnum's "Greatest Show on Earth" merges with James Anthony Bailey's circus. The combined show becomes the first famous *three ring circus*.

This same year Barnum buys a giant 6½-ton elephant named *Jumbo* from London's Royal Zoological Society, making him the star attraction of Barnum and Bailey. Jumbo probably got his name from the Gullah word *jamba*, meaning elephant, but Barnum's ballyhoo put *jumbo*, meaning large, gigantic, into the language by 1883.

1884 *The Ringling Brothers Circus* is started by the five Ringling brothers. It's known to insiders as a *Sunday school show* because it's honest and doesn't permit gambling games.

1890s The main circus tent is now called *the big top*.

1907 *Ringling Brothers, Barnum and Bailey Circus* is created when Ringling Brothers Circus buys Barnum and Bailey. This combined show is billed simply as *The Big One*.

1910 Isabella Buttes does her "Dip of Death," a loop-de-loop in a special car down an inclined plane.

1912 "The greatest bareback rider of them all," May Worth, is the first to somersault from one horse to another.

1920s Alfredo Codoma perfects his *triple somersault* from one flying trapeze to another.

His wife, Lillian Leitzel, "Queen of the Aerialists," perfects her act of pivoting 200 times while suspended from a swivel high above the crowd (she plunged to her death while doing this act in 1931, on a Friday the 13th).

1920–30s Clowns assume a bigger role during the hard times of the Depression. The earlier talking *whiteface* clowns such as the rustic wit, Dan Rice, have been joined by the silent baggy-pants ones, like sad-faced Emmett Kelly. During the Depression, too, some clowns don hobo costumes, which become a mainstay. The silent clowns' *walk around* becomes popular, Lou Jacobs riding around in his motorized bathtub and Felix Adler doing his walk around cradling and bottle feeding a pig. The *Pfunny Fhord* is also introduced into the clown act, disintegrating, exploding, or holding an impossible number of clowns.

1930s–40s *The Clyde Beatty Circus*, featuring that famous animal trainer, is a much talked-about attraction. Later it merged with the *Cole Brothers Circus* to become the *Clyde Beatty-Cole Brothers Circus*, now "the world's largest circus under canvas."

1936 Increased freight and labor costs cause Ringling Brothers, Barnum and Bailey circus to give up *tenting* and appear only in permanent halls—where the American circus started in 1785.

The Civil War

lasted from 1861 to 1865. Southerners called it *the Revolution, the War of Independence, the Second War of Independence*, and *the War of Secession* (all 1861 terms). After it was over, it was usually called by its Northern name *the Civil War* (1861) or by the names made possible only because the states were again united, *the War Between the States* and *the War Between the North and the South* (both names first popular in the 1890s).

Bad feelings between *the North* (1791) and *the South* (1781) went back to colonial days. The settlers had always been divided by two climates and two geographies, resulting in two personalities and two systems of livelihood, an industrial economy in the North and a planter-dominated, slave-based economy in the South. Slavery was not only an issue but the symbol of the divided economies and living patterns of the two regions. Thus the terms which led up to the war mainly had to do with the question of slavery:

the Mason-Dixon Line was originally called *Mason and Dixon's Line*, 1779. It was named for two English surveyors, Charles Mason and Jeremiah Dixon, who surveyed the disputed boundary between Pennsylvania and Maryland between 1763 and 1767. Their line was extended westward in 1784 and became the northern boundary of Maryland, Delaware, and part of Virginia. Before the Civil War this line and the Ohio River came to be considered the boundary between free states and slave states.

States Rights, 1798, meaning both the rights reserved to each state and the philosophy of reserving as many rights to the states as possible. *The States Rights Party*, 1840, was made up of Southern Democrats who were called *States Rights Democrats* by 1853. The South claimed that each state had the right to decide for itself whether or not to permit slavery.

slave state, 1809; *black state*, 1814, originally meaning a state with many slaves, as Virginia and South Carolina, then any state in which slavery was permitted. *Free state*, 1819; *free territory*, 1854.

the Border States, 1842. *Border free state, border slave state*, 1850s. When the war began, Lincoln's shrewdness and statesmanship kept the border slave states of Delaware, Maryland, Kentucky, and finally Missouri (after a year of intrastate civil war) in the Union.

Bleeding Kansas, Kansas during the bitter fighting of 1854–60 over whether to have slavery or not. It was admitted to the Union as a free state in January, 1861. The guerrilla bands who carried on the irregular war in Kansas were called *Jayhawkers*, though this term soon came to mean only those fighting against slavery. During the Civil War itself *Jayhawker* was a name for any guerrilla and in Kansas for a Southern sympathizer (see *copperhead* in the list below). This term *Jayhawker* seems to have come from a mythical "jayhawk," a bird of prey. Because of Kansas' antislavery Jayhawkers, any Kansan was called a *Jayhawker* by 1875 and Kansas was called *the Jayhawk State* by 1885.

A house divided against itself cannot stand. I believe this government cannot endure permanently half slave and half free. I do not expect the Union to be dissolved—I do not expect the house to fall—but I do expect it will cease to be divided. It will become all one thing, or all the other.

Abraham Lincoln, June 16, 1858, acceptance speech for the Republican state senatorial nomination, Republican State Convention, Springfield, Illinois. He was paraphrasing Mark 3:25, "If a house be divided against itself that house cannot stand."

Abraham Lincoln, 1863.

84

"*The Last Moments of John Brown,*" *Thomas Hovenden (1840-95).*

Matthew Brady in 1861. Brady had received official permission from Lincoln and the Secret Service to establish complete photographic coverage of the war. He and his photographic teams took over 7,000 pictures, ruining him by exhausting his entire $100,000 fortune, which he had earned as one of America's most popular photographers.

the Dred Scott Decision of the Supreme Court, on March 7, 1857, brought the Civil War closer by angering the North. Dred Scott was a slave whose Missouri master had taken him to the free state of Illinois and the free territory of Wisconsin. When he was returned to Missouri, Scott, supported by antislavery groups, had sued for his freedom on the grounds of his previous residency in a free state and free territory. He lost. The court held that since he was not a citizen he had no standing in court and that the *Missouri Compromise* (1820, in which Maine entered the Union as a free state, Missouri as a slave state, and slavery was prohibited in the rest of the Louisiana Territory) was unconstitutional. The court also declared that a citizen (the master) could not be deprived of his property (the slave) merely because he took it to a free territory.

John Brown's Raid brought the Civil War closer by inflaming the South. The fanatic John Brown led a raid of 13 Whites and 5 Blacks on the small town of Harpers Ferry, Virginia, holding it and the Federal arsenal there, October 16-17, 1859. Brown's object was to arm the slaves and signal a *slave rebellion* (the term had been used during the Revolutionary War in 1777; the term *slave insurrection* had been in colonial use since 1619 and was used in the Kansas conflict in 1857). Brown, who had previously killed five proslavery men at Pottawatomie, Kansas, in 1856, was captured by a government detachment led by a Colonel Robert E. Lee, Brown later being hanged for treason, December 2, 1859.

But the words, the names, that led to the final break between North and South were *Republican* and *Lincoln*. The South violently opposed the new Republican party, which was against slavery in the new territories (including those won in THE MEXICAN WAR). When this party's "secular candidate" Abraham Lincoln won the presidential election of 1860 many Southerners gave up hope for reconciliation, feeling that *secession* (1830 in its Southern use) from the Union was the only way left to preserve slavery, their economy, and their way of life.

In the five months following Lincoln's election all America had much to talk about. On December 20, 1860, South Carolina adopted the *Ordinance of Secession*, seceding from the Union, and in the next 40 days Mississippi, Florida, Alabama, Georgia, and Louisiana followed. During February 4-11, 1861, these six states met in Montgomery, Alabama, formed their own congress, adopted a provisional constitution, chose Jefferson Davis as president, and declared themselves *the Confederate States of America*. On March 4th, in his inaugural address, Lincoln asserted that the Union was indestructible, declared secession void, and urged reconciliation. On March 5th, his first full day as president, Lincoln learned that the garrison at Fort Sumpter in Charleston Harbor, South Carolina, would be starved out if not provisioned (President Buchanan's unarmed supply vessels having been turned back by South Carolina cannon fire in

I propose to fight it out on this line if it takes all summer. General U. S. Grant in a telegram to President Lincoln after the battle of Spotsylvania Court House, a town in Virginia, May 8–12, 1864, in which neither he nor Lee had won a victory. By late June he had Lee pinned to a static defense around Richmond, then began a 10½-month siege that ended the war.

January). Lincoln sent an unarmed supply expedition, but on April 12th, before it arrived, P. G. T. Beauregard ordered Confederates to fire on the fort. It surrendered April 14. The next day Lincoln called for 75,000 state militia to suppress the "insurrection"; the free states responded but Virginia, Arkansas, and Tennessee then seceded (Texas had joined the Confederacy earlier, North Carolina soon followed). The Civil War had begun.

The North began the war with 23 states, 22 million people, the navy, all the country's gold, 80% of the factories, and 70% of the railroads. The South had 11 states, 5½ million Whites and 3½ million Black slaves, and about a third of the regular army's officers (including the best, such as Robert E. Lee, who had refused the post of Commander of the Union Army). The North spoke proudly of:

General Ulysses S[impson] Grant (1822–85) and his staff at City Point, Virginia, during the winter of 1864. They were waiting for the Confederate collapse at Richmond.

the Union, applied to the entire union of colonies in 1756, to the United States since 1776, and to the Northern states since 1836. A Northern supporter had been called a *Union man* since 1837.

the Union Army, 1861. The entire U.S. Army had only 16,000 men when the war began; within two years the Union Army reached its peak of a million men (during the war a total of 2 million men served in this army).

the Grand Army of the Republic (1862), also abbreviated to *the GAR* (1867), is another name for the Union Army. The name did not become popular until it was widely used as the name of a veterans' organization in 1866.

the Blue, the Federals (both 1861), meaning both the North and its army. Northerners and Union soldiers were also called *the Feds. The Blue*, of course referred to the color of the army's uniforms. *The boys in blue*, Union soldiers, 1866 (it had also meant sailors in England since 1730 and in the U.S. since 1819). Blue had been the color of U.S. army uniforms for some time, American troops being called *blue coats* since 1833, *blue bellies* since 1851, with the term *Army blue* appearing in 1859. Calling Northern troops *the blue* or *blue bellies* was reinforced in the South by such older terms for stern or aristocratic New Englanders as *blue skins* (1776, it had also meant ardent supporters of the American Revolution), *blue-nosed* (1800s), and *blue-stocking* (1829). A Union soldier was also called a YANKEE, *Yank*, and *Billy Yank* (which had also been a term for a Revolutionary War soldier).

God's country, the Union troops' term for the North, especially when battling heat, humidity, and mosquitoes in the South. Not until the 1880s did the term mean any section of the country one loved or the open spaces of the West. The Union troops also called the American flag *God's flag*.

Loyalist, a Union sympathizer in the South, 1862.

While the above terms were used by or about the North, other terms were used by or about the South:

the *Confederacy* had meant the entire confederation of all the states, the United States, until 1829, when secession was first discussed; between then and 1861 it slowly came to mean the South and then the Confederate States of America. *Confederates* and *the Confeds* meant both Southerners and Confederate troops from 1861 on. In 1861 *Confederate* also first appeared in many combinations, as *Confederate money*, *Confederate stamps*, *the Confederate Capital*, etc. The *Confederate flag* (another 1861 term) was also called *the stars and bars*, to distinguish it from the Union's *stars and stripes*.

the *Confederate Army*, 1861. It reached a peak of 500,000 men in 1863. Two-thirds of both the Confederate and Union troops were under 22 years of age.

the *Gray*, 1861, the Confederacy or its army, from the color of its official uniforms, though these were not always available. By 1862 Confederate soldiers were also called *the boys in gray*, *graycoats*, and *graybacks*.

Butternuts, 1861, another name for Confederate soldiers, because many wore homemade uniforms dyed with butternut extract.

rebel, a Confederate or Confederate soldier, 1861. A "rebel soldier" was often called a *Reb* by 1862, with *Johnny Reb* also being a popular term. Rebel troops were famous for their blood curdling mountaineer's *rebel yell* which they gave when going into battle—Northern troops often gave a more formal "three cheers" before attacking. The North also called Southerners *seceshers*.

Dixie became a popular word for the South during the Civil War and *Dixie Land* a popular Southern song (See DIXIE for details).

The long and bloody war was a dividing line between classic warfare (Lee's defense) and modern warfare (typified by Grant's offense). It saw both classic frontal attacks and cavalry fights and also *trench warfare*, *guerrilla attacks* (diminutive of the Span-

General Robert E[dward] Lee (1807–70) with his aides at Richmond, Virginia, in the spring of 1965. Lee surrendered to Grant April 9, 1865, at Appomattox, Virginia, about 50 miles west of Richmond.

Prison pens *was the term used to describe the horrible prisons of the Civil War. Here is a view through the main gate of Andersonville,* the Confederate prison *about 50 miles south of Macon, Georgia, where 30,000 Union prisoners were jammed into a 16½-acre stockade, without sufficient food or sanitary facilities. More than 13,000 men died there. Captain Henry Wirz, Andersonville's commander, was tried by a military commission after the war and hanged.*

Admiral Farragut in Mobile Bay, 1864.

ish *guerra*, war, hence "little war"), and military *bushwackers* (1861). It was the first war in which troops were moved by steam railroads, communicated by telegraph, and wore uniforms sewn by *sewing machines* (1846). It was also the first war using ironclad naval vessels and the first to be photographed. Various aspects and moods of the war are shown in some of the terms and names it popularized or created:

admiral, in 1866, David Farragut became the first admiral in the U.S. Navy; he had been appointed the first U.S. *vice admiral* in 1864.

antebellum (Latin *ante-*, before + *bellum*, war), before the U.S. Civil War, this meaning first recorded in 1867.

A.W.O.L. became the initials for "*absent without leave*" during the Civil War (unwarranted absence of a comparatively short duration, not long enough to classify a soldier as a deserter). The South punished such offenders rather leniently, as with a reprimand or assignment to physical labor while wearing a placard with the letters AWOL on it, which helped popularize the initials. The initials were widely spoken during World War I, as "a-w-o-l," but were not used as an acronym, that is not pronounced as a word "Awol" until World War II.

brevet (Latin *breve*, letter, summary, hence a document attesting military rank) was used by the Union army as an honorary title during the Civil War, often giving officers an unearned rank. Union soldiers grew to hate many *brevet officers* and after the war used *brevet* as a sneering synonym for "honorary." Thus a *brevet child* or *brevet baby* was an illegitimate one fathered by a soldier during the war, a *brevet Northerner* was a Southerner who claimed to have been for the winning Union side all along, and by 1884 a *brevet Democrat* was one who had status in the party not because of his political work but because he had been a Confederate officer.

Confederate cruisers were the naval ships built by Britain and France for the South during the first two years of the war, before the North, looking like a sure winner in 1863, pressured these countries to stop constructing them. They destroyed over 250 Union ships. *Confederate rams* were Confederate warships fitted with an iron beak on the bow; these also did considerable damage to Union shipping.

copperhead was the name of the snake by 1775 and by 1809 meant any hostile or vindictive person, then specifically came to mean a White man who lived or fought with the Indians (*copperhead* also meant an Indian by 1838). During the Civil War a *copperhead* or *Copperhead* (1862) was the North's derogatory term for a Northerner who sympathized with the South. In Kansas such Southern sympathizers were also called *Jayhawkers* (see *Bleeding Kansas* above); in Kentucky they were called *bushwackers* (1862); in Missouri *butternuts* (see *Butternuts* above); in Illinois *guerrillas* (since 1859); and in Ohio they were also called *Vallandighamers* (1862, after an Ohio politician and Copperhead leader, Clement Vallandigham, who was finally arrested for treason in 1863 and sentenced to confine-

A Confederate soldier, 1861.

ment in Fort Warren before Lincoln commuted the sentence by banishing him to the Confederacy).

crooked shoes were first worn and complained about by many farm boys and working men as part of their Civil War uniforms. This was the term for a pair of shoes cut in the modern way, for the right and left feet, as opposed to the simpler, cheaper *straights* which fit either foot and had up to then been the type of shoe most men wore.

doughboy, a soldier. This was a fairly new and rare word at the time of the Civil War (for details see WORLD WAR I).

draftee is an American word first used in the Civil War. Nationwide conscription came to America with the confederate Conscription Act of 1862 and the Union's Draft Law of 1863. The South drafted men 18–35, the North drafted men 20–35, single men to 45. Both sides required draftees to serve for three years, find someone to serve for them, or to pay the government a fine (which was $300 in the North, 2/3rds of the average working man's annual income). Most men volunteered, many for as little as three months: only 2% of the Union Army was drafted.

draft riot, the first Union draft drawings caused riots in several cities, the worst being the *Draft Riot* in New York City, July 13–16, 1863. The mob, led by low-paid Irish immigrants, first attacked the officers drawing the names of the draftees, then the police, and finally plundered stores and warehouses, burned a Negro orphan asylum, and hanged Blacks from lampposts. The riot was finally subdued by heavy rains, the police, and troops called in from Gettysburg.

ensign first became an official U.S. naval rank in 1862, being the lowest commissioned rank. The word had meant a badge or banner in English since the 14th century (from Old French *enseigne*, insignia) and various army and navy officers in England by the 16th century (literally one leading a detachment serving under a single flag or banner).

federal income tax, although such a tax had been talked about for decades, the first one went into effect in the Union during the Civil War: a tax of 3% being levied on all incomes over $800 a year. This tax supplied about 20% of the Union's revenues by the end of the war, which was otherwise financed by currency issues, loans, and selling $511 million worth of bonds.

Black recruits boarding a train for Murfreesboro, Tennessee, to join the Northern army. By war's end there were 186,000 Black soldiers in the Federal armies, 93,000 coming from the Confederate states.

89

General of the Army, 1864, when U. S. Grant became the first American to be given this official rank.

greenbacks, *bluebacks*, and *shinplasters*. The North seized the wartime opportunity to establish a stronger centralized banking system and on February 25, 1862, Congress authorized the first U.S. legal tender bank notes—green in color, they were immediately called *greenbacks*. By the war's end the Union had issued $499 million worth of greenbacks, inflation making the $1 bill worth only 39¢ in gold.

Confederate bills were called *bluebacks* or *graybacks*, from their color. The Confederacy paid for the war by issuing over a billion dollars in paper money, raising very few funds from taxes and loans. Toward the end of the war a Confederate $1 bill was worth only 1.7¢ in gold.

Since silver coins were hoarded during the war, the North began issuing fractional paper currency of 3, 5, 10, 15, 25, and 50 cent denominations in 1862. Considered ugly and flimsy, they were derisively called *shinplasters*. They remained in use until 1876.

homeguard, 1861, Union use.

ironclads, 1867. The Confederates never had a ship named the *Merrimac*—that was a Union frigate (named after the river in Massachusetts) that had been burned and scuttled in Norfolk, Virginia's Hampton Roads Harbor. When the Confederates raised and rebuilt it as an ironclad it was officially named the *C.S.S. Virginia* (*C.S.S.*, of course, standing for *Confederate States Ship*). It was sent to clear Hampton Roads of Union blockading vessels and destroyed two Northern warships before the *U.S.S. Monitor* arrived. The two steam-powered ships fought their 5-hour "battle of the ironclads" March 9, 1862, in which the shells bounced off their iron coverings doing little damage and killing no one. The battle signaled the end of wooden warships. Because the Union's *Monitor*, built by John Ericsson in 1862, had the first revolving turret (carrying two 11-inch guns) on a deck only 18 inches above the water, many people called it *the cheesebox on a raft*. It was the first of 31 such ships built by the Union and all such ironclads became known as *monitors*. Many ironclads had only one-inch thick iron plates bolted to their wooden sides and were derisively called *tinclads*.

Two months after the "historic battle of the ironclads" between the Confederate Merrimac *(renamed the* Virginia*) and the Union* Monitor, *the former was destroyed when the South evacuated Norfolk, Virginia; ten months after the battle the* Monitor *sank in a storm off Cape Hatteras, North Carolina.*

kit bag and *kit* were 18th century English terms for a knapsack packed with a soldier's eating utensils and other necessities (from Dutch *kit*, tankard, drinking cup). The terms were in wide use by both sides during the Civil War.

the Medal of Honor, the Congressional Medal of Honor was established and named by Congress in 1862, to be given to Union heroes.

muster in, muster out were terms first used in America in the 1840s, but they didn't become well known until the Civil War. During the war *to be mustered out* was a euphemism meaning that one had been killed in action.

the Napoleon, 1862, the basic artillery piece used by both sides. A smooth-bore, muzzle-loading, brass 12-pound gun, it could shoot three rounds a minute, sending solid balls 1,500 yards and shot-filled canisters to cut down advancing troops 200 yards. It got its name because it was the field gun adopted in France around 1856 under Napoleon III. It was also called *the gun howitzer* and *the light twelve pounder.*

the Parrott gun, the Parrott, 1862, America's first rifled cannon and a major factor in the Union victory. It was named for its inventor, Robert Parker Parrott, professor of physics at West Point, who, after hearing that Germany's Krupp had produced such a gun, spent ten years working on it at the Cold Spring iron foundry.

pup tent, 1863.

Sanitary Fair. The Union's civilian *United States Sanitary Commission* cared for the sick and wounded by establishing field hospitals and helped oversee the Union troops' living conditions, especially sanitation. Its over 4,000 local branches provided extra food, clothing, and medicine for the troops. Money was raised for the Commission's work by the very popular *Sanitary Fairs,* exhibitions, art shows, teas, etc., which gave many women their first taste of work outside the home.

shelter tent, 1863, a small tent for two soldiers, it had a ridge rope supported by two poles. Not until World War II did the *shelter half* evolve.

Sherman's bummers. Grant and Sherman had agreed on a "burnt country" (we would say "scorched earth") drive from Atlanta to split the South and destroy its resources. Sherman started his "march to the sea" from Chattanooga, Tennessee, entered Georgia on May 4, 1864, and captured Atlanta on September 2nd. He left Atlanta in flames ("the burning of Atlanta") on November 14th to march on to Savannah, which surrendered December 22, then by April, 1865, Sherman and his men had marched up through South Carolina and North Carolina. His 50,000–90,000 men cut a 60-mile wide swath through the South, living off the land and destroying what they couldn't eat or carry, destroying over $100 million worth of property in Georgia alone. *Bummer* (German *bummler,* idler, loafer) had meant an army deserter by 1850 and in 1861 already meant a soldier more interested in plundering than fighting. *Sherman's bummers* were the special foragers who helped his troops live off the land. *Sherman's neckties* or *Sherman's hairpins* were railroad rails heated on bonfires of crossties and wrapped around trees while *Sherman's sentinels,* called *Sher-*

"Barbara Frietchie," by N. C. Wyeth (1882–1945).

"Shoot if you must, this old gray head,
But spare your country's flag, she said,"

are the lines from John Greenleaf Whittier's 1863 poem "Barbara Frietchie," which immortalized this old lady. She is supposed to have waved a Union flag at "Stonewall" Jackson's troops as they passed through Frederick, Maryland, in 1862, but there is no evidence the incident ever took place. She may have waved her flag at Union troops passing by a week later.

man's monuments after the war, were the standing chimneys of buildings burned down by Sherman's men.

skedaddle (from Scot and northern England dialect, probably from Greek *skedannunai*, to split up) entered American English in the 1820s but became popular during the Civil War. Union troops used the word to describe Confederate troops fleeing from battlefields.

slouch hats were a British style and term first introduced into the U.S. in the 1830s. Confederate troops made them popular.

slow bear and *mud lark* were just two of the humorous euphemisms the short-rationed, foraging troops used to refer to the farmers' pigs they killed and ate. *Confederate beef* was a term the Union troops gave the Southern cows and horses they killed and ate but, after Grant's six-weeks siege of Vicksburg, May 19–July 4, 1863, it referred to the mules the Confederate army had been forced to eat there.

Springfields, Sharps, and *Beecher's Bibles.* Various muskets and rifles made at the government armory at Springfield, Massachusetts, have been called *the Springfield (rifle)* since 1813. Both sides carried Springfields during the war, usually a one-shot muzzle loader; "rifle" was often an exaggeration, many being smooth-bore muskets, as the Union's U.S. Springfield Musket Model 1863. Both sides also had the breech-loading, lever-action, self-priming *Sharps' rifle* or *Sharp rifle* that could squeeze off 12 shots a minute. It was named for its maker, Christian Sharps, who had patented it as a .50-caliber hunting rifle in 1848 (U.S. Army *sharpshooters,* 1856, were armed with this rifle, but an accurate gun was called a *sharp shooter* long before this and the term has nothing to do with the Sharps rifle.) These Sharps' rifles were also called *Beecher's Bibles* (1856) because the abolitionist Reverend Henry Ward Beecher had preached that a Sharps' rifle in the hands of antislavery Kansas immigrants would be more convincing to proslavery forces than any argument against slavery found in the Bible—and he then used money he had raised to buy Bibles to ship Sharps' rifles to antislavery forces in Kansas.

strawfoot was Union army slang for a rural or backwoods soldier, as if he still had straw on his shoes. However, legend has it that drill sergeants found such men didn't know their left foot from their right, so taught them to march by having them tie hay to their left foot and straw to the right, then called out the marching cadence "hayfoot! strawfoot!" instead of the usual "left! right!"

Tarheel, 1864, a man from North Carolina, and *Josh,* a man from Arkansas, became popular during the Civil War. Such regional nicknames proliferated as soldiers met many men from different states for the first time.

ten acres and a mule was what many slaves talked about from 1862 on. Encouraged by some Union propagandists, they thought they would be given this after the war when their masters' plantations would be confiscated and divided up among them. This expectation increased to *forty acres and a mule* after General Sherman's special field order of January 16, 1865, stated "Every family shall have a plot of not more than forty acres of tillable ground." The federal government, of course, had made no such promise.

the Trent affair. On November 8, 1861, Captain Wilkes of the *U.S.S. San Jacinto* halted the British ship *Trent* and removed two Confederate commissioners, who were then interred in Boston (the men were J. M. Mason, Confederate commissioner to England, and John Slidell, who had played a part in events leading up to THE MEXICAN WAR and was then Confederate commissioner to France). Britain's strong protest caused Lincoln and Secretary of State Seward to disavow the act and release the two men. Since the Confederacy wasn't recognized diplomatically, it was sending *commissioners*, rather than ambassadors or ministers, to England and France to seek recognition and aid.

unconditional surrender is now associated with the Allies' World War II demands on the Axis, but General Grant used the term first. On February 16, 1862, when Fort Donelson in Tennessee was about to fall to Grant, Confederate General Simon Bolivar Buckner asked for the best terms of capitulation and Grant replied "No terms except unconditional surrender." The capture of Fort Donelson was the Union's first major victory of the war, collapsing the Confederate position in Kentucky and Tennessee. One of Grant's nicknames became "Unconditional Surrender" (matching his initials of U. S. Grant).

the Union League was a society established by staunch patriots in November, 1862, to stimulate loyalty to the Union at a time when morale was low. Later the same name was given to a secret political organization among the newly freed Blacks, many such Union Leagues being created by carpetbaggers to insure political support (see RECONSTRUCTION: CARPETBAGGERS AND THE KU KLUX KLAN).

war correspondent, 1861; *army correspondent*, 1863. The Civil War saw the development of the war correspondent. One of the best known was Winslow Homer, who accompanied the Union Army as a correspondent and artist for *Harper's Weekly*.

war widow, used during this war to mean a woman whose husband was away from home in the army or navy.

The war will be over by Christmas was a popular 1861 expression. Since then several generals and politicians have used the phrase or variations of it, in World War I, World War II, and the Korean war—and none of the wars was over by Christmas.

Zouave, 1860, a member of any of various volunteer regiments, chiefly in the North, which adopted some of the colorful Oriental uniform (including baggy pants and a short coat) and precision drill of the French Algerian Zouaves (from *Zwāwa*, an Algerian tribal name).

The Civil War changed American life and speech in many, many ways. It spurred the rapid growth of the railroads and the oil industry and the terms associated with them; it introduced many Americans to mass-produced canned foods; it saw profanity reach a peak (see GODDAMN, DARN, AND OH PERDITION!); and it sent many men to the West to avoid the war itself or its aftermath, thus helping spread eastern terms westward and popularizing western and cowboy terms.

With all the new terms, however, what Americans were really

talking about during the Civil War were the new names entering history, the names of the battles, battlefields, generals, and heroes. We talked of *Bull Run*, a little Virginia stream near *Manassas* Junction, a few miles south of Washington, D.C., and of the Northern generals McDowell and Pope and the Southern generals Beauregard and "Stonewall" Jackson and Lee who fought the two battles there; of *Shiloh*, a church near the hamlet of *Pittsburg Landing*, Tennessee and of how the Southern Commander Albert Johnston surprised Grant's forces there but was killed in the fighting; of a creek called *Antietam* near *Sharpsburg*, Maryland, where Lee was halted by McClellan; of *Fredericksburg*, Virginia, where the Union Army's newly appointed commander Ambrose Burnside was turned back by Lee and was then relieved of his command; of *Chancellorsville*, Virginia, where the Union's "Fighting Joe" Hooker failed to break through Lee's lines; of *Gettysburg*, Pennsylvania, where Lee's advancing army was turned back by General Meade and where General George Pickett led 15,000 fresh Confederate troops in parade formation in *Pickett's charge* across a half mile of open ground up *Cemetery Ridge* under withering artillery fire. We talked of *Chickamauga* creek near a southwest Georgia town of the same name, and of *Chattanooga*, Tennessee and of *the Wilderness* in northern Virginia, and next of a town called *Spotsylvania Court House*, Virginia, and then of *Cold Harbor*, Virginia—as Grant, now the commander of the Union forces, pushed Lee back toward the Confederate capital of Richmond—and then of Grant's 10½-month *Siege of Petersburg*, the railhead near Richmond, pinning Lee down while Sherman destroyed much of the South in his "march to the sea."

Lee, with only 30,000 men left, finally surrendered to Grant on April 9, 1865 at the McClean farmhouse at the little Virginia settlement of *Appomattox Court House*. The divided nation of 31 million people had suffered over a million casualties, including 350,000 Union dead and 260,000 Confederate dead, more American casualties than in any war before or since. And all

"Bull Run, Mrs. Henry's House," a famous photograph by Matthew Brady, July 21, 1861. Because the fiercest fighting at the first Battle of Bull Run centered on a hilltop near the Henry house, the battle is sometimes called "The Battle of Mrs. Henry's House."

the words, all the famous names tell the same sad story of the death of men. Finally, then, it gave us two more American terms, MEMORIAL DAY and:

Arlington National Cemetery, 1864. This 400-acre cemetery lies on the Virginia side of the Potomac on land once belonging to the adopted son of George Washington and, later, to Robert E. Lee. When Lee left it in 1861 to take command of Virginia troops, Union soldiers occupied the strategic location, using its Custis-Lee Mansion as headquarters and the grounds as a camp. It became a *military cemetery* in 1864, by order of the Secretary of War, preventing the land from becoming a postwar monument to Lee.

★ ★

John Brown's body lies amould'ring in the grave,
John Brown's body lies amould'ring in the grave,
John Brown's body lies amould'ring in the grave,
His soul is marching on.

"John Brown's Body," author unknown. Brown was hanged in 1859. When the Civil War burst in 1861 Northern soldiers spontaneously began singing this new song about John Brown, to the music of William Steffe's Georgia campmeeting song, "Say, Brothers, Will You Meet Us?"

★ ★

Yes, we'll rally round the flag, boys,
   We'll rally once again,
Shouting the battle-cry of Freedom,
We will rally from the hill-side, we'll gather from the plain,
Shouting the battle-cry of Freedom,
The Union forever, hurrah, boys, hurrah!

"The Battle Cry of Freedom," written by George Frederich Root in 1861 in response to Lincoln's call for volunteers. Over 700,000 men answered Lincoln's call, becoming the core of the Union Army.

★ ★

All quiet along the Potomac to-night,
No sound save the rush of the river.
While soft falls the dew on the face of the dead—
The picket's off duty forever.

"The Picket Guard," Ethel Lynn Beers, *Harper's Weekly,* September 30, 1861. This poem later became a song, with music by John Hill Hewitt. Mrs. Beers wrote the poem sarcastically after the phrase "All Quiet on the Potomac" was headlined in Northern newspapers during the first weeks of the war, ridiculing General McClellan's policy of delay after his defeat at Bull Run. "All Quiet on the Potomac" was the forerunner of the famous World War I phrase "All Quiet on the Western Front."

Tramp! Tramp! Tramp! the boys are marching,
Cheer up, comrades, they will come,
And beneath the starry flag
We shall breathe the air again
Of the free land in our own beloved home.
  "Tramp! Tramp! Tramp!", George Root, 1862. Besides writing this song and "The Battle-Cry of Freedom" he also wrote another popular Civil War song, "Just Before the Battle Mother."

Mine eyes have seen the glory of the coming of the Lord;
He is trampling out the vintage where the grapes of
     wrath are stored;
He hath loos'd the fateful lightning
     of His terrible swift sword;
His truth is marching on. . . .
  "The Battle Hymn of the Republic," Julia Ward Howe, the poem first appeared in *The Atlantic Monthly*, 1862. She wrote it in Washington, D.C., November, 1861, after reviewing Union troops and seeing them march away singing "John Brown's Body." Thus it was natural that when her poem became a song it used the music of "John Brown's Body." Mrs. Howe equated "the coming of the Lord" and "truth" with the Union cause.

When Johnny comes marching home again, Hurrah! Hurrah!
We'll give him a hearty welcome then, Hurrah! Hurrah.
The men will cheer, the boys will shout,
The ladies, they will all turn out,
And we'll all feel gay when
Johnny comes marching home.
  "When Johnny Comes Marching Home Again," by Union Army bandmaster Patrick S. Gilmore, under the pseudonym of Louis Lambert, 1863. A favorite song of Union troops it was also to be very popular again during the Spanish-American War.

We're tenting tonight on the old camp ground,
　Give us a song to cheer
Our weary hearts, a song of home
　And friends we love so dear.

Many are the hearts that are weary tonight,
Wishing for the war to cease;
Many are the hearts that are looking for the right,
To see the dawn of peace.
Tenting tonight, tenting tonight,
Tenting on the old camp ground.
　"Tenting on the Old Camp Ground," Walter
　Kittredge.

I am a good old rebel—
Yes, that's just what I am—
And for this land of freedom
　I do not give a dam'.
I'm glad I fit agin em'
And I only wish we'd won;
And I don't ax no pardon
For anything I've done.
　"A Good Old Rebel," Innes Randolph, 1870s

Bring the good old bugle, boys, we'll sing another song;
Sing it with a spirit that will start the world along,
Sing it as we used to sing it—fifty thousand strong,
While we were marching through Georgia.
　"Marching Through Georgia," Henry Clay Work,
　1865. He also wrote "Come Home Father" (sung in
　the melodrama *Ten Nights in a Barroom*), "Grand-
　father's Clock," Kingdom Coming" and "We're
　Coming, Sister Mary."

Wounded soldiers from the Battle of the Wilderness, Fredericksburg, Virginia, 1864. Disease killed more troops than bullets. Two famous persons associated with the Civil War wounded were Clara Barton (1821–1912) and Walt Whitman. Clara Barton collected and distributed supplies for the wounded; later she founded the American Red Cross. Whitman served as a volunteer assistant in the military hospital in Washington, D.C., and battle scenes he heard described were used in his 1865 book of poems Drum Taps.

Confidence Man

was in the American language by the 1840s (Herman Melville's novel *The Confidence-Man* was published in 1857) and *confidence game* was in use in the 1850s. These were shortened to *con man* by the 1880s and *con game* and *the con* by the 1890s. Since the 1870s and 80s smalltime confidence men have often been called *flimflammers*, and since the 90s various types of "small con" games have been called *flimflams* (akin to the Old Norse word *flim*, mockery). A typical flimflam of the 1870s and 80s, still in use, was to ask a victim to put up money to show good faith in order to share in a treasure or in the contents of an envelope of lost cash the flimflammer had "found." One of today's most popular flimflams is to ask a victim to withdraw money from his bank account and give it to the flimflammer, under the pretext that he is going to mark and redeposit it in order to trap a dishonest bank teller. The smallest con of all is probably shortchanging people; *to shortchange* was in the language by the 1890s and so was *shortchange artist*.

The "big con" (more elaborate and for much higher stakes than the "small con") gives us our word *racket* (1892), a swindle or fraud. It comes from *grabracket* (also called *grabgame*), a confidence game dating to the 1840s: in it confidence men and their victims put up large wagers, as in a poker game, then one or more of the con men stages a distraction, commotion, or racket—as a fight, mock murder, phony police raid, etc.—during which another of the con men grabs the money and disappears.

The Coochee-Coochee

became a scandalous dance in the 1890s, later called the *hootchy-kootchy* and, by 1941, simply the *cooch*. Perhaps named after the state of Cooch Behar in Bengal, though no one knows for sure, it was the first popular *muscle dance* or pseudo belly dance to reach American stag parties, theaters, and carnivals. It was sometimes billed as "the Oriental danse du ventre" by promoters who wanted to give it artistic pretensions.

The coochee-coochee is inextricably associated with its most famous practitioner, *Little Egypt* (Catherine Devine, later Mrs. Andres Spyropoulous), who made the dance and herself famous at the 1893 Chicago Columbian Exposition by performing it nude (at least that was the scandal whispered from one end of the country to the other). Both dance and dancer were again in the news in 1896 when New York police raided the famous Sherry's restaurant, where this "wicked dame" had been dancing it naked at a stag party given by one of P. T. Barnum's grandsons to celebrate the impending marriage of the other. The sponsoring grandson was indicted for "conspiring to induce the woman known as Little Egypt to commit the crime of indecent exposure"—but the police captain who led the raid was tried for invasion of privacy! (both cases were eventually dropped). Indecent exposure paid Little

*Little Egypt
1905*

Egypt well, men paid $10 apiece for her to entertain at stag parties; she died in 1908 leaving an estate of almost a quarter of a million dollars.

Corn

as we Americans know it was such a startling plant to the early explorers and colonists they didn't know what to call it or its parts. *Corn* meant any major cereal crop in Britain (wheat in England, oats in Scotland), so the British called the new plant *maize*, after the West Indian Taino word for it, *mahiz*. This maize was first called *corn* in 1608 but was still generally known as *maize, Indian maize,* or *Indian corn* (1617) by the colonists, with the term *Indian corn* still in use in America today for the coarser varieties.

Corn saved the first colonists in Virginia and Massachusetts from starvation. The Panet Indian Squanto taught the Pilgrims how to plant corn (it doesn't grow wild) with fish as fertilizer, and their first successful crop (their European crops failed in the cold, rocky soil) was 20 acres of corn, which was celebrated by the first Thanksgiving. Our present production is 125 million tons of corn a year, the largest in the world.

The parts of corn were given old words with new "corn" meanings: *ear* of corn appeared about 1622, *cornstalk* in 1645, *tassle* in 1649, *silk* in 1662, and *cob* by 1684 (*corncob pipe* is an 1820s term). The word *cob* appeared late because Captain John Smith and others had first called the cob the *core*. We never have decided if we should call the outer covering by its New England name, *husk* (1662) or by the early Virginia name, *shuck*.

Parched corn (a 1622 term) was a staple from the earliest days until the 1850s and *meal* simply meant cornmeal to the colonists until the 1740s (corn meal was first recorded in 1749, this longer, more specific term not being necessary until then). By the 1790s corn meal was being the basis of early American cooking. It was also called *Indian meal* and was so common that it didn't have to be specified by the longer term *corn meal* until 1749.

The colonists were eating and talking about *hominy* by 1629. This was originally an Indian dish of coarse-ground parched corn boiled in water, though later colonists might boil it in milk (the word comes from the Algonquian *rockahominie*, meaning parched corn). Until the Revolution, hominy was the basic American porridge or gruel, but after about 1810 it became associated with slaves and poor whites. By the 1840s the southern expression *all hominy and no ham* meant all work and no fun, all trouble and no reward. *Hominy grits* originally meant the coarsely ground parched corn used in making hominy, but the term *boiled grits* appeared in 1800 and *grits* itself soon meant a dish of boiled parched corn cooked in less liquid than hominy or drained and served like rice. The colonists also ate a lot of and talked a lot about *samp* (1643, from Algonquian *nasaump*, softened with water), which was a corn mush served with milk, butter, molasses, or maple syrup. They also ate

A corncob doll shown in an 1880s drawing used the silk for her hair and the attached husks for her dress.

"Husking the Corn in New England," Winslow Homer, 1858. Corn stalks gathered in an upland field in the Blue Ridge Mountains of Virginia (below). Before corn was harvested by machine, these corn stalks were sometimes set afire to make a spectacular display across the countryside on a fall evening.

Heap high the farmer's wintry
   hoard!
Heap high the golden corn!
   John Greenleaf Whittier
   (1807–92), "The Corn
   Song" from *The Huskers*,
   1847.

and talked about *roasting ears* by 1650 (not called *corn on the cob* until about 1753) and the corn and bean mixture *succotash* (1751, from Algonquian *misickquatash*, ear or kernel of corn.)

Special table varieties of corn were called *sweet corn* by 1810, the common varieties used for cereal and fodder then becoming known as *field corn* by 1856. People were asking for tender, sweet *Golden Chaff* by 1854, *shoepeg* by 1856 (its kernels were shaped like shoe pegs), *Country Gentleman* by 1899, and raving about *Golden Bantam* by 1909. Meantime *cornstarch* was a common term by 1853 and Americans were referring to the agricultural *corn belt* by 1882.

Wheat was scarce and expensive in early America so breadstuffs were usually of corn. *Pone* was in the language by 1612 (from Algonquian *apan*, baked) and not generally called *corn pone* until the 1800s—it was bread made only of cornmeal, water, and salt. *Corn bread* was talked about and eaten by 1750 (see BREADS); *corn dodgers* by 1834 (said to be so named because when first baked or fried they are so hard a person had better dodge if one is ever thrown at him); *corn muffins* by 1844; and *corn fritters* by 1862. *Spoon bread* or *spoon cornbread* is supposed to be an old colonial dish, but the term was not recorded until 1906 (it's a custardlike bread so named either because it is eaten with a spoon or from an Indian word *suppawn*, meaning porridge). *Hushpuppy* was in the language by 1918; it's a cornbread batter puffed in deep fat and is said to be so named because hunters tossed pieces of it to their hounds to quiet them with the admonition "hush puppy."

Other "corn" words abound in America. *Corncrib* was common by the 1680s; whiskey made from corn was called *corn spirits* in 1764, simply *corn* by 1820, and generally known as *corn whiskey* by the 1840s. *Corn huskings* were a popular social undertaking by 1786 and called *husking bees* by the 1830s. People spoke of *corn fed* pigs by 1787 and about *corncrackers* by 1844 (mills for grinding

100

corn and where "Jimmy crack corn and I don't care" cracked his corn). Nebraskans were called *Cornhuskers* by 1872, and people were discussing the merits of the new Kellogg's Toasted *Corn Flakes* in 1908. Hackneyed or countrified things and people were *corny*, and the people called *cornballs*, by 1937 (*cornball* had meant a piece of corn pone since the 1840s), and banal, outdated, or sentimental things were simply called *corn* by 1943. Thus corn has been basic to America and this is reflected by the many "corn" words in our language.

Goin' Courtin'

Men have been *wooing* (Middle English *wowen*) girls since the 11th century and *courting* them since the 16th. In colonial America some courting couples are alleged to have used a six-foot long wooden tube, called a *courting stick*, to whisper sweet nothings to each other while under the ever watchful eyes of their parents. By the 1840s a young man's best or most somber suit of clothes was called his *courting suit* and until the late 1880s a wealthy young man might keep a specially groomed *courting horse*, trained to prance so the gallant could make a fine appear-

Courting, 1860s.

ance when he went courting. Such terms are minor parts of our language of courtship, which includes many terms for what courting couples do:

bill and coo, a 17th century English term.
bundling was an English custom first reported in America in the 1630s. It was simply a courting couple's getting into bed together, he in his *small clothes*, she in her petticoats, and doing a little private talking, kissing, and fondling. In the small, cold colonial houses this was often the only way the couple could have any privacy and keep warm (the girl's family was often clustered around the fireplace in the same room). An extra mea-

sure of protection was the *bundling board*, inserted between the couple by more careful parents. Nevertheless, bundling did lead to many of the *six-month children* of colonial days (children born before a couple had been married nine months).

to spark, 1787, to court, bill and coo, earlier the term had been *to spark up to*, *to spark it*; *sparking*, 1804; *go a sparking*, 1807, go courting; *to spark a girl*, 1830s, woo her; *sparking bench*, *sparking sofa*, 1840s, where the girl and her beau sat together.

to keep company with, to court, 1830s, popular until the 1880s.

to spunk up a girl, to fondle her, make love to her, 1840s.

to spoon, late 1850s, originally this had meant to nestle against one another spoon fashion, as to keep warm, make room for others in a family bed, etc.

to lallygag, *to lollygag*, 1860s, to kiss and caress (perhaps from English dialect *lolly*, the tongue); by the 1870s *to lallygag* meant to waste time.

to mash, 1860, to flirt, try to attract a girl's attention; *masher*, 1875, a man who makes advances in public places (he was said to be *fresh* by 1906, *fresh* having meant impudent or saucy since 1848); a *mash*, 1879, the object of one's affections. *To mash* was replaced by the term *to make a pass at* in the 1920s.

to be lovey-dovey, 1870, having reached the billing and cooing stage.

to walk out with, 1870s, after the Civil War chaperoning declined and young couples began "to walk out together," the first true dating. This led to the *lovers' lane* or *lovers' walk* (both terms 1881), a secluded walk or lane where lovers could be alone; by the 1930s *lovers' lane* meant only a secluded road where a couple in a car could park and neck.

make eyes at, *make goo goo eyes*, 1890, give amorous glances, flirt; *goo goo eyes*, 1901, loving glances.

to pin, about 1900, to become engaged by pinning one's fraternity pin on a girl. By around 1935 "being pinned" no longer meant a couple was engaged but merely that they were going steady.

to date, 1902; *dating*, 1910; *heavy date*, 1923; *double date*, 1924; *blind date*, 1925. In the first decade of the 1900s, *dating* implied going steady or being almost engaged: between 1910 and 1920 the connotation changed to just going out with someone of the opposite sex, dating had changed from being a part of serious courtship to being mere intersexual fun. In fact courtship itself had changed—attentions paid the opposite sex, kissing and fondling, etc., were no longer necessarily preliminaries to marriage but could be indulged in for their own sake, for fun or sociability.

Thus the following terms apply to "courtship" in a different sense, to mating rites with or without mating—and, often enough, to mating without matrimony. Note that these concepts started before World War I and well before THE ROARING 20s.

to pet, *petting*, about 1910; *petting party*, 1914, initially as a party where much petting took place, then by the late 1920s as a private bout of petting for two. A boy frequenter of petting parties was a *snugglepup*, 1924.

to neck, *necking*, 1910, the term seems to have first been used in the South, then spread to the rest of the country during World War I, being very common from the 1920s into the early 40s. *Heavy necking*, about 1915; *necker*, 1923; *necker's knob*, early 1940s, as a knob on a car's steering wheel, allowing for *one-arm driving*, the other being used to hold one's girl tight (a *one-arm driver* was a boy more intent on squeezing his girl than in watching the road ahead).

Petting, 1950s.

Although the term *to pet* is usually considered older than *to neck*, both were in wide use from about 1910: *petting* was the milder word, almost a euphemism for *necking*, implying less ardent caresses. Thus couples admitted to *petting* and might use the word in front of their parents, leaving *necking* as somewhat of an "in" word among youths. In fact student use often confined *petting* to hands being "outside the clothing" only or to "above the waist only," while *necking* might allow much more. Necking also included *French kissing* (1920s, see FRENCH, FRENCH TOAST, AND FRENCH POSTCARDS) which was also called *soul kissing* by the late 1930s, being open-mouthed kissing with the tongues caressing. Passionate sucking kissing led to red marks, usually on the neck, called *hickies* (1920, from the 1913 *hickie*, *hickey* meaning a "doo-hickey," a small device or gadget).

> *to love up*, 1921, cuddle and caress.
> *to park*, 1920s, park a car, as on a lovers' lane, and neck.
> *to smooch*, 1920s, mainly just hugging and kissing.
> *pitch woo*, *fling woo*, 1935.
> *submarine watching*, 1960s, popularized by rock-and-roll disc jockey Murray the K, originally to sit with one's beloved holding hands and staring dreamily into space, but soon came to mean to neck.

There have been few new terms for billing and cooing since the 1930s: once nice girls didn't neck, but since the 1950s only nice girls and boys do—most others have sex.

With all these terms for courting, kissing, and fondling we also have had a lot of words for those who court, are in love, or are the object of love, including:

> *flame*, from 17th century England, a sweetheart.
> *apple of his eye*, 18th century, a beloved girl.
> *beau*, first recorded American use, 1732 (French for "fine, handsome" from Latin *bellus*, pretty, handsome, which also gives us *belle*).
> *gentleman friend*, 1829, a beau; *gentleman caller*, 1830s, a suitor.
> *young man*, 1851, a beau, as in "Sally's young man."
> *steady*, 1870s, originally as a boy's sweetheart or fiancée; 1897, as a girl's sweetheart. *Steady beau*, 1900s; *go steady*, *steady date*, 1910s.
> *girl friend*, 1881, sweetheart or fiancée; *best girl*, 1887; *girl*, 1920s, a man's sweetheart, as in "Joe's girl."
> *boy friend*, 1911, a girl's sweetheart.
> *lovebirds*, 1930s, shortened from the older "a pair of lovebirds."
> *one and only*, 1930s, one's one and only sweetheart.
> *big moment*, 1931, the major love of one's life.

The lovers themselves, of course, use more personal terms of endearment. Though *darling* had an Old English counterpart (*deorling*), our modern word is from the Middle English *dearling/derling*, with the form *dearling* in use until the 18th century (*dear* + the diminutive ending *-ling*). *Dear* itself has been in use since the 11th century and *sweetheart* since the 13th. In America both *honey* and its short form *hon* appeared in the 1880s, with *honey bun* following in the 1890s and *honey bunch* in 1904. We also shortened *sweetheart* to *sweet* in the 1880s, adding *sweetie* to the language in 1903 and *sweetie pie* in the 1930s. *Sugar* wasn't a popular term of endearment until the breezy 1920s and *kitten* wasn't an affectionate form of address to a girl until around 1935.

We've also had many terms referring to falling in love, love, or infatuation, including:

> *puppy love*, 1834; *calf love*, 1890s.
> *mushy*, 1839, sentimental, in love; *mush*, 1908, sentimental talk, love talk; *mush note*, 1927, a love note.
> *love cracked*, 1843, foolish in love.
> *crazy for*, 1850s; *crazy over*, 1889; *crazy about*, 1904; *goofy about*, 1922.
> *a case*, 1852, being in love.
> *spoony*, *spooney*, 1858, in love; *spoons on*, 1883, in love with; *spoony about*, 1904 (see *to spoon* above).
> *to be sweet on*, 1877.
> *to be mashed on* someone, 1882. In the 1880s a *mashed heart* was also a synonym for a "broken heart" (see *to mash* above).
> *to set one's eyes by* 1883, to love, esteem.
> *to be stuck on* someone, 1886, to be in love with or infatuated with someone.
> *crush*, 1884, the object of one's affection; 1895, an infatuation; *have a crush on*, 1913.
> *to fall for*, late 1890s.

Showering a bride and groom with confetti and rice is a ritual symbolizing a desire for children. The wedding veil is said to come from the full-length veil the bride kept for her burial shroud in Roman times.

to be nuts about, nuts over, 1918.
that way, 1929.
to send someone, 1950s, from the mid 1930s jive and jazz *to send*, meaning to send someone into ecstasy, as by music.

Much of this courting, especially before the 1870s, was due to parental prodding or matchmaking, but much of it was due to romantic love and to sexual urgings, which gave us also:

to have an itch, 1660, feel sexual desire; *the itch*, 1920s.
it, a euphemism for both the male and female sex organs, as well as for coitus, since at least the 18th century. *It* came to mean sex appeal in 1928 (see *the It Girl* at the entry PRETTY GIRLS).
the urge, 1890s.
sex appeal, early 1920s, popularized by publicity for movie stars, abbreviated *S.A.* by 1927; *sexy*, also 1927.
oomph, 1939, sex appeal (see *Oomph girl* at PRETTY GIRLS).

All courting was ostensibly done by the male, though the *Leap Year* custom of women proposing to men goes back at least to 1288 when a Scottish law gave this right to unmarried women (a man refusing such a proposal was subject to a fine of one pound). All this courting kept us using such terms as:

engagement, 17th century (from Old French *engager*, to pledge). *Fiancé* and *fiancée* are 19th century terms (via French *fiancer*, to betroth, from Latin *fidere*, to trust). In the 19th century a man asked for a girl's hand *on bended knee* or proposed less formally when he merely *popped the question* (1826).
wedding, the word definitely goes back to the year 1000 (Old English *weddung*) and probably to the 9th century; however, it then merely meant a pledge to marry. *Marriage* is a 13th century word (via Old French from Latin *maritus*, husband).
bride and *bridegroom* are both Old English words (*brȳd* and *brȳd-guma*, which is *brȳd* + *guma*, man). However a *brȳd/bride* originally meant both a girl or woman about to be married and one recently married. *Bridesmaid* appeared in the 16th century (initially without the *s*, as *bridemaid*) while *maid of honor* is an American term first recorded in 1906. *Groom* itself originally meant a boy or man servant in the 13th century, then especially a horse attendant, and by the 17th century was confused with the word *bridegroom* and became a short form of it. *Bridal shower* is an American term of 1891.
honeymoon has been in use since the 16th century to mean the first month of marriage. Some say the word originated because the newlyweds drank mead or honey wine during this first month, most say because the first month of marriage is the sweetest, and cynics say because affections change after the moon changes. In America a honeymoon trip was often called a *bridal tour* in the last half of the 19th century.

Marriage has also given us the New England term *to double, double up*, to get married, 1817, and our expression *to get hitched*, 1857. A wife has been called a *helpmate* since the 18th century (the word originally meant an assistant or associate), the *better half* since 1838, *the little woman* since 1881, and a *ball and chain* since 1921. A husband has been called a *hubby* in English since the 17th century, and we have used the term *henpecked* since the 1920s.

Courtship could also lead to a couple becoming *free lovers* in the 1850s, such couples being said to practice *free love* by 1870. *Trial marriage* is a term coined by Judge Benjamin Lindsey, a famous authority on juvenile law and juvenile delinquency, in a 1925 book he wrote with Wainwright Evans entitled *Revolt of Modern Youth*. He defined it as an

> informal agreement on the part of a man and woman to live together until they change their minds—usually with the intent of not changing them. . . .

Judge Lindsey advocated trial marriages as a way to reduce the crime, scandal, and tragedy involved in youthful sex and hasty marriages. His argument was that with new means of birth control such marriages would not be harmful to society: by then, in the mid 1920s, many girls were admitting to *going all the way*, and men were already calling condoms *rubbers*—they were also called *safeties* in the 1930s, which is also the decade *diaphragm* became a common word. *Birth control pill* entered the general language in the late 1950s and became simply *the pill* by the early 60s.

Thus all courting did not have the happy ending of a lifelong happy marriage, or even of any marriage at all. In fact, courting has also, indirectly, given us such terms as:

fickle, false, treacherous, inconstant, in English (Middle English *fikel*) since the 13th century.

divorce, a 14th century word (from Latin *dīvertere*, to turn aside, divert). The original charter of Plymouth Colony specifically did not give the colonists legal jurisdiction over "Life, Limb . . . Banishment, or matter of Divorce"; however, 30 years before the Declaration of Independence, an American legal definition of *decree* existed, granting independence from a spouse under certain conditions. By 1810 most of the states had passed *divorce laws* (divorce was then usually granted only for adultery or bigamy), but it wasn't until after the Civil War, in 1867, that American divorces totaled 10,000 a year—then *divorce* and the new word *divorcée* became common American words.

flirt, 18th century.

you're not the only pebble on the beach, though the term may have been often used before, the 1896 song "You're Not the Only Pebble on the Beach" by Harry Braistel made it very popular.

grass widow, around 1900, referred to a wife whose husband was away on an extended trip—but it was then often assumed he had no intention of returning or that the couple had agreed he wouldn't (earlier the term had meant an unwed mother, referring to the bed of hay or grass used in illicit lovemaking).

get the air, 1900.   *ex-wife, ex*, 1920s.   *carry a torch*, 1927.
to split up, 1903.   *to two-time*, 1926.

Covered Wagons and the Oregon Trail

In 1843 *Oregon fever* swept the Mississippi frontier and thousands of settlers moved toward the fertile Willamette Valley. They gave us our first image of *covered wagons* (1745) crossing the plains. The best known of these wagons was the *Conestoga wagon* or *prairie schooner:*

> *the Conestoga wagon.* The Delaware Indians called the famous Pennsylvania river *Susquehanna,* the Hurons called it *Kanastoge* (both meaning "muddy water"): *Kanastoge* became *Conestoga,* the name of an Iroquois tribe living along the river near Lancaster, which gave us the Conestoga Valley, Pennsylvania, which gave us *the Conestoga wagon*—the wagons being built there by the late 1740s. The Conestoga was a heavy, Pennsylvania Dutch freight wagon; but it proved ideal for carrying families, their furnishings and supplies across the continent. It was first seen on the Oregon Trail in 1843.
>
> *prairie schooner,* meaning any large wagon or coach on the prairie, as a stagecoach in Iowa, 1841; meaning a covered wagon on the Oregon trail, mid 1840s. The cloth-topped covered wagons seen above waves of wind-rippling grass did look like distant sailing ships, and some wagons even had a sail to help their progress. The image of the vast western prairie as an ocean of grass and the *prairie wagons* (1855) as ships also gave us *prairie ship* (1851) and *prairie clipper* (1870). The prairie itself was called *the prairie ocean* (1844) and forts and towns on the prairie, especially Independence, Missouri, were often called *prairie ports* (1848). For more prairie words see THE PRAIRIE.

The covered wagons traveled in *wagon trains* (1849) in charge of an elected *wagon boss* (1873), and followed a paid guide or scout who knew the trail, the country, and the Indians. Each wagon had its own *teamster* (1777), *wagoneer* (1830s), or *wagon boy* (1836)

An Ohio to Oregon wagon train is depicted in this 1830 painting by W. H. Jackson.

to drive or lead its horses, mules, or oxen over the *trail* (1807), which was soon worn to a *wagon trail* (1848). In rocky places and over mountain passes the trail might be as narrow as one wagon; on the prairie it might be ten miles wide, as wagons spread out for better grazing and to avoid each others' dust. The most famous of the western trails was:

> *the Oregon Trail*, 1820s as a trail for trappers, traders, and missionaries, early 1840s as a wagon trail. The persistent popularity of the name is due to Francis Parkman's 1847 classic *The Oregon Trail*, describing his travels over the eastern third of it while living with and studying the Sioux Indians (for the derivation of the name *Oregon* see THE STATES).
>
> The Oregon trail was a 2,000-mile trail crossing plains, deserts, mountain passes, and dangerous rivers. It took a covered wagon four to six months to travel from the *jumping off place* (1830s) near Independence, Missouri, "across the wide Missouri," through Kansas and Nebraska to Fort Kearney, then along the Platte and North Platte to Fort Laramie, over the Continental Divide through the 7,500-foot high South Pass, to Fort Hall, and along the Snake River to Fort Boise and into the Columbia River Valley to the Willamette.

The first party of 32 migrating homeseekers traveled the Oregon Trail in 1841, a party of over 100 traveled it in 1842, and then in 1843 the dam broke when the physician, missionary, and pioneer Marcus Whitman helped guide a *Great Migration* of over 900 persons to the Columbia River Valley. Whitman had President Tyler's promise to aid the immigrants once they reached Oregon: they were actually going into territory claimed by Britain's Hudson Bay Company (see 54-40 OR FIGHT!—MANIFEST DESTINY). By 1848 enough Americans had reached Oregon to warrant organizing *the Oregon Territory* and by 1850 12,000 settlers had gone over the Oregon Trail.

In the 1850s, too, 500,000 more travelers were on the eastern half of the Oregon Trail, turning off to the *California Trail* (1847) beyond Fort Hall, on their way to the California gold fields. For, although the Oregon seekers had started it all in 1843, within a few years they had been joined on "the way West" by settlers and gold prospectors going to California and by Mormons going to Utah. Within 50 years such American settlers and prospectors, plus ranchers and cowboys, would tame and populate the West, absorbing what had once been Indian land, Mexican land, Hudson Bay land, and wilderness into the United States.

When the covered wagons reached their destination in California, Oregon, or elsewhere each farm family would either buy land or settle as *squatters* (1788) on a *homestead* (1638, a tract taken from the public domain and the house and farm on it). The word *homesteader* didn't appear until after 1862, when the Homestead Act was passed, encouraging such settling by saying that any-

O, Susanna,
O, don't you cry for me,
I've come from Alabama,
Wid my banjo on my knee.
"O, Susanna," Stephen Foster, 1848. This song caught the public fancy at the time when many were on the way to the California gold fields or to Oregon to settle and was heard around many campfires. Often the words were changed to "I've come to California" or "O, Susan . . . I've come to Oregon."

one could have 160 acres (a quarter of a square mile and called a *quarter section*, *quarter*, or *section* by 1804) of public land by working and producing a going crop on 40 acres of it for five years.

Cowboys

Franciscan missionaries used mounted Indians and Mexicans to herd cattle in California by 1767, and Americans were herding cattle in Texas by 1820. But *cowboy* began to take on its legendary meaning in the spring of 1867 when the as yet uncompleted transcontinental railroad put a spur into Abilene, Kansas, and a 29-year-old livestock trader, Joe McCoy, bought most of the town for $4,250 and then advertised for ranchers and cowboys to bring the half-wild, scrawny Long Horns from Texas up the Chisholm Trail to the railhead. His lure was $40 a head, ten times the going rate for the tallow-and-hide cattle, which were to introduce plentiful beef to the East. By summer's end the first herds of 2,000–3,000 head had made the trip and McCoy was the first cattle king (perhaps even the original THE REAL MCCOY). Soon he was shipping half a million head East a year—and there were over 5,000 cowboys on the trail.

The dry summer and severe winter of 1886–87 wiped out almost 90% of the ranchers' herds, helping the homesteaders' fences and *barbed wire* (1860s) end the short 20-year rein of the cowboy. But cowboys and their legend persist, and we still talk about them often.

Cowboy may have once been a disparaging term for a colonial settler who let his cows roam or preferred raising cows to plowing. It was a Revolutionary War term for Loyalist guerrillas, who ambushed patriot farmers by ringing cowbells. Later it meant a Texan who rustled Mexican cattle. Thus the disparaging connotations we use in calling a reckless driver a *cowboy* or in the term *drugstore cowboy* (1925) are very old.

Douglas Avenue, Wichita, Kansas, 1878. The first White settlers came to Wichita in 1868, the railroad was extended there in 1872, making Wichita a principal shipping point for Texas Long Horns; and in 10 years, by 1878, it was a bustling town of 5,000 people.

The true western cowboy's average age was 24, the average working career seven years, the usual cause of death a riding accident or pneumonia. Cowboys were also called:

Rounding up horses, shown in a painting by Frederic Remington (1861–1909). Remington, who worked as a cowboy, is best known for his authentic scenes of the American West.

vaquero (Spanish, *vaca*, cow). This was the Mexican cowboy who started it all; the word was known to Americans by 1800.
buckaroo, 1827, a corruption of *vaquero*.
beef driver, 1834; *beef drover*, 1855.
cowpuncher, *cowpoke*, 1880; originally a cowboy or other worker who prodded cattle onto railroad cars with a pole.
cowhand, 1886.
bronco buster, 1888.
wrangler, 1888.
range rider, 1890.

Cow girl was first recorded in 1884, originally as a female rancher or rancher's daughter.

Much of the cowboy's clothing, equipment, methods, and special language were developed by the Mexican vaqueros; some of it came from the gold-rush days of the 1840s and 50s. Here are some major terms associated with cowboys and ranch life:

brand, 1644, a farm term. It's Old English for "torch" and related to the word "burn." George Washington's 1765 diary refers to "24 head branded on the Buttocks"; ancient Egyptians had marked their cattle this way too.
bronco, 1850 (Spanish, "rough, unruly"); *bronc*, 1893.
bull dog, 1842, to throw and tie a cow.
cattle baron, 1898; *cattle king*, 1874.
cattle drive, 1878.
cattle war, 1892; *range war*, 1912.
cayuse, 1867, an Indian horse (originally of the Cayuse tribe of Oregon), usually roan, and larger and huskier than a *cow pony* (see below).
chaps, 1870, short for *chaparejos*, 1861. This was a vaquero item that protected the legs against horse bites, rope burns, and

especially against the low, thorny shrubs called *chaparral* (Spanish *chaparra*, dwarf oak, evergreen oak, though *chaparejos* is also influenced by Spanish *aparejo* gear, equipment).
chuck wagon, a common term since the 1880s. Charles Goodnight had made the prototype from a surplus Civil War army wagon around 1867; the Studebaker Company made many of them, the average price was $75–$100.
cinch, 1859 (Spanish *cincha*, saddle girth).
corral, 1829 (Spanish, "an enclosed yard"); *cattle corral*, 1877.
cowboys and Indians Children have been playing this game by this name since 1887.
cowboy boots, an eastern term of about 1912. Cowboys just called them boots or *cowhides* (1841). Until the 1860s cow-

"Let her buck!" Cowboys would break broncos by riding them into submission.

Whoopee ti yi oh, git along, little dogies,
It's your misfortune and none of my own,
Whoopee ti yi oh, git along, little dogies,
For you know Wyoming will be your new home.
Refrain, "Git Along Little Dogies."

boys wore standard boots, then began to wear a higher heeled, pointed-toe boot which fit into stirrups better. By the 1880s cowboys were wearing fancy hand-tooled boots costing $50 a pair (two months' pay). Such fancy cowboy boots are sometimes called *Justin's*, for Joseph Justin, a famous Fort Worth bootmaker.

cowboy guns. The *Winchester* (1871, full name *Winchester repeating rifle*) is considered the cowboy's rifle. It was developed by Oliver Winchester and manufactured by his Winchester Arms Company. The *revolver* (1835) or *six shooter* (1844) was usually the *Colt* (1838), patented by Samuel Colt in 1835, but the *Smith and Wesson* (1860) seven-shot pistol and the *Remington* (1871) revolver were also Western guns. The 1873 Colt Single Action model was known as *The Peacemaker* and a favorite in the *gunplay* (1881) of the Western *gunfighters* (1894, also called *gun fanners* by 1903 because they removed or tied back the trigger of their revolvers, firing by *thumbing* or *fanning* the hammer). Real

cowboys didn't *shoot up* (1890) many towns and weren't real *gun toters* (a 1925 movie term), since carrying guns while riding was a nuisance and shooting scared both cows and horses. The Western romance writer Ned Buntline gave special long-barreled (12-inch) Colts to Wyatt Earp, Bat Masterson, and others and this gun became known as the *Buntline Special.*

cowboy hat, an eastern term of 1903. Cowboys just called it a hat, and it could be any wide-brimmed style that kept sun and rain off the face and neck. Popular models included the *sombrero* (1823, Spanish for "hat," from *sombra*, shade) and the *ten gallon hat*, which though it may have been used for carrying water, doesn't refer to capacity (the name comes from the vaquero *sombrero galón*, "hat with braids"). The *Palo Alto* was an early favorite, from California gold-rush days, while the wide-brimmed model first made by Philadelphia hat maker John Batterson Stetson around 1865 became a later favorite and was usually called a *Stetson* or a *John B.*

Frederic Remington's 1888 sketch of cowboys saddling a bucking bronc. A bronco, or bronc, is a wild, or semi-wild, horse of the West, an excellent cow pony because of its small size, endurance, and quickness. These ponies of the plains are not true wild horses, but are descended from the horses of the Spanish conquistadors, who had tamed them and brought them to America in the 15th and 16th centuries.

The cowboy as romantic hero, perhaps the most enduring of American myths, was exemplified by actor John Wayne, here shown in a still from The Cowboys *(1972), one of his many films about the West.*

cowboy saddle, 1870s. Easterners didn't generally call it a *Western saddle* until 1911. This saddle, with a high pommel and cantle, was derived by the vaqueros from the Spanish conquistadors' war saddle.

cowboy shirt, a term from the mid 1930s. Cowboys never wore them; they wore sturdy workshirts, sometimes in bright colors or having fringe. The embroidered cowboy shirts were popularized by cowboy movie star Tom Mix, and the costume grew more elaborate with Gene Autry and Roy Rogers.

cow country, 1881; *cattle country*, 1886.

cow pony, 1874, it's 12–14 hands high and weighs 700–900 pounds.

cow town, 1885; *cattle town*, 1881.

critter, a corruption of "creature." Americans have used it to mean "horse" since 1782.

cut out, 1874, separate an animal from the herd.

dogie, 1888, a motherless or weak calf.

dude, an Easterner, 1883; *dude ranch*, since about 1910.

lariat, 1831 (from Spanish *la reata*, the rope).

lasso, 1819 (from Spanish *lazo*, snare).

Levis. Cowboys wore sturdy workpants, often the blue canvas bibless overalls originally made by Levi Strauss in San Francisco in the 1850s for gold-rush prospectors. They weren't generally called *Levis* until the 1940s.

long horn, 1857; soon called *Texas Long Horn*.

maverick, 1867, an unbranded calf. Named after Samuel Maverick (1830–70), Texas pioneer, fighter for Texas independence, mayor of San Antonio, and member of the first Texas State Legislature—because he didn't brand his calves on his 385,000 acres, perhaps so he could claim all unbranded calves on the range. *Maverick* didn't mean a rootless, "different" person or a loner until 1901.

mustang, 1808 (from Spanish *mesteño*, stray).

pard, an 1850s gold-rush term. It comes from the American pronunciation of partner as "pardner," which we were saying by 1795.

pinto, 1860 (Spanish for "spotted, painted") such a spotted horse was often named "Paint."

poncho, 1826. The Mexican vaqueros got this blanketlike coat (with a slit in the middle for the head) and its name *poncho* from the Araucan Indians of Chile and Argentina.

ranch, as a building, 1808; as grazing property, 1831 (from American Spanish *rancho*, which was the Spanish word for soldiers' mess). *Rancher*, 1836; *cattle ranch*, 1857; *ranch house*, 1862.

range, as a large, open, western grazing ground, 1835. As early as 1626, however, colonists used *range* to mean public grazing land, as in forests or half-cleared pastures.

rodeo (from Spanish *rodear*, to surround) 1844, meaning a roundup. Since cowboys loved to show off to each other at the roundups, or bet on who could break a horse, throw a cow fastest, etc., the meaning of *rodeo* changed from the roundup to a cowboy contest or cowboy tournament by 1889.

roundup, 1876.

rustler, 1882; *cattle rustler*, 1903. Cowboys usually just called such a person a *cattle thief* (since 1862).

stampede, 1843 (American Spanish, *estampida*, stamp, rush, uproar).

tenderfoot, originally an 1849 gold rush term.

trail boss, 1890.

Coxey's Army

The Panic of 1893 (1893–97) was the worst depression the U.S. had ever known up to that time, with widespread unemployment and industrial unrest. Several "armies" of the unemployed marched to Washington to demand relief. Today the best known of these is *Coxey's Army*, 500 people who in 1894 marched from Ohio to the Capitol under quarry owner Jacob Coxey (1854–1951). He favored federally funded community public works and building programs as a solution to the panic. A large crowd gathered in Washington; but before Coxey could address it he was arrested for "walking on the grass" (after the march Coxey ran for various public offices, including the presidency, but only became the mayor of Massillon, Ohio, 1931–33).

Equally well known at the time was another "army" of 1500 unemployed under "General" Charles T. Kelly. It left California for the Capitol via boxcar, but so few of its members finally arrived in Washington that *Kelly's Industrial Army* is hardly remembered today.

Coyote and Mesquite

A coyote, often called a prairie wolf *(term recorded in 1804 by Lewis and Clark, who saw great numbers of coyotes during their famous expedition to the Northwest), is a member of the dog family. It habitually barks and its "evening song" is a characteristic sound of the western plains. Here one "sings away" in the winter snow.*

are two American words going back to Nahuatl, the Uto-Aztecan language of the Aztecs and related tribes of North and Central America. Both words were first recorded in American English in 1759, *coyote* being Mexican Spanish from the Nahuatl *coyotl* and *mesquite* coming via Spanish *mezquite* from the Nahuatl *mezquitl*.

The Spanish conquistadors, such as Cortés, who invaded the Aztec empire in 1519, found many new things in the New World and often took the Nahuatl words for them back to Europe, where they eventually entered English. Thus English also has the following Nahuatl or Aztec words:

avocado (via Spanish *aguacate* from Nahuatl *ahuacatl*, "testicle," from the shape of the fruit), a 17th century English word, first recorded in the U.S. in 1751.

chicle (via Spanish from Nahuatl *chictli*), 1860s.

chili (via Spanish from Nahuatl *chilli*), a 17th century English word.

chocolate (via Spanish from the Aztec *xocolatl*, literally "bitter water"), first recorded in England in 1604. *Hot chocolate* was a favorite drink of the early colonists, who brought the drink from Europe. *Chocolate fudge* is an American term dating from 1897, *chocolate cookie* an American term of 1909.

mescal (American Spanish from Nahuatl), as an agave or peyote plant, 1702.

Mexico (via Spanish *Mejico* from Nahuatl *mexihco*, literally "place or city of the Mexih") gives us our own place name *New Mexico* (see THE STATES). We were shortening the adjective *Mexican* to *Mex* by 1853.

peyote (American Spanish from Nahuatl *peyotl*), 1849; *peyote button*, dried top of the peyote, 1930; *peyote cult*, Indian religion based on hallucinations brought about by peyote, 1932.

113

shack (via American Spanish *jacal, shacal* from Aztec *xacalli,* wooden hut), 1878 in the Southwest.

tamale (American Spanish from Nahuatl *tamal*). John Smith described this Indian dish in Virginia in 1612; first recorded use of word in American English, 1691.

tomato (via Spanish *tomate* from Nahuatl *tomatl*) didn't enter English until the 18th century.

Dashing Men

is a 14th century term (before that *dashing* meant violent). Handsome or romantic men have been talked about less than PRETTY GIRLS because women talk less about men than men do about women. Like pretty girls, the most romantic men are usually of two extremes, the nice boy or the seducer, with the seducer being talked about most. Styles in male beauty and personality change, usually to follow popular models set by heroes, books, movies, ads, etc. Thus during certain periods girls may like best, and boys try to imitate, an Atlas type or a Byronic type, a cowboy or "the Arrow collar man." In the 1920s many young men copied Rudolph Valentino's *sheik;* in the early 50s they copied the intonation, slouch, and leather jacket of Marlon Brando from the movie *The Wild One* (1953); and in the late 50s and 1960s many copied the vocabulary, attitudes, and clothes of drug addicts. Literature and mythology have given us some common words for types of men, including:

"The Arrow Collar Man," 1924.

Atlas, one of the original gods of Greek mythology, condemned to support the heavens on his shoulders.

Casanova, after the Italian adventurer G. J. Casanova de Seingalt (1725–98), who in his *Memoirs* portrayed himself as an amorous adventurer, gambler, and charlatan who took Europe by storm.

Don Juan, after the legendary Spanish libertine who appears in books, plays, and poems by Dumas, Balzac, Flaubert, Molière, Byron, and Shaw and who inspired musical works by Strauss and Mozart (the opera *Don Giovanni*).

Lothario, taken from the name of the rake in the 1703 English play *The Fair Penitent* by Nicolas Rowe.

Romeo, from Shakespeare's 1596 tragedy *Romeo and Juliet* and Gounod's 1867 opera based on it.

We have had many other terms for a dashing, amorous, or appealing man and for a seducer, including:

Clark Gable, 1939.

blade, meant a gallant by the 16th century (probably because he was good with a sword or *blade,* which had meant sword since the 14th century). *Gay blade* is a term of the 1890s (so is *gay seducer;* a *gay dog,* woman chaser, dates from the 1920s).

rake, since the 17th century (from *rakehell, rakeheel, rakel,* a common word from 1542 until the 1720s, referring to the old phrase "to rake hell," meaning that one was so wicked we would have to rake hell to find his equal).

lady's man, 1814; *lady killer,* 1830s.

devil-may-care, 1847.

114

Douglas Fairbanks, Jr., 1947.

> Someday he'll come along,
>   The man I love;
> And he'll be big and strong,
>   The man I love;
> And when he comes my way,
>   I'll do my best to make him
>   stay.
>   "The Man I Love," from
> *Lady Be Good*, Ira Gershwin, 1924

Robert Redford, 1972.

he-man, 1880.

dude, as a foppish, affected man, 1881 (from German dialect *dude*, fool); as a self-confident sport, 1950s.

guy began to reach its present popularity in America in the 1890s, when it was considered much more slangy and derogatory than "fellow"; by the 1920s girls were speaking affectionately of their beaus as "my guy." The word goes back to 17th century England where a *guy* was originally an effigy of Guy Fawkes that children paraded through the streets and burned on Guy Fawkes day, November 5th, in celebration of his abortive 1605 Gunpowder Plot to assassinate King James I and the assembled Parliament in retaliation for the new and severe penal laws against Roman Catholics.

lounge lizard, 1912, originally applied to a boy who liked to pet (see GOIN' COURTIN') in the parlor but who seldom took his girl out; *parlor snake*, around 1915.

daddy, a male lover, 1912; *sugar daddy*, 1918; *big daddy*, a male who gives women a sense of security, as a protective, aggressive, older man, popularized in Tennessee Williams' 1955 Pulitzer Prize winning play *Cat on a Hot Tin Roof*, in which "Big Daddy" Pollit was an aggressive, patriarchal character; *daddy-o*, hep student use, 1940s.

sheik, see THE ROARING 20s.

bedroom eyes, 1920s, first applied to the romantic eyes of movie stars.

playboy, 1920s.

tall, dark, and handsome, late 1920s. This Hollywood term was used occasionally to refer to Rudolph Valentino (who was not exceptionally tall) but more popularly applied to Caesar Romero when he played the lead in the 1941 movie *Tall, Dark, and Handsome*.

lover boy, 1930s, almost immediately used in a mildly derogatory or humorous way.

(big) ass man, considered dashing only by some college boys, 1930s; to most girls he was a nuisance, the kind that tried to *cop a feel* (1932) on the first date. In the 1940s he was also called a *make out artist*.

smooth apple, 1930s, *smooth* had meant "great, sophisticated" since 1893; *smoothie*, 1933.

the boy next door, the nice wholesome boy, late 1930s, made more popular by Hugh Martin's song "The Boy Next Door," sung by Judy Garland in the 1947 movie *Meet Me in St. Louis*.

wolf, a woman chaser, 1940s, especially common during World War II. Around World War I a *wolf* had meant a male homosexual, then in the 1930s *to wolf* meant to try to seduce a woman. *Wolf bait*, a pretty girl, World War II use; *wolf whistle*, World War II use for an appreciative whistle made at pretty girls on the street, being two long notes, a rising one followed by a falling one.

Mr. Right, 1940s, the right, gentlemanly, loving man.

glamour boy, 1941, usually used disparagingly or humorously, based on *glamour girl* (see PRETTY GIRLS).

stud, 1950s (*stud* had meant a stallion since 1803), in the mid 1930s it had some jive and jazz use, first meaning a sporty man, then any man.

The Great Depression

An apple seller, 1932. A Chicago newspaper wryly reported that the only two growing industries in that year were apple stands *(1934) and the W.P.A.*

In earlier America most people were farmers or owned or worked for small, local businesses, often bartering food, clothing, and services. Money was always scarce and economic depressions or "hard times" merely meant less cash, not widespread suffering or industrial unemployment. Thus although both the words *panic* and *depression* had first been used in America during the Panic of 1819, it was only a financial panic, not a general depression. There were also panics in 1837; in 1857, in which *inflation* and *bread riots* were new terms; in 1869 when Jay Gould and Jim Fisk tried *to corner* (an 1849 term) the gold market and in which the term *Black Friday* was used for the first time in America; in 1873, which saw the term *stock-market crash* used for the first time; in 1893, which was followed by the worst depression until 1929 and which saw COXEY'S ARMY march on Washington; in 1901 when Edward Harriman tried to gain control of James Hill's Great Northern Railroad; and in 1907, when the *rich man's panic* saw many banks and businesses fail. But *the Panic of 1929* was to be different: now the country was bigger and more industrialized, most people depended on wages, and many average people had invested or speculated in the stock market during what was becoming known as the *Golden Twenties*.

In 1928 everyone was talking about "good times." RCA stock went from 85 to 420, Montgomery Ward from 117 to 440. There were 23 million cars on the road, and almost everyone had just bought one of those wonderful new home radios. People were singing Eddie Cantor's big hit "Makin' Whoopee" and talking about Mae West appearing in *Pleasure Man*, Vina Delmar's best-selling novel *Bad Girl*, and a bright new Hollywood star, Joan Crawford. It was a *boom* period (*boom* became an economic term in the 1870s, after its restricted use in the gold-rush days of the 1850s) and many experts said there might never be another *bust* (which had meant a bankruptcy in the 1840s and was first applied to an economic collapse in the Panic of 1893).

Then on Wednesday, October 23, 1929, stocks began to fall; the day was called *Black Wednesday*. The next day, October 24, the wave of stock selling continued and the bottom dropped out of the market; it was *Black Thursday*, the day of the stock market crash. The following Tuesday was *Black Tuesday*, with over 16 million shares being traded. A panic had been set off that destroyed $3 billion in market value; United Cigar stock fell from $113.50 to $4 in one day (the president of the firm jumped to his death from the New York Hotel). At first it was merely called a *panic*, then a *depression*, and finally *the Depression* or *the Great Depression*. It was the deepest economic depression in U.S. history: 13 million people (one-fourth of the labor force) were out of work, production was down 44%, foreign trade was at a standstill, and bank closings, bankruptcies, factory shutdowns, and farm and home mortgage foreclosures were at an all-time high. It was to last until the outbreak of World War II in 1939, when, despite the New Deal, 9½ million were still unemployed. For almost ten years the Great Depression was what all Americans talked about and worried about. It was to change the meaning of such words as *job*, *security*, *banking*, *government*, and *America* itself.

Depression terms included *Apple Annies* and *Apple Marys*, who "sold apples on street corners" to feed their families (there had been an apple surplus in 1930; one comic strip *Apple Mary*, outlived the Depression to be renamed *Mary Worth*). Many people gave *rent parties*, each "guest" bringing $2 to help pay the rent, and stood in *breadlines* (a word first used in 1900 when charities handed out loaves of bread and cups of coffee to the poor) or sought free meals in *soup kitchens* (which originally had been an 1855 army term).

In 1932 everyone was talking about the *Bonus Army*, 1,000 unemployed World War I veterans and their families who in May marched on Washington to demand immediate payment of bonus certificates granted in 1924. Another 14,000 joined them in June. When the Senate defeated the appropriation which the House had passed, many of the Bonus Army returned home on funds the government had provided, but some lingered on in shacks on the Anacosta River until President Hoover ordered their dispersal. On July 28–29th General Douglas MacArthur used tanks, bayonets, and tear gas to clear them out.

By now many people blamed President Hoover for the depression, using his famous phrase "grass will grow in the streets" against him. *Shantytowns* had long been known in the U.S.,

Bonus Army before the Capitol, Washington, D.C., 1932.

A Depression soup kitchen, with local politicians getting some publicity from the plight of the unemployed, Chicago, 1930.

A Hooverville.

originally called *shanty villages* in 1858 and *shanty towns* by 1882 (*shanty* was in use by 1820, see ERIN GO BRAGH for details). But by 1933 new shantytowns and *shed towns* of the poor and dispossessed were called *Hoovervilles*. Old newspapers that hobos slept under were called *Hoover blankets*, rabbits shot for food called *Hoover hogs*, shoes with holes in the soles called *Hoover shoes*, and in the South worn-out cars pulled by mules were called *Hoover cars*.

During the next years people didn't buy many stocks, cars, or radios, and they didn't make much whoopee—many who could afford to go to the movies went to *tin-can shows*, to which one brought a can of food to contribute to the needy. Many popular songs reflected poverty and unemployment; people were singing "Brother Can You Spare a Dime," "Shanty in Old Shanty Town," and "Time on My Hands." Other songs tried to cheer everyone up, as "Wrap Your Troubles in Dreams," "Life Is Just a Bowl of Cherries," or the ironic theme song of the Depression, "Happy Days Are Here Again" (originally written in 1929 with Jack Yellin's lyrics and Milton Ayer's music for the 1930 movie *Chasing Rainbows*). Eddie Cantor's next big hit reflected the plummeting farm prices: "Potatoes are cheaper—tomatoes are cheaper, Now's the time to fall in love." But the words now most associated with the Depression are Franklin Roosevelt's "the forgotten man" and "The only thing we have to fear is fear itself," terms such as *bank holiday* and *food stamps*, and abbreviations such as CCC and NRA. But these major Depression terms are actually part of recovery and THE NEW DEAL.

Dialects

Early Americans had more sharply differentiated dialects than we do today. The Puritans in New England spoke the English East Anglia dialect, the Quakers in Pennsylvania spoke the English midland dialect, the Scotch-Irish in the Blue Ridge Mountains spoke the Ulster dialect, etc.—and they and their speech patterns were separated by wilderness, bad roads, and lack of communications. Then our geographical and social mobility began to homogenize the language, with people from all regions moving to all others, people from all walks of life mixing and mingling. Better roads and wagons, trains, cars, moving vans, high-speed printing presses, the telegraph, the typewriter and teletype, telephones, record players, duplicating machines, radios, movies, and TV mixed and melded American speech into a more and more uniform language. In addition, our dialects were smoothed out by generations of teachers and by two crucial series of elementary school books: the various editions of Noah Webster's *The American Spelling Book*, "the Blue-Backed Speller" that sold over 80 million copies and from which generations of Americans from the 1780s to the 1880s learned to spell and pronounce the same words in the same way, and Professor William Holmes McGuffey's six series of *Eclectic Readers*, which sold over 122 million copies between 1836 and the 1920s, giving generations of Americans a shared vocabulary and literature. Thus our mobility, educational systems, and improved means of

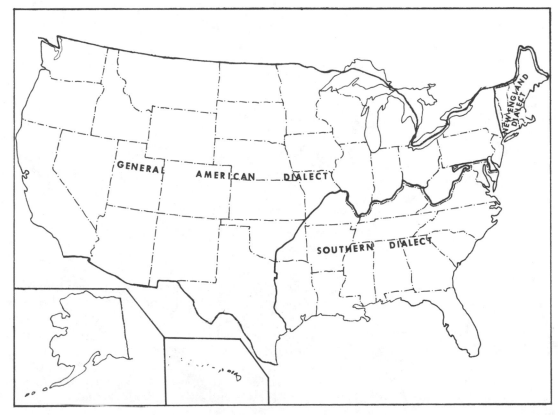

transportation and communications have given Americans an increasingly more standardized vocabulary and pronunciation. When we hear America talking today we usually hear only a touch of a regional "accent"; our dialects are fading away.

Today, those who speak with more than a touch of dialect are usually the rural, the poor, and unassimilated immigrants, those whose mobility, education, and urbanization have been limited. Dialect, like much of the speech of these groups, is often restricted to the topics and words of home and farm life, to the everyday, homey words we learned in childhood. Regional pronunciations are not apt to be found in the words we learn as college students and urban adults, the words of business, science, politics, fashions and fads, and arts and letters.

Depending on how precise one need be, one can say that America has from three to a dozen dialects. There are three overall, major ones: the New England, the Southern, and the General American (sometimes erroneously called the Midwest or Western dialect). Being more precise, we realize that New Englanders from Kennebunkport and Boston speak differently, as do Southerners from Virginia and Georgia, and General American speakers from Illinois and Oregon. Being still more precise exposes the true complexities of American dialects, for there are scattered pockets of unique dialects and local speech patterns in various valleys, counties, and city neighborhoods all over the country: the dialect of the Scotch-Irish descendants of western Pennsylvania and from the Potomac to the James River and in the Ozarks; the dialect of the Hudson River valley, influenced by the original Dutch settlers; the dialect of the Florida Keys; of the Cajuns in the Louisiana bayous; of the parts of Minnesota settled by the Swedes; of some New England coastal towns settled by Portuguese fishermen; of the boroughs of Brooklyn and the Bronx in New York City; of many city neighborhoods having large Cuban, German, Irish, Jewish, Jamaican, Mexican, Puerto Rican, Russian, and other specific populations. Some of these are true regional dialects of the American language, others are dialects of American English spoken with a foreign accent (a different kind of "dialect"), and some are merely local variations. Here are brief descriptions of our three major regional dialects:

> *New England dialect* is spoken from the Connecticut River north and eastward through Rhode Island, Massachusetts, Vermont, New Hampshire, and Maine. New England was not misnamed: between 1620 and 1640, 200 ships brought 15,000 English colonists to the region, two-thirds of them from East Anglia, the Puritan stronghold. Those colonists from East Anglia, and other parts of southern and southeastern England, gave New England its distinct dialect, first called the *New*

England dialect in 1788. It is still closer to English English than any other dialect of American English. Some of its characteristics are:

(1) pronouncing the *a* in such words as *ask*, *brass*, *can't*, *class*, *fast*, *grass*, *half*, *last*, and *path* somewhat like the broad *a* in *father*, and lengthening the *a* sound in such words as *bar*, *dark*, *far*, *farm*, and *heart* to a sound somewhat between the sound the rest of us pronounce in *hat* and *father* (this last *a* sound is also found in eastern Virginia and elsewhere in the tidewater region). Thus we tease Bostonians for saying "ahnt" (*aunt*) and "vahz" (*vase*).

(2) pronouncing the *o* in such words as *box*, *hot*, *not*, *pot*, and *top* with the lips rounded, forming an open *o* sound. The rest of us tend to pronounce this *o* more as the broad *a* sound of father.

(3) omitting, slighting, or shortening some *r* sounds, thus *car*, *dear*, and *door* sound like "cah," "deah," and "doah" to the rest of us. The broad *a* sound and the slighted *r* cause the rest of us to hear "pahk the cah in Hahvahd yahd" (park the car in Harvard yard).

(4) using such words as *angleworm* (for earthworm), *brook* (for creek or branch), *buttonwood* (for what southerners call a *sycamore*), *pail* (for bucket), and *pesky*, *scrimp*, and *snicker* (the last three words come from the Essex dialect in England). The New England uses of *clothes press* (for closet), *to home* (at home), and *trading* (for shopping) are now rarely heard.

Southern dialect could be divided into separate dialects for the upper and lower South or into several smaller dialects, such as the Virginia Tidewater, South Carolina Low Country, local dialects with Charleston and New Orleans as focal points, etc. In general, however, Southern dialect is used south and east of a line drawn along the northern boundary of Maryland and Virginia and the southern boundary of West Virginia, then along the Ohio River and past the Mississippi to include the southern part of Missouri and down through southeastern Oklahoma and eastern Texas. It is characterized by:

(1) the Southern drawl: a slower enunciation than used in the rest of the country, combined with a slow breaking, gliding, or diphthongization of stressed vowels. Thus to the rest of us the Southern *class* sounds like "clae-is"; *yes* like "yea-is" or "yea-yis"; *fine*, *I*, *ride*, and *time* like "fi-ahn," "I-ah," "ri-ahd," and "ti-ahm" (these all being long *i* sounds); *out* like "a-out"; and *due*, *new*, and *tune* like "dyu," "nyu," and "tyune" (this *y* glide of the *u* sound after *d*, *n*, and *t* is also found in some parts of New England).

(2) some of this slow dwelling on the vowel sounds weakens the following final consonants, especially *d*'s, *l*'s, *r*'s, and *t*'s, giving southerners such pronunciations as *fin(d)*, *he(l)p*, *se(l)f*, *flo(or)*, *mo(re)*, *po(or)*, *yo(ur)*, *bes(t)*, *kep(t)*, *las(t)*, *nex(t)*, and *sof(t)*.

(3) Southern pronunciation, intonation, and sentence patterns have more melody and variety than the other

American dialects, partially because the vowels are so lovingly dwelt upon.

(4) using such terms as the stereotyped Southern *honey-chil(d)* and *you all* as well as *bucket* (for pail), *heap* (for very), *raise* (for rear, children), *reckon* (think, judge), *right* (for very), *snap bean* (string bean), *spigot* (for faucet) and *tote* (for carry).

General American dialect is spoken in 4/5ths of the nation's area and by 2/3rds of the population, but is still a dialect. It is not called General American because that is what Americans should speak but because it just happens to be the dialect heard in the general regions outside of New England and the South. It is heard in the area which starts as a wedge between New England and the South, in western Connecticut, New York State, New Jersey, and Pennsylvania, then broadens out to include West Virginia, Ohio, Michigan, Indiana, Illinois, and Wisconsin, Minnesota, Iowa, northern Missouri, northwestern Oklahoma and west Texas, and finally encompasses the entire western half of the country. It actually includes at least four dialects: the North Central, the New York City Metropolitan Area dialect (including parts of Connecticut and New Jersey), the Middle Atlantic, and the Midlands dialect (Philadelphia to the Rockies and the Potomac to New Mexico, sometimes considered as separate Northern Midland and Southern Midland dialects). All these have more in common with each other than with the New England and Southern dialects, so can be grouped together as General American. It is characterized by:

(1) using the short flat *a* in such words as *ask, brass, can't, class, dance, fast, grass, half, last,* and *path.*

(2) sounding the unrounded *o* in such words as *box, hot, lot, not, pot,* and *top* almost as the broad *a* in father.

(3) the retention of a strong *r* sound in all positions, as *caR, haRd,* etc.

(4) the tendency on the part of many (but not all) speakers to pronounce certain vowels and diphthongs alike, as if only the first vowel existed; thus such pairs as *horse-hoarse, for-four,* and *morning-mourning* often sound alike.

(5) using such words as *earthworm* (for angleworm), *creek* (for brook or branch), and *string bean* (for snap bean). The Midland dialect is more apt to use window *blind* (for shade), *quarter til* (the hour, for quarter to), *sack* (for bag), and *skillet* (for frying pan). In the New York City Metropolitan Area dialect people say they *make* (rather than cook) a meal or specific dish, while Philadelphians are still apt to say *square* for a city block.

Other, less widespread dialects are also interesting. In parts of Appalachia and in the Ozarks when we hear America talking we hear the broad *a* in *barrel* and *narrow*, giving us "bahr'l" and "nahrr"; and such pronunciations as "hyar" and "yar" (*hear, ear*), "fur" (*far*), "sich" (*such*), "ontil" (*until*), and "salat" (*salad*).

The stereotyped northern Brooklyn dialect, *Brooklynese*, was first noted and joked about in the 1890s, and flourished for the next 50 years. It may stem from German and Yiddish, but may also be rooted in Gaelic, appearing soon after a wave of Irish immigrants arrived in Brooklyn and became cab drivers, policemen, and baseball fans. Its two most distinctive characteristics are: (1) the reversal of the *er* (spelled *er*, *ear*, *ir*, or *ur*) and *oi* (spelled *oi* or *oy*) diphthong sounds, and (2) pronouncing the voiced *th* as *d*. This gives us such pronunciations as:

er sound as *oi*	poil	
boid	Toidy-toid Street	voiced *th* as *d*
coil	Williamsboig	dem
oily		dese
foist	*oi* sound as *er*	dose
goil	berl	mudda (also dropping
Joisey	erl	*r* after a vowel).
moider	erster	fadda
noive	Greenpernt	brudda

"Oncet" and "twicet" (*once* and *twice*) are also considered part of the Brooklyn accent, but were first noted in Philadelphia and Baltimore, by Noah Webster, in 1789, and are also used in the Ozarks.

We Americans are still moving and communicating from one part of the country to another. As easterners and midwesterners continue to move to the *sun belt* (1950s) the local Florida and Texas speech patterns will be diluted; as people continue to leave large cities for small ones and for rural areas, pockets of local dialects will tend to weaken or disappear. Perhaps someday in the future regional dialects will be no more. Then we may have only two dialects, that of educated, urban Americans and that of rural and poor Americans. Such dialects already exist, heard mainly in grammar and usage. The rural and the poor are more apt to use such forms as *I has*, *he come*, *he knowed*, *she done*, etc., double negatives such as *He don't have none*, and words such as *ain't*, *irregardless* (1912), and *misremember* (about 1915)—as well as regional pronunciations. Educated urban speakers are more apt to add *-ly* to their adjectives (*slowly* instead of *slow*, though both are correct), use less slang, more foreign borrowings, more modifiers, longer words, and more complex sentence structures.

Perhaps, in the future, too, we will become more aware of three types of speech patterns which haven't yet received much notice: the "dialects" of the sexes and of age and personality groups. Men and women certainly have different intonations and voice timbre and have tended to use somewhat different vocabularies. In our society men have traditionally used more verbs, slang, counterwords, catchwords, words expressing strong or absolute likes, dislikes, and attitudes, more specific words and proper nouns (*Ford* for *car*), more blasphemy, obscenity, and scatology, and fewer modifiers than women. Men also tend to use such words as *dishes*, *pants*, and *visitors* while women are more apt to use *china*, *trousers*, and *house guests*. Men eschew such adjectives as *cute*, *darling*, and *lovely* as applied to inanimate objects.

There are also pronunciation and vocabulary differences between generations or decades. People who came of age in the 1940s, 50s, or 60s still tend to use the slang they learned then and the vocabulary of business, politics, science, fashions and fads, and arts and letters in vogue during their high school and college years. Thus each decade uses a somewhat different vocabulary and each also seems to have characteristic intonations and speech rhythms, speaking faster or slower, with greater or lesser emotion and tone variation. Some generations seem to shout while others mumble, some to emote while others play it cool. Also, there are the special speech patterns of related personality and psychological types, the emotional and nonemotional, the extroverts and introverts, the schizophrenic, etc. Such sexual, generation, and personality and psychological speech patterns are not true dialects, of course, but when we hear America talking we do hear such differences.

Dixie

I wish I was in de land ob cotton,
Old times dar am not forgotten,
Look away, look away,
Look away, Dixie Land!
· · ·
In Dixie land I'll took my stand,
To lib and die in Dixie;
Away, away,
Away down south in Dixie.
Daniel Decatur Emmett,
"Dixie's Land," 1859.

Romantic legend has it that a kindly 18th century slaveholder, Mr. Dixy, owned a Manhattan Island property, "Dixy's Land," which was considered an ideal place to work, giving us the names *Dixieland* and *Dixie*. However, scholars know that *Dixie* comes from the ten-dollar notes issued by the Citizens' Bank in bilingual Louisiana before the Civil War and bearing the French word *dix*, ten, on the reverse side. Soon New Orleans, then Louisiana and the entire South were called "The land of Dixie," and later *Dixieland* and *Dixie*.

The word became immensely popular with the song "Dixie" (whose actual title is "Dixie's Land"), written in 1859 as a *walk-around* (dance finale or curtain call parade) by the famous minstrel Daniel Decatur Emmett for Bryant's Minstrels in New York City. "Dixie" was popular in both the North and South, but soon the South adopted the song as an unofficial national anthem of the Confederacy. It was played at the inauguration of Confederate President Jefferson Davis on February 18, 1861, in Montgomery, Alabama and ordered sung when General George Pickett led the Southern troops into battle at Gettysburg.

The *Dixie cup* appeared in 1906 in conjunction with the American Water Supply Company's vending machine, which dispersed a drink of water in this disposable paper cup for one penny. It is supposed to have been named the *Dixie cup* because it was as reliable as that old Louisiana ten-dollar bank note.

Drunk

has more synonyms than any other word. Benjamin Franklin was the first American to publish a list of them, ending up with 228 terms in 1737. My own list in *The Dictionary of American Slang* runs to 353 terms—and I didn't exhaust the subject.

Why so many words for drunk? Because people have been getting drunk for a long time, for many different reasons, and experiencing many different reactions. We both celebrate good tidings and "drown our sorrows" in drink. Both poor immigrants and scions of first families have gotten drunk, and talked about it, to escape alienation, to reject society, or to be "one of the boys." We talk of drinking as an initiation rite, as a manly thing to do, as a sophisticated or "cute" thing to do—or we talk about it as a dastardly thing to do, the lowbrow thing to do, the bestial thing to do. We drink or overdrink from coast to coast—drinking can be funny, drinking can be sad—and both those who do and those who don't talk about it.

Words for drunk run the gamut from meaning mildly *tiddly* (a British Cockney rhyming term, from *tiddly winks* meaning "drinks") to being completely *smashed*. Many words for drunk can be grouped into one of three types: (1) words for the initial comfortable, relaxed feeling which makes us pleasantly conspicuous, as *happy, jolly, high, have a glow on,* and *lit;* (2) words for the stage of being unsteady on one's feet and not seeing clearly, as *tipsy, three sheets to the wind* (as if a boat is rolling), and *bleary eyed;* (3) words for the final stupor of being drunk, including words for punishment, oblivion, or death, as *clobbered, smashed, petrified, glassy eyed,* and *stoned,* and also including such food-preserving words as *pickled, corned,* and *soused* (which originally meant "pickled").

Here are some of the most common and typical terms we Americans have used to mean drunk:

"The Drunkard's Christmas," 1852.

drunk, 15th century England, shortened from the older *drunken. Drunk* was later used as a noun to mean a drinking bout, 1839, in the U.S., then to mean a drunk person, 1852.

inebriated, another 15th century English term (from Latin *ēbrius*, drunk, from *e*, out + *bria*, wine jar, literally "having emptied out the wine jar").

intoxicated, 16th century England (from Latin *toxicum*, poison, literally "poisoned with drink").

soused, 16th century England; *soused to the gills*, 1890s in America.

boozey, 16th century in England, 1722 in America; *boozed*, 1850; *boozed up*, 1860s.

in one's cups, 1580, England.

disguised, late 16th century England.

blind, 17th century England; *blind drunk*, 1830.

elevated, 17th century England; *high*, 1838; *high as a kite*, 1939.

foxed, 17th century England.

jolly, 1650s; *happy*, 1770.

cut, 1670s.

shot, 1670; *shot in the neck*, 1830; *half shot*, 1837.

half seas over, late 17th century in both England and America; *decks awash, half the bay over,* late 17th century; *three sheets to the wind*, 1821; *over the bay*, 1830.

wet, 1704.

oiled, 1737; *lubricated*, 1927.

stewed, 1737; *stewed to the gills*, 1925.

stiff, 1737; *stiff as a ringbolt*, 1737; *stiff as a plank*, 1932; *stiff as a goat*, 1937.

soaked, 1737.

buzzed, 1737.

bowzered, 1737.

cock-eyed, cocked, 1737; *half cocked*, 1888.

mellow, 1737.

overset, 1737.

jagged, 1737.

grogged, 1770s; *groggy*, 1818 (literally "full of grog").

fuzzy, 1770.

corned, 1785.

out, late 18th century.

blue, 1818.

half shaved, 1818; *shaved*, 1851.

snuffy, 1820.

liquored up, 1830.

bent, 1833.

slewed, 1834.

stinking, 1837; *stinking drunk*, 1926; *stinko*, 1927.

screwed, 1838.

lushy, 1840; *lush, lushed*, 1880s (*lush* first meant liquor, also around 1840).

full, 1840; *full as a goat, full as a lord, full as a tick*, 1822; *full as a goose*, 1883; *full as a fiddle*, 1905.

tight, 1843.

battered, late 1840s.

feeling good, 1850s.

pixilated, 1850s.

swizzled, 1850s.

whipped, 1851.

damaged, 1851.

primed, 1858.

balmy, 1860s.

tanglefooted, 1860s.

spiffed, 1860; *spifflicated*, 1906.

shot, 1864.

frazzled, 1870s.

D and D (drunk and disorderly), 1870.

squiffy, 1874; *squiffed*, 1880s.

These terms dated 1737 were first recorded in Benjamin Franklin's list of that year. His list also contained such terms as *have a brass eye, cherry-merry, flushed, fuzzled, glaized, gold-headed, has his flag out, lappy, limber, loose in the hilt, lordly, nimptopsical, moon-eyed, pigeon-eyed, seen the devil,* and *top heavy.*

pie-eyed, 1880; *owly-eyed*, 1900; *pot eyed*, 1901; *orie-eyed*, 1910; *wall-eyed*, 1927.

boiled, 1886.

paralyzed, 1888.

loaded, 1890s; *loaded for bear*, 1896.

packaged, 1890s.

loopy, 1890s; *looped*, 1940s.

shikker, shicker, shickered, (from the Yiddish *shikker*, drunk, Hebrew *shēkār*, strong drink), 1890s.

pickled, 1890s.

corked, 1896.

sloppy, sloppy drunk, 1896; *slopped*, 1907.

woozy, 1897.

have a bun on, 1900s; *bunned*, 1908.

pifflicated, 1900s; *piffled, piffed*, 1910s.

lit, 1900; *lit up*, 1902; *illuminated*, 1926; *lit up like a Christmas tree/a church/the Commonwealth/a lighthouse/a store window/the sky/Broadway/Times Square/Main Street*, all 1926–27; *lit up like a cathedral/Catholic Church/high mass/kite/skyscraper*, first recorded 1940–42.

ginned, 1900.

ossified, 1901.

saturated, 1902.

petrified, 1903.

tanked, 1905; *tanked up*, 1906.

blotto, 1905.

shellacked, 1905.

rosey, 1905.

jingled, 1908.

piped, 1912.
plastered, 1912.
polluted, 1912.
organized, 1914.
gassed, 1915.
hooted, 1915.
aped, 1915.
have a snoot full, 1918.
jugged, 1919.
canned, 1920s.
juiced, 1920s.
fried, 1920s; *fried to the eyebrows*, 1925; *fried to the hat*, 1927; *fried to the gills*, first recorded 1942; *fried to the eyes*, 1947.
buried, 1920s.
potted, 1922.
dead to the world, 1926 (the expression has meant "fast asleep" since 1899).

crocked, 1927.
busted, 1928.
flooey, 1930.
rum-dum, 1931. (Note that all the above terms dated from 1919 to 1933 were coined or popularized in spite of—or because of—PROHIBITION.)
bombed, 1940s (World War II was now on).
shit faced, 1940s (during the war obscenity and scatology became common, see OH SHIT!).
feeling no pain, 1940s.
swacked, 1941.
sloshed, 1950s.
boxed, 1950s.
clobbered, 1951.
crashed, late 1950s.
zonked, late 1950s.

Since the late 1950s there have been further new words for drunk, but most of them have first meant "high" on drugs and then have been applied to being "high" on liquor.

To get drunk one may "go on a drinking spree." The terms include:

a bender, 1827; *on a bender*, 1846.
a drunk, 1839.
on a bat, 1848.
to liquor up, 1850.
on a toot, 1877.
a jag, 1888.

a binge, 1889 (originally this was a British dialect word for filling a boat with water).
to hit the bottle, 1906.
a booze fight, 1922.

We also have words for those who get drunk frequently. The first *tipplers* to be recorded in history were a John Jolivet and a John Smyth (I wonder if he used his real name?), who were listed as *tipplers* when they came before authorities in England in 1396 for violating liquor laws. At that time, however, *tippler* only meant a tavern keeper; it didn't mean one of his steady customers until about 1700. We have also called a heavy drinker:

drunkard, 15th century England; *drunk* came to mean an intoxicated person in 1852.
sot, 16th century English use (before that time *sot* meant a fool).
boozer, recorded in 1611 in England, but not common in America until the 1890s; *booze fighter*, 1903; *booze hound*, 1926.
alcoholic, an 18th century English word; *alcoholist* was the fairly

common word in America in the 1880s and 90s.
dipsomaniac (Greek *dipsa*, thirst + *maniac*), a 19th century English word; *dipso*, the shortened form, 1940s.
soak, 1820.
rum sucker, 1844.
stiff, 1870s.
rummy, 1884; *rum-head*, 1914; *rum dum*, 1940s.
lush, 1890s.

The famous comedian W. C. Fields (1879–1946), whose real name was William Claude Dukenfield, is noted for his wisecracking about drinking, which made drunkenness seem funny and acceptable though also, through his skill as an actor, pitiable and futile.

Alcohol does not make people do things better, it makes them less ashamed of doing things badly.

Sir William Osler (1849–1919), famous Canadian physician and teacher of medicine in Canada, the United States, and England

souse, 1890s.
tank, a very popular word for a drunk around 1900.
stew, 1908 (a *stew* was originally a brothel or a low dive, such as is frequented by drunks); *stew-bum*, 1918.
wino, 1920s. He, of course, gets drunk frequently on cheap wine.

And with all this drunkenness we also need terms for the after-effects:

katzenjammers (German for "cat's wailing"), 1849.
the shakes, 1850s. This originally meant the trembling, fever, and chills of ague.
the D.T.'s, DTs, 1850s. An abbreviation for *delirium tremens* (Latin for "trembling delirium"), the trembling is violent and the delirium is often hallucinatory.
the jim-jams, 1852.

the horrors, 1860s.
seeing pink elephants, seeing pink spiders, 1890s. Referring to the hallucinations of the D.T.'s.
heebie-jeebies, 1910. This term was popularized, and perhaps coined, in Bill De Beck's comic strip *Barney Google*.
hangover, 1912.
the jitters, 1928.
the screaming meamies, 1941.

When you listen to all this talk you wonder if anyone stays sober in America. Most of us do, most of the time; but, since sobriety is our natural condition, we don't talk about it much. However, we do have such terms as:

sober as a judge, 1835; *sober as a deacon*, 1843; *sober as a church*, 1848; *sober as a shoemaker*, 1871; *sober as buck shad*, 1949.
cold sober, 1880s; *stone sober* is probably older, *stone* being used to mean "strong as a stone wall, stoney, completely," since the 13th century in the expression *stone dead*, with *stone deaf* and *stone blind* coming in the 14th century.
on the (water) wagon, 1905.

Other than that there is always *the cure* (the term became popular in the early 1890s, when Dr. Leslie E. Keeley's *Keeley Cure* for alcoholism and drug addiction was in vogue) or *Alcoholics' Anonymous* (abbreviated *AA*), which was founded and named in 1934.

Skid row (1944), the run-down, ramshackle part of town where live the drunks, the unemployables, the vagrants—the down-and-outers *(1917).*

The Dust Bowl

By the 1930s the Great Plains area of Kansas, Colorado, Oklahoma, New Mexico, and Texas had been farmed badly for decades, especially while trying to fill World War I demands for wheat. The *Great Drought* of 1933 destroyed crops and dried the land, and severe dust storms began in 1934, blowing huge dust clouds from this Great Plains area over Chicago and all the way to the Atlantic. Residents of the plains were talking about *dust pneumonia* by 1935 and by 1936 everyone was calling the stricken area *The Dust Bowl*.

Thousands of farm families left their unproductive land or were forced off by mortgage foreclosures. They piled their belongings on jalopies or old farm trucks and headed west, swelling the roving ranks of the unemployed during THE GREAT DEPRESSION. Since many were from Oklahoma, all were called *Okies*, the word often being used to conjure up an offensive image of these uprooted, unskilled farmers and their large, undernourished families traveling west like gypsies. Some eventually settled in shanty towns and city tenements, but many became itinerant, migratory farm workers. Other job seekers and local authorities cursed the arrival of the Okies, while those who could afford to sympathized with their plight or at least read and talked about John Steinbeck's description of it in his 1939 best-selling, Pulitzer Prize novel *The Grapes of Wrath*.

"Broke, baby sick, and car trouble!" Oakies on U.S. 99, 1937.

> *You gave us beer, now give us water.*
> Dust bowl farmers' slogan to the government (Prohibition had been repealed in 1933)

> *Okie use' to mean you was from Oklahoma. Now it means you're scum.*
> John Steinbeck, *The Grapes of Wrath*, 1939

An abandoned farm in Oklahoma's Dust Bowl, 1937, showing how dust storms cover fields and equipment.

The Dutch

have had a strong influence in America since 1609, when English sea captain Henry Hudson sailed to the New World for the Dutch East India Company on the *Halve Moon* (*Half Moon*). He didn't find a short cut to the Orient, but he did discover and sail up the *Hudson River* (he discovered *Hudson Bay* on a later trip, for English businessmen, 1610–11). The Dutch soon settled up the Hudson, at *Fort Nassau*, 1614, and at nearby *Fort Orange*, 1623 (now *Albany*, New York).

In 1624 the Dutch West India Company founded *Fort Amsterdam*, which grew into *New Amsterdam* (now New York City). This settlement was on the tip of an island the Dutch also called *New Amsterdam* but which the Indians called *Manahatin* (Algonquian *manah*, island + *atin*, hill, "hill island"). European explorers had spelled it *Manhattan* as early as 1614. History books still tell how the Dutch West India Company's director-general, Peter Minuit, purchased it from the Indians for 60 guilders worth of trinkets (about $24 worth).

In the 17th century the English-Dutch hostility over control of the seas and disputed parts of the New World was intense. In 1664 *New Netherland* fell to the English fleet under the Duke of York: Fort Orange immediately was renamed *Albany*, the town of New Amsterdam *New York*, and the island of New Amsterdam again called *Manhattan*. The anti-Dutch tradition of early English settlers persisted and gives us such terms as:

that beats the Dutch, 1775, to be unusual or surprising.
Dutch courage, 1812, false courage induced by alcohol.
Dutch fit, 1844, a fit of rage.

to talk Dutch, *it's all Dutch to me*, 1880, gibberish.
Dutch grocery, 1886, a disorderly or dirty grocery store.
Dutch treat, 1887; *go Dutch*, 1931, no treat at all, each person paying for his own meal or ticket.
to talk like a Dutch uncle, 1889, to talk bluntly, especially to upbraid or rebuke.
Dutch leave, 1898 (a popular term during the Spanish American War), to be absent from one's military unit without leave.
to do a Dutch act, 1900s, to flee, abscond, escape; 1920s, to commit suicide.
to get in Dutch, 1912, to come into disfavor; 1919, to get into trouble.

Peter Minuit (1580–1638) purchasing Manhattan Island from Indians, 1626.

In 1934 the government of the Netherlands ordered its officials to stop using the word *Dutch* because of its bad connotations and to use "Netherlands" instead!

Some of the bad connotations of *Dutch* in later American history may have been due to its confusion with *Deutsch*. These two related words have been confusing Americans for over 200 years. In the 14th century *Dutch* meant the German vernacular, as opposed to Latin. By the 16th century it meant people from the Netherlands, because they spoke a West Germanic language, "low Dutch." Then about 1740 we also began referring to the Germans as *Dutch*, from *Deutsch* (the German word

New Amsterdam, about 1667. Note the Dutch windmill.

for German). Thus the PENNSYLVANIA DUTCH are not from the Netherlands but are Pennsylvania Germans; the famous 1870s cattle and horse thief *Dutch Henry* wasn't Dutch but a Pennsylvania German; and the 1920s Chicago gangster *Dutch Schultz* was of German, not Dutch, extraction.

Although later immigrants from the Netherlands were to settle in Michigan, Minnesota, Iowa, and the Dakotas, the Dutch influence on the American language mainly stems from their early settlements between the Hudson and Delaware Rivers. Since they attempted to claim and colonize the land bounded on the north by the Hudson and on the south by the Delaware, the Dutch called the Hudson *the North River* (as some New York City residents still do, to distinguish it from the East River) and the Delaware *the South River*.

The Dutch are responsible for such American terms as:

bedpan (Dutch *beddepanne*), 1678.

bedspread (Dutch *beddesprei*), 1845.

boss (Dutch *baas*, master), 1649; *to boss*, 1856. The word *boss* spread quickly as a replacement for "master," which had bad connotations to the many English colonists who had begun their life in America as indentured servants.

bush (Dutch *bosch*, woods, forest), meaning wilderness 1657; *bush country*, 1855. *Bush ranger*, frontiersman, 1756; *bush fighter*, one who fights from behind rocks and trees, 1760; *bushwacker*, a guerrilla soldier, one who ambushes the enemy in the bush (very popular during the Civil War), 1813.

cole slaw (Dutch *koolsla*, *kool*, cabbage + *sla*, salad; it has nothing to do with being "cold"), 1792; *slaw*, 1861; *hot slaw*, 1870. Incidentally Dutch colonists near Setauket, Long Island, were the first to grow cabbage (and cauliflower) in America.

cooky, cookie (Dutch *koekje*, little cake), 1703.

cruller (Dutch *krullen*, to curl), 1805.

131

cuspidor, 1871 (see THE SPITTOON).

dope (Dutch *doop*, a dipping sauce), sauce, 1807; a mixture of unknown or suspicious ingredients, 1872; oily liquid, thick lubricant, 1876; narcotics, especially opium, 1889. Hence *dopey*, drugged, stupid, foolish, and *dope*, a stupid person, both 1896. *Dope fiend*, 1890s; *dope peddler*, 1923. *To dope up*, dilute, "doctor," 1890. *Dope* also meant inside knowledge by 1901; *to dope out*, think up, figure out, 1906.

Dutch bake oven, *Dutch oven*, 1853.

Dutch barn, 1772.

Dutch door, 17th century; the lower half of this door could be closed separately to keep out barnyard animals.

Dutch elm disease actually has nothing to do with the Dutch in America—it is so called because it was first described in the Netherlands in 1921. The fatal disease reached the U.S. in 1930, and since then we've been talking about its tragic effects on our once tree-lined streets.

Dutch turnpike, a road made of logs and tree trunks, as over marshy ground, 1818, better known as a *corduroy road*, 1780.

filibuster (via Spanish *filibustero* from Dutch *vrijbuiter*, free booter), 1851 as an American adventurer fomenting insurrection in Latin America, a soldier of fortune; 1853, both as a noun, a member of a minority in a legislature who impedes the action of the majority, and as a verb, to obstruct legislative action by parliamentary tactics, especially by speaking merely to consume time and wear down the opposition.

hunky (Dutch *honk*, the base in children's tag games) safe, fine, 1861; *hunky-dory*, fine, satisfactory, 1866.

keelboat (Dutch *kielboot*), 1786; also called a *keel*. The Dutch used it widely on the Hudson River.

Knickerbocker. By 1831 this was a popular word meaning a descendant of the Dutch settlers in New York, especially a prosperous burgher. It is from Washington Irving's 1809 *History of New York*, told through the eyes of the fictitious Dutch settler Diedrich Knickerbocker (a jesting allusion to Irving's friend Herman Knickerbocker; though Irving said the name was from Dutch *knicker*, to nod + *boeken*, book, hence one who dozes over a book). The first popular humorous book written in America, it parodied guidebooks and pedantic histories while describing the Dutch reign in New York. It caused New York to be called *Knickerbocker land*, and gave rise to such names as the once famous *Knickerbocker Hotel*, and the present day New York *Knicks* basketball team. Full Dutch-style breeches gathered and banded just below the knee also became known as *knickerbockers*, later shortened to *knickers* (following later British use it also was used to refer to long bloomer-type underwear worn by women and then to any female underpants).

landscape, as a painting (Dutch *landskip*). The word entered both American and British English in the 17th century, originally being a painter's term. We called bad landscape paintings and still lifes *Dutch dabs* by 1870.

pit, the hard seed of a fruit, as a peach pit, 1848.

pot cheese (Dutch *potkaas*), 1812; it was also called *Dutch cheese*.

Santa Claus (Dutch *Sant Klaas*), 1773. The Dutch *Kla(a)s* is a

Ichabod Crane chased by the "headless horseman," a scene from Washington Irving's famous story "The Legend of Sleepy Hollow" (1820). Sleepy Hollow is part of North Tarrytown, New York, and some of the places described in the story can still be seen there.

Santa Claus.

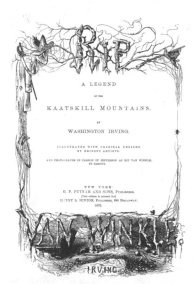

Title page for an 1870 edition of "Rip Van Winkle," Washington Irving's most famous story, first published in 1819. Note the Dutch spelling of "Catskill," which probably comes from a Dutchman named Kaat + kil, creek. Washington Irving (1783–1859), who was our first professional writer and the first to gain international recognition, often used early American-Dutch themes in his work.

short form of *Nikolaas,* thus Santa Claus is Saint Nicholas, patron saint of children. The Dutch introduced both the name and the concept of this gift-bearing Christmas figure.

scow (Dutch *schouw,* a pole boat), 1669.

a good scout, 1912, probably does not come from our English word *scout* but from Dutch *schout,* a town officer combining the duties of a mayor and sheriff.

sleigh (Dutch *slee,* sledge), 1696.

to snoop (Dutch *snoepen,* to eat sweets on the sly), to pry, spy, 1832; *a snoop, snooper,* 1880s.

span, a harnessed pair of oxen, horses, etc., 1769.

spook, ghost, specter, 1809; *spooky,* eerie, 1854; *to spook,* haunt, scare, 1867. *Spook* also meant a spy in World War II and in the Cold War between Russia and the U.S. in the 1950s.

stoop (Dutch *stoep*), 1735. It means both the front steps of a house and a small porch. In Dutch colonial days it was a small porch with a bench, usually occupied by a pipe-smoking householder.

waffle (Dutch *wafel,* wafer), 1744 (see Pancakes, Hoe Cakes, Johnny Cakes, Flapjacks—and Waffles).

Yankee, 1758 (see Yankee).

The Dutch have, of course, also given us many other words via British English. Thus *dike* (Dutch *dyk*) has been in the English language since 1531, English-speaking colonists later bringing it to America as part of the mother tongue. *Tulip* isn't a Dutch word (it comes from Turkish *tuliband,* Persian *dulban,* turban, because the flower resembles a turban), but we wouldn't use the word so much if the Dutch hadn't introduced tulips into America.

Besides *Hudson River* and *New Amsterdam,* the Dutch gave us many other place names, mainly in the Hudson River valley and along the Delaware. New York City has *Staten Island* (settled by the Dutch in 1637), the *Bronx* (settled by the Dutch in 1641, originally called the Broncks, referring to the farm of Jonas Bronck), *Brooklyn* (the area was settled by Hollanders and Walloons in 1636, the hamlet of Breuckelen established about 1646), *Flatbush* (Vlacht bosch), *Flushing* (Vlissingen), the *Canarsie Pol* (*pol* means tidal marsh in Dutch), *Yonkers, Harlem, Cortlandt, Nassau,* the *Bowery* (Dutch *bouwerij,* farm, estate, this section of New York City was originally Peter Stuyvesant's estate), *Spuyten Duyvel, Grammercy Park* (De Kromme Zee), and *New Utrecht* (Nieu Utrecht) on Long Island. In New York State and elsewhere the Dutch word *kil* (channel, creek) if found in such Dutch place names as *Catskill, Fishkill, Kill van Kull, Peekskill,* and *Schuylkill River.* The Dutch *hoek,* a bend, corner, is found respelled as *hook* (since 1670) in *Sandy Hook* and *Kinderhook;* the Dutch *gat* (a pass in a channel) is in *Barnegat* and *Hell Gate.* Farther afield we have *Rhode Island* named by the Dutch in 1644 for its red clay; *Block Island,* discovered by the Dutch navigator Adriaen Block in 1614; and, of course, *Holland,* Michigan.

133

The Erie Canal

After the Revolutionary War, far-sighted men like Franklin, Washington, Robert Fulton, and Albert Gallatin (Secretary of the Treasury under Jefferson and Madison, 1801–14) excited America with talk of building *canals* (Latin *canālis*, groove, channel) to connect towns, lakes, and rivers. By 1816, however, only 100 miles of canals existed in the U.S., and those only to bypass falls or link towns to seaports.

Then in 1825 the 363-mile long *Erie Canal* was opened, connecting Lake Erie to the Hudson (Buffalo to Albany). All Americans were proud of this 40-foot wide, 4-foot deep engineering marvel. It brought the farm products and raw materials of the Old Northwest Territory, around the eastern Great Lakes, directly to the big manufacturing centers of the East and took immigrant settlers to the vast wilderness easily. It cut the shipping rate from Buffalo to Albany from $100 to $15 a ton and reduced passenger travel from 20 to 8 days. It also eventually made New York a more important city than Boston or Philadelphia. Farmers, businessmen, and immigrants all spoke of it in glowing terms, often calling it *the Big Ditch* (a name given the Panama Canal 90 years later) or *Clinton's Ditch*, after New York Governor DeWitt Clinton who had taken the lead in getting it built, mainly by talking the state into financing it.

Even those far from the Erie Canal knew of its romance and talked of its *lock tenders* and its gaudily painted *tow boats* pulled along by steamers or two, three, or four *boat horses* or *boat mules* driven by *canal drivers* and averaging 1½ miles an hour. The brawling, hard-drinking *canalers*, usually called "canawlers," were the source of legend and scandal (especially concerning the slatternly female "cooks" who accompanied many boats). *Line boats* made regularly scheduled freight trips and might carry *deck passengers* who brought along their own food and paid 1½¢ a mile. Long, narrow *packet boats* mainly carried passengers and moved at 4 miles an hour. They charged more than the slower boats, but provided a bar, greasy meals, hinged bunks on deck for male passengers and

"Building the Erie Canal," at Lockport, New York, Anthony Imbert, 1825. Lockport refers to the locks that raise and lower boats on canals; there is another Lockport in Illinois on the Illinois and Michigan Canal.

A grain boat on the Erie Canal.

134

a separate cabin for female passengers—the canal serving everyone as toilet and well. Many of these terms, such as *deck passengers* and *packet*, were new to most Americans and were later applied to the even more glamorous Mississippi steamboats. On the Erie Canal, too, Americans first used the shout *low bridge!*, a warning that a cross-canal bridge was too low to clear a person standing on deck.

The great success of the Erie led to a canal building craze that saw over 3,000 miles built by 1840, plus many canals that were never finished. They included such famous names as the *Chesapeake and Ohio*, sometimes called "the Potomac Canal" (it follows the Potomac from Washington to Cumberland, Maryland, but was planned to go all the way to Ohio); the *Morris Canal* (60 miles, from Jersey City to the Delaware); the *Delaware and Raritan* (New York to Philadelphia); and the *Wabash and Erie* (finally completed in 1856, from Evansville, Indiana to Toledo, Ohio, 450 miles, the longest U.S. canal). But the Panic of 1837, overbuilding, and mainly the coming of THE IRON HORSE soon caused the canals to decline and a number of states defaulted on their *canal bonds* between 1844 and 1860, plunging many investors here and abroad into debt. And the Erie Canal that started it all? It's still there, more or less, now converted into the *New York State Barge Canal*.

Erin Go Bragh

The Irish were among the first immigrants to come to America. They introduced the white potato to America around 1719 and we have called it an *Irish potato* since the 1820s. We called an Irishman a *Paddy* (an ancient nickname for Patrick) by 1748, an *Irisher* by 1807, a *Pat* (also from the common first name Patrick) by 1830, and used the term *Irish American* by 1836. America had retained the English attitude of considering the Irish brawling bumpkins and thus by 1800 an *Irish hoist* meant a kick in the pants, by 1809 *to get one's Irish up* meant to get angry, and by 1840 an *Irish pennant* meant the dangling end of a sloppily tied rope (as first recorded in Richard Henry Dana's 1840 book, *Two Years Before the Mast*).

However, it was the Irish Potato Famine of 1846—actually a widespread European potato famine caused by the potato blight—which sent the wave of Irish immigrants to America that was to have a wide influence on our language. By 1860 over 1½ million Irish immigrants were in America, the largest foreign-born group then in the country. Unfortunately for them, these usually poor, uneducated immigrants found themselves competing for jobs with the well educated, urbane German immigrants of the period (see THE GERMANS), hence often had to take the more menial jobs, many Irish men working as laborers and many Irish women as servants or *Irish washer women*. Thus

135

Edward Harrigan (1845–1911) and Tony Hart (1855–1891) famous dance hall and burlesque comedians of the late 1900s, were especially known for their humorous dramatic sketches of Irish types.

in the 1850s *Mick* (from the common Irish name Michael) became a disparaging term for an Irishman, and humorous terms mocking the Irish began to multiply, as: *Irish buggy*, a wheelbarrow; *Irish confetti*, bricks (the stereotype Irishman was a brawling bricklayer and *Paddy* now also came to mean any bricklayer); *Irish nightingale*, a bullfrog (based on *the Swedish nightingale* Jenny Lind, who made a highly publicized concert tour of America 1850–52); and *Irish spoon*, a shovel, 1862. By 1870 a *biddy* meant a servant girl in America (from the common Irish name Bridget, which had also given English *biddy*, meaning chicken or any fowl in the 17th century).

The first *Saint Patrick's Day Parade* in America was held in 1779, by Irish recruits of the British army occupying New York City during the Revolutionary War, and by 1818 *Paddy* had yet another meaning, the stuffed figure of Saint Patrick carried in the *Saint Paddy's Day parade*. Saint Patrick's Day, March 17th, the traditional death date of Ireland's patron saint, also had many Americans saying *Erin Go Bragh* ("Ireland forever"), a Celtic toast that is part of the day. Other traditional toasts at 19th century Irish-American banquets celebrating the day were "Beannact Dia leat" and "To the land we left, and the land we live in," both heard long before such songs as "Mother Machree" (1910) and "When Irish Eyes Are Smiling" (1912). Incidentally *the wearing of the green* is the wearing of the *shamrock* (Irish *seamrog*, the diminutive of *seamar*, clover, hence "little clover"), associated with St. Patrick's Day because he is said to have used it to illustrate the Trinity. Other terms we associate with or have taken from the Irish include:

begorra, an Anglo-Irish euphemism for "by God."

lallapalooza, lollapalooza, a 1904 American word for something large or remarkable (said by some to be from an Irish dialect word *allayfoozee*, a sturdy fellow, from the French *allez-fusil*, "forward the musket!," though this entire etymology is doubtful).

Paddy wagon, a police van, late 1920s, referring to the many Irish or "Paddy" policemen in such cities as Boston and New York.

shanty, an 1820 American word for a shack or rough cabin (probably from Irish *sean tig*, old house, but perhaps from Canadian French *chantier*, log hut). We called a member of a logging crew a *shanty man* by 1825 and humorously called a kitchen helper in a logging camp a *shanty boss* by 1905, while a *shanty boat* was a river boat with living quarters by 1879. A *shanty village*, 1858, or *shanty town*, 1882, originally referred to a cluster of shacks built along railroad tracks to house railroad construction crews, of whom many were Irish. The term *shanty Irish* wasn't recorded until 1925, referring to lower class Irish Americans, as opposed to the *lace curtain Irish*, poor Irish who had become successful in America.

shebang, meaning a temporary shelter, hovel, or shack in English since the 18th century (from Anglo-Irish *shebeen*, an illegal drinking establishment, from the Gaelic *seibe*, mug, mugful). *The whole shebang* is an American expression of 1879.

shenanigan, trickery, mischief, an American word first recorded in 1855 (probably from Irish *sionnachuighim*, "I play the fox," I play tricks, though it could be from Spanish *chanada*, trick, deceit, or even German *schnagel*).

shillelagh, which has meant a club or cudgel in English since the 18th century, especially an oak or blackthorn one (originally it meant such a cudgel made from the famous oaks of Shillelagh, a barony and town in County Wicklow, Ireland).

smithereens, a 19th century English word, from County Mayo dialect (from Irish *smidirin*, the diminutive of *smiodar*, fragment, hence "small fragment").

Despite such words, the main contribution the Irish made to our language has been in grammar, syntax, and pronunciation. Irish immigrants introduced, or greatly increased, our use of *I seen* for "I saw" and of *shall* where "will" is the more precise and correct form. They also used the definite article and pronoun where English Americans did not, as in "She is in *the* hospital" and "He is on *his* vacation." They also gave us such pronunciations or variant forms as: *tay* for tea and *belave* for believe; *bile* for boil, 1836; *chaw* for chew, 1830; *jine* for join, 1830s; and apple-*sass* for applesauce, 1840s. Thus when we hear America talking we still hear a little bit of Ireland.

Evolution

Charles Darwin's 1859 *The Origin of Species* sold out its 1,250-copy first printing on the day it was issued in England. The 1860 dispute between Darwin's foremost advocate, biologist Thomas Henry Huxley, and Anglican Bishop Samuel Wilberforce, who defended the Bible's account of Creation, immediately spread to American intellectual and religious leaders. Within the decade a great many Americans were talking about Darwin's theory and using such expressions as *natural selection*, *survival of the fittest*, and even Darwin's 1837 term *transmutation of species*.

> I have called this principle, by which each slight variation, if useful, is preserved, by the term Natural Selection. The expression often used by Mr. Herbert Spencer, of the Survival of the Fittest, is more accurate. . . .
> Charles Darwin, *The Origin of Species*, 1859

Charles Darwin (1809–82) by well-known English portrait painter John Collier (1850–1934).

By the 1870s *evolution* had come to mean *Darwinism* or Darwin's theories (*evolution* was first used in 1662, to refer to movements of military formations, then first used in a biological context by the Swiss naturalist Charles Bonnet in 1762). Many people summed up evolution with the simplistic phrase "man is descended from monkeys" (see THE MONKEY TRIAL) and talked excitedly about the illusory *missing link* between ape and man. The Hottentots were the prime contender as the "missing link" in the public's conversation of the 70s and 80s, replaced by the *Java Man* (*Pithecanthropus erectus*) after its fossil discovery in 1891.

Thus from the 1860s to the 1890s Darwinism was a new and popular subject of conversation and contributed several new terms to the language. Until about 1940 evolution was still a scandalous topic in Fundamentalist circles (see FUNDAMENTALISM), the subject of debates, arguments, and fiery attacks. By changing our thinking about the world, Charles Darwin (1809-82) had an enormous effect on our language: he caused us to talk less about God and more about man, anthropology, and nature, making it easier for psychological terms to become popular in the early 1900s (see FREUD SAYS . . .) and perhaps, indirectly, contributed to our increasing use of blasphemy and profanity by weakening our awe of God.

Meet Me at the Fair

Americans have been going to and talking about fairs (Latin *feriae*, feast) since 1638, when *fair* simply meant a market day. By 1801 *fair* had come to mean a periodic market and exhibition and in 1810 the first annual *cattle show*, the Berkshire Cattle Show, was inaugurated in Pittsfield, Massachusetts. In the 1840s the terms *county fair*, *state fair*, and *fair grounds* were first used, the first state fair being at Syracuse, New York, in 1841. Many such fairs were to become the most widely talked about local event of the year. Today Americans talk about over 5,000 county, state, and regional fairs held annually.

In 1850 people began to use a new term, *world's fair*, referring to the London "Crystal Palace" world's fair sponsored by Prince

"Sights at the Fair Ground,"
Currier and Ives, 1888.

138

Albert and Queen Victoria and held in 1851. In 1853 we Americans were proudly talking of our own world's fair, also in a "Crystal Palace," held in New York's Reservoir Square (now Bryant Park behind the New York Public Library on 5th Avenue at 42nd Street). It covered 13 acres, cost $640,000, and 1¼ million people attended. Since then there have been at least 38 official and unofficial "world's fairs," some 15 of them in America. Those we have talked about most include:

"New York Crystal Palace," a lithograph by N. Currier, 1853. Nathaniel Currier (1813–88) and his partner J[ames] Merritt Ives (1824–95) specialized in colorful prints of American life and events. Their business name of "Currier and Ives" became a household word.

1876: Philadelphia's *Centennial Exposition*, celebrating the nation's 100th birthday, had 167 buildings and 30,000 exhibits on 236 acres and cost almost $9 million. It was called "the Mighty Cosmos" and attracted 8 million people. It had everyone talking about such exhibits as Bell's *telephone*, the *typewriter*, the improved *sewing machine*, and George Westinghouse's *air brake*. It also introduced many Americans to the exotic *banana*, sold foil-wrapped for 10¢ each.

1893: Chicago's *World's Columbian Exposition*, belatedly celebrating the 400th anniversary of Columbus' discovery of America. This fair got the whole country talking about *electricity* and the *electric light* from the dramatic moment when President Grover Cleveland pushed a "magic button" in the White House which turned on the fair's power. The fair itself was called "the White City" because of its white, classical buildings and because its 686 acres of displays were electrically lighted at night. Westinghouse's new *electric engine*, *electric dynamo*, and alternating current *generator* were prominently displayed. The less scientific minded of the over 21 million visitors talked mainly about the first *midway* (see ON THE MIDWAY) the first *Ferris-wheel*, and Little Egypt's scandalous COOCHEE-COOCHEE dance.

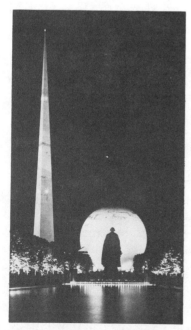

"The Perisphere and Trylon," New York World's Fair, 1939–40.

1901: Buffalo's *Pan-American Exposition* attracted 9 million visitors to its "Landscaped City," featuring a 375-foot electric tower studded with lamps and searchlights and topped with its

The "Unisphere" symbolized the New York World's Fair of 1964–65.

famous "goddess of light" statue, all power courtesy of Niagara Falls. What people talked about most was seeing their first demonstration of *wireless telegraphy*, Edison's new *storage battery*, and Niagara Falls illuminated by colored searchlights. After September 6, what most people talked about was how President McKinley had been assassinated by anarchist Leon Czolgosz while attending a reception at the fair's Temple of Music.

1904: St. Louis' *Louisiana Purchase Exposition*, the "Meet Me in St. Louie, Louie" fair, celebrating the 100th anniversary of the Louisiana Purchase and costing exactly as much as the Purchase had itself—$15 million. Its 1,240 acres was the largest of any world's fair, and its gardens, promenades, and fountains probably made it the most attractive. The almost 13 million visitors talked about the 100 automobiles on display and the futuristic *electric cooking* demonstration, but many remembered eating their first *ice cream cones* and drinking their first glass of *iced tea* there.

1915: San Francisco's *Panama-Pacific International Exposition* (and San Diego's more regional *Panama-California Exposition*) celebrated the completion of the Panama Canal. It had people talking about the fair's California *Spanish style* architecture, the *movies* shown (the first many visitors had ever seen), and the airplane rides offered to the more daring members of the public.

1933: Chicago's *Century of Progress Exposition* celebrated Chicago's 100th anniversary. Before it was opened people were talking about the fair's selling space to exhibitors, instead of giving it free, and its selling of "advanced tickets" (both necessitated by the Depression). But mainly it had us talking (especially my mother) about how cold the *air-conditioned* buildings were (the first we had ever been in) and about seeing our first demonstration of *television* (my father and other volunteers from the audience appeared in a small, totally green, picture).

Since then, of course, we have talked widely about other fairs, including the 1939–40 New York World's Fair with its 728-foot, tapering *Trylon* and 180-foot diameter *Perisphere*, Billy Rose's *Aquacade*, General Motor's *Futurama*, General Electric's *television studio*, and DuPont's *nylon stockings*. This was the "World of Tomorrow"—which turned out to be World War II. Seattle's 1962 *Century 21 Exposition* was symbolized by its 607-foot steel *Space Needle* with a revolving, glass restaurant on top. It introduced the abbreviated word *Expo* for world's fair (and later for any exposition or trade show), and popularized *monorail*. New York's 1964–65 World's Fair was mainly known for its huge open globe, *the Unisphere*, for attracting over 51 million visitors, and for costing half a billion dollars—it was a financial fiasco. Future fairs would be less elaborate and in better taste, which was true of the little-talked-about but beautiful *Expo '74* held in Spokane, Washington in 1974.

Fannie Farmer and the Level Teaspoon

... correct measurements are absolutely necessary to insure the best results.
Fannie Farmer

Fannie Farmer with a level cup-ful of flour.

Many women have become household words in America through their cookbooks. The first was Amelia Simmons, "An American Orphan," who published her 47-page *American Cookery* in Hartford, Connecticut, in 1796. It was the first American *cookerie book*, a term the British still use, our term *cook book* being an Americanism dating from about 1809 (from German *kochbuch*, Dutch *kookboek*). Early collections were also often called *culinary reviews* or simply *recipe books*, though the latter often referred to a handwritten family collection handed down from mother to daughter. In subsequent editions until the 1830s Amelia Simmons' book was talked about and used by thousands of American women, was the first to include recipes for such American dishes as cranberry sauce, pumpkin pie, watermelon pickles, and slapjacks, and was the first cookbook to use such American words as *molasses*, instead of using British words, such as *treacle*.

During the 1820s and 30s American women were talking about and comparing recipes found in books by such cooks as Lydia Child, Eliza Leslie, Sarah Hale, Ester Howland, and Mary Randolph, whose *The Virginia Housewife* of 1824 was the first American regional cookbook and the first southern one, containing recipes for Virginia ham and the like. Not only were these women and their books widely talked about, but each introduced new cooking terms and names for dishes into the American language.

In the 1840s Catharine Esther Beecher, a pioneer in women's education, gained fame with two books: *A Treatise on Domestic Economy for the Use of Young Ladies at Home and at School* (1841, a book which Emerson endorsed and used as a text) and *Miss Beecher's Domestic Receipt Book* (1846). This last, and its subsequent edition, contained not only recipes but hints on buying and storing food, using the ovens and utensils of the day, child feeding, etc. It became a tremendous best-seller, sold door-to-door "in every state of the Union"—in fact, many women talked more about Catharine Beecher and her receipt book than about her sister Harriet Beecher Stowe and her 1852 novel *Uncle Tom's Cabin*.

Fannie Farmer, officially titled *The Boston Cooking School Cook Book*, has been a watchword in American kitchens since the first 3,000 copies were printed at the author's expense and published by Little, Brown in 1896. Fannie Farmer (1857–1915) was a red-haired, iron-willed woman who, having suffered a paralytic stroke while in high school, gained neighborhood fame cooking in her family's Boston boarding house before becoming the Boston Cooking School's most famous student and then its director. After her famous cookbook appeared, she established her own Miss Farmer's School of Cooking in 1902, gave public cooking demonstrations which were widely reported in the press, wrote a cooking column for ten years in *The Woman's Home Companion*, and lectured to women's clubs from coast to coast.

All this made Fannie Farmer a household word, both as a person and as a book. Before her death she had changed American kitchen terminology from "a pinch" and "a dash" and "a heaping spoonful"—all vague terms which she detested—to her own precise, standardized, scientific terms, presenting a mode of cooking which was easy, reliable, and could be followed even by inexperienced cooks. To Fannie Farmer, "the mother of level measurement," we can attribute the popularity of such precise everyday kitchen terms as *level teaspoon*, ½ *teaspoon*, *measuring cup*, *oven thermometer*, and "bake at 350 degrees for 40 minutes."

A 1905 cooking class. Learning how to use tested recipes and standard measures makes it possible to duplicate famous dishes in a home kitchen.

54–40 Or Fight!—Manifest Destiny

[*It is*] *our manifest destiny to spread over the continent.*
Massachusetts Representative Robert C. Winthrop in a speech in Congress, January 3, 1846, speaking in favor of obtaining exclusive U.S. occupation and control of Oregon territory. This was the first use of *manifest destiny* in Congress.

54-40 or fight! (1844) was one of the most stirring political slogans in American history and *Manifest Destiny* (1845) was one of the most popular phrases and beliefs. Both grew out of the increasingly expansionist mood of the country after the 1830s and, specifically, out of Polk's presidential election campaign of 1844. That year James K. Polk and the Democrats campaigned on a platform for the "reoccupation of Oregon, the reannexation of Texas" (we had agreed to joint occupation of Oregon with Great Britain in 1818 and given up any of our Louisiana Purchase claims to Texas as part of our agreement to obtain Florida from Spain in 1819). The first part of this plat-

James Knox Polk (1795–1849).

form, the "reoccupation of Oregon" was translated into the slogan *54-40 or fight!* and the second part, "reannexation of Texas" became *Manifest Destiny.*

54-40 or fight! was first used in 1844 by William Allen in a speech before the U.S. Senate. It quickly became the slogan of hundreds of thousands of Democrats (the "war party") during that presidential election year. It meant the U.S. should resolve the *Oregon question* with Great Britain by fighting, if necessary, for sole occupancy and control of what was then called *Oregon territory* (1826) or the *Oregon country* (1831), the entire region west of the Rockies from California up to the Alaskan border, 54° 40′ North. After Polk was elected, however, he compromised with Great Britain by accepting the Oregon lands only up to the 49th parallel. He compromised because between his election campaign and the negotiations we had annexed Texas, making war with Mexico imminent—and Polk didn't want to fight two wars at once. Thus, despite the slogan *54-40 or fight!*, the boundary between the U.S. and Canada wasn't to be 54° 40′ and there was no fight. In a sense, we chose to annex Texas rather than fight for British Columbia. Congress established the official *Oregon Territory* in 1848 and made the northern part *Washington Territory* in 1853.

Manifest Destiny was the sometimes idealistic belief, some-

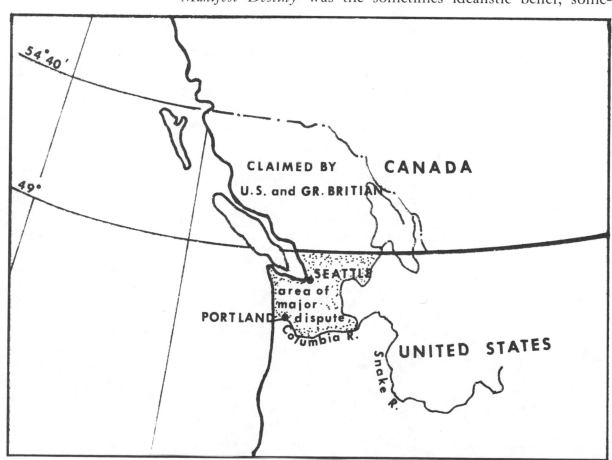

times imperialistic creed, that it was God's will (hence our obvious or manifest destiny) that the U.S. and its democratic ways spread from the Atlantic to the Pacific, from Canada to the Rio Grande. The phrase was first hinted at by Andrew Jackson in 1824 when he called the United States

> ... a country manifestly called by the Almighty to a destiny which Greece and Rome, in the days of their pride, might have envied.

However, the actual phrase *manifest destiny* was first used in the national debate over whether to annex Texas or not. It first appeared in the July–August, 1845 issue of the *United States Magazine and Democratic Review* in an article by its editor John L. O'Sullivan, then the phrase swept the country when he repeated it in a pro-annexation editorial in the *New York Morning News* on December 27, two days before the annexation of Texas. It was the last telling phrase in a ten-year debate. For no sooner had Texas declared independence from Mexico and established the Republic of Texas in 1836 (see REMEMBER THE ALAMO!) than it applied for admission to the Union; but Andrew Jackson, by then president, couldn't risk war with Mexico by approving annexation. Thus Texas remained an independent republic for almost a decade, attracting 100,000 American immigrants and supported by loans from Great Britain and France, who valued Texas cotton and wanted Texas to remain as a buffer country against further U.S. expansion westward. Meanwhile America debated *the annexation of Texas* hotly. Southerners and Democrats especially wanted annexation of the Texas lands as slave states; northern Whigs and abolitionists were against it, not wanting to tip the balance of states in favor of slavery. Thus it was not until the *Texas question* (whether Texas should be admitted as a slave or a free state) was finally resolved by the *Texas compromise* (1845, whereby Texas was admitted as a slave state but slavery was prohibited in any states formed from the Texas lands north of a continuation of the Missouri Compromise line) that Texas annexation took place, December 29, 1845.

The platform the "reoccupation of Oregon, reannexation of Texas"—*54-40 or fight!* and *manifest destiny*—won the election for Polk and the Democrats in 1844 and the austere, hard-working Polk did obtain the Oregon lands, Texas to the Rio Grande, and more. After our annexation of Texas *Manifest Destiny* was not forgotten. It was immediately applied to THE MEXICAN WAR in which we obtained California and New Mexico, and then the concept was enlarged to encompass lands beyond the continental United States, to explain our desire for Cuba in the 1850s, the purchase of Alaska in 1867, and the annexation of Hawaii in 1898.

Fletcherism

Horace Fletcher (1849–1910).

was a popular word and eating fad stemming from Horace Fletcher's 1903 book *The ABC of Nutrition*, expounding his theory that each mouthful of food should be chewed 32 times—once for each tooth. A successful San Francisco importer, Fletcher had turned to the investigation of nutrition in his middle age and soon had the whole country talking about his theory and using or kidding about the verb *to fletcherize*, to chew thoroughly. His believers included John D. Rockefeller, Sr., Thomas Edison, and, for three months, psychologist and philosopher William James, who said, "I had to give it up. It nearly killed me." The fad continued until Fletcher himself died in 1919.

The Flying Machine

Wilbur and Orville Wright received a patent for a *flying machine* in 1906. That was three years after their first 120-foot, 12-second flight made *Kitty Hawk* and "the Wright brothers" household terms. Other pioneers called their planes *aerial ships* and *aerial machines*, and Samuel P. Langley called his an *aerodrome*.

Aeroplane was first used in England in 1866 to describe a wing or (geometric) plane in the air, then in 1873 to refer to the entire craft. In the U.S. the spelling was changed to *airplane* in the late 1870s. Thus, though the Wright brothers patented the *flying machine* some Americans immediately called it an *airplane*, with the shorter word *plane* well established by 1910. *Aviator* (Latin *avis*, bird) was then the fashionable word for a flyer, but *flyer* was also in use from the start. From Kitty Hawk in 1903 until the late 1920s Americans, and most of the rest of the world, talked a great deal about airplanes and the *flying fools* who made early flying history.

By 1908 *pilot, hangar, airfield, night flying, monoplane,* and *biplane* were known to almost every man and boy. In 1910 Americans talked about Teddy Roosevelt's foolhardy stunting with a member of the famous Wright Brothers' Flying Team over St. Louis: he almost fell out of the plane while waving to the crowd below. In 1911 the talk was about the 84-day coast-to-coast "flight," actually a series of short hops, from New York City to Long Beach, California. In 1912 we marveled over stunt flyer Lincoln Beachey of the Glenn Curtis Exhibition Team and how he buzzed the gorge below Niagara Falls only two feet above the rocks—he being the same daring young man who did the first *loop-the-loop* and made the word popular. During WORLD WAR I talk about airplanes and their romantic military pilots filled the air and by 1915 made common such "technical" words as *cockpit, prop, airpocket, ceiling, take-off,* and *tailspin.*

The first powered flight, December 17, 1903, by the Wright brothers at Kitty Hawk, North Carolina (top left). Within 25 years this Boeing 40A was flying passengers and mail from San Francisco to Chicago. The pilot sat in an open cockpit so he could see the landmarks showing where he was going—there were no instruments (top right). Charles Augustus Lindbergh in 1927 when he made the first solo nonstop transatlantic flight (center left). A Fokker F-10, a Pan American Airways passenger plane. The first flight over the North Pole was made in a similar trimotor Fokker in 1929 (center right). An Eastern Air Lines DC-3 airliner, 1936 (bottom left). In 1932 Amelia Earhart (1897-1937) became the first woman to make a solo transatlantic flight. She was lost in the Pacific Ocean attempting to fly around the world.

A Capital Airlines Lockheed Constellation, *the famous "Connie" of the 1940s and 50s.*

A United Air Lines Boeing 747, *the* jumbo jet *of the 1970s.*

In 1924, four flyers, called *world cruisers* in some newspapers, had the public talking about their 25,000-mile, 175-day flight around the world in two Douglas biplanes (in 1949 the U.S. Air Force B-50, the *Lucky Lady* flew around the world nonstop in four days, refueling in the air). In 1926 the big topic was Commander Richard E. Byrd and Floyd Bennett in the Fokkar *Josephine* making the first flight over the North Pole. Then, next to the stock market crash, the most talked-about news of 1929 was the first flight over the South Pole by Byrd and three others in their Ford plane, the *Floyd Bennett* (alas, there is some doubt now that Byrd was scrupulous in claiming to have flown over the North Pole).

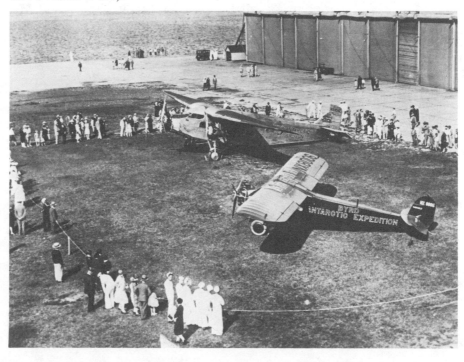

A trimotor Ford, named the Floyd Bennett *(top), and a Fairchild were two of the three planes used by Admiral Byrd on his Antarctic expedition. The third was a Fokker. The* Floyd Bennett *crossed the South Pole on November 29, 1929, with Bernt Balchen piloting and Byrd in the navigator's compartment.*

Sandwiched in between Byrd's two flights, however, was one of the most exciting, most talked-about events of the century: Charles Lindbergh's May 20–21, 1927, nonstop solo flight across the Atlantic from Roosevelt Field, Long Island to Le Bourget Air Field near Paris in 33 hours. It had all America, indeed all the world, talking about the 25-year-old *Lindy, the Lone Eagle,* and his $6,000, 27-foot plane, *The Spirit of St. Louis* (named for the St. Louis financial backers of the flight).

In 1933 the topic was Wiley Post and the plane *Winnie May* making the first around-the-world solo; two years later millions mourned Post and Will Rogers when they lost their lives in a plane crash near Point Barrow, Alaska.

Will Rogers and Wiley Post in Fairbanks, Alaska, 1935.

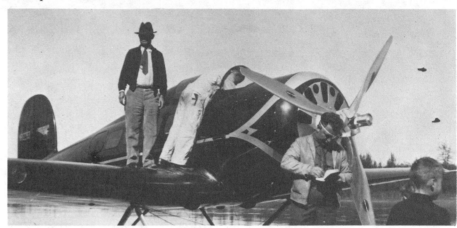

In 1937 the topic was the mysterious disappearance of Amelia Earhart in her airplane near Howland Island in the Pacific while attempting an around-the-world flight. The first woman to fly the Atlantic solo and to fly from Hawaii to California, Miss Earhart was the most famous *aviatrix* of all, and the word, which had been somewhat commonly used for a female aviator since about 1925, seemed to disappear with her. But the days of the *flying machines* and *the flying fools* who flew them had already drawn to a close toward the end of the 1920s. The future of the airplane was now with the *airline* (1914) and the *airliner* (1915).

Though a few scheduled airline flights had begun in 1914, the first major "regularly scheduled airline" in the U.S. had begun operations in 1919, between New York City and Atlantic City, with the second major one beginning flights in 1920, between Key West and Havana. However, it was 1927–31 that saw the beginning of modern airlines and some of the most famous company names. In 1927 the name *Pan American Airways* was first heard; the firm was created to carry mail from Key West to Cuba, then within the next three years expanded operations to Puerto Rico, Panama, and South America. In 1927 *Pitcairn Aviation* was started, but people didn't hear about it much until it became *Eastern Airlines* in 1938. In 1930 *TWA,* Transcontinental and Western Air, was first heard, created from Transatlantic Air Transport ("the Lindbergh Line") and Western Air Express. In 1931 *United Airlines* was a new name, operating between the West Coast and Chicago.

In 1933 people were also first talking about "coast-to-coast flights." These were TWA's Ford trimotor flights, taking 27 hours flying time and stopping at Philadelphia, Harrisburg, Pittsburgh, Columbus, Indianapolis, St. Louis, Kansas City, Wichita, Amarillo, Albuquerque, and Winslow, Arizona for fuel and passengers, all for only $160.

In 1930 Ellen Church, a registered nurse, became the first airline stewardess, choosing the name *stewardess* herself (it had been used on board ships since the 1830s). She served on a 12-passenger Boeing 80 Air Transport plane. Later some airlines briefly called their stewardesses *hostesses* and some newspapers cutely referred to them as *sky-girls*. Besides reassuring passengers and passing out chewing gum to ease pressure-plagued ears after takeoff, stewardesses aided those who had *air sickness*, a term first used by balloonists in the 1780s. They began serving free "in-flight meals" from "on-board kitchens" in 1936.

Also in 1936 *American Airways* (later known as *American Airlines*) put the twin-engined, all-metal, 21-passenger, 160-mph Douglas *DC-3* into service. As it advertised, "comfort facilities" were now available on "most planes" and "cabins . . . are comfortably heated and ventilated," so that passengers were advised to "wear regular apparel regardless of season." The DC-3 became the workhorse plane that "air travelers" grew to love and trust, the plane that most of us first flew on, introducing us to such amenities and phrases as *airline ticket*, *airline reservation*, *a seat over the wing* (said to be less bouncy than other seats, but noisier since it was near the engines), *Please fasten your seatbelts*, and the stewardess' ever-smiling question *Coffee, tea, or milk?*

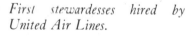

First stewardesses hired by United Air Lines.

Transatlantic service was inaugurated by Pan Am in 1939 (just 12 years after Lindbergh's solo), New York to Southampton in Boeing 314 flying boats, many people remembering the 22-passenger *Dixie Clippers* on their 24-hour flight to Lisbon. However, the popularity of the term *overseas flight* was delayed by WORLD WAR II. Toward the end of the war we heard of the latest development in German fighters, the *jet plane. Jetliner* came in the late 1940s, but by then the simpler word *jet* had already become the common word for any type of jet-powered plane. Soon conversation about air travel was, "Have you flown on a jet yet?," with "daily transatlantic jet service" introduced by Pan Am in 1953. This led to the term *jet set*, popularized and probably coined by newspaper gossip columnist "Cholly Knickerbocker" (Igor Cassini) in the late 1950s, referring to socialites and celebrities who could afford *to jet* (early 1950s) back and forth for fun and frolic on both sides of the Atlantic. In the 1960s the *DC-8, 707*, and *727* were the planes most talked about, and in 1970 Pan Am introduced the *Boeing 747*, the *jumbo jet*, with much fanfare, leading to such terms as *wide-bodied jet* and *airbus*.

About this time, too, the American public and Congress were hotly arguing about the two competing designs for a government subsidized *SST* (Super*S*onic *T*ransport), finally deciding that the money needed to develop it and the environmental hazards to the upper atmosphere and to ground-level ears were too much to bear—leaving new terms for such planes and flights to emerge from the joint British and French SST, the *Concorde*, which began regularly scheduled flights in 1976.

The Fourth of July—Independence Day

Yesterday [July 2nd]. . . . A resolution was passed . . . that these United Colonies are, and of right ought to be, free and independent States . . . The second day of July, 1776 . . . ought to be commemorated . . . by solemn acts of devotion to God Almighty. It ought to be solemnized with pomp and parade, with shows, games, sports, guns, bells, bonfires, and illuminations—from this time forward for evermore.

John Adams, letter to his wife Abigail, July 3, 1776

Adams was right about celebrating, but not about the date. The Continental Congress, meeting in Philadelphia, approved a resolution for independence on July 2nd, adopted the formal *Declaration of Independence* on July 4th, and the famous signing of "the Declaration" took place on August 2nd, after the document had been transcribed on parchment (John Hancock, the president of the Continental Congress, was the only one to sign the original on July 4th; he and 51 others signed the parchment on August 2, the

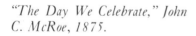

A Fourth of July Oration *in the late 1800s.*

last of the 56 signers, Thomas McKean of Delaware, didn't get around to signing it until 1781). Thus the birthday of American independence could just as fairly be celebrated each year on July 2nd, July 4th, or August 2nd. Philadelphia chose July 4th, making that date one of our most patriotic expressions.

The first *Fourth of July celebration*, of course, was on the first anniversary of the Declaration of Independence, in 1777. Boston celebrated mainly with sermons, many places celebrated not at all. But Philadelphia, the Revolutionary capital, had a major celebration, including sermons, the ringing of bells, candles lit in every window, bonfires, 13-gun salutes, speeches, an official dinner, a captured Hessian band playing—and fireworks. Here, on this very first Fourth of July celebration, the term *the Glorious Fourth* was first used. Though Philadelphia was occupied by British troops in 1778, the celebrations spread to other areas. By the late 1790s the day was also called *Independence Day*, by the 1820s it was often simply called *the Fourth*.

By the 1800s patriotic speeches, especially anti-British ones, were a tradition of the day and *Fourth of July Oration* was a widely understood expression. By the 1840s *Fourth of July picnic* was a popular term, and sports and games, such as potato races, catching a greased pig, and watermelon-eating contests, were popular. Fireworks have always been associated with the Fourth, partly because they represented the musket fire and rockets' red glare of the Revolution, partly just for the fun of it. In fact the word *fireworks* was first recorded in America in 1777 in connection with the first Fourth of July celebration (before that they had been called *rockets*, after 1820 those that were made to be heard rather than seen were called *firecrackers*). As early as 1865 people were protesting as an-

"The Day We Celebrate," John C. McRoe, 1875.

noying and dangerous the widespread use of fireworks, including:

serpents, 1701, which burned with a serpentine motion; also called *snakes*, a similar type was called *chasers*.
Roman candles, 1830s, so called because they originated in Italy.
poppers, late 1830s.
pinwheels, 1850s.
double-headers, 1860s.
punks, 1860s, slow-burning, pencil-shaped pieces for igniting other fireworks, but used by themselves as spattering, sparkling fireworks by small boys. Replaced by *sparklers* in the 1880s.

In 1954 Congress banned the transportation of fireworks into states that prohibit their sale, but debate still continues over whether they should be completely banned or not.

French, French Toast, and French Postcards

The Norman conquest of England in 1066 transformed Old English, which was almost exclusively Germanic, into Middle English by adding many French words to our vocabulary. For the next 200 years French was the language of the ruling class—the court, the merchants, and the clergy. Thus French-based words such as *nobleman*, *prince*, *baron*, *castle*, *parliament*, *palace*, *manor*, *procession*, *justice*, *crime*, *culprit*, *treason*, *chaplain*, *incense*, and *grace* entered the English language. The French conquerors and English subjects were soon one people, intermarried in fact and culture, and using many French-based words for household items, fashions, and the arts, such as *curtain*, *cushion*, *quilt*, *parlour*, *pantry*, *cape*, *lace*, *petticoat*, *plume*, *satin*, *tassel*, *art*, *dance*, *literature*, *music*, *poet*, *sculpture*, and *story*. French influence again strengthened during the Renaissance when England imported such new terms as *comrade*, *duel*, *entrance*, and *mustache*. Thus English has absorbed many French words during the last 900 years.

In addition, French has had a direct influence on American English: via French explorers, trappers, and fur traders (see VOYAGEURS, RAPIDS, AND PORTAGES and THE PRAIRIE for their words); in Louisiana (see BAYOUS, CREOLES, AND CAJUNS); and through more general contact and influence. This last gives American English such words as:

barrage (French *tir de barrage*, barrier of fire, curtain of artillery fire) entered both American and British English during World War I.
in cahoots with (perhaps from French *cahute*, cabin, but could be from Dutch or German), 1829.
camouflage (from the French slang *camoufler*, to disguise), entered both American and British English during World War I.

Chef's Selections

Filet of Sole Meuniere	6.50
Striped Bass Beurre Nantais	6.95
Frogs Legs Saute Provencale	8.50
Scampi à la Provencale	8.75
Brook Trout Amandine	6.75
Sweetbreads Maison	8.75
Coq au Vin	6.75
Canard aux Cerises	7.75
Poulet Basquaise	6.75
Tripe à la Mode de Caen	7.75
Calf Liver Lyonnaise	6.95
Beef Bourguinon	7.25
Veal Kidneys Bordelaise	6.75
Pork Chops apple sauce	6.50
Escalopine de Veau au Madère	7.50
French Lamb Chops	8.25
Sirloin Steak "Maitre d'Hotel"	8.90
Filet Mignon	8.90

all entrees include vegetables du jour and salad maison

Desserts

Tarte Maison - 1.25 ~ French Pastry - 1.25
Creme Caramel - .75 ~ Fraise au Vin - 1.25
Peach Melba - 1.25 ~ Tortoni - .90 ~ Ice Cream .90
Coupe aux Marrons - 1.25 ~ Mousse au Chocolat 1.00
Fromage Varies - 1.50

Coffee or Tea included with dinner ~ Demi Tasse - .60 ~ Milk - .60

Wine List

Vin Rouges	Full	half
Medoc	6.00	3.00
St Emilion	6.00	3.00
Chateuneuf du Pape	7.00	3.50
Nuit St. Georges	9.50	5.00
Pommard	9.50	5.00
Beaujolais	5.50	3.00
Gevrey Chambertin	8.50	4.50
Rouge Maison	6.00	3.00

Vin Blanc		
Graves	5.00	2.75
Sauternes	5.00	2.75
Pouilly Fuissé	7.00	3.50
Chablis	7.00	3.50
Vin d'Alsace	5.00	2.50

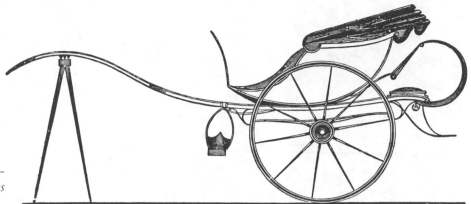

A French cabriolet, *a light one-horse carriage from which comes our* cab, *a vehicle for hire.*

carriole, a light, one-horse wagon, 1714. We soon spelled this French word as we pronounced it, *carryall*, which became confused with "carry all"; hence by 1811 we used it to mean a large, heavy carriage that could carry everything.

depot, a railroad station. The word was first recorded with this meaning in America in 1832, in a House of Representatives' document, with its French spelling *dépôt*.

détente (French for "loosening"), an easing of tensions between nations, especially between Russia and the U.S. as part of Secretary of State Kissinger's and President Nixon's foreign policy, 1973.

French boot, a lightweight dress shoe, 1850.

French church, a French Protestant or Huguenot church, 1694.

French (salad) dressing, 1884. Incidentally, *thousand island dressing* dates from the 1920s.

Frencher, a Frenchman, 1826; *Frenchy*, a Frenchman, 1883, and used after 1904 to mean capricious.

French flat, a sublet floor in a private townhouse, one of our first terms for an apartment, 1879.

French fried potatoes, 1902; *French frieds*, 1920s; *French fries*, 1930s.

French harp, a harmonica, 1883.

French monte, a popular form of the gambling card game, 1851.

French toast, 1870s.

Frog, a Frenchman, was common in England by 1870 but became well known in the U.S. only during World War I. It is probably from the French relishing frogs as a delicacy, reinforced by the toads on the coat of arms of the city of Paris.

Hugers, our 17th century term for the French Huguenots, who also gave us the place name *Huguenot* on Staten Island and *New Rochelle* in Westchester County, N.Y., and such names as New Yorker John Jay, the famous Virginia Dabney (d'Aubigny) family, Boston's Peter Faneuil and *Faneuil Hall*, and Charles Guiteau, who assassinated President Garfield.

sashay (French *chasse* from *chasser*, to chase), originally meant a sideways dance step, then to move or glide by 1836, then a trip or journey around 1900. This may have spread north from Louisiana French or elsewhere in the South, but was first recorded in Pennsylvania.

We have also used the adjective *French* in a derogatory, smirking way as a habit left over from our British colonial days: the British hated their French rivals and considered them sexually perverse. From this heritage we have:

An early French postcard picturing a classic Grecian nude. Later French postcards became pornographic and many World War I soldiers brought them back to America.

French pox, the French disease, syphilis, first used in England in 1503 and 1598, respectively. Both terms were in colonial use. In fair turnabout, the French called it "the English disease."

French letter, a birth-control device, an early form of the condom. This term was used in England and spread to America around the time of the Revolutionary War.

to take French leave, to depart abruptly or without saying enough polite goodbys, in use in England since the 18th century and in the U.S. since 1907. It has meant to be absent without leave in English military use since 1771, this meaning becoming very common with Americans during World War I.

French postcard, a pornographic photograph. Early commercial photographers often presented their work in the form of postcards and as early as the 1840s "artistic" photographs of classic Grecian nudes were circulated, originating in France. Such postcards were carried by some Civil War soldiers but the term became popular when American soldiers bought much more pornographic photographs in France during World War I.

French kiss, a passionate open-mouthed kiss with tongues caressing. This term has probably been in use since World War I, but became extremely popular with teenagers during the late 1930s.

the French way, to French, Frenching, oral sex, common terms since World War I, when American soldiers returning from France popularized them. *Sixty-nine, 69*, simultaneous cunnilingus and fellatio, so called from the figure the two participants form; the term was in rather general use by the 1930s and probably is a translation of the French term for it *soixante-neuf*, also made more widely known by returning World War I soldiers.

The French have also given us many place names, especially along the Canadian border, around the Great Lakes, down the Mississippi, throughout the old French Louisiana Territory, and in the plains and mountain regions of the West (see also MOUNTAINS, CREEKS, DESERTS, AND SWAMPS for more of these French geographical and place names). They have given us three state names, *Louisiana*, *Maine*, and *Vermont* (see THE STATES for details) and various towns—and sometimes schools and prisons—named Joliet, La Grange or Lagrange, La Salle, Marquette, Paris, and Versailles (Kentucky alone has a La Grange, a Paris, and a Versailles), as well as:

Baton Rouge, Louisiana, built as a French fort in 1719, it means "red stick," the French translation of an Indian term for a red post marking the boundary there between the hunting grounds of two tribes.

Des Moines. The river was named

154

Des Moings by the French around 1673 for the local Moingouence Indian tribe, but this name soon got confused into *Des Moines*, meaning "the monks," after which the Iowa town took its name.

Detroit, Michigan (French *de troit*, of the strait), named by French settlers in 1701 for the river or strait between Lake Erie and Lake St. Claire.

Dubuque, Iowa, named after the first settler there, the French Canadian Julien Dubuque, a lead miner.

Lake Pontchartrain, named after the Comte de Pontchartrain, Louis XIV's minister of state and patron of Antoine Cadillac, colonial governor of the French territory of Louisiana.

Little Rock, Arkansas. Originally French explorer Bernard de la Harpe named the river bluff here *La Petite Roche*, the French then establishing a trading post on it in 1722.

Louisville, Kentucky, named in 1780 for King Louis XVI of France in appreciation for his aiding America during the Revolutionary War. *Marietta*, Ohio, was named for the same reason in 1788, for Louis XVI's queen, Marie Antoinette.

New Orleans, Louisiana, named *Nouvelle Orléans* by the French governor of the colony in 1718 after the city in France and the French regent, the Duc d'Orleans; respelled *New Orleans* after the 1803 Louisiana Purchase made it part of the U.S.

the Sault Ste. Marie Ship Canal (French *sault*, rapids) bypassing St. Mary's Falls between Lake Superior and Lake Huron. The same falls also gives us *Sault Ste. Marie*, Michigan.

St. Louis, Missouri, named for the 13th century Saint Louis, Louis IX of France (who led two Crusades and built some of the great French Gothic cathedrals) by its original 1764 French settlers.

Terre Haute, Indiana, founded in 1816 on the site of an old French and Indian fur trading village; the name means "high ground," on high land above flood danger.

Vincennes, Indiana, named for Montreal-born François Marie Bissot, Sieur de Vincennes, who had built a fort and trading post there around 1731 (the Chicasaw Indians didn't appreciate this, burning him at the stake in 1736, after which the fort was given his name).

Freud Says—

> *Anyone who goes to a psychiatrist ought to have his head examined.*
> attributed to movie producer Samuel Goldwyn during the 1940s.

Around 1885 Viennese neurologist Sigmund Freud (1856–1939) worked with Josef Breuer in treating hysteria by having the patient experience *catharsis* by retelling his experiences under hypnosis. Freud replaced the hypnosis with the patient's "free association," calling this method *psychoanalysis* around 1900.

> [I] invented the term psychoanalysis. . . .
> Sigmund Freud, *Encyclopedia Britannica*, "Psychoanalysis," 1926

Between 1895 and 1900 Freud also used and gave the psychoanalytical meaning to most of the other terms we associate with him: *anxiety*, *defense mechanism*, *dream interpretation*, *ego*, *id*, *libido*, *Oedipus complex*, *superego*, *transference*, and *trauma*. His terminology began to spread rapidly in 1908 when the First International

Sigmund Freud.

Congress of Psychoanalysis met in Vienna, attended by such bright young doctors as Alfred Adler, A. A. Brill, Ernest Jones, and Carl Jung. News coverage of this meeting saw the word *psychoanalysis* appear for the first time in the U.S.

In 1920 Freud introduced his concept of the *death instinct* (popularly called *the death wish*) and *the pleasure principle*. By the mid 1920s informed people were using psychoanalytic terms and discussing Adler, Jones, Jung, Rank, Stekel, and Wundt. Interest grew in the 30s and increased after 1938, when many well-known psychoanalysts came to the U.S. to practice or teach after Hitler drove them out of Austria (Jewish-born Freud went to live with Ernest Jones in England).

By the late 1930s psychoanalysis was a prime topic of conversation and terms rightly or wrongly associated with it were part of popular American speech. We used or soon were to use frequently such terms as *behaviorist, extrovert* and *introvert* (these two words are associated with Carl Jung, who also gave us *archetype* and *collective unconscious*), *fetish, fixation, Freudian slip, gestalt, inferiority complex, inhibition, mania, masochism, masochist, neurosis, neurotic, Oedipus complex, phobia, psychiatry, psychiatrist* (also called a *head shrink* by the late 1950s and *shrink* by the 1960s, originally California terms), *psychoanalyst* (shortened to *analyst* by the 1940s), *psychopath* (shortened to *psycho* by 1942), *psychosomatic, psychosis, repression, schizophrenia, schizophrenic* (popularly called a *split personality,* then *schiz* and *schizo* by the late 1940s), *S and M* (*sadism* and *masochism,* a homosexual term of the 1950s, popularized by classified ads in pornographic magazines in the 60s), *shock treatment* (insulin shock was first used in 1933), *sublimation,* and *tabu.*

Many of these aren't Freudian terms or even from psychoanalysis at all: some are from other branches of psychiatry, others from sociology, some from the field of *sexology* (a 1902 term). But interest and awareness of Freudian theory and practice made them all popular, even when used without any true knowledge of what they really mean. Although some of the terms were used to buttress the sexual freedoms of the 1920s, by the late 1930s they were used in pseudo-psychoanalytic clichés. Thus, if Freud were listening to America, he would have heard people casually tossing off such lines as "He has an Oedipus complex," . . . "Her inferiority complex is caused by her mother," . . . "Honey, you have to overcome your inhibitions," . . . "Freud says it is not healthy to repress your desires," . . . "The pain is only psychosomatic." For better or worse, directly or indirectly, Freud had changed our way of looking at and talking about people.

Fuck and Screw

I wonder how many readers will look up these words first. Or how many will blink and quickly turn the page. They are actually very old, very common English words.

Fuck has been common in English since at least the late 15th century and was first recorded in 1503 (before that people didn't *fuck*, they *swived*). It comes from an old Germanic verb *ficken/ fucken*, to strike or penetrate, whose slang meaning was to copulate. Its root *pug-* (which also gives us *pugilist* and *puncture*) and related forms go back to prehistoric times. Thus *fuck* did not originate as a police blotter acronym for "*for unlawful carnal knowledge*" or from any such acronym or colorful modern origin as some popular stories would have us believe. *Screw* came into English via Old French from the Latin *scrōfa*, sow, which also gives us the woodworking *screw* and the word *scrofula* (the woodworking *screw* because its threads coil like a sow's tail and the word *scrofula* because the glandular swelling of this affliction is rounded like a pig's back). But this Latin word *scrōfa*, sow, was influenced by or melded with another Latin word, *scrōbis*, ditch, whose Vulgar Latin meaning was vulva—and these two words "sow—vulva" give us *screw*, to copulate.

There is, of course, no logical reason why *fuck, screw, make* (1922), or any other term (see OH SHIT!) should be "dirty," shocking, or taboo, no logical reason why they should be considered any different than such synonyms as *copulate, sexual intercourse*, or *feces*. It's a matter of conditioning and etiquette. *Fuck* appeared in poetry and scholarly dictionaries until the 18th century, then *fuck* and *screw* became strongly taboo. From then until after World War II no dictionary listed or discussed them. They became so taboo that by the 1820s *fuck* and *fucking* had developed the euphemistic synonyms *frig* and *frigging* (the English had used *frig* to mean to thrash about since the 15th century and to mean to masturbate since 1590; it probably comes from Old English *frigan*, to love). Thus *frig* came to mean *fuck* because it meant to masturbate: we have used *jerk off* to mean to masturbate since the 18th century, *jack off* since the 19th, and *beat the dummy* and *beat the meat* since around 1915.

Because of the blackout between the 18th century and the 1940s, we don't know exactly when *fuck* and *screw* were first used in certain oaths, as expletives and intensives, or when they first took on some of their extended meanings, such as to cheat (*His business partner fucked/screwed him*), to bungle or confuse (*He fucked/screwed up that job*), or to loaf or malinger (*Stop fucking/ screwing around*). We do know, however, that such uses first centered around *fuck*, with *screw* being substituted later—in fact, in many ways, *screw* is almost a euphemism for *fuck*. We also know that *fuck* probably came to mean to *bamboozle* (1712), *hornswaggle* (1829), *hoodwink* (1875), cheat, or take advantage of someone, because it is very close to the Old English *ficol*, false, treacherous, though using sex words to refer to cheating, confusion, failure, etc., is obviously psychological, implying that sexual intercourse steals our virility or innocence, or takes advantage of us or our good nature.

As explained at GODDAMN, DARN, AND OH PERDITION!, in the 1870s blasphemy began to weaken and obscenity (Latin *obscēnus*, filthy, repulsive) and scatology (Greek *skatos*, dung) began to increase. Thus the way to shock or express strong feelings was increasingly to say *fuck*, *screw*, or *shit* rather than *Goddamn*, *hell*, or *Jesus*. It is not surprising then that the 1870s saw the first widespread use of *fuck!* as an expletive of anger or annoyance, *fucked* to mean tired (*all fucked out*), the angry rejection *go fuck yourself*, or term *fuck pig* for a contemptible person, and the first recorded use of *like fuck!* and *fuck it all!*

The use of obscenity and scatology then increased greatly during World War I and became a flood during World War II. The use of the cursing modifier *fucking*, for damned, first reached epidemic proportions with British soldiers around 1915, by which time they were also using *fuck arse* (a contemptible person, American troops translated this into *fuck ass*), *fuck me gently* (literally "don't take advantage of me too much, don't cheat me too blatantly"), *fuck 'em all*, and *make a fuck up of* (to bungle, ruin). Thus popularizing the use of *fuck* was a joint British-American effort during the war. The loosening of language taboos between the wars is shown in the 1930 Canadian armed forces alliterative expression *fucked by the fickle finger of fate* and by a few daring books which represented *fuck* with the censored spelling *f**k* (this quaint form was first used in Francis Grose's 1785 *Classical Dictionary of the Vulgar Tongue*). There was then such a fantastic increase in the use of *fuck*, *screw*, and *shit* during World War II that it almost seemed no serviceman could complete a sentence without using one of them. This armed forces use and acceptance of these words spread to many segments of the population during and after the war, helped by veterans bringing their vocabulary to college campuses, a wartime and postwar lessening of social restrictions, increasing social mobility, new concepts of free speech, the "sexual revolution" of the 1950s and 60s, and the Women's Liberation movement since the late 60s. In 1959 Grove Press first printed the word *fuck* respectably in modern times, in an unexpurgated edition of D. H. Lawrence's 1928 *Lady Chatterley's Lover;* this caused a legal battle over obscenity which the publisher won in a 1960 court ruling. Beginning in World War II we frequently heard such phrases as *fucked up/screwed up* (confused, bungled), *fuck you (Charley)/screw you!* (for the now weaker "Damn you, go to hell"), and *fuck off* (as a verb, "beat it"; as a noun a shirker or loafer).

In World War II there also appeared the very popular acronym *snafu* (*s*ituation *n*ormal, *a*ll *f*ucked *u*p), meaning a mistake, bungling, or confusion, as well as other less common acronyms based on it, as: *fubar* (*fucked up beyond all recognition*), *fubb* (*fucked up beyond belief*), *tarfu* (*things are really fucked up*), *janfu* (*joint army-navy fuck up*) and *fubis* (*fuck you buddy, I'm shipping out*). There were also abbreviations such as *F.O.* (*fuck off*), *F.T.A.* (*fuck the army*), and *G.F.U.* (*general fuck up*). Later, the Korean war popularized *motherfucker*, which had been used by Blacks since the late 1930s but now spread from the army's predominantly Black construction battalions and truck drivers to general use. It soon became, and remains, the American male's strongest derogatory epithet. *Motherfucker* also produced popular euphemisms in the 1950s, including *mother-* combined with other two-syllable words substituted for *fucker*, as *mothergrabber*, *motherlover*, *mother rucker*, and *mother dangler*.

Fuck and *screw* are used far more by men than by women—probably because men have (or have been allowed to display) shorter tempers and more aggression, certainly because men have had fewer restrictions and felt it necessary to prove their masculine toughness by words as well as deeds. Perhaps greater equality for women will change this in the future: women may curse more and men may feel the need to curse less. In any case, *fuck* and *screw* were in English before America was discovered—though, beginning in the 1870s and especially since World War II, we have used them much more than the English ever have. Like it or not, when you hear America talking you hear *fuck* and *screw*.

Fundamentalism

Onward Christian soldiers,
Marching as to war,
With the Cross of Jesus
Going on before.
Sabine Baring-Gould
(1834–1924), "Onward,
Christian Soldiers"

Until 1909 most Americans were fundamentalists without knowing it. That year the words *fundamentalist* and *fundamentalism* first appeared, coming from *The Fundamentals*, the title of a very popular (250,000 copies were distributed) 12-pamphlet encyclopedia published by Lymann and Milton Stewart's Los Angeles Bible Institute. Since the 1870s some people had been attacking fundamental beliefs by saying shocking things: that the teachings of Christ and the Bible didn't work in the new industrial society, that Higher Criticism had found inconsistencies in the Bible, that geological fossils were older than Creation as described in the Bible, that Darwin's theory of EVOLUTION made sense, or that Genesis was only meant to be a metaphorical story (this last being the view of the *Modernists*). Thus Bible-reared America needed reassuring that THE KING JAMES BIBLE meant exactly what it said.

Soon the Bible had its vociferous defenders, especially among Methodists and Baptists, and a counterattack was mounted, eventually to be known as *fundamentalism*. The counterattack was based on classical Protestant orthodoxy and literal belief in the Bible, a reiteration of fundamental beliefs that began in the 1870s and that was to be heard for the next 60 years. Revivals, Bible schools, and Bible conferences flourished. People talked about

Chicago's Moody Bible Institute (founded 1889 and whose correspondence school had 10,000 students by 1919) and the Los Angeles Bible Institute (founded 1907). Believers talked about the 1900 Niagara Bible Conference and its famous *five points:* belief in the divine accuracy of the Bible and in the virgin birth, deity, and the second coming of Jesus Christ, and that He died to lift our guilt of sin. Millions heard Dwight Moody and other famous revivalists (see REVIVALS: BILLY SUNDAY AND AIMEE SEMPLE MCPHERSON) or such fundamentalist speakers as William Jennings Bryan, who in the early 1920s lectured coast-to-coast on such topics as "Tampering with the Mainspring" and "They Have Taken Away My Lord" (see THE MONKEY TRIAL).

Such revivalists and speakers were called *Bible pounders* by the 1880s and *Bible thumpers* by the 1920s. And what did the millions hear who listened to their sermons and talks? That the whale actually swallowed Jonah, the Red Sea did part for Moses, that God or the Devil had planted those fossils to tempt men into disbelief, or (during World War I) that Higher Criticism was a German plot. Such fundamentalism seemed to be particularly rampant in the South, and around 1925 H. L. Mencken coined the term *the Bible Belt* to refer to that region.

It Was a Lovely Funeral

is an American expression possible only since the 1860s, when *embalming*, the fancy *casket* for the common man, and the *funeral wreath*, then usually dyed black, all came into vogue. Embalming was popularized by Thomas Holmes, "the father of American embalming," who is reputed to have made a fortune embalming soldiers killed in the Civil War, and it was in 1863 that Nathaniel Hawthorne denounced the new euphemism *casket* as "a vile modern phrase."

The Laurel Hill Cemetery,
Ridge Ave., and Falls of the Schuylkill.

"Laurel Hill" is the oldest suburban Cemetery in the United States, with the exception of Mt. Auburn in Boston. Founded in 1835 by Nathan Dunn, Benjamin W. Richards, John J. Smith, and Frederick Brown, it has long been famous among the places of interest in Philadelphia for the natural beauty of its site and scenery embellished by much skill and labor, the magnificence and variety of its monuments, and the names of the distinguished dead who lie buried within its walls. Occupying one of the most exquisite situations in the neighborhood of Philadelphia, on the high and wooded bank of the Schuylkill adjoining East, and opposite West, Fairmount Park, it is easily reached on foot as well as by steamboat, horse-car and carriage; and, although now far within the limits of the growing city, is peculiarly and perfectly protected from encroachment by its surroundings, having Ridge Avenue on the East, the river on the West, and the Park on the remaining sides.

A large quantity of very desirable ground is to be had at reasonable prices, including some portions but recently prepared for burial purposes, and now (1876) offered for sale for the first time.

TRUSTEES:
LLOYD P. SMITH,   FREDERICK BROWN,
BENJ. W. RICHARDS,   HENRY ARMITT BROWN.

FREDERICK BROWN, *President*, 5th and Chestnut Sts. BENJ. W. RICHARDS, *Treasurer*, 524 Walnut St., Room 4. HENRY ARMITT BROWN, *Secretary*, 204 West Washington Square.

Lots may be Obtained at the Company's Office, 524 Walnut St., Room 4, Phila.

A parklike atmosphere pervades this Philadelphia cemetery, shown in an 1876 advertisement.

Embalming made the undertaker a much more important man than he had been before—until the 1860s he had shared his chores, and fees, with the local carpenter who made the simple pine box, with the livery stable owner who provided the horse-drawn hearse, and with the church sexton who rang the bell and dug the grave. By the 1890s the undertaker was calling himself a *funeral director* or a *mortician*, the latter word being officially adopted by the undertakers' association in 1917. By the 1920s these morticians were referring to the corpse as *the loved one* (Evelyn Waugh's satirical novel *The Loved One* appeared in 1947) who would be *interred* instead of buried, after a *service* instead of a funeral, in a *memorial park* instead of a graveyard. The term *memorial park* was popularized by Forest Lawn Memorial Park in Southern California, which was begun in 1917.

One's death is assumedly made easier on one's survivors by

insurance (1649, the British prefer the word *assurance*), obtained by a *policy* (1740) sold by an *insurance company* (1784) to the *policyholder* (1851) by an *insurance agent* (1869) or *insurance man* (1871). These terms all originally applied both to property and to life insurance, with the specialized terms *life insurance* appearing in America in 1841, *life insurance company* in 1847, and *life insurance policy* in 1861. Early life insurance was mainly to pay for one's funeral. However, from the 1840s on, many immigrants and others provided for this by joining a *burial society*, which often had the added advantage of serving as a fraternal organization while one was still alive. Such precautions were to keep one from being buried in a *potter's field*, a burial ground for the nameless or penniless. *Potter's field* is mentioned in Matthew 27:7 as a burial place for foreigners; however the popularity of

"The Mystery of Life," a statuary group in Forest Lawn Memorial Park, Glendale, California. One and a half million tourists visit this cemetery every year, perhaps to contemplate the mysterious ways of death.

the term in America may be due to New York City's *potter's field*, where colonial potters' built their worksheds and ovens. This field, the site of the present City Hall Park, had by 1755 also become known as the "Old Negroe's Burying-ground," then during the Revolutionary War served as a British cemetery for colonial prisoners—and ever since, New York City has had a "potter's field."

But fancy words and precautions for death are a far cry from the plain-spoken attitude of early Americans, who had no fancy caskets, funeral wreaths, or hearses—the Puritans even had no graveside religious *service*, since they scorned the Anglican Book of Common Prayer. Thus, we also have such down-to-earth terms as *kick the bucket*, to die, since 1785; *stiff*, a corpse, since 1850; and *cash/pass in one's hand/chips/checks* since 1855. *Pushing up daisies* seems to be a World War I expression, first recorded in 1918.

The Gay 90s

is a term that became popular in the not-so-gay Depression years of the 1930s, when people looked back with nostalgia to their parents' lives or their own youth of the 1890s. Since then the Gay 90s has been considered the period when *the Elegant 80s* relaxed and everyone enjoyed friendly, informal manners and fashions. In the 1890s, *gay* not only meant happy and carefree but informal, and *to get gay* with someone meant to take liberties, to be a little too brash even as Victorianism receded.

There actually was a lot of gaiety in the 90s. Our image of Gibson girls and young men wearing *flannel trousers*, *bow ties* and *straw skimmers*, humming "A Bicycle Built for Two" (1892), "The Sidewalks of New York" (1894), or Henry Sayer's minstrel show song "Ta-ra-ra-boom-de-ay" is not all wrong. People were talking about the new rages of *lawn tennis* and *roller skating*, of seeing their first automobiles and telephones, and of such innovations as *basketball*, Edison's *kinetoscopic peep show*, and the *zipper*. Chewing gum, big circuses, and houses decorated with *gingerbread* were popular. Topics of conversation included the shameless *Police Gazette*, the marvelous Chicago World's Columbian Exposition (1893), the beautiful music of John Philip Sousa's band, and the Olympic games in Athens, where the U.S. proudly won 9 of 12 track and field events (1893). Intellectuals talked about the brand new University of Chicago, John Dewey's new educational theories, and the building of Carnegie Hall in New York City. Farmers talked about the new

John Philip Sousa, 1896. Sousa was known as "the March King." He formed his own band in 1892 and in the early 1900s toured Europe and the world. But he is remembered chiefly for his lively marches, such as Semper Fidelis *(1888),* Washington Post March *(1889), and* The Stars and Stripes Forever *(1897), which won him national renown during the Gay 90s.*

Sears Roebuck mail-order business (1895), made possible by the new *Rural Free Delivery* (1892), while their young sons still wore overalls and caps to school and went barefoot on warm days.

Emily Dickinson and Edwin Arlington Robinson were leading poets, novelist William Dean Howells and psychologist-philosopher William James were writing, and 23-year-old Stephen Crane received international acclaim with his novel *The Red Badge of Courage* (1895). However, most people quoted the ex-baseball player turned evangelist, Billy Sunday, and Edwin Markham's poem "The Man with the Hoe" (which swept the country via newspapers in 1895). They read and talked about popular romances such as Sir Anthony Hope Hawkin's *Prisoner of Zenda* (1894) and Henryk Sienkiewicz's *Quo Vadis* (1896), Charles Sheldon's inspirational *In His Steps* (1896), and Edward Westcott's homey *David Harum*

An evening aboard at the "turn of the century."

(1898)—or the first American printings of *Black Beauty* and *The Adventures of Sherlock Holmes.*

People were also talking about the Sherman Antitrust Law, the new Populist Party, how Democrat Grover Cleveland beat Republican Harrison in 1892 and how Republican McKinley beat Democrat William Jennings Bryan in 1896. During the decade Idaho, Wyoming, and Utah were welcomed as new states, and people also talked about the annexation of Hawaii and of the Yukon gold rush (1896). They cursed Spain when the battleship *Maine* was blown up in Havana Harbor in 1898 and cheered the news of Admiral Dewey and of Teddy Roosevelt and his Rough Riders during the Spanish-American War that followed. Then they debated the responsibility of acquiring control of Puerto Rico and the Philippines.

There was bad news and local violence to talk about too. Sitting Bull was killed and the Dalton Gang was wiped out in Coffeyville, Kansas (1892). There were bloody strikes at the Carnegie Steel Company in Homestead, Pennsylvania (1893), in the Pennsylvania coal mines, in western silver mines, by New York City garment workers, and by the Pullman Palace Company workers, which caused a sympathy strike by Eugene Debs' American Railroad Union. People argued over the Sherman Silver Purchase Act (1890) and William Jennings Bryan's "Cross of Gold" speech. When U.S. gold reserves fell below the $100 million level there was the disastrous Panic of 1893 that lasted until 1897, seeing 600 banks and over 1500 major businesses fail, a third of the nation's railroads go bankrupt, and widespread unemployment, which led to Coxey's Army marching on Washington. In 1894 the country had its first federal deficit since the Civil War, causing our first graduated income tax (soon invalidated by the Supreme Court). At the same time millionaires wolfed down oysters at oyster bars, built mansions in Newport, and gave highly publicized parties that cost a quarter of a million dollars at the Waldorf.

Yet, despite this usual mix of good and bad and rich and poor, the 90s probably were happy, carefree times for most Americans. A great many people did relax and enjoy themselves, there were exciting and pleasant things to do and, mainly, many people seemed to *think* they were happy—something later, more sophisticated Americans have found it increasingly hard to do.

The Germans

Since English is a Germanic language it has always been full of "German" words and word elements (more precisely, English and German both belong to the same West-Germanic subfamily of the Indo-European family of languages and thus have much in common). In addition modern German has directly influenced American English through: (1) the immigration of the Pennsylvania Dutch; (2) the much larger immigration

of other Germans during much of our history; (3) World War I; and (4) World War II. German words introduced by the PENNSYL-VANIA DUTCH and during WORLD WAR I and WORLD WAR II are taken up under those entries. Here, I want to emphasize the major German influence on American English that came from the main-stream German immigration.

A small trickle of Germans arrived in America after 1640, became a small flow around 1820, increased again around 1845 when the Potato Blight struck Germany almost as hard as it did Ireland, and became a flood after the German Revolution of 1848. The earlier German immigrants were considered boorish because they drank beer on Sunday (as did later German immigrants) and didn't have the fine manners English colonists and their descendants as-cribed to themselves. However, the Germans who came to America between the German Revolution of 1848 and our own Civil War were an exceptional class of immigrants, often called the *48ers*. They were not the usual impoverished, uneducated newcomers but were middle-class city dewllers. They often arrived at our Gulf Coast ports because the ships that had delivered Southern cotton to Europe offered cheap passage back to the cotton ports: from the Gulf they came up the Mississippi and Ohio to the Mid-west, settling in such cities as St. Louis, Cincinnati, Milwaukee, and Minneapolis. By 1860 the U.S. had 28 daily German news-papers in 15 cities.

These Germans were clean, sober, literate, and law-abiding, what Americans came to call *good Germans*. Their love of educa-tion, music, gymnastics, swimming, beer, and good, solid German food influenced America and our language greatly. After the Civil War the German immigrants were again mostly poor working-class families, and New York was the main port of entry. In all, just under 7 million German immigrants have come to the U.S. since 1776. Here is a sampling of their influence on our language:

Ach (to) Louie! a catch phrase of the 1880s.

and how! (probably based on German *und wie*), 1928.

bake oven (German *Backofen*, though perhaps from Dutch *bakoven*), 1787.

bub (German *Bube*, boy, may have entered English through the Pennsylvania Dutch), 1839; *bubby*, 1841.

bummer (German *Bummler*, loafer from *bummeln*, to waste time, loaf), 1855, in the Civil War it meant a foraging soldier; *bumming*, carousing, 1857; *to bum*, to loaf, 1836, to wander, beg, 1857; *bum around*, 1863; a *bum*, 1855, a drunken loafer, 1862 as a vagabond, tramp; *on the bum*, on a spree, 1868, not in working order, 1896; *to bum a ride*, originally on a freight train, as a hobo, 1896; *a bum steer*, a false report, 1903; *to get/give the bum's rush*, throw out, eject, as from a saloon, 1922; *a bum rap*, a false charge, 1927; *beach bum*, *ski bum*, early 1960s.

check (restaurant tab, German *Zeiche*, bill for drinks), 1868. Our other meanings of *check*, as a bank check, a tally, etc., come via the English *cheque*.

coat hook (German *Kanthaken*), 1848.

concert master (German *Konzertmeister*), 1889. The British still say "concert leader."

cookbook (German *Kochbuch*), 1809. The British say *cookery book*, but we seem to have gotten our term from the German rather than from shortening the British form.

cylinder (a plug hat, German *Zylinder*, slang for plug hat), 1860s.

dachshund (German for "badger dog," because of its badgerlike shape), 19th century. The word entered British and American English simultaneously.

delicatessen (German *Delicatesse*, delicacies to eat), as preserved and cooked meats, pickles, salads, etc., 1893; as the store that sells such foods, 1903. *Delicatessen shop*, *delicatessen store*, 1890s, which Russian Jews, especially in New York City, and others who dislike things German have called *appetizing stores* since the 1890s.

dumb, meaning stupid (Old English *dumb* meant mute and, at one time, stupid, but the meaning "stupid" had dropped out and was reintroduced in America via the German *dumm*, stupid, or the Dutch *dum*), 1823; *dummy*, stupid person, 1823; *dummkopf* (German *Dummkopf* or Dutch *domkop*, "dumb head"), 1809; *dumbhead*, 1887; *dumbbell*, 1914; *dumb Dora*, 1914; *dumb Isaac*, 1916; *dumb bunny*, 1922; *dumb cluck*, 1931.

ecology, entered American English in the 19th century directly from German *Ökologie* (from Greek *oikos*, home, habitat).

frankfurter, 1890s; *wiener*, 1904 (see HOT DOGS for more information).

fresh (impertinent, German *frech*), 1848.

gabfest, 1897; *talkfest*, 1910; *slugfest*, 1916. These *-fest* words and such later forms as *funfest*, *beerfest*, etc., use the German suffix *-fest*, festival, to mean bout or session. Its evolution and use seem to be due to the American *Turners* (see below), who had an annual *Turner feast* beginning in 1856, called a *Turnerfeste* by 1871 and *Turnerfest* by 1892.

German-American, 1824.

German corn, rye, 1741.

German cotillion, an involved and very popular round dance, 1839, also called *a German; German club*, a round-dancing club, 1884.

German Jew, 1865.

German Lutheran, 1790.

German measles, mid 19th century, because there were epidemics of the disease in Germany then (and German immigrants sometimes brought the disease and epidemics to America). Its more technical name is *rubella* and it is also called *three-day measles*.

gesundheit (German *zur gesundheit*, "to your health"), to your health, God bless you, said to a person who has just sneezed.

hamburger, as ground beef, 1903; as a sandwich, 1912 (see HAMBURGERS).

hold on! (wait, stop, German *halt am*), 1835.

hoodlum (German Bavarian dialect *Hodalum*, rowdy) 1871; *hood*, 1930.

katzenjammer, 1846 (see DRUNK).

kerlush, splash, 1848; *kerswop*, 1859; *kerflop*, 1880; *kerblam*, 1884; *kerplunk, kerthump*, 1888; *kerbang*, 1909. These *ker-*words, which represent the sound of splashing, a blow, a fall, etc., are probably based on the German prefix *ge-*.

kindergarten (German for "children's garden"), 1862.

klutz (German *Klotz*, block, block of wood, figuratively a clod), a clumsy person, bungler, clod.

lager, 1840s; *bock beer*, 1856; *beer cellar*, 1732; *beergarden*, 1870; *German Garden*, 1872; *beer hall*, 1882 (for more information and related German borrowings, such as *shenkbeer*, *stein* and *seidel*; see BEER, BEERGARDENS, AND SALOONS).

Liederkranz, considered by some as an improvement on Belgian limburger, is an American cheese first made by Emil Frey in Monroe, New York in 1892, and is now a trade name owned by Borden's. Frey named it after the German-American singing societies, or men's choral groups, called *liederkranz* (first American use 1858, literally "garland of songs" in German), which not only sang but gathered to drink beer and munch rye bread and cheese.

liverwurst (German *Leberwurst*, liver sausage), 1869. The best German leberwurst came from Braunschweig and was called "Braunschweiger leberwurst";

Katzenjammer Kids, or "The Katzies," Hans and Fritz, famous cartoon characters created by Rudolph Dirks in 1897. The strip uses much Anglo-German pidgin. Katzenjammer, "hangover" in German (see DRUNK), literally means the wailing of cats; Hans and Fritz are always getting into trouble and being thrashed, with much wailing and tears.

in 1930 Swift and Company began calling its liverwurst *braunschweiger.*

loafer (German *Landläufer*, vagabond), 1830; *to loaf, loafing,* 1835. Some linguists believe this comes from the English dialect word *louper*, vagabond, or the Dutch *loof*, tired, weary, but the early U.S. spelling of the word as "laufe" points to its German origin.

nix (German *nichts*, nothing), 1815; *nixie*, a letter addressed to a nonexistent post office or to a town with no postal service (post office use) 1880s; *nixie, nixy, no!*, 1887; *nix cum arous* (German *nichts kommt heraus*), nothing comes of it, 1884; *nix on that*, nothing doing, enough of that, 1902.

ouch! (German *autsch!*), 1837.

phooey, phooie (German and Yiddish *pfui*), 1929.

pinochle (Swiss German *binokel*), 1864.

pretzel, 1824 (see BEER, BEERGARDENS, AND SALOONS for more information).

pumpernickel, 1839. This was originally a Westphalian sourdough rye bread associated with rural people; in German the word also means a lout, peasant (but it may come from German *Pumpen*, fart + *Nickel*, Devil, because it is hard to digest).

rathskeller (German *rat*, council, town hall + *keller*, cellar, town-hall cellar, often a beerhall or restaurant in Germany). The word wasn't common in America until the late 1890s, but the first such American basement restaurant was Fred Hollander's *Rathskeller*, opened in New York City in 1863.

rifle (German *riffel*, groove), 1772, first made by German gunsmiths in Pennsylvania.

sauerkraut (German "sour cabbage"), 1776, also then spelled *sourcrout*. The word had come

to England in 1617, but seems to have been reintroduced directly by German immigrants into American English, since it is not found in the writings of English colonists.

schnapps (German *Schnaps*, mouthful, dram, from *schnapper*, to snap, nip) used in England since the 19th century to mean gin and in America to mean brandy, especially a dram of brandy or other liquor drunk in one or two swallows as a toast or before a meal.

schneider (German *Schneider*, tailor) to prevent an opponent from making a score or scoring a point, especially to win a game of gin rummy before one's opponent has scored a point.

scram! (German *schrammen*, though some linguists think it may be short for *scramble*), 1920; Pig Latin *amscray*, scram, 1934. *Scram!* was very popular in the 1930s, replacing the 1906 term *beat it!*.

shoe is from Old English *scōh*, but in America *shoe* was reinforced by the German *Schuh*. This German use is why we often say *shoe* when the English would say *boot*.

shyster (probably from German *Scheisse*, shit), 1846.

slim, meaning bad, small, as in "slim chance," (German *schlimm*, bad), 1825.

smearcase (German *Schmierkase*, smear cheese), 1829.

so long (perhaps from German *so lange*, but see GOODBY, SO LONG, SEE YOU LATER), late 1850s.

spiel (German *spielen*, to play a musical instrument), to play a musical instrument, 1880s; to talk persuasively, 1894 (see BALLYHOO, PITCH, SPIEL, AND FLACK).

standpoint (point of view, German *Standpunkt*), 1870s.

Turners, Cincinnati, about 1900.

the Turners, 1850, were societies of German-American men who practiced *turnvein*, strenuous gymnastic exercises, originated by Friedrich Ludwig Jahn, "the Father of Gymnastics," in Berlin in 1811 to inspire patriotism in Prussian youth and a spirit of resistance to Napoleonic domination. The first *Turner Halls* were built in the U.S. in Cincinnati and New York City in 1850 and American Turners became a gymnastic, social, and beer-drinking society, and helped influence schools to build gyms and give physical education courses. Some Turner groups were more ominous, practicing military drills and marching.

wanderlust (German "travel lust"), 1850s.

wisenheimer, know-it-all, smart alec, 1920s. This is an American pseudo-German coinage; based on no German word but on *wise*, it's supposed to sound like a German word but isn't.

yesman (probably a translation of the German *Jaherr*, yes man), 1924.

zwieback (German for "twice baked"), 1894.

American English has scores of other German borrowings, many of them only partially naturalized, so that we still associate them with Germans or things German, as *gemütlich*, *hausfrau* (housewife), *knackwurst* (literally "sausage that cracks open when eaten") *noodle* (German *Nudel*), *prosit/prost* (via German from the Latin "may it benefit"), *sauerbraten* ("sour roast," marinated roast), *vienerschnitzel* ("Vienna cutlet"), etc. Many Yiddish words and words associated with German Jews also have a German basis, as *bagel*, *lox*, *gefilte fish*, and *kibitz* (see THE JEWS). And many American intonations, as well as our love of compounding words and word elements into even longer words, are also due to the German influence.

Our concept of the genial, beer-drinking German changed before and during World War I, giving us many derogatory names for Germans. This was due to the Kaiser's bad public relations before the war; to the German invasion of Belgium with accompanying stories of the burning of villages and universities, looting, rape, and murder; and to the sinking of the *Lusitania*, with many Americans aboard (see WORLD WAR I). But much of the anti-German feeling began because, two weeks after America entered the war, President Wilson created the *Committee on Public Information* (widely known as the *CPI*). Headed by a former muckraking newspaper editor and writer of religious and patriotic books, George Creed, the CPI rallied reporters and ministers to the Allied cause, magnified the "depravity" of the Germans, and fanned anti-German feelings. This wave of anti-German hysteria during World War I decreased the use of German terms and of the word *German* itself, creating new terms that now seem childish or humorous. Thus *sauerkraut* became *liberty cabbage*, *German measles* became *liberty measles*, *frankfurters* were increasingly called *hot dogs*, *German shepherds* became *Alsatians*, and many streets with German names were renamed *Liberty Street* or after American heroes, etc. Many Americans of German descent also now Americanized their names, with *Knoebel* becoming *Noble*, *Shoen* becoming *Shane*, and *Stein* becoming *Stone* (in England the *Battenberg* family changed its name to *Mountbatten*, the German *berg* translates to "mountain," and King George V changed his family name from *Wetlin* to *Windsor*, by royal proclamation in 1917). Such name changing was by no means universal, however, and we Americans conveniently forgot that our heroes Captain Eddie Rickenbacker and General John J. Pershing were of German descent. World War I also saw the wide use of derogatory names for Germans, a few new, most from earlier times:

Prussian, 17th century, originally just a word for a German, then increasingly for a militaristic or overbearing German (after the state in northern Germany).

Dutch (German *Deutsch*, German), 1742; *Dutchman*, 1841. A neighborhood German was often called *the Dutchman* and many German bartenders and saloonkeepers were called *the Dutchman* after the 1840s; *Dutchie*, 1880. *Dutch* was also a nickname for some men of German extraction, as the 1870s cattle and horse thief *Dutch Henry* and the 1920s Chicago gangster *Dutch Schultz*. It has often been used in a nonderogatory way.

Hessian, originally a German solider (from Hesse) sold into service to England. These *Hessians* became unwilling soldiers in the New World and in the Revolutionary War, during which many of them deserted (including one named Kuster, whose great grandson became Major General George Custer). *Hessian* thus came to mean a person of low character, and during the Civil War the South sometimes referred to Northern soldiers as *Hessians*. By 1877 the word meant a hireling or a mercenary politician.

sauerkraut, 1819, first common when General Joseph Heister ran for governor of Pennsylvania and was called "Old Sauerkraut," 1869. The shorter *kraut* had a little World War I use, but didn't become common until the mid 1920s, then had fairly wide use in World War II, which also saw the word *krauthead*.

cabbagehead, 1854, to mean a German; it had meant a stupid person since the 1660s.

Junker has been in the English language since the 16th century but became popular as meaning an arrogant, militaristic German during the mid 19th century. It originally meant a young German nobleman (from German *jung*, young + *herr*, man, literally "young master").

sausage, any German, 1880s.

Heinie, Heiney, a German soldier, 1890 (German *Heine*, a diminutive of Heinrich).

Hun, a German soldier, 1908 (from the barbarous 4th and 5th century invaders of Europe, as led by Attila).

the Boche, 1914. We got this word from the French, in which it is short for *alboche*, from *al*(lemand) + (ca)*boche*, literally "German blockhead," German thickskull, German cabbagehead.

jerry, a German soldier, 1914. We borrowed this word from English troops (*jerry* was English slang for chamber pot, the British calling German soldiers *jerry* because their helmets resembled chamber pots).

(right) Charles Proteus Steinmetz (1865–1923), electrical engineer and inventor; (from top to bottom) Jacob Henry Schiff (1847–1920), banker and philanthropist (right); Eric Von Stroheim (1885–1957), actor and cinema director; Marlene Dietrich (1904–), cinema actress and singer.

The Germans in America have also given us many place names, including various towns called *Berlin* and *Germanna*, German neighborhoods called *Germantown* and *Yorkville*, and:

Bismarck, North Dakota. Originally named Edwinton, it was renamed for the German Chancellor Otto Furst von Bismarck in 1873, in gratitude to German bondholders who helped finance the railroad reaching to this state capital.

Frankfurt, Indiana, 1830. The grandfather of the town's founder had come from Frankfurt, Germany. Incidentally, the capital of Kentucky, *Frankfort*, is not named after Frankfurt, Germany, but was originally *Frank's Ford*, named by settlers after a man named Frank who had been killed at the ford by Indians.

Frederick, Texas, 1846, named by German settlers for Frederick the Great.

the German Coast, a section along the Mississippi River about 30 miles above New Orleans, settled by Germans in 1723, now St. Charles and St. John parishes.

German Flats, a region in Herkimer County, New York, near Utica, settled by German Protestants from the Palatinate in 1723; they were the remnants of 3,000 Germans brought to America by the English Board of Trade in 1710 to make tar, pitch, etc., for the English naval stores industry.

Germantown, Pennsylvania, was settled by Germans (Pennsylvania Dutch), in 1683.

Germantown, Texas, was renamed *Schroeder* during World War I to show the citizens' dislike of Germans and to honor a local soldier killed in France (the Texans must have known that Schroeder was of German descent, but they were objective enough to recognize him as a loyal American patriot).

Hamburg, New York, 1808.

Mount Richthofen, Colorado, named around 1870 for Baron Ferdinand von Richthofen, German geographer and geologist who had worked in California.

New Bern, North Carolina, founded by Germans and German-speaking Swiss.

170

And, of course, the Germans have given us many family names, ranging from such famous ones as Altgelt, Astor, Chrysler, Eisenhower, Frick, Fritsche, Heinz, Rockefeller, Roebling, Schnabel, Singer, Steinmetz, Steinway, Studebaker, Westinghouse, Weyerhauser, and Zenger to such frequently heard names as Albrecht, Albert, Black, Block, Bowman, Gluck, Kirsch, Pepper (Pfeffer), Schroeder, Schultz, and hundreds of others.

Goddamn, Darn, and Oh Perdition!

A wonderful bird is the pelican,
His bill will hold more than his belican.
He can take in his beak
Food enough for a week,
But I'm damned if I see how the helican.
Dixon Lanier Merrith, "The Pelican," 1910. By this time *damned* and *hell* were not always taken too seriously.

Goddamn and *damn* have been used as swearwords in English since the 15th and 16th centuries respectively. Since only a small minority of the early American colonists were clean-spoken Puritans and Quakers, the majority brought *Goddamn* and *damn* to America with them, along with such other strong Elizabethan oaths as *God's Blood!*, *God's bodken!*, and *God's death!*, referring to Christ's crucifixion. Thus blasphemy has been part of the American language from its beginning. However, the majority of respectable, religious American businessmen, parents, and old maids of the past have, at least in public, preferred milder euphemisms like *darn!* and *cripes!* or even more delicate mincing terms like *Oh perdition!* and *Shucks!* Such milder terms were popular because they were acceptable to both God and man while still expressing the feelings and being naughty enough to give the speaker status as a red-blooded, down-to-earth American.

Many of the milder oaths listed below follow the old Hebraic and Middle English tradition of avoiding the use of sacred words, such as *God*, by substituting words with the same initial letter. Thus for *God* the oaths substitute *George*, *ginger*, *Godfrey*, *golly*, *gosh*, *gracious*, *gravy*, *grief*, etc. (*By God!* becomes *By George!*, *Good God!* becomes *Good Grief!*, and so on). For *Christ* we have *cracky*, *cricky*, *criminy*, *cripes*; for *Jesus* we have *gee*, *gemini*, *Jeez*, and *jeepers* (though the g of *gee* and *geminie* were originally meant to represent G——, *God*). For *Lord* we have *land* and *law*; for *damn(ed)* we have *dang*, *deuced* (though Deuce was actually a synonym for Devil, as in *What the Deuce!*), *dogged*, and *drat* (as well as *blame*, *blast*, *blowed*, *cursed*, *jiggered*, and *switched*); and for *hell* there is *heck* and *Hail Columbia!* (as well as *blazes*). However for *damnation* we often use a word suggesting it by merely ending in its final *-ation*, as *botheration*, *tarnation*, or *thunderation*; while the two-syllable *goddamn(ed)* is often merely suggested by other two-syllable words, such as *consarn(ed)*, *confound(ed)*, *doggone(d)*, and *dad-burn(ed)* (*dad*- perhaps coming from *Gad* or ——d, earlier euphemisms for *God*).

Many of our basic *curse words* (1872) can be used in three ways, as an expletive (*Darn!*), as a curse (*Darn you!*), and as an intensive or modifier (*too darn hot*). The following list of some of the most common blasphemy, mild curses, and mincing terms heard, or once heard, in America also gives the dates of first recorded use or first widespread popularity:

Zounds!, 16th century in England, from "(by) God's *wounds*," referring to Christ's crucifixion.

By Jove!, 1570 in England.

Egads!, 17th century England, for "By God!, Oh God!"

Gadzooks!, 1650s in England, probably from "God's hooks," referring to the nails in Christ's crucifixion.

Gemini!, 1660 in England, spelled *Jiminy* by the 1830s in America; *Jiminy Crickets*, 1848; *Jiminy Christmas*, 1905.

Criminy!, 1680, England.

My stars!, 1728, England.

Golly!, By golly!, both 1743, England; *goldarn*, 1832.

Gosh!, 1743; *Gosh all hemlock!*, 1865; *gosh darned*, 1884; *gosh-a-mighty*, 1888; *gosh awful, Gosh all fishhooks!*, both 1907.

a *Devil of a* (mess, fight, etc.), 1750s; *How the Devil* ——*?*, 1821; *Who the Devil* ——*?*, 1834; *Go to the Devil!*, 1840s; *What the Devil* ——*?*, 1881; *Where the Devil* ——*?*, 1922.

I swan! (I swear!), 1754.

Gracious!, 1760s; *Gracious me!*, 1831; *My gracious!, Good gracious!, Goodness gracious!, Gracious alive!*, 1840s.

infernal, 1764.

Dear me!, 1770s; *dearie me*, 1780s.

tarnal, ternal (contraction of *eternal*), early 1770s, also used as a euphemism for *damn(ed)*.

darn, mid 1770s. It was not originally a euphemistic pronunciation of *damn* but comes from *tarnal/ternal*, see above.

deuced, 1774 in England; *What the deuce!*, 1834; *take the deuce*, 1848; *The deuce!*, 1856.

hell of a ——, 1776; *hell's fire, hell-fired*, 1830s; *Hell sweat!*, 1832; *hell-bent*, 1835; *Give him hell*, 1851; *hell-to-spit*, 1871;

Hell's bells!, 1920.

tarnation (*tarn*al + *damn*ation), 1784.

Dang!, 1790; *danged*, 1875.

Botheration!, 1801.

My eyes!, 1819.

Thunderation!, 1820s; *Thunder!*, 1834; *By thunder!*, 1836; *Go to thunder*, 1855.

Ye Gods!, Ye Gods and little fishes!, both 1820s.

blame, 1829; *blamed*, 1833; *Blame my buttons!*, 1835; *Blame my cats!*, 1865.

blazes, 1830; *Where in blazes* ——*?*, 1836; *What the blazes* ——*?*, 1856; *How in blazes* ——*?*, 1883; *blue blazes*, 1885.

Cracky!, 1830; *by cracky*, 1888.

I'll be jiggered!, 1830s.

by gravy, 1831; *Good gravy!*, 1856.

all-fired, 1833.

hang, 1834; *Hang it!*, 1875.

consarn, 1834.

Land('s) sake!, 1834; *Land('s) sake('s) alive!, Sakes alive!, Good land(s)!*, all 1840s; *Land!*, 1850; *Land o' goshen!*, 1855; *Land alive!*, 1865; *Landy!*, 1877; *Good land a mercy!*, 1886; *My lands!*, 1927.

Blast!, 1835; *blasted*, 1840.

by gum, 1837; *by gummy*, 1848.

switched, 1838.

cussed, 1838.

Cricky!, 1839; *by cricky*, 1906.

Lordy!, 1839; *Good Lord!*, 1906.

What the Sam Hill?, 1839.

I'll be dogged!, Dog my cats!, both 1839.

dad-burned, 1830s; *dad-blasted, dad-blamed, dad-rat*, 1840s; *dad-gum*, 1887.

By Jupiter!, 1841.

By Judas!, 1842.

Cripes!, by Cripes, 1840s.

by George, 1842.

by the great horn spoon, 1842; *by the great horned spoon*, 1848.

blowed, 1843; *I'll be blowed*, 1878. *Drat!*, 1844.

Law Sakes!, 1844; *Law!*, 1861; *Lawsy!*, *Lawdy!*, 1870s. Although *law* may have become a way to avoid writing *Lord* in vain, in speech it was usually just a pronunciation of *Lord*.

Shucks!, 1847.

confounded, 1849; *Confound it!*, 1850s.

doggone (perhaps from Scotch *dagone*, "gone to the dogs," or maybe an alteration of *God-damn*), 1851; *doggoned*, 1857.

Jewhilliken!, 1851; *Gee whillikens!*, 1857; *Gee wiz!*, 1895, which soon became *Gee whiz(z)!*; *Gee whit(t)aker!*, 1895; *Holy gee!*, 1895; *Jeez!*, *Jees!*, 1900; *Gee!*, 1905; *Jee!*, 1909; *Jeepers!*, late 1920s; *Geez!*, 1932; *jeepers creepers*, 1934.

heck, 1850s; *by heck*, 1865; *What the heck ——?*, 1892.

Hail Columbia, 1854.

by ginger, 1856.

Great snakes!, *Great guns!*, both 1875; *Great Scott!*, 1884; *Great Caesar!*, 1888; *Great Caesar's ghost!*, 1903.

blankety, 1880; *blankety blank*, 1887; *blank*, 1888.

Holy smoke!, 1889; *Holy cats!*, *Holy mackerel!*, both 1803; *Holy Moses!*, 1906; *Holy cow!*, 1942.

By heavens!, 1890s; *Heavens!*, *Heavens to Betsy!*, both not recorded until 1914.

I don't give a damn, 1890s; *I don't give a hoot*, 1925.

Oh perdition!, a favorite mincing oath of the Gay 90s.

Good grief!, 1900.

for Pete's sake, 1903; *for the love of Mike*, 1910; *for cat's sake*, 1921; *for crying out loud*, 1924.

by gar, 1905.

Suffering cats!, *Suffering catfish!*, both 1907.

by Godfrey, 1909.

Judas Priest!, 1922.

Jesus H. Christ!, 1924.

The most recent expression on this mild list is the 1942 *Holy cow!* Until the Victorian period blasphemy was the usual break-the-taboo way to shock or express strong feelings and mild forms of blasphemy the way to express somewhat weaker or suppressed feelings. After Victorian morality began to replace God and religion as the basis for the country's moral code, however, awe of God and religion lessened so much that blasphemy and its milder offshoots didn't seem strong enough any more. Therefore after the 1870s blasphemy began to give way to an increasing use of obscenity and scatology, which overtook blasphemy in popularity during World War I and almost completely replaced it during World War II (see FUCK AND SCREW and OH SHIT!).

Thus when we hear America talking today we hear less blasphemy and fewer euphemisms and mincing expressions than we did before the 1940s: when we hear America talking tomorrow we may not hear such mild terms at all. But be it mincing expressions, mild oaths, blasphemy, obscenity, or scatology, when I hear America talking I hear America cursing—thank God! What a docile, unfeeling people we would be if we didn't have strong emotions and beliefs that needed strong words. It's good to live in a country where people give a good Goddamn.

The Gold Rush

Many early American trappers, traders, and frontier farmers looked for *gold dust* (1704) when they had the time. By 1804 a creek in Cabarra County, North Carolina, was called *gold creek*, and by 1821 the region was called *gold country*. Though it wasn't called that at the time, the first gold rush in the U.S. took place at Dahlonega and across northern Georgia in 1828, which gave us such terms as *gold digger* (1830, one who digs for gold; it didn't mean a mercenary woman who preys on men until 1915), *gold region* (1832), and the *gold belt* (1879). Gold was also found or prospected for in Illinois, Missouri, Iowa, around the Great Lakes, and westward all the way to California before the famous gold rush there. Such early finds, or excitement over gold, gave us:

bonanza (a Spanish word, literally meaning "fair weather" and figuratively meaning "prosperity," from Latin *bonus*, good, calm at sea), 1844, meaning both a lucky discovery of gold and any source of sudden wealth.

claim, stake one's claim, claim jumper, all appeared in the mid 1830s, but then referred to any land claim, not just a mining one; by 1846 the terms were almost completely associated with gold seekers. Since the earliest colonial days, land had been claimed by marking it off with *claim posts* or stakes, hence to *stake a claim* literally meant just that and as early as 1640 *to pull up stakes* or *pluck up stakes* meant to give up one's land and move on.

El Dorado (Spanish for "the gilded [land]" from Latin *dēaurāre, de-*, thoroughly + *aurum*, gold) was originally the name of the legendary Indian city or kingdom of gold sought by 16th century Spanish explorers in America. By 1827 it was used to mean a site where gold was located; it was first recorded with the one-word spelling *eldorado* in California in 1846.

lousy miner, 1830s. Since obtaining clean clothes and bedding, baths, and shaves were considered too time-consuming by many miners, they often ignored such niceties. Thus they were tormented by lice and *lousy miner* became a common expression. This helped give us such terms as: *lousy,* contemptible, 1839; *lousy with,* well supplied with, having an abundance of, 1843; *louse,* a contemptible person, 1915; and *to louse up,* to ruin or spoil something, 1938.

to pan for gold, 1833; *to pan out,* to pan gold in a river or stream, 1839, which by 1873 gave us the general term *to pan out,* meaning to produce, result, succeed. (See also *to wash,* below.)

placer (a Spanish word from *plaza,* place) 1842, as an alluvial or glacial deposit of sand or gravel containing gold or other minerals, hence a place where such deposits were washed to obtain the minerals; *placer mine, placer gold,* 1848 California use.

a prospect, a location which seems a promising place to search for gold, first used in Illinois and Missouri, 1832; *to prospect,* 1841, first recorded in Iowa; *prospector,* 1846, first recorded around Lake Superior; *prospecting,* 1848, first recorded during the California gold rush.

to wash, 1825. This means the same as *to pan* for gold (see above) but is an earlier term, because in the early days Indian baskets

Sutter's Mill, before the big *strike.*

and wooden bowls were often used instead of pans. The two words together gave us *wash pan*, a California term of the 1850s: it was a horseshoe-shaped pan with high sides, the side of the narrow end having ridges to trap the gold particles. Another way of *washing* a large quantity of sand, gravel, and gold was to run the water mixture down a *sluice* (see below).

In 1848 the pioneer Swiss trader John Sutter was living in baronial splendor on his large land grant in the Sacramento Valley, running his *Nueva Helvetia* settlement (*Helvetia* is the Latin name for Switzerland) and owning over 18,000 sheep, oxen, horses, and cows. Then on January 24th, James Marshall, a carpenter Sutter had hired to help build a sawmill, *Sutter's Mill*, on the American River, discovered grains of gold. Soon Sutter's workers quit to look for gold and other local gold seekers squatted on his land—within a few years Sutter was ruined and California was made. In July territorial governor R. B. Mason reported there was enough gold in the country drained by the Sacramento and San Joaquin Rivers to pay for the Mexican War a hundred times over and that up to $50,000 in gold was being taken every day: President Polk included this report in his message to Congress on December 5, 1848, insuring that it got wide publicity. Soon everyone had *gold fever* (1847) and the *gold rush* (1876) was on. The first *forty niners* (an 1853 term; it wasn't generally written *'49er* until the mid 1860s) reached the small village of San Francisco on the steamer *California* on February 28, 1849—by 1850 San Francisco was a bustling city of 25,000 and California became a state. By 1853 San Francisco had a population of 50,000. Between 1849 and 1853 the California gold rush had created or popularized such terms as:

Then ho, brothers, ho,
To California go;
There's plenty of gold
In the world we're told
On the banks of the Sacramento.
  Jesse Hutchsinson, Jr.,
  "Ho for California," 1848

The miners came in '49,
The whores in '51;
And when they got together
They produced the native son.
  This western song is at least partially true: the miners came in '49, planning to make a quick fortune and return home, but most of them became settlers and permanent citizens of California.

the *Barbary Coast*, 1849, as the San Francisco waterfront area notorious for its brothels, bars, and gambling houses. It was named after the Barbary Coast, the Mediterranean coast of Algeria, Morocco, Tripoli, and Tunisia, where piracy flourished until the French captured Algiers in 1830.

gold diggings, digs. Typical of the vivid, descriptive names the '49ers gave their claims and digs were *Centipede Hollow, Chucklehead Diggings, Coyote Hill, Greenhorn Canyon, Jackass Gulch, Puke Ravine,* and *Rattlesnake Bar.*

Levis and *Palo Alto* (hat) were originally articles of clothing associated with California gold rush miners but later became associated with cowboys (for more about these see Cowboys).

lode, first recorded in the U.S. in 1853, but it is a 1602 British word for a vein of ore (it is Middle English for watercourse, course, way); *mother lode*, 1870s, first used in Colorado and Nevada. The gold that the miners panned or washed along river banks had, of course, been deposited there from a more concentrated source, such as a vein of ore in a mountain; by following the traces upstream the gold seekers hoped to find the lode itself, which could then be mined.

MAKING NOTHING.   MAKING SOMETHING.

Christmas in the gold fields, 1849.

"The Luck of Roaring Camp," Bret Harte's sentimental 1868 short story in which the dying prostitute Cherokee Sal gives birth to a child who is adopted by outwardly rough-and-tough characters of the mining camp, one of the miners later dying while holding the infant in his arms when the camp is destroyed by a flood. Harte had left school for the San Francisco gold rush and later became a journalist there.

miners' law, the unwritten law of the miners concerning rights to claims, how near a man could stake a claim next to another's without a fight, etc. *Miners' meetings, miners' courts*, 1870, in Colorado; since miners were usually far from law and order they often enforced their own vigilante version, often with meetings and mock courts.

nugget, gold nugget (the diminutive of the British dialect word *nug*, block, mass).

pard and *tenderfoot* are two more terms originating in the California gold rush which later became associated with cowboys (see COWBOYS for details). A *tenderfoot* was also called a *rawheel* by the '49ers, not so much because of the walking done as because indoor eastern types weren't used to wearing boots. Elsewhere, outside of California, the early 1850s were also a time of masculine familiarity and other Americans were using the new terms *buddy* and *bud*, probably a shortening for *brother* (the word *pal* dates from 1893, *to pal around* from the 1920s, and *palsy walsy* from the early 1930s, from Romany *phal*, Sanskrit *bhrātar*, brother).

pay dirt, ore containing enough gold to justify mining. *To find pay dirt*, 1873, first recorded in Nevada; *to strike pay dirt*, 1903.

piker, a California gold rush term for a person from Pike County, Missouri, and then for anyone from Missouri, there being a large contingent of settlers from that county in California at the time. These settlers made a poor impression, perhaps because they were sober farmers rather than free-spending prospectors and miners; at any rate the whole country knew that a *piker* meant a poor sport or a cheapskate by 1898 (*cheapskate* itself is an 1896 term, *skate* meaning "chap," from a British dialect word).

sluice, a long trough, flume, or series of riffles through which a mixture of sand, gravel, gold, and water is run to deposit out the heavier gold particles. Those who panned or washed for gold might construct a small sluice, but sluices were usually used with mines, the ore being crushed and then run through.

strike, big strike, lucky strike, all first used during the California gold rush.

tailings, the debris of sand, gravel, crushed ore, etc., that has been dumped out of the end of a sluice.

After the California gold rush, gold and silver began to be discovered in large quantities in Colorado, Nevada, and Montana, then elsewhere in the West, and finally in Alaska. Thus prospectors

176

and miners continued to enliven our history and language with new names and terms, including:

A dejected 59er.

the '59ers (first recorded in 1870). Gold was discovered along Cherry Creek, Colorado, near Pike's Peak in the foothills of the Rockies, in 1858. By the end of 1859, 100,000 '59ers had reached the area either to search for gold or make their living off those who did.

Pike's Peak or Bust was a slogan first seen on the wagons of the '59ers who set out for the Colorado gold region. Unfortunately for most of them, the gold here was hard to get at, requiring rather patient and sophisticated mining. Many returned home or moved on elsewhere with the sign *Busted By Gosh!* on their wagons.

Denver, Colorado grew from a '59ers settlement called *Auraria*, uniting with two similar settlements in 1860 to become *Denver* (from J. W. Denver, governor of the Kansas Territory).

the Comstock Lode, Nevada's gold and silver lode with many bonanzas, was named for a roving, shiftless, Canadian-born prospector, Henry Tompkins Paige "Old Pancake" Comstock (1820–70). It had been discovered by the brothers Ethan and Hosea Grosh, who died before recording it; Comstock filed his claim in 1859, lived on it a while, then sold it for a pittance. Perhaps he was disappointed that the gold was hard to get out—but it turned out to be the richest silver vein the world has ever known.

Virginia City, Nevada, was named after James "Old Virginny" Fennimore, one of the earliest prospectors of the Comstock Lode. "The Comstock" made Virginia City one of the most famous mining boom towns of the West, having three-quarters of Nevada's population in the 1860s and 30,000 people and 100 saloons in the 1870s. Most of its *bonanza barons*, including the Hearst family, took their fortunes to San Francisco, where they built Victorian mansions and established many banks. By the late 1880s the mine was running out and Virginia City became a *ghost town* (an 1875 term, first used to refer to deserted California mining towns).

grubstake, 1863, the supplies and equipment needed by a prospector or the money to buy them, about $150 at this time, about $300 in the 1880s: the pick and shovel, pans, blankets, flour, sugar, coffee, side of bacon and other staples were cheap, it was the horse or mule and the mandatory rifle that were expensive. The term comes from the custom of merchants furnishing such items to prospectors in return for a percentage of any gold they found, the merchants *staking* the prospectors to equipment and *grub*. *Stake* itself meant provisions by 1738, *to stake* meant to provide another with provisions by 1853. *Grub* was first used to mean food in America in 1807, but was a 17th century British slang word for food, from grubs being considered as food for birds. Westerners used *grub wagon* by 1884 (see COWBOYS for *chuck wagon*); circus people spoke about the *grub tent* by 1891; and in the 1880s *grub wages* were just barely enough to live on, about $15 a month.

Custer's Last Stand doesn't seem to have anything to do with gold prospecting—but it does. In 1867 the Sioux had been forced to

Custer's Last Stand.

sign a treaty and accept a reservation in South Dakota. The peace was destroyed by *the Big Horn Expedition* of gold seekers of 1870 and the discovery of gold in the Black Hills in 1874, miners then overrunning the Sioux's new land. The Sioux opposed them and *the Black Hills Indian Wars* began. Lt. Col. George Armstrong Custer was detailed to end the Indian resistance, which is what he was trying to do when he and some 260 cavalrymen were surrounded and wiped out by the Sioux under Crazy Horse and Sitting Bull at the Battle of Little Bighorn, June 25-26, 1876, in what is now southern Montana. Thus gold led to Custer's Last Stand.

Tombstone, Arizona, is where prospector Ed Schieffelin made a major gold discovery in 1877. He called the site *Tombstone* because soldiers scouting the Apache had told him if he went off prospecting alone in this Indian country all he would find would be his own tombstone. By 1881, 7,000 people lived in this boom town of shacks, tents, saloons, and dance halls, including such adventurers as "Doc" Holliday and Johnny Ringo. Feuds were common, the most talked about culminating in "the gunfight at the O.K. Corral" in 1881 between Wyatt Earp's posse and the lawless Clantons. By the late 1880s rising underground water and falling silver prices closed the mines and Tombstone became a ghost town.

Boot Hill is the name given Tombstone, Arizona'a cemetery, because so many died here not in bed but of violence, with their boots on. Dodge City, Kansas, also has a Boot Hill—in fact, since 1903 writers and tour guides have referred to any cemetery associated with a violent frontier town as a *boot hill.*

the Klondike/Yukon/Alaskan gold rush started August 17, 1896, when George Carmack, his Indian wife, and their relatives discovered a large quantity of gold in the gravel of a creek three miles from Dawson; he then named the creek *Bonanza* (it's a tributary of the Klondike and Yukon Rivers in the Yukon territory of Canada). News of the strike reached the outside world in June, 1897, when the steamship *Portland* reached Seattle with a ton of gold from the region. Soon *Klondike* (probably a corrup-

An Alaskan gold prospector. Even today washing for gold attracts the hardy, independent man.

178

tion of an Athopascan word which was the name of the river) and *Yukon* (Athopascan for "big river") were place names known to all. By 1898 *Klondiker* meant both an inhabitant of the Klondike and a gold prospector. Many prospectors died from cold, starvation, and disease on the trip to Dawson, but over 30,000 made it, to pay $1 each for eggs and $10 for a plate of ham and eggs while seeking to make $1,500 a day panning for gold. In 1900 alone, $22 million in gold was taken out.

sourdough, 1902, an Alaskan prospector, from the lump of sour dough carried as a starter to make bread and pancakes (see BREADS— RYE 'N' INJUN', ANADAMA, SOURDOUGH, SLICED WHITE, etc.).

desert rat, 1907, one who has lived in the desert a long time, especially a prospector.

An army—about 100,000 altogether—of Klondikers *toiling the heights of Chilkoot Pass in Alaska, 1898, to reach the Canadian Yukon on the other side. Only about one in three made it to Dawson, the rest dying or turning back.*

Goodby, So Long, See You Later

Good day, *good afternoon*, *good night*, and *farewell* were all Old English terms before the first colonists sailed for America. Around the time the Pilgrims sailed *goodby* was a rather new English word, a contraction of "God be with you" that was still spelled "Godbwye." By the 1640s *bye-bye* seems to have been used in England, was probably known in the colonies by the early 1700s, and definitely became common in the 1840s. *Bye* and *bye now* were first popular after World War I, which was also when matrons began to use the British *toodle-oo*.

So long is probably British usage, meaning "so long as we are parted" (until we meet again), and was used in America by the late 1850s. However, one could make a case that it comes from the German *so lange* (or even the Hebrew *sholom* or the Arabic *salaam*).

I'll be seeing you and *see you later* date from the 1870s, *see you in church* was considered sporty in the 1920s, *see you around* grew popular in the early 1940s, and just *see you* in the late 40s. The cute *abyssinia* ("I'll be seeing you," pronounced like the former name of Ethiopia) saw some jive use in the 1930s as did the rhyming *see you later, alligator.*

Go West, Young Man! Go West!

Horace Greeley (1811–1872) spent his life in the East.

or words very much like them have been ringing in American ears since the Eastern Seaboard was settled. Horace Greeley didn't say these exact words. During the recession of 1837 he wrote in his weekend miscellany *The New Yorker*, "We say, then, Mechanics, artisans, laborers. . . . Fly—scatter throughout the country—go to the Great West—rather than remain here, consuming the pittance which is left of your earnings." In 1851 John Soule wrote in the *Terre Haute Express*, "Go West, young man! Go West!" and after the Civil War, in 1865, Greeley then wrote, "Go West, young man, and grow up with the country," in an editorial in his *New York Tribune*, urging young men to seek their fortunes beyond the Alleghenies.

Incidentally, *go west* was originally an Elizabethan expression meaning to die or disappear into the great unknown, as did the setting sun. In early America it was used to refer to those trappers, traders, and frontiersmen who went west into the wilderness of Pennsylvania, Ohio, Illinois, the Carolinas, etc., never to reappear again—because Indians, rapids, blizzards, rattlesnakes, disease, and broken legs had taken their silent toll. *Gone West* was used by real cowboys to refer to someone who had quit his job or deserted his family or friends, usually heading west to lose himself in new surroundings. World War I soldiers used *gone West* in a similar way, to mean that someone had deserted or gone absent without leave. However, movie cowboys misuse the expression, using it not to mean to desert, as did real cowboys, but to mean "died," harking back to the use of the Elizabethans and early American settlers.

Grizzly Bears, Rattle Snakes, and Bald Eagles

Grizzly Bear.

Foreigners are charmed with the vivid descriptive names we have given our native animals. Yet since primitive times all men have given newly seen species descriptive names, often by combining two old words. The ancient Greeks named one strange animal "river horse" and another "nose-horned," which come out as *hippopotamus* and *rhinoceros* in English. The English themselves have given us such descriptive names as *marsh hen*, *earthworm*, *firefly*, and *dragon fly* (also called a *devil's darning needle* in England and parts of New England). But American settlers did combine descriptive words to give us many vivid names for our mammals, reptiles, fish, birds, and insects—and we've continued to name animals by descriptive combinations ever since. Thus we have the:

Bald Eagle.

John James Audubon (1785–1851) was born in Haiti but lived mostly in Louisiana and Pennsylvania. Finding no publisher for his paintings of birds, Audubon himself published his famous Birds of America between 1826 and 1838. The National Audubon Society was founded and named for him in 1905.

bald eagle, 1688, because its white neck and head make it look bald. This bird was considered our national symbol before its picture was placed on the Great Seal of the United States in 1785; since then it has also been called the *American eagle,* 1798, and the *United States eagle,* 1847.

Baltimore oriole, 1771, originally called the *Baltimore bird,* 1669, because its black and orange colors were those on the coat of arms of Lord Baltimore.

barn swallow, 1790, because it often builds its nests in the eaves of barns.

blue jay, 1709. Colors often appear in our descriptive names: we also have the *bluefish,* 1622; *blue heron,* 1781; and *blue gill,* 1881. *Blue point oysters* get their name because they are found off Blue Point, Great South Bay, Long Island, New York.

bobcat, 1711, because of its stubby or "bobbed" tail (originally this name was given to the bay lynx).

bullfrog, 1698, because it makes a roaring noise like a bull.

canvas back, 1782, from the color of its back.

catbird, 1709, because its call resembles the mewing of a cat. Like many words on this list it was originally spelled with a hyphen, *cat-bird.*

catfish, 1612, the name first recorded by John Smith in Virginia, because of the fish's facial resemblance to a cat, especially its whiskers.

copperhead, 1775, because of its coppery brown color, on which are dark markings.

cottontail, 1869, because the underside of its tail has a white tuft, like a ball of cotton.

fiddler crab, 1843, originally called simply a *fiddler,* 1709, because the straighter, shorter claw resembles a violin bow about to play the longer, curved one.

garter snake, 1769, because of its size and longitudinal stripes, resembling a garter.

grizzly bear, 1791, because some of the animals have a grizzly or gray color; in fact it's sometimes called the *white bear, silver-tipped bear,* etc. Shortened to *grizzly* by the early 1800s.

ground hog, 1656 (see *woodchuck* at THE INDIANS entry). *Ground-hog day,* 1871.

ground squirrel, 1709 (see *gopher* at THE PRAIRIE entry).

hop toad, 1827.

humming bird, 1632.

jackass rabbit, 1847, from its long jackass-like ears. Shortened to *jack rabbit* by 1863. Also euphemistically called *mule rabbit,* 1857.

Kentucky cardinal, 1894, originally local use, because cardinals were so common in Kentucky.

lightning bug, 1778. The English had called this beetle a *glow worm* since the 16th century and a *firefly* since 1658.

mountain lion, 1859, mainly western use for the cougar; easterners had used *mountain cat* since 1709, originally meaning a bobcat and later a cougar. The American cougar has also been simply called *lion* (1613), *panther* (1683), *cougar* (1774, via French and Portuguese from an Amazon Tupi Indian word *suasuarana,* "like a deer" in color), and *puma* (1777, via Spanish from the Inca Quechua *puma,* which may have been a jaguar).

Passenger Pigeon.

muskrat, as *musk cat* in 1607, present form in 1642, because this aquatic rodent has musk glands (but the name may have been influenced by the Algonquian word for it, *musquash*).

passenger pigeon, 1802, earlier called *pigeon of passage* in the 1720s, because it was a migratory bird. This poor bird was so common that the first Virginia settlers simply called it *pigeon* (1612), flocks were so large that their flights darkened the sky, their nesting grounds were said to cover 100,000 acres, and flights of millions were reported. Most of the early accounts tell how easy they were to club or shoot and how good they tasted—the two things that led to their extinction. The last passenger pigeon died in the Cincinnati zoo in 1914.

prairie dog, 1774; *prairie hen*, 1804. See THE PRAIRIE for other animals named for their prairie habitat.

rattlesnake, 1630, shortened to *rattler* by 1827. *Water rattlesnake*, 1736, also called *water moccasin*, 1784, and *cotton mouth* by 1832. *Diamond snake*, 1814, which became *diamond rattlesnake* by 1835, and *diamond back rattlesnake* by 1894. *Sidewinder*, 1885.

robin redbreast, 1689, generally called merely *robin* by the 1700s.

tree frog, 1738.

tree toad, 1778.

turkey buzzard, 1672, because its red neck and head resemble that of a turkey.

We also have other two-word descriptive combinations based on the sounds birds, insects, etc., make, as the *bobwhite* (1837) and *katydid* (1751, originally spelled *Katy Did*).

We have borrowed the names of many of our other animals from the Indians and from the French and Spanish (see THE INDIANS, THE SPANISH, THE FRENCH, THE PRAIRIE, etc.). And we have even named some of our animals by mistake. After all, the settlers, frontiersmen, and farmers who named so many of them were not zoologists—many could barely read and write. Thus despite our *jack rabbit*, there are no true rabbits in the United States, they are all really hares; our *robin* is really a thrush; and our *blackbird* (1602), *hedgehog* (1605), *gar fish* (1624, *gar*, 1765, *alligator gar*, 1832), and *marsh hen* (1709) are not the same creatures as the English blackbird, hedgehog, gar fish, and marsh hen—but the first settlers who saw and named them thought they were.

> *When first my father settled here,*
> *'Twas then the frontier line:*
> *The panther's scream filled night with fear*
> *And bears preyed on the swine.*
> "The Bear Hunt," a poem by the young Abraham Lincoln, who fortunately became a politician rather than a poet

Gumption, Spunk, Grit, Sand, Guts, Balls

spirit, courage, determination, call it what you will, we have used these words admiringly throughout our history. *Gumption*, a Scottish word, was in colonial use by 1719, and later became a regional word for hard cider, the kind that would give any man courage.

Spunk has meant courage since 1753. In early colonial times *spunk* meant tinder and *to spunk up* a fire meant to kindle, stir up, or throw more wood on the fire. From this use *to get one's spunk up* came to mean to become fired with courage or anger, to take courage or get mad, as when in 1885 a cowboy wrote, "I finally spunked up and drawing my pistol proceeded. . . ." Before the Civil War *to spunk up a girl* meant to inflame her sexually, by kissing and petting.

Grit arrived in the early 1800s and was often used in combinations, as *true grit*, *pure grit*, and *clear grit*. A Civil War account of the Fifth New York Cavalry tells how "with trusty carbines and Yankee grit we boys scattered the enemy. . . ." *Sand* came into use in the 1870s, originally as a western word; *guts* appeared in 1890 and *gutsy* not until around 1950; with *backbone* taking on the meaning of gumption in 1905. The most recent word is *balls*, which has meant testicles since the 1880s and manly courage since about 1935.

Hamburgers

have come a long way since the Tartars introduced eating shredded raw meat (we still call it *tartar steak*) into the Russian Baltic provinces. Germans picked up the dish from there and soon Hamburg, Germany became famous for it, sometimes cooking it—and giving it its name. *Hamburg steak*, always cooked and served as a steak, appeared in the U.S. around 1884 and was soon called *hamburger steak*, then *hamburg* by 1903. Dr. J. H. Salisbury, himself a food faddist, helped popularize it and the term *Salisbury steak* at the turn of the century by recommending that it be eaten at least three times a day.

By 1912 enough people were finally putting their hamburger steaks on a bun so that *hamburger* came to mean the sandwich. *Hamburger with the works* (with ketchup, mustard, and a slice of tomato, onion, and pickle) was first heard in the early 1930s, soon after hamburgers began to overtake HOT DOGS as our most popular quick food. The meat shortage of World War II, and American postwar informality and backyard cookouts, increased the sandwich's popularity. The proliferation of names for hamburgers in the 1940s, depending on whim or public relations, was due to the explosion of the number of hamburger stands, advertising *beef-*

A burgerteria (hamburger + cafeteria, an American Spanish word meaning coffee store—see SPANISH*), a self-service, roadside hamburger stand serving America's favorite quick food.*

Wimpie gorging on—yes! hamburgers. Sometimes hamburgers are called wimpeyburgers.

burgers, *wimpeyburgers*, (after the hamburger-loving Wimpie in the *Popeye* comic strip), *steerburgers*, and just plain *burgers* (*cheeseburgers* appeared in the mid 1930s). The term *hamburger stand* itself first became common in 1932, about four years after the *White Castle* hamburger chain got started and some 30 years before most Americans had heard of *McDonald's*, the franchise chain with thousands of outlets and sales of billions of hamburgers, the hamburger mecca of today's children and a name heard over and over by American parents from children who wish to be dined there.

Hello, Howdy, Hi,

or words to that effect, are used by most of us several times a day. *How do you do?* (literally "how is your health?"), *good morning*, *good afternoon*, and *good evening* have been English greetings since the mid 15th century. *Howdy*, a contraction of *how do you do?*, is an Americanism popular since the 1840s. Although we consider "Howdy, stranger" a western greeting, *howdy* was originally very southern and was taken west by Civil War veterans.

Surprisingly enough, *hello* didn't become a truly common greeting until the mid 1860s. It comes from *holla!*, "stop!" (French *ho!* + *là*, there), used to attract attention, hail a coach, ferry, etc. *Hi* is just a variant of *hey!*; it had been used as a shout to attract attention for over 500 years before we began using it as a greeting in the 1880s. *What's up?* dates from the 1880s, too. *What's new?* and *What's with you?* have strong New York backgrounds, perhaps being translations of the German immigrants' *was ist los? What do you know?*, *What do you say?* ("whata-ya know?," "whata-ya say?"), and *How's tricks?* date from the mid 1920s, while *Long time, no see* is from the early 20s. *What's cookin', good lookin'?* and *Hello Joe, whata-ya know?* were jive terms of the late 1930s. The shorter *What's cooking?* dates from the 1940s.

Hicks, Rubes, and Hayseeds

Country bumpkin was an English term of 1782 (from Dutch *boomkin*, little tree, little barrel), *bumpkin* had meant a short, stumpy Dutchman since the 16th century. It joined the earlier English term *clodhopper* (1690). In America we also called a country bumpkin a *Rustic Reuben* around 1800, shortened it to *Reuben* by the 1840s and to *Rube* by the 1880s. A country bumpkin was also called a *country Jake* or simply a *Jake* in the 1850s. *Hick* first came into wide use in the 1840s, coming from Hick, then still a pet name for men named Richard. *Hick town* was a popular term by the 1920s. *Hayseed* was yet another word for a rustic, appearing around 1888.

Hey, Rube! is a shout circus people are supposed to have used around 1890-1930 to summon help in a fight against local rowdies who were about to cause trouble, demand their money back, etc. Unfortunately, most old circus people claim they never heard the term, while others claim the circus was such a wholesome, noble place that fisticuffs were never warranted. It's hard to decide which is more suspect, the term or the disclaimers. However, *Hey, Clem!*, or simply *Clem!* was definitely used as a circus shout to rally for a fight.

Horsecars, Streetcars, Els, and Buses

Horsecars, noted for good service, reached their high point by 1875.

Though some cities had local *stages* (1772) before the Revolutionary War, the first true horse-drawn city buses appeared in the 1820s. They had such names as the *Accommodation*, a 12-passenger, coachlike vehicle; the *Sociable*, so called because it had lengthwise seats with passengers facing each other; and, by the 1830s, the *omnibus* (Latin "for all"), which was often shortened to *bus* by the 1840s.

In 1832 New Yorkers were using a new term, *street railway*, horse-drawn cars on rails sunk so deep into the street that other traffic was endangered. New types of rails, almost flush with the street, were developed in the 1850s and *street railway* and *horse car* (1833) then became common terms until the 1890s. By the late 1860s everyone knew that *horsecars* (now usually one word) were kept in *carbarns*, that *bobtail cars* or *bobtails* were small, one-horse horsecars, and that larger horsecars not only had a driver but also a *conductor* to collect the *car fare* (*conductor* had originally meant the person in charge of a stagecoach's mail in the 1790s, then had been used on railroads since the 1830s). People talked about the smell of horse manure on the streets, the fetid hay on the car floors to soak up rain and mud, and   as users of public transportation still do—about overcrowding, rudeness, poor maintenance, stupid schedules, and graft and corruption giving private companies monopolies of public transportation. Nevertheless, by 1886 over 300 American cities had horsecars. Some people were also calling them *streetcars* (1862).

By the late 1870s people were talking about the new *cable cars* and the equally new *street railway* or *electric streetcar*. San Francisco had started using cable cars on its hilly streets in 1873, and others were soon in use in Chicago, New York, and elsewhere. The electric streetcar had been invented by Stephen Dudley Field and was seen in New York in 1874. By 1887 Richmond, Virginia, was boasting the nation's first complete "electric railway service" and by 1890 horsecars all across the nation were being replaced by the *electric trolley cars*, *trolley cars*, *electric cars*, or simply *electrics* or *trolleys* (Old French *troller*, to search, wander; actually the *trolley* was the grooved wheel in contact with the overhead, current-carrying wire). Thus *trolley* was the big 1890s word, though eventually that old name for a horsecar, *streetcar*, replaced it and stayed in wide use through the 1930s.

Sometimes now it was hard to hear America talking above the grinding clash of steel wheels over steel streetcar tracks, the pop-pop noise of the circuit breaker when a motorman accelerated too fast, and the electric clang-clang that had replaced the horse-car's gong. In the 1890s the *motorman* was also called a *motoreer* (*motor* + engin*eer*) and the sight of him getting out of the streetcar to reposition the trolley wheel back on the overhead wire was so common that by 1896 *to be off one's trolley*, to be crazy, was a popular expression.

There were soon open-sided *summer cars* to take people to outlying picnic grounds and amusement parks (often owned by the streetcar companies). *Interurban* (the word in use since 1883) was an exciting word in the 1890s. It was a heavy, self-propelled street-car, complete with cowcatcher and freight compartment, speeding fresh milk and farm produce to the city and city newspapers to the country, carrying businessmen and families between cities and from city to town, creating many Gay 90s resorts and suburbs. There were fast ones such as the much admired Indianapolis *Muncie Meteor* and *Marion Flyer*, and small, slow ones. In the 1920s a small, slow one was apt to be called a *Toonerville Trolley*, after Fontaine Fox's cartoon trolley which met all the trains.

Meanwhile people had been discussing the *elevated railway* since New York City built its first one in 1867, but it wasn't until the early 1880s that it was called *the elevated*, not until the late 80s that

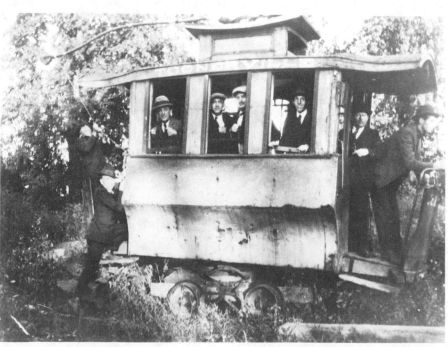

A "Toonerville Trolley," 1923, Williams Corner, Pennsylvania, photographed by a group of high-spirited mineralogists on a field trip from Philadelphia. In the 1920s many a small suburban trolley was named after the trolley in Fontaine Fox's famous cartoon.

it was called the *el*. New York's were to have gingerbread Gothic stations with stained glass windows, land speculators were to make millions controlling the rights of way, and cinder-strewn slums were to be created running the length of the city. From the mid 1920s until World War II names like *the Third Avenue El* and *the Sixth Avenue El* typified the big city's hustle, bustle, dirt, and noise.

Streetcar lines had usually ended in *loops* at the edge of town. Thus some cities and towns, such as Louisville, Kentucky, still have an area called *the Loop*, now often well in town and serving as a neighborhood shopping center. But elevated lines often looped around an entire business district, thus New Yorkers were calling the Battery *the Loop* by 1893 and Chicago's main downtown area became *the Loop* by 1897.

Subway had been in the language since 1893, but Boston didn't build America's first *underground electric train* system until 1897, New York building its first *subway* system in 1904 (it was the *Interboro Rapid Transit*, the *IRT*, from Brooklyn Bridge to 145th Street). *Rapid transit* had been applied to elevated railways in the 1880s, but from now on it was to mean subways to most people.

City *motorbus* service began in 1905 in several cities, with New York's Fifth Avenue Coach Company introducing one 24-passenger, French-made *double-decker bus* that year; it was so successful that the company replaced all its horsecars with buses by 1908, and most cities replaced streetcars with buses by the end of the 1930s. In 1913 some cities introduced buses powered by overhead electric trolley wires and these were immediately called *trackless trolleys* or *trolley buses*. The motorbuses began replacing interurban streetcars in the early 1900s, such buses usually being trucks fitted with seats or elongated or rebuilt automobiles, with the Hupmobile being a favorite. The first specially designed *long-distance buses* appeared in the early 1920s, with movie star Mary

Pickford christening the first Hollywood to San Francisco one with a bottle of grape juice in 1924, Prohibition preventing the use of champagne. In 1928 three western bus systems merged into the *Pacific Greyhound Lines*, which was eventually to give us cross-country service and the famous name *Greyhound*.

An "elegant" Greyhound long-distance bus, 1930.

Hot Dogs

The American hot dog was the most popular food at Fourth of July picnics, baseball games, and carnivals from the 1890s to the late 1920s, when the late-starting hamburger (see HAMBURGERS) began to overtake it.

Originally the larger, beef *frankfurter* (after Frankfurt, Germany) and the smaller, pork-and-beef *wienerwurst* ("Vienna wurst") were two different sausages, especially in German neighborhoods—but they soon combined to become the American hot dog. *Wienerwurst* were called *wienies* as early as 1867 and *wieners* by 1904, but meant only the sausage, never the sandwich (*wienie roast* became popular in the 1920s). The *frankfurter* is said to have been introduced both as a sausage and as a sandwich by Antoine Feuchtwanger, an immigrant from Frankfurt, Germany, in St. Louis in the 1880s. Some say that another German immigrant, a baker, Charles Feltman, introduced the frankfurter in the late 1890s; but it seems likely he was merely the one who introduced it to Coney Island, which became a mecca for frankfurter eaters. At any rate, *frankfurters* were being called for by name everywhere in the early 1890s, with the shorter *frank* not becoming common until the late 1920s.

Frankfurters were called *red hots* as early as 1896 and Harry M. Stevens, who then had a food concession at New York City's Polo Grounds, helped popularize the term around 1900 by having his vendors call "Get your red hots! Red hots!," especially on cold days. He is also credited with heating the roll and adding condiments, though Germans had been eating wurst with rolls and mustard for untold generations.

Hot dog was popularized by Hearst cartoonist T. A. ("Tad")

Red hot frankfurters, New York City, 1936.

188

Dorgan, who drew the once German sausage, now known as the red hot, as an elongated dachshund on a bun—dachshund being a facetious symbol for things German in the early 1900s, and many people suspected the mixed meats in the sausage contained dog meat, or worse. Whether in guilt, or in righteous indignation, Coney Island vendors took offense at the new name and the Coney Island Chamber of Commerce banned the use of the term "hot dogs" on signs there in 1913. By this time the main Coney Island snack was a large, spicy frankfurter on a roll, often topped with sauerkraut, this called a *Coney Island* (the term had meant fried clams in the 1870s and 80s). Also in 1913 Nathan Handwerker opened *Nathan's Famous* frankfurter stand at Coney Island, his $15 investment growing into a multimillion-dollar franchise operation in the next 50 years. By 1920 *hot dog stand* was a term heard all across America.

Hot dog!, an exclamation of approval or surprise, was in use by 1906 and the more emphatic *hot diggity dog* in the 1920s, shortened to *hot diggity* by 1939. Since the 1950s we have heard *hot dogger* as a surfing term for a show-off or daredevil, as if hoping onlookers will say "hot dog!" But *hot dogger* may come from a different source: *dogs* meant feet as early as the 1890s, and by 1895 *to hot dog* was a college term meaning to go fast, make tracks, which may have given us the later surfing term.

Today the ubiquitous, general-purpose American hot dog has grown tame and soft, as have the mustard and roll used with it. There is, however, still a difference between the bland, mass-produced *skinless* hot dog developed from beef, pork, chicken, and meal after World War II and such succulent varieties as the large, redder, all-beef, garlic-loaded kosher *special* still found in some German-Jewish neighborhoods.

Huh? and Uh-Uh

aren't in most dictionaries, whose editors probably consider them grunts rather than words. Yet all Americans know them and most use them over and over. *Huh* is used to mean "what?" or to express surprise, disbelief, or the like, while *uh-uh* repeated in a flat monotone is one of our most common expressions for "no," and with a rising tone on the second "uh," or pronounced "um-huh," is probably our most common way of saying "yes." In addition *um* means "is that so?" or "I'm thinking about it." These are among the most common "words" heard in America, and are truly native earmarks of an American. Captain Frederick Marryat, an English naval commander and writer of novels about the sea and of books for boys, had the right idea when in 1839 after a visit here he pointed out in *A Diary of America:*

> There are two syllables—*um, hu* [huh]—which are very generally used by the Americans as a sort of reply, intimating that they are attentive, and that the party may proceed with his narrative, but by inflection and intonation are made to express dissent or assent, surprize, disdain. I myself found them very convenient at times, and gradually got into the habit of using them.

I . . . I . . . I: The Most Frequently Used Words

The English language now has at least 600,000 words, over 400,000 more than when the Pilgrims landed. Depending on education, most Americans are estimated to "know" 10,000-20,000 words but actually "use" only half that number. Of these, just 10 basic words account for over 25% of all speech and 50 simple words for almost 60%, with between 1,500 and 2,000 words accounting for 99% of everything we say!

What is the most common word spoken in America—*love, God, money, sex, baseball?* Sorry—it's the word *I.* The second most common spoken word is *you* (*I* and *you* account for almost 10% of all informal conversation). The third and fourth most common words we say are the articles *the* and *a.* In fact, when we hear America talking, the 50 words heard most are the obvious, mundane ones. They are the pronouns *I, you, he, she, it, we, they, me, him, her, them, what;* the articles *the, a, an;* the prepositions *on, to, of, in, for, with, out, from, over;* the conjunction *and;* the adverbs *about, now, just, not; that* and *this* as adjectives and relative pronouns; the verbs *is, get, was, will, have, don't, do, are, want, can, would, go, think, say, be, see, know, tell;* and the vague noun *thing.*

These basic words, of course, are only the bare framework on which we hang our talk about love, God, money, sex, baseball, politics, business, philosophy, art, and science. Thus "*I* love *you*" and "O *say can you see by the* dawn's early light" contain 13 words, 8 (62%) of which are among the most common ones, yet they express deeply felt emotions. Our written language is only a little more varied than our spoken one, 70 words making up 50% of it. In writing we are more likely to qualify our words and to use *but, or, if, so, which,* and *who.* In general, too, our spoken language differs from the written in that we use shorter sentences, fewer auxiliary verbs, and more active verbs.

Ice Cream

has been eaten for 3,000 years, originally as flavored snow or ice. Marco Polo found it in China, the Aztec ruler Montezuma II is said to have liked his with hot chocolate poured over it (predating our chocolate sundae by some 400 years), and early colonists

"The Hokey Pokey Man."

poured maple syrup over snow. Both Washington and Jefferson owned a "cream machine for making ice" and Dolly Madison's White House dinner parties were talked about for the "large shining dome of pink ice cream" used as the centerpiece. Colonists had been talking about going to *ice cream houses* since the 1700s, which weren't generally called *ice cream parlours* or *ice cream stands* until the late 1870s. By 1884 people were calling the cheap ice cream sold by street vendors *hokey pokey* and children looked for the *hokey pokey man* or listened for his yell "Hokey pokey, a penny a lump!" just as today's children watch for the *Good Humor man* and listen for his bells. But since immediately after the Revolutionary War, ice cream lovers had been praising *Philadelphia ice cream*, originally made without eggs, and that city was famous for its ice cream parlors and factories for the next century and a half.

Early ice cream was prepared and hand beaten until frozen in a pot placed in a pan of ice and salt. In 1846 Nancy Johnson invented the hand-cranked *ice cream freezer*, but it was patented by William Young. The first large ice cream manufacturer and wholesaler was a Baltimore milk dealer, Jacob Russel, who began operations in 1851. *Neapolitan ice cream*, different flavored layers frozen together, and *tutti-frutti ice cream* (Italian "all fruits"), with candied fruits and nuts, were both first being talked about in the 1870s.

People began to ask each other if they had tried one of the new *ice cream sodas* soon after they were introduced at the semicentennial celebrations of Philadelphia's Franklin Institute in 1874. In the 1880s *ice cream cake* and *floats* appeared. Sometime in the 1890s the *ice cream sundae* came into being. *Sundae* is merely a respelling of "Sunday" and the dish was originally sold only on that day, some say because it was originally an ice cream soda without the soda water (see SODA POP AND SODA WATER), which some areas would not allow to be sold on Sundays, while others say the chocolate syrup made it an expensive "only on Sunday" dish. *Frappés* (French *frapper*, to ice) appeared around 1900.

Drive-in ice cream stands have replaced most ice cream parlors since World War II.

After the 1904 St. Louis World's Fair people started asking for *ice cream cones*, invented at the fair when an ice cream vendor ran out of dishes and a nearby vendor of the crisp pastry, salabria, twisted it into a cone to hold the ice cream. *Double decker* referred to a cone with two scoops of ice cream until the end of the 1930s, when the term *double dip* replaced it. The chocolate-covered ice cream bar was introduced in 1921 under the trade name of *Eskimo Pie*, while it was around 1930 that most people first heard of a *banana split* (the first bananas were brought to the U.S. in 1804, the *United Fruit Company* was founded in 1899, and we were using the term *banana boat* by 1916). Soon after World War II most people had heard of Howard Johnson's "28 flavors." However, the new postwar mobility and the growing suburbs saw a decrease in the importance of local ice cream parlors and the rise of drive-in ice cream and *frozen custard* stands and of roving *ice cream trucks*. Soon millions of children were asking to be taken to the nearest *Dairy Queen* or waiting at the curb for the *Good Humor man*.

The Immigrants

To immigrate and *immigration* are 17th century English words, first used to refer to those who came to the colonies. *Immigrant* itself is an American word of 1789 (before that *emigrant* or the French *émigré* had been used to refer both to one who left an old country and one who came to a new one). It is fitting that *immigrant* is American, because it was America's land, classless opportunity, and political and religious freedom that gave Europe's masses the idea of immigrating to improve their lot—and because all Americans, except the Indians, are immigrants or descendants of immigrants.

Ellis Island, about 1907.

To most of us today *immigrant* does not call up images of those early English, Dutch, French, Germans, Scotch-Irish, and Spanish who crossed the Atlantic on sailing vessels to settle in the wilderness or to escape religious persecution, the Potato Blight of the 1840s, or European revolutions. Our main image of *immigrants* today is of the central, eastern, and southeastern Europeans who came via the Mediterranean and Atlantic on steamships between 1865 and 1920 because they were poor and hopeless in their native lands. Historians call them *the New Immigrants.* They had to wait until steamships and the rivalry between steamship companies made passage from Mediterranean ports cheap enough for them to come. Thus the steamship created the New Immigrants and a new America.

In general, the New Immigrants arrived at the port of New York and many stayed in the large northern cities, because the wilderness was almost gone and the good free or cheap land had already been settled by the earlier arrivals—which is why the early arrivals are now called *settlers* and the later arrivals *immigrants.* By the time the New Immigrants arrived the earlier settlers had already named most of the cities, towns, rivers, mountains, animals, and plants and made their culture, ideas, customs, and language the American norm. Thus the Bohemians, Czechs, Hungarians, Italians, Lithuanians, Poles, Slavs, and other New Immigrants had less influence on our language than the earlier immigrants (for the history and words of specific immigrant groups see The Dutch; Erin Go Bragh; French, French Toast, and French Postcards; The Germans; The Italians; The Jews; The Pennsylvania Dutch; Spanish).

Between 1900 and 1920 alone 14½ million New Immigrants came to America, averaging ¾ million a year, 2,000 every day. The price of America was about $40: $15 for passage in *steerage* (literally the below-decks section of a ship near the steering gear) plus the $25 required on entering the new country to prove one wouldn't be a public charge. After 1892 most immigrants first set foot in America on *Ellis Island,* named for Samuel Ellis, a New Jersey merchant and one of its early owners (this busiest of all U.S. immigration centers was finally closed in 1943). Since many were turned back at Ellis Island, separating families, it was known as *the isle of tears.* As were all other immigrant groups, the New Immigrants were called by various disparaging names:

Bohunk (*Bo*hemian + *Hung*arian), 1890s, originally for an unskilled laborer from Austria-Hungary or Bohemia, then by 1903 for any immigrant from central or southeastern Europe, as a Czech, Slav, or Pole.
Cheskey (from Bohemian *český,* Czech), a Czech.
Hunk, 1896, *Hunky,* 1900, a poor, unskilled immigrant, especially a Hungarian, but often a Pole, Slav, Lithuanian, etc. These words

193

probably come from *Bohunk*, but could come from *Hungarian* itself and may have been influenced by *hunk* (1891) meaning a large piece, since such immigrant men were considered merely large hunks of muscle best fit for manual labor.

Litvak, a Lithuanian.

Polack, Polock (from Polish *Polak*, meaning Pole), 1879; *Polacker, Polocker*, 1883.

Rusky, a Russian. This was first used to refer to a Russian soldier in 1914, then after World War I was used to refer to any Russian.

By 1917 an immigrant was also called a *greenhorn*, which had meant an inexperienced person in English since 1785, either from the "green" or budding horns of young animals or as a corruption of the 1698 British slang *greenhead*, a stupid, inexperienced person.

According to various *naturalization acts* (1798) and *naturalization laws* (1822) an immigrant could become an American after a prescribed number of years, usually five, and meeting certain requirements for citizenship, including taking out *naturalization papers* (1856), of which the *first papers* (1912) were to become the most important. Then if the immigrant had succeeded in the American *melting pot* (from the title of Israel Zangwill's 1908 play) he or she would be indistinguishable from a *native born American* (1830s). Today with our talk of *ethnic groups* (a popular term since the 1960s, from Greek *ethnos*, people, nation) and *minority groups* (also early 1960s) this all seems far too simple. But amazingly enough it worked.

Indians

The word *Indian* comes from the most celebrated mistake in history. When Columbus discovered the Western Hemisphere he thought he had reached the Indies of Asia; hence the Caribbean Islands were called the *West Indies* and their inhabitants *Indians*. The word then spread to include all the aboriginal peoples of the Americas. When the Pilgrims landed there were a thousand unique Indian nations north of the Rio Grande, speaking 58 major languages (actually several thousand tribes and subtribes speaking thousands of languages and dialects, which linguists now group into 58 language families). Most Americans still speak some Indian words every day.

The Indian words we still use include: (1) thousands of place names; (2) scores of words about Indians used in our history and mythology; and (3) hundreds of names of plants, animals, and landscapes which have become part of our everyday speech. As for place names, 26 of our states, over 1,000 of our rivers and streams, 200 of our lakes, and untold numbers of our cities, towns, counties, hills, valleys, forests, parks, etc., have Indian names. The rivers and valleys include the *Mississippi, Ohio, Missouri, Illinois, Connecticut, Arkansas* (see THE STATES for what

A Plains Indian, "Noapeh," a Sioux of the Assiniboin tribe.

A Roanoke chief, about 1585. The large pearls and copper plate are badges of authority, the crossed arms a sign of wisdom.

these Indian words mean), *Potomac*, *Shenandoah* ("daughter of the skies"), *Susquehanna* ("muddy river"); the lakes include *Michigan* and *Huron* (after the tribe, named by the French word *huré*, "bristly, unkempt"); the *Mohave* desert ("three mountains," referring to the peaks near Needles, California); and *Yosemite* park ("grizzly bear, killer"). The cities and towns with Indian names include *Chicago* ("place of the bad smell," perhaps "wild onion place" or "skunktown"), *Miami* (the Florida tribe, "people of the peninsula"), *Poughkeepsie* ("at the little rock water," at the bottom of the waterfall), *Saginaw* ("place where the Sauks lived"), *Spokane* ("sun," "sun warrior"), *Tulsa* ("old town," in memory of an older Indian town elsewhere), *Tuscaloosa* (after Choctaw chief Tascaluca, meaning "black warrior"), *Waukeegan* ("house, trading post"), *Winnebago* ("people of the filthy water"), as well as *Cheyenne*, *Kalamazoo*, *Omaha*, *Tallahassee*, *Tacoma*, *Wichita*, and hundreds more.

The words we use in talking about Indians include some real Indian words plus others from our conceptions and misconceptions of Indians, words from our history and from our fiction:

brave (the French word for an Indian warrior), has had wide American use since 1819. Before then we usually used the term (*Indian*) *warrior*.

breech cloth, 1793. Before then it was often called a *breech clout*.

bury the ax, 1680; *bury the tomahawk*, 1705; *bury the hatchet*, 1754. This was an Indian custom, used to symbolize coming to an agreement or making peace.

council. By the 1740s in America *council* was usually used to mean a formal meeting with Indians to discuss treaties, boundaries, etc. Indians were said to have *council chiefs* (1826) who met at *council grounds* (1842) or *council camps* (1870) around *council fires* (1753).

firewater, 1817 is the earliest recorded use of this "Indian talk" word for whiskey. It may be a translation of the Algonquian *scoutiouabou*, "fire water."

good Indian, bad Indian, 1840s.

Great Spirit, the Indian *manitou*, the spirit of nature deified in the Algonquin religion, 1790.

Great White Father, the U.S. president, was popularized in western novels about 1916. The Indians did use our word *father* since 1727 to mean any friendly White man, especially one in authority. The "Great White" part seems to have been added for the benefit of readers and moviegoers.

Happy Hunting Ground, first used in 1837, in the fiction of Washington Irving.

heap big. Heap, a good deal, very, was first reported as Indian talk in 1848, in "heap hungry" and "heap thirsty." The use of *big* in Indian talk dates from the 1830s, suspiciously close to the time when Americans began to overuse "big" to mean fine or important. *Big chief* didn't appear until 1861.

Honest Indian?, "is it true?" 1851; *Honest Injun* "on my honor," 1892, originally sarcastic use, because Indians were considered dishonest.

How! actually was a western Indian greeting (Sioux *hao*, Omaha *hau*) first encountered by Whites about 1815. However, the Indians usually used it as an expression of impatience.

Indian, first used in English to refer to a native of what is now the U.S. in 1602; *Ingen*, 1680; *Injun*, 1825. The *Dictionary of Americanisms* lists over 400 American terms using the word *Indian*, referring to plants and animals, Indian clothing and customs, our beliefs about Indians, etc.

Indian Affairs, 1703; *Indian Agent*, 1712; *Indian Commissioner*, 1713; *Indian Agency*, 1822; *the Bureau of Indian Affairs*, established in 1824 under the War Department, transferred to the Department of the Interior in 1849, initially oversaw Indian trade and removing Indians to reservations; *Indian Bureau*, 1832; *Indian Office*, 1871; *Agency Indian*, an Indian living on a reservation, 1891.

Indian beads, 1640; *Indian basket*, 1642; *Indian blanket*, 1764.

Indian chief, 1641. Colonists also called a chief *sagamore* (Abnaki for chief, ruler), 1613; *sachem* (Narraganset *sachimau*, tribal chief, tribal representative), 1622; and *mugwump* (Algonquian *maqquomp*, chief), 1663.

Indian country, 1664; *Indian land*, 1658; *Indian territory*, 1677; *Indian Territory*, 1828, the territory, now Oklahoma, set aside by the government for the Five Civilized Tribes.

Indian fighter, 1832.

Indian file, 1756.

Indian gift, 1764; *Indian giver*, 1830s.

Indian nation, a tribe, 1622. *Tribe* is a 13th century English word, used to refer to the tribes of Israel and to Roman tribes long before it was used to refer to aboriginal groups in Africa and the Americas. The earliest settlers usually spoke of an Indian *nation* rather than an Indian *tribe*.

Indian pony, *Indian horse*, 1750s.

Indian school, to teach young Indians Christianity, peace, and some reading and writing, 1660. *Mission school*, for Indian children, 1822.

Indian scout, an Indian serving as a scout or guide for the settlers, 1675; a White man serving as a scout against the Indians, 1838. The change in meaning of this term aptly illustrates the change in relations between Indians and the Whites.

Indian sign, a track or indication of Indians, 1807; a signal used by Indians, 1906.

Indian summer, 1778. Probably so called because it is a "false" summer, as deceptive as most Whites considered Indians to be. But it could be so called because at this time of year Indians burned grass to clear and fertilize land and to drive animals in one last fall hunt (early accounts of Indian summer stress its smokiness or haze), or even because Indians were on the move to winter quarters or hunting grounds during these last warm days of fall.

Indian village, used in a translation of DeSoto's writings, 1544; *Indian town*, 1608; *Indian camp*, 1775.

Indian war, 1668; *Indian treaty*, 1719.

Indian wrestling, 1913.

the Long Knives, the Big Knives, first recorded in 1750 as Indian talk for settlers, especially in Virginia, and referring to the swords early settlers carried. The terms became Indian names for the U.S. Cavalry in the Indian War of 1876.

medicine dance, the term was first recorded by the Lewis and Clark Expedition, 1805; *medicine man*, 1806; *medicine*, as supernatural power or as a charm, deity, or person possessing supernatural power, 1807. *Bad medicine*, adverse magic, 1815; *big medicine*, 1846. The traveling White peddlers of various nostrums and cure-alls were called *Indian medicine men* by 1830.

moccasin (Powhatan *mockasin*, Micmac *mkussin*). Virginia colonists were using the word by 1612. *Moccasin snake*, 1765; *water moccasin*, as a poisonous swamp rattler in the South, 1784 (perhaps from the Ojibwa *massasauga*, the Indian name for a Canadian river and a type of rattlesnake found near it), by 1832 this snake was also called the *cotton mouth* (because of its whitish mouth lining). *Moccasin Rangers*, a famous Civil War rebel guerilla group active in the Allegheny Mountains. *Moccasin Joe*, the grizzly bear, because its footprints resemble those made by moccasins, 1893, as first recorded by Theodore Roosevelt. The *moccasin telegraph*, as the Indian grapevine for passing on news via travelers, wasn't called this until 1927.

paleface, 1822. James Fenimore Cooper put this term for White man into the mouths of his Indian characters. He probably invented it.

papoose (Algonquian for baby, child). Colonists were calling Indian babies this by 1633.

peace pipe, 1760; earlier it was called a *pipe of peace*, 1705. This long, decorated ceremonial pipe was first called a *calumet*, in 1678 (via Canadian French from French *calumeau*, reed, any plant with straw suitable for a pipe stem). *Calumet* is also a place name for a river, county, village, etc., in Illinois, Indiana, and Michigan, indicating places where such reeds grew.

potlatch (Chinook and Nootka *patshatl*, gift, giving, a gift-giving festival), 1845. This is a ceremonial feast of Indians in Washington State, British Columbia, and Alaska in which the host gives valuable gifts to the guests or destroys his goods and possessions to show he can afford it.

powwow (Algonquian *powwaw, powah*, sorcerer, medicine man, from a root word meaning "he dreams"). Our spelling has included *powah, powaw, pouwau*, and many others, the present *powwow* prevailing only since 1850. Whites first used this Indian word to mean an Indian medicine man, 1624; an Indian conjuring ceremony or council meeting, 1625; a conference, 1812.

redskin, 1699; *red man*, 1725; *red devil*, 1834.

reservation, 1789; *reserve*, 1805; *Indian reserve*, 1818; *Indian reservation*, 1819; *reservation Indian*, 1866. *Reservation* originally meant one for Indians and the word *Indian* did not have to be added to clarify it until later. By 1850 we had *military reservations* and by 1890 *forest reservations*. *Reservation* meaning a previously reserved room, seat, ticket, etc., was not in use until the late 1890s.

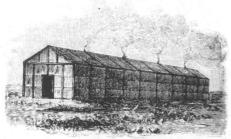

An Iroquois long house *and Comanche* typees *(below).*

to scalp, 1693; *scalp dance*, 1791; *scalp lock*, 1825. *Scalper*, one who takes scalps, 1760; one who resells tickets at an exorbitant price, 1869.

seeing Indians, drunk, 1850.

smoke signal, 1873; *signal smoke*, 1834, as a simple signal, not part of a complex message.

snake dance, an Indian ceremonial dance using live snakes, 1772; a sensuous writhing dance similar to the coochee-coochee, 1896; a zigzag Indian-file parade of students celebrating an athletic victory, 1911.

squaw (Algonquian *squa*, woman, not necessarily a married one), the colonists were using it to mean an Indian wife by 1634; *squawman*, a White man living with or married to an Indian woman, 1866.

tepee, wigwam, long house, lodge, hogan. The colonists and early frontiersmen never heard the Sioux word *tepee* (*tepe*, dwelling). It's a Plains Indian word which most Whites did not encounter before 1835. Earlier Americans knew this type of Indian house by the eastern Indian word *wigwam* (Ojibwa *wigwaum*, Delaware *waquoam*), colonists using this word by 1628. Colonists also used the terms *long house*, 1648, for the Iroquois long communal or council house, and *Indian lodge* (via the French use of the term in America, from French *loge*, summer house, hut), 1656, shortened to *lodge* by 1804. *Lodge* could refer to any type of Indian dwelling but usually meant a wigwam; *lodgepole*, 1805; *lodgepole pine*, 1859. Whites didn't encounter the Navaho *hogan* (*qoghan*, home) until 1871; it's usually a hemisphere of earth over timber supports.

tomahawk (Algonquian *tamahakan*, beater, cutter), known to Virginia colonists by 1612, also sometimes called an *Indian hatchet*, 1677. This Indian war club developed into a lighter hatchetlike weapon and tool after the Whites arrived with their examples of hatchets with sharp metal blades.

totem (Chippewa *atoteman*) a sacred identifying object or symbol, as an animal, charm, etc., first recorded in 1609, just two years after the Virginia colonists landed. *Totem post*, first recorded in Alaska, 1876; *totem pole*, 1880.

Totem poles. Some Indian totems were tattooed on the body; others were placed on weapons; these of the Haidan Indians in the Pacific Northwest are all masks carved on poles.

ugh, used in western books and movies as Indian talk for "yes" and "hello." There is no record of a real live Indian ever having said it.

wampum (Algonquian *wampanpeag*, "white string" of beads, a string or belt of shell-bead money, white beads being the least valuable, black or purple the most valuable), known to colonists by 1638; slang use for money by 1904. Another Indian word for shell beads was *roanoke*, which may give us the place name *Roanoke*, Virginia.

war dance, 1711; *war whoop*, 1715; *war party*, *war path*, 1755; *war club*, 1776; *war bonnet*, 1840. James Fenimore Cooper gave us the terms *on the war path* and *war paint* in his 1826 novel *The Last of the Mohicans.*

Indian words for plants, animals, and landscapes began to appear in our language as soon as the colonists landed and began to ask the Indians "What's that?" Most answers were in Algonquian, the most widespread family of Indian languages, spoken by most Indians of the eastern half of the U.S. Since the Indians hadn't yet invented writing, and since each local tribe might have its own pronunciation of any given word, the colonists had a hard time trying to spell and pronounce Indian words. Often they shortened the Indian word or phrase (*asquatasquash* became "squash"), tried to pronounce the parts of the word like familiar English words (a process called folk etymology, making *wejack* or *otchig* into "woodchuck"), or took a whole Indian sentence or clause and made one word out of it. Virginia's Captain John Smith introduced many such words into English, beginning with his written description of Virginia in 1608. If you had been in Jamestown, Plymouth, or on the Kentucky frontier, or had crossed the prairie in a covered wagon, you would have heard your fellow Americans using a good many Indian words. Today about 130 Algonquian words, mainly for plants and animals, are still in use, plus a sprinkling of words from other Indian language families. The most frequently heard include:

bayou (via French from Choctaw *bayuk*, stream, creek), 1766 (see BAYOUS, CREOLES, AND CAJUNS).

caribou (via Canadian French from Micmac *khalibu* or something that sounded like *maccaribpoo*, "he who paws the snow"), 1610.

catalpa tree (Creek *kutuhlpa*, "winged head," referring to the flowers), 1730; shortened to *catalpa*, 1785.

Chautauqua was originally a place name for a county, town, and lake in southwestern New York State (from the Seneca for "place of death," "place where one is lost," "foggy place"). Then in 1874 a Methodist minister, John Vincent, established a Sunday school institute on a campsite on Lake Chautauqua. Soon this became a permanent summer colony offering a wide range of religious, cultural, and recreational activities, which taken together were called a *Chautauqua.* By the 1900s groups of lecturers, musicians, physical fitness experts, etc., traveled the *Chautauqua circuit* together, giving Chautauquas, lasting from several days to several weeks and often held in tents, in many towns across the country. *Chautauqua salute*, the waving of handkerchiefs in appreciation instead of applauding a speaker or performer, originated at the 1877 Chautauqua, for a deaf speaker who had given a pantomime lecture.

chipmunk (Ojibwa or Chippewa *atchitamon*, "head first," hence a squirrel, from the way the animal descends a tree), as *chitmunk*, 1832, present spelling, 1857.

hickory (Algonquian *pawcohiccora*, a dish of pounded hickory nuts and water), as *pockerchicory*, *pokahickory*, 1618, modern spelling, 1670. *Hickory nut, 1670. Hickory switch,* 1734, for whipping children, later called a *hickory stick. Hickory* was used to mean firm, unyielding by 1800, giving us such nicknames as "Old Hickory" for Andrew Jackson and such terms as *hickory cloth* and *hickory shirt* in the 1840s, referring to a strong cotton fabric. By 1848 *hickory* also meant a hickory walking stick and by 1900 was used to mean a baseball bat.

hominy, 1629; *pone*, 1612; *samp*, 1643; *succotash*, 1751. Many of our "corn" words come from the Indians; these words are discussed in detail at the entry CORN.

menhaden (Algonquian *munnoquohatean*, "that which enriches the soil"), the fish Massachusetts Indians used to fertilize their corn crops and which they taught the Pilgrims to use, spelled *munnawhatteang* by the colonists in 1643.

moose (Passamaquoddy *moosu*, "he trims smoothly," referring to the bark moose strip and eat from trees), spelled *mus*, 1613, present spelling by 1673. *The Loyal Order of the Moose*, a charitable secret fraternal order, was founded in Louisville, Kentucky in 1888, its members called *Moose* since then.

muskellunge (Ojibwa *mashkinoje*), a variety of Great Lakes pike, 1789.

opossum (Powhatan *aposoum*, "white animal"), 1610, shortened to *possum* by 1613. *To play possum*, 1822.

pecan (Algonquian *pakan*, *pagan*, nut, the word may have come directly to us from the Indians or via earlier Spanish explorers and settlers), spelled *paccan*, 1773.

persimmon (Cree *pasiminan*, "dried fruit"), as *putchamin*, 1612, as *persimon*, 1635, present spelling by 1709. In the 1850s and 60s Americans used such expressions as *bringing down the persimmons*, and *walking off with the persimmons*, meaning to succeed or win the prize.

poke means several different plants to us because it is our final pronunciation of several different Indian words. *Poke* originally was a name for the tobacco plant (from Algonquian *uppowoc*) which we spelled *apooke* in 1618. Other *poke* plants get their name from a Virginian Indian word *puccoon*, a plant they used for dyeing. Thus we have *pokeroot* by 1687; *pokeweed*, 1751; *pokeberry*, 1774. By 1778 *poke* also meant the skunk cabbage. *Poke greens* was first recorded in 1848 and *poke salad* in 1880.

raccoon (Algonquian *arakunen*, scraper, scratcher) was first recorded in 1608, in Virginia, though early spellings included *arocoun* and *raugrougheun. Raccoon coat,* 1649. *Raccoon* was shortened to *coon* as early as 1742, though most "coon" words and

Pueblo in the Taos Reservation, New Mexico, 1936. In Spanish pueblo *means people or town; the word has come to mean a stone or adobe community dwelling developed by the Indians of our Southwest. Spanish settlers adopted the pueblo style for their own houses and towns. See* SPANISH.

meanings appeared in the 1830s and 40s, when *coon hunts* became popular and *coon* was first used to mean a rustic frontiersman (1832) and then a Black (1837). In the presidential election year of 1840 the Whig party used a raccoon as its symbol and *coon* came to mean a Whig, including the presidential candidate William Henry Harrison and such men as Henry Clay, Daniel Webster, and John Calhoun; a *coon song* then meant not a Black minstrel song but a Whig political song (for more on the racial use of *coon* see THE BLACKS).

Coonskin, as one word, 1818; *coonskin cap*, with the tail hanging down the back, 1836. *Coon dog*, 1833. *A coon's age*, a long time, 1843. *A gone coon* was a humorous Revolutionary War expression referring to a story about a backwoods spy dressed in raccoon skins who said to the British soldiers who discovered him "I'm a gone coon." This grew into a popular 1830s story many marksmen told—it was one of Davy Crockett's favorites—of treeing a raccoon only to have it say "Don't shoot, I'll come down, I know I'm a gone coon."

scuppernong (Algonquian *askuponong*, "place of the magnolias," the Scuppernong River valley in North Carolina, where this variety of grape grows), 1811.

Sequoia is named after the Cherokee Indian Sikwayi (1770–1843) who invented an 85-syllable "alphabet" for recording the Cherokee language, which was adopted by the Cherokee council in 1821. Born in Tennessee, Sikwayi (sometimes spelled *Sequoya*) took the name George Guess when he grew up, from an American trader he believed to be his father. *Sequoia* was first used as a genus name of a tree, which includes the giant California redwoods, by Hungarian botanist Stephen Endlicher in 1847.

skunk (Algonquian *skekakwa, squnck,* "mammal who urinates" or sprays), 1588 by explorers, 1634 by colonists. It has also been called a *polecat* in America since the 1600s, after a related European animal. *Skunk cabbage*, 1751. *Skunk* was used to mean a contemptible person by 1840. *To skunk*, to defeat completely, keep an opponent from scoring, appeared in 1843.

Five Sioux warriors "captured" by a small-town Dakotan photographer, 1890, 14 years after the Indian victory at Little Bighorn.

Chief Joseph, a Nez Percé of the Pacific Northwest. Though noted for their friendliness, the Nez Percé, led by Chief Joseph, attacked Whites in 1877 because of widespread treaty violations by Oregon settlers.

squash (Narragansett *asquatasquash*, "eaten raw"), 1642. *Winter squash, summer squash,* 1750s; *crook-neck squash,* 1818, from its shape; *Hubbard squash,* late 1860s, from Mrs. Elizabeth Hubbard of Massachusetts, who first cultivated it; *zucchini squash, zucchini* (the Italian diminutive of *zucchine,* squash, hence "little squash") was generally unheard of in America until the 1920s; *acorn squash* did not become popular until the 1930s.

tamarack (from an Algonquian word that sounded like *tamarack* or *hackmatack,* which is another name for this red larch), 1805, now mainly found in the names of summer camps and resorts.

terrapin (Algonquian for "little turtle"), 1672; *terrapin soup,* 1825; *terrapin stew,* 1842; *diamond-backed terrapin,* 1877.

toboggan (via Canadian French from Algonquian *tabakun,* drag, hand sled), 1829; *tobogganing,* as a sport, 1855; *toboggan slide,* a playground slide for children, 1890s; *toboggan cap,* a stocking cap, especially with ends to wrap around the neck as a muffler, 1902.

wapiti, the North American elk, named in 1806 by the American physician and naturalist Benjamin Barton (using the Shawnee word for the animal, literally meaning "white rump"). This word never replaced the less precise word *elk,* which had been used in America since 1635.

whiskey-jack (Cree *wisketjan*), the Canadian jay. This name was first recorded by John J. Audubon, in 1839.

woodchuck (Algonquian *wejack,* Chippewa *otchig,* Cree *otchek,* the fisher), 1674. This is a prime example of folk etymology, of pronouncing strange words to resemble familiar words or word elements; it has nothing to do with "wood" or "chuck" except in sound.

In addition to the above, most Americans know about 50 names for Indian tribes from *Algonquin* to *Zuni,* plus such Indian words or words associated with Indians as *caucus* (1773, probably from

The only good Indian is a dead Indian.

General Philip Henry Sheridan at Fort Cobb, Indian Territory, Jan., 1869. The general used this reply to a Comanche chief who presented himself saying "Me Toch-a-way, me good Indian." The general's actual quote was "The only good Indians I ever saw were dead."

"The Attack," by Frederic Remington, about 1907.

Sitting Bull (1831?–1890),

Algonquian *caucauasu*, counselor), *mackinaw* (1820s as a blanket, 1902 as a jacket, from Ojibway *mitchimakinak*, "great turtle," which became the name of the strait between Lake Michigan and Lake Huron, an island on this strait, and a trading post where this heavy wool, plaid blanket was common), *pemmican* (1791, Cree *pimikkan* from *pimii*, fat, grease), and *podunk* (Mohegan for "neck of land," used as a place name by Indians in Connecticut and Massachusetts, as recorded in 1666, then used by Whites to mean a small or insignificant town or rural region by 1841). And remember that all these words come only from "our own" Indians of what is now the United States. Such words as *potato* and *tobacco* are West Indies Indian words and *tomato* and *chocolate* are Aztec Indian words (see CANOES AND CANNIBALS and COYOTE AND MESQUITE for further lists). Thus language often pays history's debt: Montezuma, Massasoit, Squanto, Hiawatha, Pocahontas, Sacajawea, Cochise, Sitting Bull, Tecumseh—we still hear you talking when we hear America talking.

The Iron Horse

Rails for horse-drawn wagons with grooved wheels were in use by 1550, and by the 18th century in England were called *tracks*, *railways*, and *railroads*. The first such *railroad* chartered in the U.S. was just such a road, the 1826 *Granite Railroad* for hauling granite from Quincy, Massachusetts quarries to a wharf three miles away, the granite being used to build Bunker Hill Monument. The first U.S. passenger railroad, the 1827 *Baltimore and Ohio Railroad*, the "B&O," was also originally equipped with horse-drawn cars.

Beginning in 1804, however, steam engine locomotives were experimented with in Great Britain, the first one being used on a public railroad there in 1825 and the first truly successful one being George Stephenson's 1829 *Rocket*. In America, Peter Cooper's one-ton *Tom Thumb* (so named because it was so small) was put to the test by the B&O in 1830: although it limped to defeat in a race against a horse-drawn car it convinced that railroad to convert to steam engines, beginning "the age of steam." That same year the B&O's prize-winning *York* became the first commercially adequate steam engine built in America. *Engine* had meant any complex machine since the 17th century and the *steam engine* had been known long before its use to pull railroad cars. Thus we used the older *engine* and *steam engine* more comfortably than that strange new 19th century English word *locomotive* (from Latin *locō*, place + Middle English *motive*, causing to move, from Latin *movēre*, to move, hence that which causes something to move from place to place). Since the cars on railroads were originally pulled by horses, it was also natural to call a locomotive an *iron horse* (1830s) or even a *steam horse* (1840s).

Peter Cooper's "Tom Thumb," though defeated in an 1830 race by a horse-drawn car, had a successful run, convincing B&O to convert to steam.

"The Best Friend of Charleston," first locomotive built in U.S. for actual service, 1830.

The *steam railroads* or *steam cars* (1833) began as competition to boats, especially canal boats, and to stagecoaches—and took many terms from these older forms of transportation. Thus such railroad terms as *All aboard!*, *berth*, *caboose*, *crew*, and *gondola* come from ship and boat use and *accommodation*, *car*, *coach*, *conductor*, and *station* come from stagecoach use. Of those two 18th century horse-drawn terms *railroad* and *railway*, we preferred *railroad*, often reserving *railway* for horse-drawn and, later, electric locomotion (the British prefer *railway* as the general term). *Train* (via Middle English *trayne* from Latin *trahere*, to drag) was in use in England by 1824 for a string of cars, but it was the late 1840s and early 50s before the word took hold in America. Thus it was not until the 1840s and 50s that *wagon train* (1849), *mule train* (also 1849), and *pack train* (1853) became common American terms, that the older term *railroad conductor* was sometimes replaced by *train conductor*, and that a *railroad station* began to be called a *train station*.

The railroad changed American life and commerce forever. It also introduced or popularized many terms and gave America some of its most talked-about names, including:

accommodation train, 1835, a passenger train making stops at all stations, and often between stations for people wanting to get on or off. The name comes from the *accommodation stage*, 1811, a stagecoach operating in the same way. *Accommodation car*, *accommodation coach*, 1830s, a car on such a train, or a car reserved for local passengers, these were the cheapest, least comfortable coaches.

All aboard!, the conductor's standard call since 1837, from its use on river boats and ships.

American Standard, the standard American steam locomotive that dominated U.S. railroading until after the Civil War. It had a horizontal boiler, a four-wheel pilot truck to guide the front of the locomotive and four coupled driving wheels, with no other locomotive wheels behind them, this being called a *4-4-0* type.

the Atchison, Topeka, and Santa Fe, "the Santa Fe," was chartered in 1859, eventually connecting many parts of the West with the East.

the automatic railway coupler, patented by Eli Hamilton Janney in 1868 and made standard equipment on all railroads in 1888, and

The famous "Lightning," the first steam locomotive built at the American Locomotive Company, in 1848, Schenectady, New York.

204

An 1850 train from New York City to Portchester, New York, had to connect with old-fashioned stages to get the commuters home.

I've been workin' on the railroad, all the live-long day;
I've been workin' on the railroad, just to pass the time away;
Don't-cha hear the whistle blowin', rise up so early in the morn,
Don't-cha hear the captain shoutin', Dinah, blow your horn.
   "I've Been Workin' on the Railroad,". author unknown

A *typical* cattle car, *about 1932.*

the *air brake*, first patented by George Westinghouse in 1869, were major inventions in making high-speed rail travel safe.

baggage wagon, baggage car, 1833; *baggage check* (then a large tin disk), *baggage master,* 1845; *to check* baggage, 1846; *baggage agent,* 1858 (also called a *train agent* by 1879); *baggage truck,* 1860s, as a cart used in stations; *baggage coach,* 1878; *baggage rack,* 1889. *Baggage room* is an 1819 term, first used on excursion boats. *Baggage smasher* was first used as a name for cartmen and for baggage handlers on docks, then entered railroad use in the 1860s.

box car, 1856.

butcher, butcher boy, early 1880s as a vendor of candy, fruit, sandwiches, newspapers, etc., on trains and streetcorners, at sporting events, etc; *news butcher,* 1894; *train butcher,* 1903. Before the word *butcher* became common such a vendor was called a *train boy,* 1869.

cab (on a locomotive), 1859. Since the mid 1950s some streamlined electric and gas turbine locomotives have a raised *blister* on top, replacing the cab.

caboose (via Dutch from Low German *kabuse,* hovel) was first used in the U.S. to mean a shack (1839) and then to mean a ship's galley, as on riverboats. In 1861 it was first recorded as the last car on a freight train, containing the crew's kitchen and sleeping quarters. It was also called the *war car* by 1879 and the *conductor's car* and *train car* by 1895. We have used *caboose* figuratively to mean the seat of the pants or the buttocks since 1894.

car, railway car, 1826 (see THE CAR for the etymology); *the cars,* a train, 1831; *rail car,* 1834; *train car,* 1856. *Car house,* a building for the storage and repair of railway cars, 1833.

cattle car, cattle train, early 1850s, also called *stock car, stock train,* late 1850s. *Double decker,* a double-decked car for hogs or sheep, 1856 (the modern *automobile carrier* is a flat car with three decks).

the Chesapeake and Ohio, the "C&O," originated as the 22-mile Louisa Railroad of Virginia in 1837 but eventually connected Norfolk, Virginia (the Chesapeake part of its name) and Cincinnati (the Ohio part of its name).

club car, 1895.

coach, passenger car, 1832. *Day coach,* 1870s, to distinguish it from a coach which could be converted into night sleeping quarters (see *Pullman car*).

coal car, 1858. This is a car for carrying coal as cargo, not to be confused with the *tender* which carried wood or coal and water to "tend" to the needs of the engine. *Coal train*, 1861.

commutation, of or for passengers traveling regularly on the same route at reduced fares, 1840s; *commutation ticket*, 1840s, also called *season ticket. Commuter, to commute, commuter road*, 1865 (via Middle English from Latin *commutāre*, to exchange). Early commutation tickets were mainly from cities to popular nearby beaches and resorts; by 1865, however, people were already commuting to city offices from homes in the *suburbs* (a 14th century English word from Latin *suburbium, sub*, near + *urbs*, city).

conductor, on a stagecoach, 1790; on a horse-drawn railroad, 1826; on a steam railroad, 1832; on a city horsecar, 1860s. *Railroad conductor*, 1842; *train conductor*, 1849.

cow catcher, 1838. The original *guard* (1832) was invented by Isaac Drips of New Jersey's Camden and South Amboy Railroad after several cows had been killed by trains. Unfortunately, most early guards were too sharp and too high, impaling the cows, so soon blunter inclined planes were designed for catching or thrusting aside cattle and other obstructions, and called *cow catchers*. Railroad men usually called a cow catcher a *pilot* (1846) and the public also called it a *horse catcher* (1838) and a *cow guard* (1878).

cross tie was originally a construction term used by carpenters (1813), then was used in railroading by 1833. It was also called a *rail tie, railroad tie*, and just plain *tie* by the 1840s.

dead head has been used since the late 1830s to refer to a person allowed to ride on a public conveyance or to see a theatrical performance without a ticket. The practice was so common in the 1870s that it and the favored people who didn't have to pay were known by the slangy abbreviation *D.H.* By 1900 *deadhead* and *deadheading* referred to freight cars returning empty from a run, to a train of such cars, and to the locomotive pulling it.

depot was first recorded in 1832, in its French spelling *dépôt*—and for years pedants criticized it as an unnecessary American synonym for the perfectly good English word *station* (Longfellow thought the word *depot* rather quaint, noting in 1842 that a fellow passenger on a train pronounced it to rhyme with "teapot"). *Railroad depot*, 1836; *locomotive depot*, 1841; *railway depot*, 1863.

the Diesel engine was patented by the Paris-born German engineer Rudolph Diesel in 1892 and then perfected by him at Friedrich Krupp's works during the next five years. By 1934 large railroad *diesels* like the Burlington's *Pioneer Zephyr* were making runs in about half the time of the fastest steam engines, and between then and the 1960s diesels almost completely replaced steam engines in the U.S., ending the age of steam. Racing by the coal chutes and water tanks of the many *railroad towns* which had grown to serve steam engines, the diesel soon made ghost towns or stopped the growth of many such communities.

dining car, 1838. George Pullman built his first dining car, the *Delmonico*, in 1868 (named for the famous series of restaurants run by the Delmonico family in New York City); typical menus on the early dining cars offered buffalo, elk, antelope, beefsteak, mutton chops, or grouse dinners for $1.00. *Diner*, as a railroad

An 1895 dining car.

dining car, 1890. For decades after such cars were in service, however, many passenger trains still made *dinner stops* at *dinner stations* (both 1890s terms).

dispatcher, 1878. Before that he was often called a *train dispatcher*, 1857.

dormitory car, *lodging car*, 1880s, for railroad construction workers, though some circus troupes and other groups also used them. Such cars were much higher than ordinary cars and had tier upon tier of bunks.

double header, a long, heavy freight train drawn by two locomotives, 1878.

double track railway, *double track*, 1834, the tracks being laid side-by-side, allowing trains to run in either direction without the risk of head-on collisions.

engineer, 1832; he was also sometimes called a *pilot* and a *driver* in the early days, a *locomotive engineer* by 1843 and a *locomotive runner* in the 1880s. In the 1840s he earned the astronomical salary of $100 a month. *Engineer* was originally a 14th century word for a designer of "military engines," such as catapults.

the Erie Railroad was established in 1832 as a 6-foot gauge track from Piermont, New York, on the Hudson, to Dunkirk, on Lake Erie, then became a major New York–Chicago line. Jay Gould, Daniel Drew, and Jim Fisk waged "the Erie war" stock-market fight against Cornelius Vanderbilt over this railroad during 1866–68, Gould then looting it of its profits in 1868, then selling his securities on the eve of the Panic of 1873. It merged with the Lackawanna in 1960 to form the Erie-Lackawanna.

express car, 1839, first used to refer to such cars going from Boston to New York; *through train*, 1846.

flag man, 1856, a rear brakeman who ran back with a flag when a train stopped between stations, warning other trains not to run into the stopped one.

flat car, 1862.

freight car, *burden car*, 1833, originally a small open-topped car, with stakes, ropes, and covers used to tie down or protect the freight. *Freight train*, *freight*, mid 1840s, freight cars and trains already then being called *rattlers*. *Freight engine*, 1864; *freight yard*, 1870s. *Fast freight*, 1875.

frog, a crossing or switch plate where tracks cross or diverge, 1847.

funeral train was first used in 1865, referring to the train bearing Abraham Lincoln's body from Washington, D.C., to Springfield, Illinois, taking 12 days on a circuitous 1,700-mile route and giving all who saw it status in the eyes of their community. The term was widely used again in 1945 for the train bearing the body of Franklin D. Roosevelt from Warm Springs, Georgia, to Washington, D.C.

gandy dancer, a well-known term by 1915 and said by some to have been a hobo term for the hobos and tramps who did such work when they felt like it, it may have been used by railroaders as early as the 1860s. It's from the gooselike, or ganderlike, rhythmic movement of the workers tamping the ties and gravel and straightening rails.

Engine for Abraham Lincoln's funeral train, decorated with flags, wreaths, and portrait.

gondola, as a flatcar with low side walls, late 1880s. The word came to railroading through its earlier use to designate a type of flat-bottomed river boat, but has been known in English since the 16th century (the Italian *gondola* is, of course, a much more romantic boat, the Italian word, however, actually means "roll, rock").

gravy train, *on the gravy train*, 1940s. The term comes from the 1910 *gravy* meaning profit, illegal gain, especially through political conniving. In the 1940s *gravy boat* and *on the gravy boat* were also in use for such profitable conniving.

the Great Northern Railroad Company originated as the St. Paul and Pacific in 1862, becoming the "Great Northern" in 1889, 11 years after the Canadian James J. Hill, "the empire builder" took it over. Hill owned railroads, steamship companies, banks, and mines, all under his Northern Securities holding company. As the railroad's names implied, it ran from Duluth and St. Paul through ten states and Canada to Seattle, Washington. Hill's clash with Edward Harriman over securing an entry for his line into Chicago and St. Louis was part of the two-men's struggle for control of the railroads (see also *the Northern Pacific Railroad Company* below) which led to the Panic of 1901.

the Harvey girls were the pretty waitresses working in the *railroad eating houses* (1873) which Fred Harvey began to open in Santa Fe Railroad stations in the West and Southwest in 1879, his first being in a room over the Topeka, Kansas, station. His restaurants became known not only for their pretty waitresses but for their superior food; they evolved into the *Fred Harvey diners* (1928) and the *Harvey House* restaurants (1941).

high ball, a semaphore signal of a large ball raised high to signal railroad engineers to proceed, 1890s. By the 1930s *to high ball* was a general term meaning to move at full speed, perhaps in some confusion with *red ball* (see below).

hopper, *hopper car*, 1862, as an open-topped freight car with a hopper bottom.

hot box, a journal box overheated by friction, 1840s. A *journal* is the part of an axle or shaft supported by a bearing, a *journal box* enclosing both this journal and its bearing.

the Illinois Central Railroad, 1851, was established to serve the farmers of central Illinois but became the first U.S. *interstate railroad*, eventually going from the Great Lakes to New Orleans. It also was the first railroad to receive federal railroad *land grants* (an 1850s term).

the Interstate Commerce Commission, the *ICC*, was established in 1887 to curb railroad malpractices, fix adequate controls, and see to the adoption of the *standard gauge* (4'8½") between rails. It was especially formed to prevent the railroads from charging exorbitant prices while engaging in the discriminatory *rebate*. John D. Rockefeller had called rebates *drawbacks* in the 1870s and used them so successfully that by 1879 he had cornered 95% of the oil refining capacity of the country, other companies being forced to pay double what he did to ship oil and oil products over the railroads. Thus *Rockefeller*, *rebate*, and *Interstate Commerce Commission* entered the language, thanks to the railroads.

jerkwater town. Early steam trains had to stop frequently for the crew to *jerk water* from nearby streams or to take on water from

a *water station* (1847). Montrose, New York, became the first jerkwater town in 1870, when pans of water were set between the tracks there to fill the tender as the train moved over it. By 1897 *jerkwater town* was a slighting name for any small town, technically one where trains didn't even stop to take on water but jerked it from between the tracks (though in the public mind it meant towns where trains stopped only to take on water). Slow or local trains that stopped at such towns were called *jerkwater trains* by 1905.

local, 1879.

mail car, mail train, 1855. *Post office car*, 1857, *postal car*, 1864, in which mail was sorted en route.

milk train, 1853, such trains then having the right of way because they carried a perishable cargo. The meaning of *milk train* as a slow train stopping at every station to pick up or put off milk cans seems to have evolved around 1910. *Milk car*, first recorded in 1890.

the New York Central Railroad was created in 1853 by consolidating 11 *short lines* between the Hudson River and Buffalo, New York. Cornelius "Commodore" Vanderbilt (1794–1877) was almost 70 when he began acquiring railroads in the 1860s, doubling the New York Central lines and extending them to Chicago. Such consolidation and lengthening of lines increased *trunk lines* (1851, meaning main lines) greatly, allowing passengers to travel from New York City to Chicago without changing trains ten times as some had previously had to do. Vanderbilt completed New York's *Grand Central Station* in 1871. The New York Central built the famous locomotive *999* to pull its *Empire State Express* in 1893 and belatedly greeted the new century with its 1902 *Twentieth Century Limited*. It merged with the Pennsylvania Railroad in 1968, forming the Pennsylvania-New York Central, called "the Penn-Central."

the Norfolk and Western Railway was incorporated in Virginia in 1896 but was based on an older company. Throughout the years it acquired or leased some of the best known and some of the most interestingly named railroads, including *the Akron, Canton, and Youngstown; the Boston and Maine;* the *Buck Creek Railroad;* the *Delaware Hudson;* the *Erie-Lackawanna;* the *New York, Chicago, and St. Louis Railroad* (better known as *the Nickel Plate*); the *Sandusky Lines* of the Pennsylvania Railroad; the *Tug River and Kentucky Railroad;* and the *Wabash Railroad*, including the *Pittsburgh and West Virginia Lines*. As many of the places in the names of the lines suggest, this railroad transports a lot of bituminous coal.

the Northern Pacific Railroad Company, 1864; receiving a lavish land grant of 40 million acres, this was the first transcontinental railroad to reach the Pacific Northwest. Its failure brought about the collapse of Jay Cook's banking house, plunging the nation into the Panic of 1873. In 1881 Henry Villard captured control of this railroad, then James J. Hill and John Pierpont Morgan took it over in 1896; when Edward H. Harriman and Kuhn and Loeb tried to gain control by purchasing its shares the value was inflated grossly until the stock crashed, causing the Panic of 1901.

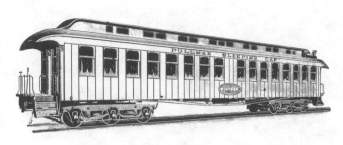

Observation car (upper left), *first Pullman sleeping car* (upper right), *Vistadome* (below).

observation car, the specially built last car on a passenger train, 1872, so called because of its *observation platform* (1880s). By the 1950s an *observation car* was also used to mean a specially built passenger car with window bays in the roof, especially a *Vistadome.*

parlor car, late 1850s, a passenger car with superior parlorlike accommodations, such as chairs and sofas, originally called a *Pullman saloon parlor car.* Also called a *saloon car*, because such cars had a main saloon, and a *chair car*, 1870s.

the Pennsylvania Railroad, "the Pennsy," was established in 1846 and soon connected Philadelphia and Pittsburgh. In 1910 it built a tunnel under the Hudson River, allowing trains to enter Manhattan directly for the first time.

private car, 1832. The most famous ones were built by the Pullman Company (see *Pullman car* below) between the 1880s and the stock-market crash of 1929 and cost about $100,000 the first year, including furnishings, crew, and food.

Pullman car, 1867. The first railroad sleeping accommodations appeared in 1836 when a Pennsylvania railroad divided a car into four sections and fitted each with three *berths.* People were talking about *sleeping cars* by 1839, and generally calling them *sleepers* by the 1870s (*sleeping train* and *sleeper train* are late 1870s terms). A hinged-shelf *upper berth* was patented by Theodore Woodruff in 1850. Cabinetmaker George M. Pullman began improving coach accommodations in the 1850s, converted a coach into a sleeping car in 1859 and built the first truly modern one, the *Pioneer*, in 1864. This palatial car then cost $20,000 to build and had painted ceilings with chandeliers, Brussels carpet, and walnut woodwork. Initially a ticket on such a car cost $2 a night, versus the $1.50 in regular *sleeping coaches. The Pullman Palace Car Company* was formed in 1867, its 47 cars staffed by Black *Pullman car porters* (1877).

railroad was originally used in 18th century England to mean a road of two parallel wooden rails for horse-drawn wagons to use, usually in a coal mine or quarry. In America *railroad* was also used to mean a road covered with planks or rails placed transversely, what we remember better as being called a *corduroy road* (1780). The full term *rail road train* came into wide use in the 1840s, when *rail road* was still often two words; *railroader* appeared in the late 1850s. *To railroad* someone, convict him falsely, appeared in 1877 and by the early 1900s a *railroad* or a *locomotive* also meant a college cheer imitating the sound of a locomotive, usually by being repeated faster and faster. The term *railroad flat*, for a row of rooms one behind the other, appeared in 1927.

Station porter, 1888.

railroad crossing, 1834, first seen that year when the Boston and Providence Railroad marked its highway crossings with large warning signs "Rail Road Crossing: Look out for the Engine." Until the railroads came most Americans knew a *crossing* (1753) as a place where a river was forded.

railroad cut, 1862, an excavation through a hill to provide a roadway for the railroad.

railroad euchre, 1889, euchre using a joker as the highest card.

railroad fever, 1852, popular and financial excitement over the building of railroads, during the rush to build them.

railroad fire, 1892, a fire caused by a train, usually from sparks from the engine. Such fires frequently destroyed thousands of acres of prairie grassland, timberland, and farms.

railroad grade, a graded portion of track, 1894. *Grade* had been used to mean the percentage of a road's slope since 1808 and an ascending or descending portion of road since 1811.

railroad iron, iron rails for the railroads, or the iron used in such rails, 1827.

railroad snow plow, used to clear tracks of snow, 1867.

railroad time, in good time, with speed, 1864. By 1880 it meant the system of time used by the railroads, the time differing from zone to zone as one traveled from east to west.

red ball, early 1900s, a fast freight or a freight car carrying perishables, usually fruit, and marked with a placard bearing a large red circle to indicate its priority to dispatchers, freight handlers, etc. Similar placards with other colors and symbols indicated other types of cargo and priority in the railroad system of *carding* or *way carding* (1890s) freight cars. By World War II *red ball* referred to any fast or priority movement, as the Army's *red ball express* of military supply trucks.

red cap, a station porter, 1919.

refrigerator car, 1868, then being a freight car with an ice compartment. It was also called a *freezer*, 1905, and a *reefer* (1909, from *refrigerator*).

right of way, the right to construct a railroad on a piece of land, 1838; the strip of land on which the railroad is built, 1850s.

the road, railroad tracks, 1832; *road bed*, 1840s, which was also called a *rail bed* by 1880.

rolling stock, 1850s.

round house, a circular building concentric with the center of a turntable on which railroad engines are turned, cleaned, and repaired, 1850s.

round trip, 1850s.

section (of track), 1855; *section agent*, 1855; *section master*, 1856; *section boss*, 1870; *section hand*, 1873; *section gang*, 1890. By 1866 *section* also meant a sleeping section of upper and lower berths in a sleeping car and a compartment in a parlor car. By 1872 two or more trains running as one were numbered as sections, the original being the *first section*, the first additional train the *second section*, etc.

a sidetrack, 1835; *to sidetrack* (a train), 1880. By 1893 *to sidetrack* was in general use to mean to divert from the main issue, course, or goal.

smoking car, 1856; *smoker*, 1882.

the Southern Pacific Company, organized in 1865 to connect San

Francisco and San Diego, it soon controlled the best mountain passes into California and by 1881 El Paso, Texas, was its eastern terminus. Colis P. Huntington replaced Leland Stanford as the road's president in 1890 and at Huntington's death in 1900 E. H. Harriman, backed by Kuhn, Loeb, and Company, acquired 45% of its stock.

the Southern Railway Company, incorporated in Virginia in 1894, and eventually joining all the large cities on the Mississippi with the Eastern seaboard.

steam car, a railroad car, 1833; *steam road*, a railroad, 1850s.

stopover, 1860s.

streamlining, 1909, in England. It was made possible by the diesel engine and led to trains with exciting names, using images of flight and air, such as *Comet*, *Flying Yankee*, *Meteor*, and *Zephyr*, while older steam engines often had speedy but bulkier names, as the *Cannonball*.

switch, originally meaning a sidetrack, 1835; *switch engine*, 1867; *switch yard*, 1888, *switch tower*, 1901.

tank car, 1874.

telescope, to collide and slide inside one another like the tubes of a telescope, first said of colliding railroad cars, 1867.

track layer, 1861, as a man; the first track-laying machine was called this in 1876. *Track force*, *track master*, 1866. *Track walker*, 1872, a man employed to walk along and inspect a specific section of track regularly. *On the track*, *off the track*, figurative use, 1870s, meaning to be on or off the right course on the way to a decision, solution, goal, etc.

T-rail, 1837, an inverted T-shaped rail developed by Robert Stevens of New Jersey's Camden and South Amboy Railroad, still the most common rail. Early rails were often of wood with metal *stringers*, dangerous because the metal strip sometimes came loose and sprang up through the wooden floors of the cars, causing death and destruction. *Welded rails*, up to a half mile in length, were first used in 1933, by the Delaware and Hudson Railroad.

trainman, 1877.

train robber, 1887.

train shed, 1892.

the transcontinental railroad was first talked about by that name in 1853, but didn't become a reality until 16 years later. *The Central Pacific Railroad* was chartered in 1861 to build tracks from Sacramento eastward until they linked with those of *the Union Pacific Railroad*, which was authorized under Congress's 1862 Pacific Railroad Act to build tracks westward from Omaha, Nebraska. The Central Pacific, using many Chinese coolies, laid 689 miles of track and the Union Pacific, using mainly Irish laborers and uprooted veterans of the Civil War, laid 1,085 miles of track, four to seven miles of track a day. The tracks were linked at a point designated by Congress and called *Promontory Point*, being near Promontory, Utah. Each blow of the sledge hammer on the final ceremonial *golden spike* on May 10, 1869 was signaled by Western Union and celebrated throughout the country by the ringing of bells. Now the United States was truly tied together as one nation from coast to coast.

Let us complete the grand design of Columbus, by putting Europe and Asia into communication. Let us give to his ships, converted into cars, a continuous course. . . .
Senator Thomas Hart Benton, speech, 1849. The transcontinental railroad was completed in 1869

way freight, as both freight to an intermediate or way station and a local freight train, 1833; *way fare*, 1846, passenger fare to a point along the way, costing more per mile than a *through fare*. This use of *way* goes back to the *way passengers* and *way stations* of stagecoach days of the 1780s.

whistle stop refers to a town too small to be a regularly scheduled stop for a train: if a passenger wants to get on there, the station master displays a flag to stop the train; if a passenger wants to get off there, the conductor signals the engineer to stop by pulling the signal cord and the engineer responds with two toots of the whistle. *Whistle stop* became a common term during the 1948 presidential campaign between Harry Truman and Robert Taft, Taft being said to have first used the term October 8, 1948, in criticizing Truman for his remarks about the Congress which he made from the platform of his campaign train at various small towns. However, the term is probably much, much older. Railroad men have called the same type of town a *flag station* since 1849 and a *flag stop* since the 1850s.

yard, *yard master*, *yard conductor*, *yard man*, early 1870s; *yard boss*, 1891.

A list of all the railroad words and names would fill a book. We have talked about such train names as the famous Los Angeles-to-San Francisco night train, the *Lark;* the *Hummingbird* between Cincinnati and New Orleans; the Hollywood-bound *Superchief;* the Washington-to-New York expresses with such names as the *Congressional, Embassy, Executive, Federal, Legislator, Patriot,* and *President;* the *Southern Belle*—the names go on and on, each region and each line having its favorites. The last major names would be the government-subsidized intercity passenger system *Amtrak* (*Am*erican + *trak*), which went into operation May 1, 1971 and the government-supported freight and commuter system *ConRail* (the *Con*solidated *Rail* Corporation), which went into operation April 1, 1976. Operating in 17 states between Boston and St. Louis, ConRail combined six bankrupt lines—the Penn Central, Reading,

Erie-Lackawanna, Central of New Jersey, Lehigh Valley, and Lehigh and Hudson River—with a total of 17,000 miles of track.

The railroads gave us many other names and words indirectly. *The Gadsden Purchase* was made by U.S. minister to Mexico James Gadsden in 1853, partially for America to build a railroad to the Pacific through what is now southern Arizona and New Mexico. The railroads created and supported many towns in the West, created such American types as the cowboy and the hobo and their words, and, with advertising, enticed immigrants from Europe to come to America to be western homesteaders. The railroads had Americans talking about railroad accidents, speed records, traveling. But mainly the railroads bridged and criss-crossed the country, letting Americans see places and people they had never seen before, shuttling goods, people, and our language from one side of the nation to the other, serving as a great stirring spoon for our people and language.

The Italians

Christopher Columbus and Amerigo Vespucci were the first Italians to sail to America and influence our language. Columbus came first, landing on San Salvador Island on October 12, 1492. His name gives us:

> *Columbia* (a Latinized version of Columbus), a name given the emerging United States in 1775; at least 39 cities and towns named *Columbia;* the *Columbia River; Columbia University*, New York City's *King's College* was renamed *Columbia College* after the Revolutionary War, in 1794, and grew into the university. *Columbian*, an American, 1789.

The District of Columbia, on land given to the nation in 1790 by Virginia and Maryland but not generally talked about until President Adams and the Congress moved to Washington from Philadelphia in 1800.

Columbus, Ohio, and at least 21 other cities and towns named *Columbus*.

The Knights of Columbus, a Catholic fraternal order founded in 1882 and instrumental in making Columbus Day a legal holiday.

Columbus Day was celebrated on October 12, 1792, the 300th anniversary of the discovery of America, and again in 1892, when New York City's *Columbus Circle* was built and a statue to Columbus erected there. It began to be observed widely on an annual basis in 1893, the year of the Chicago *World's Columbian Exposition*, which celebrated the 400th anniversary of Columbus's discovery a year late.

Amerigo Vespucci first came to America in 1497 and was the first major navigator to recognize it as a new continent rather than thinking it a part of Asia. His first name gives us *America* (see AMERICA AND THE UNITED STATES). Giovanni da Verrazano came to America in 1524 and explored our Atlantic coast. He gave us only one major name, New York's 1964 *Verrazano-Narrows Bridge*, connecting Brooklyn and Staten Island over the bay he discovered, New York Bay.

Despite these early Italian navigators, few Italians immigrated to America until after 1865. Then over 5 million Italians came to the U.S. as part of the New Immigration (see THE IMMIGRANTS). They usually settled in large northeastern cities, in sections soon called *Little Italy*. Other Americans had a confused image of them, often talking about them as stereotyped organ grinders, ice men, fruit vendors, shoemakers, boxers, politicians, opera singers, and gangsters. Most Italians, of course, were none of these things: most of them found work in American factories.

Many of the Italian words in English entered the language during the Renaissance when Italian culture was very much in vogue. Thus English has had *gondola* (from Italian *gondolar*, to rock) and *piazza* (Italian for public square, market square) since the 16th century; Italian musical terms such as *allegro*, *duet*, *opera*, *piano*, *staccato*, *trill*, and *violin;* and other words from Italian such as *balcony*, *cameo*, *granite*, *grotto*, *portico*, *stanza*, *umbrella*, and *volcano*. Words which have come directly into American English from Italian or our experience with Italians include:

fascist and *fascism* (from Italian *fascio*, political club), first heard in America in 1919 when Benito Mussolini formed his *Fascio di Combattimento*, its members were called *Fascisti* and Mussolini's brand of totalitarian government *fascism*.

pizza (an Italian word, perhaps from *pizzicare*, to pinch, prick, pluck, which also gives us the Italian musical term *pizzicato*) has had growing popularity in America since the 1940s; *pizzeria*, 1940s; *pizza parlor*, late 1940s.

Caricature of an Italian organ grinder, 1906.

spaghetti (Italian for "little string") was first common in America in the 1880s. The word entered both American and British English only in the 19th century.

tutti-frutti ice cream, 1876. It means "all fruits" (see ICE CREAM).

Many other Italian borrowings are only partially naturalized, still being associated mainly with Italians or things Italian. Thus we have dozens of Italian food terms such as *café espresso* or *espresso* (Italian, literally "pressed out," by the steam), *cannelloni* (literally "big pipe"), *dulce* ("sweet"), *lasagna* (literally "cooking pot"), *minestrone* ("to serve, dish out"), *parmesan* ("from Parma"), *pasta* ("paste, dough") and *antipasto* ("before the pasta" course), *ravioli* (literally "little turnips," from the shape), *spumone* ("spume,

Enrico Caruso (1873–1921), famous tenor (top left); Fiorello La Guardia (1882–1944), mayor of New York City, 1934–44 (top center); Eleonora Duse (1859–1924), actress (top right); Arturo Toscanini (1867–1957), symphonic conductor (bottom left); Joe Di Maggio (1914–), baseball player (bottom center); Frank Sinatra (1915–), singer and actor (bottom right).

216

*Yankee Doodle went to town
A ridin' on a pony;
He stuck a feather in his cap
And called it macaroni.*

The word *macaroni* (Italian *maccaroni*, groats) has been in the English language since the 16th century. It was 18th century slang for a fop or dandy because London's Macaroni Club was well known for its dandies.

froth"), *tortoni* (popularized by Italians but probably invented and named for a 19th century Parisian restaurateur named Tortoni), and *vermicelli* (literally "little worms"). Other not yet naturalized Italian borrowings include *arrivederci*, until we meet again; *patrone*, patron, master, employer; and *subito*, best known as a musical direction but also meaning "quick, suddenly" in other contexts.

As have all other immigrant groups, especially New Immigrants, the Italians have been called by a variety of derogatory names, most dating from the 1880s and 90s when Italian immigration was reaching its peak:

Eyetalian, 1840; *Eytie, Eyetie*, World War II.
Dago (from the common Spanish name *Diego*), this originally meant a Spaniard in 1832, then came to mean an Italian by 1887. *Dago red*, cheap Italian red wine, especially Chianti, 1900; *Dago bomb*, a round, bomblike firecracker, 1935.
guinea originally meant a Black from the Guinea coast of Africa in 1789, then came to mean an Italian in the mid 1880s; *ginny*, 1910; *ginzo*, 1920. *Guinea football*, a small bomb or hand grenade, a synonym for the gangsters' "pineapple," 1920s; *guinea red*, 1944, cheap Italian red wine, a variant of *Dago red*.
wop, mid 1890s. By the 1920s the word was used in combinations such as *wop house*, an Italian restaurant; *wop special*, an order of a plate of spaghetti; and *wop land*, Italy. It comes from the Neapolitan dialect's *guappo*, a dandy (literally a handsome man), later used as a Neapolitan greeting and by other Italians to refer to a Neapolitan. The oft-repeated story that *wop* comes from a tag attached by immigration authorities to immigrants arriving without a passport and bearing the initials W.O.P. (*With-out passport*) isn't true.
greaseball, 1935. The term has been applied to Italians, Spaniards, other southern Europeans and Latin Americans.

The Italians have also given us many famous "American" names as Ameche (Amici), Capone, Caruso, DiMaggio, Galento, Galli-Curci, Gallo, La Guardia, Landis (Landi), Lanza, Marcantonio, Romero, Sacco, Sinatra, Valentino, and Vanzetti; scores of other family names such as Alberti, Boniface (Bonifazio), Conti, Little (translation of Piccolo), Oliver (Olivieri), Pope (Pape), and Russo; as well as many Tonys (Antonio), Vincents (Vincenzo), and Richards (who are Ricardos).

Jails and Jailbirds

Jail and *gaol* are two forms of the same word (from Latin *cavea*, cave). By the 1640s the British, including our colonists, were using the *gaol* variant, but by 1776 the *jail* form was taking over in America.

Since jails were first established in the 12th century merely to hold people awaiting trial (by colonial times they were debtors' prisons), *jail* has always had a less foreboding meaning than the 11th century word *prison* (via French from Latin *prehendere*, to

217

seize). *Penitentiary* (literally "a place for penitents") is an American word dating from 1790, when the Quaker state of Pennsylvania built a special cell block to separate more serious offenders from lesser ones; thus penitentiaries were considered part of prison reform at the time. We've had a lot of other words for jails and penitentiaries, including:

workhouse, a 1533 British term, first recorded in America in 1653.

the clink, an 18th century term (originally the name of a London jail) that became popular around 1918.

calaboose, 1792, but it didn't become common until cowboys popularized it in the 1860s (from Spanish *calabozo*, dungeon).

reformatory became a common American word after the Elmira, New York, reformatory opened in 1807.

jailhouse, 1812.

the jug, 1815 (probably from Spanish *juzgado*, see *hoosegow*, below).

the lockup, 1839.

hoosegow, an 1860s cowboy term (from Spanish *juzgado*, sentenced, jailed).

pen, short for penitentiary, 1870.

the cooler, 1884, originally a special cell for "cooling off" drunks or violent prisoners.

the joint, a penitentiary, 1890s.

the big house, a penitentiary, especially Sing Sing, 1900.

the can, 1910.

the pokey, 1919 (from *pogy*, an 1891 word for a workhouse, poorhouse, or old people's home, from *poke*, to confine).

the tank, 1920s; *fish tank*, 1939, a large cell for holding suspects or new prisoners (*fish* had meant newcomer, novice since around 1900); *drunk tank*, 1943, a large cell for holding drunks overnight.

The Rock, Alcatraz penitentiary, 1930s. Located on rocklike Alcatraz Island in San Francisco Bay, this was a military prison after 1858 and a federal prison from 1933 to 1963.

the slammer, *the slam*, mid 1930s. Long before that *slammer* was the underworld slang for "door."

Alcatraz Island, about 1960. As a Federal prison, Alcatraz symbolized harsh discipline and maximum security.

Originally A RACE OF CONVICTS and *convict servants* (1651, indentured servants) and now with a prison population of well over 200,000, we Americans have always used a lot of prison terms and been fascinated by crime, jails, and convicts. Here are some of our most common terms associated with jails and convicts:

gaolbird, an habitual criminal, 17th century; *jailbird*, 1814.

yard, a prison yard, 1777; *yardbird*, a convict or ex-convict, 1920s.

jail fever, typhus, 1780. Many prisoners had it due to lice infestation in prisons.

solitary confinement, 1780s. Originally it was spoken of highly

Sing Sing, 1878, showing prisoners marching in lock step. Lock step was a part of penal management that enforced silence at all times.

as one of the Pennsylvania prison reforms, because it replaced the brutal floggings then given recalcitrant prisoners.

prison walls, 1782; *prison hospital*, 1850s. The game of *prisoner's base* dates to the 1840s.

chain gang, 1835.

do time, 1860.

take the rap, 1886; *bum rap*, 1927; *beat the rap*, 1931. *Rap* had meant blame, rebuke, a "rap on the knuckles" since 1777.

con, short for convict, 1890.

screw, jailer, prison guard, 1891. By 1851 *screw* had meant a harsh disciplinarian, figuratively one who put the thumbscrews on.

frame-up, 1900; *frame*, 1914.

fall guy, 1906.

to be sent up the river, sent to prison, 1930s. Originally this meant to be sent to Sing Sing, which is up the Hudson River from New York City, at Ossining, New York. *Sing Sing* prison was built around 1830 at *Sing Sing*, New York, which changed its name to *Ossining* in 1901 (both words are from the Delaware Indian *assinesink*, "at the place of the small stone").

two-time loser, 1930s. This means a desperate criminal because in some states a person who has been convicted twice for major crimes faces mandatory life imprisonment for a third conviction.

Sing Sing, about 1915, originally noted for its brutal discipline, was reformed by Warden Thomas Mott Osborne (1859–1926), shown here in a typical cell block.

Jesse James

Of the American BADMEN who are popular topics of conversation, ballads, and stories, Jesse James may have an excuse for being romanticized. He did have Southern sympathizers in his lifetime who helped him evade the authorities. Born on a Clay County, Missouri, farm in 1847, Jesse was to know his father's death at four, and his Southern-sympathizing household was to know two stepfathers and two Northern militia raids before the boy joined William Quantrill's guerrilla raiders at 15. He surrendered after the Civil War but was shot and became a fugitive, forming a gang with his brother, Frank, the Younger Brothers, and others, and embarking on a 15-year career of robbery.

Jesse James was a two-gun man.
William Rose Benét, poem "Jesse James: American Myth"

Jesse James

Frank James

"The James Boys'" highly publicized exploits included an 1873 robbery of a Rock Island train in Iowa and a disastrous attempt on a Northfield, Minnesota bank in August, 1876, in which all the gang but Jesse and Frank were killed or captured. Jesse is supposed to have then "retired" until 1879 when he headed a new gang while living a supposedly quiet life in St. Joseph, Missouri, under the name of Thomas Howard. On April 3, 1882, prompted by a state reward of $10,000, gang members Robert and Charles Ford shot Jesse James in the back of the head, killing him instantly. Brother Frank later surrendered, was twice tried and acquitted, and lived out his years on his Missouri farm until his natural death in 1915.

The Jews

Old Synagogue, Charleston, South Carolina.

who came to America never spoke Hebrew as their native language—Hebrew is used only in prayer and religious ceremonies (in modern times it is also the official language of the state of Israel). Thus from the first 23 Dutch Jews who came to New Amsterdam from Brazil in 1654, to the 2,500 Jews attending religious services in 1776 (mainly in such cities as New York, Philadelphia, Newport, Charleston, and Savannah), to the 200,000 German Jews who came to America between 1840 and 1860, Jewish immigrants influenced the American language by bringing the language of their native lands: English, German, Dutch, French, etc. Most of the Jewish immigrants to colonial America were *Sephardic* Jews (from Hebrew *Sephāradhi/Sephāradh*, Spanish, Spain), following the Jewish liturgy and customs developed in Spain and spread elsewhere when the Jews were exiled during the Spanish Inquisition in 1492, by edict of Ferdinand and Isabella.

The 200,000 *German Jews* (1865) who came to America between 1840 and 1860 came as part of the educated, middle class, urban German immigrant group called the *48ers* (see THE GERMANS). They settled where the other German *48ers* did, usually in the Midwest and in cities along the Ohio and Mississippi, as in Chicago, Cincinnati, Milwaukee, etc. As late as 1880 America still

220

frequently referred to its 250,000 Jews not as Jews but as *Hebrews* or *Israelites*.

Then between 1880 and 1910 almost 3 million Central and Eastern European Yiddish-speaking Jews came to America as part of that great wave of *New Immigrants* (see THE IMMIGRANTS). Though they came from many different countries, each was an *Ashkenazi*, a Central or Eastern European Jew as opposed to a Sephardic or German Jew (from *Ashkenaz*, an ancient kingdom in Armenia, named for the Biblical Ashkenaz, the grandson of Japheth and son of Gomer). Like other New Immigrants, these Jews usually first landed in New York, stayed in the big cities, and were disliked for being "different," poor, and uneducated (at least in American ways). Many of these Jews stayed in New York's *Lower East Side* (1890s), working in factories, as pushcart vendors, waiters, janitors, and, typically, in the crowded rooms, lofts, and shops called *sweatshops* (1892), wielding needles and scissors for the middlemen *sweaters* (1890s) of the garment industry. Now the Jews were called Jews and, as was true of all New Immigrant groups, derogatory terms for and about them became common, ranging from the centuries old *Christ killer* and *dirty Jew* to:

Hebe, from *Hebrew*; most common after the mid 1920s.

to jew, haggle, drive a hard bargain, 1824; *to jew down*, 1870.

Jew boy, for a man, 1861; *Jew bastard*, 1860s.

Jew butter, goose grease, 1889; *a Jewish flag*, a dollar bill, 1922.

kike, 1880s, originally a disparaging term used by the successful and assimilated American German Jews for a newly arrived Central or Eastern European Ashkenazi Jew. Most linguists say *kike* derives from the fact that many of the Jewish immigrants of 1880–1910 had Slavic names ending in *-(s)ki* or *-(s)ky*, they had "ki-key" type last names. However, in his 1968 *The Joys of Yiddish*, Leo Rosten, using an observation made by Philip Cowen, "the dean of immigration inspectors" at Ellis Island, says *kike* was born on Ellis Island where Jews who did not know the Roman-English alphabet refused to sign entry forms with the customary Christian cross or X and made a *kikel* (the Yiddish word for circle) instead. Soon immigration authorities were calling anyone who signed with a circle instead of an X a *kikel* and finally a *kike*.

mockie, late 1930s.

sheeny, 1824. Some linguists say this term is from the German *schön*, beautiful, pretty, because Jewish peddlers and merchants used the word so often in describing their merchandise; others suggest the word may come from the Yiddish expression "a miesse meshina," meaning an ugly fate or an ugly death.

Yid, 1874. This is from German *Jude*, Russian *Zhyd*, Jew, a short form of *Yehuda*, the name of the Jewish commonwealth in the period of the Second Temple (named after Yehuda, or Judah, the son of Jacob, whose descendants made up one of the tribes of Israel).

A Jewish street peddler, New York City, 1890s.

The almost 3 million Ashkenazi Jews who came to America between 1880 and 1910 had a unique influence on the American language—they spoke Yiddish, and brought Yiddish words, intonation, and syntax to America. *Yiddish* (from German *judisch*, Jewish, see *Yid* in the list above) is the 1,000-year-old language of these Central and Eastern European Jews. It began when Jews from northern France first moved into the Rhineland and began to write German words with the letters of the Hebrew alphabet (shunning the Latin alphabet of Christians and Christian monks). Eventually this led to their pronouncing the German words differently than the Germans did. Yiddish is still written in the Hebrew alphabet, from right to left, and 70–75% of its vocabulary is still based on German words, the rest of its vocabulary being about 15–20% Hebrew and a mixture of words from Polish, Russian, Rumanian, Ukranian, and Slavic dialects, added as the Jews traveled and migrated over the centuries. Yiddish was the language of the ghettos and the shtetles, those two places where so many Jews were forced by laws, edicts, and police to herd together, isolated from time and the mainstream of European culture.

ghetto was first defined in English in 1611, as a place where Jews dwell; it's from the Italian *borghetto*, little boro, the section of Italian towns to which Jews were restricted. By the late 1880s in America it meant any poor, crowded Jewish neighborhood, by the late 1950s it meant any slum section occupied by any ethnic group, and since the early 1960s it has usually meant a Black slum area.

shtetle literally means little city, village (a diminutive based on the German *Stadt*), it refers to a peasant village of Eastern European Jews, especially in Russia, where under the watchful eyes of the police and unable to own land or practice certain crafts and trades, the Jews carried on rural village life and developed an Ashkenazi liturgy and culture different from that of the Sephardic Jews and German Jews.

Pushcart vendor, Lower East Side, about 1905. This section of New York City became a Jewish ghetto and is still noted for its sidewalk shopping, bargain stores, and restaurants.

Here Yiddish flourished, many Jews, who were excluded from state schools, never learning or using the language of the country in which they lived and died.

As the Yiddish-speaking Jews met and mingled with other Americans, Yiddish words spread out of the ghetto, often via Jewish authors and comedians, first in newspapers, magazines, and vaudeville, then in radio, the movies, and television. Thus Yiddish has contributed such terms to our language as:

alter kocker (from German *alter*, old + *kocker*, excrement, shit, literally "old shit") old man, old fogey, also abbreviated as *A.K.*, mid 1930s.

bagel (via Yiddish *beygel* from German *Beugel*, round loaf of bread, from *baug-*, ring) a chewy, ring-shaped yeast roll that is dipped into boiling water before being baked.

blintz (via Yiddish *blintse* from Ukranian *blinyets*, the diminutive of *blin*, buckwheat pancake) a filled, rolled pancake with a sour cream topping.

chozzerai (from Hebrew *chazir*, pig, hence "awful food"), junk, trash, worthless articles, lies, etc.

chutzpa(h) (from Hebrew for insolence, audacity), impudence, gall, unmitigated audacity.

dreck (German *Dreck*, filth, dung), trash, junk, inferior things.

feh! (probably from German *pfui*), phooey.

fin (via Yiddish *finf*, *finif* from German *funf*, five), a $5 bill. Used in American English since before 1920.

fresser (from German *fressen*, to devour), one who eats a lot, one who snacks a lot, usually in the expression *little fresser*, applied to children.

gefilte fish, *gefulte fish* (via the Yiddish, where it is often *kafilte fish*, from German *gefullte Fische*, stuffed fish), chopped, chilled fishcakes, usually round or oval.

gelt (from German *Geld*, money), English slang since 1698, first recorded in the U.S. in 1889.

gevalt!, *Oy gevalt!* (from German *Gevalt*, powers, force), an exclamation of despair, dread, protest, or amazement (see *oy!* below).

gonif (via Yiddish *ganef* from Hebrew *gannābh*, *ganov*, thief), first recorded in England in 1835 and in the U.S. in 1845.

goy (from Hebrew *gōy*, *goi*, people, nation, non-Jews) a non-Jew, gentile.

halva, *halava* (via Yiddish and Rumanian from Turkish and Arabic) a ground sesame seed candy using honey as a binder.

ish kabible (perhaps from *es is mein diege* or a similar Yiddish expression meaning "it's my worry"), I should worry, a popular fad expression of 1910.

kibitz (via Yiddish *kibitsen* from German *kiebitzen*, to look on, hover around, from German *Kiebitz*, literally lapwing, plover, figuratively to be a busybody, watch, hover around) to watch a card game and give unwanted advice to the players, 1928; to give gratuitous advice, meddle, second guess.

knish (via Yiddish from Ukranian *knyš*, Polish *knysz*), a baked or fried dumpling filled with groats, grated potatoes, onions, cheese, or chopped liver.

kosher (via Yiddish from Hebrew *kāshēr*, right, fit, proper), ritually clean according to Jewish dietary laws, fit to eat; American slang use to mean legitimate, honest, authentic, 1924.

krechtz (from German *krächzen*, to croak), to complain, protest, groan, grumble.

kreplach (via Yiddish *kreplech*, plural of *krepel*, from German dialect *Kräppel*, fritter, German *Krapfen*, apple fritter, and akin to French *crêpe* from Latin *crīsp(us)*, curled, wrinkled), a small pocket of noodle dough filled with chopped meat, chicken livers, or cheese and served in soup, humorously called "Jewish ravioli."

landsman (from German *Lantsmann*, compatriot, fellow countryman), a person who comes from the same town or region as oneself.

latke (from Russian *latka*) a grated potato pancake.

L'chaim, *L'chayim* (from Hebrew *lehayim*), to life, cheers, used as a toast.

lox (via Yiddish *laks* from German *Lachs*, salmon), smoked salmon.

matzo, *matzah* (via Yiddish *matse* from Hebrew *massāh*), thin, flat, crackerlike unleavened bread, as eaten during Passover.

mavin (from a Hebrew word for "understanding"), an expert, connoisseur.

mazel tov (from Hebrew mazāl, luck + tov, tob, good), good luck, congratulations.

mazuma (via Yiddish mezūmen from Hebrew mezūmān, set, fixed, prepared, ready, from Chaldean "the ready necessary"), used to mean money, cash in America since 1880; the original Chaldean use is the same as our slang terms for money or cash the ready (1890), the necessary.

megillah, the whole megillah (from Hebrew megillāh, scroll, from gālal, to roll), literally one of the five scrolls in the synagogue but especially the one containing the long, rambling, detailed Book of Esther, which is read during the Purim holiday and seems even longer after a day of fasting; figuratively, a long rambling story, an account with too many details.

mensch, mensh (from German Mensch, man, person), a manly, purposeful man, one who stands up for his rights or the rights of others.

meshuga, meshugge (from Hebrew meshuggā, crazy), crazy, insane, foolish, in American use since the 1880s. Meshugass, craziness, nonsense, foolishness, insanity; meshugana, a crazy or foolhardy person, though sometimes now used for meshuga, crazy.

momzer, mamzer (from Hebrew mamzēr bastard, more precisely a child born of a marriage forbidden by Judaism, which could include a child born of an incestuous marriage, of a mixed marriage, etc.), a detestable man.

nebbish (may be from the Czech neboky or from some old Yiddish neb/nib word meaning beginner), an ineffectual person, an insignificant, apologetic person.

nosh (from German naschen, to nibble, eat on the sly), to snack, a snack; nosher, one who snacks habitually; nosheri, snacks, as potato chips, nuts, etc.

nu? (German dialect and Russian nu), well? so? so what?

nudnik (from Russian nudna) a pest, annoying person, boring person.

oy!, oy vay! an exclamation of despair, fear, surprise, etc. Oy vay! translates, "woe is me." Exclamations such as aha! and ai-yi-yi! are sometimes given a Yiddish pronunciation or intonation and their popularity has been influenced by Yiddish-speaking people, but aha! (a + ha!) is a cry of discovery or surprise from 18th century England and ay! a cry of surprise, sorrow, or pity used in English since the 14th century. Hoo ha!, an exclamation of envy, scorn, or admiration, certainly has Yiddish intonation and was first widely heard as used by comedian Arnold Stang on the Henry Morgan radio show of the late 1940s (Stang there also popularized the Yiddish-sounding, rising and falling, "I tell him yes—he tells me no").

schlemiel, schlemiehl (via Yiddish schlemiel, this may come from the name Shelīmīel or Shlumiel, a general and son of a leader of the tribe of Simeon, mentioned in Numbers 2, who always seemed to lose his military battles, or it may be a variant of schlimazel or come from the Hebrew she-lu-m-el, s-l-msl, that which is not luck, one who is worthless), a foolish, gullible, unlucky, clumsy person, a fainthearted person,

"Shylock," portrayed by Jacob Adler in The Merchant of Venice. A money-lender who thinks more of his treasures than of even his daughter, Shylock is nevertheless a tragic figure: "Hath not a Jew eyes? If you prick us, do we not bleed? If you tickle us, do we not laugh? If you poison us, do we not die?" Shylock has passed into the language to mean a heartless, money-loving man and many Jews so resent Shakespeare's vivid and relentless portrait that they question the value of teaching this play in our schools.

Al Capp's shmoo, *that bountiful creature of the 1940s, gives milk, lays eggs, tastes like chicken, and has eyes that make fine suspender buttons.*

a social misfit, used in English since the 1890s. A classic distinction is that the *schlemiel* spills the soup on the *schlimazel* and the *nebbish* cleans it up.

schlep(p) (via Yiddish *shlep* from German *schleppen,* to drag), to drag, lug, carry, also to lag behind; one who is always dragging behind, a slow, lazy, untidy person. *Schlep(p)er,* one who carries or drags something; one who lags behind or is slow, lazy, and untidy.

schlimazel (via Yiddish *shlimazel,* bad luck, which may come from German *schlimm,* bad + Hebrew *mazāl,* luck or from the Hebrew *she-lu-m-el, s-l-msl,* that which is not luck, one who is worthless) a born loser, an unlucky person.

schlock (via Yiddish *shlock* from German *Schlag,* a blow, literally referring to damaged merchandise) a shoddy, cheaply made, fake, or defective article. *Schlock house,* a store that sells such articles.

schmaltz (via Yiddish *shmaltz* from German *Schmaltz,* grease, fat, drippings) grease, fat, especially rendered chicken fat; used in American English to mean excessive sentimentality, banality, "corn" since the late 1930s.

schmeer (via Yiddish *shmeer* from German *Schmiere,* literally grease, that which can be smeared, figuratively flattery, bribe) to bribe, "to grease one's palm" with a bribe or tip; *the whole schmeer,* the entire amount, the whole package, the whole deal.

schmooz(e), schmoos (via Yiddish *shmues* from Hebrew *shemu'oth,* heard things, rumor, gossip, idle talk) to have a talk, to gossip; a talk, a chat. Used in American English since the early 1940s.

schmuck (via Yiddish *shmuck,* penis, from German *Schmuck,* ornament, jewelry), a dumb, clumsy, bumbling person, a detestable person. Calling a person a *schmuck* is the same as calling him a *prick* (1932).

schnook (via Yiddish *shnok, shmok* from Slovenian *smok*) one who gets the blame, a gullible person, fall guy or goat, American use, 1948; a dumb and hapless person. *Schmo* is a variant of *schnook* (coming from Yiddish *shmok* rather than its variant *shnok*). In Al Capp's comic strip *L'il Abner* the *shmoo* was a lovable egg-shaped creature that loved to be kicked, gave milk to drink, and when fried tasted like chicken.

schnorrer (via Yiddish *shnorrer* from German *schnorrer,* beggar, one who begs in the street while playing a pipe or horn, from German *snurrer,* to hum, whir) a beggar, chronic borrower, or cheapskate.

schnoz, schnozzle, schnozzola (Yiddish *shnoits,* snout, and its affectionate diminutive *shnoitsl* from German *Schnauze,* snout) nose, especially a large one, 1930. *Schnozzola* was also an affectionate nickname for the large-nosed comedian Jimmy Durante.

schvartz(er), schwartz(er) (via Yiddish *shvartz, shvartzer* from German *schwarz,* black) a Black person, Black; gloomy, black.

shamus (from Hebrew *shamash, shomus,* servant, a synagogue caretaker or sexton), a hotel detective, a private detective, 1934.

shekel (via Hebrew *sheqel,* weight, coin, from an ancient Babylonian unit of weight equal to about 2/3 of an ounce, then a silver coin weighing this amount, the most important silver coin in Biblical times, mentioned in Genesis 33:12–16 and Exodus 30:13), a coin, a dollar, 1871; *shekels,* money, cash.

Rabbi Isaac Mayer Wise (1819–1900), born in Bohemia, helped organize the Union Hebrew Congregation in 1873 and the first U.S. rabbinical seminary, the Hebrew Union College, in 1875. He was instrumental in introducing Reform Judaism to America around 1885.

Abraham Cahan (1860–1951) set a precedent in the U.S. in 1882, the year he arrived from Vilna, by addressing an American Jewish audience in pure Yiddish. He then made a lasting contribution to the use of Yiddish in America by founding the Yiddish Jewish Daily Forward in 1897. This daily had a peak circulation of 237,000 in 1917, leading to a favorite Jewish immigrant expression, "It must be true—I read it in the Forward."

shikker (from Hebrew *shēkār*, strong drink, intoxicating beverage) drunk, 1890s. The same Hebrew word *shēkār* also gives us our word *cider* (by way of Greek, Latin, Old French, and Middle English).

shiksa (via Yiddish *shikse*, the feminine of *shegetz*, a Jew with gentile attitudes and behavior, hence it came to mean a non-Jew, from Hebrew *sheques*, blemish) a non-Jewish woman, especially a pretty, young one who might entice a "nice Jewish boy" away from his religion.

shtick (via Yiddish *shtik* from German *Stück*, piece) a piece; a piece of clowning, prank, trick; a characteristic piece of business used by an actor, hence a characteristic trait, gesture, detail, way of doing something, etc.; the essence, core, benefit, attraction.

toches, *tuches* (Hebrew *tokheth*, buttocks, ass), buttocks, ass, in American use since the 1880s. *T.L.* (abbreviation for *toches*/*epper* or *toches* *licker*) an "ass kisser," syncophant.

trayf (Hebrew *teref*, torn asunder; figuratively, of an animal, not slain or butchered in accord with ritual law, hence not kosher) not kosher, not eatable according to ritual law.

tsuris (Hebrew *tsarah*) trouble, distress, worries, woe, suffering.

tummeler, *tummler* (from German *Tummel*, tumult, commotion, sport, romping, in German a *Tummelplatz* is a playground), a social director and entertainer, as at a Catskill resort in the *Borscht Belt* (1935) near New York City, who sees that everyone has a good time by acting as the general buffoon, heckler, leader of group games, master of ceremonies, matchmaker, etc; a person who makes a lot of commotion but accomplishes little.

yarmulke, *yamulkah* (via Polish from a Tartar word for skullcap) a skullcap, worn especially during prayer and religious study by Orthodox and Conservative Jewish men.

yenta, *yente* (said to be taken humorously from the Italian *gentile*, French *gentille*, lady, well-bred), gossip, busybody; low-bred woman; shrew.

yontif (from Hebrew *yom*, day + *tov*, *tob*, good) religious holiday, celebration.

zaftig, *zoftig* (from German for "juicy") buxom, plump, well-rounded, said of a sexually appealing girl, 1940.

zhlub (from Slavic *zhlob*, a coarse, gauche fellow) a boorish slob.

The intonations and syntax of Yiddish (and the scornful fatalism developed in the ghetto and shtetle) have also given America such expressions as *Get lost*, *Give a look*, *He don't know from nothing*, *If you'll excuse the expression*, *I'm telling you*, *I need it like a hole in the head*, *I should live so long*, and *I should worry* (1915). It has also given us the prefix *schm-*, added to a word repeated to convey sarcasm or a "who cares?" attitude, as in *actor-schmactor*, *fancy-schmancy*, etc., and the noun-forming suffix *-nik* (from the Russian diminutive *-nik*) as in *nudnik* and *no goodnik*, though the popular *beatnik* of the late 1950s was probably influenced more by the first Russian manmade satellite, the Sput*nik*, than by the Yiddish use of *-nik*. Other words which we sometimes associate with Yiddish speakers actually come directly from German, Russian, Polish, etc., thus *bialystock* or *bialy*, a bagel-type roll with onions, may be Polish (from the Polish city of Bialystock where it originated), and *borscht* entered English from Russian (Russian *borshch*, cow parsnip, from which this soup was originally made, though it is now a beet soup).

Though the major influence of Jews on the American language has been Yiddish, most Americans know some Jewish religious terms, names of Jewish organizations, etc. Most such Jewish religious terms are from Hebrew and have been in English a long time, including *Sabbath*, in English since the 7th century, and *Jehovah*, first used in English in a translation made of the Bible in 1530 (*Sabbath* entered English on the lips of early Christian monks, the word coming via Greek and Latin from Hebrew *shābbāt/shābhāth*, to rest; *Jehovah* comes from the sacred tetragrammaton, or four-letter word, JHVH or YHWH, used for the inutterably sacred name of the Almighty, with the insertion of the vowel points of *Adonis*, lord). Thus besides the Yiddish borrowings listed above, other terms which Jews have added to our language (usually from Hebrew) include:

Justice Louis Brandeis (1856–1941) is remembered especially for his promotion of social and economic reform and for his judicial liberalism. Appointed by President Wilson, Brandeis served as Justice of the Supreme Court from 1916 to 1939.

bar mitzvah (Hebrew "son of the commandment") the confirmation ceremony at which a 13-year-old Jewish boy takes on the duties and status of a man.

B'nai Brith (Hebrew for "sons of the covenant") a fraternal and philanthropic Jewish society and community action group, a division of which is the *Anti-Defamation League*, organized in 1843.

bris (Hebrew *brith milah*, *brith* means covenant) the Jewish circumcision ceremony.

challah (Hebrew *hallāh*) the Sabbath and holiday loaf of braided white bread with an egg-white glaze.

Chanukah, Hanuk(k)ah (Hebrew *hanakkāh*, dedication), the "Feast of Lights" commemorating the victory of the Maccabees over the Syrians in 165 B.C. and the rededication of the Temple in Jerusalem.

Hadassah (after the New Hebrew for the Biblical Queen Esther), a women's Zionist organization, originally founded in New York City in 1912 by Henrietta Szold to improve health and educational conditions in Palestine.

Kaddish (from Aramaic *qaddīsh*, holy, holy one) one of the oldest, most solemn Jewish prayers, glorifying God and recited at given points during daily worship; also a five-verse form of this prayer recited by mourners.

menorah (Hebrew for "candlestick"), a candlabrum, especially the nine-branched one used in celebrating Chanukah or a seven-branched one celebrating the seven days of Creation.

mezuzah (Hebrew for "doorpost"), a small oblong container affixed to the right of the front doorjamb to consecrate a Jewish home; it contains a small rolled parchment of verses from Deuteronomy 6:4–9 and 11:13–21.

minyan (Hebrew for "number, reckoning") the minimum number of ten adult Jewish males necessary to begin certain ceremonies and religious services.

Passover (a combination of English *pass* + *over*) or *Pesach* (Hebrew *pesah*, a passing over), the seven or eight day festival

227

commemorating the Exodus of the ancient Jews from Egypt.

rabbi (used in English since the 14th century, via Latin and Greek from Hebrew *rabbī*, *rabh*, teacher, master + -*i*, my) the chief ordained religious leader and official of a synagogue; a title of respect to a Jewish scholar or teacher.

Rosh Hashanah (Hebrew for "beginning of the year"), the high holy day marking the beginning of the Jewish New Year.

sabra (New Hebrew, from the state of Israel, *sābrāh*, prickly pear, a plant common in the Negev) a native-born Israeli.

Seder (Hebrew for "order, division"), the ceremonial feast celebrated on the first night or first and second nights of Passover, including the eating of certain symbolic foods and the reading of the Haggadah, including stylized questions and answers, hymns, and prayers.

shofar (Hebrew for "trumpet, horn," especially a ram's horn), the ram's horn blown in the synagogue at Rosh Hashanah and Yom Kippur.

sholom, *sholem* (Hebrew for "whole, entire, peace"), peace, said as a salutation to mean both hello and good-by. The full traditional salutation is *Sholom aleichem*, "peace unto you," and the response is *Aleichem sholom*, "and to you, peace." Sholem Aleichem is also the penname of the Russian Jewish writer and humorist Solomon Rabinowitz (1859–1916) who lived in the U.S. the last ten years of his life; he is sometimes called "the Jewish Mark Twain," though it is said that on at least one occasion Mark Twain referred to himself as "the American Sholem Aleichem."

(Above, top to bottom) Solomon R. Guggenheim (1861–1949), financier and philanthropist; George Gershwin (1898–1937), Richard Tucker (1914–1975), tenor; (right top, left to right) Clifford Odets (1906–1963), playwright; Norman Mailer (1923–), writer; (below from left to right) the Marx brothers, Groucho (1895–), Chico (1891–1961), Harpo (1893–1964), and Zeppo (1901–), comedians.

228

synagogue, *shul*, and *temple* all mean a Jewish house of worship. *Synagogue* (from Greek *synagōgē*, assembly, congregation) meant a Jewish congregation in English by the 12th century and a Jewish house of worship by the 13th. *Shul* is a Yiddish word (from German *Schule*, school, since the Jewish houses of worship also traditionally served as the home of religious scholarship and instruction). *Temple* (via French from Latin *templum*, sanctuary) has been in English since before the year 1000. Reform Jews usually refer to their houses of worship as *temples* and Orthodox and Conservative Jews in the Yiddish-speaking Ashkenazi tradition often refer to theirs as *shules;* *synagogue* is the more general word to both Jews and non-Jews.

tallith, tallis (Hebrew for "cover") the fringed prayer shawl worn by Orthodox and Conservative Jewish men at prayer and for certain solemn occasions.

Talmud (Hebrew for "learning, instruction"), the massive compendium of 63 books containing the learned dialogues, debates, and commentaries of the scholars who interpreted the Torah.

Torah (Hebrew for "law") the Pentateuch, the first five books of the Old Testament, especially the scroll containing them and read in the synagogue on the Sabbath, festival days, and on Mondays and Thursdays.

United Jewish Appeal, abbreviated as the *UJA*, a Jewish fund-raising group originally formed in 1936 to help Nazi-persecuted Jews escape Germany. After World War II it helped Jews in displaced persons' camps and in assisting in their resettlement in Europe, America, and Israel, then continued helping such Jews with aid to Israel.

yeshiva (Hebrew for "academy," literally a place where one sits and studies), an Orthodox rabbinical seminary; an Orthodox Jewish school teaching both religious and secular subjects to children of elementary school age.

Yom Kippur (Hebrew for "the Day of Atonement"), the holiest Jewish holiday, in which fasting and prayer are prescribed for the atonement of one's sins.

As have all other immigrant groups, the Jews contributed many family names to America which have been widely heard, some because they belong to Americans who became famous, some because they have become so common. These include such last names as Berle, Cantor, Cohen, Copeland, Gershwin, Green, Heifetz, Horowitz, Jolson, Lehman, Lewisohn, Mailer, Morgenthau, Odets, Pearce, Schiff, Stein, Stern, Tucker, etc. However, no name can truly be said to be typically Jewish—because most American Jews have last names that are typical of their country of origin, German names, French names, Russian names, Polish names, Spanish names, etc. In fact, many Jews, especially descendants of New Immigrants, have typically English names, many original European names having been shortened, translated, or changed by immigration officials to American pronunciations and spellings.

The Korean Conflict

Before the end of World War II, the Allies agreed that Korea, which had been under Japanese rule for over 40 years, would be freed as an independent nation. For symbolic reasons we also agreed that Russian troops would accept the Japanese surrender of Korea north of the 38th parallel and American troops would accept the surrender south of this line. Once the surrender was completed, however, the Soviets claimed that the 38th parallel was a political boundary which divided Korea into two "occupation zones," and severed all communications between the two.

After two years of trying to get the Soviets to allow Korea to become a unified and free nation, the U.S. referred the "Korean problem" to the United Nations, which attempted to hold elections throughout all of Korea. However, the USSR refused to let its part of Korea participate in the elections, or even to allow UN representatives to enter it. Thus in 1948 the UN supervised free elections in the American zone only and these established the Republic of Korea (unofficially *South Korea*), with its capital at Seoul. We talked proudly of the new nation we had helped form. The Russians declared the UN actions illegal and established a Communist government in their zone, declaring it the People's Democratic Republic of Korea (unofficially *North Korea*), with Pyongyang as the capital. All occupation troops were withdrawn by mid 1949, with the Russian trained and equipped North Korean troops making frequent guerrilla raids on South Korea, which was defended by its own U.S. trained and equipped army.

On June 25, 1950, with the full approval of Stalin and Mao Tse-tung, North Korean troops, led by 100 Russian-built T-34 medium tanks, crossed the 38th parallel and invaded South Korea. The U.S. immediately sponsored a resolution in an emergency session of the UN Security Council which declared North Korea an aggressor and, on June 27, the Council called upon the UN's 52 member nations to repel the invasion. As a member of the Security Council the Soviet Union would have vetoed any such UN action, but its delegation was not there, having staged one of its widely talked-about *walkouts* earlier, temporarily boycotting the UN to protest its refusal to eject Chiang Kai-shek's Nationalist China after the Chinese Communists drove him from the mainland to Formosa (now Taiwan). The day the UN called for action, June 27, President Truman ordered the U.S. Air Force and the 7th Fleet to aid South Korea and to protect Nationalist Chinese occupied Formosa against possible Chinese Communist attack. Although 15 other UN countries sent at least a token number of combat troops to aid South Korea, it was understood that the U.S. would conduct the war and provide almost all the *United Na-*

South Korean child crying on the streets in Inchon.

United Nations forces fighting in the streets of Seoul.

tions forces, including naval and air support. The UN Security Council also asked Truman to name a Supreme Commander of the UN forces in Korea and he appointed World War II hero and commander of the occupation of Japan, General Douglas MacArthur.

At his first news conference after the fighting began, President Truman emphasized that we were not at war but were engaged in a *police action* under UN authority. Since we never declared war, Congress referred to it as *the Korean Conflict* in passing various military appropriations to fight it, though within a year most Americans called it *the Korean war*.

The North Korean forces took Seoul on June 29, 1950, four days after the invasion began, and by August had pushed the South Korean and newly arrived United Nations forces back to a perimeter defense at Pusan on the tip of the Korean peninsula—but we mainly talked about the brave delaying tactics of our captured General William F. Dean. Soon, enough troops and supplies arrived in Korea for MacArthur to counter-attack: on September 15 the U.S. 10th Army Corps surprised the North Korean army with a daring daylight amphibious landing at its rear at Inchon (30 miles north of Seoul), while the U.S. 8th Army launched an offensive from the Pusan perimeter. The UN forces pushed the North Koreans back to the 38th parallel by early October and, with the approval of the UN General Assembly, drove into North Korea, capturing Pyongyang October 20, and then, with the U.S. 7th Division leading the way, raced north, reaching the Yalu River, China's Manchurian border, on November 20. The war seemed almost over and we talked of an easy victory.

But as UN troops had moved north, there had been reports of Chinese Communist forces fighting with the North Koreans. In a November 6 communiqué MacArthur had complained of the Chinese who aided the North from their "privileged sanctuary" beyond the Yalu, where his observation planes and bombers were not allowed to go. The Chinese did have 850,000 troops massed behind the Yalu, and on November 26, 200,000 of

Medics carrying a wounded soldier. Two Korean laborers have stacked their "A" frames to watch.

them crossed the river and attacked the UN forces in the bitter cold. The Chinese said these troops were merely "volunteers" who wanted to help the North Koreans. Thus the tide turned again. The North Koreans and Chinese pushed the UN forces back toward the south—as Truman put the U.S. on a war basis, the UN General Assembly named Communist China an aggressor, and the Chinese called the U.S. a *paper tiger* (a term Mao Tse-tung had first begun to use to refer to the U.S. in 1946). The UN forces evacuated 100,000 troops and 98,000 refugees from Hungnam, North Korea, on December 24 and by early 1951 the UN forces had been driven back 70 miles below the 38th parallel. There the Communist advance was stopped and reversed, and by late April 200,000 South Korean and UN troops had forced the 500,000 Communist troops back again to the 38th parallel (almost 50% of the troops defending South Korea were American and almost half were South Korean, with a sprinkling of other UN troops; about 75% of the Communist troops were Chinese).

Meanwhile MacArthur publicly advocated blockading China, pursuing the North Korean Russian-built fighter planes across the Yalu to their bases in Manchuria, and permitting Chiang Kai-shek's Chinese Nationalist troops to join in the war against the Communists. President Truman, however, was determined not to risk World War III with China and Russia over Korea (especially since both sides would have atomic bombs, Russia having developed hers in 1949). He decided to settle for a Korea divided at the 38th parallel and to fight only a *limited war*, a new term at that time. MacArthur forced a showdown with the president on March 24 by allowing a Congressman to publish a letter in which the general threatened Communist China

"Long Toms" firing on Communist targets near Munema.

232

Marines land near Inchon Harbor.

with air and naval attacks. Truman then relieved MacArthur of his command on April 11—for publicly challenging the authority of the president, his commander in chief, specifically for disregarding the president's order to clear policy statements through the Defense Department.

General Matthew Ridgway succeeded MacArthur and the UN troops stopped a Communist "spring offensive" by mowing down its "human wave" attacks with infantry and artillery fire. After that defeat the Communists asked the UN for cease-fire talks, which began in July, 1951, but were broken off and begun again many times over the next two years. During those two years the fighting continued near the 38th parallel as the two sides fought small but bloody battles for control of strategic hill positions in central Korea and we continued heavy air and naval attacks on North Korean ports and bases.

In the summer of 1952 we talked about the main truce talks at Panmunjom near the 38th parallel and how the Communists rejected the UN proposal of *voluntary repatriation*—because over half of the 170,000 Communist prisoners of war were violently opposed to being sent home (eventually over 15,000 Chinese prisoners of war chose to go to Formosa and 8,000 North Korean ones chose to stay in South Korea, but to make a truce we forced 50,000 Communist prisoners to return home with the 75,000 who wanted to do so). Finally on July 27, 1953, a cease-fire was signed at Panmunjom and an uneasy peace prevailed, with joint UN and Communist *truce teams* policing the *DMZ* (see below). The Korean Conflict was over. U.S. losses were over 38,000 killed or missing in action and over 100,000 wounded; 70,000 South Koreans and 4,786 other UN troops had been killed in action, while the Communists had suffered a million and a half killed or wounded. Korea was still divided at the 38th parallel.

One of the obvious things shown by any list of Korean war terms is that there aren't many of them: the war made little impact here at home, we were not emotionally involved, and we talked about it as something far away and not very important. Rightly or wrongly, in our hearts and minds it was a "limited war." The new words used by our armed forces include several from the Japanese (such as *honcho* and *moose* in the list below) because at the beginning of the war U.S. troops were rushed into Korea from Japan, where they had been serving as part of our occupation forces after World War II—such terms became well known during the Korean war but are really from our postwar occupation of Japan. If you had heard America talking during the Korean war you would have heard such new terms as:

brainwashing, a new word of 1950, first used to refer to a combination of physical torture, threats, intimidation, promises, and around-the-clock indoctrination used by Communists to break down the loyalties of anti-Communist resistance fighters (it seems to be a direct translation of the Chinese Communist term for it, the Mandarin Chinese *hsi nao*, *hsi* meaning wash and *nao* brain). We used it widely at the end of the Korean war when all America was shocked to learn that some American prisoners had been successfully *brainwashed:* the term was first commonly heard when 21 American prisoners of war threw in their lot with the Chinese and remained in China; it was in the news soon again when we learned that American pilots who had falsely confessed to carrying out *germ warfare* (see below) had done so after brainwashing. By 1962 *brainwashing* had simply come to mean any changing of an alliance, belief, or opinion and *to brainwash* merely meant to convince thoroughly.

Chopper carrying wounded from the battlefield.

chopper, *whirly bird*, and *egg beater* all became common terms for a helicopter during the Korean war, the first war in which helicopters were used extensively to transport troops and supplies. *Helicopter* (from Greek *helix*, spiral + *pteros*, wing) had been in the language since the early 1900s (the Wright brothers built and experimented with helicopters), and the synonym *gyroplane* had been popular in the 1930s. Helicopters came into increasing use when Igor Sikorsky, a Russian engineer who came to the U.S. after the Russian Revolution, perfected the *single-rotor helicopter* in 1940, just in time for its use in observation and rescue work during World War II, which was when helicopters were first called *'copters*. Incidentally, the words *helipad* and *heliport* (*heli*copter + air*port*), had come into use in the 1940s.

DMZ, the abbreviation of *de*militarized *z*one, referred to the area on both sides of the 38th parallel, separating North and South Korean troops. Many Americans also used it to mean the 38th parallel itself. In the Vietnam war *the DMZ* meant the demilitarized zone centered on the 17th parallel, and the letters were also sometimes used to mean that dividing line between North and South Vietnam itself.

germ warfare had been a science fiction term until early 1952 when it appeared in newspaper headlines. Serious epidemics swept North Korea early that year and the population blamed the Communists for lack of proper medical care, food, and shelter. The Communists tried to shift the blame by charging the United Nations with "germ warfare," torturing and brainwashing 78 captured American pilots for four months until 38 of them confessed to dropping loads of cholera-infested

On guard in a foxhole while his buddy sleeps.

insects on North Korea. After the war the UN proved the charges false and all the pilots repudiated their confessions.

honcho saw wide U.S. armed forces use in Korea to mean leader, boss, man in charge, and soon entered general American slang (it's from Japanese *han*, squad + *cho*, leader, literally "squad leader," a corporal or sergeant).

Mama-san, literally "boss mother," was used by U.S. troops to mean a brothel madam. *Papa-san*, "boss man," the man in charge, was also used, the suffix *-san* being added to many English and pidgin words in imitation of Japanese use.

MIG alley was our term for the airspace over a chain of North Korean valleys where Soviet MIG-15 jet fighters from Manchuria often intercepted U.S. planes attacking North Korea from the south. The MIG-15 (*MIG* being series of Soviet jet fighters named after its designers *Mi*koyan and *G*urevich) was first used in the war in 1950 and was the newest and best Soviet fighter of the time, easily outflying our obsolete F-80 *Shooting Star*, being notably superior to our Republic F-84 *Thunderstreak*, and in some ways superior to our own latest F-86. However, U.S. pilots were vastly superior to whoever flew the Soviet planes (the Russians always denied that any Russian pilots were involved in the war) and we kept air superiority, using vast quantities of air power to support our troops and disrupt Communist supply lines. Even though U.S. fighter pilots were forbidden *hot pursuit* of the MIGs north of the Yalu as they fled to their home bases in Manchuria, in air-to-air combat they destroyed 1,108 Communist planes, including 838 MIG-15s, with a loss of only 114 American fighter planes.

moose (from Japanese *musume*, girl), our armed forces use in Korea for a native prostitute or sometimes for any girl or woman. Native women were also called *slant eyes* and, in opposition, Occidental women were referred to as *round eyes*. A Korean prostitute's shack, house, or room was called a *hooch* (from Japanese *uchi*, house) as was any house where a serviceman set up housekeeping with a native woman (for later uses of *hooch* see The Vietnam War).

mother fucker first achieved wide use during the Korean war, as explained at Fuck and Screw.

number 1 became a slang term among our troops, meaning the best, good. *Number 10* was then used to mean the worst, bad.

ROK was first used in 1948 as an abbreviation for the new *R*epublic *o*f *K*orea, then that same year was used as an adjective in the expression "ROK troops," and by 1949 was an acronym (pronounced as "rock" by our troops but sometimes as "rook" by civilians in the U.S.) used to refer to the South Korean army or any of its soldiers. We also used the acronym *katusa* (*K*orean *a*ttached *t*o the *U.S. A*rmy), which was also sometimes used to mean any South Korean soldier. South Korean troops were also called *friendlies* (see The Vietnam War for more about this use).

slant, meaning an Oriental or Asiatic, was in very common use with U.S. troops during the Korean war; it's from the older *slant eye*, which was also in wide use during the Korean war, as it had been in World War II (it was first used in the 1930s). We also called Orientals or Asiatics *gooks* (for details on this word see World War II).

A tired American soldier.

235

The Law West of the Pecos

was the name Justice of the Peace "Judge" Roy Bean (1825–1903) gave himself when he held court, with the aid of a single law book and a six-shooter, in his saloon in Vinegaroon (later Langtry), Texas, on the lower Pecos River. He opened his saloon in 1882, shortly after being appointed justice of the peace, and named it *Jersey Lily*, which was the nickname of the beautiful and popular English actress Lily Langtry, who had been born on the island of Jersey.

Leopold and Loeb

was the sensational topic of 1924. Everyone was talking about the two youths from wealthy, respected Chicago families, 18-year-old Nathan Leopold and 17-year-old Richard Loeb who had killed a friend and neighbor, 14-year-old Bobbie Franks. Leopold did it to prove he could commit a perfect crime, involving kidnaping, ransom, and

Nathan Leopold, Jr. (1906–71), Clarence Darrow (1857–1938), and Richard A. Loeb (1907–1936).

236

murder: they picked up young Franks after school, Leopold driving the car with the victim sitting next to him in front, Loeb sitting in back and killing Bobbie by hitting him on the head with a chisel. Many newspapers described the pair sensationally as wealthy young "thrill seekers," and the youths' lawyer, the famous Clarence Darrow, added to the interest. Darrow saved his clients from the death sentence, ending the sensational "Leopold-Loeb case" (they were sentenced to life imprisonment, Loeb dying in prison, Leopold paroled in 1958 and working with underprivileged children in Puerto Rico until his death).

Lickety Split, *lickety brindle, lickety-click, lickety cut,* and *lickety-switch* were terms of the 1830s and 40s for moving fast or doing something quickly. Many such expressions for speed or speeding up come from this period of the Industrial Revolution, when cities were growing, steam engines and trains were proliferating, and household clocks were first common. Some of our most common such expressions include:

as quick as lightning, 1763; *quick as greased lightning,* 1840s; *like a streak (of lightning)* 1890s. *Quick as a wink,* 1836; *quick as powder,* 1840; *quick as dust,* 1875; *quick as scat,* 1889.

I'll do it as soon as say Jack Robinson, 1778; *before you can say Jack Robinson,* 1832. This is attributed to a Jack Robinson who was so changeable that when calling on a neighbor he would often leave before he was announced.

to hustle, to move or work rapidly, energetically, or aggressively, 1830.

in a jiffy, in a jiff, 1830s.

pronto (Spanish for "quickly"), 1830s.

full chisel, full split, like split, mid 1830s; *hell to split,* 1867.

like smoke, 1833; *like a house afire,* late 1830s; *like 60,* 1869; *like jehu,* 1842; *like a shot,* 1840s; *like hell,* 1860s; *like mad,* 1895.

hell bent, 1835; *hell bent for leather,* late 1920s; *hell bent for breakfast,* 1931.

quicker than hell would scorch a feather, 1840s.

immediately if not sooner, 1840s.

shake a leg, 1840s.

lickety split, 1843. Puritans are said to have used this expression in the 17th century, but it became popular only in the 1840s.

zip, to go fast, 1852.

in less than a pig's whistle, 1859.

like hotcakes, 1859, applied only to the fast selling or "moving" of merchandise.

full blast, 1863; in the 1830s it meant "in the extreme."

P.D.Q., p.d.q., an abbreviation for "pretty damned quick," said to have been coined by the Boston Stock Company comedian Dan Maginnis around 1867.

get a move on, 1890s.

hot foot it, 1896.

make it snappy, 1915.

on the double, early 1940s, originally army use, from double-time marching.

The Lindbergh Kidnaping

was the most talked about crime of the 1930s. In March, 1932, German-born Bruno Hauptmann kidnaped two-year-old Charles Augustus Lindbergh, Jr., from his home in Hopewell, New Jersey, and later murdered him. That the infant

was the son of two of the nation's best-loved celebrities, aviation hero Charles Lindbergh and his wife Anne Morrow Lindbergh, led to sensational newspaper coverage of the crime and of Hauptmann's capture and trial. Hauptmann was electrocuted in 1936; the Lindberghs, shocked by the tragedy and the publicity, retired to Europe to lead more secluded lives; and kidnaping laws were tightened. *Kidnaping* became a fearful word to all American parents, and has remained so ever since.

Bruno Hauptmann and his wife during his trial.

Lynching

comes from Captain William Lynch, who in 1760 drew up a compact, the first *Lynch Law*, with his neighbors in Pittsylvania County, Virginia, to deal summarily with unsavory characters who seemed to them to be beyond the reach of the law. The word is said to have spread quickly, however, through the practices of another Lynch, also of Virginia, a Charles Lynch, planter and justice of the peace, who dispersed his own harsh *Lynch law* in the late 18th century.

By 1800 *lynching* was a common term that usually referred to tarring and feathering and to horsewhipping, but occasionally to shooting or hanging. It was the practice of such groups as the Regulators of New York, the Rangers of Pennsylvania, and various others who by the late 1850s were called *vigilantes* and *vigilante committees.*

It was not until after the Civil War that *lynching* came to mean vengeful, often public, executions, particularly by southern *lynch*

238

mobs, who between 1882 and 1936 killed over 3000 Blacks, often for the supposed crimes of being concerned with their rights or of "insulting" White women. In the West lynching was still applied mostly against lawless White men, though it had come to be a hanging matter there also, often at *necktie parties* (1837). But the term *to string up* seems to have come from books and movies, since it was not recorded until 1931. There were 87 such lynchings during Montana's frontier days—and other territories were much more lawless.

Mad!—Mad!—Mad!

Some Englishmen had used *mad* to mean angry since the 13th century, but after the 1750s this archaic use was condemned as a new and vulgar Americanism. John Witherspoon criticized it in 1781 and John Pickering listed it as American in his 1816 dictionary of Americanisms. By the 1840s, however, *mad* meaning angry was accepted and becoming standard, formal English. We also have a lot of other informal expressions for being angry, including:

have an ax to grind, 1815, originally used to mean being angry.

mad as a wet hen, 1821; *mad as a hornet*, 1833.

get one's dander up (perhaps from Scottish *dunder*, to ferment), 1830s; *get one's back up* (as a cat does when angry), 1840s.

in a huff (breathing heavily, huffing and puffing), 1830s; *huffy*, 1840s.

hot, 1846; *hot under the collar*, 1910s; *hot and bothered*, 1920s.

sour on, 1862.

peeved (from *peevish*), about 1915, *pet peeve*, 1918; *peeved off*, 1920s.

pee'd off, late 1930s; *pissed off*, common during World War II. It's possible that *pee'd off* comes from "*peeved off*" rather than *pee*, then was strengthened into *pissed off* by mistake.

ticked off, t'd off, tee'd off, 1940s.

Of course, *mad* also continues to mean insane or crazy; this had been a new English use when the first colonists came to America (*madhouse* dates from 1687 in England). We've had a lot of expressions referring to insanity and insane people since, many of them also used figuratively to refer to an eccentric, nonconformist, or one who is "insane" only on one subject. These include:

funny, meaning odd, 1806.

cracked, 1825; *crackbrain*, 1838; *crackbrained*, 1855; *crack-up*, mental or nervous breakdown, 1850s; *crackpot*, 1860s.

insane hospital, 1828; *insane asylum*, 1830.

crazy as a bedbug, 1832; *crazy as a loon*, 1845; *a crazy*, an insane person, 1870s; *crazy house*, an insane asylum, 1887; *crazy in the head*, 1912.

loco, 1840s in the West, 1880s generally (see SAGEBRUSH, LOCOWEED, TUMBLEWEED—AND JIMSON WEED).

pixilated (from British dialect *pixy-led*, led astray by pixies, hence confused, bewildered, senile), 1840s.

half-baked, 1842; half-cooked, 1877.

touched in the head, 1846; out of one's head, 1870s; wrong in the head, 1880s.

off one's head, 1850s; off one's chump, off one's nut, 1891; off, 1901; off one's trolley, 1896; off one's rocker, 1930s.

have a screw loose, 1860s; screwy, screwball, early 1930s.

looney (from lunatic), 1860s; looney bin, 1880s.

crank, 1870s.

nut, 1880s; nutty, nuts, 1890s; nut house, insane asylum, 1905; nutty as a fruitcake, 1935.

meshuga (via Yiddish from the Hebrew), 1880s. See THE JEWS.

daffy (from Scottish dialect daff, fool), 1890s.

bughouse, an insane asylum, 1890; meaning a crazy person, 1891.

booby hatch (perhaps from Spanish bobo, fool), insane asylum, 1897.

cuckoo, 1918.

funny house, funny farm, insane asylum, 1920s.

not all there, 1920s.

wacky (probably from the 1730s whack, a blow on the head), 1936.

weird, weirdie, early 1940s; weirdo, 1950s.

Marshal, Vigilante, and Posse

are words which are part of both the reality and the myth of the American West—yet none of them were originally western words. *Marshal* (Old High German *marah*, horse, which also gives us "mare" + *scalh* servant, hence horse servant) was first used in the colonies in 1642 to refer to an officer who served writs and collected fines. The first *federal* or *U.S. marshal* was appointed in 1789 and the term *city marshal* appeared in 1830. The word took on its western connotation in 1866 when the governor of the Oklahoma Territories appointed a *territorial marshal* having many of the duties of a sheriff.

A vigilante "court" in the West, with the rope being strung up before the "trial" was over.

240

"Peace Commissioners" of Dodge City, Kansas, early 1870s. Bat (William Barclay) Masterson (1853–1921) became a well-known sports writer in New York City after his days on the frontier were over. Wyatt Earp (1848–1929) was a notorious gunfighter, gaining fame in the battle at the O.K. Corral (bottom left center).

Vigilante is a Spanish word for vigilant (from Latin *vigilāns*, kept awake, wide awake) and was in common use in America by the 1830s when many communities, especially in the South, had "Committees of Vigilance" or "Vigilanty Associations." These not only maintained order by hanging murderers and horse thieves, but helped maintain conformity by intimidating anyone suspected of immorality or what was considered wrong thinking. The Vigilantes spread westward with southerners, the most successful group in the West being the San Francisco Vigilance Committee which curbed Barbary Coast desperadoes in the gold-mining days of the 1850s. In the South before the Civil War *vigilantes* came to mean organizations for intimidating Blacks and abolitionists, forerunners of the Ku Klux Klan and other "night riders." As late as the 1880s *vigilante man* and *vigilante police* were fairly common terms in the South. .

Posse may sound western, but it comes from a Medieval Latin and legal term *posse comitātūs* (power of the country, armed force). Long before the first American settlement it referred to a body of men a sheriff called to assist him. It became associated with the American West during the 1860s.

Memorial Day

was originally set aside to remember the Civil War dead by decorating their graves with flowers; hence the two names *Memorial Day* and *Decoration Day*. Although Boalsburg, Pennsylvania claims to have had a Memorial Day in 1864, Waterloo, New York is usually credited with having the first true Memorial Day observance, on May 5, 1866, which included flying the village flags at half-staff, a veterans' parade, and a march to the village cemeteries where speeches were made. The first nationwide *Decoration Day* was planned and held in 1868 by *the Grand Army of the Republic*, formed by Union Army veterans in 1866 (primarily to get Congress to provide veterans' pensions and aid to soldiers' widows and orphans). It was

In Flanders fields the poppies blow
Between the crosses, row on row.

"In Flanders Fields," a very popular World War I poem written for the London *Punch*, December 8, 1915, by John McCrae, a Canadian who commanded a dressing station at the Second Battle of Ypres and who was later killed in the war. The American War Cemetery in Flanders, at Waereghem, Belgium, contains 368 American graves.

for the purpose of strewing with flowers or otherwise decorating the graves of the Comrades who died in defense of their country during the late rebellion and whose bodies lie in almost every city, village or hamlet churchyard in the land.

Order sent to local posts of the Grand Army of the Republic by its commander-in-chief General John A. Logan, for observing May 30th, 1868 as Decoration Day.

The date, May 30th, had no real significance, though it is roughly the anniversary of the surrender of the last Confederate Army (General Kirby Smith's, on May 26, 1865). A *Confederate Memorial Day* was soon observed in some southern states, varying from April 26th (the date of the surrender of Gen. Joseph

241

Johnson at Durham Station, North Carolina, 1865) to June 3rd (Jefferson Davis' birthday).

After World War I *the American Legion* (chartered in 1919) took over planning the observance, which became a memorial day for American servicemen from all wars. Soon, however, it was also known as *Poppy Day*, these flowers having become the symbol of the tragedy of World War I because they bloomed profusely in French battlefield graveyards. Poppies had originally been sold on street corners during World War I for the benefit of French and Belgian war orphans; then in 1922 the Veterans of Foreign Wars conducted the first nationwide "poppy sale" for disabled and destitute American war veterans. In 1971 Memorial Day was changed to the last Monday in May, making it one of several official three-day weekends.

Decoration Day, 1876, America's centennial year. Orphans are placing flags on their fathers' graves in Glenwood Cemetery, Philadelphia.

The Mexican War,

*They jest want this Californy
So's to lug new slave-States in
To abuse ye, an' to scorn ye, An' to plunder ye like sin.*
James Russell Lowell, *The Biglow Papers*, 1st series, written 1846-48. Other abolitionists who were against Texas annexation and the Mexican War wrote pamphlets for the *Anti-Texass Legion*, delighting in spelling Texas as Tex*ass*.

1846-48, was called that from the beginning. It was necessitated by our belief in manifest destiny—we wanted the Mexican territories of New Mexico and California—but its direct cause was our annexation of Texas, December 29, 1845, which Mexico had never recognized as an independent republic (see REMEMBER THE ALAMO! and 54-40 OR FIGHT!—MANIFEST DESTINY). Upon the annexation, the U.S. pressed Texas' claims against Mexico for damages suffered in its war for independence and the assertion that its southern boundary was the Rio Grande, not the Nueces River. President Polk sent John Slidell to negotiate these claims with Mexico and, if possible, to purchase the New Mexico and California lands. When Mexico refused to negotiate, Polk sent General Zachary Taylor to Texas, in January, 1846, with a 3,000-man "army of observation." In March this army moved into the disputed area between the Rio Grande and the Nueces and on April 25th the Mexicans ambushed one of its scouting parties, claiming it was on Mexican soil. Polk said the Mexicans had "invaded our territory ... [and] shed American blood on American soil." Congress declared war on Mexico, May 13, 1846.

Throughout its entire two years the Mexican War was as hotly debated by Americans as had been the annexation of Texas itself, and for the same reasons. Southerners and Democrats wanted Texas, and the New Mexico and California lands, because they hoped they would become slave states, tipping the delicate balance of the Union in favor of slavery: abolitionists and New England Whigs had been vehemently against Texas annexation and were against the Mexican War because they considered them Southern plots. For example, in 1847, a year after the war was declared, a freshman Congressman from Illinois attacked Polk's statement that Mexico had started the war on American soil and asked that the spot where the first blood had been shed be identified. His resolutions for more information were sarcastically called the *Spot Resolutions* and his antiwar stand put him into political oblivion for years: when this man, Abraham Lincoln, ran for the Senate in 1858 his opponent, the incumbent Stephen Douglas, still referred to him as "Spot Lincoln."

All the talk about whether the war was just or unjust was soon obscured by the string of American victories. Five days before war was declared Zachary Taylor had defeated Mexican forces at the *Battle of Palo Alto* (the name of a waterhole near Brownsville) and the following day crushed the Mexicans at Resaca de la Palma. After war was declared Taylor's forces crossed the Rio Grande and occupied Matamorros, May 17th, after which his widely talked-about 6,000-man *Army of the Rio Grande* captured Monterrey, September 24th, ending what was known as the *campaign of the Rio Grande*.

Because Taylor failed to pursue the Mexicans vigorously enough and was beginning to loom as a political figure, President Polk told him to hold his line in Mexico and ordered General Winfield Scott, the popular hero of the War of 1812 and now General-in-Chief of the U.S. Army, to take troops by sea to capture Veracruz and march inland to Mexico City. Taylor then disobeyed orders and crossed the mountains to Saltillo, defeating Santa Anna's 16,000-man army at the *Battle of Buena Vista* (near Buena Vista ranch), February 22–23, 1847. Now America talked about the scandal of General Taylor's disobedience but, since he had won the battle, most Americans approved. The following month, on March 10th, Scott's 12,000-man force, the first U.S. troops to be transported by steamships, made its naval-supported amphibious landing, taking Veracruz on March 27th and then pushing Santa Anna back toward Mexico City.

General Winfield Scott entering Mexico City, September 14, 1847.

Antonio Lopez de Santa Anna was president of Mexico and commander-in-chief during the Mexican War. But he is remembered by Americans chiefly for his brutality during the War of Texas Independence (see Remember the Alamo!*).*

BEAR FLAG

From the halls of Montezuma, To the shores of Tripoli, We fight our country's battles On the land as on the sea. "The Marines' Hymn," 1850s, in which "the halls of Montezuma" refers to the capture of Mexico City in the Mexican War ("the shores of Tripoli" refers to the war in 1805 against the Barbary pirates).

Scott's troops won the *Battle of Cerro Gordo* (a mountain pass) April 18th, won both the *Battle of Contreras* and a fight at Churubusco on August 20th, and the *Battle of Molino del Rey* on September 8th. On September 12–13 they gained the gates of Mexico City by storming and scaling the fortified hill at the *Battle of Chapultepec* (an Aztec word meaning "grasshopper hill," its final defenders were young military cadets schooled there, some of whom leaped to their death rather than surrender). The American troops then occupied Mexico City September 14, 1847. Thus despite the hot debates over the war, from May, 1846 through September, 1847 most Americans talked proudly of how our outnumbered and inexperienced troops, using daring tactics under two bold generals, won victory after victory over the badly led and ill-equipped Mexicans.

Meanwhile on June 14th, 1846, a month after the war began, some of the 700 Americans in California staged the *Bear Flag revolt*, occupied Sonora, and established the *Republic of California*, "the Bear Flag Republic" (so called because its flag showed a grizzly bear facing the red star of its standard). This revolt had been prompted by fear that Mexico would force Americans to leave California, by the U.S. Consul at Monterey, and by army captain and explorer John Frémont, "the Pathfinder," and his party of mountain men who just happened to be "exploring" in California when the war began. On July 7th, a U.S. naval expedition under Commodore John Sloat landed at Monterey, proclaiming California part of the U.S., absorbing the Bear Flag Republic and securing northern California. By January, 1847 the Commander of the Army of the West, General Stephen Watts Kearny, had occupied New Mexico and then joined with the small Pacific Squadron force of Commodore Robert Stockton (for whom *Stockton*, California is named) in securing southern California.

Thus by September 14, 1847, northern Mexico, Mexico City, and the Mexican territories of New Mexico and California were in American hands: Mexico was beaten. The Treaty of Guadalupe Hidalgo was signed in that village, a suburb of Mexico City, on February 2, 1848, establishing the Rio Grande as the boundary between the U.S. and Mexico, and ceding the New Mexico and California lands to the U.S. for $15 million (present-day California, New Mexico, Arizona, Nevada, Utah, and western Colorado were part of this territory). The U.S. had settled the border dispute, gained a new hero in General Zachary Taylor (he was elected president the following year, in 1849), and acquired over half a million square miles of new territory from the Gulf of Mexico to the Pacific, assuring the fulfillment of its Manifest Destiny from ocean to ocean. All this at a cost of 17,435 American casualties.

Buried under all this important history is the first widespread

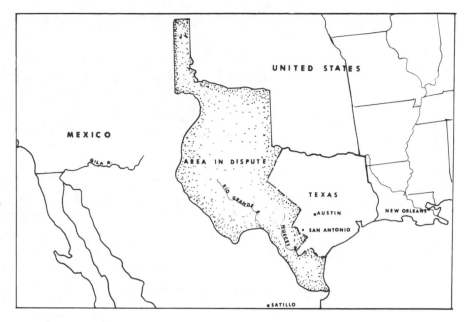

The Mexicans said the Texas border was the Nueces River; the Americans claimed territory to the Rio Grande. The Treaty of Guadalupe Hildago, which ended the Mexican war, established the Rio Grande as the border between U.S. and Mexico and ceded to the U.S. all lands north and west of the Gila River.

[In American history the Mexican War was] *the most unjust war.*
Ulysses S. Grant, *Personal Memoirs*, 1885. Grant had been a second lieutenant in the Mexican War.

American military use of the word *chevrons*. They were first worn on the coat-sleeves of U.S. noncommissioned officers during the Mexican War. The word was first recorded as meaning the decorative, ornamental design in England in 1605, from a 14th century English word for "rafters" (going back to Latin *capra*, goat, since rafters were raised on end resembling butting goats). The war also gave us *Fort Worth*, Texas, named after General William Jenkins Worth, who fought both under Taylor in the north and under Scott in central Mexico.

On the Midway—Merry-Go-Rounds and Kewpie Dolls

The *Midway Plaisance*, a boulevard connecting Chicago's Washington and Jackson Parks, contained the amusement section of the 1893 World's Columbian Exposition. Even while the fair was being built this *Midway Plaisance* was simply being called *the Midway*, and fairs and carnivals have had *midways* ever since (see Meet Me at the Fair).

On that first midway was the first *Ferris wheel*, designed for the exposition by George Washington Ferris. A *merry-go-round* (a 1729 British term) was at that time usually called a *carousel* in America (Italian *carosello*, tournament, as by knights on horseback). Originally we had called a merry-go-round a *whirligig*, which once meant a child's spinning top (when Thomas Jefferson invented a chair that swiveled he called it a "whirligig chair," and it wasn't popularly called a *swivel chair* until the 1850s). Thus we have gone from *whirligig* to *carousel* to *merry-go-round* in the names of this midway ride.

Midways also have *side shows* (a circus term from 1846), and *concessionaires* (a 1910 word), who sell *cotton candy* (a 1920s term),

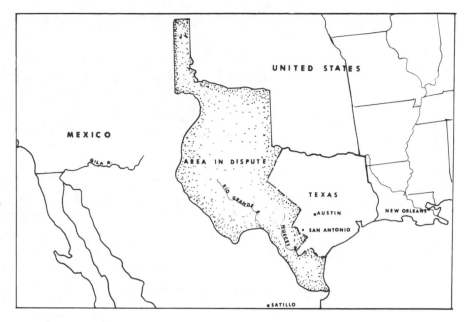

The first Ferris wheel.

popcorn, hot dogs, etc. They also have games where one can win a *Kewpie doll*, originally the trademark name of a doll first popular in 1913 and patterned on a 1909 drawing by Rose O'Neill (it was a chubby, winged doll, part elf, part Cupid, with a topknot).

The word *carnival* itself (from Latin *carnis*, meat + *levāre*, to remove) originally referred to the merrymaking preceding meatless Lent. The shortened form *carney* appeared in the 1920s.

The Monkey Trial—Scopes, Bryan, and Darrow

[It is] unlawful for any teacher in any of the . . . public schools of the state, to teach any theory that denies the story of the Divine creation of man as taught in the Bible, and to teach instead that man has descended from a lower order of animals.

State of Tennessee anti-evolution law, passed by the legislature and signed by the governor, March 13, 1925

The Monkey Trial was one of the most sensational, most talked-about trials in American history. It was the major battle between the evolutionists (see EVOLUTION) and the Fundamentalists (see FUNDAMENTALISM). It all really began in 1921 when the Baptist Rev. Dr. J. W. Porter, head of the Anti-Evolution League of America, had a bill introduced in the Kentucky state legislature banning "the teaching of Darwinism, atheisim, agnosticism, and evolution . . ." in state-supported schools. The press called it "the monkey bill."

It became a national issue: William Jennings Bryan urged its passage "to drive Darwinism from our schools," Billy Sunday praised it, and so did the violent, ranting Rev. J. Frank Norris, leader of the largest Fundamentalist congregation in America, the 10,000-strong First Baptist Church of Fort Worth, Texas. Kentucky's House of Representatives defeated the bill by one vote, but it started a trend, and similar "monkey bills" were passed into law in Oklahoma, Texas, and Tennessee.

Next, the American Civil Liberties Union publicly offered to help anyone challenging one of these "monkey laws." George Rapplyea, a drugstore owner in Dayton, Tennessee, a county seat of 3,000 souls, thought such a challenge would put Dayton on the map. He recruited John T. Scopes, a teacher of general science and athletic coach of Rhea County High School, to initiate the test case by claiming that he had taught Darwinism. The prosecution had the eager services of the rural Fundamentalist idol William Jennings Bryan: The ACLU led the defense with the big-city agnostic Clarence Darrow, fresh from the LEOPOLD AND LOEB trial in Chicago. Since the trial was of John Scopes and was about "monkey bills" and "monkey laws," it was called *the*

> *That hell-born, Bible-destroying, deity-of-Christ-denying German rationalism . . . evolution.*
> Rev. J. Frank Norris of the First Baptist Church of Fort Worth, Texas

> *My theology is a simple muddle. I cannot look at the universe as the result of blind chance, yet I can see no evidence of beneficient [Godly] design.*
> Charles Darwin

Scopes Trail and *the Monkey Trial*. It was a raucous carnival lasting from July 10 to 21, 1925. The judge loved to be photographed; people clamored to be jurors and to get front-row seats; some sessions of the hot, crowded court were held outdoors. Dayton teemed with special correspondents, including H. L. Mencken of the *Baltimore Sun*, newsreel teams, hot dog vendors, and souvenir sellers. The American Association for the Advancement of Science sent expert witnesses to defend evolution—and two showmen exhibited trained chimpanzees in town, the defense lawyers inviting one of the chimps to lunch! Dayton was on the map, the whole world was talking about it.

The trial ended after Bryan had taken the stand himself, as an expert witness on the infallibility of the Bible. The shirt-sleeved Darrow in cross-examination took him apart "like a dollar watch." But the judge had announced that he would not consider any testimony on the validity of evolution, the case was merely to decide whether Scopes had violated the state law or not. By all testimony he had, and the jurors found him "guilty as charged." The judge imposed a $100 fine. And the aftermath? The state supreme court set aside the fine, saying the judge could not impose one in excess of $50; the judge lost a reelection bid and became a Fundamentalist organizer; Scopes' notoriety won him a graduate school scholarship in geology and some lecture fees; Bryan died a beaten man five days after the trial—and Arkansas and Mississippi passed "monkey law" bills the following year! Tennessee didn't repeal its law until 1967, and the last state monkey law, in Mississippi, was repealed in 1972. But both evolutionists and Fundamentalists had had their say, free speech won a moral victory—and people had something to talk about all summer long.

Clarence Darrow, in shirt sleeves and wearing suspenders, at the Scopes trial, July, 1925. He took William Jennings Bryan apart "like a dollar watch."

Mountains, Creeks, Deserts, and Swamps

England is a gently rolling plain; its tallest mountain, Sca Fell, is 3,210 feet; its largest lake, Lake Windermere, is 10½ miles long; there are no deserts or canyons, no swamps, or thundering waterfalls or rapids as we know them. California's tallest mountain, Mount Whitney, is 14,490 feet high; Lake Superior is 360 miles long; and here colonists and westward-surging settlers found mountain chains, flat grasslands, tidewater regions, swamps, canyons, deserts—a new and awesome variety of landscapes and geographical features that demanded naming. For some of the features and types of land we borrowed Indian words, Spanish words, French words, Dutch words; for others we made common words out of words that were to become obsolete in England or had been but local dialect terms there. Many of these terms are now typically or uniquely American. The most important and interesting ones include:

Badlands National Park, South Dakota.

A typical butte, *with its sloping sides and flat top, Capitol Reef National Park, Utah.*

the Appalachians. This 1600-mile mountain chain was given its Indian name (Choctaw *appalachee*, "people on the other side") by a French explorer in 1567. *Appalachia*, the region, 1705; the *Blue Hills* of Virginia, 1753, soon changed to the *Blue Ridge Mountains. Mountaineer*, 1834, first applied to one who hunted, wandered, or lived in the Appalachians; *hillbilly* (1900, as *Hill-Billy*).

arroyo (Spanish for brook or creek, influenced by Spanish *arroyo seco*, dried-up creekbed, gully), written as a foreign word, in italics, 1806; used as an American word, 1860s.

Bad Lands (the translation of an Indian term meaning bad lands to cross), the region in South Dakota and Nebraska where erosion has created intricate landscapes of buttes and rock formations, 1851.

barren, a track of barren or infertile land, 1651; *pine barren*, 1731.

bluff (perhaps from Dutch *blaf*, flat, broad), 1687, originally used in South Carolina and Georgia to mean a steep river bank or its top, especially the bank on which Savannah, Georgia, is located (see THE AMERICAN LANGUAGE). It may be a short form of the earlier *bluffland*, 1666, steeply rising land. *Pine bluff*, 1766; *Council Bluffs*, Iowa, established as a trading post in 1820. A bluff is also called a *knob* and Americans were talking about *the knobs*, high river bluffs or prominent hills, by 1817.

bottom (a British dialect word), 1634, fertile lowland, as along a river or creek. *Bottom land*, 1728; *timber bottom*, 1836, a southern term for timbered bottom land.

branch, a tributary, 1624; a stream or brook, 1663 (see *creek* below). *Branch water*, 1850; *bourbon and branch* (bourbon whiskey and branch water), 1850s.

butte (French from Old French *but*, target, mound behind a target), 1659, in a Rhode Island place name; first western use by the Lewis and Clark expedition in 1805. *Butte*, Montana, founded 1864.

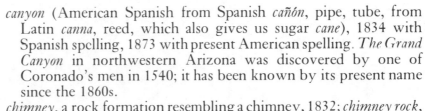

The Grand Canyon, *Arizona, with a view of the Colorado River at its bottom, seen from the south rim.*

canyon (American Spanish from Spanish *cañón*, pipe, tube, from Latin *canna*, reed, which also gives us sugar *cane*), 1834 with Spanish spelling, 1873 with present American spelling. *The Grand Canyon* in northwestern Arizona was discovered by one of Coronado's men in 1540; it has been known by its present name since the 1860s.

chimney, a rock formation resembling a chimney, 1832; *chimney rock*, 1847.

creek is an English word meaning tidal inlet, and is still so used in parts of Virginia, Georgia, etc. Our more general use of the word to mean any stream or brook (perhaps influenced by the Dutch *kreek*, bend) dates to 1622. *Crick* was an English dialect pronunciation for *creek* and Captain John Smith of the Virginia Colony used it in 1608—thus *crick* was recorded in America 14 years before *creek* and was probably the more common pronunciation in the colonial South.

A creek is also called a *brook* in New England and a *branch* in the South. In colonial days it was also called a *run* (place where water runs), as in *mill run*, 1652, and the name *Bull Run*, the stream in northeastern Virginia that was the scene of two important Civil War battles.

desert has been in the English language since the 13th century, but in America the word took on new reality. We have *the Great Desert* (part of the Great Plains), 1784, which became *the Great American Desert* by 1834. *The Mohave (Mojave) Desert* of Southern California gets its name from the Mohave Indians (*hamok avi*, "three mountains," referring to the peaks near Needles, California). *The Painted Desert* of Arizona was so called by the 1860s, while *Death Valley* has been known by that name since the 1870s. *Desert rat*, a person living in the desert, dates from 1907.

divide, mountains or a mountain ridge forming a watershed between two river systems, is a word first recorded by the exploring General Zebulon Pike in 1806. *The Great Divide*, 1861; *the Continental Divide*, 1868.

everglade (*ever* probably meaning vast, unending), 1823, when the word first appeared on a map of Florida. *The Everglades*, 1893; *Everglade National Park*, established 1947.

fall and its full form *waterfall* were both in the English language by the 14th century. Americans seem to prefer the plural *falls*, first recorded here in 1634. The first European to see *Niagara Falls* (*Niagara* is an Iroquoian word meaning "neck" of land) was a French missionary, in 1678; by the 1840s we were using *Niagara* metaphorically to mean any deluge. *Falls City*, a nickname for Louisville, Kentucky, 1859, because it is located at the falls of the Ohio. The *fall line*, 1882, was important to early colonists: it's the line between the Appalachian uplands and the coastal plain where rivers drop sharply, forming falls or rapids. Here coastal settlements stopped, trading goods from the interior had to be transferred from canoes to ships, and water power was available. Thus the earliest settlements were at the mouths of rivers, as was Jamestown, the second line of settlements was at the fall line, as are Richmond, Virginia; Raleigh, North Carolina; Columbus, Georgia; and Columbia, South Carolina.

Yosemite Falls in Yosemite National Park, California. The 1,430-foot drop dwarfs the huge boulders at the bottom.

Two great figures of American conservation, President Theodore Roosevelt (1858–1919) and John Muir (1838–1914) standing on Glacier Point, Yosemite Valley, 1904. Muir, a naturalist and campaigner for the preservation of our forests, helped persuade Congress to establish the Yosemite National Park (1890), and Roosevelt was a strong advocate of conservation at a time when most Americans did not understand that our natural resources are finite. The term National Park was first widely used in the 1890s after Yosemite National Park was established. See THE WILDERNESS AND THE FRONTIER.

flat, a tract of high, level land, 1773. The word is also in many place names, as *French Flats* and *German Flats*, and Bret Harte's 1869 short story "The Outcasts of Poker Flats."

foothill, 1850, first used in reference to the foothills of the Rockies.

fork, the point where two streams meet, 1646; either of the two streams, 1697. Uesd to mean the point where two roads meet, 1779; either of the two roads, a side road, 1806.

gap (a rare or obsolete English word that became common in America), American use, 1635, also called a *notch* in New England by 1718. *Water gap*, 1756, referring to what was to be known as the *Delaware Watergap; river gap* by 1834. *The Cumberland gap*, through the Appalachians between Virginia and Kentucky, was discovered in 1750; Daniel Boone first traveled it in 1769, and then he and others blazed a trail through it in 1775. It made possible and became part of the *Wilderness Road, Wilderness Trace,* or *Boone's Trace* (all 1830s terms) which pioneers took westward.

The Great Basin, named by explorer John Frémont in 1843.

The Great Lakes were discovered by the French between 1615 and 1669, the name *the Great Lakes* first being recorded by William Penn in 1683. *Lake Superior* is named for its size (it's the largest body of fresh water in the world); *Huron* is named for the Indian tribe (named by the French *huré*, bristly, savage, unkempt); *Michigan* is from the Chippewa *mica gama*, big water; *Erie* is named for that Iroquois tribe (from an Iroquois term meaning people of the panther); and *Ontario* is also an Iroquois word (meaning fine lake, the French originally named it *Lake Frontenac* after the Canadian governor).

gulch (an English dialect verb meaning to sink in, cave in, said of land), recorded in Newfoundland in 1835; first recorded in the American West in 1842. *Dry gulch*, 1870.

gully (an obsolete 16th century English word, literally gullet, "little throat"), American use, 1637. *Gully washer*, a hard rain, 1823. *Gully keeper* (a variant of *goal(ie)-keeper*, a name for the child's game of prisoner's base), 1876.

hollow, in England this meant a low meadow; it was first used with this meaning in America in 1649 (it still may have meant a low meadow in Washington Irving's 1819 tale, *The Legend of Sleepy Hollow*). By the 1840s we were using the word almost exclusively to mean a small valley or dell.

hummock originally meant a parcel of land a little less than an acre in size, which is the way the English and many colonists used it. The meaning of a tract or knoll of high ground, especially in a swamp, was first used by an explorer on the American continent in 1589.

lick, salt lick, deer lick, buffalo lick, etc., were all first recorded in the 1740s and 50s. *Lick* also gives us many place names, as various *Licking Creeks* and *French Lick*, Indiana, originally a French trading post.

mesa (Spanish for table and tableland), 1759 as a foreign word, in italics; 1840 as an American word. *Tableland* was a late 17th century English word, not common in America until the 1820s.

natural bridge, 1775. This and all other early uses of the term refer to the *Natural Bridge* near Lexington, Virginia.

neck of land, 1663. This New England term originally referred not so much to a narrow projection of land as to a specific parcel of land.

Great chunks of petrified wood, 150 million years old, lie in the Petrified Forest National Park in northern Arizona.

oxbow (from the U-shaped piece of wood of an ox yoke), common in New Hampshire and Vermont by the 1780s. The word was popularized and associated with the West by William van Tilburg Clark's 1940 novel of the lynching of three innocent men suspected of cattle rustling, *The Ox-Bow Incident* (and further popularized by the 1943 movie based on it).

panhandle, first used to refer to parts of Virginia in the 1850s, becoming part of West Virginia when it seceded from Virginia during the Civil War. *The Panhandle State*, West Virginia, 1894. The *Texas panhandle*, 1873.

pass (used in England to mean a passage between mountains but its American use has been influenced by the French explorers' and trappers' *pas d'une montagne* and *pas d'une rivière*), American use, 1720. *The Donner Pass* is named after an elderly Illinois farmer, George Donner, who attempted to lead a group of 87 ill-equipped, inexperienced settlers to California through this Sierra Nevada pass, north of Lake Tahoe, in the winter of 1846: the *Donner party* was caught in the pass by blizzards and 41 of them died of cold and starvation, the rest surviving by eating the bodies of their dead companions, including that of George Donner. Despite this, over 40,000 people used this pass to California in the 1849-50 gold rush.

petrified forest (via Old French *petrifier* from Latin *petra*, stone + *facere*, to make), 1830, the early references are to petrified forests in Illinois and Missouri. *The Petrified Forest*, in the Painted Desert of Arizona, 1906.

Pike's Peak, discovered by General Zebulon Pike in 1806.

plain (Middle English from Latin *plānus*, flat, clear), 1775; *the Great Plains*, 1806.

pond (Middle English *ponde*, enclosure) is used in England to mean only a man-made pool or lake, as an artificial fish pond. In America it has meant any pool or small lake since 1622, such as Thoreau's beloved *Walden Pond* near Cambridge, Massachusetts. I wonder if the change in meaning was not due to the American beaver, whose *beaver ponds* (1640) are artificial yet natural.

prairie (French, literally "little meadow"), 1691. See the entry THE PRAIRIE.

rapids (from Canadian French *rapide*, swift, a running descent in a river), 1765. See VOYAGEURS, RAPIDS, AND PORTAGES.

ravine (French for "mountain torrent," but in English as a violent rush, as of water, by the 15th century), used in America to mean a deep gorge or mountain cleft, 1781, in George Washington's diary.

ridge, 1624, but not common until the 1780s.

the Rocky Mountains, known by this descriptive name since 1802; *the Rockies*, 1827. *Rocky Mountain sheep*, 1804; *Rocky Mountain goat*, 1842; *Rocky Mountain spotted fever*, 1934. *Mountainman*, a hunter, guide, or wanderer in the western mountains, 1840s.

savanna (via Spanish from the Taino *zabana*, grassy plain, lowland), 1671. See the entry CANOES AND CANNIBALS.

scrubland, land covered with scrub trees, 1779; *scrub hills*, 1788. *Scrub* is a 16th century English word for stunted trees and dwarf cattle, hence our *scrub oak*, 1766, and *scrub pine*, 1791. From stunted, dwarf, *scrub* came to mean inferior in America, hence *scrub race* (1831, a race between inferior horses) and *scrub team* (1893, a makeshift team or team of second-rate players).

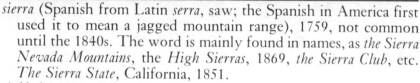

The beautiful Cascade Range, Washington. These mountains, an extension of the Sierra Nevada of California, show the same characteristic "sawlike" peaks.

sierra (Spanish from Latin *serra*, saw; the Spanish in America first used it to mean a jagged mountain range), 1759, not common until the 1840s. The word is mainly found in names, as *the Sierra Nevada Mountains*, the *High Sierras*, 1869, *the Sierra Club*, etc. *The Sierra State*, California, 1851.

sinkhole, 1709; *sink*, 1791.

spring has been in the English language since the 13th century, but the variety and importance of springs in America gave the word new reality to the settlers. It also gives us many place names, as *Springfield* (Massachusetts, 1636; Ohio, 1799; Illinois, 1818; Missouri, 1835); *Saratoga Springs*, New York; *Hot Springs*, Arkansas; *Warm Springs*, Georgia; *Cold Spring Harbor*, New York; and *Palm Springs*, California, as well as various *Springvilles*, *Spring Valleys*, *Spring Hills*, etc. *Warm springs*, 1748; *hot springs*, 1806.

swamp. This English dialect word first came into wide American use in colonial Virginia, first being recorded there by Captain John Smith in 1624. *Swampy*, 1649; *swampland*, 1663; *swamper*, one who lives in a swamp, 1725, also called a *swamp angel* by 1857. *To swamp*, to mire down in a swamp, 1646; to mire down with work, duties, etc., 1740s.

the Tetons, range of mountains in western Wyoming, 1830s (from French *téton*, woman's breast, from the shape); *Grand Teton*, 1860s.

the tidewater, 1722, the coastal rivers and fertile coastal plain below the *fall line* (see *fall* above) in Virginia, the Carolinas, and Maryland. Early settlers came here and it became the center of the 18th century plantation aristocracy. *Tidewater country of Virginia*, 1832.

wash, an eroded area or place, 1835; a dry watercourse, 1861, both originally western uses.

watershed, 1874.

Okefenokee Swamp, Georgia.

252

Carry Nation

(1846-1911) had Kansas talking in the 1890s and all America talking by 1900. Alone or with other temperate Christian women she would walk into a bar to sing psalms and pray—then, unlike Women's Christian Temperance Union crusaders, she would smash the saloon's stock, furniture, and fixtures with her hatchet. She became so famous she earned $300 a week on the lecture stage and by selling souvenir hatchets—and spent the money getting out of jail and paying her fines. This almost six-foot woman was also frequently clubbed and shot at by irate saloon keepers and their patrons. Well she might be, for besides wielding her hatchet, she lambasted barkeeps and customers with harsh words, calling all saloons *joints*, and their habitués *rummies* (helping popularize these two words). She called her method of closing saloons "hatchetation."

In Kansas Carry Nation claimed that any citizen had a right to destroy whiskey and saloons because they were against the law in that dry state. But there was more to her hatred of drink. Born Carry Amelia Moore in Garrard County, Kentucky, she had obtained a teaching certificate from Missouri State Normal School before marrying her first husband, Dr. Charles Gloyd, when she was 21. The marriage was soon ruined by her husband's alcoholism. Thus, though she was also against tobacco, foreign foods, corsets, and lewd paintings (such as were found in saloons behind the bar), her main hatred was alcohol. When she had time she was also for woman's suffrage. Alas, just as alcohol ruined her first marriage, her temperance work ruined her second: David Nation, a lawyer and minister, divorced her after 24 years of marriage, because she was too busy breaking bottles to be his wife.

An 1890s cartoon shows the implacable Carry Nation at work in a Kansas saloon.

The New Deal

was a phrase taken from Franklin Delano Roosevelt's acceptance speech at the Democratic National Convention in Chicago on July 2, 1932:

> I pledge you, I pledge myself, to a new deal for the American people.

The only thing we have to fear is fear itself.
Franklin Delano Roosevelt, First Inaugural Address, March 4, 1933

With these words Roosevelt had not only a campaign slogan but named the first five years of his presidency and an era of American life. The GREAT DEPRESSION was in its third year and Democrats were calling Hoover's Republican party "the Depression Party" and using the song "Happy Days Are Here Again" as their theme for a new beginning. Roosevelt won the 1933 presidential election promising "a new deal" for "the forgotten man," and in his inaugural address told the nation, "The only thing we have to fear is fear itself."

Where did these oft-quoted words come from? *New deal* was probably a combination of Wilson's "New Freedom" slogan and Teddy Roosevelt's "Square Deal," and was coined either by Judge Samuel Rosenman or Columbia professor Raymond Moley, both of whom worked on Roosevelt's acceptance speech. *The forgotten man* was a term that William Graham Sumner (1840–1910), an influential political and social scientist at Yale, had popularized in his speeches and in his 1883 book *What the Social Classes Owe to Each Other*. "The only thing we have to fear is fear itself" was probably based on "Nothing is so much to be feared as fear," from Thoreau's *Journal*, 1851. In any event, the nation now had an educated, articulate, energetic president, and recovery from the Depression seemed about to begin. Roosevelt and his New Deal were to have Americans talking for years and introduced many new ideas and phrases.

Franklin Delano Roosevelt taking the presidential oath of office on March 4, 1933 (it was the last March inauguration). He was 51 years old. Twelve years later, on April 12, 1945, he died after being elected to an unprecedented fourth term as president.

Brain trust was the first new term used. It was coined by James Kieran, president of Hunter College, to describe the group of professors who advised Roosevelt during that 1932 election campaign. It was soon applied to all the new president's close intellectual advisers, who included professor of government and law Raymond Moley, law professor Adolph Berle, economist Rexford Tugwell, and social-welfare organizer Harry Hopkins (whose programs introduced the terms *underprivileged*, *social worker*, *welfare*, *welfare worker*, and *welfare recipient* to millions of Americans).

Next began what came to be called *the hundred days*, the first hundred days of the New Deal. These hundred days began on March 5th, 1933, the day after Roosevelt's inauguration, when he called a special session of the 73rd Congress, and ended June 16th when the session ended. Never had so many reforms and sweeping legislative programs been put into effect in such a sh rt time. Attempting to provide quick recovery from the Depression, the government created vast relief and public works measures, new banking regulations, and agricultural subsidies, and in the process formed the FERA, AAA, HOLC, TVA and many other of the alphabet agencies.

On March 6th, two days after his inauguration, Roosevelt declared the famous four-day *bank holiday*. Bank "runs" and failures had abounded early in the Depression and most banks had already been closed by state action. Now the new president suspended all banking and gold transactions while Congress rushed through the Emergency Banking Act on March 9th, ratifying Roosevelt's bank holiday and providing for the reopening of sound banks.

After the four-day bank holiday and a two-day weekend, on March 12, 1933, the new president gave his first evening radio talk. It was to announce that the banks would be reopening the next day and was entitled "An Intimate Talk with the People of the United States on Banking." It was the first of the famous *fireside chats*, a name used in promoting the second radio talk and suggested by Harry Butcher, head of CBS's Washington office. In the 12 years of his presidency Roosevelt was to give exactly 30 of these fireside chats, the early ones to calm the Depression fears of the nation and to win support of his New Deal recovery policies, the later ones to encourage and inform the nation during World War II. Each began with Roosevelt's familiar salutation "My friends...," which he had used in speeches since 1910 when, running for a seat in the New York State senate, he had heard U.S. Congressional candidate Richard Connell use it (Jefferson had addressed audiences as "Friends and fellow citizens" and Lincoln had used "My friends...," in his departure speech to the citizens of Springfield, Illinois, when he left for Washington).

A fireside chat. Wilson was the first president to address the nation by radio; Roosevelt the first to use TV.

To comprehend the rapid changes taking place under Roosevelt and the New Deal one has only to note the rapid additions to the language: *New Deal*, July 2, 1932; "The only thing we have to fear is fear itself," March 4, 1933; *the hundred days*, beginning March 5, 1933; *bank holiday*, March 6, 1933; *fireside chat*, sometime after March 12, 1933. Roosevelt's enthusiasm and energy turned the dull, drab days of the Depression into exciting times and gave America a future again. If the New Deal didn't cure all the problems of the Depression, at least it took America's mind off it and had Americans talking about present plans and future hopes.

During the early days of the New Deal people began to talk about the succession of new *alphabet agencies* (government agencies, administrations, authorities, offices, and corporations created for relief and recovery), their *coordinators* and the *directives* they issued, and the *paperwork* and other work they *expedited*, *implemented*, and *processed*. Thus the alphabet agencies created a large *bureaucracy* and many of its terms. Sometimes called *alphabetical agencies* when the term was new in 1933, many of these agencies' initials, especially CCC, WPA, and NRA, were the most talked-about, beloved, debated, or hated "words" of the period. They included the:

AAA (*A*gricultural *A*djustment *A*dministration, 1933) which provided subsidies to farmers for reducing the acreage of certain crops, though not until 1941 did farm income regain 1929 levels.

CCC (Civilian Conservation Corps, 1933–41), in which over 2 million unemployed youths aged 18–25 lived in *work camps* and earned $30 a month (of which $22 was automatically sent home to their families) while working on conservation projects, such as reforestation, forest-fire prevention, mosquito control, dam and road building, etc.

These unhappy times call for the building of plans ... that build from the bottom up and not from the top down, that put their faith once more in the forgotten man at the bottom of the economic pyramid.

Franklin Delano Roosevelt, radio speech, April 7, 1932

A CCC crew planting trees in Olympic National Forest, 1936.

256

FCA (*Farm Credit Administration*), which refinanced 1/5 of the nation's farm mortgages.

FDIC (*Federal Deposit Insurance Corporation*, 1933), which still insures deposits in member banks.

FERA (*Federal Emergency Relief Administration*, 1933) which spent over $2¾ billion providing direct relief to states and localities, and absorbed the *CWA* (*Civil Works Administration*), which put 4 million unemployed men to work on *public works*, improving schools, roads, and parks, paying workers "on relief" 30¢ an hour.

FHA (*Federal Housing Administration*, 1934), for insuring mortgages for new construction and repair of houses, farm buildings, and small business plants.

HOLC (*Home Owners Loan Corporation*, 1933), which aided 1/6th of the nation's home owners, who were threatened by mortgage foreclosures.

NRA (*National Recovery Administration*, 1933), created to administer codes of fair business practice, such as a 35–40-hour work week and a 30-40¢ minimum hourly wage (jobs were so scarce that some businessmen were paying 25¢ an hour again). Businessmen displayed and cursed "The Blue Eagle," the poster symbol indicating acceptance of the NRA's "code of fair competition." Its 765 codes were ineffective and the Supreme Court declared the code system invalid in 1935.

NYA (*National Youth Administration*, 1935), giving students 16–25 years of age part-time jobs in schools and colleges to help them complete their education.

REA (*Rural Electrification Administration*, 1935), which made loans to public bodies and cooperatives to bring electric service to rural areas.

RFC (*Reconstruction Finance Corporation*, 1932), created under Hoover, had lent over $1½ billion to over 5,000 banks, railroads, insurance companies, and other large businesses to keep them from going bankrupt before Roosevelt became president and expanded it to make loans to small businesses as well. It eventually lent $15 billion to businesses to see them through the Depression.

SEC (*Securities and Exchange Commission*, 1934), to regulate the stock market and insure that investors were provided with full, accurate information.

TVA (*Tennessee Valley Authority*, 1933), which was created to build 30 dams along the Tennessee and its tributaries in a seven-state area (Tennessee, Kentucky, Virginia, North Carolina, Georgia, Alabama, Mississippi). It also promoted navigation and supplied hydroelectric power to the region, where the average resident had not had electricity before.

WPA (*Work Progress Administration*, 1935, which became the Work Projects Administration, 1939-43, without changing its initials). Paying more than FERA relief work but less than private industry, and only for men over CCC age, it gave 8 million unemployed men work building sewage plants, power plants, waterworks, schools, streets, bridges, etc., cleared slums, and employed people in the arts to paint murals in post offices, write state guides, give plays, etc.

257

Other widely talked about New Deal initials, though not alphabet agencies, included the *NIRA* (*N*ational *I*ndustrial *R*ecovery *A*ct, 1933) which spent $3½ billion for public works and included the *PWA* (*P*ublic *W*orks *A*dministration, not to be confused with the WPA); the *NLRB* (*N*ational *L*abor *R*elations *B*oard) to adjust labor disputes; and *OASI* (*O*ld *A*ge and *S*urvivors *I*nsurance), better known as *Social Security*.

But probably the best-known initials of all were *FDR*, widely used in referring to Franklin Delano Roosevelt by the mid 1930s (newspaper headlines, needing to fit limited space, always help popularize such abbreviations). Although Teddy Roosevelt had been known as *TR*, FDR's initials were the first president's to be widely used. This familiar use seems to have become a tradition with all subsequent Democratic presidents, with Truman well known as *HST*, Kennedy as *JFK*, and Lyndon Johnson as *LBJ* (although Eisenhower was "Ike," other Republicans have not been so familiarly referred to, Nixon seeming too cold and remote and Gerald Ford not projecting a personality).

But many people didn't like FDR, his New Deal, or his alphabet agencies. There was even a new offensive verb, *to boondoggle*, which meant to work at the trifling, inconsequential tasks created by some of FDR's alphabet agencies to give employment to the needy. This verb came from the *boondoggle*, the braided leather lanyard Boy Scouts wore around their neck, the word said to have been coined by a Rochester, New York scoutmaster, Robert Link, in 1925 and which had come to mean a piece of unnecessarily time-consuming handicraft (but there is some indication that cowboys had earlier used *to boondoggle* to mean to make saddle trappings out of odds and ends of leather when there was nothing else to do). So boondoggling and excess bureaucracy led to the forming of the anti-Roosevelt *American Liberty League* in 1934, and dissident Democrat Al Smith, who led the league in 1936, said the New Deal was submerged in "alphabet soup."

Although conservatives hated "that man in the White House," when Roosevelt ran for his second term in 1936 he had farmers, labor, and the poor behind him. He swamped Alfred M. Landon, despite the Republican slogan "Landon by a Landslide," and carried every state but Maine and Vermont. And the New Deal continued. Although the Depression was not to end until the onset of World War II in 1939, "New Deal" was used less and less, and by 1937 it is considered to have ended. Many of its terms are still with us, such as *relief*, *case worker* (a social worker investigator), *farm subsidy*, the *FDIC*, the *SEC*, *TVA*, *Social Security*, and *food stamps* (introduced in 1939 as one of the last anti-Depression relief measures, each family on relief qualified to buy $1.50 worth of *orange stamps* for $1 for each family member every week, and for each $1 of orange stamps was also given an additional 50¢ of *blue stamps* to buy farm surplus). Thus the New Deal changed the American language and American life forever.

Nonsense!

Throughout our history we've used many different words and retorts to show a speaker we don't believe his lies, flattery, boasting, bombast, or exaggerations, to show him *I'm from Missouri* (1899). Perhaps this is because we just don't like to be taken for fools, because we Americans like to think of ourselves as pragmatic truth seekers who want the *lowdown* (an 1880s expression), want everything to be *on the level* (1923), want a speaker to *tell it like it is* (mid 1960s). Or perhaps it's because in this big country there are a lot of *big talkers* (1870s).

Nonsense! (1614), *far-fetched* (early 1600s), and *cock and bull story* (1607), entered English around the time the first colonists were setting sail for Virginia and Massachusetts. Since then, we've added many similar terms:

all my eye!, 1768; *all my eye and Betty Martin*, popular in the 1780s (no one seems to know who or what Betty Martin was); this soon became *my eye!*
fish story, 1819.
humbug, common in the U.S. since the 1820s.
folderol, 1820s. "Fol-de-rol" was originally a meaningless refrain in old songs, similar to "la-la-la" or "tum-de-dum."
buncombe, bunkum, mid 1820s. Felix Walker, congressman from Buncombe County, North Carolina, 1817–23, made an empty, rambling speech in Congress and refused to cut it short, telling his colleagues it wasn't really meant for them but for his constituents, "for Buncombe." The expression soon caught on among politicians and then the general public. It was shortened to *bunk* by the 1850s. *De-bunk* is from the early 1920s.
soft soap, 1830s
Go tell it to the Marines!, is an expression of incredulity used in England in the early 19th century and in America by the 1830s. It means "The Marines may have a strong enough stomach to believe you but I don't." The Marine Corps had been in existence in America since 1798.
You can't pull the wool over my eyes, 1830s.
tall, 1834; *tall story*, 1845; *tall talk*, 1850s; *tall tale*, 1920s.
flummery, flumdiddle, 1840s. *Flummery* was originally a pap-like oatmeal (Welsh *llymru*) before it came to mean flattery.
twaddle, 1842 (probably from a Scandinavian word meaning to babble).
moonshine, 1843.
Fiddlesticks!, 1846; *fiddle-faddle*, 1863; *fiddle-de-dee*, 1880s. These are all based on *fiddle*, referring to loud homemade fiddles or various noisemakers called *horsefiddles* since the 1800s.
Pshaw!, 1851.

flapdoodle, 1850s.

bosh!, 1850s.

Oh fudge!, 1850s. *Fudge* had meant a hoax, swindle, or nonsense since the early 1830s.

whopper, a big lie, gross exaggeration, 1858.

fib, 1860s. This may have had earlier British use and come from *fable*.

poppycock, 1865. Dutch settlers may have used it much earlier. It comes from the Dutch *pappekak*, soft dung, which goes back to the Latin baby-talk word for soft food *pappa* (which gives us *pap*) and Latin *cacāre*, to defecate (which gives us our baby-talk *caca* for excrement, bowel movement).

hot air, 1873.

stuff, stuff and nonsense!, 1870s. *Stuff* had meant a hoax or a deception by the 1830s.

guff, 1880s. Used in England since the 1820s.

In a pig's eye!, 1880s.

eyewash, 1880s.

Tommyrot, 1880s; *rot*, 1890s.

Do you think I was born yesterday?, *I wasn't born yesterday*, 1880s.

My ass!, 1880s. As many other such terms, this is probably much older but was considered too vulgar to be recorded earlier.

blarney, not popular in America until the 1890s, but known in Britain since the 18th century. It's from the stone in a 15th century Blarney, Ireland, castle, said to give the gift of flattery to any who kiss it.

balderdash, a popular Gay 90s term. The word meant froth in 16th century English and a drink of mixed liquors in the 17th century.

truck, 1890s.

sour grapes, also popular in the 1890s.

full of prunes, 1890s, originally meant full of mistakes.

Balls!, a not-so-gay Gay 90s expression.

balloon juice, 1901, a snappy synonym for the 1873 *hot air*.

hogwash, 1904. Before that it merely meant swill, garbage fed to pigs.

Applesauce!, 1910. Said to have come to mean flattery because boarding houses served plenty of cheap applesauce to disguise the fact that fancier food wasn't served.

Bananas!, *banana oil*, around 1910.

full of beans, 1911. This had meant full of energy since the 1870s. *Full of hops* dates from the 1870s.

Bull!, 1911. Since the 1830s there had been expressions such as "I wouldn't trust him as far as I could sling/fling/throw a bull." These may have helped popularize *bull*; but obviously it's a shortening for *bullshit*, which was too taboo to be recorded before 1928, though its abbreviation *B.S.* was recorded in 1915! *Shit* itself was first recorded as meaning lies or exaggeration in the 1870s, *shit*, *horseshit*, and *crap* having fairly wide World War I use with this meaning and becoming very common during World War II (see OH SHIT!).

hokum, very popular after 1917. It could come from *hocus pocus* (England 1624, as a mock Latin conjuring formula used by jugglers, sometimes said to be based on the Eucharistic mass formula *hoc est corpus*, "this is my body," but probably based on some string of impressive-sounding Latin words like *hax pax max* used as a joke by Medieval students).

baloney, bologna, boloney, early 1920s.
malarkey, 1920s.
Rubbish!, 1921.
blah, 1921.
tripe, 1924.
hooey, 1924.
line, popular by the mid 1920s, though had some use in the early
　　1900s.
Horsefeathers!, late 1920s, may have originally been a euphemism
　　for *horseshit*.
spinach, 1929. This seems to be from a famous 1928 Carl Rose *New
　　Yorker* magazine cartoon showing a mother telling her child,
　　"It's broccoli," and the child replying, "I say it's spinach and
　　the hell with it."
Vanilla!, early 1930s. This seems to come from soda fountain use,
　　where "vanilla" when shouted by a waiter to the kitchen help
　　was code for "Hey, come out here and look at this pretty girl."
　　Maybe the kitchen help was fooled or disappointed once too
　　often.
jive, 1930s.
jazz, 1940s.
snow job, to snow someone, early 1940s, very popular during and
　　after World War II. From the 1880s *to snow under*, to overwhelm.
put on, You're putting me on, mid 1960s. From the 1850s "to put the
　　joke on someone."

OK

is the most popular typical American expression. Short, slangy,
and affirmative, this abbreviation is used millions of times a day
in America, while foreigners around the world identify Americans
by it—and use it themselves.

Contrary to some popular myths, *OK* does *not* come from the
initials or abbreviation of (1) a railroad freight agent *O*badiah
*K*elly who initialed bills of lading, (2) an Indian chief *O*ld *K*eokuk
who wrote his initials on treaties, (3) "*o*uter *k*eel" that shipbuilders
once put on some of their timbers, (4) the teachers' comment
"*o*mnis *k*orrectes" written on perfect exam papers, (5) boxes of
*O*rrins-*K*endall crackers which were popular with Union troops
during the Civil War. It also does *not* come from (6) an English
farm word *hoacky*, meaning the last load of the harvest, (7) a Fin-
nish word *oikea* meaning "correct," (8) a Choctaw work *okeh* or
hoke, or (9, 10, 11, 12, and 13) any French, German, Norwegian,
Scotch, or Cockney word or phrase. Allen Walker Read nailed
down the origin of *OK* in an article in the *Saturday Review of
Literature* in 1941 and sealed its history in a series of articles in
American Speech in 1963-64. Here's the real story:

OK started out as part of a humorous fad or game of abbreviating
phrases in an outrageous way (sometimes humorously misspelled
to add to the fun) among a few Boston and New York writers,
journalists, and wits in the summer of 1838 (*O.K.* meant "oll
*k*orrect"; *O.W.* or *A.R.* meant "Oll Wright"; *K.Y.* meant "know

yuse"; *N.S.M.J.* meant "'nuf said (a)mong jintlemen"; and so on). *O.K.* was a Boston coinage and first appeared in print in the *Boston Morning Post*, March 23, 1839. Meaning "oll korrect," it had moved to New York City by March 11, 1840, when a Tammany newspaper *The New York Era* advertised the forming of a new Tammany social club, the *Democratic O.K. Club.* On March 27th the same paper printed *O.K.* in the large letters of a heading to a piece giving indirect support to a suggestion to break up a scheduled Whig meeting—which Tammany supporters and thugs did on the 28th, using the cheer *O.K.!* During the rest of that presidential campaign year of 1840 "oll korrect" and *O.K.* became Democratic rallying cries, strongly reinforced by the fact that Democratic president and candidate for reelection, Martin Van Buren, was called "*Old Kinderhook*" (as well as "the Kinderhook Fox/ Sage/Wizzard"—he was from Kinderhook, New York, near Albany). Supporters of the Whig candidate, William Henry Harrison, countered by reminding the public that Van Buren had been Andrew Jackson's hand-picked successor and spread the story that *O.K.* had been Jackson's uneducated way of abbreviating "all correct." But "Old Kinderhook" and Jackson's misspellings were all stories spread after the fact—*O.K.* is from "oll korrect," a humorous Boston use of 1838. Before the end of 1840 it was in wide use, found in popular songs, and soon had swept the country. Incidentally, that presidential campaign was a good year for new terms: Van Buren and his *O.K.* lost to Harrison and his slogan "Tippecanoe and Tyler Too."

By the 1880s *O.K.* was a verb, *to O.K.*, and the lowercase *o.k.* was in use. Another president, Woodrow Wilson, popularized the spelling *okey* around 1918 by using it on documents (helping to popularize the Choctaw okeh story), and by the early 1930s such cute forms as *oke, okey-dokey, okie-doke,* and *okle-dokle* were popular. By the mid 40s *OK*, without periods, was the most popular form.

A-1 is an 1830s term stemming from its use by Lloyd's Register to designate ships in first-class condition. It was combined with *OK* in 1961 and introduced into millions of American homes as *A-OK* during the televised splashdown of astronaut Alan B. Shepard's space capsule when he reported "Everything's AOK— dye marker out."

The Overland Stage

By the mid 1830s *overland* meant just one exciting thing to Americans, over the Great Plains to the far West, from the Mississippi to the Pacific by land—as opposed to the water route around Cape Horn or via ships and across the yellow-fever trap of the Isthmus of

A western stagecoach.

Panama. The post office was speaking of slow *overland mail* by 1848, but not until 1858 did it contract with expressman John Butterfield to carry overland mail and packages from Missouri to California fast—within 25 days. To do it, Butterfield started the *Overland Mail Company*, which also carried passengers and became the widely talked about *overland stage*.

Butterfield started two *stagecoaches* (a 1640 British term) or *stages* (1772) each way every week, but his mail, freight, and passenger service grew until he eventually had 160 *stage stations*, over 250 vehicles, and 1,800 horses—employing over a thousand drivers, horse herders, blacksmiths, veterinarians, and wheelwrights to take care of them, plus hostelers to feed the passengers. His stations were scattered along a 2,800-mile route from St. Louis to San Francisco, a route sagging south through Fort Smith, Arkansas, and El Paso, Texas, to avoid northern winters and satisfy southern politicians (during the Civil War the route was straightened out). Most trips took 22-24 days, passengers paid $200 westward and $150 eastward (there was never enough eastbound traffic), including 40 pounds of baggage free.

Butterfield used *Concord coaches* much of the way and it is this coach we think about when we say *stagecoach*. It was a 9-passenger, 4-6-horse (sometimes mule) coach with springs, weighing 2,500 pounds and costing about $1,250. It got its name because it was first made in Concord, New Hampshire, about 1827; it was respectfully and affectionately called *the Concord wagon*, *the Concord stage*, or just *the Concord*.

In 1860 the overland stage was indirectly responsible for creating another much talked-about American term, THE PONY EXPRESS, which was created to compete with it in carrying mail. In 1866

263

Butterfield sold the Overland Mail Company to an old business associate, Henry Wells, who had formed *the American Express Company* in 1850 and organized *Wells, Fargo & Company* in 1852. Thus the overland stage became known to millions as *Wells, Fargo* (the passenger service was discontinued soon after the completion of the transcontinental railroad in 1869).

Incidentally, the *shot gun* (1776) was originally considered by most Americans as the weapon carried by express riders and messengers. Thus it was fitting that such a messenger or an armed guard on a stagecoach was called a *shotgun* in the 1880s, the guard riding beside the stage driver said to be *riding shotgun*. The term *double-barrel(ed) shotgun* dates from 1848, *sawed-off shotgun* from 1898, and *shotgun wedding* is a term of the 1920s (meaning the bride's father is forcing the groom to the altar, as with a gun at his back, to protect his pregnant daughter's reputation).

The Panama Canal

The 50-mile wide Isthmus of Panama is such a logical place for connecting the Atlantic and Pacific that Columbus looked for a natural waterway there on his fourth voyage in 1502, Balboa saw both oceans from a high point there in 1513, and Philip II of Spain sent surveyors there in 1567 to study the possibility of building a canal. Thus the idea had been talked about for centuries before the French 1881 attempt to build it under Ferdinand de Lesseps failed. This French attempt had the world using the name *Panama Canal* 25 years before Panama was a country and 35 years before the first ship used it (the isthmus was still sometimes called *the Isthmus of Darien* and the canal *the Pacific Canal* in the 1900s).

Although the commercial need for the canal had long been realized, its military need became obvious to the U.S. during the Spanish-American War (1898) when the battleship *Oregon* took 66 days to make its way around Cape Horn in its dash from San Francisco to Cuba. We purchased the French rights for $40 million despite the opposition of Colombia, the country that owned the land. President Theodore Roosevelt then grew exasperated negotiating with Colombia, aided a New York planned "revolution" led by two of the French Panama Company's members, and had a cruiser off Colón the evening before the revolution started. The cruiser held back Colombian forces, and three hours after the revolution began we recognized the new nation, *Panama*. This was in November, 1903; we began building the canal in 1904. The abortive French attempt to build the canal, our involvement in the Panamanian revolution, and the engineering marvels and progress in building the canal, 1904–14, kept Americans talking about it for 35 years. We were also talking about the army medical officer William C. Gorgas who made digging the canal possible by clean-

Theodore Roosevelt (1858–1919).

Marines have landed and the situation is well in hand.
Cablegram sent from Panama by war correspondent and reporter Richard Harding Davis in 1885 and giving us our expression "the Marines have landed."

ing the area of *yellow fever*, also called *Panamas fever* (Gorgas had been in charge of *yellow-fever camps* in Cuba and freed Havana of the disease during the American occupation after the Spanish-American War).

Theodore Roosevelt's methods may not have been subtle, but *the Big Ditch* was completed a few days after World War I began, served us well in two world wars, and cut 7,873 miles and three weeks from the San Francisco to New York trip. It also added the name *Canal Zone* to geography books and introduced the term *electric mule* (a trolley-fed electric locomotive first used to tow ships through the locks). And all the scheming, treaties, money, and work also explains something quite minor—the popularity of the term *Panama hat*.

Two 1908 snapshots joined to give a panoramic view of the construction of the Panama Canal.

Pancakes, Hoe Cakes, Johnny Cakes, Flapjacks—and Waffles

Early American Pancakes were made of ground parched corn or cornmeal, fried versions of the early corn breads (see CORN). The earliest was the *Indian cake* (1607), made of parched cornmeal, water, and salt, and also called a *no cake* (1634, from Narragansett *nokehick*, "it is soft," the soft batter being thrown and shaped from one hand to the other). *No cake* had become *hoe cake* by 1745, perhaps a mispronunciation of *no cake* or perhaps because it was sometimes cooked on a hoe blade. If cooked in the ashes of a fire, this parched cornmeal, water, and salt cake was also called an *ashcake* or *ashpone* (1810).

265

From a 1934 advertisement of Aunt Jemima Pancake Flour.

By 1739 people were eating and talking about the somewhat fancier, sweeter *Johnny cake*, made with cornmeal, salt, sugar, and boiling water. Its name probably comes from *joniken*, an Indian dish of flat, thin cornmeal cakes fried in grease, but the name could be a corruption of *Shawnee cake* or even of *journey cake*, since travelers carried them on long trips. Johnny cakes were so popular in New England that New England was called *the land of johnnycake* before the Civil War. Both the earlier, simple hoe cakes and the fancier Johnny cakes were sometimes called *pancakes*, but this name did not begin replacing all the others until the 1870s.

Meanwhile by the 1740s Dutch-style *buckwheat cakes* had come to the colonies—they were America's first wheat pancake. We were calling both our cornmeal and wheat cakes *slapjacks* by 1796 (one slapped them into shape or into a skillet) and this became *flapjacks* by the 1830s (they were flapped or turned over once in the pan). Pancakes were also called *flap cakes* and *battercakes* by the 1830s and *griddle cakes* by 1840, the 1830s seeing the big change from cornmeal to wheat flour. *Flannel cakes* and *a string of flats* are lumber camp terms for pancakes, from their consistency (lumberjacks wore flannel shirts) and flat shape.

The commercial brand of self-rising pancake mix *Aunt Jemima* was developed by Chris Rutt in 1889 and named after a popular vaudeville song, "Aunt Jemima." The Davis Milling Company acquired it, and at the 1893 Columbia Exposition had a popular exhibit with Nancy Green, an outstanding Black cook from Kentucky, making pancakes as "Aunt Jemima." For years after that she appeared as "Aunt Jemima" in advertising and on tours.

Waffles (Dutch *wafel*, wafer) were known to the *Mayflower* pilgrims from their stay in Holland and were later popularized in New Amsterdam by the Dutch themselves. Waffles had been a popular food in Holland, Belgium, Germany, and France since medieval times, often sold from stalls at fairs. Colonists had waffles and hot chocolate for supper or at evening *waffle frolics* (1744) or *waffle parties* (1808). The early spelling was often *woffle* and *woffle iron* was a well-known term in America by the 1790s (it had a long handle and was placed in or over the fire, users being cautioned to turn it over to "bake the woffle on both sides"). *Waffle wagons* were familiar to many Americans in the last half of the 19th century, being handcarts and horse-drawn wagons from which street vendors sold hot waffles. Around 1910 *waffle* was slang for a hard or dangerous task and in the 1960s *to waffle* came to mean to vacillate or to claim to be on both sides of a controversy in order to try to please everyone. In 1973 heavy hiking shoes or boots whose thick nonskid soles had a gridlike tread resembling the pattern made by waffle irons were called *waffle stompers*.

Flapjacks.

The Pennsylvania Dutch — The Plain People

Pennsylvania Dutch means the Mennonites, Amish, Dunkers, Moravians, Schwenkfelders, and other settlers (and their descendants) who fled religious persecution in southern Germany and Switzerland to settle in southeastern Pennsylvania between the 1680s and 1740s (especially Germans from the Palatinate who settled in Berks, Lancaster, Lebanon, Lehigh, Northampton, and York counties, Pennsylvania). These people and their language, a Palatinate dialect of High German with some English mixed in, have both commonly been called *Pennsylvania Dutch* since the 1850s. The *Dutch* in *Pennsylvania Dutch* has nothing to do with Holland, but is from *Deutsch*, meaning German (the people and their language have also been called *Pennsylvania German* since the 1850s).

That these Germans settled in Pennsylvania was no accident. William Penn obtained proprietary rights and founded the colony in 1681, then peopled it with his English Quakers and with these somewhat Quakerlike German people he considered compatible with them. He encouraged these godly, hard-working Germans to immigrate to his colony by having propaganda pamphlets distributed to them, describing Pennsylvania as a land of milk and honey free from religious persecution. By 1776, the Pennsylvania Dutch numbered about 100,000, one-third of Pennsylvania's population. The names of these religious groups have become part of America's history and vocabulary.

William Penn (1644–1718) persuaded Charles II to grant a tract of wilderness west of the Delaware River between New York and Maryland, which Penn, himself a Quaker preacher and writer, opened to settlement by English Quakers, who were then being severely persecuted at home. These Quakers were joined by members of other compatible religious sects from Germany, the Netherlands, and Switzerland, who became known as the Pennsylvania Dutch.

The Mennonites were a Swiss Anabaptist denomination originally called *The Swiss Brethren*. They were renamed *Mennonites* for the Dutch religious reformer Menno Simons (1496–1561), who led them in Holland and Germany. The first Mennonites came to America from Germany in 1683, just two years after Pennsylvania was founded, and established *Germantown*, Pennsylvania. By 1771 they were also called by their Dutch name, *Mennists*. There are about 200,000 Mennonites in the U.S. today.

Amish traveling the Lancaster (Pennsylvania) Pike in their rockaways (1845), four-wheeled wagons with canopies and side curtains (named after Rockaway, New Jersey, where they were made).

267

The Amish, full name the *Old Order Amish*, are a conservative sect of the Mennonites. They are named after a 17th century Swiss Mennonite bishop, Jacob Ammann (sometimes spelled *Amen*), who insisted on strict literalism.

The Dunkers originated in Germany, then first came to America in 1719. Their name comes from German *Tunker* (dipper, dunker), from their belief in *trine emersion* (triple immersion, symbolizing death, burial, and resurrection). In America they were originally called *Tunkers* or *The Brethren; Dunker* was first recorded in 1744, *Dunkard* in 1750, and other Pennsylvania Dutch sometimes called them *Donkelaars*. Their church was named the *Church of the Brethren* until 1904, when it was renamed the *German Baptist Brethren*. Their 200,000 American members are divided into several sects, including the *New Dunkers* (1848, the most conservative), *Old Order Dunkers* (1881), and *Progressive Dunkers* (1882).

The Moravians are members of the Moravian Church, officially called the *Renewed Church of the Brethren* or *Unita Fratrum*, which was founded in the province of Moravia in the 15th century (Moravia was then part of Bohemia, later of Czechoslovakia). Some members fled to Germany after the Thirty Years' War and found refuge in 1722 on Graf von Zinzendorf's Saxony estate at Herrnhut, hence the Moravians are also called *herrnhuters*. In the New World they first settled, unsuccessfully, in the West Indies and Georgia to convert the slaves and Indians, then settled successfully in Pennsylvania in 1740, founding *Bethlehem, Nazareth,* and *Lititz*. By 1756 their towns were called *Moravian towns*, as were villages of their converted Indians, who by 1779 were called *Moravian Indians*.

The Schwenkfelders are spiritual descendants of Kasper Schwenkfelder (1489-1561), a German leader of the Reformation and founder of the *Reformation of the Middle Way*. His middle way between Catholics and Lutherans caused him and the various "brotherhoods" he founded to be persecuted by both sides. As late as 1719 a group of his followers had to flee to Saxony and 200 of these soon came to America. In 1782 his American followers organized the *Society of Schwenkfelders*, which was incorporated into the *Schwenkfelder Church* in 1909, there now being around 2,500 members, mostly in the Philadelphia area.

A Dunker barn displays hex signs *across the front.*

The major Pennsylvania Dutch groups established prosperous farming communities, while preserving their own religion and customs. Like the Quakers, they were to oppose slavery, bearing arms, taking legal oaths, and state-run schools. In simple obedience to the Bible, they insisted on plain living and dress (based on their familiar 17th century rural costumes). Thus the earliest Pennsylvania Dutch (and Quakers) called themselves *the plain people* as early as the 1680s and called the Pennsylvania Calvinists and Lutherans *the gay people.*

The Pennsylvania Dutch influenced our language in many ways. First they introduced a number of things we still talk about, including German *stoves* in the 1700s, *flatboats*, the *Conestoga Wagon*, and *mashed potatoes*. They also introduced *sauerkraut* (1776) into the language and *hex* (German *hexe*, witch), with tourists talking about the *hex signs* or *hex marks* on Pennsylvania Dutch barns ever since touring by car became popular. However, it is often difficult to pinpoint which words were introduced by the Pennsylvania Dutch and which by other German immigrants (see THE GERMANS).

Not until around 1850 did some of the Pennsylvania Dutch groups make English their first language. Some Pennsylvania Dutch words, uses, and intonations still persist, including *Belsnickel* for Santa Claus and *(paper) tut* for paper bag; *spritzen* for "to sprinkle"; the use of *that* for "so that" ("Heat the water that it boils"), *leave* for "let" ("Leave him have the book"), *all* for "all gone" ("The cheese is all"), and *look* for "be seemly, look right" ("It wouldn't look for a girl to travel alone"). Their intonation includes raising the voice at the beginning of a question and lowering it at the end.

Incidentally, many of the quaint names of Pennsylvania Dutch towns, such as the Lancaster County Amish towns of *Intercourse* and *Bird in Hand*, weren't given them by these religious people but by earlier frontiersmen.

The Pilgrims and the Mayflower

They knew they were pilgrims.
William Bradford, *Of Plimoth Plantation*, written 1620–47. A leader of the Mayflower Company, Bradford was governor of Plymouth Plantation for all but five years during 1621–56.

This passage, first printed in 1669, gave the members of the Mayflower Company the name *Pilgrims*. The word had meant "wayfarer, traveler" since the 12th century and a traveler to a sacred place, as a shrine, since the 13th (from Latin *pelegrīnus/peregrīnus*, a foreigner, wanderer, which also gives us the name *peregrine* falcon). The term *Pilgrim Fathers* didn't appear until 1799. The Pilgrims were also called:

> *the Puritans*, a name assumed by the 16th century Church of England reformers who wanted to purify the church by simplifying its creed and ceremonies and who advocated strict religious discipline.
>
> *Separatists*, a 17th century name for those Puritans who had come to feel that changing the Church of England was impossible and withdrew from it to form their own groups.
>
> *Congregationalists* or *Brownists*, because the Pilgrims were Separatists who followed the ideas of the nonconformist ex-clergyman of the Church of England Robert Browne, who around 1580 had advocated a system of church government following a *congregational* pattern, claiming each local congregation was free to manage its own beliefs and affairs without bishops and other church officials coming between its members and Christ. For all practical purposes *Congregationalism* (a 17th century word) became the state religion of early New England.
>
> *the Scrooby Group*, because the original group of Separatists who became the Pilgrims had come from the village of Scrooby in Nottinghamshire.

Why did Bradford and the other Pilgrims speak and write of Plymouth *plantation* instead of Plymouth *colony*? *Plantation* had meant a planted area or farm in England since the 15th century (from Latin *plantāre*, to plant, literally "to thrust in with the sole of the foot"). The word was widely used to mean any homestead or small farm by the early settlers—it wasn't until 1780 that *plantation* was considered a southern word for what New Englanders had meanwhile come to call a farm; not until the 1830s did *plantation* usually mean a large southern rice, sugar, cotton, or tobacco farm worked by slaves. The English, however, had also used the word *plantation* to mean a colony since 1558, actually talking of "planting" settlers in new areas. Thus *plantation* also meant colony and *Plymouth Plantation* (still spelled *Plimoth*) is what the English and early settlers called the first successful New England Colony. As late as 1790 Rhode Island entered the union under the official name of *the State of Rhode Island and Providence Plantations*.

The word *colony* (spelled *colonie* by the settlers) had been used in England since 1548 (from Latin *colōnia*, farm, settlement, since it was farmers who settled new lands). Thus *colony* and *plantation* were both used in early America. The verb *to colonize* was coined by Sir Francis Bacon in 1622, two years after the Pilgrims landed. All immigrants to the New World were sometimes called *pilgrims* from the 1670s to the 1750s, the word *colonist* not being generally used until around 1700. In 1776 the word *colonial* suddenly took on a new meaning and all Americans immediately used it to refer to pre-Revolutionary days.

The *Mayflower* was named after the *mayflower*, a 16th century name for the hawthorn blossom, so called because it was collected and used as a decoration to celebrate May Day. By coincidence this 90-foot long cargo ship did smell sweet, it had transported wine for years before it took on its cargo of Pilgrims. After living 12 years in Holland, the Pilgrims bought the small, old *Speedwell* (which didn't) and sailed it back to England. There they made an agreement with the London merchants of the Virginia Company of Plymouth, England to buy the bigger and better *Mayflower* and provision both ships for the voyage to Virginia—the Pilgrims agreeing to work seven years for the company and thereafter to split their profits from the fur, lumber, and fishing trade with it 50–50. The two ships sailed on August 5, 1620, but turned back when the *Speedwell* proved too leaky for the long voyage. Some of its passengers transferred to the *Mayflower* and it sailed again, dangerously alone, from Plymouth on September 6, with 102 passengers (including 34 children) and about 30 crewmen. Only about a third of the passengers were leaving England for religious reasons, the rest were seeking adventure, hoping to improve their financial lot, or were servants accompanying their masters or employers.

What did the Pilgrims talk about on the 66-day voyage? Probably about those left behind, about missing their possessions (each family was allowed only one chest of personal belongings, cooking utensils, tools and weapons, a cradle for each baby, and a *Bible box* with the family Bible). They probably also talked about what their new life would be like in Virginia, about the baby born on board and appropriately named Oceanus, about the sailors who hated them and called them *puke stockings* because they got seasick, especially the 80 or so who slept in the dark airless hold. They may have grumbled about the 20 most prosperous and important passengers whom Captain Jones had given his cabin. They certainly talked about farming, weaving, and shopkeeping, since most followed these occupations; about the salt horse and hardtack they ate, along with dried beans and peas; the increasingly rancid butter and moldy cheese; and about the water going bad and everyone, including children, having to drink beer (the beer soon ran low, which is one reason they landed in Massachusetts instead of following the coast to Virginia). They certainly talked about the two big storms in October, especially the second which broke the ship's main beam, which was repaired with a heavy iron screw they had brought from Holland; about Dr. Fuller's young servant Will Butten dying of ship's fever; of the two dogs and the ship's rat-catching cat; of the small fire one of the children, Francis Billington, started; and of how good it was to have not only a doctor but a professional soldier (Miles Standish), a blacksmith, a cooper, and a shoemaker with them to start their new life.

The Puritans nobly fled from a land of despotism to a land of freedom, where they could not only enjoy their own religion, but could prevent everybody else from enjoin' his.
Artemus Ward in "The London Punch Letters," 1866.

They also read their Bibles, sang psalms, and talked about God.

Finally on November 9th the Pilgrims sighted Cape Cod. They then began using the names that we have been talking about as part of our history ever since:

Cape Cod, named by the British navigator Bartholomew Gosnold in 1602 (he had also been second in command of the expedition that took the Virginia settlers to Jamestown in 1607). The Pilgrims first went ashore on the site that later became *Provincetown*, where the women washed the clothes and bedding, the children played on the beach, and many of the men argued about whether all need stay together or whether they could split up into several groups once they found a suitable landing place to start settlements.

the Mayflower Compact. The arguments about whether or not to stay together reached their peak on Cape Cod, leading to the November 11th meeting in the "Great Cabin" of the *Mayflower*, where 41 adult male passengers signed the Mayflower Compact, in which all agreed to stick together, abide by majority rule, and have a right to choose their own leader. This was the beginning of democracy in America.

Plymouth. The Pilgrims made three exploring expeditions in the ship's shallop, looking for a place to live, the exploring party reaching Plymouth on December 21st (it had been named *Plymouth* by Captain John Smith in 1614; the Indian name for it was *Patuxet*, but the Patuxet Indians who had lived there had been wiped out by disease just four years before the Pilgrims landed). Plymouth was chosen as the place to settle because it had a reasonably safe harbor, two freshwater brooks, and even fields cleared by the Indians (the exploring party had previously found a basket of Indian corn, seen Indians whaling, and had a brief skirmish with another group of Indians).

Plymouth Rock isn't mentioned in the early chronicles. The name, and the legend that the Pilgrims stepped from their shallop onto it, seem to have become common only after the 1820 bicentennial celebration of the Pilgrims' landing.

the Common House was built in 26 days, including Christmas Monday of 1620 (Puritans didn't believe in celebrations),

An exploring party steps ashore at Plymouth Rock on December 21, 1620. Many of the Pilgrims disembarked five days later after some rough thatched huts had been built; others stayed aboard the Mayflower *until March. Weakened by exposure at sea, poor food, and inadequate housing 50 of the 101 settlers died during this first winter. Exactly where the Pilgrims landed is not known; Plymouth Rock was apparently mentioned first in 1741 and not really accepted as the landing spot until the 1820s.*

with everyone living on board the *Mayflower*. Built as a storehouse for tools and guns, it housed many of the men while they built homes; later it was used as a church and hospital. The men also made one pathlike street from the shore to the top of the hill where the cannon and lookout were, and named it *First Street*, which indeed it was.

Samoset, *Squanto*, and *Massasoit*. The Indian *Samoset* first greeted the Pilgrims on March 16, 1621. His greeting was the first words the Pilgrims ever heard an Indian say; it was—"Welcome Englishmen." He had learned English from fishermen who visited the coast, sometimes staying long periods to take on wood, fresh water, and meat; to dry or smoke their catch; and even to wait for good spring weather before the long voyage home. Samoset visited the Pilgrims several times, bringing *Squanto*, who lived with them the rest of his life, teaching them how to plant corn and showing them the best places to hunt, fish, and gather wild plants and herbs. Samoset also introduced the Pilgrims to *Chief Massasoit* with whom they made a verbal peace treaty and mutual assistance pact that was to last 54 years.

Not until March, four months after they had landed at Plymouth, had the Pilgrim men built enough one-room, thatched-roof houses so that all could sleep ashore. Then finally, on April 5, 1621, the *Mayflower* left to return to England. That first winter, half of the Pilgrims and sailors had died in the New World, most buried secretly in unmarked graves so the Indians wouldn't know that now only some 50 Pilgrims were left on shore.

Far north of the boundary of the Virginia Company, the Pilgrims soon gained the right to settle *Plymouth Plantation* from the Council for New England, an offshoot of the Virginia Company. The *Massachusetts Bay Colony* wasn't founded until 1630 and Plymouth Plantation wasn't absorbed into it until 1691 (the land of the original Plymouth Plantation then being called *the Old Colony*).

Americans, like most peoples of the world, talk about winners or survivors. Have you ever talked about the *Popham Colony*? Named for its sponsor Sir John Popham, Chief Justice of England, and led by his brother George Popham, it was actually the first settlement in New England, composed of 120 colonists who settled at the mouth of the Kennebec River in Maine in 1607-08. But during that severe winter a ship came and about 60 returned to England (after the first hard winter at Plymouth, the *Mayflower*'s captain had offered to take any of the Pilgrims back to England who wanted to go—none went). Next, George Popham died and then, soon after, the second in command, Raleigh Gilbert, returned to England to assume a large inheritance. Without leaders and short of supplies, the remaining Popham settlers abandoned their colony in 1608. Did they fail because they lacked religious zeal, a democratic way to ensure continuing leadership, or merely due to circumstances? At any rate, few remember the Popham Colony today. When we talk of the first New England settlers we talk of the Pilgrims, the *Mayflower*, and Plymouth Plantation.

Pissing and Peeing

According to the written records, Americans have been *pissing* since 1760 and *peeing* since 1788. It seems doubtful that earlier colonists held their water or merely used the word "urinate." *Piss* has actually been part of the English language since the 13th century (via Old French from Vulgar Latin *pissiãre*), the problem of its late recording in America being that people didn't write such words, even though they said them. *Piss pot* was a 15th century word for chamber pot and the expression "He hasn't got a pot to piss in" (is too poor to own a chamber pot) probably predates the sailing of the *Mayflower*. Because of delicacy and censorship, such terms as *pisser*, someone or something extraordinary; *pissed-off*, angry; *to be full of piss and vinegar*, full of energy; and *piss call*, the first call to get out of bed in the morning, especially in the Navy, didn't generally appear in writing until the late 1930s, and it is impossible to tell how long they had been in the spoken language before that.

Pee is a much later word than *piss*, first being used in the 18th century as a children's euphemism for *piss*, formed by merely saying the first letter, *p*. It was first popular in America about the time of the Revolutionary War. The children's terms *pee pee* and *wee wee* both appeared in the 19th century, as did the adult euphemism *go see a man (about a dog)*, which appeared in 1867.

Call the Police!

We have been calling on the police for help—and calling the police by various names—almost since the first colonists landed, though people didn't actually use the word *police* until the 1780s. At first many settlements used a "watch and ward" system, in which private citizens patrolled at night, primarily to raise an alarm against fire and Indian attack. The first real policeman in the colonies was the *constable* (a 13th century English word via French from Latin *comes stabulī*, officer of the stable, chief groom), which was recorded in Massachusetts in 1630 as a man paid to organize a "constable's watch." *Constable* was a common word for any policeman well into the 1890s.

By 1646 the word *sheriff* was recorded in Massachusetts, as a chief officer of a court charged with preserving the peace. *Sheriffs*, however, have existed for over 1,000 years, since Anglo-Saxon times (Old English *scīr-gerēfa*, the "reeve" or royal officer of a "shire," hence a *shire reeve* or *sheriff*). By the late 1640s constables,

New York City police, about 1855. They did not carry firearms.

274

The full regalia of a 1929 "trooper."

sheriffs, and sheriffs' *deputies* were all being called *officer* (Latin *officium*, service, duty). The first real police force in the New World was an eight-man guard established by the Dutch in New Amsterdam in 1658; New York City then provided the first complete uniforms for its guard in 1693. By the 1780s Americans were beginning to use the word *police*, with *policeman* being in wide use by the 1830s—*police forces* growing with the new industrial cities.

Since 1780 words associated with the police and their work have come thick and fast, including:

frisk, 1781 (the word once meant "lively, fresh").

police power, 1827.

nab (arrest), 1827; *pinch*, 1845; *collar*, 1879; *bust*, meaning a police raid, 1930s, coming to mean a police dispersal of a youth gang by 1949 (this was also called a *hassle*), and meaning to arrest by the early 1960s, originally by rebellious students.

Black Maria, 1840; *patrol wagon*, 1887; *paddy wagon*, 1920s.

chief of police, 1840s.

police station, *stationhouse*, late 1840s.

police commissioner, 1850s.

patrolman, 1860s.

traffic police, 1860, the year New York's famous "Broadway Squad" was formed to help people cross the street and direct horse-drawn traffic; *traffic cop*, 1915.

police surgeon, 1868.

harbor police, 1870.

third degree, 1890s.

desk sergeant, 1890s.

police captain, 1890s.

police blotter, 1900.

lineup (of suspects), 1907.

squad car, 1930s; *highway patrol*, and *road block*, late 1930s.

tactical police, late 1960s.

Police and policemen have also frequently been called by other more colorful and less respectful names, such as:

New York City police parading, about 1910.

the law, 1835.

copper, 1846; *cop*, 1859. These probably come from Latin *capere*, to catch, capture, but some people believe they come from the copper buttons on police uniforms or the copper star-shaped badges many police once wore (the badge is now made of tin and is called a *tin*). It has also been suggested that *cop* comes from "constable on patrol," but it doesn't.

pig, 1848. This was obsolete throughout the first half of this century but had a resurgence in the 1960s when first Blacks, then radical students, made it a common derisive word.

Modern riot police, with guns, billy clubs, and hard hats.

bull, 1893 (from the Spanish Gypsy *bul*, policeman; *fly bull*, a detective or special duty policeman, 1907; *cinder bull*, a railroad detective or guard, 1910; *harness bull*, uniformed policeman, from the Sam Brown belt, 1915; *yard bull*, originally a railroad detective or guard, now a prison guard, 1915.

flatfoot (flatfooted from walking the beat), 1913.

fuzz, 1931, probably from the 1920s *fuzzie*, a strict or mean policeman, from the 1920s *fussytail*, a person hard to please.

We have also called policemen by the French *gendarme* (French *gens d'arms*, men at arms) and have even used the informal British *bobby* (from Sir Robert "Bobby" Peel, 1788–1850, British statesman and reformer who instituted the Irish constabulary, called "peelers," and reorganized the London police force).

Detectives have been part of American police forces since about 1840 (from Latin *dē-*, away, off + *tegere*, to cover, hence one who uncovers a crime or criminal). *Private detectives* became well known with the Pinkertons, especially in the 1860s. Detectives have been called by various names too:

shadow, 1859, coming before the verb *to shadow* (follow), 1865; *to tail* dates from 1904.

fly cop, 1860.

plainclothesman, 1880s.

dick, 1900 (from condensing "detective").

gumshoe, 1900s, because a detective moves quietly as if wearing gum-soled shoes.

shamus, 1934, originally it meant any policeman but especially a hotel detective (from Hebrew *shamash*, synagogue caretaker and watchman, pronounced to rhyme with "Thomas" but is influenced by the Irish name Shamus/Seamus and is sometimes pronounced to rhyme with "Amos").

private eye, 1942, a shortening of *private i*(nvestigator), popularized by such writers as Raymond Chandler.

Americans were reading and talking about *detective stories* by 1883 and calling them *whodunits* in the early 1930s (the term *whodunit* was probably coined by Donald Gordon in the *American News of Books*, July, 1930).

The Pony Express

From the late 1840s until the mid 1890s the general term *pony express* was used proudly by newspapers, business firms, and express companies, such as Wells Fargo, to mean any fast, direct service for dispatches, mail, and parcels. But *the Pony Express*, that name so frequently talked about and so often romanticized in Western movies and novels, lasted only 19 months, from April 3, 1860 to October 24, 1861. Affectionately called *the Pony Post* or simply *the Pony*, its full name was *the Central Overland Pony Express Company*. It was established by the stagecoach and freighting firm of Russell, Majors, and Waddell in an attempt to win a mail contract by out-

performing THE OVERLAND STAGE and thus stave off bankruptcy. It failed when the telegraph connected the East and West Coasts.

The Pony Express went from St. Joseph, Missouri to Sacramento, California, with 190 *stations* along its 1,830-mile route. The object: to carry a letter along the route in ten days. The 80 *Pony Express riders*, including "Buffalo Bill" Cody and "Pony Bob" Haslan, were often boys or small men chosen for their light weight. Each man rode about 75 miles and changed his fast Indian pony at each station, approximately every ten miles. Horse corrals were kept at *horse stations*, about a hundred miles apart. To change horses within two minutes the riders carried the letters in four leather *cantinas* (boxes, Spanish, "rooms, storage rooms") attached to a specially designed *mochila* (Spanish, roughly "saddle blanket"), a leather square thrown over the saddle. Many horses and riders were used on each trip but the mochila was passed along from one end of the line to the other and was the true symbol of this brief service.

News of Abraham Lincoln's election on November 6, 1860, was carried to The Rocky Mountain News *in Denver by* Pony Express, *the dispatch being delayed two days until the electoral vote was counted (Lincoln won only 40% of the popular vote but an overwhelming percentage of the electoral vote). It was not until October, 1861, that the transcontinental telegraph line began operation, dooming the Pony Express.*

A Pony Express rider carrying the mochila, *which to save time was passed on from rider to rider. It is said the fastest trip was 2,000 miles in 7 days, 17 hours, carrying Lincoln's first message to Congress.*

Emily Post Says---

has been an American expression ever since the Baltimore-born, New York socialite Emily Post (1872–1960), became the arbiter of polite manners with the publication of her book *Etiquette* (often called "The Blue Book of Social Usage") in 1922. Daughter of the eminent architect Bruce Price, she married Edwin Post at 20 and soon found it necessary to supplement her income, which she did by writing light, polite magazine pieces and several novels about Americans in Europe (her 1904 *The Flight of a Moth* is her best known).

After her *Etiquette* appeared the many letters she received asking for advice about specific social situations led to her writing a popular syndicated newspaper column and giving a successful radio show. Her book became very popular because it came out during a time of increasing prosperity, when millions of Americans felt themselves moving up the social ladder, and also because it was the first modern etiquette book written for the average person rather than for the upper classes. Her oft-quoted underlying rule was the democratic "consideration for others." Thus, since 1922 we have been settling etiquette debates by saying "Emily Post says ---."

Emily Post shows a young lady how to repair an electric plug, 1943. During World War II Miss Post relaxed her standards of correct comportment. She urged young women to work in defense plants and said that, under such circumstances, wearing slacks makes good sense.

Powder and Paint

has been a term for cosmetics since the 16th century. Early cosmetics were used to absorb perspiration and to cover dirt, rashes, and skin blemishes, as well as to produce a smooth, white complexion or to paint cheeks and lips red. Although women were reported seen wearing make-up on the Boston Commons in the 1660s, Puritan ministers then warned that *painted ladies* could not enter heaven. As late as 1770 Pennsylvania adopted an edict

> That all women ... whether virgins, maids, or widows, that shall ... impose upon, seduce, and betray into matrimony any ... subjects by the scents, paints, cosmetic washes, artificial teeth, false hair ... shall incur the penalty of the law against witchcraft.

The word *cosmetics* (Greek *kosmatikos*, skilled in decorating, the root *kosmos* meaning "order") was in wide use by the 1720s, and the word *make-up* became popular after the War of 1812. By the 1830s and 40s rice powder, rose water, cucumber cream, and lemon juice were common complexion aids, with *cold cream* (a word that came in around 1710) being fairly common.

Not until aniline dyes were invented in the mid 19th century, increasing the color range of cosmetics, did the modern cosmetic industry begin to flourish. In 1886 "Avon calling" was first heard, the first "Avon lady," Mrs. P. F. A. Allre, being employed by

A 1914 advertisement for a beauty cream.

278

Theda Bara in her role as Cleopatra, 1917. Noted for her use of eye make-up, she helped popularize mascara in the 20s.

Clara Bow with her lips painted in a Cupid's bow.

the firm's founder, D. H. McConnell, to visit and sell cosmetics in the home. In the 1905 Sears Roebuck catalog *rouge de théâtre* was offered for sale, though *rouge* (the French word for "red") still bore some of the stigma associated with actresses and *painted ladies of the street*, who had been using it for over a hundred years. It was not until after World War I, however, that the ideal white-and-pink female face changed, due mainly to Theda Bara's artificial *vamp look* of the 1920s. Her make-up was created by Helena Rubenstein, using colored powders, eye shading, *mascara* (Arabic *mask-harah*, buffoon, clown, referring to the make-up that clowns have worn for centuries), and bright lip coloring. Actually *lip rouge* or *lipstick* had been in use by actresses and Black minstrels before 1880 but had just become easily accessible with the invention of the metal lipstick container by Maurice Levy in 1915—just in time to provide the lips for the vamp look and for the *Cupid's bow* mouth as seen on Clara Bow, Lillian Gish, and millions of less famous women. By the 1920s, too, *Elizabeth Arden* was promoting *cold cream* heavily as did *Pond's* in the 1930s, often with the endorsements of society women, to create respectability, which is what cosmetics lacked until after the first World War.

Meanwhile, the hands were not forgotten. *Jergen's* lotion appeared in 1901, advertising "the Jergen's girl," and liquid *cuticle remover* was introduced in 1907. This was soon made by pharmacist Northam Warren who then went on to produce the first liquid *nail polish* in 1916, calling it *Cutex*.

The Prairie, that great American grassland, was named by French explorers, trappers, and fur traders spilling west from the Mississippi and eastern Canada (see VOYAGEURS, RAPIDS, AND PORTAGES). We first used the French word *prairie* ("large

meadow") in 1691; it is also widely used in Canada, where western Canada's Manitoba, Saskatchewan, and Alberta are called *the Prairie Provinces*. The same French who first explored the prairie also gave us other words we associate with it:

bois de vache (literally "cow wood"), buffalo chips, as used for campfires, 1843, also called *prairie chips* and humorously known as *prairie coal*.

butte, a hill, 1659; first U.S. western use recorded by the Lewis and Clark expedition in 1805.

cache (French, from *cacher*, to hide), first U.S. use also recorded by the Lewis and Clark expedition, 1805.

gopher (French, from *gaufre*, honeycomb, from the animal's complex burrows), 1814; *gopher hole*, 1837; *pocket gopher*, 1873. *Prairie gopher*, 1875, also called a *prairie chipmunk*, 1888. Minnesota was called *The Gopher State* by 1880. *Gopher man*, a miner who "burrows" into the earth by digging or using explosives, 1880, which by 1901 became a slang term for a safeblower or safecracker.

The prairie played a large role in American history, being loved or hated by our explorers, trappers, and hunters, by those who crossed it, and by those who finally settled and farmed it. *The Dictionary of Americanisms* lists 227 American terms using the word *prairie*, of which the most common include:

Since wood was scarce on the prairie, pioneer homes were often built partly underground, as shown by this Nebraska dugout, 1888, or were constructed of layers of sod baked hard by the sun. Prairie farmers even made their fences of sod.

prairie chicken, 1691; *prairie hen*, *prairie fowl*, first recorded by the Lewis and Clark expedition in 1804; *prairie grouse*, 1852. The Lewis and Clark expedition, 1804–06, was also the first to record *prairie bird*, *prairie cock*, *prairie bear*, *prairie buffalo*, *prairie wolf* (coyote), and many other terms for animals, plants, geological features, and customs of the prairie.

prairie cocktail, raw egg with pepper and salt drunk in vinegar or whiskey, 1890; called a *prairie oyster* by 1905 (to earlier hunters *prairie oysters* were buffalo testicles, considered a delicacy).

prairie dog, 1774. Also called *prairie squirrel*, *prairie marmoset*, 1808; *prairie ground squirrel*, 1844. *Prairie dog village*, 1823; *prairie dog town*, 1843; *prairie dog city*, 1850: note that as the U.S. grew from villages to cities the name given prairie-dog colonies kept pace. *Prairie dog hole*, 1871.

prairie farm, 1838.

prairie fire, 1824.

prairie fox, the kit fox, 1838.

prairie grass, 1812.

prairie Indian, 1829.

prairie land, 1807; *prairie region*, 1826.

prairie law, *law of the prairie*, 1823, the rules for survival in the prairie as necessitated by nature and the Indians.

prairie life, 1843, the way of life of westward migrants and settlers on the prairie.

prairie rabbit, a white rabbit, 1840; the western jack rabbit, 1846.

prairie rattlesnake, 1817.

prairie rose, 1822.

Prairie schooners *carrying immigrants to Kansas.*

Prairie schooner, 1841; *prairie wagon*, 1855; *prairie clipper*, 1870. For more details see COVERED WAGONS AND THE OREGON TRAIL.
Prairie State, Illinois, 1842; any state in the prairie region, 1852; specifically, North Dakota, 1900.

As always, our language can tell us a lot about our history. Note that before 1838 most of the new prairie words were names for the plants, animals, and Indians on the prairie, for things of interest to the explorers, hunters, and trappers. After 1838 the new *prairie* words generally have to do with farms, westward wagon trains, and even states.

Oh, bury me not on the lone prairie,
Where wild coyotes will howl o'er me,
Where the rattlers hiss, and the crow flies free,
Oh, bury me not on the lone prairie.
"The Lone Prairie." This cowboy song is based on an old sailors' song, "Oh Bury Me Not In the Deep, Deep Sea."

A prairie fire *(1824) was a frequent and terrible calamity for the pioneer. Here an 1870s farmer is running his* fire guard *(1874).*

Pretty Girls

The Gibson Girl *of the 1890s.*

Calling a young woman *girl* isn't an insult: the word *girl* entered the English language in the 13th century as meaning "maiden, young woman" and has meant that ever since; its additional meaning of "female child" didn't appear until 300 years later. It's probably no coincidence that *pretty* originally meant "crafty, wily" in English, then came to mean "beautiful, dainty"—because men always seem to have been attracted most to two diametrically opposed types of girls, the angelic, wholesome *nice girls* and the daring, crafty vampirelike *coquettes* (*nice* has meant coy, shy since the 13th century, before that it meant "foolish, stupid," also no coincidence; *coquette* is a 17th century English word, the feminine form of the French *coquet*, show off, flirt, the diminutive of French *coq*, cock). Whether nice or coquettes, girls have been the topic of millions of American conversations—and pretty girls get talked about most, both by

281

men and by other women. Here's a list of words we have used for pretty girls, many being used almost exclusively by men:

angel is a 15th century word; it has always had some figurative use meaning an angelic person. *Angel face*, 1931; *angel puss*, some mocking use since 1936.

gal, 1790s (a corruption of the word *girl*, perhaps influenced by the Celtic *caile*, girl).

beauty, 1820s; *Baltimore beauty, Baltimore belle*, 1840s, a delicate, fragile beauty, the kind for which Baltimore was then famous; *a beaut*, 1866 (*a beaut* had been slang for anything remarkable since about 1860).

chicken, 1859; *chick*, 1927; *hip chick, slick chick*, late 1930s (*slick* has meant "smooth," attractive since 1842; *hip* has been a variant of *hep*, aware, since 1931). The names of almost all birds have been used to designate a girl or woman, *pigeon* since the 16th century (it also meant a dupe by 1590), *quail* by 1859 in America (it may also have been influenced by Celtic *caile*, girl), and even *bird* itself, which we have used since 1940, but which became truly popular as imported British slang in the 1960s with the British singing group the Beatles (*bird* had meant an admirable person in the U.S. by 1830 and a fellow or guy by 1914). Incidentally a *San Quentin quail* was a 1930s term for a sexually attractive but underaged girl, a *quail* young enough that carnal knowledge of her could lead to a term of imprisonment; such a girl was also called *jail bait* in the 30s. Since the late 1950s such a young girl has been called a *Lolita* (a diminutive of *Lola*, which itself is a diminutive of *Dolores*, which means "sorrow" in Spanish), from the precocious heroine in Vladimir Nabokov's 1955 novel *Lolita*.

stunner, 1862.

peach, 1865; *peacherine, peacherino*, 1900.

piece of dry goods, 1869; *piece of calico*, 1880, both terms usually referring to a healthy, rosey-cheeked, pert girl. *Piece* took on the sole meaning of sex object around 1891 with *piece of ass* not recorded until World War II, though the term is probably much older.

fairy, fairey, 1880s. It was not until 1908 that *fairy* took on its homosexual meaning.

good looker, 1894; *looker*, 1902.

queen, 1894, originally for a regal beauty.

dream, 1896; *dreamboat*, popularized by the 1936 song "When My Dreamboat Comes Home," by Cliff Friend and Dave Franklin, the word could apply to both girls and boys; *dream girl*, late 1930s; *dreamy*, 1940s, also applied to both girls and boys.

pippin, 1899; *pip*, 1912. By 1880 *pippin* had meant any remarkable thing and *pip* was used in that way since about 1910, the words, of course, come from the *pippin* variety of apple (*pippin* meant a seedling apple or seed in English long before America was discovered).

adorable, first used to refer to girls around 1900. The word had been in general use soon after the Pilgrims landed.

baby, 1901; *babe*, 1915.

doll, 1904.

The It Girl, *Clara Bow, 1920s.*

282

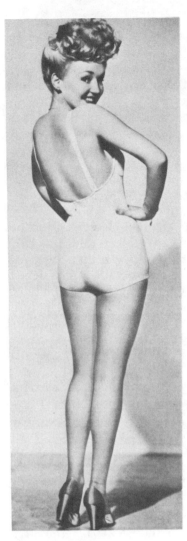

The Pin-up Girl, *Betty Grable, 1940s.*

cutie, 1919, pretty girls had been called *cute* since 1906; *cutie pie,* 1930s; *cute trick,* 1939.

an eyeful, 1920s, referring to a girl's figure more than her face; *easy on the eyes,* 1936.

an armful, 1930s, one of many terms for attractive women popularized by Hollywood gossip columnists.

a lovely, 1930s, another term popularized by the newspapers. *Lovely* had been used since the 1750s to refer to a virtuous or "nice" person.

mouse, 1930s, usually a small, cute, or passive girl, popularized by its use by tough guys in books and movies.

filly, 1930s.

dish, 1936.

fox, a pert girl, originally Black use and first known to most other Americans when heavyweight boxer Muhammad Ali used it in an interview in *Time* magazine in 1963.

Though female beauties may be fair and delicate, dark and passionate, tall and slim, or plump and bouncy, each age has its own typical beauty and personality type, for styles of beauty and personality change too. Famous or infamous women, and magazines, books, newspapers, and especially movies, have created the models women imitate and men desire. The dream girl of the Revolutionary War soldier is unknown to us, indeed, without the romantic and sexual stimulus of mass media he may have had none. Many Civil War soldiers, however, carried drawings of pretty girls clipped from fashion magazines of the day, and by the 1880s such actresses as Lillian Russell, "airy, fairy Lillian, the American Beauty" set the style for pretty girls. In the 1890s Charles Dana Gibson's *Gibson girl* was the mode. The early *flappers* (see THE ROARING 20s for details) bobbed their hair in imitation of the French prostitutes so highly advertised in World War I, molded their personality on the girls in F. Scott Fitzgerald's stories, and took other aspects of their *jazz baby* look and personality from John Held Junior's drawings and movie roles about flaming youth as portrayed by such movie stars as Madge Bellamy, Colleen Moore, Betty Compson, and Clara Bow. For by the 1920s the movies controlled American taste in beauty, giving us such virginal but vulnerable types as Lillian Gish, Mary Pickford, and Norma Talmadge and such man-destroying femme fatales as Theda Bara. The World War II *oomph girls, sweater girls,* and *pinup girls* were also products of the movies, while later American women followed such fads, fashions, and advertising as appeared in *Vogue, Harper's Bazaar,* or even the *Ladies' Home Journal* or took President John F. Kennedy's wife Jacqueline as their model. Here are some major types of pretty or alluring girls we have talked about:

the Gibson girl, the typical, idealized 1890s girl as portrayed by (and in a large measure created by) illustrator Charles Dana Gibson in his many drawings for such popular magazines as

Rita Hayworth, 1950s.

the old *Life, Century, Harper's, Scribners,* and *Collier's Weekly.* The Gibson girl's soft, wide pompadour, parasol, and clothing influenced styles until the 1930s. Gibson drew her in what became known as a *Gibson girl blouse,* a starched, tailored *shirt-waist* (an 1879 word) with leg-of-mutton sleeves and a high collar with an ascot tie at the neck; a dark skirt skimming the floor and worn over *Gibson girl petticoats* (she wore a *divided skirt* when riding a BICYCLE); and a *Breton sailor hat.* Of course she had the 1890s *hourglass figure.*

the Ziegfeld girl, 1907. Florenz Ziegfeld's *Follies of 1907 was a* new type of musical *revue,* featuring "the most beautiful girls ever to walk across an American stage," each personally chosen by Ziegfeld himself. By the time of the last annual *Ziegfeld Follies* in 1931, the typical Ziegfeld girl had changed a lot, but America had gotten used to calling any tall, statuesque girl a *Ziegfeld girl.* Ziegfeld's main contribution was that he chose slender girls for his Follies, thus *show girls* became more slender and the trend toward pretty girls being slender was accelerated. Other revues featuring girls in opulent costumes also became popular before World War I, and Americans were also talking about *Earl Carroll girls* or saying a girl was as pretty as a *George White girl;* but the best compliment was to be called "a regular Ziegfeld girl."

the vamp and *to vamp* were in the language by 1910, referring to an unscrupulous, seductive woman who exploited men. However, as a type of heavily made-up, mysteriously exotic woman, the word and type were popularized by Theda Bara in the 1914 movie *A Fool There Was,* and later by Pola Negri in the 1919 German-made film *Passion. Vamp,* of course, is a shortening of the 17th century word *vampire* (via German from the Tartar *ubyr,* witch).

the flapper. See *flapper* at THE ROARING 20s.

bathing beauty was popularized before the 1920s by the *Mack Sennett Bathing Beauties.* This was the first term for a girl which admitted that to be "pretty" she had to have a good figure as well as a pretty face. In the 20s *bathing beauty contest* also became a popular term, though *beauty contest* dates from the 1890s.

Miss America, literally the girl chosen as the most beautiful in America at an annual national beauty contest. The first winner was Margaret Gorman of Washington in 1921, who was first called "Miss America" the following year. Since the late 1930s any pretty, typically American girl has been called "a regular Miss America."

the It Girl. People began talking about *it* (sex appeal) and *the It Girl* in 1928, both due to the 1928 Hollywood movie based on Elinor Glyn's lush, titillating, mildly daring, best-selling 1927 novel *It.* The star of the movie was Clara Bow, billed as *the It Girl;* an *it girl* then came to mean any girl who was full of sex appeal and vivacious gaiety.

sex kitten, 1940, usually in newspaper gossip columns.

glamour girl, 1941, popularized by Hollywood gossip columnists; *glamour puss,* a humorous or disparaging term for a pretentiously glamorous person of either sex.

oomph girl, early 1940s, popularized by Hollywood press agentry. *Oomph* had been Hollywood use for sex appeal since 1939.

sweater girl, early 1940s, originally Hollywood press agent use for a sexually attractive girl whose ample, firm, and well-defined breasts looked good in a sweater. Two things were happening during World War II that popularized this term: women, including defense plant workers, were wearing tight sweaters over hard, tight brassieres, and Hollywood studios and press agents were trying to come up with new sex-appeal words to describe specific stars. The *oomph girl*, *sweater girl*, and *pinup girl* all applied to the same type of healthy, sexy girl, and several Hollywood stars and starlets claimed to be "the original oomph girl" or "the original sweater girl."

pin-up girl, *pinup girl* entered the general language toward the end of World War II, first appearing in the Armed Forces newspaper *Yank* on April 30, 1943. It became a popular term thanks to U.S. soldiers, sailors, pilots, and marines, who had pinned, glued, and taped free publicity photographs of movie actresses and models in footlockers, barracks, crews' quarters, airplane cockpits, military truck cabs, and bars all over the world, making respectable the sexy photos of scantily clad girls that had been popular since the 1930s. Betty Grable was probably the most popular *pinup* and Rita Hayworth's most famous pinup photo probably the most artistic (a copy is said to have been attached to the first atomic bomb dropped on Hiroshima in 1945). Comparatively obscure models and actresses also had their sexually appealing photographs distributed by the hundreds of thousands, as Chili Williams, *the Polka-Dot Girl*, whose popular pinup shot in a polka-dot bathing suit was known to all.

sex symbol, mid 1950s. A term first used to explain why certain Hollywood stars were so popular, it was soon used by newspapers to describe the most famous Hollywood glamour girls, especially Marilyn Monroe.

playmate had been used since the 1920s to refer to a *good time girl* (1928) who "seeks men only as playmates." It became a popular term with *Playboy* magazine's monthly *foldout* photograph of a sexy, scantily clad girl (nude since the early 1970s) called "the Playmate of the Month." The term was well known soon after *Playboy's* first issue, December, 1953. As had *Esquire* magazine's famous *Petty girl* drawings since before World War II, Playboy's *playmate* catered to male sexual fantasies, showing unbelievably long-legged, large-breasted women. Besides its *playmates*, *Playboy* magazine, and later its *Playboy Clubs*, also featured scantily clad *bunnies*, the club's waitresses' scanty uniforms even being equipped with white cotton tails. By the mid 1960s *bunny* meant a sexually attractive girl, especially one who attached herself to a sport because she enjoyed the social life and the men found with it, giving us terms such as *ski bunny* and *beach bunny*.

Playboy bunnies, *1960s*.

Besides talking about pretty girls, men have been whistling (*wolf whistle*, late 1930s) and calling out to them on the street since about the 1880s, usually just to express appreciation but sometimes as an opening gambit or *come on* (a sexual invitation,

1940s; an allurement, or bait, for a customer in a store, 1902). Thus pretty girls have heard:

Does your mother know you're out?, around 1900.
(I love my wife but) oh you kid, 1908, also considered a snappy remark.
Oh you beautiful doll/baby/babe, 1920.
Hi, beautiful, 1925.
Hubba-hubba, 1941, wide armed forces use in World War II. It's from the Chinese greeting "how-pu-how" and was first used by air force personnel, who got it from Chinese pilots being trained at an air force base in Florida. It was made very popular by radio comedian Bob Hope, who broadcast his weekly show from military bases during the war, using armed forces terms and references to get laughs.

Of course, all girls are not pretty. By the 1820s in America there were enough girls to go around so that men could openly refer to the ugly or unpopular ones they rejected. Thus in the 1820s such American expressions as *ugly as sin* and *ugly enough to tree a wolf* were heard and the word *wallflower* entered the language (perhaps because such a shy or unpopular woman sat or stood near the wall during a party, waiting to be talked to or asked to dance). The words *cow* and *bag* for ungainly or ugly women appeared in the 1920s. Other ungentlemanly but not necessarily insulting words for a girl or woman include *twist*, *twirl* (1890s, from the English Cockney rhyming slang of *twist and twirl*, girl); *skirt* (1895); *dame* (1900); *frail* (1908); and *broad* (1910), almost assuredly because broad hips and buttocks are a sexual characteristic of women, but the word could have been influenced by *bawd*). But don't despair—people, even men, also talked about THE NEW WOMAN, and women also got even by talking about DASHING MEN.

Prohibition—Joe Sent Me

The manufacture, sale, or transportation of intoxicating liquors ... is hereby prohibited.
18th Amendment to the U.S. Constitution, 1919

Thus began *the Prohibition Era*, the *dry era*, the *Noble Experiment* (President Herbert Hoover's 1928 term) which lasted from 1919 to 1933. It was brought about by THE TEMPERANCE MOVEMENT and postwar idealism—and ratified by the states while hundreds of thousands of thirsty men who would have been against it were still overseas with the AEF. The 18th Amendment was immediately followed by legislation to enforce it, the *Volstead Act* (also 1919), named after its Congressional sponsor, Minnesota Representative Andrew Volstead. This act legally defined *intoxicating liquor* as "any beverage containing ½ of 1% alcohol," thus including

Andrew J. Volstead (1860–1947).

wine and beer. Congress overrode President Wilson's veto and the Volstead Act went into effect on January 16, 1920. Sixteen days later, on February 1st, Federal agents made the first *raid* on a *speakeasy*, the Red Lantern, a basement bar in Chicago. Suddenly all America was talking about its new life style—illegal drinking—and about its new industry—bootlegging. During the next 13 years we used such terms as:

bathtub gin, homemade or inferior bootleg gin, usually drunk with ginger ale or orange juice to kill the taste.

blind pig, 1840; *blind tiger*, 1857, any unlicensed saloon.

bootlegger, 1850, a smuggler of illegal whiskey, because he hid the bottle in the leg of his tall boots. The word became popular in the dry states of Oklahoma and Kansas in the late 1880s. *Bootleg whiskey*, 1904; *to bootleg*, 1906.

Budweiser was introduced by Anheuser-Busch as a *near beer* (see below) during Prohibition. It became so popular that it was made into a real beer afterwards, becoming one of our best-known brand names.

highjacker, 1890, said to be from the robber's stopping his victim by calling out "High, Jack!" Often spelled *hijacker* by 1921; *to hijack*, 1923, referring only to robbing bootleggers and rumrunners of their stock.

home brew, though beer had always been made at home, this beverage and term became very popular during Prohibition. Hardware stores did a thriving business selling *bottle cappers* at $2.50 each and the sound of bottles of home brew exploding in the basement was heard throughout the land. The verb *brew* (Old English *brēowan*) was probably first used as a noun meaning "beer" in the 17th century.

hospital alcohol is what bootleggers always told their customers they were getting, good, pure alcohol, not cheap denatured industrial alcohol.

Jake, Jamaica ginger, a liquor made from Jamaica ginger. *Jake* (or *jake-leg*) also meant a form of paralysis caused by drinking *Jake* or denatured alcohol.

near beer, 1909, as an imitation beer or beerlike soft drink containing less than 4/10 of 1% alcohol (in the 1900s *near* was first used to mean "nearly, almost," hence combinations such as *near beer*, *near accident*, etc., came into vogue). During Prohibition near beer was made by reducing the alcohol content of real beer to the legal level of less than ½ of 1% (sauerkraut contains more alcohol than this). Many drinkers added grain alcohol to it before drinking.

needle beer, *needled beer*, near beer or 3.2 beer into which grain alcohol had been illegally injected.

Prohibition, as specifically meaning the prohibiting of alcoholic beverages, was first recorded in the 1851 annual report of the American Temperance Union, in lauding Vermont's struggle toward "entire prohibition."

raid (Old English *rād*, ride, road, later a Scottish Highlanders' word for forays into the lowlands) had long been a military and police word. During Prohibition, however, it meant only one thing,

Philadelphia's Public Safety Director "Duckboards" Butler smashing kegs of beer and pouring it into the Schuylkill River, 1924.

the invading and closing of a still, liquor cache, or speakeasy by federal or local officers.

red ink, homemade wine. During Prohibition heads of households were legally allowed to make 200 gallons of wine yearly for home consumption. California and New York vineyards did a booming business, with a sevenfold increase in acreage and a tenfold increase in wine-grape prices. They sold bricks of compressed grapes for winemaking and also an enormous quantity of grape juice in bottles and kegs, which was not ostensibly for winemaking—but with which they thoughtfully provided detailed instructions on how *not* to make wine!

rum row, the line of liquor-laden schooners sitting offshore near most East Coast cities, supplying the rumrunner fleets of small motorboats. The ships carried Scotch and other whiskey from Canada and Bermuda, rye from Nova Scotia, and rum and alcohol from the West Indies and Cuba. Rum row was 30 miles off the coast, a new limit established during Prohibition to help the Coast Guard curtail the trade, increasing the usual three or twelve mile limit. The ships were called the *rum fleet* (*rum* had been a general word for any alcoholic beverage since colonial days).

rumrunner, any person, ship, boat, car, truck, etc., engaged in smuggling whiskey. The overpowered motorboats unloading rum-row ships carried up to 70 cases at a time and could speed at 35 knots. The cars were often souped-up, oversprung, eight-cylinder touring cars, carrying up to 200 gallons. Rum-row schooners brought in 40,000 cases of whiskey monthly, with another 20,000 cases coming from Canada via the Great Lakes, the Niagara River, and by road and rail, over which booze was shipped as "lumber."

Seagram's became a famous brand name during Prohibition. The company then began its growth from a Canadian mail-order liquor house and local distillery into an international giant by increasing its Canadian production and selling to all comers for cash, no questions asked. Its label soon became a guarantee of "the real stuff"—though this wasn't necessarily true, since Seagram's, Beefeater's, and all other desired labels were beautifully counterfeited during Prohibition. Some illegal distilleries also had their own famous brand names, as *Old Orchard Beach.*

speakeasy, 1889, in the dry state of Kansas; sometimes shortened to *speak* during Prohibition. The word may come from the English underworld *speak-softly shop* (1823), a smuggler's home or place of business. Many Prohibition speakeasies were "clubs," some charged a 50¢ entrance or membership fee; some issued much-sought-after identification cards to their regulars, which could be flashed at the peephole or at the doorman; others were "key clubs," giving door keys to regular patrons. It was the first time many Americans talked about *clubs, key clubs, identification cards,* or even *peepholes.* If you weren't known, a simple "Joe sent me" would often do. Some of the better "clubs" became legitimate *nightclubs* after Prohibition, or successful restaurants, such as Sherman Billingsley's *Stork Club* and *The 21.*

Texas Guinan Clubs were the most talked-about speakeasy clubs. By 1928 the colorful Mary Louise Cecilia "Texas" Guinan had a string of her fashionably sporty clubs (they were the "Playboy

A bootlegger's Packard and its contents of liquor, disguised in mason jars, confiscated in Washington, D.C., 1922.

288

"Texas" Guinan, 1921. In 1928 Tex Guinan's Portable Night Club was located in the Hotel Harding on West 54th Street, New York. It was estimated that by 1930 there were over 22,000 speakeasies in New York City.

Clubs" of THE ROARING 20s). She wore a gold police whistle around her neck to mock local police and federal *Prohibition agents* and greeted customers with her famous phrase, "Hello sucker."

3.2 beer, a fairly weak beer containing 3.2% alcohol. Though it was sometimes confused with *near beer*, it was actually real beer by definition (3–6% alcohol). It was legalized April 7, 1933, a little before Prohibition ended, giving beer drinkers something to shout about and breweries a head start in resuming production.

Virginia Dare was an extremely popular Prohibition tonic, supposedly for anemia, containing 22% alcohol; later it became the name of a legitimate wine. The original Virginia Dare, of course, was the first child born in America of English parents, in 1587, on Roanoke Island, Virginia, now part of North Carolina. She was the granddaughter of the colony's founder and governor, John White, who sailed to England for aid and supplies nine days after her birth—but the Spanish war prevented a rescue ship being sent until 1591, by which time the *Lost Colony* had vanished.

wildcat beer, beer made by illegal breweries during Prohibition.

In addition to the above terms, many old words for cheap, inferior, or fiery whiskey again became popular during Prohibition, such as *bust head* (1860s), *hooch* (1898), *rot gut* (1819), and *smoke* (1904), as well as new terms like *a belt*, *the sauce*, and *moon* for the older *moonshine*. Besides alcoholic beverages, people drank bay rum (60% alcohol), hair tonic, perfume, antifreeze, and heating and cooking alcohol (*smoke* and *canned heat*). Many of the words meaning drunk were used more frequently than ever before, and new terms were added, such as *buried*, *busted*, *canned*, *crocked*, *flooey*, *fried*, *juiced*, *jugged*, *polluted*, and *rum-dum* (see DRUNK for the dates and a further list).

Did people really talk so much about illegal drinking and bootlegging during Prohibition? Yes. By the mid 1920s bootlegging was a $2 billion a year industry employing half a million people. If you wanted the real stuff, Canada alone was producing over seven million gallons of whiskey a year, most of it coming into the U.S. If you wanted the cheap illegally made stuff—well, in 1925 over 170,000 illegal stills were raided and the government assumed that was only one-tenth of the total number in operation.

One of the lasting results of Prohibition was widespread organized crime, giving all America a terrifying new topic of conversation and a new vocabulary of violence. As early as 1919 Johnny Torrio and Al Capone entered bootlegging in Chicago, and soon America was reading about and talking about *the mob*, *crime syndicates*, *gang wars*, *rods*, *torpedoes*, *gorillas*, *trigger men*, people being *taken for a one-way ride*, and *the St. Valentine's Day Massacre* (see AL CAPONE). There was so much crime and corruption it was a relief when in 1931 people started talking about an aggressive, incorruptible Chicago police detective—but, unfortunately, he only appeared in a comic strip, Chester Gould's *Dick Tracy*, whose first case was solving a speakeasy murder.

People also talked about a new movie actor, James Cagney, who in 1931 appeared in a popular movie, *Public Enemy*, portraying the rise and fall of a bootlegger.

By the late 1920s Prohibition was in shambles: liquor flowed, crime and corruption flourished, enforcement was lax or non-existent. Referendums showed the public was disgusted with the experiment—Prohibition was no longer noble, it wasn't fun any more, and it didn't work. Americans had already had one major *Repeal*, the colonists having used the word widely to refer to the repeal of the British Stamp Act in 1766. Now the second major *Repeal* in American history occurred, the *21st Amendment*, repealing the 18th. It went into effect in December, 1933, Franklin D. Roosevelt's first presidential year. But to many Americans the end of Prohibition was almost lost in more pressing concerns, for by now people were talking about THE GREAT DEPRESSION and THE NEW DEAL.

Public Enemy Number One

Dillinger was the name that struck terror throughout the Midwest in 1933. John Dillinger had been born in Indianapolis, went to school until he was 17, worked four years as a machinist, and then joined the Navy—he seems to have led a normal life until he was 22. Then he deserted from the Navy, robbed a grocery, and was sent to a reformatory in 1924, later trying to break out and being sent to state prison until paroled in 1933. Now his name became one of the most talked-about in America. Within a month he and his gang were robbing banks and killing people in Illinois, Indiana, and Ohio. He was caught, escaped, raided police stations for guns, committed more robberies and murders, and was named *Public Enemy Number One* by Attorney General Homer Cummings. He was the first officially designated Public Enemy Number One; in fact, he was the only one (others were merely at the top of the FBI's "ten most wanted" list).

John Dillinger (1903–34).

He and his gang continued to terrorize Illinois, Indiana, and Wisconsin until he and six others were caught in Tucson, Arizona, in January 1934. Dillinger escaped from the Crown Point, Indiana jail with a mock gun whittled from wood, was wounded by police in St. Paul in March, and by May had a $50,000 reward on his head. Then a mysterious girl friend, whom millions knew only as *the woman in red*, betrayed him, and he was shot and killed by FBI agents while he was leaving Chicago's Biograph Theater on July 22, 1934. Since his release from prison in 1933, he had shot 17 people, killing 10 of them.

A Race of Convicts

was a term that angered the colonists and was a fairly common insulting sobriquet used by the British. It is traced to Dr. Samuel Johnson's statement, quoted in Boswell's *Life of Johnson*, that the Revolutionary colonists were "a race of convicts [who] ought to be thankful for anything we allow them short of hanging." It was an awful thing to say, especially insulting because it contained a lot of truth: between 1607 and 1776 about 40% of the English who came to the colonies were convicts, drunks, runaways, debtors, and others who had less than idealistic reasons for starting over in a new land.

The Real McCoy

is one of those tantalizing terms that many Americans have used but no scholar can trace—no one knows for sure who the real Mr. McCoy was, or if there ever was one. We do know that there was a phrase *the clear McCoy*, used to describe good whiskey as early as 1908, and that when *the real McCoy* became popular in the Prohibition days of the early 1920s it was usually used in describing whiskey or beer. Thus "real McCoy" seems to have grown out of "clear McCoy," and both were drinking men's terms. It follows that McCoy should be the name of a whiskey or beer, moonshiner, drinker, saloon, or bartender before 1908.

The people and words usually given as the basis for "the real McCoy," however, have nothing to do with drinking before 1908, which makes all these explanations suspicious: (1) it comes from an Irishman or an old Irish ballad; (2) it comes from Joseph McCoy, who promoted Abilene into the first cow town around 1867 (see COWBOYS); (3) it comes from Kid McCoy, welterweight champion 1898-1900, who was said to prove his identity by throwing punches at doubters until they admitted, "It's the real McCoy"; (4) it comes from a Prohibition rumrunner, Bill McCoy; (5) "McCoy" comes from "Macao," whose uncut heroin had drug addicts in the 1930s asking for "the real Macao." All of these are interesting possibilities—and one of them may even be true.

Reconstruction—Carpetbaggers and The Ku Klux Klan

Even before the Civil War was over, the Union began talking about *Reconstruction* (1863) of the South. Thus *Reconstruction* and the *Reconstruction Period* came to mean the 12 years 1865-77 when the Federal government controlled and Federal troops occupied the South, making the war-ravaged southern states change their political and social institutions before being readmitted to the Union (all southern states were readmitted before the end of 1870 but Federal control and troops remained for seven more years).

During the 1860s and 70s *Reconstruction* meant different things to different people. To Presidents Lincoln and Johnson it meant a quick and compassionate reunion of North and South, "With malice toward none; with charity for all," as Lincoln said in his Second Inaugural Address, March 14, 1865. To the northern Republicans who ruled Congress and were to have the final say in the matter, Reconstruction meant Federal control of the South until its political, social, and economic institutions were crushed and, in appreciation, the newly freed Blacks would make it a Republican stronghold. To the Black South it meant an opportunity to step from slavery into full citizenship, to vote, get an education, own land, and earn a living. To the White South Reconstruction was a humiliating word, a synonym for submission, and many resisted it. These four conflicting attitudes helped create some of the events and groups we have talked about ever since. The most widely talked-about topics and common terms associated with the Reconstruction period include:

the assassination of Lincoln. Thirty-one days after his second inauguration and five days after Lee surrendered to Grant, President Lincoln was shot in the back of the head at 10:13 P.M. on Good Friday, April 14, 1865, while attending a performance of *Our American Cousin* at Ford's Theater in Washington, D.C. He was carried to a nearby rooming house and died at 7:22 A.M. April 15. The Maryland-born actor John Wilkes Booth had organized the conspiracy to assassinate the president, vice president, and certain cabinet members (Secretary of State Seward was severely wounded in his home that evening) and had shot Lincoln himself.

Thomas Nast's view of the cruelties of slavery and the blessings of emancipation, 1865.

Booth broke his leg when he jumped from Lincoln's theater box, but escaped, finally being traced to a barn near Bowling Green, Virginia, on April 26. When he refused to surrender the barn was set afire and Booth either shot himself or was shot. A military commission tried nine others implicated in the plot and on July 7 four of them, including one woman, were hanged; four of the others were convicted and one was freed.

Black Codes, 1866, were the laws southern states passed after the Civil War to keep the former slaves "in their place," as by denying them the right to vote or hold office, bear arms, work at certain trades and professions, etc. These codes helped convince Congress that the defeated South was untrustworthy and that stricter Federal control was necessary, as under the Reconstruction Act of 1867.

carpetbagger, 1868, was a northerner who went to the South to gain political power, business advantages, cheap land, etc., during the political and social upheaval of Reconstruction. Such carpetbaggers were really created by Congress's Reconstruction Act of 1867, which disqualified many southern white voters because of their treasonous Confederate activities and divided the South into five military districts: thus carpetbaggers could gain control by winning Black support and votes, sometimes backed up by Federal troops and local *Black militia*.

The *carpetbag* was the common lightweight handbag of 1840–70 and consisted of two squares of carpeting sewn together. Thus since the 1850s *carpetbagger* had meant anyone who traveled fast and light, from carefree vacationers to itinerant businessmen, bankers, and gamblers who moved on before their goods and schemes were found to be fraudulent.

freedman, 1863, a Black freed by the Emancipation Proclamation and the Civil War. A Black who was born into freedom after the Civil War was called a *free-issue Black*.

Freed slaves were called *freedmen* rather than *freemen* because since 1839 *freeman* had meant an ex-slave who had escaped to the North or bought his freedom, and since 1640 in America had meant a White man with full citizenship, including the right to vote and hold office, which in various colonies had depended on his owning property, belonging to the established church, etc.

the Freedmen's Bureau was the popular name of the Bureau of Refugees, Freedmen, and Abandoned Lands, created by Congress as part of the War Department, March 3, 1865, to issue food and clothing to war refugees and destitute freedmen and to rent abandoned or confiscated southern land. The Bureau helped displaced southerners return home and was soon providing shelter, medical care, and food for as many as 150,000 freedmen daily.

The Freedmen's Bureau accomplished a great deal, especially by building over a thousand *Freedmen's schools* (1865) and establishing Black teacher-training institutes. It had its failures too: it failed to gain much abandoned and confiscated lands for the Blacks and to obtain full civil rights for them, due to southern resistance.

Howard University, established by Congress and opened by the Freedmen's Bureau in 1867, with special responsibility for training Black students. It was named in honor of the commissioner of the Freedmen's Bureau, General Oliver O. Howard, who had served with the Union in many battles of the Civil War, in which he lost his right arm, and who also served as the third president of Howard University, 1869–73, later becoming the superintendent of the U.S. Military Academy at West Point.

impeachment. Except for lawyers and a few others, most Americans had never heard this word until the House of Representatives voted articles of impeachment against President Andrew Johnson in 1868. It's a 14th century English word (meaning to impede, accuse, via French from Latin *impedicāre,* to entangle, put in fetters) and is used in the Constitution:

> The President, Vice President, and all civil officers of the United States shall be removed from office on impeachment for and conviction of treason, bribery, or other high crimes and misdemeanors.

President Johnson had tried to follow Lincoln's wishes in his compassionate amnesty and Reconstruction proclamation of May 29, 1865, and thus people were already talking about *reconstructed states* and *reconstructed rebels* in 1866. But as soon as Congress reconvened in December the Radical Republicans had refused to seat the "Confederate Brigadiers" the South had elected and created its own Joint Committee on Reconstruction, ending Johnson's "soft peace" and "Presidential Reconstruction."

Johnson fought Congress bitterly but after the election of 1866 it passed the Reconstruction Act of 1867, dividing the "conquered provinces" into five military districts, each under a general and all under the Secretary of War. To be sure that Johnson didn't gain control of the five southern military districts by replacing Secretary of War Stanton with one of his own followers, Congress passed the Tenure of Office Act, preventing him from removing a cabinet officer without Senate consent. When Johnson removed Stanton anyway, Congress was delighted to get rid of the soft-on-the-South president by impeaching him. The House did impeach, but on May 26, 1868, after a two-month debate, the Senate finally failed to convict him, falling just one vote short of the 2/3 majority necessary to remove Johnson from office. After that the Radical Republicans in Congress carried out their "Congressional Reconstruction" without much presidential interference.

Ku Klux Klan, 1865. During Reconstruction some southern Whites tried to regain power and reassert *white supremacy* (1867) by forming secret groups that intimidated, flogged, tarred and feathered, lynched, murdered, and burned Blacks (and sometimes carpetbaggers and other Whites) who were active in Liberty and Union Leagues or otherwise seeking full civil and human rights. Thus, in addition to the Ku Klux Klan, between 1865 and 1870 such new organizations and names appeared as the *Invisible Cane, Pale Faces, Red Shirts of South Carolina, Knights of the Green Circle, Knights of the White Brotherhood,* and *Knights of the White Camelia.* This last group was larger and more active than the Klan in the lower South, but technically merged with the Klan in 1867 to form "The Invisible Empire of the South." Some of these

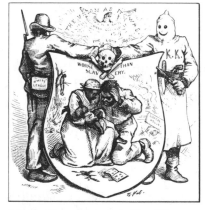

White Leaguers and Ku Klux Klanners join forces over prostrated Blacks, a Nast cartoon of about 1868 after the Knights of the White Camelia officially joined the Klan to form "The Invisible Empire of the South."

An 1868 portrait of two Ku Kluxers in their robes.

White Leagues were less violent than others, with *White Line* groups claiming to be only secret political organizations.

Ku Klux Klan comes from the Greek word *Kuklos*, circle, cycle + "clan," with the simplified spelling of *k* for the hard *c* (this was a vogue at the time, Walt Whitman spelling Canada as *Kanada*, etc.). There have actually been three groups named *Ku Klux Klan*: (1) the original small group in 1865, (2) the historic *Klan* formed in 1867, and (3) another national *Klan* formed in 1915.

(1) The original Ku Klux Klan was formed as a social club by six young Confederate veterans in Pulaski, Tennessee, on Christmas Eve, 1865. It was soon called *The Klan* and *The Ku Klux* and its members soon found that its Halloweenlike robes and mock Greek-Christian-mythical names and rituals frightened the Blacks. Within two years it developed into or inspired a much larger group.

(2) The historic Ku Klux Klan was founded in Nashville, Tennessee, in 1867. Its members were called *Ku Kluxers* and *Kluxers* and it was simply called the *KKK* by 1872, with the word *Klansman* appearing in the late 70s. Some officers had elaborate robes, the rank-and-file white ones or sheets, so they could ride forth at night claiming to be ghosts of the Confederate dead. The robes and masks and the elaborate titles given the members served to disguise them, to scare ignorant southern Blacks, and to attract ignorant southern Whites. When formed in 1867 its organization included such names and titles as:

An 1872 depiction of a night visit of hooded Ku Kluxers. Note the goblin hood at the window.

Grand Wizard, the leader of the entire Klan. The first Grand Wizard was the Confederate Cavalry hero General Nathan B. Forrest. To his credit, he felt the violence was getting out of hand and ordered the Klan disbanded in 1869, to no avail.

Grand Dragons, the heads of state-wide Klan *Realms*.

Grand Giants, the heads of countywide Klan *Provinces*.

Cyclops, the heads of the local Klan *Dens*, each composed of 12 *Terrors* and two *Night Hawks*, who were couriers and scouts.

There were also grand titles for those who collected dues at meetings, kept the minutes and records, acted as guards, etc., as *Grand Exchequers*, *Grand Scribes*, and *Grand Sentinels*, as well as *Grand Ensigns*, *Grand Magi*, *Grand Monks*, *Grand Turks*, *Furies*, *Genii*, *Goblins*, and *Hydras*. This Klan was very active throughout Reconstruction and operated on a smaller, more local scale into the 20th century.

(3) The third Klan, the *Knights of the Ku Klux Klan* was founded on Stone Mountain, near Atlanta, Georgia, in 1915 by Colonel William J. Simmons, a preacher who earned a good living

A 1957 KKK poster.

promoting fraternal organizations. He proclaimed it a "high class mystic, social and patriotic" society devoted to the protection of womanhood and the supremacy of White Protestants, but personally considered it a money-making venture (he later sold out his share in the Klan to a Texas dentist for $90,000). Its membership reached a peak of 4 million in 1924, mainly in small towns in the South and Midwest (especially Indiana). It carried on the old Ku Klux Klan tradition of hate, intimidation, and violence against Blacks, and also against Catholics, Jews, and foreigners, and in the 1930s against labor unions, "internationalists," and Communists. It was this Klan that became famous for its *cross burning* as a warning. It retained much of the terminology of the historic Reconstruction Klan but added or changed some terms, using:

Kleagle or *King Kleagle* (*Kl*an + eagle), instead of Grand Dragon, as the head of a state-wide Klan *Realm.*

Grand Goblin, the head of a countywide Klan *Dominion* (the historic Klan had had

Grand Giants as heads of countywide *Provinces*).

Klavern (*Kl*an + *cavern*), a local Klan group, which the old Klan had called a *Den.*

Kloran (*Kl*an + *K*oran), this Klan's sacred book of duties, obligations, passwords, prayers, etc.

Civil rights organizations finally prompted the Federal government to act against this Klan in the 1940s, shattering it into local fragments.

The Loyal League was a secret political organization formed in the North during the Civil War to help Blacks secure and protect their new rights. Many local branches were formed in the South during Reconstruction, but most were in the hands of carpetbaggers who used the leagues to teach Blacks to vote Republican. The *Union League* (*of America*), often abbreviated ULA, was a similar secret organization in the South, also used by carpetbaggers to control Black votes. Also during Reconstruction carpetbaggers formed many *Republican Clubs* to organize Black voters.

night riders, 1875, members of any Ku Klux Klan type group who rode at night to flog, burn, kill, etc. The term was also later used to refer to a group of Kentucky tobacco growers who between 1906 and 1909 rode at night to burn tobacco barns, warehouses, and factories and sometimes to flog and kill those who resisted their organization.

Radical Republicans, 1865, northern Republicans who demanded that the southern states meet stiff requirements before readmission to the Union. Many of them had been strongly against slavery and staunch supporters of the Civil War (*radical* had been used since 1847 to refer to anyone strongly against slavery), others wanted a harsh Reconstruction to bolster northern influence, win Black support, and leave the South Republican. The Radical Republicans in Congress assumed control of Reconstruction.

Black Republican (late 1850s) was originally a contemptuous southern term for a Republican against spreading slavery to the territories; by 1860 *Black Republican* and *Black and Brown Republican* meant one who favored proportional representation of

On September 1, 1868, the Tuscaloosa *(Alabama)* Independent Monitor *ran this woodcut showing what would happen to "those great pests of Southern society—the* carpetbagger *and* scalawag. . . . [The] scalawag *is the local leper of the community. Unlike the carpetbagger, he is native, which is so much the worse."*

Blacks in the party; and by 1868 *Black Republican* was used to mean one who seemed to favor Blacks over Whites in the South, especially to get Black votes.

scalawag, 1868, was the name southern Democrats and unreconstructed rebels threw at White southern Republicans, planters, and businessmen who accepted Reconstruction and cooperated with northern politicians, officials, and troops for their own political and financial gain. The word had actually meant a rascal or rogue since the 1840s and may come from the Gaelic *sgalag*, servant, rustic, or from *Scalloway* in the Shetland Islands, which is known for its dwarf ponies and cattle and thus might have come to mean a morally dwarfed person.

sharecropping, 1867, also then called the *share of the crop system* and the *share crop system.* This system developed naturally on large southern farms and plantations after the Civil War: planters had lost their slaves and had no money to pay workers, the freed slaves needed work and food, the nation needed the southern crops, especially raw cotton for nothern mills. Blacks who took up sharecropping were usually called *share hands* (late 1860s) while Whites who later took it up were often called *share tenants* (1911), with the term *sharecropper* becoming common for both Blacks and Whites around 1915.

the Solid South, 1876, was originally used to refer both to the solid Republican Black vote and to the solid Democratic White vote in the South during Reconstruction. As soon as Reconstruction ended and the Whites regained full political power, the *Solid South* came to mean only the solid Democratic vote. The South generally voted Democratic from 1877 to 1952, when the landslide election for Eisenhower finally broke the pattern (anti-Catholic prejudice against Democrat Al Smith had interrupted the pattern in 1928, causing five southern states to vote for Republican Hoover).

wave the bloody shirt was what Democrats charged the Republicans of doing throughout Reconstruction and until the 1890s, by which they meant Republicans tried to get votes by waving the bloody shirt of the Civil War, equating the Democrats with the Confederacy and slavery.

A National Convention of Blacks, held in Nashville, 1878. In 1880 the first Black to chair a major political party presided temporarily over the Republican National Convention at Chicago. Political emancipation for Blacks was started on its long, slow journey during the Reconstruction era.

Even though we now usually talk about Reconstruction as a time when night riders rode and corrupt carpetbaggers and new Black officeholders ran up huge debts for the southern taxpayer, many good things were accomplished. The Freedmen's Bureau did start many Blacks toward an education and Blacks did begin to vote—and the southern state legislatures, the carpetbaggers and Black legislators whom people made so much fun of, did set up free, tax-supported schools; gave women property rights; helped the small farmer and businessman by passing laws protecting property from foreclosure; did away with imprisonment for debt; and spread taxation more evenly. In any event, all the states were back in the Union by 1870, the Freedmen's Bureau closed in 1872, and Federal troops withdrew from the South in 1877—Reconstruction was over.

Relativity, $E = mc^2$

and Space Is Curved were terms bandied about in intellectual conversations in the 1920s, 30s, and 40s, first after Albert Einstein won the Nobel Prize in 1921 and more commonly after this lovable, pixyish-looking theoretical physicist fled Nazi Germany in 1933 and graced America by joining Princeton's Institute for Advanced Study.

> There was a young lady named Bright,
> Whose speed was far faster than light:
> She set out one day
> In a relative way,
> And returned home the previous night.
> Popular limerick by Arthur Buller; it first appeared in *Punch* in 1923.

The term *quantum theory* comes from his 1905 postulation of light *quanta*, or *photons*, to explain the photoelectric effect, developing "the quantum theory of specific heat." Also in 1905 he set forth his "special theory of relativity," expanded into the "general theory of relativity" around 1911, and giving the equivalence of mass and mechanical energy, which the public knew as *relativity* and $E = mc^2$. In 1916 Einstein completed the mathematical formulation of this theory, which included gravitation as a field rather than a force, giving science the term *gravitational field*, and stating that it was a determiner of curvature of the *space-time continuum*—which gave the public the confusing but heady expression *space is curved*.

Remember the Alamo!

is one of the most famous battle cries in American history, but was used only in the final month of the brief War of Texas Independence, and in only one major battle.

It all really began in 1821 when Stephen Austin, who was to become known as "the father of Texas" and is the man for whom *Austin*, Texas is named, brought the first 300 American settlers to Texas. That was the same year Mexico revolted from Spain, making Texas Mexican territory (*Texas*, from a local Indian word for "friend, ally," then referred to an area which included not only present-day Texas but also parts of Oklahoma, New Mexico,

The Alamo, with the state flag of Texas flying overhead.

Colorado, and Wyoming). After Mexican independence *Texas fever* gripped thousands of Americans, especially southerners, who moved to the cotton land of east Texas with their slaves, settling on large Mexican land grants. Mexico tried to keep these Americans in Texas under control by abolishing slavery there and imposing duties and taxes. Then in 1835 a Spanish priest, Miguel Hidalgo y Castillo, led a revolt of Mexicans in Texas against Mexico and its dictatorial president, General Antonio Lopez de Santa Anna. The Americans in Texas joined the revolt, took it over (there were then about 30,000 Americans and only 7,500 Mexicans in Texas), and by October were fighting for independence.

Texas troops captured San Antonio on December 11, 1835, but Santa Anna soon arrived with about 4,000 troops and counter-attacked. On February 23, 1836, the remaining 150 Texas defenders of San Antonio withdrew behind the walls of an old Spanish mission, the *Alamo* (so called after the cottonwood trees growing nearby, from Spanish *álamo*, cottonwood tree) and, with 32 reinforcements who had slipped through Santa Anna's lines, held out until March 6th, when they were overcome and massacred. The dead included the commander, Lt. Col. William B. Travis, and the widely talked-about American folk heroes, Davy Crockett and Jim Bowie (who was then a naturalized Mexican citizen). Three weeks later, on March 27th, an even greater massacre occurred, when 330 Texans who had surrendered after fighting a brief battle while retreating from Goliad eight days earlier were shot by order of Santa Anna. Then *Remember the Alamo!*, or simply *Alamo!*, and *Remember Goliad!* became Texas battle cries.

299

On April 21, 1836, Colonel Sidney Sherman's regiment shouted *Remember the Alamo!* as it led the attack in the final battle of the war, the *Battle of San Jacinto* (the name of a small river), near present-day Houston. Here the commander of the Texas army, General Sam Houston (for whom *Houston*, Texas, is named) and his retreating 1,600 troops suddenly turned and made a surprise attack during the Mexicans' siesta, killing, wounding, or capturing all but a dozen of Santa Anna's army. Santa Anna himself was captured and forced to guarantee Texas independence. Though the Mexican congress repudiated this guarantee, the defeat of Santa Anna made Texas independence a fact.

Even as the Alamo was being besieged, Texas had declared its independence and established the *Republic of Texas*. Houston, who had once been governor of Tennessee, defeated Austin in the election and on October 22, 1836, took the oath of office as the first president of the Republic of Texas.

The War of Texas Independence also led to the name *Texas Rangers;* they were first organized in 1835 as a quasimilitary, nonuniformed, civilian group to protect Texas against raiding Indians and Mexicans. "The Rangers" were mustered into Federal service during the Mexican War, served with the Confederates in the Civil War, then became most famous as mounted police against cattle thieves and desperadoes, and finally merged with the Texas state highway patrol in 1935. Two other events and terms which later grew out of Texas independence were, of course, *the annexation of Texas* (see 54–40 OR FIGHT!—MANIFEST DESTINY) and THE MEXICAN WAR.

Incidentally, the term *bowie knife* was first recorded the same year that Jim Bowie was killed at the Alamo, in 1836. Though his fame popularized the knife's name, it was actually first made by, and named for, his brother, Rezin P. Bowie. It was a heavy 9–12-inch sheath knife, often made by local blacksmiths out of large files and rasps for frontiersmen and soldiers, who boasted it was the best skinning, stabbing, throwing, and eating knife ever made.

Revivals: Billy Sunday and Aimee Semple McPherson

[The sinfulness of the] cocktail-drinking, gambling, indecently-dressed, automobile-driving, degenerate, God-forsaken gang you call society.
Billy Sunday, sermon

Revival and *camp meeting* were both first used in Logan County, Kentucky in 1799, to refer to the three- and four-day religious meetings Presbyterian James McGready held along the river banks there. Though Americans had talked about *ministers* since 1619 and *preachers* since 1648, itinerant preachers were in short supply along the frontier and many families didn't see one all year. Thus people came from as far as 40 miles to camp meetings, to camp under the trees, sit on log benches in the open-air church, have

Dwight Moody (1837–99) and Ira D. Sankey (1840–1908) waving farewell after their tour of England, 1873–75. Moody was the first nationally known revivalist. Born in East North-field, Massachusetts, he prospered in the boot and shoe business before devoting his life to religion after 1860. Traveling with the popular hymn writer, organist, and singer Ira Sankey, he attracted huge crowds in the U.S. and England.

their weddings and baptisms performed, and partake in the almost nonstop preaching, praying, hymn singing, and socializing. The idea and the terms spread so rapidly that by 1811 there were 400 *camp meetings* or *revivals* held along the frontier from Georgia to Michigan.

By the 1820s even city people knew that a front row *anxious seat* or *anxious bench* was set aside at revival meetings for those anxious souls ready to come to the altar *to get religion* (1772, to be con-verted) or to repent. By the 1830s *circuit preacher* and *circuit rider* were well-known terms but many small-town and rural people still talked about the annual camp meeting held by the *revival man* at the local *preaching grounds* as the highlight of the year. City folk and easterners might sneer at these revivals, but in the 1730s and 40s they too had experienced their *Great Awakening* (1736), led by Jonathan Edwards.

By the 1870s camp meetings were often called *tented meetings* or *tent meetings*, because they were now held in large tents instead of in the open air; in this form they had also spread to the cities. By the 1870s, too, such meetings were often highly organized Fundamentalist revivals (see FUNDAMENTALISM) featuring nation-ally known revivalists. Between 1875 and 1899 Dwight Moody was the most talked-about revivalist star, preaching what he called "the Old Fashioned Gospel" and founding Chicago's famous Moody's Bible Institute in 1889.

Next came Billy Sunday (William Ashley Sunday, 1862–1935) who was raised in a log cabin near Ames, Iowa and in an orphans' home, then became a hard-drinking, woman-chasing, base-stealing outfielder for the Chicago White Stockings during 1883–90, before he got religion, reformed, married, and became a YMCA worker. By 1896 he was a Fundamentalist revivalist, Presbyterian variety, and during the next 30 years crisscrossed the country holding over 300 revival meetings. Sunday, the most popular of the 700 traveling evangelists of his day, changed revival meetings forever. He introduced: more zealous audience participation; large choirs; and circus-style parades, led by big marching bands, to his meet-ings. He also greatly influenced the American language: over 100 million Americans heard his slangy, wisecracking, emotional sermons and tirades, in which he mixed slang, baseball terms, and strings of adjectives and clauses with his hatred of rum, prostitutes, and card playing. His speaking style influenced the sermons mil-lions of Americans have heard since. Billy Sunday also coined or popularized such terms as:

free-will offering, Billy Sunday's term for a contribution.
hit the sawdust trail, *walk the sawdust trail*, to walk down the sawdust-covered aisle of a revival meeting to the altar to repent or be con-verted. Sunday got the term from Dwight Moody who had first used it in a rented circus tent he used to hold a revival meet-ing during the 1893 Columbian World's Fair in Chicago; it had been in circus use since the 1880s.

Billy Sunday hamming it up.

301

Aimee Semple McPherson, 1931.

tabernacle, a revivalist or evangelical church. Billy Sunday took the revival meetings out of tents and put them into what he called "tabernacles," his specially built, temporary, wooden churchlike arenas.

boy evangelist, girl evangelist, cowboy evangelist, Billy Sunday had up to 20 people in his on-stage troupe, at times featuring a five- or six-year-old *child evangelist*. The first man he billed as "the Cowboy Evangelist" was Fred Seibert.

After Billy Sunday the next highly talked-about revivalist was "Sister" Aimee Semple McPherson (1890–1944), a tall, attractive, red-headed dynamo from Canada who kept the American public gossiping about her personal life. According to "Sister Aimee" she had converted to Pentecostal evangelicalism at 17, then had been a missionary in China with her first husband, Robert Semple, who died there after fathering her daughter, then had married and divorced Harold McPherson (she later married and divorced again). At any rate, she did come to the U.S. from Canada in 1917 with a daughter, her mother (who was also her manager), one leaky tent, and a reputation as a faith healer. She held her first really big-time revival in Los Angeles in 1918, then during the next five years crisscrossed America by Pullman with her revival troupe, holding meetings in most large cities. On January 1, 1923, she opened her famous Angelus Temple in Los Angeles, a temple with 5,000 seats, two balconies, a sky-blue ceiling, and a dome glistening with crushed seashells. It was the center of her *Foursquare Gospel*, which by 1926 was the International Church of the Foursquare Gospel with over 80 branches in the U.S. and Britain. "Are you foursquare?" is still the greeting and slogan of her followers.

Special streetcars filled her Angelus Temple nightly with the faithful and the curious. They saw colorful tableaux and winsome Aimee Semple McPherson herself appearing in costume in front of theatrical sets: wearing a slicker and at a ship's wheel while the chorus of 100 sang "Throw out the lifeline! Someone is sinking today!"; wearing a southern belle costume against a backdrop of cotton fields as she preached on "Slavery Days"; etc. And she had the whole country talking about her in 1926 when she

Are we downhearted? No! No! No!
Troubles may come and troubles may go;
We'll trust in Jesus, come weal or woe.
Are we downhearted? [everyone whistles] No! No! No!
rallying song of Aimee Semple McPherson's Foursquare Gospel

"Camp Meeting," by Worthington Whittredge (1820–1910), American landscape painter noted for his New York and New England scenes.

disappeared while swimming off Santa Monica, California and was believed to have drowned; we talked about her again when she emerged in the desert near Douglas, Arizona with a story of having been kidnaped—then talked about her again when reporters found no evidence of a kidnaping but attributed her absence to a lovers' vacation with her radio station manager-announcer. She died of an overdose of sedatives in 1944.

"Sister Aimee" changed revivals from traveling shows to institutions with permanent homes, reaching out to the audience through radio (she had her own station, KFSG, Los Angeles), through her own magazine, through pamphlets and books, through bible schools, and through social work. Today when you turn on a radio and hear a rousing sermon by a *radio evangelist* (early 1930s), followed by a zealous hymn and a plea to send in a contribution, you are hearing America talking, and you are still hearing Aimee Semple McPherson. She, of course, has been followed by other widely known revivalists, including (Granville) Oral Roberts, who began his career in 1935, and Billy Graham, who, since 1943, has popularized the term "Decide for Christ" and bills his revivals as *Crusades.*

The Revolutionary War

began on April 19, 1775, when colonial minutemen and militia lined up on the village green to fight the British at *the Battle of Lexington*, Massachusetts. It ended at *the Battle of Yorktown*, October 19, 1781, when Cornwallis surrendered, his 7,000 men besieged by a combined American and French force of 16,000 men, Lafayette cutting off the British escape by land and a French fleet preventing escape by sea. The final Treaty of Paris was signed September 3, 1783, with the last British troops leaving New York City on November 25.

The war was first called *the Revolution*, then *the Revolutionary War*, and only after it was won and the new nation well established was it called *the War of Independence* (1832). It was also called an *insurrection* and *the Civil War*, especially by the Loyalists. Both Loyalists and Patriots called believers on the other side *traitors* or *turncoats* (a 1557 English word for traitor, from the idea of a coat being word right-side or wrong-side out according to circumstances, especially for renovating an old worn coat by turning it).

"The British are coming!" Paul Revere didn't shout this on his famous midnight ride—his cry was, "The regulars are out." It was the night of April 18, 1775, and he rode from Boston to Lexington where he woke, among others, the patriots John Hancock and Samuel Adams, who thus escaped the British.

The British side had the:

redcoats (English use since 1520, American use since 1674), also called *lobsters* (England, 1643; America, 1770), *lobsterbacks* and *bloody backs* (American use since 1770). All these, of course, referred to the British soldiers' bright red uniform jackets. Both sides also called the members of the regular standing British army *regulars* (English use since 1706, American use since 1714).

the Brown Bess, the musket the British troops used, called that since 1708 by the troops themselves, probably because it had a brown walnut stock; it was also called the *brown musket*.

Loyalists, Tories, Friends of the King, those Americans who opposed separation from England and remained loyal to the crown. They called themselves *Loyalists* and were often called that by the Patriots. The more conservative or disliked Loyalists were called *Tories*. Some New York Tories called themselves "the friends of the king" or "king's friends" which the Patriots spelled backward to get the derogatory *Sgnik Sdneirf*. The word *Tory* is from Old Irish *tōir*, pursuit, and originally meant the Irishmen who had become bandits after being dispossessed by the English in the mid 17th century; by 1689 it was applied to Irish Catholic royalists, especially the Irish supporters of James II after he accepted the Catholic faith, and later to the English party faithful to him and the Church over William and Mary. Thus *Tory* started off meaning a rebellious bandit and ended meaning a conservative.

The British Loyalists numbered about 500,000 Americans (20–33% of the colonists); about 40 thousand of them fought in the 70 *Loyalist Regiments* of the British army. Tens of thousands of *Negro Loyalists* remained faithful to their Loyalist masters or took the war offered opportunity to desert their "rebel masters." Several thousand of these fought on the British side, some of them in the Black fighting corps *the Black Pioneers* (both White and Black Loyalists were offered Canadian land grants for serving with the British). During the Paris Peace Treaty negotiations, many Loyalists talked hopefully of *the spring fleet*, *the June fleet*, and *the fall fleet*, the three British flotillas which carried thousands of uprooted Loyalists from their New York bastion to Nova Scotia. Over 100,000 Loyalists fled, were evacuated by the British, or were ordered out of America: we euphemistically called them *absentees* and our new country confiscated millions of dollars worth of their property under various *absentee acts*.

Ethan Allen and his Green Mountain Boys demanding the surrender of Fort Ticonderoga: "By what authority?" "In the name of the Great Jehovah and the Continental Congress."

On our side, we had:

the Continental Army, authorized and named by the Continental Congress in June, 1775, when it appropriated $6,000 for its support and appointed George Washington its *Commander in Chief* (the *War Department* was not established until the war was over, in 1789). Soldiers of the Continental Army were also called *continentalers.*

the Continental Navy, also established by the Continental Congress in 1775. It was called the *new Navy* to distinguish it from the *Colonial Navy* which had been in operation since 1631. This new Continental Navy started with 53 ships, appointed Esek Hopkins its first *Commodore* (a 1695 English word) in 1776, and was to be followed by the formation of *the United States Navy* in 1794. By 1777 a pistol used by the Continental Navy was called a *navy* (it was usually smaller than an army pistol), which later gave us the term *Navy pistol* (1849) and the Civil War's *Navy Colt* (1861, a .36 caliber Colt), *Navy revolver*, and *Navy six.*

Minute Men, also authorized by the Continental Congress in 1775, as a special force of militia. However, Massachusetts and other colonies had already organized such groups, the word being well known by 1774.

the Green Mountain Boys of Vermont (originally part of the New Hampshire grants) became famous in 1770 when Green Mountain land was granted to New York and settlers who had received land from New Hampshire had to repurchase it. "The Boys," spurred on by their leaders, the brothers Ethan and Levi Allen, refused to do this and fought New York settlers and resisted dispossession by New York sheriffs. They sided with the Patriots during the Revolution and won a victory at Fort Ticonderoga, May 17, 1775.

rifle (1772), *rifleman*, *rifler* (1775), As were the British, the Patriots were mainly armed with muskets, often the *Charlesville*, a French-made flint-lock. We did have some companies of *riflemen* or *riflers* armed with the new "rifled musket" or *rifle*. The extremely accurate *long rifle* saw very little use: its length made it too difficult to load and aim quickly for military service.

the Patriots (1775) were those Americans who supported the Revolution; of the 2½ million colonists 67–80% were Patriots. They also called themselves *Yankees* or *Yanks*. They were also called *Whigs*, which had been used in America since 1711 to refer to those who opposed various measures of the Royal Governors. The Loyalists also called the Patriots *rebels*, "the rabble," and *Brother Jonathan* (see Yankee).

the Continental Congress. Continental was first recorded as meaning the collective or united colonies in 1774. The First Continental Congress met in Philadelphia during September and October in 1774 to proclaim colonial grievances; the Second Continental Congress met in May, 1775, and created the *Continental Army* (see above). Later the Continental Congress coordinated the war effort, moved toward a Declaration of Independence, and drafted the *Articles of Confederation* (1777). It served as the American government throughout the Revolution, representing the country for 13 years before calling the *Constitutional Convention* in 1787.

"Don't fire unless fired upon; but if they mean to have a war, let it begin here," were the words uttered April 19, 1775, by John Parker, commander of the force of Minutemen at the Battle of Lexington. *Someone did fire first, no one knows who,* and the war began. *It was called "the shot heard around the world,"* by Ralph Waldo Emerson in "The Concord Hymn," 1836.

The American Revolution was the most successful in history. Not only did it create a new, independent country with its own leaders (as other revolutions have done), but it succeeded in creating an organized democracy (as very few have done).

The Revolution, of course, led to nearly all of our later words having to do with American democracy, government, and politics. It was also the first time that we Americans used our own military terms, although most such terms were borrowed from the English or had earlier been used in Indian fighting, as:

... which is better—to be ruled by one tyrant three thousand miles away, or by three thousand tyrants not a mile away?
Boston Loyalist and Congregational Minister, Mather Byles. This statement sums up a basic Loyalist belief about the Revolutionary War.

barracks (from French *baraque*, soldier's tent, Spanish *barraca*, mud hut), the English had used the word since 1686 for a temporary shelter for soldiers, Americans had used it since 1697 in *hay barrack*, for storing hay. In 1775 Americans first used it to mean soldiers' quarters.

bounty and the *draft*. The British had attracted new soldiers by offering *bounties* (1702 English use, literally "something good") and the Continental Army did likewise. New Jersey offered up

"Don't fire until you see the whites of their eyes," cautioned Colonel William Prescott, commander of the redoubt at Breed's Hill, where the Battle of Bunker Hill was actually fought, June 17, 1775. The British dislodged the Minutemen only after their powder ran out.

to $1,000 for each *enlistee* and Virginia offered a choice of 300 acres of land and a "prime Negro slave" or 60 pounds (still using English currency terms). Some New England colonies even had a *draft. Bounties* were also offered in the War of 1812, the war with Mexico, and the Civil War. Since 1972 the new all-volunteer army has offered "bonuses" for enlistment of from $1,500 to $2,500, avoiding the obsolete word *bounty.*

discharge from military service, used in England since 1548.

furlough (from Middle High German *verlouben,* to permit), used in England since 1625.

military academy, 1776; *military school,* 1777, when suggestions were made for creating one in America.

militia (Latin for "warfare" from *mīles,* soldier), used in America since 1705, when it referred to each colony's own defense force against the Indians. In the Revolution *militia* meant all able-bodied males between the ages of 16 and 60 but especially those serving in colonial regiments.

outpost meant only an outlying settlement in 1759. During the Revolution we first used it to mean a wilderness stockade or outlying *military outpost.*

rangers, a group of armed mounted men protecting the West from Indians; *colonial rangers,* a special force of provincial troops used by England to defend the colonies against Indians. In the Revolutionary War, both sides called their special, most mobile units "rangers."

stockade (French *estocade,* Spanish *estacada,* from *estaca,* stake) had been used in America since 1668 to mean a defense barrier or wall of stakes; *stockade fort,* 1742; *fort,* 1776, as a stockaded trading post fortified against Indians and the British.

And, of course, during the Revolutionary War many Americans first learned what drilling and marching really meant, and also first found themselves referring to American military rank, as:

commissioned, noncommissioned, applied to officers in the Revolutionary War. Commissioned officers originally held their commissions from the Continental Congress, later from the president with the consent of the Senate.

general, 1775, first applied to George Washington.

lieutenant general, used in America since 1630 to refer to a deputy proprietor of a province. Not in wide American military use until 1790.

brigadier general, in the Revolution a commander of a local brigade, also called a *brigadier* in America by 1780.

sergeant, used in America since 1683 to mean a town official who attended court and carried out ordinances.

"The Spirit of '76," Archibald Willard's famous painting, 1876. The expression, which gained wide popularity in the early 1800s, became a favorite name for newspapers after the Revolution.

All other major ranks from *captain* to *corporal* and *private* were also first widely used as American terms in 1775.

During the war people also first widely spoke of: *hunting shirts* (1774) which many backwoods soldiers brought with them as part of their own uniform; *tickens* (1780), overalls made of ticking, the official work dress of both the army and navy; *Kevenhullers,* the Swiss soldiers' hat, named after an Austrian field marshal and worn by many American soldiers; and of the *officers' cockades*, a badge of ribbons worn in the hat to indicate rank (via French *cocarde*, a jaunty hat, from *coq*, cock, since the ribbons resembled a cock's tail).

"Surrender of Lord Cornwallis at Yorktown," by John Trumbull (1756–1843). Benjamin Lincoln takes the surrender, George Washington remains in the background; Cornwallis, pleading indisposition, did not attend. During the ceremonies the American bands played "Yankee Doodle" to the mortification of the British, who had used the tune to deride the patriots during the war (see YANKEE*).*

The Roaring 20s

The 1920s was a complex decade. It has been called:

Zelda and F[rancis] Scott Fitzgerald (1896–1940) represented to many Americans the liberation in manners and morals of the Roaring 20s.

the Golden 20s, emphasizing post World War I prosperity and rising stock-market prices before the 1929 crash.

the Prohibition Era, the Dry Era, the Dry Decade, the Lawless Decade, emphasizing prohibition, its bootlegging, speakeasies, and gang warfare (see PROHIBITION and AL CAPONE).

the Jazz Age, a name F. Scott Fitzgerald gave the period in his 1922 *Tales of the Jazz Age*. The word *jazz* itself was first reported in the New Orleans area in the mid 1870s, as used by Blacks to mean to speed up and as a primitive form of syncopated music. By 1913 Blacks and Whites were using *jazz* to refer to a style of ragtime music having syncopated rhythm and by the end of 1917 American *jazz music* and *jazz bands* were a major attraction in New York, London, and Paris. Because of its early New Orleans Black use, most linguists believe the word *jazz* is of West African or Creole origin, though a specific etymology or African source word has never been pinpointed.

the Roaring 20s, combining all the above, since the 1920s roared with prosperity, sporty cars, wide-open speakeasies, gangland machine guns (James Cagney's 1939 movie *The Roaring 20s* was about bootleggers), jazz music, and jazz-age youth shouting its independence. The 1840s had been called "the roaring 40s," a term coined by historian George Bancroft (1800–1891) in referring to its political and social changes, and Bancroft's phrase caused others to refer to various turbulent decades as "roaring."

The typical flapper, *with swinging beads, rolled stockings, and a short skirt, drawn by John Held, Jr., 1926.*

Our main image of the period is of its *flaming youth*, a term first used by the muckraking magazine writer Samuel Hopkins Adams. For after World War I, war-jaded youth did go on a rampage, releasing pent-up emotions and reacting to the dazzling new stimuli of peacetime prosperity, speakeasies, movies, cars, radios, and the newly popular *Sunday supplements* and *confession magazines*. It was the first young generation to take itself seriously as a separate, distinct group—and the first to be analyzed, egged on, and exploited by the books, movies, newspapers, and magazines of its own day, which shocked and titillated the public with stories of *flappers* and *sheiks*.

the flapper was the wild, drinking, smoking, necking, jazz dancing girl who tossed away her corsets and restraints to become the symbol of the Roaring 20s. The word probably comes from the 1770s British *flapper*, meaning a duck still too young to fly; by the late 1880s in England it meant a young girl who had not yet put up her hair, while in the U.S. it then meant a girl prostitute; by 1910 *flapper* meant any pert, headstrong woman, especially one supporting women's rights and the new *painless childbirth;* in 1919 it finally came to mean the type of girl we associate it with today. In the 1920s such a flapper was also called a *jazz baby* and sometimes a *mama* (1925), *whoopee mama*, or *hot mama* (the Black term *big mama* for a passionate, bold, or staunch woman dates from the 1950s).

sheik, the flapper's typical boyfriend of the Roaring 20s, took his slicked-back hair and his name from Rudolph Valentino and his role in the 1921 movie *The Sheik*. The sheik was also called a *jazz bo* or, if he were a typical college boy, a *Joe College, Joe Yale,* or *Joe Zilch*.

The flapper and the sheik were originally Ivy League student types, soon copied by other students and then by working girls and young salesmen, clerks, and office boys. Shocking as they were supposed to be, they were actually created by their times, by commercial products, and by books, newspapers, movies, and magazines. They learned what to wear, say, think, and feel from the cartoons, articles, and stories in *College Humor*, from John Held Junior's illustrations in the old *Life*, from ads and articles in *Harper's Bazaar*, and from Fitzgerald's 1920 novel *This Side of Paradise*, Maxwell Anderson's and Lawrence Stalling's 1924 play *What Price Glory*, and Percy Mark's 1925 book *The Plastic Age*. Thus the flapper was talked about as a *long-legged girl* with a *boyish figure, bobbed hair*, and a *cigarette holder*—but didn't create this image herself. She looked long-legged only because she wore scandalously thigh-high *short skirts* and *rolled stockings* (stockings rolled below the knee—because she had thrown away her corset and didn't have anything dependable to attach them to, garters being passé and garter belts not yet common). She had that much-talked-about *boyish figure* both because she had thrown away her corset

Rudolph Valentino (1895–1926) in a scene from The Sheik, *a 1921 film.*

and because she wore the popular *Boyishform brassiere* (first widely advertised in 1918). Her *cigarette holder* was to emphasize that she dared smoke, though women had been smoking for a hundred years. Her make-up owed much to Theda Bara's *vamp* (see PRETTY GIRLS), and her bright red lipstick had just been made easily accessible by the invention of the *lipstick tube*. All this make-up meant the flapper had to carry a large *compact*, which now became a popular word. She and her sheik drank because Prohibition was in effect and because speakeasies were the place to go.

The sheik might wear a *raccoon coat* (a 1649 term now very much in vogue), carry a *hip flask*, and like to *jazz around* looking for girls or other fun and excitement. The flapper called him her *boyfriend* (1911, but very popular in the 20s) and he called her his *girlfriend* (1881). They liked their lives *jazzed up* (1917) with excitement and went to *wild parties* (patterned after the *studio parties* in Greenwich Village of the 1910s). They *made love* or talked about it; but, though some girls did *go all the way*, to many flappers and sheiks *making love* still meant only *petting* and *necking* (see GOIN' COURTIN'). Whatever they did they preferred to *do it* in a Stutz Bearcat, but usually did it on a porch swing or sofa in the popular fraternity houses or country clubs of this prosperous decade. Being Jazz Age youth, they danced to *jazz* and also to the *Charleston* (popular by 1925), the *black bottom* (popular by 1926), and the *Fox trot* (a name first listed in the Victor Record Catalog in 1915). They used a lot of slangy, cynical terms like *Oh yeah!* (1924) and *nerts!* (late 1920s from the 1905 *nuts!*). They expressed wonder and joy by saying *oh boy!* (1906) and called something or someone so special as to be *unreal:*

> *the cat's pajamas*, 1920 (popular because pajamas were still new enough to be considered daring).
> *the cat's meow*, 1922.
> *the cat's whiskers*, 1923.
> *the bee's knees*, 1923, and also *the snake's hips, the clam's garter, the eel's ankle, the elephant's instep, the tiger's spots, the leopard's stripes, the sardine's whiskers, the pig's wings*, and just about any combination of an animal, fish, or fowl with a part of the body or article of clothing that was inappropriate for it.

With all the flappers and sheiks, jazz and speakeasies, people were also talking about baseball players Babe Ruth, Tris Speaker, and Ty Cobb; prizefighters Jack Dempsey and Gene Tunney; Gertrude Ederle, the first woman to swim the English Channel (August 6, 1926); golfer Bobby Jones; tennis player Bill Tilden, Admiral Byrd; Charles Lindbergh; the League of Nations; the Scopes Monkey Trial; Sacco and Vanzetti; Janet Gaynor and Charles Farrell in the movie *Seventh Heaven* and Tom Mix in *Riders of the Purple Sage;* and Rudy Vallee crooning over the radio—the 20s weren't all roaring. In fact some people even talked about those unlikely Jazz Age presidents, Warren G. Harding and Calvin Coolidge, before the Roaring 20s plunged to its death in the Great Depression.

Sacco and Vanzetti

"The Passion of Sacco and Vanzetti" by Ben Shahn (1898–1969), one of a series of Sacco and Vanzetti paintings, 1931–32.

had all America talking in the 1920s. Were they murderers or martyrs? Nicola Sacco and Bartolomeo Vanzetti were Italian anarchists who had immigrated to America in 1908, one a shoe worker, the other a fish peddler. In 1920 they were arrested for murder and robbery, charged with having killed a shoe-factory paymaster and his guard in South Braintree, Massachusetts, while taking the $16,000 payroll.

Sacco and Vanzetti were convicted in Judge Webster Thayer's court after a six-week jury trial in the summer of 1921. Socialists and radicals claimed the trial was not fair and many others felt the two men had been convicted for their radical beliefs rather than for any crimes they had committed. Supporters claimed the two men had been falsely identified, and in 1925 a convicted murderer, Celestino Madeiros, confessed that he had taken part in the crime with the Joe Morelli gang. Now came a worldwide stream of protests and mass meetings. In June, 1927, Governor A. T. Fuller of Massachusetts appointed Harvard President A. Lawrence Lowell, MIT President Samuel W. Stratton, and a former judge, Robert Grant, to review the case. They found the trial fair, both men guilty, and advised the governor not to exercise clemency. Demonstrations again took place and radicals set off bombs in New York City and Philadelphia. Sacco and Vanzetti were executed on August 23, 1927, still protesting their innocence.

Sagebrush, Locoweed, Tumbleweed— and Jimson Weed

Sagebrush, locoweed, and *tumbleweed* are words that evoke the American West. *Sagebrush,* a shrub of the western plains, is the most common of the three plants and was known and named first. It was simply called *sage,* after the garden herb, in the 1800s, then *sagebrush* by the 1830s (*sage* is from the Latin *salvus,* safe, because the garden herb was thought to have medicinal properties). Sagebrush is so abundant in the dry, alkaline area of Nevada that the region was called *sagebrush country* by the 1840s and Nevada was called *the Sagebrush State* by 1894. Sage was also used to name a species of large western grouse, the *sage hen* (1850s) and *Sage Hen* was a nickname for a native of Nevada by 1863, with Nevada also being called *the Sage Hen State* since the 1890s.

Loco (Spanish for "insane, crazy") was part of the American language in the Southwest by the late 1830s. It then meant both crazy and any of several plants which, if eaten in small amounts, makes animals act crazy, as if drugged or drunk (it is fatal to livestock if eaten in large quantities). By the 1870s, however, *loco* was used only to mean "crazy" and the plants were called *locoweed* (or sometimes *crazyweed*). Thus our word *loco* is 40 years older than *locoweed*, which is based on it.

The *tumbleweed* is any of several plants, especially an amaranth, which when it dries and breaks from its roots, spreads its seeds by being blown across the plains by the wind. It was first widely known as *tumbleweed* in the 1870s, when it was also sometimes called *rolling weed*.

Jimson weed is not primarily a western plant. It's a tall, coarse, vile-smelling poisonous member of the nightshade family that colonists first saw around Jamestown, Virginia, in the 1620s. In fact, its original name was *Jamestown weed*, which over the years was pronounced first as *jims'ton weed* and finally *jimson weed*, being spelled *jimson weed* by 1800. This probably means the colonists pronounced Jamestown, Virginia, as *Jims'ton*, just as some Englishmen still pronounce "Saint James Palace" as "Sin Jim's Palace."

The Salem Witch Trials

... More than twenty-one have confessed that they [have] ... engaged in ... bewitching and ruining our land.... The devil has made a dreadful knot of witches in the country.
Cotton Mather, *Wonders of the Invisible World*, 1693.

There have been ways of trying witches ... which the righteous God never approved of, but which ... were invented by the devil that ... innocent persons might be condemned and some notorious witches escape....
Increase Mather, *Cases of Conscience Concerning Evil Spirits*, 1693.

You shall not permit a sorceress to live.
Exodus 22:18. These words were quoted at many witch trials and were the basis for putting witches to death.

The Salem Witch Trials are among the most talked-about events of our colonial history, yet witch trials themselves were never common in America. The term *witch trial* had been in use in England since the 13th century, and witchcraft was punishable by death according to English law from long before the Pilgrims landed until 1736.

In the late 17th century, English excitement over witches spread to the colonies, especially after the most famous Puritan clergyman and statesman, and president of Harvard college, Increase Mather (1639–1723), and his famous son Cotton Mather (1663–1728), both published books "proving" the existence of witches. Then in 1692 two girls had fits in Salem Village (now Danvers), Massachusetts, and accused townspeople of bewitching them. Mass hysteria prevailed and soon 150 men and women had been accused of being possessed by the devil. A special commission led by jurist Samuel Sewall investigated and conducted the *Salem Witch Trials:* 19 "witches and wizards" were hanged

Increase Mather (left) and his son Cotton Mather.

(none were burned) and one was pressed to death between weighted planks for refusing to plead guilty or not guilty, while ten others were convicted but not executed.

Increase Mather himself was the first to criticize the trials and helped halt them; his son Cotton never protested, though he did call for fairer rules of evidence; and Judge Sewall later repented the part he had played as presiding judge. Salem is still called *Witch City*.

After this one witch-hunting orgy, Salem came to its senses and witch trials virtually disappeared from the colonies.

Ducking stool, in which common scolds and witches were submerged in water as a punishment. The number of duckings was determined by the severity of the woman's sentence.

313

Scotch-Irish

is wrongly used by some people to mean a person of half Scotch, half Irish descent. The true Scotch-Irish were originally Lowland Scots Presbyterians (small farmers, cottagers, and, mainly, weavers) who had been settled by the English in the turbulent Northern Ireland counties, collectively called Ulster, to replace the rebellious Irish in the 1600s. Hating both the low-class Irish Catholics and the upper-class Church of England English landlords, and suffering from harassment by the British textile industry and a series of crop failures in the 1720s, these Scots who had lived in Ireland flocked to the American colonies. In fact, between 1730 and 1770 almost half of Ulster sailed to the New World, and by 1776 one out of every seven colonists was Scotch-Irish.

Scram, Skedaddle, Take a Powder

To hear us talk, we Americans are always in a hurry to leave one place to get to another. Here are some of the words we've used for leaving:

cut and run, 1704; *cut out*, 1775, originally used to mean to be replaced in a dance, game, etc.; *cut for*, *cut*, 1839. Cowboys didn't *cut* a cow out of a herd until the 1870s and *cut it out!* didn't mean "stop it!" until the 1900s.

split, 1787. This was again considered very modern slang in the 1940s and 50s.

skip, 1815.

skedaddle, 1820s, but see more about this word at the entry THE CIVIL WAR; *skidoo*, 1904.

make tracks (footprints), 1827.

make oneself scarce, 1831.

vamoose (Spanish *vamos*, let's go), 1840s.

shove off, 1844; *shove*, 1856.

get, *get on*, 1860s. Since the 1840s "get on" had been a command to a horse to start moving or giddyap.

light out, *lit out*, 1870.

pull out, to leave, 1887; for a train to leave a station, 1891.

high tail (it out of here), 1890.

blow, 1902.

beat it, 1906.

go while the going's good, 1912.

head out, 1913.

take a run out powder, early 1920s; *take a powder*, late 1920s.

scram (see THE GERMANS), 1920; *amscray* (Pig Latin for *scram*), 1934.

take off, late 1930s.

Oh Shit!

has to be any scholar's cry of exasperation when he tries to pin down the use and popularity of such taboo words as *shit*. Even though people said such words, they usually didn't write them down before the late 1930s—and early lexicographers ignored them (see FUCK AND SCREW). We do know that the Old English *scītan*, to defecate, befoul, was spelled *shite* by the 14th century and *shit* by the 16th century. Until the late 19th century, however, written uses are so few that we don't know what expressions *shit* was used in. Then, in the 1870s, such terms as *to fall in the shit* (to get into trouble) and the exclamation *shit and corruption!* were recorded. Also in wide use between the 1870s and 1890s were such seemingly modern terms as *shit* and *bullshit* meaning "nonsense, rubbish, lies" (*chicken shit* and *horseshit* were first recorded in the 1930s); *the shits*, diarrhea; *shit pot* and *shit face*, both referring to a contemptible person (followed by *shit head* around 1915); *to shit on someone*, to treat someone badly; and *to beat the shit out of* someone. By 1910 *shit or bust*, to do or die, was common and so was *shit or get off the pot*, a vulgar rephrasing of the old New England "fish or cut bait," meaning to do something or let someone else try, do something or give up. By 1918 *S.O.L.* was a common abbreviation for the older *shit out of luck*.

In World War I the old rural term *shithouse* (see WHERE'S THE BATHROOM?) became a popular soldiers' term for latrine, while *shit alley* was a particularly dangerous battlefield or position and *shit pan alley* was a military hospital (a pun on the 1914 *tin-pan alley*). World War II introduced such expressions as *shit list*, a blacklist, a mental list of disliked people; *shit on a shingle*, creamed chipped beef on toast; and saw the increasing popularity of all obscenity and scatology, including *shit heel* for a contemptible person, and the abbreviation *S.O.S.*, "same old shit," the same old lies, exaggerations, chores, or procedures, especially military ones (a pun on the international Morse Code distress signal S.O.S.).

Thus *shit* has been in English for a long, long time, both as a verb and as a noun; it is popular not only in American expressions but in Canadian and Australian ones as well. *Crap* (from Middle English *crappe*, residue, rubbish) is used more in America than in other English-speaking countries. It had wide American use, both as a verb and as a noun, by the Civil War and was used to mean "nonsense, rubbish, lies" by 1910. *Crap house* (outhouse) and *crapper* (toilet) were first recorded in the 1930s but are much older than that.

Poop meant the buttocks when it was first used in America, around 1640, but is an old English word (via Old French from Latin *puppis*, stern of a ship, hence our *poop deck*). The English also used *poop* as a verb meaning to break wind (*fart* is an Old English word, in use before the 10th century), and it probably meant feces by the 16th century. *Pooped* has also meant tired since before 1890 and was originally a sailors' term, referring to a ship that was disabled or forced to proceed slowly because a following sea was coming over the stern or poop. By 1920 *poop* also meant information or facts (perhaps referring to the "shit" of rules or regulations) and by 1935 a *poop sheet* meant a fact sheet. The childish *poo* or *poo poo* for shit comes from a 19th century term for chamber pot, *po pou*, a reduplication of the French word *pot*, pot.

315

Soda Pop and Soda Water

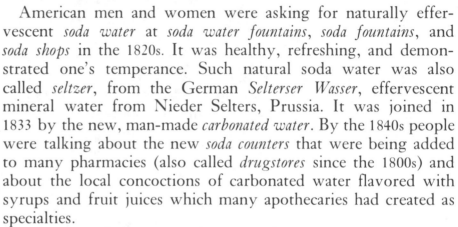

Let us have wine and women, mirth and laughter, Sermons and soda water the day after.   Byron, *Don Juan*, written 1819–24

American men and women were asking for naturally effervescent *soda water* at *soda water fountains*, *soda fountains*, and *soda shops* in the 1820s. It was healthy, refreshing, and demonstrated one's temperance. Such natural soda water was also called *seltzer*, from the German *Selterser Wasser*, effervescent mineral water from Nieder Selters, Prussia. It was joined in 1833 by the new, man-made *carbonated water*. By the 1840s people were talking about the new *soda counters* that were being added to many pharmacies (also called *drugstores* since the 1800s) and about the local concoctions of carbonated water flavored with syrups and fruit juices which many apothecaries had created as specialties.

One of the first two big favorites of the 1840s used the Simlat plant or other ginger flavoring and was called *sarsaparilla* (Spanish *zarzaparilla*, *zarza*, bramble + *parilla*, little vine), *sarsaparilla soda*, *ginger pop* (the first use of the word *pop*), *ginger champagne*, or even *ginger ale*. The other 1840s favorite was *root beer*, a general name given to various drinks flavored with roots and herbs; a somewhat similar drink was called *birch beer* in the 1880s, but this originally had been a slightly alcoholic drink containing fermented birch sap. By the 1880s, too, *soda jerker* was a well-known term, known somewhat humorously as a *soda squirt* in the 1890s, and commonly called a *soda jerk* by 1915. *Soda pop* and a *bottle of pop* were still considered somewhat slangy when used by the flappers and sheiks of the 1920s.

A pharmacist in Atlanta, Georgia, Dr. John S. Pemberton, developed a carbonated water and syrup concoction in 1886 that local customers seemed to like. He and his partner, Frank M. Robinson, who made the syrup at their Pemberton Chemical Co., Inc., named it *Coca-Cola* in 1887 and registered the trademark in 1893. The name, of course, was from its original ingredients, derived from coca leaves and cola nuts. The nick-

name *Coke* was at first shunned by the company (a minute quantity of cocaine, also called *coke*, was in the early formulas but was eliminated around 1906 with the appearance of the Pure Food and Drug Act). Nevertheless, by 1909 *Coke* meant *Coca-Cola*, in 1930 the Supreme Court ruled that the company had exclusive use of the shorter name, it was registered as a trademark in 1945, and *Coke* has been used in advertising since 1955. During World War II the term *Coke machine* became common (the first *soft-drink vending machine* had appeared in 1927). *Cola* has come to mean any soft drink based on the cola nut and in 1938 the Supreme Court ruled it to be a generic word and not the *Coca-Cola* Company's exclusive property. In the 1930s a popular Coca-Cola advertising slogan was "The drink that makes a pause refreshing," which later became "The pause that refreshes."

Americans have also talked about many other carbonated soft drinks, such as the Armour Company's grape drink *Vin Fiz* around 1911, Anheuser Busch's nonalcoholic but beerlike *Bevo* introduced in 1916 (made from a yeast by-product of

beer brewing, it disappeared when beer production was stopped during Prohibition), *Moxie* around 1927 (the word has meant shrewdness or initiative since 1939), *Orange Crush*, *7-Up* (also the name of a card game since the 1820s), *RC* (*Royal Crown Cola*), and especially *Pepsi-Cola*. *Pepsi-Cola* challenged *Coca-Cola's*

317

6-ounce bottle in the 1930s with its 12-ounce bottle, offering twice as much for the same nickel in one of the earliest, most popular singing commercials in America, with a tune based on the English hunting song "O'ye Ken John Peel" and with those immortal lyrics by Alan Kent:

> Pepsi-Cola hits the spot,
> Twelve full ounces, that's a lot.
> Twice as much for a nickel, too.
> Pepsi-Cola is the drink for you.
> Nickel, nickel, nickel, nickel,
> Trickle, trickle, trickle, trickle. . . .

Son of a Bitch

was first recorded in England in 1712, *bitch* (Old English *bicce*) having meant female dog since before the 10th century and an immoral woman since the 15th. By the 1780s *son of a bitch* was one of the most offensive and common American insults. By the 1890s, however, American men could also use the term familiarly, as in calling an old friend "You old son of a bitch you." The euphemism *son of a gun* was common by the 1750s while *son of a sea cook* appeared in 1825.

Son of a bitch was used so often by World War I American soldiers as an expletive or intensive (meaning *God damn* or *goddamned*), that Frenchmen called them "les sommobiches." The abbreviation *S.O.B.* also appeared during World War I. It was widely discussed during President Harry Truman's administration, first in 1948 when "Give 'em Hell, Harry" Truman used *s.o.b.* to refer to his critics, especially columnist Drew Pearson, and later when he used the term in a White House letter giving his opinion of a music critic who had criticized the singing of Truman's daughter, Margaret. Many Americans found the president's use of the term shocking, while others found it admirable in its straightforwardness.

> *I was wakened this morning . . . [by] the landlord ordering his Negroes. . . . In his orders . . . son-of-a-bitch was often repeated.*
> Alexander Hamilton (1757–1804), from a diary entry while stopping at a New Jersey inn.

> *Come on you sons of bitches! Do you want to live forever?*
> World War I American battle cry, coined by Marine Sergeant Daniel Daly during the Battle of Belleau Wood, June, 1918.

Spanish

Are the following words Spanish or American?

aficionado, 1940s.   *hacienda*, 1808.   *playa*, 1854.
bodega, 1849; 1950s.   *hombre*, 1836.   *presidio*, 1808.
cabaña, 1890; 1940s.   *macho*, 1960s.   *señorita*, 1823.
embarcadero, 1846.   *mañana*, 1885.   *siesta*, 17th century.
fiesta, 1844.   *padre*, 1792.   *tequila*, 1849.
frijole, 1759.   *peon*, 1826.   *tortilla*, 1831.

They are both. They are Spanish borrowings or loan words used in American English. With one exception, the dates above are the first time the words were recorded as Americanisms, that is, written without italics or translations (all but *aficionado*, *macho*, and *siesta* are listed in the 1951 *Dictionary of Americanisms*). The one word on the list which did not enter English through America is *siesta*, which was known in England even before it was recorded here. *Bodega* and *cabaña* have two dates: in 1849 *bodega* meant wine shop, liquor store in American English (directly from the Spanish), in the 1950s it came to mean a small neighborhood grocery store (from the Puerto Rican use); in 1890 *cabaña* was used in American English to mean cabin (the original Spanish meaning), in the 1940s it came to mean a beach dressing room or tent. Unless you live in the West you may not know that *embarcadero* means wharf, landing place, and *presidio* garrison, fort, the hub of many early Spanish-American towns. A *playa* is a beach and *macho* means manly, full of manly pride.

American English has borrowed more words from Spanish than from any other language, and is still borrowing them—there are hundreds of thousands of Mexicans living in the Southwest; 650,000 Puerto Ricans in New York City; and 100,000 Cubans in New Orleans, plus several hundred thousand more in the Miami area. It all started with the 16th century Spanish explorers and *conquistadors* (another Spanish loan word). Men such as Coronado, Cortés, Ponce de León, Pizarro, and de Soto were the first Europeans to see many of the plants, animals, tribes, customs, and geological features of the Americas. They used Spanish names or borrowed the local Indian names for them, spreading their own Spanish words and their Spanish version of the Indian words to Europe and eventually into English. Thus through the Spanish in *New Spain* (1535) the English language absorbed words from the Caribbean Indians (see Canoes and Cannibals for a list of them) and from the Aztec Nahuatl language (see Coyote and Mesquite). From the Spanish conquest of Mexico, including much of our own Southwest, we have many Mexican Spanish words in American English. Many of these, such as *bronco*, *corral*, *lasso*, *ranch*, *rodeo*, and *stampede*, are now associated with American cowboys (see Cowboys for a list of them). Spain also ruled Puerto Rico, Cuba, and the Philippines, and our relations with these countries, immigration from them, and our own tourists who visited them, have given us more Spanish words. Thus, from the early Spanish explorers to the exodus of Cubans from Castro's Cuba to the U.S. after 1959, Spanish has given American English many, many words. The most common ones include:

Mission San Juan Bautista, California, 1797. It is the largest of the Spanish missions in California and attracts thousands of tourists each year.

> *adobe* (Spanish for plaster, from Arabic *al-tōba*, the brick), sun-dried clay brick, 1759; a house made of this, 1821. Also shortened to *dobie*, *doby* since 1838.

319

General Pancho Villa (1877–1923), Mexican revolutionary leader.

Cesar Chavez, labor leader.

alfalfa (Spanish from Arabic *al-fasfasah*, good fodder), 1655.

alligator (Spanish *el lagarto*, the lizard), English use, 1597; first recorded in America, 1682.

arroyo, gully or brook, 1806, but not in wide American use until the 1860s.

bonanza, 1844, see THE GOLD RUSH for details.

bracero (Spanish for manual labor, from *brazo*, arm). This term came into wide American use during World War II to designate Mexican farm laborers legally entering the U.S. for a limited period of time to help harvest crops during the wartime emergency and labor shortage. Such legal entries continued by act of Congress until 1964. Since the beginning of World War II Mexican laborers who enter the U.S. illegally have been called *wetbacks*, because many of them swim or wade across the Rio Grande.

breeze (Spanish *brisa*, a northeast wind, especially a northern trade wind), as a cool wind from the sea, 16th century in English, then came to mean any light wind in the 17th century. American English also has *breezy*, impudent, informal, or full of pep, 1872; *to breeze along*, *breeze by*, *breeze through*, to proceed quickly or easily, 1907; *a breeze*, an easy task, a cinch, 1930s; and *breezeway*, 1931.

buffalo (this is the Italian spelling, Spanish and Portuguese spell it *bufalo*), the Spanish probably first took this name for a type of wild ox and applied it to the American bison, de Soto calling the American animal *bufalo* as early as 1544 (see THE BUFFALO).

burro (Spanish *borrico*, donkey), 1844.

cafeteria (Spanish American for coffee house, coffee store), meaning coffee house, 1830; self-service restaurant, 1893.

calaboose (via Louisiana French from Spanish *calabozo*, dungeon), 1792. See JAILS AND JAILBIRDS.

canyon (American Spanish *cañon*), 1834.

Chicano (from Mexican *chico*, fellow, and the nickname Chico), originally a Mexican migratory farm worker, first widespread use during Cesar Chavez's United Farm Workers 1965 California vineyard strike. Now means a Mexican-American.

chinch bug, *chinch* (Spanish *chinche*, bug), as a specific hemipterous insect destructive of wheat and corn, 1785; meaning bedbug, 1819.

cockroach (Spanish *cucaracha*), recorded in Virginia by Captain John Smith in 1624.

hoosegow (Spanish *juzgado*, court, tribunal, hence sentenced, jailed), 1860s. The same Spanish word probably gives us *jug*, meaning jail, 1815. See JAILS AND JAILBIRDS.

incommunicado (Spanish *incomunicado*), 1844.

junta (a Spanish word for legislative council), used in 17th century England for a Spanish or Italian legislative council. Later, especially in Latin America, it came to mean a secret political faction intriguing to overthrow a government, then came into wide American use during the Spanish-American War.

key, *cay*, a low island, a coral island (Spanish *cayo*). The Spanish may have gotten their word from the Taino tribe of the West Indies or it may be related to the English *quay*, French *quai*. In

Xavier Cugat, band leader.

Carmen Miranda (1917–55), dancer, actress.

any event our word *key* comes to us via the Spanish. It gives us such place names as *Key West* and *The Florida Keys.*

loco (Spanish for insane), 1840s. See SAGEBRUSH, LOCOWEED, TUMBLEWEED—AND JIMSON WEED.

machete (via American Spanish, the diminutive of Spanish *macho*, ax, club, mace), first recorded in American English in the writings of the ornithologist and artist John James Audubon, 1839.

marijuana (American Spanish *marihuana*), 1894.

mesa (Spanish for table and tableland), 1759. It also gives us such place names as *Mesa Verde.*

mosey, 1829. Many linguists think this comes from Spanish *vamos*, let's go (see *vamoose* below). However, English dialect had two terms, *to mose about*, meaning to go about in a stupor, and *to mouse*, *to mousey*, to run about like a mouse, which seem the more probable origin. Until the 1890s our *mosey* was used both to mean to move slowly along and to go quickly, seeming to confuse the two English terms. Since the 1890s our *mosey* has meant only to walk slowly, amble.

mosquito (Spanish diminutive of *mosca*, fly, hence little fly), in 16th century English, first recorded in America in the writings of William Bradford, governor of Plymouth Colony, 1656. Mosquitoes plagued early Americans all along the Atlantic Coast, giving us such names for protective gauzelike curtains as: *mosquito bar*, from South Carolina, 1682; *mosquito curtain*, from Virginia, 1770; *mosquito veil*, from New York State, 1843. By 1921 we were talking about repellent *mosquito dope.*

patio (Spanish for courtyard), 1827.

pickaninny, *piccanniny* was introduced into America by slaves from the West Indies, first recorded here in 1653. It was the slaves' way of pronouncing either Portuguese *pequenino*, little, or Spanish *pequeño niño*, little child. The slaves may have gotten this pronunciation in the West Indies or brought it there from African use in Guinea.

placer (Spanish for a deposit of sand or gravel), 1842; *placer mine*, 1848, both terms first recorded in California. See THE GOLD RUSH.

plaza, 1836.

pronto, 1850.

quadroon (from Spanish *cuarterón*), 17th century. By 1805 the New Orleans *quadroon balls*, for White men and their quadroon mistresses, were famous.

sassafras (Spanish *sasafrás*), explorers in America were using the word by 1577, its English spelling was first recorded in America in 1602. Spanish may have gotten the name for this aromatic tree of the laurel family from an Indian word or confused the tree with the *Saxifrage* genus of plant. In early America strong homemade lye soap was often called *sassafras soap*, because it was stirred with a sassafras stick or otherwise scented with sassafras. *Sassafras tea* was so common as a beverage, considered to have medicinal properties, that it was familiarly called *sass tea* by 1847.

savvy (Spanish *saber*, to know, understand, may have come into American English through the phrase ¿*Sabe usted*?, "Do you

Roberto Clemente, baseball player.

know?"), 1850. It was often spelled *sabe* in English until the 1870s.

sierra (Spanish from Latin *serra*, saw, which also gives us our word *serrated*, the Spanish in America first used *sierra* to mean a jagged mountain range), 1759, not common until the 1840s. See MOUNTAINS, CREEKS, DESERTS, AND SWAMPS.

tornado (Spanish *tronada*, thunderstorm, influenced by the Spanish *tornar*, to turn, twist), 1804. See BLIZZARDS, TORNADOES, AND HURRICANES.

vamoose (Spanish *vamos*, "let's go"), 1840s.

vigilante (Spanish for vigilant), 1850s.

American English also has its derogatory words for Spanish-speaking people, as it does for all other groups. These include:

Dago (from the common Spanish name *Diego*), a Spaniard or person of Spanish descent, 1832. By the late 1880s, however, this word was primarily used to mean an Italian.

greaser, a Mexican, 1836. Note that *Dago* and *greaser* appeared in the 1830s, when Americans were swarming into Texas and the Southwest, competing with Mexicans for land, leading up to the Mexican War in 1846. *Greaseball*, 1935, a derogatory term applied to Latin Americans, Spaniards, Italians, and Southern Europeans.

conch, originally a native of the Bahamas living in Key West, 1852 (because such natives were known for their skill in diving for conch shells). By the 1860s the word was used to apply to a poor White in Florida; by the 1920s it was used to refer to any West Indian, including both Spanish and French speaking ones.

Spick, spic, 1915. This may come from the expression "no spicka Engleesh," but the word was originally *spig* and may have come from *spag*hetti, since until 1915 *spig* was used to refer to an Italian.

In turn, Spanish-speaking people and Spanish-Americans have their own derogatory words for Americans of Anglo-Saxon descent, including:

gringo (American Spanish for "gibberish," from Spanish *griego*, Greek, literally one whose language is "all Greek to me"), first used by Mexicans during THE MEXICAN WAR, now common throughout Latin America.

Anglo, 1941.

Yanqui, the Mexican pronunciation of YANKEE, now used throughout Latin America. It first came into wide use in the 1820s but most Americans first heard it in the anti-American phrase "Yanqui go home" in the 1950s.

We have also used the words *Mexican* and *Spanish* in many combinations, including:

Mexican dollar, a peso, 1820s.

Mexican jumping bean, 1880s.

Joseph Montoya, U.S. Senator.

322

Herman Badillo, U.S. Representative.

Spanish America, 1789.

Spanish American, a North American of Spanish descent, 1811.

Spanish bayonet, 1843; *Spanish dagger*, 1859, both for various species of *Yucca*.

Spanish Creole, 1807.

Spanish dance, 1827.

Spanish fever, a cattle disease transmitted by ticks, 1858, also called *Texas fever* by 1866.

Spanish fly, a bright green blister beetle of the Mediterranean, formerly used for making a counter irritant for blisters and an aphrodisiac called cantharides, which is popularly known as *Spanish fly*. The term was in English by the 15th century, so it is not an Americanism.

Spanish (land) grant, 1826.

Spanish Indian, Latin American Indians under Spanish rule, 1715.

Spanish Mexican, 1848.

Spanish moss, 1823; this moss, which grows on or hangs from trees in the South, was first called *Spanish beard*, 1763.

Spanish quarter, a Spanish section of an American town, 1872, first used in California.

Spanish trail, the trail between Santa Fe, New Mexico and Los Angeles, California, 1857. Other routes to California were also called "the Spanish Trail," including one from Salt Lake City to San Bernardino and a long one from New Orleans via El Paso to Los Angeles.

Spanish has also given us many, many American place names, including the names of six states (see THE STATES), over 2,000 names of U.S. cities and towns, and thousands of names of rivers, mountains, valleys, etc. A brief sampling includes: *Alhambra*, *Eldorado*, *El Paso* (the full original name of the city was *El Paso del Norte*, the crossing of the river of the north, after Juan de Oñate forded the Rio Grande there in 1598; the city began to grow up on this site in the 1820s), *Hermosa Beach* (beautiful beach), *Key West*, *Los Angeles* (a shortening of the name the Spanish gave it in 1769, *El Pueblo de Nuestra Señora la Reina de Los Angeles de la Porciuncula*, the town of our Lady, Queen of the Angels of the Porciuncula, which was a Franciscan shrine near Assisi), *Las Vegas* (originally built by the Mormons in 1855, using the Spanish word *vega*, meadow, in its name), *Monterey* (*Monterey Bay* was named for the Conde de Monterey in 1602, the city then grew from a presidio and Junipero Serra mission, which were established in 1770), *Palo Alto*, *Pueblo* (Spanish for town, literally "the town," when it was first established in 1842 it was the only trading post in the area), *Raton Pass*, the *Rio Grande*, *Sacramento*, *St. Augustine* (founded 1565), *San Antonio* (the river so named because it was discovered on the Day of Saint Anthony in 1691; a presidio and mission were founded along the river and called San Antonio in 1718), *San Bernardino, San Diego, San Francisco, San José* (named after San José de Guadaloupe), *San Luis Obispo* (another of the nine mis-

Joan Baez, singer.

sions established by Father Junipero Serra between San Diego and San Francisco), *San Pedro, Santa Clara* (after Santa Clara de Assisi), *Santa Monica, Santa Fé* (the full original name was *Villa Real de Santa Fé de San Francisco*), and *Toledo* (named after the Spanish city in 1833). The list goes on and on. In fact, California alone has over 400 cities and towns with Spanish names, 80 of which are saints' names. But be it place names or words from our general vocabulary, when we hear America talking we hear many, many words that were originally Spanish.

The Spanish-American War

was fought from late April to mid August, 1898. During those four months it was called *the Cuban War* and *the War with Spain*. President William McKinley called it *the Spanish-American War* in 1899, when urging the Senate to ratify the peace treaty; during the debate over the treaty the Senate called it *the Spanish-Cuban War*. John Hay, U.S. Ambassador to Great Britain, called it that "splendid little war," because we fought it for both idealistic and imperialistic reasons and won an easy victory. Its object was to liberate Cuba from Spain.

Cuban rebels had fought the Ten Years' War against Spanish rule between 1868 and 1878; widespread fighting broke out again in 1895. This had Americans talking sympathetically about the Cuban *insurgentes* (a Spanish borrowing which had been in the English language since the 18th century). After January, 1896, we talked with anger about the new and ruthless Spanish commander of Cuba, General Valeriano Weyler y Nicolau, "the Butcher," who herded Cubans into *reconcentration camps* where they could be watched and controlled and where thousands of the *reconcentrados* died of disease, hunger, and exposure (Spain recalled "the Butcher" in 1897). American sympathy for the rebels and hatred of Spain were whipped to a high pitch by several things which added new terms to the American language and our history:

> *yellow journalism, yellow journal, the yellow press, the yellows,* all 1898 terms. William Randolph Hearst had purchased the *New York Journal* in 1895 and set out to outdo Joseph Pulitzer's sensational *New York World*. Soon the two papers were competing with each other in carrying sensational, often exaggerated, stories of Spanish atrocities in Cuba, while antiwar Americans and publications deplored the two papers' *yellow journalism.*
>
> A popular misconception is that the term *yellow journalism* comes from the yellow-nightgowned slum waif "the Yellow

William Randolph Hearst (1863–1951). Hearst treated the Spanish-American War as a circus; from a press boat off Cuba he issued orders to his correspondents and, in New York City, as many as 40 editions of the New York Journal appeared in a day.

Please remain [in Cuba]. You furnish the pictures and I'll furnish the war.

William Randolph Hearst cable to artist Frederic Remington in Cuba. Hearst had sent reporter Richard Harding Davis and artist Remington to Cuba to write and draw scenes of the Cuban revolution, but Remington had cabled Hearst he wished to return home as there was no war.

Kid" in Richard Outcault's pioneer *Shantytown* comic strip, which appeared in the *World* and later in the *Journal* during this period. However, *yellow* had been used to refer to sensational publications for 50 years before this, being recorded in 1846 as referring to sensational books and magazines in inexpensive yellow covers and later that same year to newspapers which tried to attract readers by sensational reporting.

the De Lôme letter. Hearst's *New York Journal* brought American war fever to an almost uncontrollable frenzy on February 9, 1898, when it published a private letter written to a Cuban friend by Dupuy de Lôme, the Spanish minister to Washington, in which he described President McKinley as "weak and a mere popularity-seeker." Cuban revolutionaries had gotten hold of the letter and Hearst used it to show that America must fight Spain to gain self-respect for itself and the President, who didn't want war.

Remember the Maine! On February 15, 1898, just six days after the *Journal* published the De Lôme letter, the U.S. battleship *Maine* exploded and sank in Havana harbor, taking 258 American lives (the ship had been sent to Havana to protect U.S. residents and property during the Cuban revolution). A U.S. Navy board found evidence that an initial explosion outside the ship's hull had touched off the battleship's magazine—but it was never determined if that initial explosion had been caused by a Spanish mine or torpedo, by Cuban rebels wanting to force the U.S. into the war, or by some spontaneous sparks. Nevertheless, "Remember the *Maine*" became the rallying cry of Americans—at least that's what history says, but the full cry of every red-blooded American male was:

Remember the *Maine*—the hell with Spain!

Soon American mothers were talking about and dressing their little boys in the new *sailor suits*, which both remembered the *Maine* and celebrated the successful American Navy—and thousands of boys were to curse those cute little sailor suits for years to come.

"Destruction of U.S. Battleship Maine," published in 1898 shortly after the event.

On March 27, the State Department sent Spain an ultimatum demanding the closing of the Cuban reconcentration camps, an armistice with the rebels, and the accepting of the U.S. as peace mediator; on April 9, Spain agreed to these terms and it seemed war might be averted. But many prominent Republicans, such as Assistant Secretary of the Navy Theodore Roosevelt, Ambassador to Great Britain John Hay, and Senator Henry Cabot Lodge, forced McKinley to ask Congress for a resolve to use the army and navy to free Cuba from Spanish rule. McKinley did this on April 11, Spain broke off diplomatic relations on April 20, we blockaded Cuban ports on April 22, Spain declared war on April 24, and we declared war on April 25—ten weeks after the *Maine* had sunk.

Our small army was ridiculously unprepared for war, but our navy was well trained and supplied, thanks in part to Assistant Secretary of the Navy Roosevelt. Fortunately, most of the decisive battles of the war were naval battles and our forces easily defeated the weak resistance of the tottering Spanish monarchy. Thus we were soon talking about our victories, including: landing our troops in Puerto Rico and capturing it with little resistance; the U.S. Marines' defeat of the Spanish at the Battle of Guantánamo Bay, Cuba, on June 15; and Guam's surrendering to the USS *Charleston* on July 20 (the Spanish commander of the island had thought the ship's barrage was a salute and apologized for not returning it, having no ammunition). But the most talked-about victories were the first naval battle and the last major land battle, giving us two new terms:

> *Like Dewey took Manila*, meaning very easily. Two months before the war began, Assistant Secretary of the Navy Roosevelt had told his own new, hand-picked commodore of our Asiatic squadron, George Dewey (1837–1917), that if and when hostilities broke out, he was immediately to engage the Spanish fleet in the Philippines. Thus Dewey, as soon as he heard war had been declared, steamed from Hong Kong to Manila Bay, arriving there on May 1st. Then in an almost leisurely seven-hour battle beginning at dawn on that day, Dewey's fleet destroyed or crippled all 10 ships of Spain's Pacific fleet, which had been anchored there.
>
> Dewey, however, didn't have enough men to "take Manila." After his victory his fleet blocked Manila Bay. Filipinos, who had carried on anti-Spanish activity for 100 years, had started a revolt in 1896; then, after Dewey's victory, declared independence and laid siege to Manila. On July 25, 11,000 American troops arrived and later joined the Filipino rebels in taking the city in the Battle of Manila, on August 13–14 (not knowing that the U.S. and Spain had agreed to an armistice on August 12).
>
> *the Rough Riders. Roughrider* had meant a cowboy ever since Theodore Roosevelt coined the word in an 1888 article in the *Century Magazine*. Shortly before war was declared, Roose-

Admiral George Dewey on the bridge of his flagship during the Battle of Manila Bay. Not a single American was lost in the engagement.

velt hurriedly resigned as Assistant Secretary of the Navy and helped his friend Colonel Leonard Wood organize the First U.S. Volunteer Cavalry Regiment. Since Roosevelt recruited many of its men through his western rancher and cowboy friends (he had lived on his North Dakota ranch 1884–86), the men said they were joining *Roosevelt's Rough Riders;* thus this regiment became known as *the Rough Riders* and Roosevelt became Lieutenant Colonel Roosevelt and its commander.

On June 22, 17,000 U.S. troops began landing in Cuba, then captured El Cuney on July 1. Also on July 1, Teddy Roosevelt led his Rough Riders in an impetuous charge up Kettle Hill, as part of a successful attack on San Juan Hill overlooking Santiago de Cuba (the Rough Riders didn't "charge up San Juan Hill," but helped win the Battle of San Juan Hill by charging up and capturing Kettle Hill). The Battle of San Juan Hill made the *Rough Riders* a popular name and Roosevelt a popular hero: he was idolized in the press, became governor of New York in 1899, then became Vice President of the United States in 1901, succeeding to the presidency on McKinley's assassination that same year.

Our capture of San Juan Hill was important because it commanded the heights overlooking the harbor of Santiago de Cuba, threatening the Spanish fleet there with artillery fire (a U.S. naval force from Key West had bottled up the Spanish Atlantic fleet in Santiago harbor since May 29). On July 3, two days after San Juan Hill was captured, the Spanish fleet tried to break out of Santiago harbor, and in a four-hour battle along the coast, the seven-vessel American fleet destroyed the seven-vessel Spanish fleet, all Spanish ships being beached while sink-

The Rough Riders, *and their commander, Colonel Theodore Roosevelt, at the top of San Juan Hill. In the battle Black troops under Lieutenant John J. Pershing distinguished themselves.*

Battle of Santiago Harbor.

ing or burning. Before this battle the U.S. battleship *Oregon* had made one of the most remarkable runs ever made by a steam vessel, racing from Mare's Island Navy Yard in San Francisco and around Cape Horn to reach Cuba in 66 days, in time to help defeat the Spanish fleet. A remarkable feat, but that 66-day trip convinced America that THE PANAMA CANAL had to be built (some Americans, such as ex-Assistant Secretary of the Navy Roosevelt, didn't need convincing; they had been convinced long before and had welcomed the Spanish-American War as a way of keeping Spain and Cuba from interfering with the projected canal).

Other terms which came out of or were popularized by the Spanish-American War or its aftermath include:

> *belly robber*, an army cook or mess sergeant.
> *boondocks* (via the Philippine Tagalog *bundok*, mountain), first used by U.S. Marines during our own fighting against the Filipino guerrillas (during 1899-1902) to refer to isolated or outlying mountain country (U.S. troops shortened *boondocks* to *boonies* during the Vietnam war). Soon after the U.S. occupation of the Philippines began, the Filipino guerrillas who had fought Spain for independence began to fight us, with each side using about 70,000 men. We now called the "ungrateful" Filipino guerrillas under Emilio Aguinaldo *insurrectos* and put many Filipinos in *relocation camps* (which were somewhat more humane than the Cuban *reconcentration camps* that had helped start the Spanish-American War in the first place).
>
> *boot* first came to mean a navy or marine recruit during the Spanish-American War, from the leggings sailors used to wear (since colonial days we had used *boot* to mean footwear reaching to the knee). *Boot camp*, a training camp for new recruits, became a popular term by World War I.

the brass, the war brass was first used during the Spanish-American War to mean high-ranking officers, referring to the insignia on their uniforms. It comes from the 1887 *brass button brigade*, meaning those officers who ruled the military from their desks in Washington (see also *brass hat* at WORLD WAR I).

to bust, to reduce in rank, was also a new U.S. military use in the Spanish-American War.

campaign hat, was the name given the khaki-colored felt hat worn by the Rough Riders. Considered dashing, similar *campaign hats* were then to be adopted by other military units, police units, forest rangers, etc.

embalmed beef was a term popularized by Teddy Roosevelt during the war and discussed with horror as one of America's biggest scandals. It referred to tainted canned beef of uncertain age which caused more casualties to American troops than the war itself—the U.S. lost 5,462 men in the war, 279 of them in combat and the rest killed by accidents, embalmed beef, and disease (see *yellow jack* below). The scandal over the tainted embalmed beef was a major cause of the passage of the 1906 Pure Food and Drug Act and also prompted Upton Sinclair to write his 1906 *The Jungle*, one of the most widely discussed books ever written in America, a grim, realistic account of life in the Chicago stockyards and its debasing effects on a Slavic immigrant and his wife. It also led to Roosevelt's hatred of the *Beef Trust* which, as President, he tried to bust in the early 1900s.

the Gatling gun, a light, rapid-fire "revolving gun battery" that fired 350 rounds a minute and was the forerunner of the machine gun, was patented by Richard Jordan Gatling on November 4, 1862. Although some historians believe Union troops used it during the Civil War, the U.S. Army Ordnance Department didn't adopt it until the war was over, in 1866. It then saw some use against Indians in the West, but came into wide use only in the Spanish-American War, which is when most Americans first heard of it. It was simply called a *gatling* by 1880 and probably gives us the word *gat*, handgun, first used by New York and Boston gangsters around 1904 (by the 1920s those who robbed at gunpoint were sometimes called *gat men* or *cat men* and such robbery was called *gatting up* or *catting up*, *cat* in this use perhaps being a slurred pronunciation of *gat*).

goo-goo, gu-gu was the disparaging word for a Filipino that American soldiers and marines used after our occupation of the Philippines and during our fighting against the Philippine guerrillas in 1899–1902 (see *boondocks* above). The term could have been a way of mocking the sounds made by the Tagalog-speaking Filipinos or perhaps a reference to Oriental slanted eyes, *goo-goo eyes* meaning loving glances in the U.S. in the 1890s and *goo-goo* then being a slang term for eye (see *slanteye* at WORLD WAR II AND G.I. JOE). This *goo-goo* may also be the word that gave us *gook* in World War II.

a message to Garcia, to carry a message to Garcia. Shortly before we declared war on Spain, Andrew Summers Rowan, a young lieutenant in the Bureau of Military Intelligence, was sent to communicate with the Cuban insurgent leader General Calixto García Íñiguez and to obtain from him information on the size and dispersal of the Spanish and Cuban forces. Rowan landed in an open boat in Cuba on April 24, 1898, the date Spain declared war, and completed his mission successfully, bringing back the wanted information—thus he didn't so much deliver a message to García as bring back information to our military intelligence. His exploit was popularized in Elbert Hubbard's inspirational essay "A Message to Garcia," which was published in Hubbard's *The Philistine* in its March issue in 1899, the essay extolling young men to be loyal and trustworthy and to act promptly to do what is necessary. Thus Rowan's successful mission and Hubbard's essay added the expressions "a message to Garcia" and "to carry a message to Garcia" to our language, used figuratively to mean an important message and to accomplish what one has been entrusted to do.

sergeant clerk was a new army rank in 1895, first generally known during the Spanish-American War; such a sergeant had formerly been called a *brigade sergeant major*.

shavetail meant a mule or ass among farmers and in the army mule corps by 1846 (because the mule has a less hairy tail than the horse). By the 1890s it meant an inexperienced person, then during the Spanish-American War was first used to mean an inexperienced or newly commissioned lieutenant. Some say this use is from the U.S. Military Academy, because seniors figuratively had their coattails shaved when they graduated as second lieutenants, going from West Point's long-tailed uniform coat to the shorter service coat. However, *shavetail* means a second lieutenant for only one reason—it was the army mule corps word for "ass."

war record was first used in a general way in 1890 to mean war experience, but people didn't talk about a veteran's specific *war record* until immediately after the Spanish-American War.

the White Fleet, the Great White Fleet. The Spanish-American War generated great enthusiasm for our victorious navy, made us realize its importance, and gave us possessions in the Caribbean and Pacific which needed a large navy for their protection. Thus soon after the war our navy grew to be the second largest in the world. To stress our new naval might and show we were indeed now a world power, in 1907 the navy sent 16 battleships and 4 destroyers on a world cruise, all 20 ships being painted white. Thus Americans were talking proudly about our *White Fleet* or *Great White Fleet*.

yellow jack was first recorded in 1836 as a West Indies name for yellow fever, then became a very common name for this disease as our troops contracted it fighting in Cuba during the Spanish-American War. Yellow fever, an infectious "tropical fever" characterized by jaundice (hence *yellow fever*), hemorrhaging, and vomiting, was no stranger to Americans. It had been called *yellow bilious fever* during a Boston epidemic in 1739, then *yellow fever* during a Charleston epidemic in 1740. Epidemics were annual summer tragedies in the South, with cities such as Charleston, Mobile, and New Orleans becoming summer death traps: the wealthy southern city dwellers retreated to isolated estates, and steamboats often curtailed summer trips below St. Louis. Long after the Civil War *yellow-fever con-*

certs and *yellow-fever balls* were given to aid the victims of the disease, or their survivors. We also called yellow fever *dock fever* (1796), *stranger's fever* (1824), *the vomito* (1836, a Texas name for it, from the Spanish, though this name often referred to a particularly violent form of the disease accompanied by black vomit), *New Orleans fever* or *Orleans fever* (1843), *Panama fever* (1850, though this name was also used to mean malaria), and *bronze John* (1869).

On August 4, 1898, eight days before the armistice, the U.S. War Department ordered our Cuban Expeditionary Force back to the U.S. so that it would escape the further spread of yellow fever, malaria, and food poisoning: over 1,000 troops then had food poisoning (see *embalmed beef* above), and 3,000 had yellow fever. During the Cuban occupation Major Walter Reed of the U.S. Army Medical Corps and a group of heroic enlisted men serving as guinea pigs proved Cuban physician Dr. Carlos Finlay's theory that the yellow fever virus was transmitted by the bite of a specific type of mosquito (British Dr. Ronald Ross in India has recently found that other mosquitoes transmitted malaria). This led to the draining of swamps and the cleaning up of city dumps to destroy mosquito breeding sites. Such efforts also made the other Caribbean Islands and southern U.S. cities safer places to live and visit. The control of yellow fever and malaria also made possible the building of the Panama Canal.

The armistice was declared on August 12th and the Treaty of Paris signed December 10, 1898, stipulating that Spain was to free Cuba and cede Guam, the Philippines, and Puerto Rico to the U.S., the U.S. to pay $20 million for the "improvements" Spain had made in the Philippines. Thus Spain lost all that remained of her once great empire in the New World and the U.S. emerged as a world power, making the Caribbean an "American lake" and giving us a strategic interest across the Pacific (we had also agreed to annex the Republic of Hawaii in 1898 because the war made its strategic value increasingly evident).

Before we ratified the peace treaty there was a major nationwide debate concerning *imperialism* and *anti-imperialism*, the first time the two terms had been widely used in the U.S. (*imperial* was a 1603 English word, *imperialism* had been used in 1858 in England to mean the despotic rule of an emperor and in 1881 to mean the policy of seeking to extend the empire or its influence). American *anti-imperialists* argued that acquiring the Spanish colonies was against U.S. tradition and deprived others of freedom—though many were mainly worried about acquiring territories peopled by "alien races." Liberal leaders from all parties formed the Anti-Imperialist League in early 1899 to oppose the peace treaty and expansion of the U.S. beyond the continental borders. However, others argued that if we didn't take over the Spanish possessions, "foreign powers" would soon gobble them up and U.S. expansion would be forever limited, while such men as Theodore Roosevelt and Senator Lodge wanted the Philippines so Manila Bay could be used to protect American interests against European powers in the Pacific and China, and some Protestant churches saw the obtaining of the new territories as a divine summons for missionary work. Most Americans joined in the debate—we had never expected to win any colonies in the war and didn't know what to do with them. The Senate ratified the Treaty of Paris in February, 1899, with a bare two-vote majority, thus entangling the U.S. in the Caribbean and Latin American affairs and tying us much more closely to the course of future events all across the Pacific. The Spanish-American War was to lead to much dramatic American history and talk—concerning Cuba, Guam, the Philippines, and Puerto Rico, and World War II, Korea, and Vietnam.

Come along get you ready, wear your bran, bran new gown,
For dere's gwine to be a meeting in that good, good old town,
When you hear that the preaching does begin,
Bend down low for to drive away your sin,
And when you gets religion you want to shout and sing,
There'll be a hot time in the old town tonight, my baby,
There'll be a hot time in the old town tonight.

"A Hot Time in the Old Town Tonight," music written by Theodore A. Metz, orchestra leader of McIntyre and Heath's Southern Minstrels, in 1886, and words by Joseph Hayden. This was the rallying song of Roosevelt's *Rough Riders* and so popular with American troops during the Spanish-American War that many Spanish and Cubans thought it was our national anthem. Teddy Roosevelt later used it as his political campaign song.

332

Oh the moonlight's fair to-night along the Wabash
From the fields there comes the breath of new-mown hay.
Thro' the sycamores the candle lights are gleaming,
On the banks of the Wabash far away.

"On the Banks of the Wabash," written by Paul Dresser, brother of novelist Theodore Dreiser, in 1896. It became a popular sentimental song with the homesick soldiers. The first verse and this chorus are supposed to have been written by Theodore Dreiser.

Over hill, over dale, we have hit the dusty trail
And those caissons go rolling along.
Countermarch! Right about! hear those wagon soldiers shout
While those caissons go rolling along.
Oh it's hi-hi-yee! for the field artilleree,
Shout out your numbers loud and strong,
And where'er we go, you will always know
That those caissons are rolling along.

"The Caisson Song," written by Lieutenant (later Major) Edmund L. Gruber of the 5th Field Artillery in the Philippines on the reuniting of its 1st and 2nd battalions in April, 1908. *Wagon-soldier* had meant a light or field artilleryman since before the Civil War and remained in use through World War I. A *caisson* has meant an ammunition chest and ammunition wagon, as well as a watertight compartment, in English since the 18th century (via Old French *casson*, Italian *cassa* from Latin *capsa*, box, chest).

The Spittoon

Amerigo Vespucci was the first to note that Caribbean Indians chewed and spat tobacco. Sailors to the West Indies adopted the habit and it reached epidemic proportions in our colonies, where tobacco was homegrown and plentiful. By 1700 *chewing* was already condemned as a low-class colonial habit—gentlemen smoked pipes in public. But as the Revolution approached, red-blooded American chewing increased and spitting became patriotic, the antithesis of *sniffing* snuff which was associated with the British gentry and Royalists.

Thus the term *chewing tobacco* and *a chew* were widespread by 1776, with the lower class and rustics saying *chaw tobacco* and *a chaw* ("chaw" for *chew* is a British dialectical pronunciation dating back to 1600 and was brought to America by the Irish). *Twist*

> *Spit not in the room but in the corner.*
> *The School of Good Manners, 1784*

333

has meant a thick, intertwined rope of tobacco since the 1740s and was the first form chewed widely. The *plug*, a flat rectangular cake of pressed tobacco, became common around 1818; associated with sailors it was known as *Navy Plug* by 1869, as *Navy* by 1876. By the 1820s and 30s *spitting contests* were in vogue and President Andrew Jackson was said to be pretty good at them.

From before the Revolution until about 1900 one thing you would have heard over and over in America would have been women and foreign visitors decrying the disgusting, yellow tobacco stains covering rugs, floors, windows, stoves, shirt fronts, shoes, chins, and beards from the humblest frontier cabin to the White House. After all, as late as 1860 95% of all domestic tobacco was used for chewing tobacco.

In colonial America *sandbox* didn't mean a large box filled with sand for children to play in but a smaller wooden box of sand in the corner or by the fireplace to spit into. *Spittoons* (*spit* + the common suffix *-oon*) didn't grace most hotel lobbies, taverns, post offices, or stores until after 1800. Despite the signs begging "Use the spittoon" these were never exactly where needed, and many men considered using them somewhat effete anyway. The *cuspidor*, a fancy name for a fancy spittoon, was a late arrival in America. It first appeared as *cusperdore* in an 1871 patent; the word and item come from the Portuguese *cuspidor*, literally "spitter," and had been used in Portuguese colonies since the 1770s (the word may have come to us via its Dutch version *kurspedoor*, spitbox). Cuspidors often were nickel plated, bore mottoes such as "In God We Trust," and were found in some of the fanciest railroad cars, barbershops, hotel lobbies, and homes in the land. But by the time cuspidors were introduced people were already complaining less about tobacco juice and more about cigar smoke—and within 20 years would be troubled by the increasing amount of cigarette smoke. It was a question of out of the spittoon, into the fire.

The Star-Spangled Banner

When the Jamestown and Plymouth colonists said "our flag" they meant a white square with the red cross of St. George extending its full length and width. It, along with the British Union Flag, was flown on the ships that brought them to America and from the flagpoles of their settlements. New England Puritans always objected to this cross as an idolatrous relic given England by the Pope; thus from about 1700 on many local New England flags displayed one of God's own native trees. Since then America has had many flags and many names and expressions associated with them:

Grand Union Flag 1775?–1777

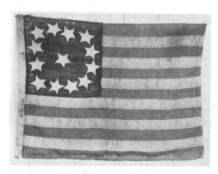

The flag adopted in 1779 had no official arrangement for the stars. This early hand-woven, hand-sewn flag has 12 stars around a center star; the most common arrangement was all thirteen in a circle, thus showing that each state was the equal of the other states.

the *Pine Tree Flag* was popular in New England from about 1700 on, was the Massachusetts state flag during the Revolutionary War, and was our first naval ensign, in 1775. It often had the words "An Appeal to Heaven" on it. Though called *the Pine Tree Flag*, many such flags actually pictured oak trees. These flags also evolved into the *Liberty Tree Flag* of 1775, which often bore the words "An Appeal to God" (for the term *Liberty Tree* itself see TAXATION WITHOUT REPRESENTATION).

the *Rattlesnake Flag* became popular during the French and Indian War, 1754–63, the native rattlesnake representing the colonists as dangerous-when-aroused. South Carolina's state flag featured a rattlesnake during the Revolutionary War and by then the rattlesnake was a common American decoration, often accompanied by the inscription "Don't tread on me." One reason for the rattlesnake's popularity then was that it was usually pictured with 13 rattles, one for each colony or state.

the *Grand Union*, 1776. In the first week of January, 1776, the new Continental Army besieging Boston and the new Continental Navy began to fly a new flag: it had a field of seven red and six white stripes with the British Grand Union flag and its crosses of St. George (for England) and St. Andrew (for Scotland) in the canton—this canton still showing our loyalty to the crown. Many Americans disliked this British identification and rather contemptuously called this flag the *continental flag* or the *congress colours*, referring to the Continental Congress as being too weak in opposing the British. Its true name, however, was the *Grand Union*, taken from the British name, though "union" also meant the union of the colonies. It was also called the *Cambridge flag* since it was first flown around Boston. Americans were to fight the British under this British-inspired flag for a year and a half.

the *Stars and Stripes.* On June 14, 1777, the Continental Congress resolved that

The flag of the United States shall be thirteen stripes, alternate red and white, with a union of thirteen stars of white on a blue field, representing a new constellation.

The only change from the Grand Union flag (see above) was that the union of the St. George and St. Andrew's crosses in the canton was replaced with a union of stars. The colors and overall design of the flag thus followed British tradition: there was no suggestion that the red and white colors represented

E pluribus unum, *"one out of many,"* was chosen in 1776 by Benjamin Franklin, Thomas Jefferson, and John Adams as the U.S. motto. At the same time they chose the design of The Great Seal of the United States, which bears this motto, as do all U.S. coins and dollar bills.

Oh, say, can you see, by the
    dawn's early light,
  What so proudly we hailed at
    the twilight's last
    gleaming,
Whose broad stripes and bright
    stars through the perilous
    fight,
  O'er the ramparts we
    watched were so gallantly
    streaming?
And the rockets' red glare, the
    bombs bursting in air,
Gave proof through the night
    that our flag was still
    there.
Oh, say, does that star-
    spangled banner yet wave
  O'er the land of the free, and
    the home of the brave?
    "The Star-Spangled Ban-
    ner," Francis Scott Key,
    1814

anything (such as the red representing the blood being spilled during the Revolutionary War) nor that the stripes derived from Washington's coat of arms (which theory was presented much later).

Since Congress had made no rule as to how the stars should be arranged, there was no uniformity: some of these flags had 12 stars in a circle around the 13th, some had horizontal rows of 4, 5, and 4 stars, some arranged them in an outline pattern of the two crosses on the British flag. However, having all 13 stars in a circle became the most common arrangement, probably from the original design by artist Francis Hopkins, a signer of the Declaration of Independence and a member of the naval committee of the Continental Congress. By 1782 *The Stars and Stripes* was a popular name for such flags.

the Continental Flag (1775), *the National Flag* (1777) don't refer to any specific flags. Various flags used from 1775–77 were called *the Continental Flag,* including the Grand Union and a white Liberty Tree flag. We have called a variety of flags *the National Flag,* each has had a stars and stripes design but the number and arrangement of stars has changed as new states have been added to the Union. In fact, from 1795 to 1818 our national flag contained 15 stars and 15 stripes, both standing for the 15 states; in 1818 the stars increased to 20, but Congress then decided to revert to the original 13 stripes and keep them that number no matter how many states and stars were added.

The Star-Spangled Banner. Since at least 1806 the American flag has been called "star spangled," but it was the 35-year-old Baltimore lawyer Francis Scott Key who gave us the popular name for the flag, *the Star-Spangled Banner.* On September 13, 1814, during the War of 1812, he and a friend set out in a small boat to deliver a letter from President Madison demanding the release of a prominent Baltimore physician, Dr. William Beames, who was being held prisoner aboard a British ship in Baltimore Harbor. Key and his friend arrived at the British ship just as the British attack on Fort McHenry in the harbor began; they were detained on their boat and watched the 25-hour bombardment. When Key saw the American flag still flying at dawn on September 14th he took an envelope from his pocket and wrote down the first words of a poem, "Oh, say, can you see, by the dawn's early light...," describing what he had seen and felt.

This poem, entitled "Defence of Fort M'Henry," was printed on handbills and then published in the Baltimore *Patriot* on September 20th, becoming an immediate sensation in the city where the bombardment had taken place. Soon it was sung to the tune of the English song "To Anacreon in Heaven," which had been written by John Stafford Smith for the Anacreontis Society of London (founded in honor of the Greek poet Anacreon who lived from about 572–488 B.C. and is famous for writing in praise of love and of wine and is reputed to have died choking on a grape seed). A phrase from Key's poem "star-spangled banner," had almost immediately come to mean our flag; now *The Star-Spangled Banner* became the title of the song, which by 1843 was called "our national ballad." It didn't

The Pledge of Allegiance to the Flag by Francis Bellamy, based on an earlier version by James B. Upham. Bellamy, a Baptist minister, was chairman of a committee for a national school program to celebrate the 400th anniversary of the discovery of America; this "Pledge of Allegiance" was written to be presented at the Chicago World's Fair in October, 1892, but was first published in the Boston weekly magazine *Youth's Companion*, September 8, 1892. Millions of American children have recited this pledge daily at the beginning of school since the 1890s. It was officially amended to read "one nation under God" by Congress in 1954.

become our national anthem until March 3, 1931, 117 years after Francis Scott Key wrote his famous poem.

Old Glory was originally the name of a specific large American flag presented to Salem, Massachusetts ship captain William Driver of the brig *Charles Daggett* on August 10, 1831. As this flag was hoisted to the masthead Captain Driver proclaimed, "I name thee Old Glory." Most sources say the flag was presented to him by friends when he took command of this ship; some say it was presented him by a group of women in recognition of his having returned some mutineers of the British ship *Bounty* from Tahiti to their chosen home on Pitcairn Island. In any case, his Old Glory was well known and by the 1850s *Old Glory* had come to mean the American flag in general.

Betsy Ross (Elizabeth Griscom Ross, 1752-1836) was never talked about as being the maker of the first American flag until after March 14, 1870. On that date her grandson William J. Camby read a paper before the history society of Pennsylvania which presented the story based on his aunt's memories of what Betsy Ross had told her. The story is that in June, 1776, George Washington and two others representing a committee of the Continental Congress came to Betsy Ross's upholstery shop in Arch Street in Philadelphia, showed her a rough draft of the flag and asked if she could make one; she did and it was taken to Congress and adopted. This story could be true, even though it was first presented 96 years after the fact—but there is no record of such a committee or of the adoption of the flag until a year later. She did make some flags for the Pennsylvania navy, in 1777, but these were neither original nor unique.

Flag Day was first talked about in the 1890s, especially after Dr. B. J. Cigrand founded a society in 1895 to promote such a day. The first nationwide one was proclaimed by President Wilson for June 14, 1916, June 14th being the day the Continental Congress had passed the resolution concerning the first American flag back in 1777.

The States

In 1792 Americans spoke proudly of "the 15 states," in 1837 of "these 26 states," during the centennial of 1876 of "the 38 states," from 1912 to 1959 of "the 48 states," and since 1959 we have talked of "the 50 states." These 50 states get their names from six basic sources: (1) 28 state names come from native words, of which 26 come from Indian words, one from Eskimo, and one from Hawaiian; (2) eleven state names are English; (3) six come from the Spanish; (4) three come from the French; (5) one, *Rhode Island*, comes from the Dutch; (6) and one, *Washington*, comes from American history. Here is a list of our state names with their meanings, dates of the states' admissions to the Union, previous names for the areas (of which a state may have been only a part), and the major nicknames for the states.

Alabama, 1819, 22nd state—from Choctaw *alba ayamule*, "I open the thicket," literally one who clears the land and gathers food from it. Previously *Alabama Territory*; also called *the Cotton State, the Heart of Dixie.*

Alaska, 1959, 49th state—the Russian version of the Eskimo *Alakshak* or *Alayeksa*, "great land, mainland." Previously called *Russian America;* also called *the Last Frontier*.

Arizona, 1912, 48th state—from Papago *Arizonac*, "place of the small spring." Also called *the Grand Canyon State*.

Arkansas, 1836, 25th state—Sioux for "south wind people, land of the south wind people." Previously spelled *Arkansaw;* also called *the Wonder State*, *the Land of Opportunity*.

California, 1850, 31st state—Spanish name for "an earthly paradise," an imaginary island in Spanish lore. Previously called *Alta California* (Upper California, in opposition to *Baja California*); also called *the Golden State*.

Colorado, 1876, 38th state—Spanish word for "red," literally "red land, red earth." Previously *Colorado Territory;* also called *the Centennial State*, because of the year it entered the Union.

Connecticut, 1788, 5th state—from Mohican *quinnitukqut*, "at the long tidal river," referring to the Connecticut River. Also called *the Nutmeg State*, *the Constitution State*.

Delaware, 1787, the 1st state—named in 1644 for English governor Lord de la Warr. Previously called *New Sweden*, *South River;* also called *the First State*, *the Diamond State*.

Florida, 1845, 27th state—Spanish "land of flowers," but Ponce de Leon named it on Easter Sunday 1513 to mean "flowery Easter." Previously *Florida Territory;* also called *the Sunshine State*.

Georgia, 1788, 4th state—named in 1732 for King George II of England. Also called *the Peach State*, *the Empire State of the South*.

Hawaii, 1959, the 50th state—native name *Hawaiki* or *Owykee*, "homeland." Previously *the Sandwich Islands;* also called *the Aloha State*.

Idaho, 1890, 43rd state—from a Shoshone term meaning "light on the mountains." Also called *the Gem State*.

Illinois, 1818, 21st state—via French from Algonquian *iliniwek*, "men, warriors." Also called *the Prairie State*.

Indiana, 1816, 19th state—*Indian* + *a*, hence "land of the Indians." Previously *Indian Territory;* also called *the Hoosier State*, *hoosier* being a dialect word for big, hence "big man, mountaineer" (the area was settled by mountaineers from Kentucky).

Iowa, 1846, 29th state—from Dakota *Ayuba*, "the sleepy one," a derogatory name for the Indian tribe. Also called *the Hawkeye State* (allegedly from the name of a sharpsighted Indian chief).

Kansas, 1861, 34th state—from Sioux for "south wind people, land of the south wind people," via French *Kansas* (1673) and Spanish *Escansque* (1601). Previously *Kansas Territory;* also called *the Sunflower State*.

Kentucky, 1792, 15th state—from Iroquois *Kentake*, "meadow land." Previously *Kentucky County*, Virginia; also called *the Blue Grass State*. Sometimes historically called *the Dark and Bloody Ground* because several hostile Indian tribes used it as a hunting and burial ground, making it an Indian no man's land.

Louisiana, 1812, 18th state—named in 1681 for King Louis XIV of France. Previously *Louisiane;* also called *the Pelican State*, *the Creole State*, *the Sugar State*.

Maine, 1820, 23rd state—the name of a French province.

Previously *the Province of Maine;* also called *the Pine Tree State.*

Maryland, 1788, 7th state—named for Henrietta Maria, Queen Consort of Charles I of England (and sister of Louis XIII of France). Previously *Marieland;* also called *the Old Line State.*

Massachusetts, 1788, 6th state (officially as *the Commonwealth of Massachusetts*)—Algonquian for "at the big hill, place of the big hill." Previously *Massachusetts Bay Colony;* also called *the Bay State.*

Michigan, 1837, 26th state—Chippewa *mica gama,* "big water," referring to Lake Michigan. Previously *Michigan Territory;* also called *the Wolverine State.*

Minnesota, 1858, 32nd state—from Dakota Sioux meaning "sky-tinted water," which can be translated either as "cloudy water," or as "sky-blue water." Previously *Minnesota Territory;* also called *the Gopher State, the North Star State.*

Mississippi, 1817, 20th state—Chippewa *mici sibi,* "big river," for the Mississippi River. Also called *the Magnolia State.*

Missouri, 1821, 24th state—via the French from Algonquian "muddy water," referring to the river; however, the name could be from a completely different Indian term, somewhat similar in sound, meaning "people of the big canoes." Previously *Missouri Territory;* also called *the Show Me State.*

Montana, 1889, 41st state—Spanish for "mountainous." Previously *Montana Territory;* also called *the Treasure State.*

Nebraska, 1867, 37th state—from the Omaha *ni-bthaska,* "river in the flatness," referring to the Platte River. Previously *Territory of Nebraska;* also called *the Cornhusker State.*

Nevada, 1864, 36th state—Spanish for "snowy, snowed upon." Previously part of *Washoe Territory;* also called the *Sagebrush State, the Silver State.*

New Hampshire, 1788, 9th state—named by Captain John Mason for Hampshire County, England, in 1622 when he was granted the land, which then also included present-day Maine and parts of Vermont. Also called *the Granite State.*

New Jersey, 1787, 3rd state—part of the area the British seized from the Dutch in 1664, it was renamed *New Jersey* for the Isle of Jersey off the English coast, where one of the two Englishmen to whom the land was granted had been governor. Also called *the Garden State.*

New Mexico, 1912, 47th state—named by Spanish explorers from Mexico in 1562. Previously *Nuevo Mexico, New Mexico Territory;* also called *the Land of Enchantment.*

New York, 1788, 11th state—part of the area named *New Netherland* by the Dutch in 1621, it was seized by British forces under the Duke of York in 1664, then renamed *New York* when the land was granted to this Duke of York by his brother, Charles II of England. Previously *New Netherland* (*Niew Netherland*); also called *the Empire State.*

North Carolina, 1789, 12th state—Named the *Province of Carolina* after King Charles II of England (Latinized as Carolina) in 1619; divided into North and South Carolina in 1710. Previously part of the *Province of Carolina;* also called *the Tar Heel State, Old North State.*

North Dakota, 1889, 39th state—*Dakota* is the Sioux name for themselves, meaning "friend, ally." Previously part of *Dakota Territory;* also called *the Flickertail State, the Sioux State.*

Ohio, 1803, 17th state—from Iroquois *Oheo*, "beautiful, beautiful water," referring to the Ohio River. Also called *the Buckeye State* (*buckeye* being the horse chestnut).

Oklahoma, 1907, 46th state—Choctaw for "the red people." Previously *Indian Territory;* also called *the Sooner State* (a *sooner* being one who "jumped the gun" before the last big tract of Indian land was officially thrown open for settlement on April 22, 1889, hence one who grabbed choice land "sooner" than the time legally set for staking one's claim).

Oregon, 1850, 33rd state—either from an Indian word for the Colorado River (which may have been the Algonquian *Wauregan*, "beautiful water") or from an Indian word sounding something like "Wisconsin," which was misspelled on a French map (*Wisconsin* being the Algonquian word for "grassy place" or "place of the beaver"). Also called *the Beaver State.*

Pennsylvania, 1787, 2nd state—named in 1681 for the owner of the land grant, William *Penn* + *sylvania* (Latin *sylva*, wood, woodland). Also called *the Keystone State.*

Rhode Island, 1790, 13th state (officially as *the State of Rhode Island and Providence Plantation*)—from the Dutch, literally "red clay island." Previously *Isle of Rhodes;* also called *Little Rhody.*

South Carolina, 1788, 8th state—the *Province of Carolina* was named after King Charles II of England (Latinized as Carolina) in 1619; divided into North and South Carolina in 1710. Previously part of the *Province of Carolina;* also called *the Free State; the Palmetto State.*

South Dakota, 1889, 40th state—*Dakota* is the Sioux name for

themselves, meaning "friend, ally." Previously part of *Dakota Territory;* also called *the Coyote State, the Sunshine State.*

Tennessee, 1796, 16th state—the name of a Cherokee settlement with no known meaning. The Spanish called it *Tenaqui* as early as 1567. Previously *the State of Franklin* (1784–88), *Franklin;* also called the *Volunteer State* (from the large number of men, 30,000 who volunteered to serve in the Mexican War).

Texas, 1845, 28th state—via Spanish *tejas*, allies, from a local Indian word *texia* for "friend, ally," applied to the numerous tribes allied against the Apaches. So called by the Spaniards as early as 1541. Previously *the Republic of Texas* (1836–45); also called *the Lone Star State.*

Utah, 1896, 45th state—said to be Navaho for "higher up, the upper land," but probably means "land of the Ute," the Indian tribe. Previously *Utah Territory;* also called *the Beehive State*, from that Mormon symbol of communal cooperation.

Vermont, 1791, 14th state—French *vert*, green + *mont*, mountain. Previously *New Connecticut;* also called *the Green Mountain State.*

Virginia, 1788, 10th state—named in 1607 for the Virgin Queen, Elizabeth I, of England. Also called *Old Dominion.*

Washington, 1889, 42nd state—named in 1853 for George Washington. Previously *Washington Territory;* also called *the Evergreen State.*

West Virginia, 1863, 35th state—from the English-named state of Virginia, formed when the western counties of Virginia broke away from that state after it seceded from the Union during the Civil War. Also called *the Mountain State.*

Wisconsin, 1848, 30th state—perhaps from the Algonquian name of a river (meaning "grassy place" or "place of the beaver"). As with Oregon and many other Indian place names, all we know for sure is that it is from an Indian word or expression, we are not sure of exactly which one or what it means. Also called *the Badger State*.

Wyoming, 1890, 44th state—from Algonquian *mache-weaming*, "at the big flats." Also called *the Equality State*.

Thus the states got their names. The word *state* itself had originally been used to refer to a British colony in America in 1634; Revolutionary War Americans were calling all the United States *The States* in 1776.

Besides state names America has many regional or area names. The Spanish called parts of America *New Spain* by 1535, the French called their Canadian lands *New France* by 1608, and the Dutch called their lands along the Hudson River *New Netherland* by 1621. Thus it is not surprising that Captain John Smith put the name *New England* on his map in 1616, explaining that "That part we call New England ... betwixt the degree 41. and 45." looked like old England. Later names for our regions and geographical areas were not always so precise: *the North West* and *the West* kept moving westward as the colonies and then the United States grew. Thus when we say *the North West* today we mean Oregon and Washington and nearby areas, but originally it referred to *the North West Territory*, the lands ceded to us by Great Britain after the Revolutionary War and encompassing the present states of Ohio, Indiana, Illinois,

Michigan, and Wisconsin. Similarly when we say *the West* today we usually mean Colorado and beyond, but during much of our history it meant the land west of the settlements, which at one time was merely over the Appalachians, and later was west of the Mississippi, as Missouri or Kansas. In early Virginia *western* meant on the western side of Chesapeake Bay, giving us the term *the Western Shore* (1634), the parts of Maryland and Virginia on the western side of that bay. Yet, 200 years later a Californian was referring to the Dakotas as "the East"! Thus many such terms are relative. Here are the names and dates for our major regions:

the Atlantic States, 1789; *the Atlantic seaboard*, 1852 (*seaboard* is an American word of 1788, when it meant only the Atlantic seaboard).

the East, 1654; *Easterner*, 1840. *Back East*, 1876.

the Gulf States, 1870s. *Gulf Coast*, 1889 (the name *the Gulf Stream* dates from 1769).

the Middle Colonies, being those between New England and the South, 1775; *the Middle States*, being New York, New Jersey, Pennsylvania, Delaware, and sometimes Maryland, 1784.

the Middle West, 1898, this presupposes there is a *far west* (see *Western* below); *Middle Western*, 1909; *Middle Westerner*, 1921. *Middle America*, the central U.S., 1926. The short forms *Mid West* and *Mid Western* date only from the 1920s.

New England, 1616; *New Englander*, 1638; *New England States*, 1787. *Down East*, 1819 for New England, later it primarily came to mean Maine.

the North, 1792, then referring to New England; *Northern*, 1724; *Northerner*, 1831. *The far North*, referring to the Northern U.S., especially to the heavily wooded areas of Wisconsin and Michigan, 1903; *the North Woods*, the Adirondacks, 1881.

the North East, 1789.

the North West, 1690; *Northwestern*, 1789. *Northwestern Territory*, 1796; *Northwest Territory*, 1802, the old northwestern portion of the eastern half of the U.S., between the Ohio and Mississippi rivers south of Canada.

the Pacific States, 1820; *Pacific Coast*, 1872; *the Pacific North West*, 1889.

the South, 1781; *Southern*, 1780s; *Southern gentleman*, 1787; *Southern hospitality*, 1819; *Southerner*, 1828. *The Southland*, 1812; *the Sunny South*, 1846. *The far South*, 1835; *way down South*, 1851; *the Sweet South*, 1859; *the deep South*, 1920s, these being the southernmost parts of Georgia, Alabama, Mississippi, and Louisiana. *The Old South*, 1873, meaning the South before the Civil War. See also Dixie.

the South East, 1857.

Southwestern, 1806; *the South West*, 1853; *Southwesterner*, 1867.

Western, 1713; *the West*, 1798, in these days before the Louisiana Purchase "the West" was the land bordering the eastern side of the Mississippi River. *Westerner*, 1837. *The West Country*, 1829; *the far West*, 1830; *the wild West*, because it was regarded as lawless and primitive, 1851; *the wild and woolly West*, 1886. *The West Coast*, 1850.

Other names for American regions and places are given at Mountains, Creeks, Deserts, and Swamps.

342

Steamboat 'a Comin'

was the exciting shout at scores of small *landings* (1790s) and large *river towns* (1853) along the Mississippi during the heyday of steamboats, 1820–70. Yelled as soon as an approaching boat's whistle was heard, it sent a crowd racing to the river bank to watch the *boat hands* (1821) bring the ship in, see who arrived, hear *up river* or *down river* (both 1830s as adjectives) news and gossip, and see what cargo was dragged on and off by the *roustabouts* (1868).

The 2,340-mile-long Mississippi, with its 250 tributaries, including the Ohio and Missouri, had served as the continent's major highway system long before de Soto "discovered" it in 1541. The Chippewa *mici sibi,* "big river," not only gives us the name Mississippi but has also been translated into some of our other names for it, including *Father of Waters* (1763), *Father of Floods* (1809), and *Great River* (1842). We have also called it *the Nile of America* (1813), *Old Muddy* (a name also given the Missouri), and *Ol' Man River.* It has shaped and carried our life and language from the Great Lakes to the Gulf and from the Alleghenies to the Rockies. But until the steamboat came the Mississippi was a one-way river—downstream.

Settlers, farmers, and merchants all floated, poled, and rowed down the Ohio, Missouri, and Mississippi to get to market or move on. Their major transportation was large, clumsy rafts and boats, up to 150 feet long and 25 feet wide, often with a roofed section, lean-to, or cabin, and sometimes with animal stalls built in, and manned by from four to ten men. These ark-like boats were the:

> *keelboat, keel* (from Dutch *keel boot*), mid 1780s, a large flat-bottomed boat with a keel and pointed prow, in wide use on the Hudson, Ohio, and Mississippi.
> *flatboat,* 1822, a square-ended, flat-bottomed, boxlike boat, with a rudder or sweeps for steering.
> *broadhorn,* sometimes known as the *Kentucky broadhorn* or *Mississippi broadhorn,* about 1819. This was a large flatboat with a giant sweep projecting from either side for steering, these hornlike sweeps giving the boat its name. It was so common along the Ohio that boatsmen were called *broadhorns* and were said to speak the *broadhorn dialect.*

There was no way to get these large rafts and boats back upstream. When the travelers reached New Orleans they broke them up and sold the wood for lumber before beginning the long and dangerous trip back home via coastal ships to eastern cities or striking off overland through the wilderness.

But two new words were emerging: in 1779 a 14-year-old boy named Robert Fulton had devised a successful *paddle-wheel* for his little fishing boat; and by 1785 a few far-sighted busi-

The Clermont, *shown here with open paddle wheels as it was originally designed, was the first steamboat to achieve financial success in the U.S. It used a British-built engine, a proven success, designed by James Watt. With its narrow hull and two masts, the* Clermont *looked much like a sailing ship, except for its stack. Its top speed was about 5 m.p.h.*

nessmen were talking about the *steamboat*. Then on August 17, 1807, a boat Fulton designed and called simply "The Steamboat," and which his critics had called *Fulton's Folly*, made its historic 150-mile trip up the Hudson, against the current, from New York City to Albany in 32 hours. It soon began regularly scheduled trips under the name *The North River Steamboat* (see THE DUTCH for why the Hudson is called *the North River*), then in 1808 was rebuilt, lengthened, and renamed *The North River Steamboat of Clermont*, which the newspapers soon shortened to *The Clermont*. In 1811 Fulton and his backer, ex-U.S. minister to France, Robert Livingston, who now had a monopoly on *steamboat navigation* on the Hudson, had Nicholas Roosevelt oversee the building of the steamboat *New Orleans* in Pittsburgh for use in "the Western waters," meaning the Ohio and Mississipi. Though this steamboat might have served well on a lake or the gentler Hudson, it took eight repair-ridden months for it to reach New Orleans—and its progress upstream against the Mississippi current and over the Mississippi *shoals* (a 16th century English word for shallows), *sandbars* (1781), and *snags* (1804) was even more painful.

Then in 1816 the engineer-inventor-boatman Henry Shreve (who was to found *Shreveport*, Louisiana, in 1835) launched his specially designed *Washington*, a new type of steamboat he called a *Mississippi river boat*, soon called a *Mississippi river steamboat* (1832), and finally a *Mississippi steamer* (1845). It was really just a shallow-draft barge with a high-pressure boiler on top, which got improved drive by having its paddle wheel mounted on the side. River men said it could "skim a mile on the foam from a keg of beer." Its design gave us the terms *boiler deck* (1830, it was usually located above the main deck), *side wheel* (1835), and *side wheeler* (1836). Many steamboats, especially slower ones such as workboats, retained the *stern-wheel* (1819) and were called *stern-wheelers* (1836) or, because of the appearance the stern wheel gave them, *wheelbarrow boats* or *wheelbarrows* (both 1877 terms, used especially in the far West, mainly in Oregon). Shreve's *Washington* could steam upstream, New Orleans to Louisville, against the Mississippi and Ohio current in just 25 days (in 1853 the *Eclipse* made this same trip in 4½ days).

The Mississippi river steamboat soon dominated the economy and social life of the Ohio-Mississippi-Missouri system, the entire midsection of America, bringing prosperity, jobs, and immigrants to scores of cities and towns, including Pittsburgh, Cincinnati, and Louisville to the East; Kansas City to the West; and, of course, to Minneapolis, St. Paul, La Crosse, Dubuque, and Davenport in the North; while making household words out of St. Louis, Cairo, Memphis, Vicksburg, Baton Rouge, and New Orleans. It took settlers westward, opened up new markets for western farmers and eastern factories, and ushered in the golden era of the South—it had northerners, southerners, easterners, and westerners moving and meeting, mingling their dialects and vocabularies. Now, too, all along the lower reaches of the Mississippi, cotton, sugar, tobacco, and slaves became extremely valuable and large plantations possible, because they could be supplied upstream from New Orleans and could depend on regularly scheduled downstream boats to take their products to market. Thus steamboat owners who controlled *steamboat lines* (1816) and plantation owners in the South's interior and on its western edges grew wealthy together; cotton became *king cotton* (1860, from the title of David Christy's 1855 book *Cotton Is King or The Economical Relations of Slavery*)—and the southern

A Mississippi steamboat glides through the bayous, the way lighted by torches extending from either side of the bow.

345

The pilot house of the Grand Republic, *1867, perched high above the water in order to command a view of the snags and shoals ahead. The* Grand Republic *was the legendary "calendar steamboat": it was said to be 365 feet long, 52 feet wide, 12 feet in hull depth, 7 decks high, and constructed at a cost of $365,000.*

economy became worth fighting a Civil War for. Within a decade after the Mississippi steamboat appeared, the population of New Orleans had doubled: by 1835 New Orleans rivaled New York City as a port and banking center, with 30 steamboats landing a week, lining the river bank along a five-mile stretch.

The most lavish, expensive, and talked-about Mississippi steamboats, such as the *Grand Republic, Natchez, Robert E. Lee, Western World,* and "The White," the *J. M. White,* carried up to a thousand passengers and were gilded, flowered, and knobbed on the inside and covered with gingerbread on the outside (giving us the name *steamboat Gothic* for the gingerbread-loaded architectural style, which retired steamboat captains preferred because it reminded them of their former glory). People spoke with awe of the best cabins and public rooms of the more lavish boats, which were furnished with ornate Victorian furniture, elaborate chandeliers, Turkish carpets, marble-topped tables, gilded looking glasses, velvet drapes, and fringed curtains ("mosquito bars" also covered all windows). Such boats had ornately painted *paddle boxes,* a large gilded star or other ornament between their *double smokestacks,* and on the forward deck an ornamental *steamboat gun* (1845), which could be fired for special occasions.

Such lavish ships were called *floating palaces* (1819, first applied to the fancy excursion boats on the Hudson), *palaces on paddle wheels,* and *floating wedding cakes.* Their many tiers were topped with the *hurricane deck* (1833), the promenade deck where affluent passengers strolled and watched the shore flow by (no one knows why this was called the *hurricane deck,* though passengers standing there feeling the breeze in their faces when a ship was going full speed felt it was aptly named). *The Texas deck* or *Texas* (both 1850s terms) was behind the *pilot house* (1846, *river pilot* in an 1838 term). It was the deck, often part of the hurricane deck, on which the officers' quarters were located. It was called *the Texas deck* because staterooms were often named for the states of the Union and the largest, the captain's quarters, was named *Texas,* thus *Texas deck* literally means the deck where the *Texas stateroom* or captain's quarters is located. The fastest boats could average 14 knots and made record runs of over 325 miles a day. They held much talked-about match races for a prize of buckhorns, which the winning captain hung between his smokestacks.

All river steamboats, lavish and dingy, took on *deck passengers,* a term of the mid 1820s, first popular on the Erie Canal (this canal gave us many terms used on Mississippi steamboats, see THE ERIE CANAL). Deck passage was also later called *steerage,* though there was no true below-deck steerage on a riverboat. The deck passengers were sometimes called *standees* (1830), since they stood, sat, and slept on the deck, huddling in the heat and rain among the cotton bales and other cargo. Many were poor immigrants who had arrived at New Orleans or other Gulf ports and were headed upriver to find friends, relatives, or jobs, while others were small businessmen and poor farmers who had floated down river with their products on rafts, keelboats, flatboats, and broadhorns and were returning home after making their yearly sales. Many bought their tickets from *steam boat runners* (1847), who solicited business for the owners and captains in all the river towns, waging cutthroat competition to fill up every square inch on the ships.

Rich and poor ships also carried the notorious *Mississippi river gamblers* or *river gamblers* (both terms common by the late 1840s), ranging from the professional poker players who fleeced plantation owners of their year's profits to sleight-of-hand artists and con men who preyed on the poorer innocents. Both lavish and poor boats also gave special moonlight rides to *steamboat parties* (1821). All boats made frequent stops at *wooding places*, *wooding stations*, or *wood yards* (all 1820s terms), which were small towns, plantation landings, and clearings along the river, to *take in wood* to feed the ever-hungry boilers. Passengers welcomed these stops, where they could stretch their legs and snack on shore (*to wood up* soon came to mean to have a drink or get drunk).

Even the most lavish steamboats were dangerous. That's why the Fulton Company ran two *safety barges* (1825) on the Hudson, these being passenger barges towed far enough behind steamboats to afford the passengers complete safety if a boiler exploded. The *swimming volcanoes* on the Mississippi exploded, burned, collided, went aground on sandbars and mud flats, and had their bottoms torn out by drowned trees. The average life of a Mississippi river steamboat was only four years: such famous names as the *Robert E. Lee* and the *Natchez* were not just given to one ship but to a succession of ships over the years. Between 1816 and 1849 alone, 235 Mississippi steamboats sank, taking 2,500 lives (in 1865 the *Sultana's* boiler exploded above Memphis and 1,400 newly exchanged Union soldier prisoners of war were killed). Such carnage would have been even greater if it hadn't been for the *steamboat inspectors* (1834) who inspected the ships' boilers; the double-bottomed or watertight compartments called *snag chambers* or *snag rooms* (1820s) that some boats had; and the heavy, often double-bottomed *snag-boats* (1832) that used winches to remove obstacles from the river.

Two of the last and most important names the Mississippi steamboats made popular were *showboat* and *Mark Twain:*

> *showboat*, 1869. The first one wasn't a steamboat and wasn't called a *showboat*, it was *The Floating Theatre* built by the

On January 13, 1840, in the icy waters of Long Island Sound, the steamboat Lexington *caught fire from sparks that ignited bales of cotton on its deck. Steamboats carried no lifeboats and there were only three survivors—it is estimated that 119 persons, both passengers and crew, lost their lives. This lithograph by Nathaniel Currier appeared in 1840, shortly after the tragedy.*

British-born actor William Chapman in Pittsburgh in 1831. He and his family floated it from town to town down to New Orleans performing *The Taming of the Shrew* and other dramas, with music and dance acts added. Chapman and his family junked the boat in New Orleans and returned to Pittsburgh by steamer, repeating the same venture in 1832. The next two famous "floating theaters" were actually circus boats, built for Gilbert R. Spalding in the 1850s. The first of these, the *Floating Palace* was 255 feet long and had a 60 foot beam, seating 3,000 spectators around a regulation 42-foot circus ring. It was actually a huge barge that had to be towed from port to port and by 1860 was permanently anchored at New Orleans. Spalding's second circus boat, the 244-ton, 177-foot *James Raymond* was a sidewheeler originally built to tow the *Floating Palace*, but served as a floating circus sideshow, featuring fire eaters, sword swallowers, bearded ladies (see THE CIRCUS IS COMING TO TOWN), stuffed animals and other curios and had a concert hall with cane-bottomed seats. The *James Raymond* was owned by the patriotic circusman Dan Rice at the outbreak of the Civil War and ran the Southern blockade at New Orleans to steam up the Mississippi to St. Louis, where the Union transformed it into a *tinclad* gunboat (having one-inch thick iron protective plating) which patrolled the Ohio River with flags flying and calliope playing!

Only after the Civil War did true steamboat showboats emerge: by 1878 dozens of boats, such as the *New Era*, *New Sensation*, *The Princess*, and *The Water Queen*, seating 100 to 300 patrons, plied the rivers, presenting melodramas and vaudeville and featuring the songs of Stephen Foster. In the 1900s larger, more elaborate showboats were built, including such famous ones as the *Cotton Blossom*, *The New Showboat*, *The Sunny South*, and the *Goldenrod*, which made the last true showboat run in 1943.

mark twain, as every schoolboy still knows, means two fathoms deep, as shouted by the leadsman taking soundings on Mississippi riverboats. Samuel Langhorne Clemens (1835–1910), who had lived in Hannibal, Missouri, on the Mississippi, from the age of four until he was fourteen and had been a Mississippi river pilot from 1857 to 1861, took the pen name *Mark Twain* in 1862, when he became a reporter in Virginia City, Nevada.

In his books Mark Twain helped make *the Mississippi* mean what it does to us today and, in turn, the river made him rich and famous. He described life along and on the river in three of the most read and talked about books written in America, *The Adventures of Tom Sawyer* (1876), *Life on the Mississippi* (1883), and *The Adventures of Huckleberry Finn* (1884). *Tom Sawyer* gets some of his last name from the word *sawyer* (1625, a sawer of wood), which by 1815 meant one who worked in a sawmill but along the river meant especially one of the highly paid wood sawyers who provided fuel for the steamboats (and gave us the expression "saucy as a sawyer"). But Tom also gets some of his last name from a 1790 river word *sawyer*, an uprooted tree sawing up and down in the current.

Tarring and Feathering

was common in pre-Revolutionary days and the fear-inspiring expression "He ought to be tarred and feathered" was often applied to Tories or others who refused to join the Revolution. Often the main punishment was the humiliating experience of being stripped in front of the mob—but it could be a cruel torture, as sometimes the pine tar was applied blistering hot from the scalp to the soles of the feet, the goose feathers sprinkled on the soft tar ignited, and the victim stoned or beaten with clubs as he was paraded through the streets. When he finally peeled the tar from his blistered body much of his skin tore away with it. An early instance occurred in Salem, Massachusetts, in 1768, when a British informer "was stripped, tarred and feathered and placed on a hogshead under the Tree of Liberty on the Common." It was so much a part of pre-Revolutionary times that *The Liberty Boys* (see TAXATION WITHOUT REPRESENTATION), were often referred to as "the tarring and feathering gentlemen."

By the 1830s the punishment was a favorite method of LYNCHING (which didn't necessarily mean hanging until after the Civil War) in the West as well as the East, and it was usually followed by *riding out of town on a rail* (a common practice since the 1770s but not a common term until the 1830s), in which the tarred and feathered victim was hog-tied to a split rail, its sharp, splintery side up, and paraded through the streets, then deposited outside the town, often in a pond, bog, or bramble bush.

> *Old Floyd Ireson for his hard heart,*
> *Tarred and feathered and carried in a cart*
> *By the women of Marblehead.*
> John Greenleaf Whittier, "Skipper Ireson's Ride," 1860

Taxation Without Representation

In 1763 Britain began to pass a series of Parliamentary acts that turned the majority of her loyal American subjects into dissidents and revolutionaries. These acts, which historians now call *the War Arousing Acts*, and our reactions to them gave America many terms which were widely used at the time and which are an important part of our history.

> *Caesar had his Brutus; Charles the First had his Cromwell; and George the Third |"Treason!" cried the Speaker of the House]—may profit by their example. If this be treason, make the most of it.*
> Closing lines of Patrick Henry's speech opposing the Stamp Act in the House of Burgesses, Williamsburg, Virginia, May 29, 1765.

    the Acts of 1763, the first of which authorized the maintaining of a standing British army in America, ostensibly to defend the colonies against the Indians. Colonists objected to these "foreign" soldiers, especially when new taxes were imposed on them to pay for this force. Another of the Parliamentary Acts of 1763 prohibited colonists from settling west of the Appalachians, angering the settlers, traders, and trappers who were already there and the colonies that claimed land there.

    taxation without representation is attributed to the American lawyer and statesman James Otis (1725–83) who is supposed to have said, "Taxation without representation is tyranny" in 1763—after he resigned as the king's advocate general in Boston to act as counsel for local merchants opposed to British taxation on the ground that the colonies were not represented in the House of Commons. There is no written evidence of Otis having said these exact words, but in his 1764 *Rights of the Colonies* he did write, "No parts of His Majesty's dominions can be taxed without their consent."

the Sugar Act was part of Parliament's broad *Revenue Act of 1764*. It reduced to three pence a gallon the tax on molasses imported into the colonies from countries other than Britain, but raised duties on foreign refined sugar. This increased tax on sugar was to defray the cost of the standing British army protecting the colonies. It dealt a severe blow to colonial trade with the non-British West Indies and made "taxation without representation" a common complaint.

the Quartering Act, 1765, required the American colonies to house British troops in public inns or private barns in areas without British barracks, the cost to be borne by each colony in which such troops were stationed. It also ordered the colonies to provide fuel, candles, and cider or beer to the British troops. This made those "foreign" soldiers of the British standing army in America even more unpopular.

the Stamp Act, passed April 11, 1765, was a revenue act imposing a stamp tax on publications and legal and commercial documents in the American colonies. Thus such things as newspapers, pamphlets, almanacs, playing cards, and liquor permits, as well as most documents, had to bear a stamp bought from a distributor serving as a tax collector. This tax angered the most vocal forces in the colonies—printers, editors, lawyers, and tavern owners, just the people best equipped to take their case to the public and stir up trouble for the British. Nine colonies sent delegates to a *Stamp Act Congress* in New York City in October, 1765; as expected, this congress attacked the Stamp Act as unconstitutional taxation without representation.

Committee of Correspondence, 1765, meaning any official committee appointed by a colony or town to communicate and coordinate means taken among the colonies to get Britain to redress grievances. After *the Boston Massacre* (see below) in 1772 Samuel Adams established the famous Massachusetts Committee of Correspondence. These committees fomented anti-British words and deeds and laid the groundwork for the Continental Congress.

the Sons of Liberty was originally formed in 1765 as a New York City Committee of Correspondence to oppose the Stamp Act, but on November 1st, the day the act went into effect, hanged Lt. Gov. Colden in effigy on Bowling Green. Thus it became the first and one of the most radical groups to agitate against the British. It took its name, "the Sons of Liberty" from a phrase used in a pro-American, anti-taxation speech delivered in the House of Parliament on February 6, 1765, by the Irish M. P. Colonel Isaac Barré.

Liberty became the watchword of the American Revolution and of America itself, mainly due to its use in the name *the Sons of Liberty*. Other *Sons of Liberty* were formed elsewhere in the colonies, notably in Boston where Samuel Adams was the leader and Paul Revere often served as the group's courier (some sim-

The Sons of Liberty *in Boston tarring and feathering an excise man under the* Liberty Tree.

ilar groups took the name *the Sons of America*). Such groups rioted, looted, and hounded the British stamp-tax collectors until most abandoned their task. The Stamp Act was soon repealed, on March 18, 1766, but by then the Sons of Liberty were strong and pressing for independence. The Sons of Liberty and the wide use of the word *liberty* gave us such names and terms as:

the Liberty Tree, an elm tree in Boston on which the first *Stamp Act mob* there had hanged the Secretary of Massachusetts Colony, Andrew Oliver, in effigy after he had agreed to distribute the stamps. Feelings were so high that, four months after he had resigned, his house was vandalized and he was dragged to the tree and forced to recant publicly. Other unpopular pro-British were also hanged in effigy from this tree, which was "officially" consecrated as *The Tree of Liberty* August 14, 1765. The area around it was called *Liberty Hall* (1768) for the many patriotic rallies held there; it was also called the *Liberty Elm* by 1769; and finally its stump even became known as *Liberty Stump* (1782). Other cities and towns soon designated dominant trees on their village greens or market squares as "Liberty Trees" and well into the 19th century Americans planted or designated symbolic "Trees of Liberty."

Liberty pole, 1766, was another name for a Liberty Tree but usually meant a pole with a cap or banner on it, serving as a rallying place for the Sons of Liberty and as a protest against British rule. British troops sometimes tried to cut down these poles and in 1766 and 1770 such attempts led to rioting and bloodshed in New York City.

Liberty songs, 1766, the very popular anti-British, pro-Revolutionary songs sung at rallies and meetings and to mock British soldiers.

Liberty Boys, 1774, a general term for the active supporters of the Revolution, whether a member of a Sons of Liberty group or not; a supporter of Independence was also called a *Liberty man*. *The Liberty Boys* took on a further political connotation when they controlled the Whig party after the Revolutionary War.

the Liberty Bell was originally a symbol of religious liberty, being ordered from London by the Pennsylvania Assembly in 1752 to commemorate the state's 50 years of religious freedom under Penn's Charter of Liberties. It cracked while being tested after its arrival in America but was melted and recast here and hung in the steeple of the Pennsylvania State House in 1753. It rang out in defiance of the Stamp Act, tolling the death of liberty and calling the people together to resolve not to allow the stamps to be sold. It rang out again against the *tea tax* (see below), to announce the battles of Lexington and Concord, and when the Continental Congress first met in Philadelphia, which is when it was first considered as the emerging nation's *Liberty Bell*. This name was solidified when it called the townspeople together on July 8, 1776, to hear the Declaration of Independence read aloud. It later announced the surrender of Cornwallis at Yorktown in 1783 and tolled the deaths of Washington, Jefferson, Adams, and French General Lafayette, before it cracked again in 1835 announcing the death of Chief Justice John Marshall. It was placed in Independence Hall in Philadelphia in 1917.

After the Stamp Act and the Sons of Liberty, new names and terms continued to lead us from the "taxation without representation" complaint to the Revolutionary War, including:

the Townshend Acts, 1767, a series of acts named for the British Chancellor of the Exchequer Charles Townshend who convinced Parliament that although the American colonies objected to taxes to regulate trade, such as the Sugar Act, and to "internal" taxes, such as the Stamp Act, we would accept "external" taxes on imports. He was wrong. The Townshend Acts levied a three pence per pound tax on tea and also taxed paper, glass, lead, and paint imported into the colonies. The colonists' boycott of such goods caused the acts to be repealed in 1770, except for the tax on tea.

the Boston Massacre, March 5, 1770, was due to colonial unrest against the Townshend Acts and the British soldiers sent to America to enforce them. It started when a boy threw snowballs at a British sentry on duty in front of the Boston Customs House. Soon a mob armed with stones and clubs collected and the sentry called out the soldiers, who panicked and fired, killing six men and wounding five. A patriotic leader of the mob, Crispus Attucks, a Black, was the first to die. John Adams defended the soldiers, who were acquitted of murder charges. Henry Pelham (1749–1806) made an engraving of the shooting, The Fruits of Arbitrary Power, which scene Paul Revere pirated, issuing his engraving under the more sensational title The Bloody Massacre (1770). Revere's popular engraving caused a sensation, giving the incident the name "the bloody (Boston) massacre." Samuel Adams then kept the term the Boston Massacre alive in his anti-British oratory.

the Tea Act, 1773, was passed by Parliament to enable the British East India Company to pay the Townshend tea tax and still sell tea cheaper to the colonies than the Dutch. This threatened to give the British company a monopoly on tea, which interfered with the colonial merchants' lucrative tea business and seemed to portend that other British monopolies might be established by taxes on other imported items. Tea became a symbol of hatred for the British and of American resistance.

the Boston Tea Party, December 16, 1773, was a reaction to the Tea Act. "Certain British citizens," partly disguised as Mohawk Indians, boarded three recently arrived British East India Company tea ships and threw 342 chests of tea into Boston harbor, partially to enforce the nonimportation resolve of the colonies. Similar acts were carried out by other tea mobs in other coastal cities, the New York Sons of Liberty having its tea party in April, 1774, dumping 18 cases of tea from the London into New York harbor, and the Providence Tea Party taking place in 1775.

the Intolerable Acts, 1774, sometimes called the Coercive Acts, were Parliament's reply to the Boston Tea Party. They were a series of five acts which closed the port of Boston until the

"The Bloody Massacre," Paul Revere.

"The Boston Tea Party," Howard Pyle (1853–1911). Pyle, one of America's best-known illustrators and art teachers, was noted for his drawings of events of American history.

352

tea was paid for, abrogated Massachusetts' charter, declared that some officials formerly elected locally were now to be appointed by the king and that officials indicted in Massachusetts while enforcing English laws were to be tried in England, imposed a new Quartering Act on all the colonies to house British troops, and nullified many western claims of the coastal colonies (this is the Quebec Act, to appease Canada). Massachusetts refused to pay for the tea and called for a Continental Congress. The British appointed General Gage Govenor to restore order and he declared Massachusetts in revolt.

The Intolerable Acts were followed on March 30, 1775, by *the Restraining Act*, in which Parliament cut off colonial commerce to other countries and closed North Atlantic fisheries to New England fishermen. By now, however, such acts had little meaning to many Americans. The first *Continental Congress* had already met in Philadelphia, September 5–October 26, 1774, to list colonial grievances in a petition to the king—and its members resolved to meet again if George III didn't redress their grievances. He didn't. They did. On May 10th, 1775, the second Continental Congress met, appointed George Washington as Commander in Chief of the Continental Armies, and moved toward a Declaration of Independence (see THE FOURTH OF JULY and THE REVOLUTIONARY WAR).

Teapot Dome,

with its Senate investigating committee, sensational courtroom trials, and the sudden death of a president, shared the headlines with Al Capone and the glamorous sports' stars of THE ROARING 20s. It was in the news from 1922 to 1929 and became the most talked-about political scandal until Watergate. The name refers to the Teapot Dome Reserve, a 9,321-acre oilfield on public land near Casper, Wyoming, which was set aside in 1915 as an oil reserve for the U.S. Navy. Twelve weeks after his inauguration in 1921, President Warren G. Harding, at the insistence of his Secretary of the Interior Albert B. Fall, signed an executive order transferring the naval petroleum reserves from the Navy to Fall's Department of the Interior. Fall then entered into secret negotiations to lease Teapot Dome to Harry Sinclair's Mammoth Oil Company and to lease another naval oilfield, the 38,000-acre Elk Hills Reserve in California, to Edward Doheny's Pan American Petroleum Company. For these favors Fall received $223,000 in Liberty Bonds and a herd of cattle for his ranch from Sinclair, and a $100,000 cash "loan" from Doheny.

The public began talking about Teapot Dome on April 15, 1922, when Wyoming Senator John Kendrick said he had learned from his home state that its naval reserve oilfield had been leased to Sinclair and asked Fall to explain. In 1923 a Senate committee under Senator Thomas J. Walsh began investigating Teapot Dome

Albert B. Fall, 1929, the year he was fined $100,000 and sentenced to one year in prison for his part in Teapot Dome.

and the country was soon rife with rumors of other corruption in the Harding administration. In June, President Harding, while in Alaska on a transcontinental speaking tour with his wife and an entourage of 65, received a long coded message from Washington, apparently informing him of the widespread corruption about to be exposed. He never recovered from the shock and the shame, took suddenly ill when he reached San Francisco, and died there on August 2, reportedly due to complications from ptomaine poisoning, though the cause of his death was never completely clear.

In February, 1924, the Senate investigating committee's work was done and in a joint resolution Congress stated that the oil and gas leases negotiated by Fall with Sinclair and Doheny indicated fraud and corruption and directed President Coolidge, who had succeeded Harding, to begin civil and criminal prosecution of those involved. The final results of Teapot Dome: the fraudulently made oil leases were declared void by the Supreme Court; Secretary of the Navy Edwin Demby, who had signed the leases without full awareness of their contents, resigned; Sinclair and Doheny were tried and acquitted on charges of bribery and conspiracy to defraud the government, though Sinclair spent three months in prison for contempt of the Senate in refusing to testify; and Fall was finally convicted of accepting bribery and sentenced to a year in prison in 1929.

Harry F. Sinclair (second from right) with his team of attorneys at the Senate hearings, 1924.

The Temperance Movement—The Saloon Must Go!

Almost all the early colonists drank alcoholic beverages heavily—there was not much else they considered safe to drink. This tradition of drinking soon led to agitation against "the sin of drink" and "demon rum" (*rum* was a general term for all alcoholic beverages). Many early Americans

Temperance crusaders at work in New York City, 1870s.

talked about drink as we talked about drugs in the 1950s and 60s—as leading to crime, violence, poverty, prostitution, insanity, and broken health. Worst of all, many thought it led to Hell. Soon "tippling" was a crime in many places and drunkenness punished by time in the stocks or by public whipping. But the temperance movement's main war was to be a war of words. Its history can be told by its words, the names of its groups, and the titles of its books and plays.

licensing. In the 1650s New Amsterdam limited taverns by licensing them; soon the word and practice spread to all the colonies.

Inquiry into the Effects of Ardent Spirits Upon the Human Mind and Body was published by Benjamin Rush in 1784 and became one of the first widely talked-about books in the new nation. America's most famous doctor, Rush had been a signer of the Declaration of Independence and official Surgeon of the Continental Army: he and his book took a stand against alcoholism not as a sin but as a health hazard. His book had an effect similar to that of the reports linking cigarette smoking and cancer in the 1950s and 60s.

the pledge, to take the pledge. Since religion and science agreed that alcohol was bad, by 1800 people were talking about signing *the pledge* to abstain from drinking *ardent spirits* (hard liquor).

Temperance Society was a name first used in 1808, referring to a group formed in Saratoga, New York, by a country doctor, Billy James Clark. He formed it after reading Benjamin Rush's book.

the American Temperance Society, the American Temperance Union, 1826. Beginning around 1813 various church groups and Bible and Tract Societies were formed for "the suppression of intemperance" or for "the promotion of temperance." Some of these developed into the American Temperance Society, which became the American Temperance Union. By the early 1830s the Union had 6,000 branches and a million members.

temperance had meant moderation, self-restraint, since the 14th century, but by 1830 the American Temperance Society defined *temperance* as "the moderate . . . use of things beneficial and abstinence from things harmful," going on to call hard liquor "poison." Thus, in regard to liquor, the American Temperance Society changed the meaning of *temperance* to *abstinence*.

teetotaler and *the New Pledge*. In 1836 the American Temperance Union decided that abstinence from hard liquor was not enough. It introduced *the New Pledge*, requiring signers to abstain not only from hard liquor but from beer, wine, and hard cider as well. Those who abstained from all alcoholic beverages were now called *teetotalers*, emphasizing the initial *t* of *total*, *T-total*, complete total abstinence, or as we would say "total with a capital T." *Teetotally* (T-totally) had first been used by Parson Mason Locke Weems in 1807 in America, but *teetotal* meaning total abstinence from all alcoholic drink is said to have first been used by Richard Turner of Preston, England, in 1833.

the Washington Temperance Society was a nonreligious, grassroots temperance society that started among craftsmen in the 1840s

Taste not, touch not, handle not.
The New Pledge, American Temperance Society, 1836, applied to all alcoholic drinks including wine, cider, and beer

and by the 1850s had spread to laborers and then just about everyone. Members helped each other stay sober and held weekly meetings admitting "We were all drunks" before recounting their personal stories of drink and its horrors and then their successes and pleasure in teetotaling (the modern *Alcoholics Anonymous*, founded in 1934, owes much to this group). Soon the *Washingtonians* and their ladies' auxiliary, the *Martha Washingtons*, had 8,000 local clubs and a million and a half members.

Joining the Washington Temperance Society became a fad, a way to moral uplift, and almost a business, political, and social necessity. Many who had no drinking problem joined, including Abraham Lincoln. Soon the temperance movement became a big fraternal organization for teetotalers, who gathered in lodges, greeted each other with secret passwords, and gave their officers ornate Eastern titles. Thus in mid-century men joined and talked about such teetotaling groups as *the Order of Good Templars* (1851), *the Order of Templars of Honor and Temperance*, and *the Society of Good Samaritans*. Even Congressmen had their own society, *the Congressional Temperance Society*, while Sunday School children could join *the Cold Water Army*. Thus in the 1850s and early 60s temperance was both serious business and fun, second only to abolition in being the most talked-about subject in America. New terms and names continued:

temperance hotel, temperance steamboat, temperance merchant ship were typical terms of the 1850s and early 60s, indicating places where one could relax or work safe from the evil influence of alcohol.

Ten Nights in a Bar-Room and What I Saw There, Timothy Shay Arthur's 1854 book that remained a best seller for the next 20 years. In 1858 William Pratt dramatized it into the melodrama *Ten Nights in a Barroom* and soon everyone could recite the climax, little Mary's song at the saloon door, "Father, Dear Father, Come Home with Me Now." The book did for the temperance movement what *Uncle Tom's Cabin* (1852) had done

> *Father, dear father, come home with me now,*
> *The clock in the belfrey strikes one;*
> *You said you were coming right home from the shop As soon as your day's work was done.*
> "Come Home Father," Henry Clay Work, 1862

Illustrations from the play Ten Nights in a Barroom.

356

Prohibitionists, perhaps members of the WCTU, parade and sing before sneering taverners, late 1900s.

WCTU's Pledge Card, *1934, which includes forswearing wine, beer, and cider as well as hard liquor. Many children, at the urging of their parents and teachers, signed Pledge Cards before they were old enough to understand what they were doing.*

for the abolition movement—popularized and sentimentalized it. The play was one of the most popular and best loved of the period, second in popularity only to the dramatization of *Uncle Tom's Cabin*. Other temperance melodramas were also immensely popular, including *The Drunkard, or The Fallen Saved* (1874).

the Prohibition Party, 1869, is now America's oldest third party, though it has never won a single electoral vote. After the Civil War the temperance movement became increasingly political. This had started in the late 1830s when temperance societies turned to seeking legal prohibition. Massachusetts forbade selling retail quantities of liquor in 1838, Maine prohibited all liquor selling in 1841, by 1851 13 northern states were dry, and before the Civil War the army and navy abolished their daily ration of spirits. Each of these prohibitions had caused widespread debate. By 1858 11 of those 13 states were wet again, because prohibition hadn't worked or cured crime, corruption, poverty, etc., as it was supposed to—but temperance leaders didn't talk about that, the nation would have to find out the pitfalls of prohibition for itself later. Now, getting towns, counties, and states to vote in prohibition was still the goal of many, and thus the Prohibition Party was formed.

wet, dry, 1870; *go dry*, 1888; *vote dry*, 1904. *Local option*, 1884. These terms were part of the new political thrust of the temperance movement, trying to vote the country dry. If anyone were listening, however, he would have heard two other new terms in the dry areas of the late 1880s, *bootlegger* and *speakeasy*.

the Woman's Christian Temperance Union, formed in Cleveland, Ohio, in 1874 by members of *the Woman's Crusade*, a group of militant and exemplary housewives who were for temperance, morality, and women's rights. Called the *WCTU* from the beginning, the new group was run by small-town elite who believed in Protestant Fundamentalism and were against drink, *the Social Evil* (a popular 19th century euphemism for prostitution), tobacco, and "coarseness." The WCTU was widely talked about for its members who invaded bars to sing hymns, pray, and pressure barkeeps to close (see CARRY NATION for an extreme case). Not only could children join the WCTU's *Loyal Temperance League* but the WCTU got schools to adopt temperance literature, teaching the bad physical effects of alcohol to every child.

the Anti-Saloon League (widely known as the *ASL* until the 1920s) was founded in 1893, at a time when proliferating saloons (see BEER, BEERGARDENS, AND SALOONS) were a noisy, smelly annoyance. Its slogan, "The Saloon Must Go," was one of the most popular in American history. Those who were for saloons were now called *saloonists* (1890s, it had meant a saloon keeper since the 1870s). Well organized, the ASL used shrewd political pressure to bring the temperance movement to a successful climax—Prohibition.

By 1902 the WCTU had made temperance literature part of every child's education in every state. By the early 1900s, too, the WCTU and ASL had gotten many major magazines to ban liquor ads and to print temperance editorials, made anti-liquor lectures part of almost every revival meeting and Chautauqua, and

357

Leaders of the WCTU at the New York World's Fair, 1939, 20 years after Prohibition became law of the land and 5 years after its repeal.

gotten the public support of the American Medical Association as well as the General Federation of Women's Clubs. They had also recruited businessmen and industrialists like John Wanamaker, H. J. Heinz, S. S. Kresge, Andrew Carnegie, and John D. Rockefeller to give vast sums to the temperance cause, and writers like Upton Sinclair, Floyd Dell, and reformed alcoholic Jack London to speak out for temperance.

In 1913 the Anti-Saloon League finally publicly announced that its goal was no longer merely closing the saloons but nationwide prohibition. In 1914 Congress defeated the ASL-sponsored prohibition amendment. But 24 states now had prohibition, and the ASL soon pushed for War Prohibition to keep our innocent young soldiers pure, devote full industrial effort to the war, and conserve scarce grain. Congress did pass *War Prohibition*, prohibiting the use of grain for manufacturing intoxicating beverages, but this was mainly the ASL's wedge for nationwide peacetime prohibition— the ASL's sponsored prohibition amendment passed Congress in 1918, just ten days after the Armistice. It was then sent to the states for ratification as the 18th Amendment. Thus the temperance movement and World War I finally turned *temperance* into nationwide PROHIBITION.

The *Titanic*

Ever since April 15, 1912, America and England have talked about "the *Titanic* disaster," one of the most spectacular, most shocking maritime disasters of all time. It all began shortly before midnight on April 14, 1912, when the 45,000-ton British White Star liner the *Titanic*, the world's newest, largest, and most luxurious passenger ship, speeding at 12 knots on its maiden voyage from Liverpool to New York, struck an iceberg in the North Atlantic, 95 miles off the Grand Banks of Newfoundland.

The Titanic *going down bow first in the waters of the North Atlantic. The unsinkable ship sank less than three hours after striking an iceberg.*

The iceberg ripped a 300-foot gash in the ship's right side, rupturing five of its 16 watertight compartments: the "unsinkable" ship sank at 2:20 A.M., April 15th. The Leland liner *California* was less than 20 miles away but its radio operator was off duty and didn't receive the *Titanic*'s distress call. Twenty minutes after the *Titanic* sank, however, the Cunard line's *Carpathia* arrived on the scene and rescued 706 of the *Titanic*'s 2,223 passengers and crew— 1,517 were drowned in the icy water.

In 1912 and 1913 the *Titanic* disaster was mainly talked about in anger, the public raising an outcry because the ship had been ordered to speed in iceberg-infested waters, because it had lifeboat space for only about half its number of passengers, and because the *California* could have heard its distress signal but didn't. The disaster and the resulting U.S. inquiry and first International Convention for Safety of Life at Sea, held in London in 1913, then had many Americans talking about such comparatively new terms as *iceberg belt*, *iceberg patrol*, and *lifeboat drills*. The London convention did draw up rules requiring that every ship have lifeboat space for all passengers, that lifeboat drills be held during each voyage, and that all ships maintain a 24-hour *radio watch*. The disaster also led to the establishment of the International Ice Patrol to warn ships of icebergs in the North Atlantic shipping lanes.

The *Titanic*'s sinking also had America discussing the distress signals used at sea. The Morse Code letters *SOS* (··· --- ···) had been adopted as the international radiotelegraph distress signal in 1908, solely because they were easy to transmit and distinguish— the letters were not chosen as standing for "save our ship" or "save our soul." After the *Titanic* disaster, a new Morse Code

Titanic *survivors aboard the* Carpathia—*less than a third of the passengers and crew were rescued.*

distress signal, *CQD*, was introduced, and the U.S. Attorney General said it meant "*c*ome *q*uick, *d*anger," but this signal never replaced SOS. Incidentally, the later international distress call, *Mayday*, does not replace the radiotelegraph's SOS, but is the spoken distress call used over radiotelephones. It has nothing to do with May Day but is a rendering of the French *m'aidez*, help me.

Tits, Bellies, Rumps, Gams, and Meathooks

We talk quite a bit about our own bodies—and other people's bodies. Because certain parts of the body weren't talked about in polite conversation, and certain words not recorded, until the 1880s or 90s (or even until the 1930s), we tend to think that many Old English words for parts of the body are new and American. But most of these words have been in English for a long time, with a smattering of informal Americanisms added later. For example, for *hands* (Old English *hænd*), we have:

> *dukes*, 1870s, from Cockney rhyming slang *Duke of Yorks* for "forks," meaning fingers.
> *mitts*, 1880s, short for *mitten* in Britain and America since the 18th century.
> *lily whites*, since about 1910 (this is an American term).
> *meathooks*, late 1920s (an American term).

In America part of the elbow has been called the *funny bone* since the 1840s and the *crazy bone* since the 1850s, and the little finger has been called the *pinkie* since the 1860s (from the obsolete *pink*, meaning "small"). We've called left-handed baseball players and boxers *southpaws* since 1918.

For the *legs* (a 13th century word) and *feet* (Old English *fōt*) we also use:

limb, a 17th century word for arm or leg that became a euphemism for leg during the Victorian period.
tootsie, an 1850s British term (based on the babytalk *footsie*) that originally meant the small foot of a child or woman.
stems, used to mean legs in America since about 1870.

gams, a slang word for legs, especially shapely female ones, since about 1900 (from the obsolete *gamb*, leg of an animal, which goes back to Latin *gamba*, leg, hook, to Greek *kampē*, bend, curve).
dogs, an Americanism for feet, since about 1910.

For *head* (Old English *hēaford*) we have the slangy:

knob, 1720s.
nut, 1850s.

noggin, a British word popular in the U.S. by the 1870s.

bean, 1880s.
noodle, 1900s.

And for *face* (13th century):

phiz, a 1680s British word, short for *physiognomy*.
mug, 1840s.
kisser, 1860s, originally meaning the mouth.

puss, 1880s.
map, 1902.
pan, 1910.

A mouth has been a *fly trap* since the 1790s, simply a *trap* since the 1830s, and a *yap* since the early 1900s. A nose has been a *snoot* since 1866 and a *schnoz, schnozzle, schnozzola* since the early 1930s (see THE JEWS for the history of these words). The point of the chin has been called the *button* since about 1920. *Orb* is a 17th centurn English word for *eye*, while we Americans have been calling a black eye a *mouse* since 1847 and a *shiner* since 1904.

The *stomach* (Middle English *stomak*) has been called the *gut* and the *belly* (Old English *belig*, bag) since the 14th century, with Americans also calling it the *breadbasket* since the 1820s. We have also added such combinations as *belly button* (1877), *pot belly* (1890s), *belly robber* (1890s, a cook or commissary steward, as in the Army or Navy), *beer belly* (early 1900s), and *belly laugh* (1932). *Tummy* was an 1860s British euphemism for stomach, with *tum-tum* coming around 1904. We've been calling a roll of fat around the waist a *spare tire* since the 1920s. Incidentally, *ticker* has meant the heart since the 1880s (since the 1840s it had meant a clock or watch).

Bosom, *breast*, and *tit* (meaning teat) all date from Old English, before the Norman invasion of 1066. Calling the complete female breasts, especially well-developed ones, *tits, melons, breastworks, boobs, boobies, knobs,* and *knockers* may be fairly old, but such words were seldom batted about widely until World War II, when pin-up pictures and the American male's "breast fixation" made them a very popular part of the language. *Headlights* definitely comes from the early 1940s when the shape of the female breasts in the *uplift brassieres* of the time seemed to match the protruding style of automobile headlights.

Penis (Latin, tail), *cock, prick, member, organ, vagina* (Latin, sheath, scabbard), and *pussy* were all common 17th century words, which tells us something of what Elizabethans talked about—and the early colonists were Elizabethans, though the Puritans may not have shared all their interests. *Jock* and *jack* have meant the penis since the 16th century (from the familiar names for *John*), hence such terms as *jocker* and *jock* (1915) for sodomite, *jock strap,* and *jack off. Prick* was considered a standard word until the 18th century, when it began to be considered a vulgar one. *Dick* became a common word for penis around the time of the Civil War and men commonly called the testicles the *balls* by the 1880s. *Cunt* goes back to Middle English (literally a hollow space, empty container), while *clitoris* is a 17th century word (Greek *kleitoris*, small hill).

That leaves the part of the body which seems to have the most synonyms, the *arse* (Old English *ærs*), whose variant *ass* is the basic American word. The first colonists brought with them such Old English synonyms for it as *fundament, buttocks, tail, rump, rear, backside,* and *prat. Posterior* was a new British word for it during the early colonial days, then Americans popularized *behind* in the 1780s, *fanny* in the 1860s (from the name Fanny, no one knows which Fanny gave the *fanny* her name), *beam* and *backporch* in the 1880s (houses didn't have *back porches* until the 1840s), and *can, rear end,* and *rumble seat* in the early 1930s, soon after cars had rumble seats. To show how difficult it is to date words which may be considered vulgar, *buttocks* has been in English since the 13th century, but its short form *butt* is first recorded as having been written in America in 1859!—and it just doesn't seem logical that it took 600 years for this short form to appear. Often Americans said words we were too timid to write.

The Tweed Ring

In the early 1870s most Americans were talking about the Tweed Ring, a group of corrupt New York City politicians led by William Marcy Tweed (1823–78), better known as *Boss Tweed.* He had been a leader of Tammany Hall, the New York City Democratic political organization, since 1859 and had absolute power in the party after 1868, controlling patronage and dictating the Democratic candidates for New York City's mayoral and New York State's gubernatorial elections. He was content to take for himself such positions as New York City School Commissioner, Deputy Street Commissioner, Deputy Commissioner of Public Works, and member of the Board of Supervisors—positions that gave him power and graft.

"Boss" [William Marcy] Tweed.

Then in 1869–72 Boss Tweed's *Tweed Ring,* including New York's Mayor Hall, City Comptroller Connolly, City Chamberlain Sweeny, and others, milked the city of from $50 to $300 million. Besides taking kickbacks, the ring used faked leases, false vouchers, and padded bills to steal city money. Tweed himself owned one company that did all the city's printing and another that supplied marble for its public buildings. He bribed judges, legislators, and reporters, and he silenced opponents with political jobs and patronage. But the people liked him—he gave handouts to the poor and helped immigrants obtain their naturalization papers.

Finally the New York State reform Democratic leader Samuel Tilden, *The New York Times,* and Thomas Nast's political cartoons in *Harper's Weekly* rallied some citizens and law-enforcement agents against Tweed. He was jailed for forgery and larceny 1873–75. Upon his release New York City arrested him on civil charges in an attempt to retrieve some of the money he had stolen. He escaped and fled to Cuba and Spain, was caught and returned to New York City, and died in the city's Ludlow Street jail in

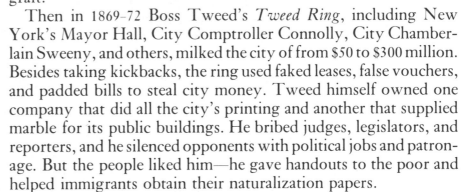

Americans . . . are ruled by the Boss and the Trust.
William Ralph Inge, *Outspoken Essays, First Series,* 1919.

1878. Though people had spoken of *political bosses* since the 1850s, Boss Tweed gave the term new life, and by the early 1880s *bossism* and *bossdom* were in wide use.

Uncle Sam

originated during the War of 1812 at Elbert Anderson's store-yard at Troy on Hudson (now Troy), New York. The name comes from the yard's inspecting superintendent, "Uncle Sam" (Samuel) Wilson. Each of his approved cases of the storeyard's military provisions was marked "EA—U.S.," meaning "Elbert Anderson—United States." However, the workers and longshoremen joked that the initials "U.S." stood for the inspector "Uncle Sam." Thus "Uncle Sam" and the United States became one. *Uncle Sam* then spread quickly as a personification of the United States during the war, partly to counter the British enemy's symbol of John Bull (the personification of England or the typical Englishman, based on the character named John Bull, a bluff, bullheaded English farmer, in John Arbuthnot's 1712 satirical political allegory *Law in a Bottomless Pit*, later retitled *The History of John Bull*). It wasn't until 1868, however, that Thomas Nast, the cartoonist for *Harper's Weekly*, drew Uncle Sam as we would recognize him today, adding the beard and putting stars on his vest, copying some of the details from a drawing he had made of the famous circus clown Dan Rice in his red, white, and blue striped "flag suit," top hat, and goatee (Rice wore this suit as part of his publicity hoax that he was running for the presidency).

A Thomas Nast (1840–1902) cartoon of Uncle Sam, John Bull, and Kaiser Wilhelm I, 1872. Nast was the most famous political cartoonist in the country. During the Civil War Lincoln called him "our best recruiting sergeant." He invented the symbols of the political parties: the donkey of the Democrats and the elephant of the Republicans.

The Vietnam War

We usually spelled and pronounced *Vietnam* as *Viet Nam* until the early 1960s. The name is from the Ancient Chinese *ywet nam*, the land "south of ywet" (*ywet* being an area in southern China and *nam* meaning south), and this region first became a country with the name *Viet Nam* in 1802. After many years of fighting, the French finally conquered Vietnam in 1885 and combined it with Cambodia and Laos into what became *French Indochina* (a name first used in the U.S. in 1887, originally spelled *French Indo-China*, *Indo-* meaning Indian or East Indian).

The Japanese occupied Indochina in 1940 and the major guerrilla resistance force that fought against them in Vietnam during World War II was a Communist-formed coalition called the *Viet Minh* (1941, a Vietnamese shortening of *Viet Nam Doc Lap Dong Minh Hoi*, the Vietnam League for National Independence). This was led by the Vietnamese-born, Moscow-trained Communist, Ho Chi Minh (1890–1969), his original name being Nguyen That Thanh but—after using the name Nguyen Ai Quoc, "Nguyen the Patriot," while working for the Communists in France, China, and Hong Kong in the 1920s and 30s—he took the name Ho Chi Minh, "He Who Shines," while organizing the Viet Minh, in 1941.

After the Japanese rule collapsed in 1945, Ho and the Viet Minh proclaimed the Democratic Republic of Viet Nam, with Ho as president. But the French returned in force after World War II and established their own regime, which the Viet Minh began fighting in December, 1946, receiving military aid from the Chinese after the Communists took over China in 1949. During the early 1950s we considered this Vietnam fighting and THE KOREAN CONFLICT as related, both parts of an overall Communist plan to take over as much of Asia as possible, and thus we began sending economic aid, arms, and supplies to the French in Vietnam. But not until the Viet Minh besieged the last French stronghold, Dien Bien Phu, for 55 days, capturing it on May 7, 1954, did most Americans begin talking about Vietnam.

After Dien Bien Phu fell, an international *Geneva Conference* worked out a series of agreements, *the Geneva agreements* or *Geneva accords*, between the French and the Viet Minh. These agreements partitioned Vietnam into two parts, divided roughly at the 17th parallel: the Democratic Republic of Viet Minh to the north, with Ho Chi Minh as president, and the capital at Hanoi, and the Republic of Viet Nam to the south, with a French-supported government and the capital at Saigon. Before the end of 1954 these two countries were known unofficially as *North Vietnam* and *South Vietnam* (later, when we spoke of "the war in Vietnam" we meant South Vietnam, where the ground fighting took place, and our troops called it simply *Nam*).

In 1955 the American-backed anti-Communist Ngo Dinh Diem became president of the Republic of South Vietnam in a rigged election, then in 1956 refused to hold the free elections to unify the two parts of Vietnam as called for by the Geneva agreements (both north and south were preparing for blatantly dishonest, terror-filled elections, which Ho Chi Minh would probably have won). The Viet Minh and its Communist supporters in the south then launched a campaign of assassination and terrorism against southern village chiefs and others loyal to Diem. We didn't know it then, but the war in Vietnam had begun. The Viet Minh terrorism increased to full-scale guerrilla warfare by North Vietnam against South Vietnam and in 1960 the Viet Minh formed the *Viet Cong* (see the list below) in South Vietnam to join them in waging it. The U.S. countered each increase in the Communist war effort by sending more economic aid, weapons, and supplies to the South Vietnamese, and finally sent combat troops to fight for South Vietnam. By this time the autocratic Diem had been overthrown and killed by a military coup (in November, 1963) and, after several unstable governments, General Nguyen Van Thieu had assumed command of a military government in South Vietnam (in June, 1965) with Nguyen Cao Ky as premier (Thieu became president in 1967).

The war in Vietnam lasted almost 20 years (from 1956 to 1975) and American combat troops fought in it for eight years (from 1965 to 1973, though our Air Force began bombing North Vietnam in 1964 and continued in action after our ground troops left). Between the late 1950s and 1965 we talked about *the war in Viet Nam*, but once our ground troops began fighting there in 1965 most Americans called it *the Vietnam War*. Since war was never officially declared, however, some politicians called it by such euphemisms as *the Vietnam conflict* (in analogy with THE KOREAN CONFLICT)—but it was a war, with more U.S. troops involved than in Korea and more tons of U.S. bombs dropped than during all of World War II.

The war familiarized Americans with many new place names in what commonly became known as *Southeast Asia* (including Cambodia, Laos, and Thailand as well as Vietnam); it introduced many new political and military terms as we fought it, talked about it, and saw and heard it on nightly television newscasts; and finally it created a new vocabulary of protest as many Americans turned against it. The most important names and terms of the Vietnam War include:

> *advisers, military advisers.* As the Communist pressure on South Vietnam increased through the late 1950s President Eisenhower sent more and more aid to South Vietnam and finally agreed to help train its troops. In 1961, after the *Viet Cong*

365

An American infantry adviser alongside South Vietnamese troops, 1964.

(see below) had entered the fighting, South Vietnam asked for still more help and our new president, John F. Kennedy, sent U.S. pilots and helicopters to ferry South Vietnamese troops into battle and our *Special Forces* as *military advisers*, often simply called *advisers*, to direct the South Vietnamese defense of villages and military outposts. By the end of 1961 we had 2,000 troops serving as "advisers" in South Vietnam and by mid 1965, when our troops first entered combat, we had 23,000.

airmobile, used to refer to U.S. infantry units equipped with their own transport planes and helicopters to fly them into battle.

angel, an unexplainable or false image on a radar screen, as caused by a malfunction, unique atmospheric conditions, etc.

ARVN (pronounced "Arvin"), an acronym for the *A*rmy of the *R*epublic of *V*iet *N*am, the South Vietnamese army that fought against the Communists. Its soldiers were called "Arvins" and we also called South Vietnamese *Viets*.

birdfarm became the new slang term for an aircraft carrier, replacing the World War II word *flattop*. *Bird* had been used as an obvious metaphor for an airplane since the early days of flight and had been widely used by our servicemen to mean an airplane during the Korean War.

bombing pause, a temporary cessation of bombing to entice the North Vietnamese to negotiate or to create a more friendly atmosphere for negotiations, while at the same time appeasing antiwar factions here at home. The term was first used by Canadian Prime Minister and Nobel Peace Prize winner Lester Pearson in an April 2, 1965 talk in Philadelphia, in which he suggested that President Johnson order such a pause to initiate peace talks, the first such bombing pause then taking place the next month, May 13–19, 1965, with others following throughout the war.

choi oy, used by U.S. troops as an expression of disgust or negation, one of the few words they adopted from the Vietnamese.

click, late 1960s, U.S. military use for a kilometer (approximately 0.6 mile), perhaps referring to the sound of the letter *k*, the abbreviation for kilometer, reinforced by the clicks made by a gunsight when it is adjusted for distance.

counterinsurgency was a new word in 1961, the year we established a Counter-Insurgency Committee to devise ways to meet the unconventional warfare being waged by the Communists in Southeast Asia. In the early 60s it was often spelled with a hyphen, *counter-insurgency*, and the acronym *COIN* (from *co*unter-*in*surgency) was sometimes used. Originally the concept included psychological warfare and political reforms as ways to fight insurgency, but soon the word merely meant fighting guerrillas with guerrillas of one's own.

defoliate, to spray chemicals or use incendiary bombs on enemy territory to destroy trees or crops, so as to deprive enemy forces of concealment or food. This military term became well known during the 1964 presidential campaign when the Republican candidate Barry Goldwater horrified many Americans by suggesting that small atomic bombs might be used to destroy areas of the Vietnamese jungle so the Communist guerrillas and supply columns would have no place to hide.

the DMZ, the abbreviation for the *de*militarized zone between North and South Vietnam along both sides of the 17th parallel. The abbreviation had been widely used in the Korean War to refer to such a zone between North and South Korea along the 38th parallel.

the domino theory was the basis of much official U.S. thinking during the 1950s and 60s. It was the theory or belief that if Vietnam fell to the Communists, its neighbors in Southeast Asia would then fall one by one, like a row of standing dominoes. The old metaphor "like a stack of dominoes" (ready to fall, easy to push over) was first used in this Vietnamese context by political columnist Joseph Alsop in 1954. The domino theory was forgotten by the war's end, but during the last two weeks of South Vietnam's collapse Cambodia did fall to the Communist Khmer Rouge and within four months Laos fell to the Communist-led Pathet Lao.

escalation. As the Communists continued to make gains in South Vietnam, President Lyndon Johnson decided he must increase the U.S. effort there beyond what President Kennedy had done (see *advisers* above). After *the Gulf of Tonkin incident* (see below) he ordered U.S. planes to bomb specific military targets in North Vietnam, then in February, 1965, allowed continued bombing of targets in both North Vietnam and Communist-held areas of South Vietnam. Finally on June 8, 1965, he authorized the 23,000 military advisers then in South Vietnam to enter combat. Thus in 1964 and 65 President Johnson began what he called a reluctant but necessary *escalation* of the war (from the 1900 word *escalator*, taken from the trademark name for a "moving staircase," this name itself being a blend of *escal*ade, to scale with a ladder + elev*ator*). As Johnson continued this escalation, we had 184,000 troops in Vietnam by the end of 1965, over 335,000 by the end of 1966, over 470,000 by the end of 1967, and finally over 540,000 by early 1969, when Nixon became president.

[There are] some Nervous Nellies . . . who will . . . break ranks under the strain [of the Vietnam war]. And some will turn on their own leaders and their own country, and on our own fighting men.

President Lyndon Johnson, May 17, 1966

President Lyndon Baines Johnson (1908–73).

fire base, late 1960s, a military position established to deliver heavy gunfire, as an artillery emplacement with its own troop protection, ammunition and supply dumps, etc. Such bases were often established around or near strategic cities, supply lines, mountain passes, etc., there being no true front lines at which to mass fire power.

fire fight, used in U.S. military communiqués to replace the 14th century English word *skirmish*.

fragging, originally the killing of an officer by his own men by rolling a *fragmentation grenade* (hence *to frag*, *fragging*) into his tent, but by the late 1960s the killing of one's officer by any means. The U.S. officers *fragged* in Vietnam were usually those the troops considered overzealous in seeking out and pursuing the Viet Cong, especially after mid 1969, when U.S. troops were being withdrawn and no soldier wanted to be made to take any unnecessary risks when he would soon be sent home.

free-fire zone, late 1960s, an area designated on U.S. military maps as being deserted by civilians or held by hostile forces and thus one in which no prior clearance was needed to commence firing. Since control of the patchwork of rural hamlets and jungle areas of South Vietnam changed hands frequently, the designation of such free-fire zones was logical, but led to tragic mistakes of firing on friendly troops and civilians.

friendly had seen some World War II and Korean use for an allied soldier or civilian (from the term "friendly troops") but during the Vietnam War saw wide use to refer to units and soldiers of the South Vietnamese army and civil guard.

the Green Berets were a select, commandolike American military unit originally sent to South Vietnam as advisers to help train its troops in jungle warfare. With their distinctive green berets and highly publicized special training and esprit de corps they were America's romantic heroes of the early years of the war. Berets had been worn by peasants and peasant soldiers since the Middle Ages, with red berets being a part of the uniform of various fascist and Communist groups since the 1930s (hence perhaps our choice of green berets), then became part of the dashing uniform of various special commando and paratroop units during World War II.

grunt, late 1960s, was originally used by U.S. Marines in Vietnam to refer to an infantryman, then became widely used by the foot soldiers themselves, referring to the usual complaints grunted by soldiers as well as to the hard work of hiking and fighting in the jungle. The troops also referred to an infantryman as a *snuff*, because his job was to kill or *snuff out* (a 1920s gangster term, though it may have originated in World War I), and as a *hump* because soldiers had *to hump*, to make a long march, carry a heavy load; (*get a hump on*, to hurry, work harder, dates from 1892).

the Gulf of Tonkin incident, sometimes called *the Tonkin Gulf incident*, occurred on August 2, 1964, when after South Vietnamese naval craft had raided an island north of the 17th parallel in the Gulf of Tonkin, two nearby U.S. destroyers, the *Maddox* and the *C. Turner Joy*, were reportedly attacked by North Vietnamese PT boats. Although it was never explained why the U.S. ships were nearby and though the attack seems to have been but the sighting of the North Vietnamese PT boats (and perhaps the wake of torpedoes) on the destroyers' radar screens, President Johnson immediately ordered a retaliatory bombing raid on the PT boats' base. Five days after the supposed attack on the U.S. destroyers, Congress passed the Gulf of Tonkin Resolution giving the U.S. president power to

> . . . take all necessary measures to repel any armed attack against the forces of the United States and to prevent further aggression.

This resolution was as close as the U.S. ever came to making a declaration of war.

gun ship, an old Navy term, was used since the mid 1960s to mean a large helicopter armed with cannons and rockets and serving as flying artillery to support ground troops or bombard enemy positions.

hack it, to be able to stand up to opposition, criticism, etc., an updating of *to cut it*, *to cut the mustard* (used since the first decade of the 1900s), meaning to come up to expectations, to succeed. *Hack it* became truly well known when President Nixon used it in his March 4, 1971, news conference, saying that General Creighton Abrams had reported to him that the South Vietnamese could "hack it," thus reassuring the American people that withdrawing American troops and turning the war back to the South Vietnamese might still lead to victory (see *Vietnamization* below).

hard hat, early 1960s, as meaning a full-time, uniformed Viet Cong soldier (wearing a helmet) as opposed to a part-time, nonuniformed guerrilla. By the late 1960s we also used it to mean a construction worker, because such workers wear hard protective helmets. Then, because there were several instances in which construction workers fought with antiwar student demonstrators and because the construction workers' union vehemently supported Nixon and his Vietnam policy, *hard hat* came by 1970 to mean a staunch supporter of the war and a political conservative. Incidentally, in earlier America *hard hat* (1880s) had been a slang term for a derby hat and for the bankers, businessmen, gamblers, and detectives who habitually wore them.

the Ho Chi Minh trail, late 1950s. Named for the Viet Minh and North Vietnamese leader Ho Chi Minh, this was a network of jungle trails leading from North Vietnam through Cambodia and Laos into South Vietnam, being the main Communist supply route to the Viet Minh and Viet Cong fighting in the south.

hooch (from Japanese *uchi*, house) had been used by our troops in the Korean War primarily to mean the hut, house, or room of a prostitute or a house where a serviceman set up housekeeping with his native girlfriend. In the Vietnam War our troops first used it to mean a typical Vietnamese jungle hut, then later to mean any living quarters, especially a barracks or Quonset hut.

Huey, *Huey the helicopter*, originally our Helicopter, Utility Model 1-B but later in the war any of our UH1 (*Utility*

Helicopter) helicopters. The Huey was the workhorse of the war, used to transport troops and supplies, as an *air ambulance* (a World War II term), and sometimes as a *gun ship* (see above). The nickname *Huey* comes from our military designation "*H*elicopter, *U*tility," reinforced by the familiar name *Huey* (for Hugh, Hubert), especially as the name of one of the three mischievous young nephews (Huey, Louie, and Dewey) of Walt Disney's comic strip character Donald Duck.

KIA and *MIA* had long been military abbreviations for *k*illed *in* *a*ction and *m*issing *in* *a*ction but now came into wide use in news reports and conversation. The abbreviations also were now used as nouns, a serviceman being said to be a *KIA* or *MIA* if he were killed or missing in action.

kill ratio, the ratio of the number of enemy killed to the number of American or American and South Vietnamese troops killed. This was a term frequently used by the U.S. military during the war, usually to point out that though a battle had been lost the kill ratio was high (the enemy had lost more troops than we had). The number of dead enemy troops was determined by what the Defense Department called a *body count*.

My Lai or *the My Lai massacre* was widely talked about during March, 1971, when Lieutenant William Calley, Jr., was court-martialed for massacring 22 South Vietnamese men, women, and children in the hamlet of My Lai on March 16, 1968 (his court-martial conviction was later overturned by a Federal Court). We had long known that Communist troops executed civilians whom they hated or distrusted as helping us, but this was the major instance in which it seemed that our troops might also kill civilians they hated or distrusted as working with the enemy.

napalm (from the chemical name *na*phthene *palm*itate), an incendiary jellylike mixture containing gasoline, had been used in flame throwers and incendiary bombs since World War II, but became widely talked about in the Vietnam War when antiwar groups denounced its widespread use on enemy troops and Communist-controlled hamlets.

pacification was in wide use by 1967 to mean the eradication of Communist influence in a South Vietnamese area or hamlet. Originally President Johnson's administration used it to mean the bringing of peace to an area by persuading the population to support the South Vietnamese government, but at times the Defense Department seemed to use the word as a euphemism for the wiping out of armed resistance.

to pop had meant to shoot a gun since the 18th century, but became very common in the war; it was also now used to mean to kill an enemy.

protective reaction. Soon after Congress passed the Gulf of Tonkin resolution (see *the Gulf of Tonkin incident* above) giving the president power to repel armed attacks and prevent further aggression, U.S. bombing attacks began against Communist bases if they fired on our military observation planes, our military and government officials sometimes announcing such a bombing as a *protective reaction*. Many Americans found the term offensively euphemistic.

A pacification mission, 1967. Here American soldiers destroy Communist bunkers on a hilltop near Dak To.

An American cordon moves through a stream near Saigon on a search-and-destroy *mission, 1969.*

SAM had been the abbreviation for *surface-to-air missile* since the 1950s, but during the Vietnam War it became an acronym for such a missile, especially in talking about the Russian-built SAMs used to defend Hanoi and other major targets in North Vietnam, the word being used frequently after these SAMs shot down 15 of our mightiest B-52 bombers when they were used for the first time against Hanoi on March 18, 1972. Our pilots also called these Russian missiles *telephone poles*, which they resembled.

search-and-destroy mission, late 1960s, was originally a U.S. military term for a combat operation to find a Communist main force and engage it in a pitched battle, where our superior fire power could be used effectively. The Communists avoided such pitched battles, however, and soon our troops and news reporters used the term merely to refer to any patrol mission to find and fight small enemy units in the jungle.

slope, *dink*, *slant*, *slant-eye*, *gook*, and *zip* were the major derogatory terms used by our servicemen in Vietnam to refer to the natives, or to any Oriental or Asian. *Slope* was a new term of the war, referring to Oriental eyes, being an updating of *slant*, which was still in wide use and had been common in the Korean War, and of *slant-eye*, which also had wide use in the Vietnam War, just as it had in both World War II and the Korean War (it dates back to the 1930s). *Dink* and *zip* were also new Vietnam War terms. *Dink* may have come from the 1858 English dialect and 1887 U.S. use of *dinky/dinkey*, insignificant (though this origin is dubious). *Zip* had been used since 1900 to mean zero, especially as a score in sports or a mark in school, but the war saw its first use as applied to a person (it probably comes from the psychologists' acronym *zip* for *zero intelligence potential*). *Gook* was also still common (see WORLD WAR II).

smart bomb, early 1970s, a bomb that, after being released from an aircraft, seeks out its target by following a radar or laser beam, by being attracted to a heat source, etc.

the Tet offensive, a Communist offensive against 30 provincial South Vietnamese capitals that began January 30, 1968, and in which the Communists held Hue for 25 days of bitter street fighting. *Tet* is the three-day Vietnamese New Year festival, during which the offensive began.

tiger cage, a torture cage in which the Viet Minh sometimes kept prisoners of war, being a cage too small for a man to stand up or lie down in, forcing a prisoner to maintain a painful and often crippling squatting or stooped position.

titi, used by U.S. troops to mean "a little, not much" (from the Vietnamese for "very little").

the Viet Cong, *V.C.*, and *Charlie*. In 1960 North Vietnam announced the formation of the National Liberation Front of South Vietnam Communists. This South Vietnamese organization and its members were often called the *NLF* (from *National Liberation Front*) in the early 1960s but soon it, its members, and especially its uniformed soldiers and nonuniformed guerrillas, were

An anti-war protest at the Capitol, Washington, D.C.

Robert Kennedy (1925–68) surrounded by anti-war students during the Democratic primaries, 1968. Kennedy announced his candidacy for president after Eugene McCarthy had demonstrated in earlier primaries that the Democratic party was badly split by Johnson's hawkish policies. After winning six primaries, Kennedy was assassinated in Los Angeles just after winning the important California primary.

called the *Viet Cong* (a short form of the Vietnamese for "Vietnamese Communist"), or simply *the Cong*. The Viet Cong was recruited, trained, supplied, and led by the Viet Minh, but became the major Communist fighting force as the war continued.

We abbreviated *Viet Cong* to *V.C.*, then since our military communication code word for the letter *V* is *Victor* and for *C* is *Charlie*, also called the Viet Cong or V.C. *Victor Charlie*, or simply *Charlie*, and also used these terms to refer to any enemy South Vietnamese soldier or guerrilla.

Vietnamization. In 1967 some American politicians began to talk of the "de-Americanization" of the war, the *phasing out* or withdrawal of American forces while strengthening the South Vietnamese so they could defend their country themselves. By 1968 the Johnson administration called this approach the *Vietnamization* of the war, but the word was to be popularized by President Nixon's administration. In his famous *Silent Majority* (see the list below) television speech on November 3, 1969, President Nixon announced:

> The Vietnamization Plan [has been] launched . . . we will withdraw all of our forces on a schedule in accordance with our program, as the South Vietnamese become strong enough to defend their own freedom.

Willie Fudd, the propeller-driven Grumman WF-2 airplane with a radar dome or *radome*. Though this nickname was based on the designating letters WF, it also had connotations of the plane's awkward appearance, being reinforced by Elmer Fudd, the name of the plump, lisping protagonist in the well-known animated cartoon series *Bugs Bunny*. We also talked about our F-105 *Thunderchief* jet fighter-bomber (which our troops called "the thud" because so many crashed or were shot down), the Navy's carrier-based McDonnell F-4B *Phantom*, and the Air Force's giant Lockheed C-130 *Hercules* transport plane.

The two most important effects the Vietnam War had on our language may have been the brazen increase in deceitful and purposely vague words used by our high-ranking military and government officials (see WATERGATE) and the creation of a new vocabulary of protest by antiwar groups. For, as the war escalated, so did antiwar protests. Opposition to the war began in 1962, with college students being in the vanguard throughout and bringing to this new cause some of their organizations and rhetoric from the Civil Rights movement of the 1950s and early 60s. After President Johnson escalated the war in 1964–65, the *peace movement* spread from the students to other segments of the population, especially liberals and intellectuals, and an antiwar faction developed in Congress, with such senators as J. William Fulbright, Wayne Morse, Eugene McCarthy, Mike Mansfield, Frank Church, and Robert Kennedy among its spokesmen. The peace movement erupted into vehement antiwar protests and demonstrations in 1967, convincing President Johnson he could not campaign for re-election without causing major demonstrations against him and the war and, thus, in a television address on March 31, 1968, he sur-

Eugene McCarthy, the most effective of the anti-war campaigners, won the 1968 New Hampshire Democratic primary and thus helped convince President Johnson not to run for reelection. McCarthy lost the nomination to Vice-President Hubert Humphrey, to the deep disappointment of thousands of students and others who had rallied to his campaign.

We are pursuing neither law nor peace in Southeast Asia. We are not even pursuing freedom.
 Senator Wayne Morse, 1966

prised the nation by announcing that he would not seek reelection.

Even though only a small percentage of Americans ever outwardly protested or demonstrated against the Vietnam War, most of us argued with friends and neighbors for or against it from the mid 1960s through the early 1970s. The antiwar movement gave rise to many terms which, in roughly chronological order, included:

hawk, an advocate or staunch supporter of the war, from Thomas Jefferson's 1798 term *War Hawk* (see *War Hawk* at THE WAR OF 1812 for details). The first use of *hawk* in modern times had been to refer to those advisers who urged President Kennedy to take a belligerent stance during *the Cuban Missile Crisis* of 1962 (a Soviet–U.S. confrontation on the placing of Russian missiles in Cuba, just 90 miles from the U.S.). The term then remained in use and was soon applied to advocates of the Vietnam War.

dove was first used to mean the opposite of a *hawk* (see above) during the Cuban Missile Crisis of 1962, then soon came to mean one who wanted peace in Vietnam. The dove had long been a symbol of peace, but its use in the 1960s was strongly reinforced by a famous Picasso drawing of a dove which the Communists had used on posters as a peace symbol since the 1950s and which was often seen on antiwar posters and placards after 1965.

peace movement, the various groups and individuals who protested against the war, using such methods as *peace marches*, *peace demonstrations*, and *teach-ins* (see below). One of the largest student protest groups was the *SDS* (*S*tudents for a *D*emocratic *S*ociety), organized in 1962 on college campuses to protest the war. One of the leading groups among nonstudents was *SANE* (the National Committee for a *Sane* Nuclear Policy) which had been founded in 1957 to create public pressure for a nuclear test ban treaty and, after this goal was achieved in 1963, turned to working for worldwide disarmament and to opposing the war.

draft-card burner, any draft-aged male who signified he would refuse to be drafted into the armed forces by burning his draft card publicly at an antiwar demonstration.

A Hunter College student burns his draft card during an anti-war rally in New York City.

draft evader, any draft-aged male who evaded the draft, as by fleeing to Canada or Sweden. Antiwar groups coined this new term to distinguish those who evaded the draft for idealistic, antiwar reasons from those old-fashioned *draft dodgers* who dodged the draft because of cowardice. By the war's end, 137,000 Americans were officially listed as being sought by authorities as draft evaders or military deserters. On September 16, 1974, President Ford offered such men *conditional amnesty*, amnesty on the condition that they serve the country for up to two years in public service jobs; however, draft evaders in exile in Canada and Sweden condemned the program as assigning guilt, and fewer than 10,000 applied for it.

teach-in, 1965. Based on the *sit-in* of the Civil Rights movement (see THE BLACKS), a *teach-in* was an all-night session in a college or university classroom at which students, professors, and guest speakers argued against the war.

Vietnik (1966) and *peacenik* (1967) were derogatory names that prowar writers and speakers used for student antiwar demonstrators and protesters, the implication being that they were but anti-establishment or radical *beatniks* (a 1958 word, see THE JEWS for *nudnik* and more about the *-nik* suffix).

The Yippies. During the August 26–29, 1968, Democratic National Convention in Chicago (which chose President Johnson's vice president, Hubert Humphrey, to run against Republican Richard Nixon) over 10,000 antiwar student demonstrators clashed with Mayor Richard J. Daley's police, who clubbed some demonstrators and bystanders. The most publicized of the demonstrators was the small group led by Abbie Hoffman and Jerry Rubin and which they somewhat humorously called the *Yippies* (an acronym for members of the *Youth International Party*, but also based on the 1957 word *hippie* and the 1930 exclamation of delight *yippee!*). Seven leaders of the demonstration were tried as "the Chicago seven" for conspiracy to incite riots; all were found innocent of conspiracy but five were convicted of crossing state lines with intent to incite riots.

moratorium has meant a legal authorization to postpone payment of a debt since 1875 (from Latin *morātōrius*, delaying), then in 1963 was used to mean a temporary halt in Civil Rights demonstrations, and after mid 1965 was sometimes used by President Johnson's administration to refer to a *bombing pause* (see the list above) in the Vietnam War. On October 15, 1969, antiwar groups held *Moratorium Day* or *the Moratorium*, during which hundreds of thousands of people throughout the country halted school, work, and other activities to take part in demonstrations or otherwise protest the war: after that, *moratorium* was sometimes used to refer to any peace demonstration and sometimes to refer to planned general strikes against the war, none of which were ever carried out.

the Silent Majority was originally used to mean that majority of Americans who didn't protest or demonstrate against the war and later to mean average, middle-class Americans. It became a popular term when it was used by President Nixon in a television address on November 3, 1969, just 19 days after the major antiwar *moratorium* (see above). The purpose of the president's address was to counter or subdue the mounting dissent against the war. He said:

> If a vocal minority . . . prevails over reason and the will of the majority, this Nation has no future as a free society. . . . And so tonight—to you, the great silent majority of my fellow Americans—I ask for your support.

Actually, Vice President Spiro Agnew had used *silent majority* six months before Nixon popularized it. On May 9, 1969, Agnew had said:

> It is time for America's silent majority to stand up for its rights. . . . America's silent majority is bewildered by irrational protest—and looking at the sullen, scruffy minority of student protesters . . . [who seem to] prefer the totalitarian ideas of Mao or Ho Chi Minh. . . .

Silent majority goes back even further than that: the ancient Greeks and Romans used it and "the great majority" to refer to the dead.

Kent State refers to the May 4, 1970, incident at Kent State University in which four students were killed and nine injured when Ohio National Guardsmen fired at students demonstrating against our Vietnam War invasion of Cambodia 30 days earlier (the Communists had been using some border areas of Cambodia as troop staging areas and supply bases for the war in Vietnam).

trashing originally meant emptying trash cans and strewing garbage in college buildings as a student protest against the war, especially against colleges and faculties that obtained research grants from the Defense Department to conduct war-related research. By 1972, however, *trashing* had come to mean any vandalism, such as breaking windows and defacing buildings.

There is no substitute for victory in South Vietnam.
Richard Nixon criticizing President Johnson's Vietnam policy in 1964, five years before Nixon became president. In 1951, during the Korean war, General MacArthur had said "In war . . . there can be no substitute for victory."

the Pentagon Papers. On June 13, 1971, *The New York Times*, soon followed by *The Washington Post*, began publishing a series of excerpts from the Department of Defense's classified 47-volume history of the origins of the Vietnam war and of the U.S. involvement and policy in it. Though *The Times* entitled its series the "Vietnam Archives," all America immediately called it and the full 47 volumes *the Pentagon Papers*, the Department of Defense having been called *the Pentagon* ever since it was formed after World War II—because it is housed in "the Pentagon," a 34-acre pentagon-shaped building in Arlington, Virginia, built for the old War Department in 1942.

The Pentagon Papers had been obtained and *leaked* to the press by Daniel Ellsberg, a former Deputy Secretary of Defense who had come to think the war immoral (Ellsberg and the word *leak* were also to be involved in WATERGATE). The papers were also published in book form, becoming a best seller and convincing many Americans that the government had been devious in its actions in Vietnam and in its refusal to keep the American people informed of our involvement there.

Peace talks between the U.S. and the North Vietnamese began in Paris in May, 1968, and seemed as futile and confusing as the war itself, being broken off and resumed several times and with presidential adviser Henry Kissinger beginning a secret series of peace negotiations with the Communists in June, 1971. Though some U.S. troops began to be withdrawn from Vietnam on July 8, 1969, the war continued during the peace talks. After the last U.S. combat troops left Vietnam, on August 11, 1972, peace talks broke down again, and in December Nixon ordered the heaviest bombing raids of the war against the north. A peace pact was then finally signed in Paris on January 27, 1973, supposedly ending the war and definitely ending direct American involvement. American troops had been fighting longer than in any previous war in our history and had suffered over 46,000 combat deaths and 150,000 wounded.

But the war wasn't over for the Vietnamese. Both the Communists and non-Communists in South Vietnam broke the peace agreement by building up their military forces and supplies, the North Vietnamese supplying the Viet Cong and the U.S. supplying Thieu's armies. In January, 1975, the North Vietnamese and Viet Cong launched a major offensive, forcing Thieu's army to withdraw from the northern part of South Vietnam in March, the withdrawal soon becoming a race of South Vietnamese soldiers and refugees southward along the coast. As the coastal provinces collapsed the Communists intensified attacks in the Mekong Delta in the south and began to encircle Saigon. On April 30, U.S. helicopters evacuated the last 395 American diplomats and advisers from Saigon to U.S. warships waiting offshore. Within hours after the evacuation, South Vietnam announced its unconditional surrender.

Voodoo, Zombie, and Gris-Gris

A zombie, *from a 1943 movie.*

Voodoo comes from the African Ewe word *vodu*, meaning god, spirit. African slaves brought the word to Haiti and other parts of the Caribbean, from where the French brought it to New Orleans. Voodoo itself is mainly a rural religion of Haiti, based on the African religion of the people of Dahomey. In voodoo, sorcerers work magic by curse charms and create zombies: however, the religion is based on divine *loa* (gods or deified ancestors acting within the bodies of those they have put in a trance) who dance, feast, perform fire feats, and accept animal sacrifices. Although *voodoo* is very old, the word was first recorded in the U.S. in the 1820s, at which time it already meant the religion, a loa deity, and various forms of Black sorcery with its charms and spells. It was first spelled in various Frenchified ways, as *voudo, voudou, voodeux*, etc., with the variant *hoodoo* first recorded in 1875.

After the Civil War, some journalists delighted in sensational, often fictionalized, accounts of the customs of the recently freed slaves. Thus stories of backwoods and swampland voodoo rites with cannibalism, human sacrifices, and sexual orgies sent a chill or thrill down many White spines, and terms such as *voodoo queen* (1870), *voodoo doctor* (1875) (based on "witch doctor") and *voodoo dance* (1882) emerged. *Zombi*, often spelled *zombie*, was also now first recorded (in 1871). It's from Kongo, the Bantu language of the lower Congo river (either from its *zumbi*, fettish, or *zambi*, god, or a combination of the two). *Zombie* was both the name of a snake god and of a spell that could animate a dead body, and was later used to refer to a corpse animated by such a spell, though still dead and not inhabited by its original spirit. After several horror movies were made about such zombies in the 1940s, students began using *zombie* to mean any dull-eyed, eccentric, or disliked person, while bartenders started naming tall cocktails of rum, liquors, and fruit juice

A voodoo dance. The sorceress, or houngan, *sits in a trance; the dancers are possessed by* loa *and, as here, commonly appear hysterical.*

377

zombies (implying that they would put the drinker into a zombie-like stupor).

Gris-gris was first recorded in America in 1763, 60 years before *voodoo;* this first reference calls them superstitious "toys" that Blacks carried. Sometimes spelled as it is pronounced, as *grigri* or *gree-gree*, the word still means amulet, charm, or fetish in Senegal and is also found in Spain, the Moors having used it to mean a small scroll containing the names of saints and worn as a talisman. The word itself goes all the way back to Arabic *hirz acihr*, amulet used for enchanting, and came to America both from African slaves via the West Indies and directly from Spain.

Voyageurs, Rapids, and Portages

French explorers, *trappers* (1621) and *fur traders* (1819) in Canada and in our own North from Maine to Oregon gave early America many useful terms. Some of these are now found only in history books, while others are still heard every day. They include:

batteau, a light, tapering, flat-bottomed boat, 1711.

boisbrûlé, boise brûlé (literally "burnt wood"), forest-dwelling Indians, from the color of their skin, first recorded in American English by the Lewis and Clark expedition, 1805; a Canadian-French and Indian halfbreed, especially a trapper, canoe-paddler, or guide, 1851.

brûlé, brulé, brooly (literally "burnt"), burnt-over grassland, 1793; a burnt-out forest area, 1925.

Canuck, Kanuck, a French Canadian, 1835. This may be from "Connaught," a nickname originally given by French Canadians to the Irish and later applied to the French Canadians themselves, but it could be from the Indian pronunciation of "Canadian."

chowder (from the French *chaudière*, kettle, cauldron) came to us from the French Canadians in Nova Scotia and was well known by the late 1740s.

chute, falls, rapids, 1804; as a slide or sluice for grain, ore, or logs, 1892; as an amusement-park slide or ride, 1895 (sliding down it was called "shooting the chute" which gave us *chute-the-chute* by 1922).

coulee (French *coulée* from *couler*, to flow), a deep gulch, a stream that dries up in summer, 1807. This gives us the name of Washington State's *Grand Coulee Dam*.

coureur de bois (literally "traveler of the woods"), a French Canadian or Canadian-French and Indian halfbreed boatsman, fur trader, or hunter, 1672.

French fur traders bargaining with Indians, Claude Joseph Sauthier, 1777.

flume (via French from Latin *flūmen*, river), 1748.

French Canadian, 1775.

French Indian, 1696.

portage (French from *porter*, to carry), 1698.

rapids (Canadian French *rapides*), 1765.

voyageur (Canadian French), originally a boatsman employed by the Hudson Bay Company to carry men and supplies between trading posts, but by 1809 Americans were calling any Canadian fur trader or boatsman a *voyageur*. When Americans, such as Zebulon Pike in 1806–07 or John Frémont in 1841, engaged such men to help guide or transport their expeditions they called them *engagés*.

As they moved westward these French trappers and fur traders gave us many terms we associate with THE PRAIRIE. They also were the first to contact various Indian tribes, passing on to us such Indian words as *toboggan, caribou, Sioux, Iroquois, Illinois,* and *Nez Percé,* which we still spell and pronounce in the French way. In addition, they also used some French words for Indian things, such as *brave, calumet,* and *lodge* (see THE INDIANS).

The War of 1812

lasted from 1812 to 1815. It included famous naval battles from the New England coast to the Great Lakes to the South Atlantic and bloody land battles with the British and their Indian allies from Canada to New Orleans. The 7½ million Americans talked about the battles of Detroit and Lake Erie, our invasion of Canada, our burning of Toronto (then called York), and the British burning of Buffalo and Washington, D.C. We also talked about two new military heroes, General William Henry Harrison and Andrew Jackson, "the hero of New Orleans," both of whom were to become presidents. The war also gave us UNCLE SAM, THE STAR-SPANGLED BANNER, and such terms as "Don't give up the ship," *leatherneck,* and *war hawk.*

New England Federalists opposed the war: some New England governors and militia refused to fight at all, while others refused to fight outside their own state borders. Such New Englanders called the war *the War of Iniquity* or *Mr. Madison's War,* a bitter reference to President Madison who had previously been called "the Father of the Constitution." Historians have called it "the unnecessary war" and "the war of faulty communications," because (1) two days before the U.S. declared war, Britain said she would repeal the offending laws that caused it, but the U.S. didn't receive this news in time, and (2) the greatest battle of the war, the Battle of New Orleans, January 8, 1815, also called the "unnecessary battle," was fought 15 days after the Treaty of Ghent had been signed.

It all began with the war between England and France, 1793–

The mortally wounded Captain James Lawrence (1781–1813) is said to have shouted his famous command as he was being carried below deck. The Americans were defeated in spite of Lawrence's order.

Don't give up the ship.
Commander James Lawrence, June 1, 1813. The dying Commander is said to have screamed these words aboard his badly damaged U.S. frigate *Chesapeake* when he saw his crew lowering the flag in surrender to the British frigate *Shannon*, off the coast near Boston. Commander Lawrence actually said "Tell the men to fire faster and not give up the ship; fight her till she sinks."

Dear Gen'l:
We have met the enemy and they are ours, two ships, two brigs, one schooner, and one sloop.
Yours with great respect and esteem,
O. H. Perry
"We have met the enemy and they are ours" comes from this message 28-year-old Captain Oliver Hazard Perry sent General William Henry Harrison, commander of the American Army of the Northwest, after winning the Battle of Lake Erie, September 10, 1813. This cleared the lakes of the British "Lake Squadron," making possible the recapture of Detroit. Perry's flagship, the *Lawrence*, flew James Lawrence's famous words "Don't give up the ship," from the masthead.

1815, with the U.S. desperately trying to remain neutral in order to maintain its foreign trade and its shipping industry. Things got bad during President Jefferson's administration, 1801–09, especially in 1806 when Britain declared a general blockade of all European ports and Napoleon retaliated by declaring a blockade of the British Isles. Terms leading up to the war include:

the paper blockade, the contemptuous American term for the British and French blockades preventing U.S. ships from trading with either country. Congress first used this term in 1803, claiming such blockades only existed on paper and could not be enforced. Congress was wrong: the British navy enforced it and goods piled up and rotted in American warehouses; the French navy enforced it and seized $10 million of U.S. cargoes and vessels in 1808–09. We went to war with Britain after Napoleon pretended to lift the French blockade.

impressment, 1787, was the word that aroused our anger in the 1800s. The British navy claimed British merchant sailors serving on American ships were rightfully theirs, stopping our ships to remove them and often taking American seamen "by mistake," then impressing them into British service. This was one of Britain's ways of being a bad loser after the Revolutionary War.

free ships, *free goods*, the American rallying cry, meaning that all goods carried on neutral ships should be free from being captured.

the O-grab-me Acts. To prevent hostilities, Congress passed the Embargo Acts of 1807, authorizing President Jefferson to restrict the departures of American ships. This caused more hardships for New England shipowners and exporting southern planters than it did the British or French. Since the embargo had an effect which was the reverse of the one intended, some Americans spelled "embargo" backwards to get "o-grab-me" and called the acts "the o-grab-me acts."

The main term to be popularized by the War of 1812, however, was *War Hawks*. It had been coined by Jefferson in 1798 to refer to those Federalists who wanted war with France, but as 1812 approached *war hawks*, *war birds*, and *war dogs* were what easterners called "war Republicans," Congressmen from the South and West who had *war fever* (1812) and wanted war with Britain, such as South Carolina's John C. Calhoun and Kentucky's Henry Clay. The South wanted war so its cotton and other products could again be sold and shipped to Europe and so the rest of Florida could be seized from Britain's ally Spain (we had annexed part of Florida's panhandle in 1810). The West wanted war to make the frontier safe from British-inspired Indian attacks, to discourage the British from preventing our westward expansion, and to capture Canada and its fur trade. These western *war hawks* kept their name after the war: in the 1840s the term was applied to the Democrats who wanted the U.S. to claim the entire Oregon region up to Alaska (see 54–40 OR FIGHT!—MANIFEST DESTINY). Generations later, during the Cuban Missile Crisis of President Kennedy's administration and during THE VIETNAM WAR, supporters of a belligerent national stance were still to be called *war hawks*, though by then the term was usually shortened to *hawks*.

The War of 1812 also popularized the terms:

> *artillery*, *infantry*. *Artillery* had been in the English language since 1386 (Old French *artillerie*, to fortify) and *infantry* since 1579 (Italian *infanteria*, foot soldiery, related to *infant*, a youth, especially a knight's page). However, the words first saw widespread American use during the War of 1812, when we first began to develop separate, specialized military units.
>
> *blue lights*, New England Federalists who opposed the war, so called from Commodore Decatur's claim that on December 12, 1813, pro-British Americans had used blue lights as a signal to warn British ships that his two frigates were about to sail out of New London, Connecticut, the British then preventing the American frigates from doing so. Until the 1850s *blue lights* continued in general use to mean traitors.
>
> *gunboat*. President Jefferson had preferred the local *gunboat system*, as defense for American harbors, that is using small armed craft manned by local seamen. The New England Federalist shipowners and shipbuilders mocked this system, favoring a strong navy. Fortunately, we had both a regular navy and local gunboats during the War of 1812, the latter delaying the British from attacking New Orleans in full force until Andrew Jackson arrived.
>
> *leathernecks*, *sailor collars*, and *shakos*. *Leatherneck* wasn't recorded to mean a U.S. Marine until 1830, but the War of 1812 was the first in which Marines wore a black leather stock at the neck of their uniforms, which gives us the word. This Marine uniform, adopted in 1804, included a "claw-hammered" *coatee* (1757, a short, close-fitting military coat) with a black leather neck stock for the men and a black silk one for officers. This war was also

the first in which U.S. seamen wore *sailor collars* and a black neckerchief. The army now introduced its plumed, visored, cylindrical dress hat called a *shako* (via the British army word, from German *Zachen*, peak, showy headdress).

Old Ironsides, 1815. The frigate *Constitution* earned this nickname in the War of 1812. She was "Old" merely as a familiar nickname (she was launched October 21, 1797, and was one of six new American naval ships with heavy guns used in the war); she was "Ironsides" because of her indestructible performance in the war, it being said a seaman first called her that when he saw an enemy shot rebound from her oak sides. Oliver Wendell Holmes wrote his poem "Old Ironsides" in 1830 when he read of plans to scrap the ship; it aroused public opinion and she was rebuilt, saw Civil War service, was rebuilt again by public subscription in 1925, and is now preserved as a national monument in Boston harbor.

the U.S. Military Academy at West Point had opened in 1802, but the War of 1812 was the first in which its graduates saw action. The academy was not generally called *West Point* until the 1820s.

warrant officer, 1815, was a new American military rank of the War of 1812.

Watergate

(the word means "gateway to the water" as well as floodgate) was only the name of a modern apartment building and office complex overlooking the Potomac in Washington, D.C., until the summer of 1972. Then it became the name of the biggest American political scandal since TEAPOT DOME, resulting in impeachment proceedings against President Richard M. Nixon and in his subsequent resignation, the first resignation of a president in the history of the United States.

It all began the night of June 17, 1972, a presidential election year, when five burglars were arrested at the Watergate offices

The Watergate complex of hotels, apartments, and offices in Washington, D.C.

of the Democratic National Committee. But they weren't really burglars at all: led by undercover agent James McCord they had *CIA* (*C*entral *I*ntelligence *A*gency) connections and had been paid to break into the Democratic headquarters by the Committee for the Re-election of the President (Republican President Nixon) to plant *bugs* or *taps*.

> *bug*, late 1940s, a concealed recording device. Since 1889 cardsharps had used the word to mean a card or group of cards stuck to the underside of a gambling table, for substitution into one's hand when profitable—the image remained one of concealment and small size.
>
> *tap*, early 1960s, from the 1950s police and FBI use of *wire-tap*, an electronic device attached to a phone or telephone wire that taps, or siphons off, its signal so conversation can be secretly heard or recorded. Since 1894 gamblers and confidence men had used *to wire tap* to mean to attach a line to a telegraph or telephone wire to get, or pretend to get, information on race results before bookies did and thus to be able to, or pretend to be able to, bet on a sure thing (con men pretended they could do it in order to convince a victim to give them money to bet).

It was never proved that President Nixon planned the Watergate break-in or that he even knew about it beforehand—but the break-in was obviously to gain information for the Committee for the Re-election of the President (which punsters called by the acronym *CREEP*), and the President's top White House aides and his most trusted advisor, Attorney General John Mitchell, were closely involved with it (Mitchell resigned to run the president's re-election campaign). What Nixon was found guilty of was a massive effort to avoid Watergate investigations and disclosures. As reporters, lawyers, special prosecutors, and a Senate committee uncovered more and more of the episode, all America talked about the latest Watergate news and argued whether Nixon was guilty or not, especially after Nixon was re-elected to a second term in November, 1972.

First, beginning in late 1972, we talked about Judge John Sirica's *Watergate trial* of the five men who had broken into Watergate and of the two *plumbers* (see the list below) who had helped organize the break-in. Most of the talk concerned the trial's revelations that Nixon's two top aides, H. R. Haldeman and John Ehrlichman, White House counsel John Dean, and Attorney General John Mitchell were involved. After the trial Nixon announced that he had begun his own Watergate investigation, accepted the resignations of Haldeman and Ehrlichman, dismissed Dean, and had the new Attorney General, Elliot Richardson, select a Special Watergate Prosecutor, Archibald Cox, to investigate the whole affair for the Executive Branch.

This White House move, however, did not stop the Senate Select Committee on Presidential Campaign Activities, under the chairmanship of North Carolina's Bible-quoting Senator Sam Ervin, from beginning its *Watergate hearings* in July, 1973. America watched these televised hearings with fascination and saw and heard witnesses: accuse Nixon of a *cover-up* (see the list below); testify that evidence had been *deep sixed* (thrown into the ocean or a river, the Potomac in this case); reveal the ways the funds intended to buy the silence of the Watergate "burglars" had been *laundered* (passed back and forth between various countries and bank accounts to conceal its source); declare under oath that McCord, the leader of the break-in, had been offered "executive clemency" by *the White House* (a vague metaphor Nixon used often in his *stonewalling* tactics, so the public never knew for sure if "the White House" meant the president himself or merely his aides acting without his authority). Most surprising of all, the Watergate hearings revealed that Nixon had made tape recordings of many of his meetings and telephone calls (as had Presidents Kennedy and Johnson before him) and that these recordings could prove or disprove his involvement in the cover-up. These tapes were immediately called *the White House tapes*, *the Nixon tapes*, and *the Watergate tapes*. In news releases and a special nationwide television address the president denied personal involvement in Watergate, claimed the Senate committee's witnesses were mistaken or malicious—and refused to turn the tapes over to either the Senate committee or the Special Watergate Prosecutor, even after being subpoenaed to do so. He claimed "executive privilege," a tradition that communications within the Executive Branch of the government are privileged or protected from public disclosure and derived from the Constitution's separation of the three branches of government.

[*Nixon*] *never told the truth in his life.*
Harry S Truman, while campaigning for John F. Kennedy against Nixon in 1960.

NIXON RESIGNS

Acts in 'Interest of Nation,' Asks for End to Bitterness

Ford Will Take Oath at Noon, Kissinger Agrees to Stay On

I hereby resign the office of the President of the United States.

The full text of President Richard M. Nixon's letter of resignation to Secretary of State Henry Kissinger, August 7, 1974.

Now, toward the end of 1973, the scandal unfolded rapidly and seemed to be the only thing America talked about. When Special Watergate Prosecutor Cox persisted in demanding the White House tapes, Nixon had him fired, after Attorney General Richardson and his assistant had resigned rather than do so. The Saturday resignations and firings immediately became known as "the Saturday Night Massacre." There was such a public outcry over it that Nixon released his own highly censored transcripts of some of the tapes, claiming these contained all the pertinent information. But the new Special Watergate Prosecutor, Leon Jaworski, asked for all the tapes, and finally, in July, 1974, the Supreme Court ruled that Nixon's claim of executive privilege could not be used to withhold evidence in a criminal case (various criminal cases were being pressed against those already indicted in the break-in and its cover-up). At the same time the House of Representatives' Judiciary Committee began its nationally televised "Nixon Impeachment Hearings" and by the end of July passed articles of impeachment against the president—for obstructing justice, failing to uphold the nation's laws, and unconstitutionally defying lawful subpoenas.

Though Nixon had again appeared on nationwide television proclaiming his innocence and his right to "executive privilege," on August 5 he did release the last of the transcripts of the tapes, except for an 18-minute gap which had been mysteriously erased from the tapes. Among other things, these tapes showed that the FBI had been pressured by the White House to drop its Watergate investigation, by being told it might lead to revelations of CIA activity being undertaken in the national interest. By now even Nixon's staunchest supporters in the House and Senate were convinced that Nixon had been involved in the Watergate cover-up and had tried to obstruct justice (in the mind's of many Americans, however, the president's one unforgivable sin was that he had lied to the American people). Knowing that he would certainly be impeached and found guilty in the Senate, Nixon resigned on August 7, 1974.

Thus for almost two years our newspapers and television screens were full of Watergate news and Americans talked about it daily. During these two years we often heard and used such terms as:

cover-up, the overall attempt by Nixon, his aides, and his cronies, to avoid disclosures of who was responsible for ordering the Watergate break-in, who paid the participants, and finally who was directly involved in the lies and deliberate obstruction of justice in the earlier stages of the cover-up itself. *Cover-up* had been used since 1942 to mean an excuse or false story to conceal a real plan or action.

385

dirty tricks, incidents of political espionage or any illegal or un-
ethical acts to gain a political advantage in the 1972 presidential
election campaign, as exemplified by the Watergate break-in.
The dirty tricks department had been used since 1967 as the nickname for the CIA's division that plans espionage and other covert
operations: some who planned the Watergate break-in had
worked for the CIA (see *plumbers* below), and the term's political use during the Watergate scandal probably originated
with them. In general use, however, *dirty trick* had meant a
malicious or unfair act since 1868.

game plan had been used by the Nixon administration to mean
"strategy" since 1969; during the televised hearings by the
Senate committee investigating Watergate witnesses often used
the term to describe the carefully laid plans to cover up the scandal. *Game plan* is mainly a football term of the 1960s, meaning
the overall plan a coach has for winning a game (whether to
concentrate on passing or running, which plays to use most in
a particular game, etc.). Nixon was a fan of the Washington
Redskins, the Washington, D.C., professional football team; thus
he, or some other politician who was a football fan, probably
heard the word used in television broadcasts of football games
and then introduced it to mean "strategy" in general.

leak, 1955, an unofficial or improper disclosure of government
or political secrets, as by a government official or politician
to a reporter. The leaking of *the Pentagon Papers* (see THE VIET-
NAM WAR for details), June 13, 1971, had upset Nixon and his
administration, leading to the creating of the *plumbers* (see below), who organized the Watergate break-in.

the plumbers, the nickname for the secret Special Investigation
Unit Nixon established in 1971 to stop or plug *leaks* (see above)
after Daniel Ellsberg leaked the Pentagon Papers. These plumbers included two men who had worked for the CIA, E. Howard
Hunt and G. Gordon Liddy. The Watergate investigations
disclosed that, as plumbers for Nixon, these two had been involved in breaking into the offices of Ellsberg's psychiatrist
in September, 1971, in search of material that might discredit
Ellsberg, and had organized or planned the details of the Watergate break-in.

to stonewall, *stonewalling*, to resist, or the act of resisting, all investigation or inquiry, as by refusing to disclose information,
making deliberately vague or misleading statements, etc. The
words were frequently used by Nixon and his associates, and
stonewalling was the keynote of their *game plan* (see above) in
the Watergate affair. One of the White House tapes even contains a passage in which Nixon himself explains to a confederate
how to "stonewall" while testifying before a grand jury. *Stonewall* is a cricket term (first noted in Australia in the 1950s) used
with contempt to describe the actions of a player or team concentrating on delaying or defensive tactics; however, *stonewall*
had long been used in America as a metaphor for steadfastness,
Confederate General Thomas J. Jackson earning his nickname
"Stonewall" for standing firm at the first Battle of Bull Run in
1861.

"Wild Bill" Hickok

"Wild Bill" Hickok (1837–76), dressed up for this rare photograph (he usually wore a frontiersman's costume).

(James Butler Hickok), an expert marksman and a stage driver on the Santa Fe and Oregon trails, was only 24 when he began to earn his famous nickname by killing David McCanles and two of his gang at Rock Creek Station, Nebraska, in 1861. He next was a Union army scout during the Civil War, then solidified his "Wild Bill" name by serving as deputy U.S. Marshal at Fort Riley and later Hays City, Kansas, before becoming the famous marshal who brought law and order to Abilene in 1871.

Besides "Wild Bill," he also gave us a poker term, *dead man's hand* (a pair of aces and a pair of eights together, "aces over eights"). A lover of gambling, Hickok was holding such a hand when he was shot and killed from behind by Jack McCall at Deadwood, Dakota Territory, in 1876.

The Wilderness and the Frontier

Soon after the first colonists gained a tenuous foothold on the wooded seacoast of America they were calling the entire country *the Wilderness* (1632). The wilderness seemed to be unending forest and it hemmed them in, threatened them, awed them. They had to conquer the wilderness, to cut, kill, and burn trees for their very survival. They talked about and desperately needed more open land to make room for themselves, their pastures, and their plows.

As had the Indians before them, the colonists practiced slash-and-burn agriculture. They spent much time *girdling* trees (1650, later called *deadening*, 1785), notching the bark all around so the trees would die and, leafless, let sunlight through to the corn crops and grazing grass below. Later they would burn the dead trees. Thus even their *clearings* (1678) were choked with stumps and dead or burnt-out trees (completely cleared land was a time-consuming luxury to all but the efficient Pennsylvania Dutch, who were the only early Americans to pull tree stumps).

Meanwhile, as land was cleared, *settlements* (1707) built, and the best land taken, some *settlers* (1739) decided to *pluck up stakes* (1640) or *pull up stakes* (1658, the early colonists used boundary stakes to mark off their land allotments) and move inland, back into the wilderness. By 1654 *frontier* meant the cutting edge of civilization, the line of settlers between civilization and the wilderness (in England *frontier* had meant only the border or border area between two countries). As these settlers or *pioneers* (from Old French *peonier*, foot soldier, later meaning explorer and settler) moved into the interior they

> *Woodman, spare that tree! Touch not a single bough! In youth it sheltered me, And I'll protect it now.* Woodman, Spare That Tree," 1830, George Pope Morris

A settler's clearing, surrounded by wilderness. The stumps are from trees killed by girdling *and then burned.*

Frederick Jackson Turner (1861–1932), American historian. His essay "The Significance of the Frontier in American Life," 1893, sets forth his famous "frontier hypothesis," that the form and spirit of American democracy were products of the open frontier, which stimulated American ingenuity and individualism.

moved "back" from the original settlements along the seacoast. Thus the colonists spoke of the:

> *backlands*, 1681; *backwoods*, 1709; *back country*, 1746; *back frontier*, 1755. In these backlands were soon *back settlements*, 1758; *back farms* or *back plantations*, both 1770; and eventually *back towns*, 1778. The people there were called *backwoodsmen*, 1710 or *back countrymen*, 1796 (the term *backwoods woman* did not appear until 1840).

Since the interior was not only "back" from the coast but, especially in the South, "up" into the highlands, hills, and mountains beyond the coastal plain, these frontiersmen were also said to move *upland* (to high ground, 1637, to the backwoods, 1656) or later *upcountry* (1815). The remote virgin forests or unsettled regions were thus called *wilderness*, *backwoods*, *upcountry*, and also:

> *timberland* 1654; *the timber*, 1792; *the tall timber*, 1831. In England *timber* usually meant what we call *lumber*, wood for building, but even in the 1620s colonists used *timber* to mean trees, leading us to such terms as *timber slash*, 1665, and eventually *timber line*, 1867.
>
> *the bush* (Dutch *bosch*, forest, woods), 1657. *Bush country*, 1855. *The bush* also gave us the terms *bush fighting*, 1758, and *bush fighter*, 1760.
>
> *the brush* (an obsolete English word), any region of small trees and shrubs in the wilderness, 1775; *brush land*, 1853; *brush country*, 1923. *Brush* also gives us *underbrush* and *brushfire*, both 1775.

Not until after the Civil War did the wilderness, the forest, the land, lose their status as admired enemies that had to be overcome. By then they had been tamed and seemed almost benign; then people first began to talk of protecting them. Thus:

forest reserve, 1882; *National Forest*, 1883; *forest reservation*, 1890; *forest management*, 1896; *forest ranger*, 1904.

wilderness, which in 1632 had seemed to encompass the whole country had come to designate only specific areas by the 1790s. *The Wilderness* was used to refer to a specific unsettled region along the eastern border of Kentucky in 1792 and to a forested region south of Virginia's Rapidan River in 1799, which became famous as the site of a Civil War battle. By 1890 *wilderness* was officially defined as a region having two persons or less per square mile; by 1934 a *wilderness area* was defined as a national forest at least 100,000 acres in size set aside for recreational and other uses. Thus by the 1960s the *wilderness* had roads and motels, logging camps, and ski lifts—at which point it was determined that some true wilderness must be preserved in its natural state without these things.

The New Woman

We have used many different words for woman, many of them reflecting society's concept of her as a mere extension of man or as a childbearer, cook, and sex object (see PRETTY GIRLS):

female, from Latin *fēmina*, woman, but literally "the suckling one," the sex that suckles children. It was spelled *femelle* until the 14th century, then became *female* through confusion with *male*.

lady, from Old English *hlǣfdīge*, "loaf kneader," bread maker. It has meant the mistress of a household and a wife since the 13th century, when it was also first used as a title of rank. Not until the 19th century did it come to mean any woman of refinement.

woman, from Old English *wifmann*, *wīf* then meaning woman, before it meant wife, and *mann* then meaning person, before it meant man, hence "woman person." Note that the Old English word for person (*mann*) grew into *man*, a man was a person, while the Old English word for woman (*wīf*) grew into *wife*, a woman was not a person but only a wife.

mistress, Miss, Mrs., Ms. Mistress (Old French *maistresse*) became the female correlative of *master* in the 14th century (it didn't mean a female paramour until 100 years later). *Master* itself became *mister* and was first abbreviated as a title *Mr.* in the 16th century, while the word *mistress* was first shortened to *miss* and the title *Miss* in the 17th century, then abbreviated to *Mrs. Mr.* didn't indicate marital status, he was a man, a person (see *woman* above); but *Miss* and *Mrs.* did, she was either a wife or not, her identity depending on marital status. To break this 300-year-old distinction, some members of the modern Women's Liberation Movement coined and began to use the general, nonmarital title *Ms.* (*Miss* + *Mrs.*) in the late 1960s.

poetess, sculptress, conductress, etc. The *-ess* suffix (from Latin and Greek *-issa*) that denotes females was in use by the 12th century. However, it wasn't until the mid 17th century that such words as *actress, adventuress, murderess, poetess, sculptress*, and *traitress* came into common use. This -*ess* suffix has resulted in some far-fetched formations: the English coined the nonpolitical *presidentress* in 1782 and it was recorded in America in 1819, while James Fenimore Cooper gave us *Americaness* in 1838. Between 1855 and 1875 the -*ess* feminine ending was fairly popular with woman's rights advocates and they then spoke proudly of any woman who was a *conductress* (on a horsecar), *doctress*, *lecturess*, or even a *rebeless* (in the Civil War).

bachelorette and *farmerette*. The -*ette* suffix (from Old French) entered English as a feminine diminutive, as used in *cigarette*, *statuette*, etc. However, it also came to be used to designate a woman, sometimes seeming to imply that women were trying to be small, cute men, as in such early 20th century Americanisms as *bachelorette* (1904), *drum majorette*, *farmerette* (a World War I word), and *usherette*.

English common law, with the full sanction of religion and society, kept colonial women subservient to men. In many ways a wife had the same legal status as her minor children—she couldn't sue (or be sued) in court; her money, lands, possessions, even her clothes, belonged to her husband, who had the legal right to punish her in the same way he did any of their children; and in many places the wife couldn't get a job or even leave the house without her husband's consent. Yet early American farm and village women shared more in the everyday affairs of life than did city women of the 19th century. Their husbands worked at or near home and the wives were in fact, though never legally, partners in what was really the family occupation, working in the fields or becoming the cooper, miller, potter, etc. in their husbands' absence or when the husbands died. Women innkeepers, ferry tenders, printers, even merchants and shipowners were not freaks, and the average housewife was a gardener, poultry farmer, cheese and butter maker, broom–candle–soap–clothing–rug manufacturer, teacher, and family doctor. She and her husband ran a joint self-supporting venture and gained their maturity and identity from it.

Then around the 1820s, as business and cities grew, more and more men began leaving the joint venture to be employed all day in offices, factories, and shops where they broadened their horizons and from which they obtained their identity. The woman was now left alone at home to do the "woman's work" of cooking, cleaning, and raising the children. Now besides her legal, religious, and social restrictions she was also cut off from many of the affairs of daily life, and her identity was merely that of being the wife of an office or factory worker or of a shop clerk. Under these conditions some women in America began to fight for woman's rights, often after having first gained experience and their own emancipation working for the temperance or abolition movements. In the 1820s and 30s America began talking about such women as the tall, well-bred Scots immigrant Fanny Wright (1795–1852), who scandalized us by lecturing against slavery and for woman's rights and birth control before mixed audiences. Then we talked about the Grimké sisters, Sarah (1792–1873) and Angelina (1805–79), Quaker converts who first lectured against slavery but, finding they were then denounced as mere "female reformers," became pioneers for woman's rights. From the 1820s until the Civil War Americans heard and used such new terms as:

The Female Academy of Clarksville, Tennessee.

> *female academy* and *female seminary*, both being private boarding schools for women (*academy* had meant a school of arts and sciences and *seminary* a place of education, not just religious education, since the 16th century). Emma Willard (1787–1870) made these terms popular in America, first by establishing the pioneering Middlebury (Vermont) Female Seminary in 1814 and the Waterford (New York) Academy for women in 1819, then by showing others how to establish such schools. In the 25 years before the Civil War almost 60 institutions of higher learning for women were opened, and we were speaking about such famous names as Mary Lyon's 1837 Mount Holyoke Seminary, Vassar, Wellesley, Smith, and Bryn Mawr. *Coeducation* and *coeducational* didn't enter the language until the early 1850s (though Ohio's Oberlin had opened as the first college to admit both men and women in 1833). *College girl* wasn't recorded until 1882.
>
> *business woman*, 1844.
>
> *woman's rights* was first widely used in the late 1840s. It was popularized by the first "woman's rights convention," held at Seneca Falls, New York, July 19–20, 1848. This convention was organized by the Quaker leader and abolitionist Lucretia Mott (1793–1880) and abolitionist lecturer Elizabeth Cady Stanton (1815–1902), who was to spend over 40 years working in partnership with Susan B. Anthony in the cause of woman suffrage. About 260 women and 40 men attended the convention, which became known as *the Seneca Falls Convention* or *Seneca Falls Conference*. It issued a "Declaration of Independence for Women," written by Elizabeth Cady Stanton and declaring that all women as well as all men are created equal and that women must be given the right to a thorough education, the right to vote, to hold property in their own name, and to work at any job or profession they choose. This convention and declaration marked the beginning of the organized woman's rights movement in America.
>
> *bloomers*, 1850, and *the bloomer costume* got their name from Amelia Bloomer (1818–1914) after she joined abolitionist Gerrit Smith's dress-reform movement against the hoopskirt and began wearing this costume of his design to her own Seneca Falls, New York, woman's rights lectures and on the street, then published patterns for the costume in her temperance magazine *The Lily*. The costume itself was a short skirt over wide, often ruffled, pantaloons gathered at the ankles and was usually worn with a loose coat and a broad-brimmed hat, the *bloomer hat* (1859). The pantaloons were the *bloomers*, which were also called *pantalets*. In 1851 all America began arguing about the new fashion, some considering it classically simple and charming, many others considering it evil, ugly, and perverse.

An 1851 caricature of bloomerism, with masculine-looking, cigar-smoking women dressed in the typical ruffled bloomers, short skirts, and broad-brimmed hats.

Since some leading woman's rights advocates, notably Lucy Stone (see *the Lucy Stone League* below), wore bloomer costumes as a symbol of their cause, woman's rights meetings were soon called *bloomer meetings* (mid 1850s). During the Civil War Mrs. Bloomer and other women forgot about bloomers as they devoted themselves to patriotic activities, but a simpler form of bloomer finally became popular in the 1890s, as an accepted garb for women bicycle riders.

sales lady, 1856; *sales woman*, 1870s; *sales girl*, 1887.

woman suffrage, *female suffrage*, though advocated by woman's rights groups since the late 1840s, did not become common terms until the early 1860s. The word *suffrage* itself (Latin *suffrāgium*, ballot, right to vote) entered English around 1500 and was first recorded in America in 1787, in the Constitution. The Constitution never denied women suffrage, but left to each territory and state the right to set its own voter qualifications.

> *female suffragist*, early 1870s; *suffragist*, 1880s. *Suffragette* was an English word of around 1905 and was seldom used seriously in America. It was coined by the *London Daily Mail* reporter Charles Hand and was meant to be disparaging, but the militant English suffragist Emmeline Pankhurst adopted it and made it respectable among her *sisters* in the cause.

A woman suffrage parade, 1915. Five years later the 19th Amendment granting nation wide suffrage to women was ratified by the states.

After the Civil War the woman's rights movement gained momentum: society was less rigid, women who had worked for abolition now had time for their own cause, and many people felt that, since Blacks had been emancipated and given the vote, women should be too. Also, expanding industry and cities now offered more jobs and rights to women. Many more women now became clerks, teachers, and nurses, and others took the new jobs available to women, including that of *typewriter girl* (1884), *telephone girl* (1893) or *telephone operator* (1894), and *stenog*

(1906). Between the Civil War and 1900 we had the following new terms and names:

equal rights, meaning equal rights for women, 1867.

the National Woman's Suffrage Association (the *NWSA*), with Elizabeth Cady Stanton as president and Susan B. Anthony (1820–1906) as chairman of the executive committee, and *the American Woman's Suffrage Association* (the *AWSA*), with Henry Ward Beecher as president and Lucy Stone, Julia Ward Howe, and Mary Livermore among its leaders. Both these associations were formed in 1869. The NWSA was to work for a constitutional amendment securing woman suffrage and the AWSA was to work for woman suffrage on the state level. In 1890 the two groups joined to become *the National American Woman's Suffrage Association* (the *NAWSA*) with Susan B. Anthony as its best-known leader, but with much of the work carried on by Carrie Chapman Catt (1859–1947), an Iowa high-school principal and superintendent of schools, and the British-born American minister and doctor Anna Howard Shaw (1847–1919). After helping women win the right to vote, the National American Woman's Suffrage Association was replaced by *the National League of Women Voters*, better known as *the League of Women Voters*, established in 1920.

the National Radical Reformers broke away from the National Woman's Suffrage Association in 1872 and nominated the spiritualist, stockbroker, free-love advocate, and newspaper publisher Victoria Claflin Woodhull for president of the U.S., making her the first woman to be so nominated (her running mate was the ex-slave Frederick Douglass).

the Equal Rights Party was what Mrs. Belva Lockwood, the first woman lawyer to be admitted to practice before the U.S. Supreme Court, called her followers when she nominated herself for the presidency of the U.S. on a woman suffrage platform in the 1884 and 1888 elections. She polled less than 2,000 votes in each.

club woman, 1895. The club woman's activities were written up in the *woman's department* (an 1875 term) of the local newspaper, and both she and the newspaper brought women's activities, both serious and frivolous, to public attention.

the new woman and *the emancipated woman* were both 1890s terms. Such a woman might wear *trouserettes* (full-cut men's-style trousers), discuss woman's rights at *emancipation teas*, smoke, and indulge in strenuous sports. *Emancipation* was used increasingly by woman's rights advocates after the 1870s, being popularized by the emancipation of the slaves.

In 1898 the newest states, Wyoming (which as a territory had been the first to grant women suffrage, in 1869), Colorado, Utah, and Idaho had granted full voting rights to women, and by 1918 some 18 states had granted or were about to grant women the right to vote. World War I had given women greater freedom and a chance to show their equality and usefulness in the war effort, making easier the National American Woman's Suffrage

Mary Anderson (1872–1964) was born in Sweden and came to the U.S. in 1888. She worked in factories for many years, then became a labor organizer and one of the founders of the National Women's Trade Union League. From 1919 to 1944 Ms. Anderson was Director of the Women's Bureau, U.S. Department of Labor.

Association's congressional committee's campaign for a constitutional amendment on woman suffrage. The year after the war, Congress passed the 19th Amendment, "the Equal Rights Amendment," "the Susan B. Anthony Amendment," by a narrow margin (it was twice defeated in the Senate before President Wilson called a special session to pass it). It was ratified by the states in time for all women to vote in the presidential election of 1920—thus, after a very long, hard struggle, many women cast their first vote for the winning Republican ticket of Warren G. Harding and Calvin Coolidge. Winning the right to vote gave some women the courage to form:

the *Lucy Stone League*, founded in 1921 to advocate the keeping of their own (maiden) names by married women; its members were called *Lucy Stoners*. It was named after the first well-known American woman to retain her name after marriage, the abolitionist and national woman's rights leader Lucy Stone (1818–93): she did so with the full agreement of her husband and co-worker Henry Brown Blackwell, whom she had married in 1855 (after marriage she called herself "Mrs. Lucy Stone," using the Mrs. to show she was married but keeping her own name to show she retained her identity).

In the early 20th century women truly entered the work force in large numbers: by 1935 some 25% of working-age women, well over 11 million, were working, mainly in low-paying jobs in factories and retail stores. Great strides were made during the male labor shortage of World War II when all offices, stores, and especially defense plants welcomed women workers. "Rosie the Riveter" was a popular patriotic song and, better yet, the government established a policy of "equal pay for equal work" for women. Also in the first part of the 20th century, a major woman's revolution took place on the doctor's examining table and in the bedroom, the liberation of women from being mere childbearing, child-raising factories. America was talking about:

> *birth control*, a term coined by Margaret Sanger in 1914. She also made *contraceptives* and *planned parenthood* common and acceptable terms in the 1920s and 30s. While working as a maternity nurse on New York's Lower East Side, Margaret Sanger (1883–1966) had seen the unhappiness and financial burden having too many children could cause, and had been shocked by the many deaths from self-induced abortions. She opened her first *birth-control clinic* in 1916 and formed the National Birth Control League in 1917, which grew into the Planned Parenthood Federation in 1942. More important, after being arrested

(top) Elizabeth Cady Stanton (1815–1902) and Susan B. Anthony (1820–1906) worked together from 1851 to 1902 as leaders of the woman suffrage movement. (bottom) Julia Ward Howe (1819–1910), active feminist, a founder of the American Woman's Suffrage Association, was the first woman elected to the National Academy of Arts and Letters, and Margaret Sanger (1883–1966), pioneer in America's birth control movement.

several times, she won her battle to allow doctors to dispense birth control information and finally, in 1936, to prescribe contraceptive devices. *Contraceptives* itself is a 19th century word; before that they were called *anticonceptives* and *contraception* was called *anticonception*.

diaphragm, 1880s, when it was invented. Margaret Sanger popularized the word in the 1920s and 30s by making the device the basis of her birth control program; it was what millions of women meant by birth control until the late 1950s. Incidentally, sheathlike devices had been worn by men to prevent venereal disease since the 16th century but were reinvented as a birth control device by an 18th century English physician, Dr. Condom or Conton, after whom they were then called *condoms*.

intrauterine device, 1920s, but the device wasn't perfected until the mid 1960s, the term then becoming generally known in 1966 and abbreviated in both writing and speaking as *IUD*.

birth control pills, late 1950s, even though they were then introduced by the formal name of *oral contraceptives*. By the early 1960s everyone was calling this method and the pills *the pill*.

The modern *Women's Liberation Movement* (a 1967 term) was born when female college students marched, picketed, and demonstrated as equals with male students in militant Civil Rights and anti-Vietnam war groups in the 1950s and 60s but found themselves not treated as equals within these groups. These women brought much of the militant rhetoric of the Civil Rights and antiwar movements to the woman's rights movement (as well as the word *movement* itself). They found support and cooperation in older women who had become interested in woman's rights after reading Betty Friedan's 1963 best-selling book *The Feminine Mystique*, which punctured the post-World War II myth that women were happy and fulfilled as suburban housewives and attacked the attitudes that kept women inferior, passive, and dependent (its impact was reinforced by the popular writing of Gloria Steinem and by Kate Millet's 1970 book *Sexual Politics*). This modern movement has given us such terms as:

bra burner, early 1970s, to mean any militant woman's rights advocate (after a few militant women had burned their brassieres publicly at woman's rights demonstrations, the term then being formed in analogy to the Vietnam war's *draft-card burner*). *Bra* had been a common shortening for brassiere since the early 1940s.

The bras were burned, and other women stopped wearing brassieres, girdles, make-up, etc., because they were considered demeaning symbols of the way women had dressed and lived to appeal to men, in which they became mere *sex objects* for men. Since many young women discarded their

"Babe" [*Mildred*] *Didrikson (1914–1956) at the Olympics in Los Angeles, 1932, where she established a record in the 80-meter hurdles and captured two gold medals (one in the javelin throw). Billie Jean King (right), professional tennis player since 1967, winner of many tournaments, is a strong advocate of woman's rights and of equal pay for men and women athletes.*

bras to proclaim their liberation, the *no-bra look* became a fashion of the early 70s, often achieved by wearing a soft, non-constricting brassiere.

consciousness raising, consciousness changing, 1970, making women aware of their oppression and of ways to combat it and overcome feelings of inferiority, passiveness, and dependency. Consciousness raising is often done through women's discussion groups called *consciousness raising groups.*

the Equal Rights Amendment, often abbreviated in speech and writing as *ERA*, was passed by Congress in 1972 and sent to the states for ratification. It forbids discrimination against women. The name *Equal Rights Amendment* first appeared in the 1870s, then referring to the contemplated constitutional amendment giving women the right to vote (such a bill was first voted on in Congress in 1878, and was defeated).

male chauvinist pig, 1970, sometimes abbreviated *MCP*, a male who thinks men are superior to women, is prejudiced or discriminates against them, or who considers women as mere sex objects. Literally it means a man superpatriotic to the idea of male supremacy, *chauvinist* having meant a superpatriot since 1870 (via the French word *chauvinisme*, from the name of Nicolas Chauvin, a legendary French army veteran blindly patriotic to Napoleon and parodied in an 1831 French play). *Pig* comes from the Civil Rights movement and radical student use of the 1960s (see *pig* at CALL THE POLICE).

NOW, the acronym for the National Organization of Women, which Betty Friedan helped organize in 1966.

NWPC, the National Women's Political Caucus, established in 1971.

sexism, 1970, prejudice or discrimination against women, or the belief that one sex is superior to the other; a person who practices or believes in sexism is called a *sexist.*

WEAL, the Women's Equity Action League, formed in 1968.

Women's Lib, 1970, a short form for *Women's Liberation Movement*. It made *Lib* a common shortening of *Liberation* or *Liberation Movement*, giving us such terms as *Gay Lib* for the Gay Liberation Movement among homosexuals; *Libber*, a member or advocate of the Women's Liberation Movement, 1973.

The modern Women's Liberation Movement is no longer just a movement among women or of a few groups, it is now something of a general American trend. It is working to help make women self-motivated, self-reliant, self-fulfilled human beings, each in charge of her own destiny, not relying on spouse, children, or the home for complete fulfillment or identity any more than men do. It wants complete equality for women in all things, a single standard of acceptance and judgment for both men and women. This means that women must be able to enter and reach the highest rank of any activity, occupation, business, or profession. Since over 50% of the population are women, this means that one day women may make up at least half of the number of our presidents, legislators, generals, executives, ministers—and police officers, baseball players, truck drivers, and coal miners. In order to free any woman as much as she desires from having her life restricted by home, children, and husband, it also works to eradicate any remaining stigma of being a single woman or a childless woman, favors legalized abortion, and advocates child care centers for working mothers. These things will have a permanent influence on the family, work force, politics—on every aspect of our private lives and our society, including our language.

In eradicating some of the superficial distinctions between men and women—in what they can be and do, in the roles they play in society—women's liberation advocates have attacked such terms as *chairman*, *fireman*, and *policeman*, and also *woman doctor* and *chairwoman*. American English has always tended to use *woman* more than *lady*: we say *woman doctor*, *women's clothing*, and *women's doubles* (in tennis) while the British still tend to say *lady doctor*, *ladies' clothing*, and *ladies' doubles*. From the 1850s to the 1960s this American tendency pleased woman's rights advocates, who encouraged the use of *woman* rather than *lady* or *female*. They encouraged the use of the 14th century *womankind* (though not of the condescending 1904 Americanism *women folk*) and of replacing *man* with *woman* when applicable: as in the 1890s when Susan B. Anthony addressed her audiences as "My fellow countrywomen;" in asking to be called a *chairwoman* rather than addressed as "Madam Chairman;" and in getting us to use *Congresswoman* (late 1920s).

Now, however, some women's liberation advocates feel that the use of both *man* and *woman* in certain contexts is sexist,

emphasizing one's sex rather than one's position or ability (some thus object to *woman doctor* and to both *chairman* and *chairwoman* as implying that sex makes a difference, they prefer simply *doctor* and the neuter *chairperson*). The major problem, however, is with that Old English word *mann* that once meant "person" but came to mean "man." What, if anything, is to be done with *fireman* and *policeman*? Some equal rights advocates feel that such words have "men only" connotations and should be replaced. Their suggestions for substitutes include some readily available neuter synonyms, as:

camera operator for *cameraman* (of the movies and TV, a 1920s term).

chess piece, which has been around since the 15th century, for *chessman*.

fire fighter for *fireman* (a term that became very popular in the 1830s).

human beings or *people* for *mankind*.

insurance agent for *insurance man*.

mail carrier or *letter carrier* for *mailman*.

Other "man" terms, however, have no obvious and simple neuter synonyms. In the early 1970s some equal rights advocates began coining new terms to replace them, often by simply substituting *person* for *man*. Thus we have had such forms as *midship-person*, *police person*, *person-at-arms*, *person-eating lion*, *personhole*, and *personslaughter*. Suggestions have even been made for replacing the words *boy* and *girl*, resulting in such coinages as *Youth Scouts* and *batchild*, who is not an offspring of the comics' and TV's Batman but is a *bat boy* (1925) or *bat girl* (1940s) for a baseball team. Whether or not such terms become a permanent part of our language, women's increasing equality and growing role in all aspects of our life will have a great influence on the American language of the future.

Two famous women in American politics were Frances Perkins (1882–1965) and (below) Jeannette Rankin (1880–1973). Ms. Perkins was appointed Secretary of Labor in 1933 by President Roosevelt, the first woman to serve in the Cabinet, and during her 12 years in office helped forge New Deal legislation. Ms. Rankin became the first woman elected to the House of Representatives, from Montana in 1916, after that state had granted full woman suffrage in 1914 but before the 19th Amendment was ratified in 1920. A lifelong pacifist, she voted against our entry into World War I and World War II.

World War I

was caused by the bitter economic and territorial rivalries between Europe's major empires, Germany, France, England, Russia, and Austria-Hungary. On June 28, 1914, the whole world was talking about the assassination in Sarajevo (now in Yugoslavia) of the heir to the Austrian throne, Archduke Francis Ferdinand, by Gavrilo Princip, a 21-year-old student and revolutionary Serbian nationalist. Within hours of the assassination Austria-Hungary declared war on Serbia: by the end of the summer most of Europe was at war.

On August 19, 1914, President Woodrow Wilson proclaimed U.S. neutrality, asking Americans to be "impartial in thought

HEIR TO AUSTRIAN THRONE AND HIS WIFE ASSASSINATED IN BOSNIA; SECOND ATTACK SUCCEEDS AFTER HE WARDS OFF BOMB.

> *He kept us out of war!*
> President Woodrow Wilson's 1916 reelection campaign slogan

> *Armed neutrality is ineffectual enough at best....The world must be made safe for democracy.*
> President Woodrow Wilson, address to Congress calling for a declaration of war, April 2, 1917.

as well as in action." *Neutrality* was the official American watchword, but many Americans agitated for *preparedness* and the two together became our *armed neutrality*. But even that was finally impossible. Though both sides violated American neutrality, American talk about "the war in Europe" became ever more pro-Allies and anti-German, with a growing hatred of *the Kaiser* (first recorded in English in 1871, German *kaiser*, emperor, is from the Latin surname Caesar). The three most talked-about names or events which led us into war were:

the Lusitania, the British Cunard luxury liner sunk by a German U-boat off the coast of Ireland, May 7, 1915, with a loss of 128 American lives, among the 1,198 men. women, and children who drowned.

the Black Tom Explosion, at a munitions plant on Black Tom Island (part of Jersey City, New Jersey) on July 30, 1916. It killed 7, injured 35, did $40 million worth of damage—and was traced to German saboteurs.

the Zimmerman telegram, sometimes called *the Zimmerman note*, a telegram sent by German Foreign Secretary Alfred Zimmerman to the German minister in Mexico, advising an alliance between Germany and Mexico in the event the U.S. entered the war and promising to support Mexico in recovering "her lost territory in New Mexico, Texas, and Arizona" in return for her help. British naval intelligence intercepted the telegram and gave it to the U.S., where President Wilson made it public in March, 1917.

LUSITANIA SUNK BY A SUBMARINE, PROBABLY 1,260 DEAD; TWICE TORPEDOED OFF IRISH COAST; SINKS IN 15 MINUTES; CAPT. TURNER SAVED, FROHMAN AND VANDERBILT MISSING; WASHINGTON BELIEVES THAT A GRAVE CRISIS IS AT HAND

On April 6, 1917, the United States declared war against Germany. We joined the *Allies* who, in decreasing order of the total number of men mobilized, included Russia (until the Russian Revolution of March, 1917), France, the British Commonwealth, Italy, the United States, Japan, Rumania, Serbia (defeated by October 7, 1915), Belgium, Greece (from July, 1917), Portugal, and Montenegro (defeated by the end of 1915). The Allies were finally led by *the Big Four*, England, France, Italy, and the United States. They opposed the *Central Powers*, so called because of their location in Central Europe, consisting of Germany, Austria-Hungary, Turkey, and Bulgaria.

Friedrich Wilhelm Viktor Albert, Kaiser William II (1859–1941), emperor of Germany and king of Prussia 1888–1918, a 1915 photograph.

Initially we followed the British lead in calling the conflict *the European War* (1914), but increasingly we called it *the World War*. We also called it "the war to end all wars," a phrase erroneously associated with Woodrow Wilson (and perhaps from H. G. Wells' 1914 book *The War That Will End War*), and "the last war." We spoke of it idealistically as "the war for the freedom of Europe," for "the overthrow of militarism," and for "the cause of civilization," and finally it became "the war to make the world safe for democracy," which was Wilson's phrase. Later, millions of American veterans were to refer to it as *the Great War*.

The war changed our life and our vocabulary forever. Many of the war's attitudes, life styles, even its gadgets and bureaucracies, were never to disappear. Wrist watches and factory-made cigarettes, being easy to use by the men in trenches, increased in popularity; we got used to many new federal agencies and to such abbreviations as *C.O.*, *KP*, and *MP;* women gained more freedom; the use of obscenity increased greatly (see OH SHIT! and FUCK AND SCREW). Of course we talked about many things besides the war, including the terrible *flu epidemic* of 1918, which by autumn had affected about 30% of the population and was to take the lives of 548,000 Americans, causing more deaths than the war itself (the word *influenza* had first appeared in English in 1743, in news from Rome about an epidemic there, *influenza* being the Italian word for "influence," figuratively an intangible visitation; it was shortened to *flu* in the 19th century). People called this flu the *Spanish flu*, because it had started in Spain, and many called the epidemic a *pandemic* (a widespread epidemic, from Greek *pandēmos*, *pan-*, all + *dēmos*, people).

But it was the war that shaped our language. Many of the terms we used were old ones, *furlough* and *discharge* from THE REVOLUTIONARY WAR, and *AWOL*, *draftee*, *kit bag*, and *pup tent* from THE CIVIL WAR. Many World War I terms entered our language even before the U.S. itself entered the war—we learned much of our wartime vocabulary from the British via our newspapers. Among the most common and representative terms and names Americans read, heard, and used were:

President Woodrow Wilson (1856–1924) and General John J. Pershing (1860–1948).

> *the AEF*, the *American Expeditionary Force*, led by General John J. "Black Jack" Pershing, which first reached France on June 25, 1917, only 11 weeks after the U.S. entered the war. Eventually over two million U.S. soldiers saw service in France. The name *AEF* followed that of the *BEF*, the *British Expeditionary Force*, which had landed in France on August 7, 1914. Eventually all Allied troops were responsible to Marshal Foch, who became the *Supreme Allied Commander*.
>
> *the air war* and many other of our air warfare terms were coined or popularized by the British in 1915, including: *war ace* or *ace*, a pilot who had shot down at least five enemy planes (*ace* didn't

401

Captain Eddie V. Rickenbacker (1890–1973), 1918.

come to mean an expert in general American use until after the war); *antiaircraft gun* and *ack-ack* (British telephone code for the letters *A A*, the abbreviation for *antiaircraft*), as well as *Archie*, British slang for an antiaircraft gun or battery; *aero squadron* and *squadron; air drop*, of supplies; and *bail out*, from a plane in a *parachute* (French *para-*, protecting against, preventing + *chute*, fall). The first successful *parachute jump* from an airplane had been made in 1912; during the war observers first used parachutes to descend from their balloons, then German pilots began to use them—parachutes weren't issued to U.S. military pilots until 1919, after the war was over.

Also in 1915 the British gave us the air warfare terms *bomber*, *bombing plane*, and *drop bomb*, a bomb for dropping from an airplane; *bombproof*, though in the Civil War we had used *bomb proof* to mean a person in a safe place, away from the fighting; *dawn patrol; dogfight; fighter plane* and *fighter; flight; formation* and *formation flying; hedgehopping*, flying low to avoid detection and antiaircraft fire; *incendiary bomb;* and *war plane*. And, of course, Americans were talking about England's *Sopworth Camel* and *De Haviland* scout plane and Germany's *Fokker* and its *Gotha* bomber, along with many other planes.

Before we entered the war we also talked about our *Lafayette Escadrille* (see below) and after we entered the war our most talked-about hero was our top ace, the former automobile racer Captain Eddie Rickenbacker. He was commander of our 94th Aero Pursuit Squadron, which accounted for 69 German planes, 26 of them credited to "Captain Eddie" personally. We also talked about Brigadier General "Billy" (William) Mitchell who commanded the AEF air force. The most talked-about German ace was Baron Manfred von Richthofen, known as *the Red Baron, the Bloody Red Baron,* and *the Red Knight,* because his Albatross biplane was painted crimson; he had 80 air victories before being killed in 1918 at the age of 26.

Aussie (a short form for *Australian*, used since about 1895), *Digger*, and *Anzac* all became popular words for Australian soldiers during World War I. *Digger* may have been an Australian gold-rush term of the 1850s (referring to the gold diggers) or may come from the gallant Australian soldiers who "shoveled Gallipoli into sandbags" during the ill-fated Gallipoli campaign, April, 1915—January, 1916, in which the Allies attempted to gain the Dardanelles, capture Constantinople, and join up with the Russian troops via the Black Sea, but were turned back by the Turks. *Anzac* definitely first became known to Americans during this Gallipoli campaign, in newspaper accounts of Australian and New Zealand bravery. It's the acronym of *A*ustralian–*N*ew Zealand *A*rmy *C*orps, first used in military communications in 1915.

back home is how overseas American troops referred to the United States. English troops expressed their yearning for England by calling it *Blighty* (from India, where the Hindu word *bilāyatī*, foreign, had come to mean "English").

Bangalor torpedo. This metal pipe filled with TNT was used to cut a path through barbed wire and mine fields. The British named it from the place they had first experimented with the device, Bangalore, India. Incidentally TNT's use in the Bangalor torpedo and elsewhere in the war made *TNT* (*tri*ni*trotoluene) a common term.

barrage, camouflage, see FRENCH, FRENCH TOAST, AND FRENCH POSTCARDS.

basket case, a quadruple amputee, originally British Army slang.

Big Bertha, Fat Bertha, Bertha, a German long-range gun, first used near Liège, Belgium, in 1914, then used to shell Paris from 75 miles away in 1918. These names are from the German name for it, *dicke Bertha,* fat Bertha, after Frau Bertha Krupp von Bohlen und Halback, the proprietress of the Krupp steel works where the cannon was made. Naming a large cannon after a female follows an old tradition: our word *gun* itself is from an Old Norse nickname for Gunnhildr, and originally referred to a large catapult named Dame Gunidda in the year 1330.

blimp and *zeppelin. Blimp* comes from the designation of a World War I British design for a dirigible, the type *B-limp,* limp meaning nonrigid, the gas bag supported solely by internal gas pressure. Such blimps were used in both World War I and II for antisubmarine and coastal patrol. *Dirigibles* are steerable balloons (it's an English word from the 1550s, from Latin *dīrigere,* to steer); they were also being called *airships* by the 1880s. Germany's Count Ferdinand von Zeppelin perfected his cigar-shaped *rigid dirigible* in 1900 ("rigid" because the gas bag is supported by a rigid framework rather than solely by internal gas pressure) and such craft were immediately called *zeppelins.* These zeppelins were widely talked about during World War I when the Germans used 88 of them to bomb London and other cities.

Boche, Hun, Kraut, Jerry, and *Fritz* were what we called Germans and German soldiers in World War I. Of these, *Boche, Jerry,* and *Fritz* (sometimes *Fritzie*) originated during the war (for an explanation of such terms see THE GERMANS).

brass hat was a common American World War I term for a high-ranking officer. It goes back to the 1887 *brass button brigade*, referring to top Army and Navy officials in Washington, who became *the brass* or *the war brass* during the Spanish-American War. The change seems only to be from referring to the buttons on high-ranking officers' uniforms to the braid on their hats.

bridgehead, originally used by the British to mean a fort commanding the end of a bridge.

buck private, first recorded in 1918.

chief of staff was first generally heard during World War I. It dates from 1907, following Secretary of War Elihu Root's reorganization of the army, replacing *commanding general of the army*.

chow had been a slang word for food since 1856, when it partially replaced the older word *grub* (1807). However, *chow*, meaning a meal or mealtime; *chowhound*, originally meaning the one who was always first in the food line; *chow line*; and *chow time* were all made common by World War I U.S. servicemen (in World War II *chow* almost completely replaced the word "food" in the speech of servicemen). *Chow* seems to have originated on the Pacific Coast where it was associated first with sailors and then with Chinese railroad workers in the 1850s. This almost certainly means that it comes from the Mandarin Chinese *ch'ao*, to stir, fry, cook. Incidentally, *chow-chow*, chopped mixed pickles or similar relishes, was also first used in the 1850s on the Pacific Coast and is probably pidgin English from the Mandarin Chinese *cha*, mixed.

civvies, civilian dress as opposed to a military uniform, 1918. The British had used the word *mufti* since 1816 to refer to the civilian dress of an off-duty officer, and some Americans affected this word during World War I. This *mufti* actually means the dressing gown, cap, and slippers of a Mohammedan mufti as seen on the stage, in drawings, etc., a *mufti* being a Mohammedan priest or expounder of the law.

C.O. was used as the abbreviation for both *c*ommanding *o*fficer and *c*onscientious *o*bjector.

convoy had meant to accompany, escort in English since the 15th century. Now it came to mean a fleet of merchant and troop ships protected from submarines by cruisers and destroyers.

Devil Dogs. At the Battle of Belleau Wood, June 2–July 7, 1918, a French major told American Captain Lloyd Williams to retreat; Williams replied "Retreat, hell! We just got here." "Retreat, hell!" then became one of the most famous utterances of the war. In that battle the 4th U.S. Marine Brigade's fierce attack caused the Germans to call them *Teufelhunden*, devil dogs, which has been a nickname for the U.S. Marines ever since.

dog tag, a government-issue metal identification disc worn on a thin chain around a serviceman's neck, for identification in case of injury or death, so called because it resembles a license tag on a dog's collar. This is sometimes said to have been a Civil War term, but isn't. What the Civil War soldier often did was pin a slip of paper on his uniform with his name and address on it before going into battle, so his family could be notified if he were killed or wounded.

A Red Cross canteen, France, 1918.

dollar-a-year-man, an executive working for Bernard Baruch's War Industries Board, which mobilized industry and labor for the war effort. Such men were paid a dollar a year because it was illegal to pay them nothing.

doughboys, *Tommies*, and *poilus*. An American soldier was called a *doughboy*, *Yank*, *trooper*, or *Sammy*. *Sammy* was mainly a British use (based on UNCLE SAM) to match Britain's own *Tommy;* it didn't really catch on in American speech. *Trooper* had meant a horse soldier in English since the 17th century and seemed to be more romantic than the simple word "soldier" (*to swear like a trooper* dates from 1839). *Yank* became a very common term and Europeans probably used it more than "American" or "American soldier," while we Americans spoke with pride of "our Yanks overseas" (see YANKEE).

The big World War I word, however, was *doughboy*, which had first seen some use during the Civil War. No one knows for sure where the word comes from, it may come from: (1) *doughboy*, which meant a fried sweet cornmeal cake by 1770, then a small globular biscuit served to sailors, was then used as a name for the globular brass buttons on some Civil War infantry uniforms, and was finally used as a name for the soldiers themselves; (2) the fact that the U.S. infantry once wore white belts which had to be cleaned with pipe clay "dough," causing the cavalry to call mere infantrymen *doughboys;* (3) from *adobe*, a slighting name for soldiers used by Spanish speakers in the Southwest since the late 1840s, because the soldiers were sometimes comfortably quartered in adobe buildings. About 40% of the doughboys were volunteers, the rest were drafted under the Selective Service Act passed on May 18, 1917, six weeks after the U.S. entered the war, and which registered 24 million men between 18 and 45 years of age. Five million doughboys were enrolled for military training.

A British soldier was *Tommy Atkins* (since 1893 in Britain) or a *Tommy*, Tommy Atkins being a British synonym for "John Doe" and used on sample recruiting forms. An English soldier, or any Englishman, was also called a *Limey* (since at least 1910, from the 1880s term *lime juicer*, from the limes issued British sailors to prevent scurvy).

405

We often called a French soldier a *Poilu* (bearded one) or sometimes a *Didonk*. The French sometimes called our doughboys *les sommombiches*, because our troops used SON OF A BITCH so often in their speech.

dreadnought, dreadnaught was a common World War I term for any of the largest, heaviest battleships. The word came from the British *Dreadnaught* (literally "fear nothing"), the name of the first large modern battleship, put into service in the Royal Navy in 1906. *Battleships*, an 18th century English word, were important in World War I, but proved so vulnerable to planes and submarines during World War II that the U.S. withdrew its last one from active service in 1950.

dud, a shell or bomb that failed to explode. The word probably comes from the 14th century *dud/dudde*, a coarse cloak, which gave English the 16th century word *duds*, rags, tatters. By 1919 we were already using *dud* to refer to any person or thing that didn't come up to expectations. *Live shell*, the opposite of a dud, was also a new term of World War I.

Dum-Dum bullet, an 1897 British term for soft-nosed bullet that spread on impact. Outlawed by the Geneva Convention, such bullets were in use anyway, especially by French troops; all troops made them by blunting and slitting the tips of regular bullets. They are called *Dum-Dum bullets* because they were first tested by the British at their military station and arsenal in Dumdum, India, near Calcutta.

the duration came to mean "until the end of the war." It was originally British army slang for the duration of one's enlistment.

entente was used before and during the war to mean understanding between nations to refer to various agreements, pacts, etc. (it's the French word for "understanding"). The British had used the French term *entente cordiale* since 1840.

farmerette was an English word for a woman farmer helping supply food during the war. In America by 1918 it usually meant a member of our Woman's Land Army, often a college girl, secretary, etc., who spent her summer vacation or a leave of absence tending farm crops, chaperoned by older women and earning two dollars a day.

flame throwers (a translation of the German *flammenwerfer*) were first used, by the Germans, at the Battle of Verdun, on February 21, 1916. Initially the British called them *flame projectors* and we sometimes used this term too.

gas came to mean the horrifying poison gases used in the war. Since the Hague Conference of 1907 forbade such poison weapons, the Allies were unprepared when the Germans used chlorine gas for the first time on the Eastern Front, January 31, 1915, against the Russians at the Battle of Masurian Lakes, then let loose a dense cloud of this greenish yellow gas at the junction of the French and British lines at the Second Battle of Ypres on April 22, 1915. *To gas, gas alert, gas bomb*, and *gas mask* were thus 1915 terms, known to millions of Americans through our newspapers. Initially a *gas mask* was also called an *anti-poison gas mask*, a *box respirator*, or a *respirator*, British terms which Americans used; there were even *horse masks* for horses and mules.

Artillery men wearing gas masks at the front.

Everyone also talked about the various types of gases used, *phosgene*, *tear gas* (also sometimes called *lachrymator gas*) which irritated the eyes, and even *sneezing gas* and *vomiting gas*. The term *mustard gas* appeared in 1917, so called because it had a mustardlike odor; it was also called *blister gas*. It was the most potent gas used and took a long time to recover from, if one did recover. Since it was used late in the war it was the gas most often encountered by American troops and the most feared and talked about.

get it, to be killed, originally a British army term.

gobs, *swabbies*, and *bluejackets* are what we called sailors in World War I. *Gob* was used in the U.S. Navy by 1909; it probably comes from *gobby*, which had meant a coastguardsman since 1890 (no one knows why, *gobs* had meant a large amount since 1839 and *gob* the mouth since 1859). *Swabby* comes from *swab/swabber*, used since the 18th century to mean a merchant seaman, with *swab* then coming to mean a naval officer, which is how Herman Melville used the word in his 1850 novel *White Jacket, or Life in a Man-of-War*. *Swab*, of course, comes from the sailors' routine task of swabbing the decks (*swab* meant to mop by the 16th century, probably from Middle Dutch *swabbe*, mop). In the 1920s *swabo* was a Navy term for zero, literally as clean or blank as a swabbed deck. *Bluejacket* means an enlisted sailor in both the British and U.S. Navy, the British use dating from 1859 and the U.S. use dating only from World War I. We also still called sailors *tars* and by the name *Jack*, both 17th century English words for sailors, the two being combined into *Jack-tar* in England in the 18th century (*tar* probably coming from *tarpaulin*).

Incidentally, a *skipper* (from Middle Dutch *schipper*, ship's captain, from *schip*, ship) meant the captain of a small merchant vessel in English by 1390. In World War I soldiers used it to refer to any commander.

goldbrick had meant a brick or bar of gold in the U.S. by 1853, then a valueless brick appearing to be made of gold by the 1880s (*to sell someone a gold brick* meant to cheat or swindle him by 1887). By 1914 a *goldbrick* meant an army lieutenant appointed from civilian life, without training or experience; then by the end of the war it came to mean anyone who didn't do his share and also became a verb *to goldbrick*, to do less than one's share.

hand grenade became a common term during the war, because such grenades were used extensively in the trenches (see *trench warfare* below). *Grenade* had long been both the French and English word for pomegranate (from Old French *pome grenate*, which also gives us *grenadine*, a syrup and a liquor made from pomegranates) before it came to mean a small explosive shell in English in the 16th century. The shell was called a *grenade* because it resembled the fruit—thus the Chicago gangsters who called a grenade a *pineapple* in the 1920s (see AL CAPONE) were actually using the original fruit image that gave us *grenade* in the first place! Soldiers who carried grenades were called *grenadiers* by the 17th century, and the term *hand grenade* entered English by 1661, over 250 years before World War I made it common. German hand grenades were flat at one end and had a handle at the other, and were called *potato mashers*, which they resembled.

H-hour, the exact time a military operation or attack is to begin. The British term for this was *zero hour*, which Americans also used.

hitch, a serviceman's period of enlistment.

Holy Joe had been soldiers' slang for an Army chaplain since 1900 but became well known during World War I.

iron ration, emergency rations, especially as carried by soldiers, originally British use.

khaki (via Urdu *khakī*, dusty, from Persian *khāk*, dust) meant a dull brownish yellow color in England by 1863. The British Army clothed its Indian troops in worsted uniforms of this color while putting down the Indian Mutiny or Sepoy Rebellion in 1857–58, then found the uniform suitable for the climate, and as camouflage, in South Africa. The U.S. Army adopted what it called a *khaki uniform* for field wear in 1902 and by World War I *khakis* had come to mean this uniform. Incidentally *olive drab*, meaning both the color and the uniform, was first shortened to *O.D.* during World War I.

Kamerad, meaning comrade in German, was the word used by German soldiers in surrendering. American troops used it in a humorous way, to mean captured or friendly Germans or a sycophantic friend.

KP became the common abbreviation for the army's kitchen police, the detail assigned to kitchen chores and cleanup, and for such duty itself.

the Lafayette Escadrille, sometimes known by its French name *Escadrille Americaine*, was one of the most romantic names of the war. It was named after the French General and Statesman Lafayette who joined Washington's army as a major general and served at Brandywine, Valley Forge, and in the Yorktown campaign, as well as negotiating for French aid in France (*escadrille* is the French word for squadron). This famous "aero squadron" of American volunteers was formed under Captain George Thenault in April, 1916, a year before America entered the war, and suffered nearly a third of its fliers as casualties while

The famous recruiting poster painted by James Montgomery Flagg (1877–1960).

shooting down 199 German planes between the time it arrived in France in 1917 and January, 1918, when it was absorbed into the U.S. Army as its 103rd Pursuit Squadron.

Composed mainly of wealthy or socially prominent American young men, who proudly wore the escadrille's red-bonneted American Indian insignia, it glamourized such things in America as the white silk scarves and goggles we still associate with World War I flying. It also helped make the *Sam Browne belt* a romantic part of a flyer's uniform (named after its inventor the British Brigadier General Sir Samuel Browne, 1824–1901), since the belt was worn in the war only by officers and by decorated aviators. It also popularized such words as *crate* for airplane and *egg* for bomb (in the war *egg* was also used to mean a hand grenade, a naval mine, and even a newly arrived member of the AEF, as new as a freshly laid egg). The Lafayette Escadrille also adopted the British use of *Kiwi*, often spelled *keewee*, as a poor unfortunate serviceman not lucky or good enough to be in the flying service (the word *kiwi* was later used in the U.S. to refer to cadets at flying schools and is still used as the name of a group of retired airline stewardesses, all from the *kiwi*, the flightless bird of New Zealand).

Liberty Bonds, interest-bearing bonds issued by the government to help finance the war. They were sold through schools, by door-to-door sales efforts, and by *Four Minute Men*, war heroes, executives, and local politicians who gave four-minute sales talks at factories, stores, mass meetings, etc. Douglas Fairbanks, Mary Pickford, Charles Chaplin, and other stars also promoted them heavily across the country, and John Philip Sousa even wrote a *Liberty Bond March*. Standard stocks and bonds which rose rapidly in value during the war were called *war babies*.

Liberty cabbage was what super patriots called sauerkraut during the war, with German measles being renamed *Liberty measles*, etc. (for more such terms and our attitudes toward Germans during the war see THE GERMANS).

Mary Pickford (second from left) in a patriotic play supporting a Liberty Bond drive, 1918.

Looey/Looie, First Looey, Second Looey all became popular terms for lieutenant during World War I, though *Looey* was restricted to referring to a second lieutenant by many. *Loot* was sometimes also used (the written abbreviation *Lieut.* dates from 1843).

the Lost Battalion, the 1st Battalion, 308th Infantry of the U.S. 77th Division, was never lost; it was surrounded by the Germans after breaking through to its objective in the Meuse-Argonne offensive in the last month of the war and lost 400 of its 600 men before other American troops reached it.

merchants of death was not a war term for munitions manufacturers; the term came from the title of a book by H. C. Engelbrecht and F. D. Hanighan, one of several exposés published in the 1920s attempting to prove that munitions makers and others who profited from U.S. involvement in the war had been prime causes of it.

MG, often pronounced as "emm-gee," became the abbreviation for both *machine gun* and *machine gunner* during the war.

MP was first recorded as the abbreviation for *Military Police* in 1918 (it had been used since the 1850s as an abbreviation for *Metropolitan Police*).

overseas and *sent overseas* meant only one thing during World War I, in the armed forces in Europe. The army's elongated, brimless, peakless *overseas cap* was adopted from the Scots' Glengarry and considered so dashing it was often called a *go-to-hell-cap*.

pom-pom, a type of heavy machine gun firing one-pound shells. It may have gotten its name from the French *pompom*, the ball or tuft atop French sailors' caps, but it more probably was named for the pom-pom-pom sound it made in firing. In World War II a *pom-pom* was a rapid-fire antiaircraft gun mounted on ships in twos, fours, or even eights.

puttees (via Hindu *pattī* from Sanskrit *patta*, cloth band) entered the English language via the British Army in India in 1875. They were made part of the uniform of the *New Army* created by U.S. Secretary of War Elihu Root in the early 1900s, replacing the laced canvas leggings of the *old army*. World War I soldiers said, only half humorously, that most of their basic training was spent in learning how to wind their puttees properly.

the Rainbow Division, the 42nd Division, the first to land in France, was so called because it was composed of National Guard units from many states. One of its battalions was *the Fighting 69th*, a Manhattan regiment with many Irish-Americans, who originally called themselves *the fighting Irish*.

red tape became a common wartime term, probably taken from the English, who used such tape on government documents. However, we had previously used *red tapist* (1853) and *red tapy* (1889) in referring to timid or cheap people or inferior things.

rookie (from *recruit*) had seen some use in the 1890s, especially for a new athlete, but its first wide army use began in World War I.

sabotage had been used since 1870 in France to mean the clatter of shoes, to do something badly, and to refer to the willful

Sergeant Alvin C. York.

English tanks near Amiens, France.

and organized destruction of tools, machinery, etc., by workers (from French *sabot*, wooden shoe, *savate*, shoe, old shoe). This French word soon entered English and saw wide use during the war to refer to destruction of war equipment, factories, transportation facilities, etc., by enemy agents and sympathizers.

sector is a 16th century math term for a plane contained by two radii and the arc of a circle they interrupt (that's math talk for a pie-shaped wedge). During the war everyone knew it was the part of the front line occupied by a battalion.

Sergeant York was probably the most talked-about infantryman of World War I. Alvin C. York (1887–1964), once a conscientious objector, had been an excellent marksman back home in Tennessee before he became a sergeant in the U.S. Army and led a detachment in the Battle of Argonne where, on October 8, 1918, after most of his men were killed or wounded, he charged a German machine-gun nest, capturing 90 Germans, then captured a second German machine-gun position and took 42 more prisoners.

shell shock was originally a British wartime term. Americans used it widely, but our military preferred the term *battle fatigue* instead.

shelter half, half a *shelter tent* (which was a Civil War term).

shock troops was another World War I term, though *shock* had meant the encounter of troops since the 16th century.

slacker, one who tries to avoid military service. We got this word from the British but as the war went on we came to call such a person a *shirker* (*to shirk* is an Americanism of 1833).

tank was British Colonel Sir Ernest Swinton's secret code name for this new weapon when it was being built and tested (the workers who assembled the first ones were told they were working on a new type of portable water tank for use in Mesopotamia). The parts of a tank, *turret*, *hatch*, *hull*, etc., have nautical names because this new weapon was originally sponsored by the British Admiralty, rather than the War Office. The British used the tank for the first time at the Battle of Flers-Courcelette (part of the Battle of the Somme) on September 15, 1916. *Anti-tank gun* and *tank trap* are also World War I terms and the best-known English tank was probably the *Whippet*, a light, mobile tank named after the fast English breed of dog that resembles a small greyhound.

top sergeant became the common term for a first sergeant during the war (he had formerly been a *sergeant major*, since 1840).

tracer bullet, fired from World War I rifles and machine guns, including machine guns mounted on airplanes.

trench warfare. At the beginning of the war the Western Front was mobile, with the Germans attacking France and Luxembourg and capturing most of the Belgian channel ports in *the race to the sea.* Then in early 1915 Sir John French ordered the BEF to entrench and the Germans, who had fallen back behind the Aisne after the First Battle of the Marne in 1914, did likewise, beginning the bloody, grueling three years of war *in the trenches. No-man's land* was the land between the two lines, between the crossfire of the two sides (the term had once

"Over the top."

been used in America to refer to the strip of land ceded to the U.S. by Texas after its admission to the Union in 1845, which *no-man's land* remained without government and law until it became a part of Oklahoma in 1890).

Trench warfare gave us such terms as *trench fever*, an acute infectious relapsing fever transmitted through lice; *trench foot*, originally a form of frostbite caused by standing in cold water; *trench mouth*, a form of gingivitis; the short double-bladed *trench knife;* and *trench mortar*, a mortar, a muzzle-loaded cannon firing short-range, low-velocity shells at a high projectory, of which the British *Livern projector* and the *Stokes mortar*, and the German *Minnie* (German *Minenwerfer*, "mine thrower") were widely talked about. And, of course, dashing British officers wore a new style of coat, called a *trench coat*.

Trench warfare and its no-man's land also led to the wide use of old terms like *land mine; barbed wire, wire* (American terms of the 1860s), and *wire cutter* (1876); and the new term *wire entanglement*. This type of warfare also led to such new terms as *forward listening post*, for detecting enemy movements into

German soldiers attack across the trenches with the support of their planes.

412

no-man's land; *pillbox*, the boxlike concrete machine-gun shelter built by the Germans; *smoke screen*, to screen advancing troops; and *star shell*, to light up no-man's land and enemy trenches at night.

The British called a small *shelter trench* for a few men a *pit*, *Belgium pit* (it was first used widely in Belgium), or *foxhole*— of these terms *foxhole* became the American favorite. The British and some American troops also called a small *dugout* or foxhole a *funkhole* (*funk* meaning fright or panic to the British, originally as 18th century university slang for *smoke*, which also was slang for fear). When they were going to charge out of the trenches in an attack the British said they were going to *jump off* while we Americans said we were going *over the top*.

troop ship, troop train. Ships had carried troops for centuries but our image of *troop ship* as a large ship with throbbing engines loaded with khaki-clad soldiers and zigzagging through submarine-infested waters comes from World War I. *Troop trains* had also been used before, as when the South rushed in reinforcements by train to save the day at the first Battle of Bull Run, July 21, 1861, but the term *troop train* became common in World War I.

U-boats, submarines, and **torpedoes.** *Submarine* has meant "under the sea" in English since 1684 and an *underseas boat* since the 1890s, long after David Bushnell's first American underseas boat, the 1775 *American Turtle*, and some 30 years after the Confederate *Hunley* sank a Union ship in the Civil War. *Submarine* was shortened to *sub* in 1914 (the U.S. Navy names its subs after fish and other marine creatures, such as the *Turtle* and the *Nautilus*, and its ballistic-missile submarines after American heroes).

Periscope (*peri*, near + *scope*, an instrument for observing, both from the Greek) was in English by 1822, then used to see over hills and brush, but *periscope* and the command *Up periscope!* became completely associated with submarines during the war. Then also a periscope's wake became known as a *feather* and a crippled or destroyed sub was said to leave an *oil slick*.

A German U-boat *stops a steamer, 1917.*

The Germans were the first to use submarines on a large scale and during World War I a German submarine was usually called a *U-boat* (1913, from the German *Unterseeboot*, underseas boat). A submarine was also frequently called a *pig-boat*, because it resembled a suckling pig when nosed against a *submarine tender*, and sometimes called a *tin can* (which had meant a Ford car since 1910), *tin fish*, *tin shark*, or *Navy shark*. However, *tin can* was usually reserved to mean a depth charge (in World War II it meant a depth charge and, more often, a destroyer, the smallest, least armored battle ship, while *tin fish* meant only a torpedo). The British coined the term *depth charge*, also calling it a *depth bomb* in World War I; but we liked to call it an *ash can* (which had meant a can for ashes since 1910, replacing the older *ash barrel*, 1846, as metal containers had grown more common). A cruising U-boat could be detected by a primitive World War I British version of sonar called *Asdic* (for *A*nti-*S*ubmarine *D*etection and *I*nvestigation *C*ommittee) which gave a *fix* on the enemy boat.

Torpēdo was the Latin name for a dangerous raylike fish which has a numbing electrical charge (from Latin *torpēre*, to be stiff, numb, which also gives us *torpor*). The English used *torpedo* as the name of the fish by 1520, then in America, in 1786, a *torpedo* came to mean a percussion shell, then by 1807 a device for blowing up ships (as a mine or an explosive charge for attaching to a ship, Admiral Farragut was using *torpedo* to mean mine when he shouted "Damn the torpedoes! Full speed ahead" at Mobile Bay in 1864). By 1886 a *torpedo* also meant a booby trap of concealed explosives and in 1900 came to mean a small charge placed on railroad tracks to signal an engineer by exploding under a locomotive's wheels. The *self-propelled torpedo* was first used in World War I, and soon became what most people meant when they said *torpedo* (the word wasn't shortened to *torp* until World War II). World War I also popularized the term *torpedo boat* (an American term of 1810) and gave us *torpedo plane*.

whizzbang, a small-caliber, high-velocity, flat-trajectory shrapnel shell, so named by British soldiers from the whizzing sound of its flight, followed almost immediately by the bang of its explosion. Our doughboys talked a lot about *Captain Billy's Whiz Bang*, which originally appeared as a mimeographed joke sheet to cheer up the wounded in hospitals, next became a favorite of all the troops, and finally became a publication sold on newsstands (Captain Billy was William Fawcett of Fawcett Publications). Incidentally, a *whiz* had meant an expert since 1908.

the Western Front was the 600-mile front from Switzerland to the English Channel, especially during the trench warfare that began in 1915 (*front* had meant the foremost battle line since the 14th century). The Germans called their line the *Siegfried line* but the Allies preferred to call it the *Hindenburg line*, after Field Marshal Paul von Hindenburg who withdrew to it after the Battle of the Somme in 1916—this is the same Hindenburg who was reelected president of Germany in 1932, then forced to appoint as chancellor the man he had beaten in the election, Adolf Hitler.

A trench on the Hindenburg Line.

All quiet on the Western front became a cliché in military communiqués and newspaper reports during much of the trench warfare, a rather cynical phrase to the troops who were stagnating or dying there, as shown by Erich Maria Remarque's 1929 novel about the war, *All Quiet on the Western Front*.

The Eastern Front was the 1,100-mile front from Riga on the Baltic to the shores of the Black Sea; here the Germans under Hindenburg and Ludendorf finally defeated the Russians after a series of see-saw battles over Poland.

The Southern Front referred to the 320-mile front from Switzerland along the Italian frontier to Trieste.

From the time the war began to draw to a close until the Great Depression, new terms kept emerging, some due to treaties and attempts to establish a permanent peace, others due to the accounts of the war that emerged slowly as the men returned and began to talk and write about their experiences. President Wilson presented his famous *fourteen points* offering a "just and generous" peace on January 8, 1918, the fourteenth point proposing the formation of a *League of Nations*. The *Treaty of Versailles* was signed there on June 28, 1919, with a *war-guilt* clause blaming the Germans for the war and officially calling for Wilson's League of Nations to be established to settle international disputes (but Wilson was unsuccessful in obtaining the two-thirds Senate majority necessary to ratify the treaty). *The Peace Palace* became the name of a building built in The Hague in the Netherlands between 1907 and 1913, the seat of the Permanent Court of International Justice created by "the League" in 1922. America also soon had two tragic postwar terms:

Armistice Day, first proclaimed by President Wilson as November 11 in 1919, to remind Americans of the tragedies of the war on the anniversary of its end. That day was observed with special church services, patriotic parades, and a nationwide two minutes of silence at 11 A.M., the time the firing had stopped in the trenches. Perhaps on that first Armistice Day, too, many still remembered the *false armistice* of November 7, 1918, when rumors that the war was over had sent millions of Americans into the streets to celebrate. Although set aside by presidential proclamation since 1919, not until 1938 was a law adopted making Armistice Day a federal holiday. In 1954 Congress changed the name to *Veteran's Day*, to honor all U.S. veterans, including those of World War II and the Korean War. *Veteran* had been used in America since the Revolutionary War, with the shortened *vet* first being used after the Civil War.

the Tomb of the Unknown Soldier. In 1921 four caskets of unknown American soldiers were disinterred from war cemeteries in France and America's most decorated World War I enlisted man, Sergeant Edward Younger, placed a spray of roses on one of them at the city hall in Chalons-sur-Marne. Thus *the Unknown Soldier* was chosen (Britain had brought home an *Unknown Warrior* from Flanders in 1920, to be interred at Westminster Abbey). Representing all American soldiers of World

War I whose graves were unknown, the Unknown Soldier was returned to the U.S. and lay in state for two days in the Capitol rotunda. On November 11, 1921, the casket was placed in *the Tomb of the Unknown Soldier* in Arlington National Cemetery. On Memorial Day 1958 the bodies of two more unknown soldiers, one from World War II and one from the Korean War, were buried beside the original and the tomb was briefly designated as *the Tomb of the Unknowns.*

What Price Glory? was asked by the title of a 1924 play about the ugliness, brutality, and profanity of the war, written by Lawrence Stallings (who had lost a leg in combat) and Maxwell Anderson. For the Allies the price of victory had been some 40 million men in uniform, of whom 16 million were killed or wounded (the total for both sides is estimated as 9-million dead, 20 million wounded, including the 125,000 American troops killed and 200,000 wounded). In monetary terms, the U.S. had spent $22 billion on its own war effort and sent its allies $10 billion more in supplies and materials (Britain owed the U.S. almost $5 billion and France $4 billion, never to be repaid). The losers were to pay *reparations* (until 1921 *reparation* had meant reconciliation).

A Farewell to Arms was Ernest Hemingway's 1929 novel describing the Italian rout at Caporetto in 1917 (which occurred the year before he went overseas as an ambulance driver, where he observed three weeks of bloody fighting before a trench-mortar shell put him out of action). But for the world it wasn't a farewell to arms or "the Last War." It was merely to be *World War I*, a term used as early as 1918 by a few cynics, implying that it was not to be the last major war and that the terms of its ending would not lead to lasting peace. By 1939 everyone sadly knew that indeed it merely had been *World War I.*

Pack up your troubles in your old kit bag
  And smile, smile, smile.
While you've a lucifer to light your fag,
  Smile, boys, that's the style.
What's the use of worrying?
  It never was worth while,
So, pack up your troubles in your old kit bag,
  And smile, smile, smile.
    "Pack Up Your Troubles In Your Old Kit Bag," by "George Asaf" (George and Felix Powell) in 1915 for the London show *Her Soldier Boy*

Mademoiselle from Armentières, parlay-voo,
Mademoiselle from Armentières, parlay-voo,
Mademoiselle from Armentières,
She never heard of underwear.
Hinky dinky parlay-voo.

"Mademoiselle from Armentières," the popular soldiers' song of the war had innumerable versions. It was based on an old song by "Harry Wincott" (Alfred Walden) and beloved by the British Army even before "Red" Rowley updated it around 1915.

Keep the home fires burning
While your hearts are yearning,
Tho' your lads are far away
They dream of home.
There's a silver lining
Thro' the dark cloud shining,
Turn the dark cloud inside out,
Till the boys come home.

"Keep the Home Fires Burning," Lena Guilbert Ford, with music by Ivor Novello, 1915.

It's a long way to Tipperary,
It's a long way to go.
It's a long way to Tipperary
To the sweetest girl I know.
Goodbye, Piccadilly,
Farewell, Leicester Square,
It's a long way to Tipperary
But my heart's right there
Yearning for home.

"It's a Long Way to Tipperary." Written several years before the war began, it was about an Irishman longing for his beloved Tipperary County in Southern Ireland, but became a popular soldier's song.

Over there, over there,
Send the word, send the word, over there.
That the Yanks are coming, the Yanks are coming,
The drums rum-tumming everywhere. . . .

"Over There," written by George M. Cohan on April 6, 1917, after reading the newspaper headline that the U.S. had entered the war. It became America's major World War I song and Cohan received a Congressional Medal for having written it. Other American war songs ranged from "I Didn't Raise My Boy to be a Soldier," written before the U.S. entered the war, to "Hello, Central, Give Me No-Man's Land," "If He Can Fight Like He Can Love," Irving Berlin's 1917 "Oh, How I Hate To Get Up in the Morning," (written for the all-soldier show *Yip, Yip, Yaphank*), and "There's a Long, Long Trail Awinding."

World War II and GI Joe

World War II followed World War I by 21 years. Both got their names in 1918 when critics of the Treaty of Versailles said that the war that had just ended would be but World War I and that a second would follow—thus World War II was named 21 years before it began (though the U.S. armed forces didn't officially use the name until 1942, when there was indeed fighting around the world, in Europe, Africa, Asia, and in the Atlantic and the Pacific). The critics were right: the unrealistic Treaty of Versailles, plus the weakness of the League of Nations, a worldwide depression, and the promises of the Japanese Emperor, of Hitler, and of Mussolini to return nationalistic glory to their people, brought about the second world war.

The long Chinese-Japanese war began in 1931 when Japan

invaded Manchuria (after Pearl Harbor this long war merely became part of World War II); Mussolini attacked Ethiopia in October, 1935, and seized Albania in April, 1939; Hitler marched into the Rhineland in March, 1936, and into Austria in March, 1938, then was given Czechoslovakia's northern region of the Sudetenland by British Prime Minister Neville Chamberlain and French Premier Édouard Daladier in the Munich Pact of September 30, 1938. When the umbrella-carrying Chamberlain returned from Munich, many praised him for trying to obtain "peace at any price" and he triumphantly announced that he had won "peace with honor . . . peace for our time."

NEW AUSTRO-GERMAN EMPIRE

Hitler Crosses Border on Way to Capital; 3,000 German Troops Fly Into Vienna

'No Power Can Drive Us Out,' Fuehrer Tells Cheering 250,000

German tanks, flying the Nazi swastika, cross into the remaining territory of independent Czechoslovakia on March 15, 1939. There were no cheering crowds to greet them as there were in Austria. Germany had already annexed the Sudetenland in September, 1938.

peace at any price was a phrase coined by French Minister of Foreign Affairs Alphonse de Lamartine in 1848. It had then become an American political slogan of the Know Nothings who supported Millard Fillmore for president in 1856 (they used it to mean they were willing to accept slavery for Blacks in order to avoid a civil war).

418

peace with honor was used by Chamberlain to compare himself to Disraeli, who had coined the phrase upon his return from Berlin in 1878 where, after the last of the Russo-Turkish wars and the Treaty of San Stefano, he had acquired Cyprus for England and forced Russia to give Macedonia back to the Turks.

As can be heard from the above, the key words of world policy during the rise of the Japanese empire, Mussolini, and Hitler were *nonintervention* and *appeasement* (a word first used in this pre-World War II political context by *The London Times* in 1934). Some American appeasers even said England and France had offered Hitler "too little, too late" (1935, the expression was to be widely used in 1941–42 to explain our unpreparedness for war and our early defeats). Meantime, however, President Roosevelt called those Americans who said that nothing could be done either to stop the depression here at home or Hitler abroad *defeatists* (1936). America also had:

> *isolationists* (an 1862 Americanism) who preached *isolationism*, originally used in 1922 during the nationwide debate on whether or not to join the League of Nations. The isolationists America talked about most in the 1930s included the two anti-labor, anti-Roosevelt, anti-Semitic spokesmen, the Reverend Gerald L. K. Smith and "Father Coughlin," the Reverend Charles Coughlin, famous as "the radio priest" with 30 million listeners. Both they and more respected isolationists believed that the U.S. should not defend other countries because, regardless of what happened in Europe, Hitler would never cross the Atlantic to attack *fortress America*.
>
> *interventionists* (a World War I English word of 1915), those who wanted the U.S. to intervene against *totalitarianism* in the 1930s. The isolationists often called them *warmongers* (a 1590 English word), especially after the war in Europe began in 1939.
>
> *America Firsters*, 1940, members of the America First Committee, whose best-known spokesman, our hero Charles Lindbergh (who had lived in Germany in the late 1930s and been vastly impressed by German air power) urged America to stay out of the war because the Nazis were invincible in Europe. Other America Firsters said we should not oppose Hitler or Mussolini because fascism was "the wave of the future" (a term popularized by Lindbergh's wife, Anne Morrow Lindbergh, in her controversial 1940 book *The Wave of the Future*, which seemed to be an apology for fascism).
>
> *the Neutrality Acts*, a series of acts Congress passed in 1935–37 to help keep the U.S. out of war by forbidding the selling or transporting of weapons to belligerents (as Italy and Ethiopia in 1935).

After concluding a firm military alliance with Italy in May, 1939, and a ten-year nonaggression pact with Russia in August (giving Russia a free hand in the Baltic states and Germany a free hand in Poland), Hitler again demanded the return of the free Baltic port city of Danzig and the creation of a German corridor through the Polish corridor, which had been created by the Treaty of Versailles to divide East Prussia from the rest of Germany and give Poland an outlet to the Baltic. These demands finally brought an end to England's and France's appeasement and they declared they would fight for Poland if it were attacked. On September 1, 1939, Hitler attacked Poland. Two days later France and England declared war on Germany. World War II had begun.

Most Americans had read about World War I in their newspapers, but we heard World War II on the radio—and Vietnam was to be the war we were to see on television. Because we heard it reported as it happened on nightly newscasts, World War II seemed more immediate than World War I and, perhaps because we didn't see it, more personal and glamorous than Vietnam (television took the glamour out of war). First we listened to our radios tell of the children being sent out of London and other large English cities to the countryside to escape the expected German bombings. Then we heard and talked about the *Western Front* and of France's supposedly invincible Maginot Line, then in the spring of 1940 of how Germany flanked it and invaded the Low Countries. After "the miracle of *Dunkirk*" in May, 1940, and the "tragic fall of France" in June (see *the Free French* in the list below) it became obvious that if Germany were to be halted, we would have to give up our policy of neutrality and at least become "The Arsenal of

Nazi leaders at rally in Nuremberg, Germany. Nuremberg was an important city to Nazi Germany: the National Socialist party held its annual meetings here; the Nuremberg Laws, depriving Jews of their civil rights, were announced here; and, a center for the manufacture of war materiel, it was heavily bombed by the Allies. After the war the major war crime trials were held in Nuremberg. Adolf Hitler (1889–1945) stands third from right; on his left Herman Goering (1893–1946), founder of the Gestapo or German secret police, and Heinrich Himmler (1900–45), third from left, fanatic racist and ruthless head of the Gestapo after Goering, the man primarily responsible for setting up the infamous concentration camps. All three escaped execution after the war by committing suicide.

420

Yesterday, December 7, 1941—a day that will live in infamy—the United States of America was suddenly and deliberately attacked by naval and air forces of the Empire of Japan.

Franklin D. Roosevelt, war message to Congress, December 8, 1941. The "Day of Infamy" then became a popular reference to December 7 and the Japanese bombing of Pearl Harbor.

Democracy" (see *Lend Lease* in the list below). Next we listened to our radios for nightly scores of the RAF and Luftwaffe planes downed and talked with love and gratitude of "brave little England" standing alone in *the Battle of Britain*. We rooted for Greece and its hill-fighting guerrillas after Italy invaded it from Albania in October, 1940, and for Yugoslavia and its partisans under General Mihailovic and Marshal Tito after Germany, Italy, Hungary, and Bulgaria attacked and occupied it in April, 1941. Most Americans talked with relief of Hitler's invasion of Russia on June 22, 1941—since Russia had signed the nonaggression pact which freed Germany to attack Poland on September 1, 1939, and then on September 17 had joined Germany by invading Poland from the east, we had feared Russia was on Germany's side. Now we began to forgive Russia for the Russo-Finnish War and were glad that England had a fighting ally.

We were frightened and confused by the first radio bulletins about "the sneak attack" of the Japanese on Pearl Harbor and the Philippines on Sunday, December 7, 1941, then talked about how "the dirty Japs" had crippled our Pacific fleet in the attack, but were somewhat relieved and even exhilarated finally to be in the war and fighting with *the Allies* against *the Axis*. Then all America talked in a sad whisper about Bataan and the fall of Corregidor on May 6, 1942. The war news had all been depressing until two days after Corregidor fell, when a British and American fleet defeated the Japanese at the Battle of the Coral Sea, then that same month U.S. planes started bombing Hitler's Europe (see *the B-17* in the list below). In June we gleefully talked of the Battle of Midway and in August of our first offensive: the Marines had landed at Guadalcanal, beginning the slow, bloody *island hopping* strategy under General Douglas MacArthur. It seemed that in less than a year of effort America had built up its military strength to fight back. However, the Japanese had taken all of Southeast Asia and many

U.S. Marines raise the American flag on Guadalcanal, October, 1942. It took six months of bitter fighting to capture the island.

421

Pacific islands and the Germans had reached Moscow and Leningrad (which withstood a 900-day siege, August, 1941–January, 1944).

Even before *the Battle of the Atlantic* was won, however, Roosevelt and Churchill had agreed on an attack on "the soft underbelly of the Axis," as Churchill called it, and in November, 1942, General Eisenhower led the greatest massing of land, sea, and air power up to that time in the amphibious landings at Casablanca, Oran, and Algiers in North Africa. This invasion caught the German and Italian troops in a giant pincers as British forces under Field Marshal Montgomery pushed eastward and Eisenhower's westward; all Axis troops in North Africa surrendered in May, 1943 (see *the Afrika Korps* in the list below). From our newly won bases in Africa we launched an offensive against Italy in July (see *Anzio* below), Italy surrendering in September but German troops fighting on there so that Rome was not taken until June, 1944. From our new Italian bases we bombed southern Germany and the German-held Balkans. While we amassed troops and supplies in England for a final invasion of Western Europe itself, all America speculated when this "second front," which Russia had so long demanded, would begin. It began on June 6, 1944, *D-Day*, when General Eisenhower, Supreme Commander of the invasion forces, sent its 4,000 warships, transports, and landing craft with their British and American troops across the English Channel, landing at Normandy in northeastern France. We talked with mounting excitement as our invasion force liberated France and Belgium by late 1944, moving ever eastward despite desperate German resistance, including a December counterattack (see *the Battle of the Bulge* below).

Meanwhile, since the Battle of Stalingrad (August, 1942–February, 1943), Russia had turned the tide against the Germans, forcing the Axis out of the Balkans and driving deep into Poland and Hungary, advancing all along *the Eastern Front*. Now Germany itself was caught in a giant pincers with the Russians to the east and the Americans and British to the west, beginning "a race to Berlin" and meeting at the Elbe River on April 25, 1945, with Berlin falling to the Russians. Hitler and his mistress, Eva Braun, committed suicide in the burning ruins of Berlin on the night of April 30 and on the night of May 7 the German High Command accepted *unconditional surrender*. The war in Europe was over (see *V-day* in the list below).

Also in that spring and summer of 1945 the U.S. Marines finished their island hopping, taking Iwo Jima (only 750 miles from Tokyo) in March and, after a three-month battle, capturing Okinawa (only 360 miles from the main Japanese islands) in June. American troops were poised for the final massive invasion of Japan when, on the morning of August 6, a solitary American plane flew over the city of Hiroshima and dropped one atomic bomb (see the entry THE ATOMIC BOMB). Japan surrendered on August 14.

During World War II we still used such words as *furlough* and *discharge* from THE REVOLUTIONARY WAR; *AWOL* and *draftee* from THE CIVIL WAR; and *convoy*, *dog tag*, *the duration*, *foxhole*, *KP*, and *U-boat* from WORLD WAR I. Other terms and names that we used over and over were new. Such new terms that came out of World War II or the events leading up to it include:

Abel, *Baker*, and *Charlie*, the military designations given the three squads of an Army platoon and later the three platoons of a company. The names are from the Signal Corps radio communication words for the letters A, B, and C.

the Afrika Korps, Germany's motorized, armored army in North Africa, led by Marshal Erwin Rommel, who earned the name "the Desert Fox" in 1942 for his quick attacks and elusive retreats. Beginning in September, 1940, Italian forces from Libya and British forces from Egypt began waging a seesaw desert war for control of North Africa (and the Mediterranean). By December the British had chased the Italians into Libya, but then Rommel and his Afrika Korps arrived and North Africa became a scene of huge armored battles as British and German tanks fought back and forth across hundreds of miles of desert. Finally, in May, 1942, with his faster, heavier tanks, Rommel drove the British 250 miles into Egypt, all the way to El Alamein. Then, using his new U.S. *Sherman tanks*, Field Marshal Montgomery won the Battle of El Alamein and in October, 1942, led the British 8th Army in a drive that forced the Axis troops all the way back through Libya and Tunisia. In November, 1942, the Allied land, sea, and air task force under General Eisenhower made landings in Casablanca, Oran, and Algiers, catching the Axis forces between Eisenhower in the west and Montgomery in the east. The pincers closed and all Axis forces in North Africa surrendered on May 12, 1943.

the Allies included 46 countries, ranging from Costa Rica with its 500-man fighting force to the United States and Russia with 12 million troops each. The name was a continuation of *the Allies* of World War I.

the Big Three were the leaders of the Allies: England, Russia, and the U.S. The name echoed *the Big Four* of World War I.

amphibious landing, an invasion by sea. Troops and vehicles were brought close to shore by large *landing ships*, then usually transferred to smaller *landing craft* which took them to the beach. Our best-known transports for this purpose included the *LSD* (*Landing Ship, Deck*), a landing ship carrying smaller landing craft in a large inner compartment which was flooded to launch them. Two of the better-known landing craft were the *LCI* (*Landing Craft Infantry*, to carry troops

Marine tanks reinforce the beach-head *on Iwo Jima.*

to the beach) and the *LCT* (*L*anding *C*raft *T*ank, to land tanks on the beach).

> *beachhead*, the initial amphibious landing site which had to be "secured" from its defenders before additional troops and supplies were landed.

Anzio, Cassino. After winning North Africa in May, 1943, the Allies landed in Sicily in July and began an invasion of Italy. Italy surrendered in September, but the Germans continued to fight there and had to be driven up the Italian peninsula. They held out against heavy bombings and artillery fire at the 6th century abbey of *Monte Cassino* (which they used as a fortress), half way between Naples and Rome, from January to May, 1944. At the same time, 33 miles to the south, at the small central Italian bathing resort of *Anzio*, the Allied beachhead forces were pinned down in long, bloody fighting.

> *open city.* The Italians declared Rome an "open city," a city left open to enemy occupation, in order to gain its immunity from bombardment. Rome was thus often referred to as "the Open City."

the Axis originally meant only Germany and Italy but finally included Germany, Italy, Japan, Bulgaria, Hungary, Rumania, and Finland (though Finland never declared war on the U.S.). The name was coined and made common by Mussolini who, after signing an agreement with Hitler in 1936, called Berlin and Rome "an axis around which all European states . . . can . . . assemble."

the B-17—bombers and fighters. In December, 1941, the month the U.S. entered the war and six months after *the Battle of Britain* (see below) ended, Britain's *RAF* (the *R*oyal *A*ir *F*orce) started its own small-scale bombing of Germany. Allied *air power* increased greatly as the U.S. built up its forces, producing hundreds of thousands of planes (see *defense plant* under *Lend Lease* below) and trained hundreds of thousands of airmen. Allied bombers became one of the heroes of the war and, as air raids on the Axis continued, we used such new names and terms as:

strategic bombing. The first RAF bombing raids on Germany in December, 1941, had specific strategic targets (German factories), as opposed to the massive bombing raids on British cities during the Battle of Britain—to point out this difference the British called these raids *strategic bombing raids*. Throughout the rest of the war *strategic bombing* meant the bombing of specific targets (the opposite was soon called *saturation bombing*, see below).

saturation bombing. On the night of May 30–31, 1942, some 1,000 British bombers dropped 2,000 tons of bombs in 90 minutes on Cologne, Germany; on the following night 1,000 planes bombed Essen; and on June 25, some 1,000 planes bombed Bremen (these were the only "1,000 plane raids" of the war). The very first of these raids introduced the term *saturation bombing*, the term the British used to describe it. This became a military term for any raid of massed bombers on target areas rather than on a specific target. Such raids were almost always made at night and led by *pathfinder* planes which dropped flares on or around the target area.

blockbuster. The RAF's early saturation bombings used 1,000 planes because each carried only a limited number of small bombs. To make bombing more effective the size of the bombs and of the bomb loads (and of bombers) were constantly increased. In June, 1942, the RAF dropped the first 4,000-pound bomb and in September the first 8,000-pound one, these 8,000-pound bombs immediately being dubbed *blockbusters*, since they could destroy an entire city block. By the time the war in Europe ended England and the U.S. had 22,000-pound bombs.

the Norden bombsight was talked of with awe during the war as a "secret weapon" which made the success of our strategic bombing raids possible. It was popularly known as a "gyroscopic bombsight" which could be used effectively despite the roll and yaw of a plane. The device was named after its Java-born Dutch inventor, Carl Lukas Norden (1880–1965), who had come to America in 1904. It was tested by the army in 1931 and the Sperry Gyroscope Company received a contract to manufacture it in 1933.

the B-17 (*B* for bomber, *17* was the model number) first went into action from England in early 1942. It was a four-engine (radial piston engines) *heavy bomber*, the largest bomber anyone had ever seen up to that time. It eventually had a crew of ten, including six machine gunners (the *tail gunner* was called *butt-end Charlie* by the air crews). It was called *the Flying Fortress* as soon as its presence was announced.

around-the-clock bombing. The B-17 with its Norden bombsight was initially used for specialized *precision bombing* in daylight raids on German targets while the smaller,

A bomb crater in a London street, 1944.

425

less protected British four-engine *Lancasters* and *Halifaxes* continued their night raids of less precise strategic and saturation bombing—creating the *around-the-clock bombing* of enemy targets (the small, fast British de Havilland *Mosquito bomber* was used both in daylight and at night).

the B-29. In 1943-44 most of us were awed by our first sight of the mammoth B-29, the Boeing *Superfortress* with a range of 4,000 miles. The bigger bombers were necessary not only to carry more bombs and more machine gunners, but as *long-range bombers*, to carry enough fuel to cross the vast reaches of the Pacific to bomb Japan from our island bases (see *island hopping* below). *Superfortress* and its *-fortress* ending were later applied to the ever larger, more complex *intercontinental bombers* built by the U.S. after the war, including the B-50 *Jet Superfortress* and the high-flying, eight-jet B-52 *Stratofortress*, put into service in 1955.

the P-37, the P-40, the P-47, and *the P-51* (P for pursuit) were just several of the American fighters, *fighter-bombers*, and bomber *escort planes* we talked about widely during the war. The Republic P-47 *Thunderbolt* was a fighter-bomber; North America's P-51 *Mustang* was equipped with *wing-drop tanks* (later known as *wing-tip tanks*) that were jettisoned after their fuel was consumed, giving the plane a 2,000-mile range to escort long-range bombers.

the Battle of the Atlantic was the long battle by British and U.S. cargo ships, convoys, destroyers, and planes against German submarines and bombers to keep the Atlantic shipping lanes between the U.S. and England open, so that weapons and supplies could reach England from America. The term was coined by the First Lord of the Admiralty, A. V. Alexander, on March 15, 1941. The battle for the control of the North Atlantic began in September, 1939, and was all but over by

A U.N. convoy follows behind a U.S. destroyer in the North Atlantic. During the war United Nations *referred to* the Allies.

London after the Blitz. *St. Paul's Cathedral is in the foreground.*

A German incendiary bomb *started this fire in London, November, 1940.*

1943, when Allied detecting devices, destroyers, and planes stopped our heavy losses to the Germans. German submarines were still often called *U-boats* (see WORLD WAR I); in World War II we destroyed 781 Axis submarines, 400 of them by aircraft.

the Battle of Britain. After Dunkirk and the fall of France in the summer of 1940 Britain stood alone, bracing for Hitler's expected *cross-channel invasion.* Instead of invading Britain, however, Hitler began an air attack to bring Britain to its knees. The bombing of British cities began with a *daylight raid* on London in September, 1940, with about 100 of the 400 German planes being shot down; the Germans then concentrated on *night raids* on London, Birmingham, Bristol, Coventry, Liverpool, and other English cities, using up to 450 bombers on London a night and destroying much of the city by the end of the year. The concentrated, almost nightly, bombings of English cities lasted almost two years, against the defense of the RAF and antiaircraft guns, and was called *the Battle of Britain, the London Blitz,* or simply *the Blitz.* From the beginning this air war over Britain had us using such terms as *air raid, air-raid shelter, air raid warden, blackout, bomb shelter* (more common than *air-raid shelter* in 1940), and *incendiary bomb.*

Hitler began the Battle of Britain with about 3,000 planes against Britain's 800 fighter planes, but Britain's fighters included many well-armored, 8-gun planes flown by well-trained RAF pilots, soon supported by effective radar. Late every night or at breakfast in the morning Americans listened to radio newscasts of which cities had been bombed and how many RAF or Luftwaffe planes had been downed. We talked about Germany's *Messerschmitt* fighter planes (named after German aircraft designer Willy Messerschmitt) and of the brave and daring RAF pilots in their *Spitfires* and Hawker *Hurricanes* who somehow

427

managed against seemingly overwhelming odds to hold Hitler at bay (the Hawker *Hurricane* was the first British fighter to exceed 300 miles per hour, and it shot down more German planes in the Battle of Britain than all other defenses combined). Finally Hitler, like Napoleon before him, decided to attack Russia and with this attack, in June, 1941, diverted German bombers from England—the Battle of Britain was over.

the Battle of the Bulge—Nuts! After D-Day the Allied invading forces advanced steadily into Europe. Then on December 16, 1944, the Germans launched their final counterattack of the war. This attack created a "bulge" 60 miles deep in the Belgium-Luxembourg sector of the Allied lines, trapping U.S. forces in the snow-filled Ardennes forest: the fighting during this German counterattack became known as *the Battle of the Bulge*, the 28 German divisions fighting to break through the bulge they had made in the weak center of the Allied lines, the U.S. forces fighting to contain and eliminate the bulge. We set up a defense at the important road junction at Bastogne, Belgium and were soon outnumbered and surrounded. There, on December 21, German officers bore a message to American General Anthony "Old Crock" McAuliffe, acting commander of our 101st Airborne Division, telling him his position was hopeless and asking him to surrender. Knowing that he must prevent the Germans from bursting through the bulge, McAuliffe gave his instantly famous one-word reply "Nuts!" The German officer wasn't used to American slang, he asked McAuliffe's aide what "Nuts!" meant and the aide told him "It means 'go to hell.'" McAuliffe's men held their ground for a week, until heavy fog lifted and our air raids made a shambles of the German supply roads, then the 80th Infantry and 3rd Armored Division broke through the German line. The "bulge" was straightened in January, 1945, and the Allied advance continued (77,000 Americans and 120,000 Germans had been casualties in this German counterattack: Bastogne renamed its main square after McAuliffe).

battlewagon, 1935, became a common World War II word for battleship (*battleship* itself was a name for the U.S. Navy first used officially as a designation for a type of ship in 1794).

the bazooka was originally a homemade trombone made from two pieces of stove pipe and a whiskey funnel by one of the last famous *Arkansas traveler* comedians, Bob Burns (he made and named it around 1905). It became his well-known laugh-getting prop on stage and radio in the late 1930s. Some linguists believe the word is related to the Dutch *bazuim*, trumpet, trombone, others say it comes from the slang *bazoo*, which has meant a big or loud mouth since 1860—but Burns meant the name to be comical and took it from the spitting ba-zoo, ba-zoo sound the instrument made. Then in 1943 Major Zeb Hastings named the infantry's new antitank rocket gun after Bob Burns' comical musical instrument. Soon the *bazooka* was being widely talked about as the infantryman's godsend against Hitler's tanks. The small, steel tube, about five feet long and three inches in diameter, could be carried by one man and fired from a shoulder rest. As Burns said about his musical

Hitler's blitzkrieg *rolls through shattered Poland, September, 1939.*

instrument and the antitank weapon named after it, "both have a more or less devastating effect."

B-girl. Bar girl was first recorded in 1938, meaning a girl employed or encouraged by a bar owner to talk and drink with the male customers. She earned a commission on the drinks bought and could also solicit the customers as a prostitute. During World War II the bar girl grew into the *B-girl* (shortened from *bar girl* but also having the connotation of being "grade B"). Bars didn't have to pay B-girls, they earned their money as local prostitutes and drank their way from one bar to another looking for customers.

V-girls (a short form of *Victory girl*) weren't prostitutes, they "gave it away," helping the war effort by "being nice" to men in uniform. They were promiscuous with men in uniform because they found servicemen glamorous, because their own men were away at war, or simply because of wartime opportunity.

the black market, as originally used during World War II meant the market in buying and selling stolen military supplies, such as clothing, blankets, food, and truck tires. It soon came to mean the illegal market in buying and selling rationed, scarce, or price-controlled items of any kind, ranging from cigarettes and silk stockings (which could sometimes be purchased "under the counter" from merchants who saved such items for favored customers or to sell at exorbitant prices) through guns and tractors to contraband such as drugs. The term had also seen some use in World War I, when it entered English as a translation of the German *Schwarzmarkt.*

blitzkrieg (a German word, from *Blitz*, lightning + *Krieg*, war), an overpowering, high-speed armored attack, first heard in connection with Hitler's overwhelming *panzer* attack (see below) on Poland that began the war, on September 1, 1939. By 1940 the word was shortened to *blitz.*

bookburners now means self-appointed censors, as those who seek to ban books they consider immoral or unpatriotic. The word originally referred to the thousands of pro-Nazi students who on May 10, 1933, ended a torchlight parade at the University of Berlin by burning a pile of 20,000 books while Nazi Propaganda Minister Joseph Goebbels proclaimed "The soul of the German people can express itself. These flames . . . illuminate the . . . end of an old era [and] light up the new." Throughout their reign the Nazis continued to destroy or suppress books which did not conform to their ideas of Germany's preeminent place in culture and history or to their social and economic theories.

the Bund, the common name for *the German-American Bund* (itself a translation of *Deutschamericanische Volkbund*, literally "the German-American People's League") was established in the U.S. in 1936 by Fritz Lieber Kuhn. It and the American branch of the Nazi party, the National Socialist Party, founded in 1924, were active in some German neighborhoods in America in the 1930s, especially in New York City's Yorkville section, marching, drilling, staging pro-Hitler rallies, attacking Jews and those who opposed German expansion, etc. Both groups were sometimes called *Brownshirts* or "our own Brown-

A German-American Bund parade in Yorkville, New York City, 1939.

shirts" (see *Storm trooper* below). The basic, pre-Nazi word *bund*, a German borrowing meaning group, league, club, was first recorded in America in 1867.

Bundles for Britain was originally an organization founded by Mrs. Wales Latham (and sponsored by Mrs. Winston Churchill) in New York City on January 15, 1940, to send bundles of food and clothing to English civilians. Soon a "bundle for Britain" came to mean any package of food or clothing sent to needy friends or relatives in Britain and was even used humorously to refer to Lend Lease (see below).

the Burma Road was a 700-mile military supply road built in 1937–38 between Lashio, Burma and Kunming, China. In 1943, a year after Burma fell to the Japanese, the Allies began to re-open an overland route to China with two jungle-fighting units, *Merrill's Marauders* (under Brigadier General Frank Merrill) and *Wingate's Raiders* (under General Orde Wingate). These guerrillas hacked a new road through the jungle from Ledo, India to Myitkyina, Burma (this road was named after General "Vinegar Joe" Stilwell, commander of the Chinese-Burma forces and best remembered for *Stilwell's march*, in which he led a group of soldiers and civilians out of Burma into India).

buzz bombs were the "flying bombs" Germany began launching from Europe against London and other English cities beginning in September, 1944, three months after D-Day. We called the two types of buzz bombs the *V-1* and the *V-2*, which was their German designation, shortened from *Vergeltungswaffe eins* and *Vergeltungswaffe zwei* (literally "retaliation weapon one" and "retaliation weapon two"). The V-1, the first type of buzz bomb, was launched from German-occupied France between September, 1944 and March, 1945, and was actually a small pilotless plane, hence was also called a *robot bomb*; it used Germany's newly developed *pulsejet* engine, which gave the bomb its buzzing noise and name. The V-2 bombs were launched from German-occupied Belgium; they were true *liquid-fuel rockets* which descended almost vertically at supersonic speeds (they were developed by Germany's Werner Von Braun, who later played a key role in the U.S. space program).

430

commando (from Afrikaans *kommando*, a unit of troops under one command) entered the English language during the Boer War, 1899–1902, to refer to the South African Republic and Orange Free State guerrilla units, led by such men as Smuts, who fought Kitchener's troops. However, many Americans first heard and used the word to refer to specially trained British troops who made daring raids on occupied Europe early in World War II, its first use then being in radio and newspaper accounts of England's first *commando raid*, made on March 7, 1941, at the head of the Vest fjord near Narvik, Norway, to destroy a fish-oil plant making glycerine. The largest such commando raid was the "reconnaissance in force" by 7,000 men on Dieppe, August 19, 1942, using 1,000 Allied fighter planes as air protection. This protective air armada was called an *umbrella*, the first time the word was used in this way.

Ranger, the U.S. counterpart of a British commando.

concentration camp is still mainly used to refer to the unspeakably brutal German prison camps where millions of civilians were imprisoned, killed, tortured, and starved during World War II, because they opposed the Nazis or simply weren't members of Hitler's "master race." The term was an old one, originally meaning a detention camp where civilians who might help rebels or guerrillas were "concentrated" under the watchful eyes of government or colonial troops. Thus Spain had its notorious "reconcentration camps" in Cuba in the 1890s (see The Spanish-American War) and Lord Kitchener established *concentration camps* for South Africans in 1902, during the Boer War. As early as 1934 an American Inquiry Commission headed by Clarence Darrow collected evidence and heard testimony about concentration camps being built by the Nazis in Germany to hold political prisoners. However, it was not until early 1945, when Allied troops captured areas where major Nazi concentration camps were located, that we learned the full horrors of the *death camps* and *gas chambers* where six million Jews and hundreds of thousands of Gypsies, political prisoners, physical and mental defectives, etc., were systematically put to death (gas, starvation, and other methods were used because there simply weren't enough bullets to kill all the people the Nazis wanted killed). In 1945, too, the word *genocide* entered the language (from Greek *genos*, race + *-cide*, killing, killer), referring to Germany's attempt to wipe out the Jews.

D-Day was June 6, 1944, the day the long-awaited Allied invasion of Hitler's Europe began. Planned under the code name *Operation Overlord*, 4,000 transports and landing craft protected by 600 warships and 11,000 planes landed 175,000 British and American troops along a 50-mile *beachhead* (see above) on the beaches of Normandy. The invasion was under the *Supreme Commander* of *the Allied Expeditionary Force*, General Dwight D. Eisenhower. *D-Day* and *H-hour*, meaning the exact day and hour a military operation is to take place, were first used in the Saint Mihiel offense by the Allies on September 17, 1918, in World War I.

June 6, 1944 is also called *the Longest Day* because of both its bloody fighting and the waiting to see if this, the most im-

A landing was made this morning on the coast of France by the troops of the Allied Expeditionary Force. This landing is part of the concerted United Nations plan for the liberation of Europe. . . .
General Dwight D. Eisenhower, radio broadcast to the people of Western Europe, D-Day, June 6, 1944.

D-Day, *France. American troops pouring from* LCI's *establish a* beachhead *in Normandy under heavy enemy fire.*

I walked around what seemed to be a couple of pieces of driftwood sticking out of the sand. But they weren't driftwood. They were a soldier's two feet . . . the toes of his G.I. shoes pointing toward the land he had come so far to see, and which he saw so briefly.

A description of a dead American soldier on Normandy beachhead, June, 1944, written by the beloved World War II war correspondent Ernie Pyle in his 1944 book *Brave Men.* Pyle himself was killed by Japanese gunfire on a small island off the coast of Okinawa in 1945.

portant action of the war, would succeed or fail. The Allied troops were invading Hitler's *Fortress Europe* (from German *Festung Europe*) and had to breach *the Atlantic Wall*, the strong German defenses along the coast. The Russians had long been demanding a *Second Front* in Europe to divert German strength from their own *Eastern Front* (see below).

Dear John (*letter*), early 1940s, a letter to a soldier from his sweetheart, fiancée, or wife that she was breaking with him, usually because she had found another in his absence.

Dunkirk (the French and British spell it *Dunkerque*). In April and May of 1940 Germany flanked the Maginot Line on *the Western Front* (see below) and overran Denmark, Norway, the Netherlands, Belgium, and parts of France in a race to encircle all Allied troops in Europe. The British had to evacuate their *British Expeditionary Force* and other Allied troops from Dunkirk, the last escape port open. In a race against the closing German pincers the Admiralty collected all available military and pleasure craft to shuttle the troops from Dunkirk to England. Between May 26 and June 3 and under heavy German bombing attacks about 345,000 troops (about 2/3 of them British and most of the rest French) were evacuated.

the Eastern Front was the front in Eastern Europe along which the Germans and Russians fought. During the major German offensive it moved from Poland eastward all the way to Moscow, Leningrad, and Stalingrad; after the Battle of Stalingrad it moved westward as the Russians pushed the Germans back across Europe into Germany.

Eisenhower jacket, a short, fitted army jacket reaching only to the waist and having a self belt, first worn by General Eisenhower during the war.

ersatz is a German word meaning compensation, replacement. We borrowed it into English by 1940 and used it as did the

Germans, to refer to artificial foods and synthetic items used to replace war-scarce natural ones. Thus *ersatz coffee* was made from something other than coffee, the Germans made *ersatz bread* from potato peelings, etc.

fascist, fascism (from Italian *fascio*, political club) were first heard when Benito Mussolini formed his *Fascio di Combattimento* in 1919, its members being called *Fascisti* and Mussolini's brand of totalitarianism *fascism*.

Il Duce (Italian for leader, commander, chief) was the title Mussolini gave himself in 1922 when, at the age of 39, he became dictator of Italy.

field ration (from the 1702 British use of *ration* to mean a fixed allowance of food for a soldier or sailor) was any ration issued to troops to carry onto the battlefield.

K-ration, an emergency field ration containing all necessary nutrition in a single package. The *K* is for Ancel Keys, the American physiologist who devised this ration.

five star general, a new rank created by Congress December 15, 1944, for Generals Eisenhower, MacArthur, George C. Marshall, and Henry "Hap" Arnold.

flak, antiaircraft fire, 1940 (from the German acronym for *Fl*ieger *A*bwehr *K*anone, aircraft defense gun). *Flak jacket*, a padded vest worn by air crews as body protection against flak. By the end of the war our servicemen were using *flak* or *flack* as a slang word to mean any barrage of words, lies, complaints, etc., that came at one as fast and thick as antiaircraft fire. After the war the word came to mean criticism, nagging, etc., and a *flak* came to mean one whose work is to put out a barrage of words, as in advertising or public relations.

flattop, a World War II term for an aircraft carrier. *Aircraft carrier* itself was a new term around 1910, when the first ones were being planned and designed, though not completed in time for use in World War I. The first U.S. *carrier* was the *Langley*, commissioned in 1922 (it was a converted coal ship). In the vast Pacific battles of World War II aircraft carriers replaced battleships as the main fleet vessel: we built 150 carriers during the war and our *carrier-based planes* destroyed 168 enemy warships, 359 merchant vessels, and 12,000 enemy planes. See also *task force*.

Comin' in on a Wing and a Prayer.
Title of a popular World War II song about a pilot, written by Harold Adamson and Jimmy McHugh (lyrics) in 1943.

A Wildcat fighter plane takes off from an American flattop, *1944.*

flyboy, a glamorous pilot, usually used ironically.

the Flying Tigers, the American Volunteer Group of civilian flyers formed and led by General Claire Chennault to defend China against bombing attacks. It began operations in August, 1941. After the U.S. entered the war it became the Fourteenth Air Force and, though outnumbered and badly supplied, served as the main Chinese fighter force against Japanese bombers until the end of the war.

the Free French, *Vichy*, *puppet government*, and *occupation* all appeared as new terms soon after the fall of Paris to the Germans on June 14, 1940, or the armistice between France and Germany on June 22.

> *Free France.* On June 18, 1940, in England (some two weeks after *Dunkirk*, see above) General Charles de Gaulle started the *Fighting French* movement, composed both of French troops who had escaped at Dunkirk and of French troops who were stationed in the French colonies. The movement became known as *Free France* because that was the name of its press, information service, and fortnightly magazine (an English-language edition of which was published in New York). Members of this Free France movement were then called *the Free French*. They fought with the Allies throughout the war and, of course, it was de Gaulle who became France's best-known postwar leader.

> *Vichy* or *Unoccupied France.* After Dunkirk, what was left of the French army in France fought on for about three weeks. France then signed an armistice with Germany on June 22, 1940, putting the northern half of France under German occupation (this part known as *Occupied France*) and leaving the rest unoccupied and with a French government at Vichy, this part known as *Unoccupied France*, *Vichy*, or *Vichy France*. Although unoccupied, Vichy France was under German influence, and former French premier Henri Pétain, who set up the Vichy government, was called a *puppet* of the Nazis and the Vichy government a *puppet government*, the first widespread use of this term.

> *the occupation* was first widely used in World War II to refer to the occupation of northern France. Later it was used to refer to the period of German occupation of any country—and after the war to refer to the Allied occupation of Germany and our occupation of Japan.

Geronimo! was the shout of U.S. paratroopers on jumping; it was first used in combat during the North African invasion of November, 1942. The yell was coined and popularized by the many American Indians, especially Yakis and Cherokee, in our paratroop units. Geronimo (1829–1909), of course, was the Apache renegade, the prototype of the savage Indian killer to the U.S. Army, which had called him "the Human Tiger" (he was captured in 1866 and by 1904 was on exhibit at the St. Louis World's Fair). After the war *Geronimo!* became a popular exclamation of surprise or delight.

GI Joe. In the 1920s *G.I.* began to be used as the abbreviation for *galvanized iron* in the army and a *G.I.* was a heavy galvanized-iron army garbage can. By 1935, however, *G.I.* stood for *General Issue* (some say *Government Issue*), the initials stamped or stenciled on everything issued to soldiers from underwear to trucks. Meanwhile, from the 1920s through the 1940s *Joe* began to rival *John* as the popular name for any typical guy (*Joe Zilch* was a 1920s term, *Joe College* and *Joe Blow* are from the 1930s, and "a good Joe," "an ordinary Joe," and *Joe Doakes* reached their peak popularity in the 1940s). *G.I.* and *Joe* were combined and first appeared as *G.I. Joe* on June 17, 1942, in Lieutenant Dave Berger's comic strip for *Yank*, the army weekly. Soon *G.I. Joe* became the name for any American soldier, but was most often shortened back to just *GI* (soldiers themselves felt *GI* implied solidarity and didn't usually object to it, but they often felt the *Joe* part was condescending, even though civilians both here and abroad often called them just *Joe*).

> the *GI Bill* (*of Rights*) was the popular name for the Serviceman's Readjustment Act of 1944, passed before the end of the war and entitling veterans to unemployment insurance after discharge, home loans, and payment for part of the costs of college or vocational school education.

> *dogface* also meant a U.S. soldier, or any infantryman, in World War II. The old words *Yank* and sometimes even *doughboy* were used, but *GI* was so common that other terms were relatively little used (though our occupation troops were usually called *Yanks*). See also *sad sack* below.

gizmo, gismo, a gadget or contrivance whose name is unknown; the word seems to have originally been used in the navy.

gobbledygook, meaning verbose, obscure, bureaucratic jargon, was coined by Maury Maverick, chairman of the Smaller War Plant Corporation, in a 1944 memo after attending a wordy committee meeting. He later said the word just came to him but that perhaps he was thinking of the turkey gobblers back in his native Texas and of the "gobbledygobbling" sound they made while strutting so pompously, and that their gobbling ended in a "gook" sound. Gobbledygook was just a continuation of the New Deal's bureaucratic *officialese,* which delighted in such terms as *activation, clearance, coordinator, inplementation, objective, to process* (this verb use dates back to 1884), and *roll-back.* By the early 1950s such talk or writing was also called *bafflegab* and by the early 60s *Pentagonese.*

gook, gooney, or *gooney bird* was what our troops called a native of the Pacific Islands, sometimes any Oriental, and occasionally any non-Anglo-Saxon. *Gook* may come from *goo-goo,* a Spanish-American War term for a Filipino (see THE SPANISH-AMERICAN WAR). *Gooney bird* and *gooney* were originally used in the Pacific to mean an albatross, probably from the 1895 dialect word *gooney, gony* meaning a simpleton. However, *gooney* was certainly influenced by E. C. Segar's comic strip character Alice the Goon, a large, stupid creature who appeared in his *Popeye, the Thimble Theater* around 1935–38, caus-

Bill Mauldin, who became famous for his cartoons of the infantryman's life, won Pulitzer Prizes in 1944 and 1958.

ing any stupid person to be called a *goon* by the late 1930s. Incidentally the famous DC-3, "the three" (see THE FLYING MACHINE) was called *the Gooney Bird* by pilots, another reference to the albatross, which is known for its powers of flight.

gremlin, an imaginary imp causing mechanical problems in an airplane. *Bug* later came to mean a defect or cause of trouble, especially in a new plane, ship, tank, etc. After the war the word *gremlin* disappeared but *bug* remained very much a part of the language.

gung ho (from Chinese *keng ho*, literally "more fiery," fierce, awesome) became a very popular war term meaning eager, full of zeal, devoted.

the home front referred to the civilians here at home, their life, and their contribution to *the war effort*. A major job on the home front was saving old newspapers and magazines for (*waste*) *paper drives* and saving and flattening tin cans for *scrap metal drives*.

hubba-hubba, 1941. See PRETTY GIRLS for details.

island hopping, the U.S. strategy, carried out by General MacArthur, to capture key Pacific Islands that would bring our bombers and troops ever closer to Japan. Our island-hopping offensive began when U.S. Marines "stormed ashore" at Guadalcanal in the Solomon Islands in August, 1942, in the first major amphibious landing in the Pacific, continued through New Guinea, Bougainville, Saipan, and Guam (only 1,300 miles from Tokyo, a 16-hour round trip by B-29 bombers), and ended with the bloody battles for Iwo Jima (750 miles from Tokyo) and Okinawa (360 miles from the Japanese main islands) in the spring and early summer of 1945.

the Japs are what we called the Japanese during World War II, often in the phrase "the dirty Japs" (*Jap* had been a slighting term for a Japanese since 1902). Our troops called a Japanese a *slanteye*, a disparaging term for an Oriental since the 1930s and

I shall return.
General Douglas MacArthur on leaving Corregidor, March 11, 1942, after being ordered by President Roosevelt to escape before Bataan fell.
This is the Voice of Freedom, General MacArthur speaking. People of the Philippines: I have returned.
General Douglas MacArthur on landing at Leyte Island in the Philippines, October 20, 1944.

General Douglas MacArthur (1880–1964) and a group of U.S. Army and Philippine officers wade ashore at Leyte Island.

U.S. military police parade in their Jeeps, *1941. These rugged vehicles were often called* Bugs.

increasingly common through World War II, the Korean war, and the Vietnam war. We also spoke with hatred of "The Rising Sun," the Japanese empire, as symbolized by the rising red sun on its white flag, and of Tojo and Hirohito. Tojo was General Hideki Tojo, the leader of the Japanese extremist military group, who had become premier of Japan in October, 1941, planned the attack on Pearl Harbor, and led the Japanese during most of the war (he was executed for war crimes after the war). Hirohito was the Japanese emperor, the 124th emperor of Japan in a line of direct lineage (he publicly rejected the concept of imperial divinity after the war, in 1946).

Jeep was an army word which the rest of America first heard on February 22, 1941, the day the vehicle was exhibited climbing the steps of the Capitol in Washington, D.C., newspapers all over the country carrying the story and reproducing a photograph of this feat. The car had first been projected by Captain R. G. Howie of the army tank corps in 1932, and the first 70 were made by the Bantam Car Company in 1940. The name *Jeep* came either from: (1) the Ford Motor Company's initials for such a military vehicle, *GP*, for general *p*urpose; or (2) E. C. Segar's Eugene the Jeep, and animal which first appeared in his *Popeye, the Thimble Theater* comic strip on March 16, 1936, made the peeping noise "jeep, jeep," and could do almost anything.

Any *bantam car* designed for the military before and during World War II might be called a *blitz buggy, leaping Lena, puddle jumper,* or *scout car.* The *Jeep,* sometimes also called *the Willy(s)* after it was mass produced by the Willys-Overland Motors Company of Toledo, and the *Peep* were the most famous American ones. The Germans had a famous bantam car too, originally designed for civilian use but found extremely useful by Rommel's Afrika Korps—it was *the Volkswagen* ("the people's car").

the K-9 Corps (a pun on "canine") was the corps of army guard dogs or "war dogs." It was originally known as *D4D* (*D*ogs *for* *D*efense) and sometimes called *the Wags.*

kamikaze, kamikaze pilot (a Japanese word from *kami,* divine, godlike + *kaze,* wind) was one of a group of Japanese *suicide pilots* happy to die for their emperor-god and the glory of Japan. They flew *kamikaze planes*, actually obsolete planes, each carrying a 550-pound bomb, into American ships and other targets. The word *kamikaze* first became known to us in October, 1944, when the pilots were first used to attack U.S. Navy ships in the Battle of Leyte Gulf, the ships protecting the American troops landing at Leyte in the recapture of the Philippines. During the war, 475 kamikaze planes hit Allied ships and 1,500 more were shot down by protective fire. At the war's end 9,000 kamikaze pilots were ready to attack the invasion fleet which Japan was expecting.

Kilroy was here was written on fences, buildings, sidewalks, and restroom walls all over the world by 1942 and had also become a fad expression. This most popular piece of graffiti of all time meant "a U.S. serviceman was here" and "a stranger was here." It first began to appear on a few docks and ships and in large ports in late 1939, which probably means it originated in the merchant marine or the U.S. Navy. There have been dozens of stories about who the original Kilroy was or what "Kilroy" meant to its originators—so many stories that no one knows for sure who or what the original Kilroy was. Many graffiti writers made a drawing to accompany the phrase "Kilroy was here," showing a wide-eyed, bald-headed face peering over a fence which hid everything below his nose, except for his fingers, which were shown gripping the top of the fence—Kilroy was the mischievous outsider, staring at, and probably laughing at, the world.

Lend Lease, cash and carry, the Arsenal of Democracy, and even *defense plant* were all terms that appeared as we supplied the Allies with war equipment even before we enterd the war.

cash and carry. The Neutrality Act of 1939 lifted the arms embargoes of earlier neutrality acts so that we could provide arms to England and France in their fight against Germany. However, this 1939 act had a provision known as the "cash and carry" provision, that England and France had to pay cash for the arms and carry them in their own vessels.

Lend Lease. After Dunkirk and the fall of France it became obvious that if Hitler were to be stopped short of the Western Hemisphere, we would have to offer England more than "cash and carry" aid. On December 29, 1940, President Roosevelt told the nation, "We must become the great arsenal of democracy" and asked Congress for the power to sell, transfer, "lend or lease" to those countries whose defense was vital to the U.S. any weapons or war supplies they needed ("the arsenal of democracy" had been a phrase originally used by French Ambassador to the U.S. Jean Monnet). Congress gave the president the power he wanted in the Lend-Lease Act of March, 1941, our merchant ships were then armed and carried the war cargoes, our destroyers convoyed the merchant ships—and U.S. troops landed in Greenland to safeguard the North Atlantic against Nazi submarine and air attacks.

defense plants are what we called the factories producing war materiel. They truly made us "the arsenal of democracy" by producing between 1940 and the end of the war in 1945: 300,000 planes, 7,000 naval vessels, 2½ million trucks, 1,100,000 light vehicles such as Jeeps and scout cars, 86,000 tanks, 16,000 armored cars, 18 million rifles and sidearms, 2½ million machine guns, and 315,000 pieces of artillery. Much of this was produced for our own war effort, but we provided Great Britain with over $35 billion worth of war equipment and France with over $12 billion.

liberate and *liberation*. At a press conference in May,1944, a month before D-Day, President Roosevelt said that when our expected invasion of Europe began we would be using the word "liberation—not invasion." Thus in word as well as in fact our ridding Western Europe of the Nazis was called "the liberation," and we talked of our troops' "liberating" cities rather than of capturing or occupying them. Our servicemen used *liberate* in another way, to mean to take the spoils of war; thus they "liberated" many bottles of French wine, "liberated" watches from captured German soldiers, etc.

liberty, sailor use for "shore leave," a period of time spent ashore for one's own amusement "at liberty" while a ship is in port.

Liberty ship, the standardized World War II cargo ship of 11,000 tons deadweight capacity built by Henry J. Kaiser's West Coast shipyards, using assembly-line methods. By June, 1942, such a ship could be built in from four to six days.

Victory ship, a faster, turbine-powered version of the Liberty ship.

Loose talk costs lives and *Idle gossip sinks ships* were two of many popular slogans seen on posters and signs in many defense plants, offices, bars, etc., warning everyone not to talk about war-related work, since such talk might eventually give the enemy valuable information: these two messages were printed on envelopes furnished soldiers at USO clubs. Similar messages and slogans included, "The slip of a lip may sink a ship," and, "Enemy ears are listening," used on a poster of the Office of War Information.

the Luftwaffe (German for "air force," literally "air weapon"), the German air force before and during the war.

the M1 and *the Garand* were the popular names of the standard U.S. infantry rifle in World War II, a semiautomatic gas-operated, clip-loaded, .30 caliber rifle weighing approximately 8½ pounds. Its official name was the *M1 Garand*, the *M1* for Model *1* and *Garand* from John Garand (1883-1974) who developed it around 1930 (it was adopted by the army in 1936 and replaced by Garand's fully automatic *M16* in 1957).

> *the BAR* or *the Browning* was what our troops called the Browning Automatic Rifle, an automatic, gas-operated, air-cooled, magazine-fed, .30 caliber rifle firing 200-300 rounds per minute. Invented by John Moses Brown, the BAR had seen some World War I use, but it wasn't widely used and talked about until World War II. A .50 caliber model, *the Browning .50*, was mounted on airplanes.

> *the Sten gun* was a British-made "light submachinegun," actually a machine carbine, named by the initials of its two inventors and their country (*S*heppard + *T*urpin + *En*gland).

Mae West, a canvas and rubber inflatable life vest worn by air crews. The name was first bestowed on it by Royal Air Force aviators in 1939—because wearing this bulky life vest gave one a chest measurement similar to that of the entertainer Mae West.

the Murmansk run, the cargo-ship route to Russia's ice-free Arctic port of Murmansk. Russia began receiving quantities of British and U.S. military supplies in 1941, much of it being taken over the dangerous Murmansk run, within easy range of Germany's North Atlantic submarines and bombers. The name of the route became well-known in 1943 when the number of cargo ships taking it reached a peak and newspapers and movies romanticized the merchant sailors who traveled it.

the Nazis were what we called the Germans in World War II. *Nazi* is the German shortening of *Nationalen Sozialisten*, the National Socialist German Workers' Party, founded in 1919 by Hitler and six others. The German word seems to have first appeared in English in *The London Times* in 1930. We also often called the German enemy *Jerry* and sometimes *Kraut*, but seldom used *Hun* and *Boche* in World War II (see THE GERMANS for details of these words).

    Der Führer (German for "leader") meant Adolf Hitler. In 1933 Hindenburg had appointed Hitler Chancellor of Germany, then on Hindenburg's death in 1934 Hitler united the offices of chancellor and president (with the approval of 80% of the German voters) and took the title *Der Führer*. We also called Hitler by Napoleon's sobriquet *the Little Corporal* (both were short and had been corporals, Hitler in the Bavarian army in World War I), *the Little Napoleon*, *the Little Dictator*, *the Paperhanger* (he had been a house painter for a brief period), and *Schickelgruber*. This last name was originally given Hitler by his political opponents in Vienna in the 1930s to point out that his father was a bastard—his father had borne the mother's family name, Schickelgruber, before winning the right to be called by the father's family name, Hitler.

    the master race. Hitler first called "the Aryan race" the super race in his 1924 *Mein Kampf* ("My Battle"), the book he dictated to his secretary Rudolph Hess while imprisoned for plotting the November, 1920, *beer-hall putsch* to take over Bavaria. By 1929 his propaganda chief Goebbels was calling this supposed Aryan race *the master race*, promising a millenium for "pure-blooded Germans" and blaming all the ills of Germany's 1929 depression on the Treaty of Versailles, communism, and "Jewish capitalism" (Hitler had become a socialist and violent anti-Semite around 1907 when Vienna failed to recognize him as the budding art genius which he and his mother agreed he was).

    the Third Reich (*Reich* is German for empire, republic) was the name of Hitler's Germany. The First Reich had been the Holy Roman Empire (lasting from the 9th century to 1806), the Second Reich had been the German Empire (1871-1919), and the Third Reich was established by Hindenburg in 1933.

90-day wonder, an officer commissioned after only three months of officer's training at an *OCS* (*Officer Candidate School*), as opposed to one who had come up through the ranks or been graduated from West Point or Annapolis. The term was sometimes meant to be derogatory, sometimes only to be humorous.

nylon was invented and named by E. I. du Pont de Nemours and Company in 1938. The trademark name has no meaning but the material has a long-chain molecule which contains the recurring amide group CONH, and the NH may have suggested the name. Women's full-length sheer stockings made of nylon were introduced and called simply *nylons* in 1939: they were to replace silk stockings but both silk and nylon stockings were so scarce in the war (often obtained only "under the counter," see *black market* above) that many women wore tan *leg makeup* to give the impression of wearing such stockings. In fact most of us first heard of nylon when it replaced silk in our World War II airmen's parachutes, which is why nylon was usually called *parachute silk* in the early 1940s.

the OPA (the *O*ffice of *P*rice *A*dministration and Civilian Supply) was established in April, 1941, eight months before Pearl Harbor, to combat the already rampant war-inspired inflation and to see that scarce consumer goods were distributed fairly. It was to combat inflation by recommending specific *price ceilings*, *controls*, or *freezes* on consumer goods (President Roosevelt had first used *freeze* in this way, to refer to a "tax freeze," in 1937). Later, in September, 1942, the president was also given the power to impose *wage freezes* and on July 1, 1943, rents were *frozen*. Besides recommending price ceilings, the OPA was in charge of *rationing* (see below).

There were hundreds of other wartime abbreviations. President Roosevelt had started many *alphabet agencies* (see THE NEW DEAL) in the 1930s and additional government agencies, offices, departments, and corporations continued to proliferate during the war, each with its own abbreviation. Thus we heard such abbreviations as:

OCDM, the *O*ffice of *C*ivil and *D*efense *M*obilization.

ODT, the *O*ffice of *D*efense *T*ransportation.

OEM, the *O*ffice of *E*mergency *M*anagement.

OES, the *O*ffice of *E*conomic *S*tability.

OSS, the *O*ffice of *S*trategic *S*ervices, which trained spies and saboteurs to work with underground movements in Nazi-occupied Europe. This was one of the best known and most romantic sets of wartime initials, conjuring up images of brave men parachuting at night into Europe to blow up Nazi bridges and gather information that saved the lives of thousands of Allied troops. This office was a forerunner of our present *CIA* (*C*entral *I*ntelligence *A*gency).

OWI, the *O*ffice of *W*ar *I*nformation, established in 1942 to consolidate the information activities of the various government agencies, disseminating to the public such information as policy changes, production figures, etc. The prominent radio news broadcaster Elmer Davis became its director.

OWM, the *O*ffice of *W*ar *M*obilization.

WMC, the *W*ar *M*anpower *C*ommission, which froze workers to their jobs in essential industries.

WPB, the *War Production Board*, established in June, 1942, to be in charge of all war production and supply, mobilizing the nation's resources to war production and curtailing nonessential expenditures of materials. It absorbed the *OPM*, the *Office of Production Management*.

WSA, the *War Shipping Administration*, established in February, 1942, to ensure the most effective use of U.S. shipping.

If such abbreviations seem confusing and repetitious, rest assured that they were to most Americans during World War II too. The war also saw the proliferation of military abbreviations, such as *AMGOT* (the *Allied Military Government of Occupied Territory*), *OCS* (see *90-day wonder* above), *SHAEF* (*Supreme Headquarters Allied Expeditionary Force*), *WAC* (see below), and hundreds of others. If there was a trend it was that government offices and agencies usually had abbreviations of three letters while the military used three or more letter abbreviations and preferred those that could be pronounced together as words, as acronyms.

operation had meant a military movement in English since 1744 and *mission* the performance of a duty since 1805, but both words became very common in World War II. *Combined operations*, a joint army, navy, and air force attack, was first used in April, 1940, to refer to the surprise attack the Nazis made on Norway, landing by sea and air to win "the race for Norway" even as British troops approached by sea alone. *Theater of operations*, the largest area of the war under one command, often being as large as a continent, as the European Theater of Operations (usually just called the *ETO*) or "the European Theater."

outfit, a military unit, as a regiment, battalion, company, etc.

Panzer division, *Panzers*, Germany's powerful, fast armored divisions, the terms first being widely used during Hitler's *blitzkrieg* (see above) of Poland which began the war on September 1, 1939. *Panzer* comes from the German *Panzerwagen*, armored vehicle (German *Panzer*, armor, from Middle High German *Panzier*, body armor). By 1941 Germany's Panzer divisions were equipped with the heavy *Tiger tank*, which Rommel used in North Africa; to counter "the Tiger" we began to build our 30-ton *Sherman tank* in 1942, introducing the even heavier, more powerful *M26 Pershing tank* toward the end of the war (both these American tanks, of course, being named for famous American generals).

parachute troops, *air-borne troops*, and *glider troops* were all first widely used from December, 1939, to March, 1940 during the Russo-Finnish War (which also gave us *ski troops* and *ski patrol*) and then again during the Nazi attack on Norway in April, 1940. *Air-borne campaign* was first used when the Germans captured Crete in May, 1941, using only *paratroops* and *glider troops* (also called *air infantry*). Note that betewen 1940 and 1941 *parachute troops* had been replaced by the portmanteau word *paratroops*, with *paratrooper* also becoming a common word in 1941. By 1942 we spoke of the *paratroop boots* paratroopers wore, which were later to be called *jump boots*.

penicillin (from the genus of molds *Penicillium*, from the Latin *pēnicillus*, brush, to which our word *pencil* is related) was a sensational new word to most Americans in the early 1940s. Although discovered by Alexander Fleming, its antibacterial powers were first firmly established by Sir Howard Florey who, after working on its large-scale manufacture in England, came to the U.S. in December, 1941, to persuade American drug manufacturers of its value as an *antibiotic* against disease and infection. Thus penicillin became the much talked-about "miracle drug" of the war, used on battlefield wounds to prevent infections and saving many lives.

PFC became the well-known abbreviation of *Private First Class* during the war.

pin-up girl, *pinup*, 1943. See PRETTY GIRLS for details.

pontoon bridge, a bridge supported by boats or other floating structures. Such bridges were widely talked about during the war, as used by troops and vehicles when regular bridges had been destroyed; however, the term wasn't new at all, having been in English since 1704 (via French *pontoon*, floating bridge, from Latin *pontis*, bridge).

POW became the common abbreviation for *prisoner of war* during World War II, giving us the term *POW camp*. Incidentally, the German word for a prisoner-of-war camp was *Stalag* (the German shortening of their word *Stammlager*, literally "group camp"); since these German camps were numbered rather than named we might speak of an American POW being in Stalag 17, Stalag 18, etc.

propaganda comes to us from Latin in the Roman Catholic title *Sacra Congregatio de Propaganda Fide*, The Sacred Congregation for Propagating the Faith, the Roman Curia having authority in preaching and charged with foreign missions. By the 1820s the word *propaganda* was being used in the political sense, to mean persuasion by faith rather than fact. Then in the mid 1930s the Nazi Minister of Propaganda Paul Joseph Goebbels made propaganda an instrument of

POWs *guarded by American soldiers in France.*

national policy, having said as early as 1923 "It is the . . . right of the state to supervise the forming of public opinion."

    the big lie is a lie so big and audacious it influences public opinion even if completely unsupported. The idea and the term came out of Hitler's *Mein Kampf*, in which he wrote "The size of a lie is a definite factor in causing it to be believed. . . . The primitive simplicity of [the minds of the masses] renders them a more easy prey to a big lie than a small one. . . ."

PT boat (*p*atrol *t*orpedo *boat*), 1941. Because of its noise, small size, and its use to sting enemy shipping with torpedoes, a PT boat was also called a *mosquito boat*.

PX, 1941, as a pseudo abbreviation for *p*ost e*x*change.

Quisling, a traitor, comes from Vidkun Quisling, a Norwegian major and head of the Nazi party in Norway. He persuaded Hitler to attack his own country, helped plan the April, 1940, invasion, and then became head of its puppet government under the German occupation. On May 11, 1940, just a month after Germany invaded Norway, the *London Daily Express* used *Quisling* to mean any traitor, writing "Two thousand Quislings had been rounded up. . . ."

Quonset hut, the prefabricated corrugated metal building having a semicircular roof that curves down to form the walls, was given its trademark name after Quonset Point, Rhode Island, where it was first manufactured. The British used a similar building during the war, the *Nissen hut*, designed before 1930 by British mining engineer Lieutenant Colonel Peter Nissen.

radar, one of the most important inventions of the war, was developed by Scotland's Robert Alexander Watson Watt, an Air Ministry advisor on telecommunications. It was first used by the British in the Battle of Britain—but the British called the device, which uses high-frequency radio waves, a *radiolocator*. The U.S. Navy called it *radar* (an acronym for *ra*dio *d*etecting *a*nd *r*anging) when it publicly revealed the device in the spring of 1943.

    sonar was also developed during World War II. Using high-frequency sound waves to locate submerged objects, *sonar* is also an acronym (for *so*und *na*vigation and *r*anging), influenced by the Latin *sonus/sonāre*, sound, to sound.

R and R, *r*est *and r*otation. In World War II it meant removing a soldier from a fighting unit for a week or so and sending him to a base or rest area, often a tent city, removed from the front lines. In the Korean war it came to mean a furlough, especially one to Japan.

rationing and *hoarding* (a 1593 English word) were major topics of conversation during the war. The *OPA* (see above) announced tire rationing December 26, 1941, and eventually rationed gasoline, sugar, coffee, butter, meat, canned foods, shoes, fuel oils, fat, and oils. Rationing introduced such items and terms as *ration(ing) book*, *(ration) stamps*, and the *A*, *B*, and *C* stickers for car windshields, showing how much gas the owner could buy. Rationed items, of course, became major staples of the *black market* (see above).

refugee (via the 14th century *refuge*, shelter, from Latin *refugere*, to retreat) was first widely used in English in 1685, to refer to French Huguenots who fled to England after the revocation of the Edict of Nantes. In the late 1930s we first saw refugees in newsreels, as Chinese fleeing the Japanese or as Spanish families fleeing a battle area during the Spanish Civil War, usually carrying or wheeling their possessions on roads which were under threat of bombing attack. *Refugee camp* became a common term by 1940, though it first entered English in 1906.

displaced person. Many refugees eventually became *displaced persons* living in *displaced person camps* run by various governments and international organizations. The camps became commonly known as *DP camps* after the war and the people in them as *DPs.* Millions of DPs returned home after the war, others emigrated elsewhere, and some lived out their lives in the DP camps.

Remember Pearl Harbor! became the initial war slogan and battle cry of the U.S. after the bombing of Pearl Harbor. It was in a long line of American "Remember——" battle cries, including *Remember the Maine!* (1898), *Remember the Alamo!* (1836) and *Remember the River Raisin!* (1813, the war cry of Kentucky soldiers in the War of 1812 after the Raisin River Massacre, in which 700 Kentuckians who had been badly beaten trying to capture Detroit had their wounded scalped and butchered by the Indians who were allies of the British).

Pearl Harbor came to mean the surprise attack by 360 Japanese planes on our Pearl Harbor naval base at 7:55 Sunday morning December 7, 1941, finally bringing us into the war. America first heard of the attack via a mid-morning radio news bulletin:

> The Japanese have attacked Pearl Harbor, the United States naval base on Oahu Island in the Hawaiian Islands.

Pearl Harbor, December 7, 1941.

445

The Japanese caught most U.S. warships docked or at anchor: 19 of our ships, including eight battleships, were sunk or disabled and 177 U.S. planes were destroyed on the ground. On the same day Japan declared war on the U.S. and Great Britain and on the next day the U.S. and most of the Allies (with the notable exception of Russia) declared war on Japan.

In his December 8 war message to Congress President Roosevelt said that December 7, 1941 would be remembered in history as a "day of infamy," which phrase became a synonym for the day and the Japanese attack. Actually the attack on Pearl Harbor was but part of an overall Japanese attack to win the Pacific: by December 25th the Japanese had captured or invaded the Philippines, Guam, Wake Island, Hong Kong, Malaya, and other U.S. and British bases and islands.

roger!, a code word used by pilots to mean "your message received and understood" in response to radio communications; later it came into general use to mean "all right, OK." *Roger* was the radio communications code word for the letter *R*, which in this case represented the word "received." *Roger Wilco* was the reply to "Roger" from the original transmitter of the radio message, meaning "I have received your message that you have received my message and am signing off."

sack almost completely replaced the word "bed" among our servicemen in World War II (*bed sack* had meant a sack to carry bedding in since 1661 and colonial beds were often just long sacks of corncobs, hay, leaves, etc.). By 1943 *to hit the sack*, *to sack out*, and *to sack in* all meant to go to bed, to sleep, and tired soldiers spoke longingly of *sack time*, *sack duty*, and *sack drill*, time spent sleeping, and envied the *sack artist*, one who managed to avoid extra duty and spend a lot of time in bed.

sad sack was originally a 1930s student term for a blundering, unpopular student, then became a common World War II term for the typical confused, put upon, unkempt soldier, the citizen as a misfit in military life. George Baker began his *The Sad Sack* comic strip for armed forces publications during the war.

scorched earth policy, late 1930s, comes from the war of Japan against China. The Chinese adopted a policy of leaving nothing behind for the invading Japanese, burning everything from crops to cities as they retreated, leaving the Japanese only scorched earth.

scuttlebutt, shipboard rumors, navy gossip, 1935. Originally a *scuttlebutt* (1840) was a butt (cask) of water with a small scuttle (opening) for dipping out the contents—of course navy crews gathered around a ship's scuttlebutt to have a drink and gossip and eventually the word took on its modern meaning of rumor, gossip (the office worker's equivalent is "water cooler talk").

the Seabees appeared in 1942 as members of special construction battalions to handle Navy construction in combat zones. The word is an acronym, pronounced "cee-bees," from the initials *CB* of Construction Battalion, the "cee" being spelled *sea* because the battalions were attached to the Navy. The Seabees made two other words well known, *air strip* and *bulldozer:* they constructed the *air strips* (runways, simple landing fields) on many Pacific islands and used *bulldozers* to do the job quickly. *Bulldozer* had

If it moves, salute it;
If it doesn't move, pick it up;
If you can't pick it up, paint it.
World War II humorous saying known to all draftees as they learned how to behave at an army base. It was sometimes called "the sad sack's catechism."

A local draft board. *This one, before Pearl Harbor, in New York City, registers men in the first peacetime draft in America.*

meant a Caterpillar tractor with a scraper or blade for clearing or leveling land since 1930, but most Americans never heard the word until the Seabees made the bulldozer a somewhat glamorous wartime item (*to bulldoze* had meant to intimidate since 1876, first being recorded in New Orleans to refer to Whites who "bulldozed" Blacks to keep them from voting).

selectee and *trainee* first appeared in the Selective Training and Service Act of 1940 (*draftee* was a Civil War word). During World War II over 10 million men were selected to be drafted by a lottery system, were then *inducted* into the army at *induction centers* and became *inductees*, until they were sent to *basic training camps* where they became *trainees* as they went through six weeks of *basic* (basic training as soldiers).

All men 18–45 years of age were "eligible for the draft," carried wallet-sized *draft cards* issued by their *local draft boards*, and wondered if they would be classified *1-A* (physically fit to serve) or *4-F* (not meeting physical requirements to serve) after a *pre-induction physical* examination. The World War II draft expired in 1947, two years after the war ended, but between 1948 and 1972 was replaced by the Selective Service Act of 1948.

shack up, 1940, to set up housekeeping and live with a local woman near one's military base; a woman a man shacked up with was called a *shack job. Shack up* (which may have been a truck drivers' term before the war) remained in use after the war, meaning simply to live together or to have a fairly permanent sexual liaison.

sky pilot had been a hobo and western slang term for a clergyman since 1891 and saw some use by our troops in World War I— but *pilot* meant a navigator and the image was of a clergyman guiding one toward Heaven. In World War II the term became very common for an armed forces chaplain—but *pilot* now meant an aviator and the image was of a clergyman flying one to Heaven. *Chaplain* had meant an army or navy clergyman in English since 1704 and *Holy Joe* had been a new American term

447

for a chaplain in World War I. *Go tell it to the chaplain* was a World War II army phrase meaning "stop complaining, shut up," literally "take your problems to the chaplain and stop bothering me."

snafu. See FUCK AND SCREW for this and related terms such as *fubar, janfu,* etc.

snorkel (German *Schnorchel*, air intake, spiral) was introduced during World War II, when it meant a retractable tube for ventilating a submarine as it cruised slightly below the surface. By the late 1940s it came to mean a tube through which a person may breathe while swimming face down in the water on or close to the surface.

stateside replaced the World War I "back home."

storm troopers, members of the Nazi party's *Sturmabteilung* or *SA* (*Sturm*, storm, attack + *Abteilung* division, department), organized in 1921 as the party's strong-arm squad, to protect party meetings and break up meetings of the opposition. By the early 1930s the SA was known for its violence and terrorism against Jews and those who opposed the Nazis; in 1934 it was reorganized as the instrument of physical (military) training and political indoctrination of German men and by 1936 had reached its full strength of 1½ million well-disciplined troops. Storm troopers wore brown shirts as part of their uniform and were thus also called the *Brownshirts*, which also came to mean any group of fascists.

SS troops, members of Hitler's *Schutzstaffel* ("protective echelon"), formed around 1923 as an elite corps of storm troopers who served as bodyguards for Nazi leaders. Under Heinrich Himmler the SS men were Hitler's "secret police," the men who assassinated for Hitler, tortured prisoners into making confessions, and arrested and shipped non-Aryans to concentration and death camps, which the SS built and ran. They wore black shirts as part of their uniform and thus were called the *Black Shirts*.

Stuka was the German shortening from *Sturzkampfflugzeug*, literally "dive fighter." The name was first widely used in 1937, during the Spanish Civil War, when the *Junker Ju87 Stuka* dive

A German army unit goose steps during a parade in Berlin, 1939.

bomber (with a top speed of 210 miles an hour) was used by the Condor Legion, the air force Hitler sent to help Franco. It was widely used again when the German Stukas played a large role in the invasion of Poland in September, 1939. *Dive bombers* were used by both sides at the beginning of the war because the bombs they released in their dive had a greater velocity than bombs released from level flight. Though effective and frightening, the dive bombers proved to be too vulnerable to ground fire and saw less and less use as the war progressed.

task force meant a naval attack force on a special mission or patrol. The public first heard the term in news reports of the task force carrying out the amphibious landings in North Africa in November, 1942 (see *Afrika Korps* above).

> *the task force system.* In the Battle of the Coral Sea, May 7–8, 1942, carrier-based planes of a British-American naval force sank part of a Japanese fleet, halting its advance toward Australia. This was our first major naval victory of the war and the first naval battle in history in which surface ships did not exchange a shot, U.S. planes from the carriers *Yorktown* and *Lexington* sinking seven major enemy warships (our *Lexington* was sunk by the Japanese). The following month we won the Battle of Midway, June 3–6, 1942, the turning point in the naval war in the Pacific, ending the Japanese threat to Hawaii and putting the Japanese on the defensive. In this battle Admiral Chester W. Nimitz' fleet never came within sight of Admiral Yamamoto's fleet, the battle again being fought by carrier-based planes (and submarines): the Japanese lost four carriers, a heavy cruiser, and 322 planes, while the U.S. lost the carrier *Yorktown* to a submarine, one destroyer, and 147 planes. These two battles conclusively proved the value of aircraft carriers (see *flattop* above). Our navy then officially adopted *the task force system*, in which task forces were built around aircraft carriers as the main attack force using other ships to protect them. Before this aircraft carriers had mainly been used to protect battleships.

tin can, see *U-boats* at WORLD WAR I. Destroyers were called *tin cans* because they were the smallest fleet vessels and had the thinnest armor. A *rust bucket* meant any old ship but in World War II it especially meant a destroyer.

Tokyo Rose and *Axis Sally* were heard and talked about by every American soldier overseas. They broadcast popular American music for our troops to listen to, combined with propaganda for them to quit and go home. Japan's best-known *Tokyo Rose* was Iva D'aquino, a 29-year-old Nisei from Los Angeles who was also billed as *Orphan Annie* and who claimed she took the job working for the Japanese for the experience (after the war she was sentenced to ten years imprisonment and a fine of $10,000). The Nazi *Axis Sally* was really Mildred Gillars, a frustrated actress from Portland, Maine, who got her job in Germany through her lover and former Hunter College professor Max Koischurtz. At least one larger American talent was also involved in Axis propaganda: poet Ezra Pound broadcast Fascist propaganda to the U.S. from Italy under Mussolini, was

---

Sighted sub, sank same.
Radio message from U.S. navy flyer Donald Mason, January 28, 1942, after he had dropped a depth charge on a surfaced Japanese submarine in the South Pacific. This concise message was one of the first pieces of good news to come after Pearl Harbor and was given wide publicity as showing the good spirit of our armed forces.

tried for treason after the war, judged insane in 1946, and spent 12 years in a Washington, D.C., mental hospital.

torpedo juice, originally sailors' use, raw homemade whiskey, such as that made from alcohol drained from a Navy torpedo.

total war, meaning general mobilization of a nation's entire population, resources, and economy, the destruction of the enemy's production capacity, and waging economic and psychological warfare along with military attacks, was a term taken from the title of General Erich Ludendorff's 1935 book *Der Totale Krieg*, which advocated these things for Germany. Ludendorff had been the chief German strategist in World War I and was a Nazi general in World War II.

unconditional surrender. At the Casablanca Conference in January, 1943, Roosevelt and Churchill first called for the "unconditional surrender of the Axis," declaring such a surrender the only one the Allies would accept. The phrase had first become famous in General Grant's message to General Buckner, the commander of Fort Donelson, in 1862, when Grant flatly declared "No terms except unconditional surrender."

the underground was the loose network of small groups throughout Nazi-occupied Europe that continued to resist the Germans, with sabotage, by providing military information to the Allies, by helping Allied airmen who had been shot down to escape capture, etc. The French underground was the largest and was called *the resistance*, its members often being called *resistance fighters*. Guerrilla groups that continued to fight against the Axis after their countries were defeated, especially in Greece and Yugoslavia, were called *partisans*. Those who accepted and worked with the Nazi conquerors were called *collaborators*.

the USO (the United Service Organization) was a voluntary organization begun in 1941 to supply social, recreation, welfare, and spiritual facilities to servicemen. It was best known for its *USO clubs*, located in cities and towns near military bases, where servicemen away from home could relax, eat, drink, make friends, and dance with local girls at the weekly *USO dances*. It also provided *USO shows* or *camp shows* for which professional entertainers made tours of U.S. military camps and bases all over the world (there were 80 such companies overseas in 1944). They brought Broadway and Hollywood entertainers to servicemen in the jungle and the Arctic, with comedian Bob Hope's troupe being the favorite and most widely traveled. It also provided the famous *stage door canteens*, staffed by theatrical and movie celebrities.

V.D. was the well-known abbreviation for venereal disease by 1942. The armed forces used the abbreviation in their anti-venereal-disease campaign, on posters in military camps and in millions of pamphlets and booklets issued to servicemen. As part of the campaign, servicemen were also shown *Mickey Mouse movies*, depicting the ways young soldiers could be enticed into exposing themselves to V.D. through the greed of prostitutes, ways to avoid, recognize, and seek treatment for the disease, and—mainly—showing in gruesome detail the effects of syphilis and gonorrhea (the euphemism *Mickey Mouse movie* was, of course, meant to be funny).

I left my heart at the stage door canteen,
I left it there with a girl named Irene. . . .
"I Left My Heart at the Stage Door Canteen," by Irving Berlin for the 1942 all-soldier review *This Is the Army*.

Winston Churchill (1874–1965), at 80 years of age, flashes his famous V-for-Victory, *1954.*

V-for-Victory. Just as *Liberty* was the key word of the Revolutionary War (see TAXATION WITHOUT REPRESENTATION) and of World War I, *Victory* was the key word of World War II. "Victory" meant the end of the war, the liberation of Europe, the end of totalitarianism. It was represented by the letter *V* on posters, in slogans, and in the *V-for-Victory* hand sign, made by raising the index and middle fingers into a V. Using the letter *V* for Victory was originated January 14, 1941, by Victor De Lavelege, a member of the Belgian parliament in exile in London: in a radio broadcast to his homeland on that day he used the letter V as a symbol of passive resistance against the Nazis—in his native Flemish the V stood for *Vrieherd/Vrijherd*, freedom. Soon the V was used by all the Allies, meaning V for Victory in America and throughout the British Empire and V for *Victoire* to the Free French. Winston Churchill made the V-for-Victory hand sign famous, using it frequently, as seen in newspaper photos and in the newsreels. *Victory* and its *V* also gave us:

> *V-Day*, Victory day, the day the war would end. We began to use this term frequently after D-Day, later talking about the separate *V-E Day* and *V-J Day. V-E Day*, Victory-in-Europe Day, was celebrated May 8, 1945 (the Germans had agreed to an unconditional surrender on the night of May 7). *V-J Day*, Victory-in-Japan Day, or Victory-over-Japan Day, was celebrated August 15, 1945, the day the Japanese agreed to unconditional surrender (President Truman also made September 2 a more formal V-J Day, that being the day the formal surrender was signed aboard the battleship *Missouri* in Tokyo Bay).
>
> *V-girl*, Victory girl. See under *B-girl* above.
>
> *Victory garden*, late 1942, a home garden as planted by Americans during the war, to help the war effort by growing their own vegetables, leaving more farm land free for wheat and other major crops and using home-grown and processed vegetables in place of canned ones (tin, tin cans, and canned goods were scarce).
>
> *Victory ship.* See *Liberty ship* above.
>
> *V-mail*, a system used for armed forces mail in which letters written on special writing paper were microfilmed and sent forward for printing in full size on photographic paper before being delivered. Often the special V-mail letters weren't actually microfilmed but merely forwarded, resembling the self-sealing combination letter-envelopes still used in overseas correspondence.

WAACs, WAVES, SPARs, and *WAFS* were the women's "auxiliary" or branch of the U.S. Army, Navy, Coast Guard, and Air Force respectively. This was the first time in our history that the American armed forces had such branches (Britain had them in World War I), the women were well segregated into their own units and usually doing clerical work at military bases.

> the *WAACs*, the *Women's Army Auxiliary Corps*, was authorized by Congress on May 15, 1942, allowing women to volunteer to relieve the manpower shortage in the armed forces (every woman who did clerical work, drove a truck,

451

Red Cross girls saw service at home and overseas. Here they give the taste-test to their famous sinkers, *which were served directly to the troops from* Clubmobiles *located behind the front lines.*

etc., released a man for combat duty). The "Auxiliary" was dropped in 1943, to indicate that women were full-fledged members of the armed services, the *WAACs* then becoming the *WACs, Women's Army Corps,* and each of its 250,000 members then became a *WAC* instead of a *WAAC.* Incidentally, the acronym *WAACs* had been used by the British in World War I, for *Women's Auxiliary Army Corps.*

the WAVES, Womes Accepted for Voluntary Emergency Service (in the Navy), was established July 31, 1942 (many World War II organizations were given a rather awkward name in order to produce a pleasing, meaningful acronym). A member of the WAVES was called a *WAVE.* The British counterpart of the WAVES was the *WRENS, Women's Royal Naval Service* (whose abbreviation was actually WRNS, the E being added to make it pronounceable as a word); it had been organized in World War I, in 1917, then was re-created for World War II in 1939.

the SPARs was established for the Coast Guard, the acronym coming from the Coast Guard motto and its translation "*Semper Paratus: Always Ready.*" A member of this organization was called a *SPAR.*

the WAFS was originally known as the *Women's Auxiliary Ferrying Squadron,* helping ferry planes from defense plants to military bases in the U.S. and overseas. In 1940, when the Army Air Force became a separate service, the Air Force, it took over the organization and its acronym WAFS, but gave it a new name to fit the old initials, the *Women in the Air Force,* which also included women in clerical and other Air Force jobs. A member of either of these groups was called a *WAF.*

Women Marines didn't have a catchy name, their corps was the Women's Reserve of the Marine Corps. Long before these groups were established in World War II women had gained regular status in the armed forces in the Army Nurses Corps, established in 1901.

BUY WAR BONDS

walkie-talkie, a radiotelephone combining a receiver and transmitter in one unit light enough to be carried by one man (thus it both "walked" and "talked"). It was developed by the Signal Corps in 1933 and the name was used in the army before the war. Another type of portable radio set sent out an automatic SOS signal only and was called a *coffee grinder*, because working its generating crank resembled grinding coffee in a tabletop coffee mill.

war bonds were interest-bearing bonds sold by the government to raise money to help pay for the war effort. The best-known ones were the cheapest, the $18.75 ones that returned $25 at maturity. As with Liberty Bonds during World War I, War Bonds were advertised, promoted, and sold widely, at schools, offices, post offices, by celebrities, etc., especially during the special *War Bond Drives*. Phil Baker's sign-off slogan for his Sunday night radio programs during 1942–44 was "By-by, buy bonds," which became a somewhat cute way of saying "goodby."

war bride, a European bride of a U.S. serviceman stationed overseas, especially one who came to the U.S. to live.

the Wehrmacht (a German word from *Wehr*, defense + *Macht*, force), Germany's armed forces under Hitler.

the Western Front originally meant the front between France and Germany, from the beginning of the war in 1939 until German forces went around the French lines into the Low Countries in the spring of 1940. After D-Day there was again a Western Front, the front between the advancing Allies and the retreating Nazis, which moved slowly eastward toward Berlin.

the Maginot Line was the supposedly impregnable system of French fortifications built along the original Western Front from Switzerland to Belgium (it was named after the French Minister of War André Maginot, who had started it in 1929). After an initial attack on the Germans at the very beginning of the war the French (and British) spent seven months in the Maginot Line, lacking modern weapons for an offensive, while the Germans remained behind their Siegfried Line making new plans and waiting for spring weather. In December, 1939, French Premier Daladier called this period of inactivity *the phony war*, others called it the *Sitzkrieg* (a pun on *blitzkrieg*).

the Zero, the Japanese Mitsubishi Zero, a highly maneuverable, single-engine Japanese fighter plane.

The war that began with a *blitzkrieg* ended with the Atomic Bomb. Between December 7, 1941, and September 2, 1945, the day the Japanese formally surrendered, the U.S. had over 16 million men in uniform, of whom 400,000 were dead and 700,000 wounded as a result of the war (casualties almost three times that of World War I); we had spent $350 billion on war materiel—yet every other major nation envied us for the easy time we had had. From September 1, 1939, the day Hitler invaded Poland, until September 2, 1945, the world had seen the bloodiest six years in its history. Over 15 million men had been killed in com-

Prime Minister Clement Attlee (1883–1967), President Harry Truman (1884–1972), and Chairman Joseph Stalin (1875–1953) at the Potsdam Conference.

bat (10½ million on the Allied side, 4½ million on the Axis); untold millions of civilians had been killed by bombs, extermination (Hitler exterminated 6 million Jews alone), *slave labor camps*, starvation, and disease. Ten million refugees who had fled their own countries had become displaced persons, two million of them never to return home again. Entire nations were in ashes and near starvation.

The postwar period saw many new names and terms. We talked about the Potsdam Conference of Truman, Churchill, and Stalin near Potsdam, Germany July 17–August 2, 1945 and used the new terms that originated there:

> *occupied zone*. The participants of the Potsdam Conference agreed that Germany was to be divided into four *occupied zones*, administered by France, Great Britain, the U.S., and the Soviet Union, these occupied zones later being called simply *zones* or *sectors*.
>
> *de-Nazification* was also a term first used at the Potsdam Conference, when it was agreed that all traces of Nazism must be erased from Germany.
>
> *war criminal* was another new term of the conference, all agreeing that Axis war criminals must be punished for their *war crimes*. The U.S., the Soviet Union, and Great Britain established an International Military Tribunal which conducted *the Nuremberg Trials* of 22 Nazi leaders at Nuremberg, Germany, beginning in November, 1945—11 of these top Nazis, including Goering, Ribbentrop, and Streicher, were sentenced to death in September, 1946. The trials presented voluminous evidence which revealed for the first time the full story of Nazi barbarism. Similar trials were held in Tokyo, resulting in the execution of Premier Tojo and six other Japanese war leaders. In all a half-million Germans and 4,000 Japanese were eventually found guilty of war crimes.

'WE GIVE UP!'
TOKYO RADIOS

Hideki Tojo (1885–1948), Prime Minister of Japan during the war. He was hanged as a war criminal.

We also talked of the new international alliance that was to help insure peace:

> the United Nations was first hinted at in the August, 1941, Atlantic Charter, signed by Roosevelt and Churchill four months before the U.S. entered the war and calling for a "final destruction of the Nazi tyranny" and a permanent postwar system of general security. President Roosevelt is said to have then coined the name *United Nations* during Churchill's December, 1941, visit to Washington, when the two leaders discussed a name for both the wartime and postwar alliance. The name was first officially used January 2, 1942, when 26 Allied nations pledged to continue the war effort jointly and not make any separate peace agreements (thus *the United Nations* was originally a synonym for *the Allies*).

China, Great Britain, the U.S., and the USSR then drafted a proposal for *the United Nations Charter* at the Dumbarton Oaks conference in the fall of 1944. At the Yalta Conference in February, 1945, Great Britain, the U.S., and the USSR agreed on a *veto system* in the *Security Council* and, with China and France, called a conference of all nations that were at war with Germany and Japan to meet in San Francisco in the spring of 1946. There 51 countries approved the United Nations charter, which was signed and ratified by the required number of countries by October 24, which became *United Nations Day*. Both *the General Assembly*

War criminals on trial at Nuremberg, 1945. (bottom, left to right) Herman Goering, Rudolph Hess, Joachim von Ribbentrop, Wilhelm Keitel; (top, left to right) Karl Doenitz, Erich Raeder, Baldur von Schirach, and Fritz Sauckel. Of this group of Nazis in the dock, Goering committed suicide in jail; Ribbentrop, Keitel, and Sauckel were hanged in 1946; Hess and Raeder were sentenced to life imprisonment; and Schirach was sentenced to 20 years' imprisonment.

of the 51 nations and the Security Council held their first meetings in London in January, 1948; the organization occupied its headquarters in New York City in 1952. Around this time the abbreviation *UN* became very common for *United Nations* (we had previously used *UNO*, for the *United Nations Organization*). We also talked a great deal about *the Secretariat*, *the Big 5* (the five permanent members of the Security Council, China, France, Great Britain, the U.S., and the USSR) each of whom had *veto power* over Security Council proceedings), and *UNESCO* (the *United Nations Educational, Scientific, and Cultural Organization*).

Beginning in 1945 we had also talked about *CARE* (the Cooperative for American Relief in Europe) and the *CARE packages* we sent to help those in distress. In 1947 we started talking of our projected European Recovery Plan for aiding European nations in their economic recovery from the war—but by the time it went into effect in 1948 it was better known as *the Marshall Plan*, since it had been proposed by our Secretary of State, the former General George C. Marshall (who won the Nobel peace prize for the program in 1953).

We also used new terms such as *surplus*, *war surplus*, and *Army surplus*, referring to surplus war goods left over from the war, and of the new *Army-Navy (Surplus) Stores* which sold war surplus clothing, tents, and battlefield items which could be used as camping equipment. There were *GI students* going to college on the *GI Bill* (see *GI Joe* in the list above) and *Fulbright scholars* going to schools in European countries in return for the military equipment we had left them.

The aftereffects of World War II still continue to permeate our lives and our language. After the war the U.S. and Russia accepted the surrender of North and South Korea from Japan separately, eventually leading to THE KOREAN CONFLICT; during the war a Communist-led group of guerrillas fought the Japanese in French Indochina, grew strong, and eventually took over Vietnam (see THE VIETNAM WAR); the USSR and the U.S. emerged from the war as the two major *superpowers*, leading *the Communist bloc* and *the free world* in *the Cold War*, which ranged from the USSR's construction of *the Berlin Wall* to a "race for space" that resulted in *the space age*, and research and diplomacy to give one's side the advantage in *the nuclear arms race*. One chapter in history leads to another—and one word leads to another. In general, however, due perhaps to the Cold War and the constant atomic threat, ever since World War II we have continued to live in a wartime atmosphere—our philosophy, attitudes, lifestyles and language have remained on a wartime level of quick change and tension. In some ways it seems that only now, over 30 years after the war, is America returning to a peacetime respect for the environment and "the quality of life."

Off we go into the wild blue yonder,
Climbing high into the sun;
Here they come, zooming to meet our thunder,
At 'em boys, give 'er the gun!
Down we dive, spouting our flame from under,
Off with one helluva roar!
We live in fame, or go down in flame.
Nothing'll stop the Army Air Corps!

"The Army Air Corps," written in 1939 by Robert Crawford in response to a prize offered by the Army Air Force for a song.

Anchor's aweigh, my boys, anchor's aweigh.
Farewell to college joys, we sail at break of day!
Through our last night on shore,
Drink to the foam,
Until we meet once more
Here's wishing you a happy voyage home.

"Anchor's Aweigh," the official marching song of the U.S. Navy, composed for the 1906 Army-Navy football game, by Charles A. Zimmerman (music) and Alfred H. Miles (lyrics). These lyrics are the familiar ones sung during World War II and are very different from the original football song.

Yankee

probably comes from the Dutch *Jan Kees*, "John Cheese," a disparaging European nickname for the cheese-making, cheese-eating Hollanders since the 1650s (it may also be from Dutch *Janhe*, "little John" or even from an Indian pronunciation of the word "English"). By 1863 the Dutch settlers in New York seemed to have turned the term *Yankee* around, using it as a derisive name for their neighboring English settlers to the north in Connecticut (who thus became the first *Connecticut Yankees* and the first northerners to be called Yankees). Soon British soldiers, who had been calling English settlers *Brother Jonathans*, implying a rustic simpleness or stupidity, were calling them all *Yankees*, as when General Wolfe used the word in referring to his New England colonial troops in a 1758 letter to another British officer:

> My posts are now so fortified that I can offer you two companies of Yankees and the more, as they are better for ranging and scouting than either work or vigilance.

Southern colonists, who felt that their northern counterparts were too shrewd and calculating, also took to calling them Yankees; but New Englanders saw the word as a tribute to their ingenuity and cunning, and so proudly adopted it, though the term *Yankee pedlar* didn't appear until the early 1800s.

Yankee Doodle was probably introduced to America by a British surgeon shortly before the Revolutionary War, in mockery of the poorly clad colonial troops, and was played by British drum and fife corps to annoy the colonists. After the Battle of Lexington in 1775, however, colonial troops proudly took up the name Yankee, now sometimes shortened to *Yank*, changed the lyrics of *Yankee Doodle*, and used it as their own marching song.

After the war, the stage Yankee became the most popular character in the American theater, first appearing as a servant named Jonathan (perhaps a reference to the earlier *Brother Jonathan*) in Royall Tyler's 1787 *The Contrast*, the first true American drama. The stage Yankee was always deceptively simple, honest, shrewd, and full of homespun humor—and always got the best of any snobbish Anglophile or other city slicker. In face and dress he was a forerunner of UNCLE SAM.

During the Civil War, the South used *Yankee* (and also occasionally *doodle*) as an expression of contempt for a Union soldier, and *Yankee Doodle* was considered a pro-Union song, hence banned in Mobile, Alabama, and elsewhere in the Confederacy. *Damn Yankee*, by the way, wasn't originally a Southern term, but was first used around 1812 in referring to a New Englander.

By World War I all American troops were again *Yankees* or *Yanks* and in 1917 were singing George M. Cohan's *Over There:*

A "Yankee" of the Revolutionary War.

458

"Over there, over there, the Yanks are coming, the Yanks are coming and we won't be back till it's over, over there." From then onward *Yank* and *Yankee* have been popular European terms for any American, soldier or civilian, or for UNCLE SAM or America itself. In Latin America the spelling is often *Yanqui* and the sign "Yanqui go home" (1950s) referred not only to American soldiers but also to American business interests and American political influence. Incidentally, in 1903 the word first used by the Dutch in New York returned to New York, in the name of a baseball team, when the New York Highlanders became the *New York Yankees*.

"Yanks" of World War I.

Yes and No

The first colonists brought with them the English *yea*, the more emphatic *yes*, and the newly popular *aye*, which is still used to indicate an affirmative vote in both the British House of Commons and the U.S. Congress. *Right* also meant "yes," *affirmative* was just coming to mean "yes" in England in the 1620s (the astronauts popularized this use again in the 1960s), and the later British colonists of the 18th century were to bring *correct* with them. Since then we have added other ways to say yes or to express positive feelings, including such expressions as:

bet your boots, 1820; *bet your hat*, 1839; *bet your life*, 1848, *you bet your sweet life*, 1909; *bet your bottom dollar*, 1866.
I don't care if I do (as acceptance), 1831.
uh-huh, 1830s (see HUH? AND UH HUH).
that's a fact, 1834.

like anything!, 1835.
and no mistake (about it), 1839.
O.K., 1840 (see OK).
yes sir-ee, yes sir-ee Bob, mid 1840s.
as sure as shooting, 1853.
yes indeedy, indeedy, 1856.
you bet, you bet you, 1866.
I should say so!, 1879.

sure (meaning "yes"), *Sure, Mike!*, *sure thing*, 1896.

yep, yup (variants of "yes"), 1890s. *Yep* seems to be from the late 1880s, a few years older than *yup*.

all right—all right, all rightee, late 1890s. *All reet,* jive use of the late 1930s.

And then some!, 1906.

It's jake with me, 1910.

You and me both!, 1918.

I'll tell the cockeyed world!, 1918.

You said it!, 1919; *You said a mouthful,* early 1920s.

absolutely!, 1922.

yea, Bo, a fad term of the 1920s.

You're damn tootin', 1920s.

And how!, 1924.

You tell 'em, Harry, I stutter, the snappy line of 1926, which gave us *You tell 'em.*

I don't mean maybe, 1926.

yeah, this quick way of saying "yes" surged to popularity in the mid 1920s.

You're the doctor, 1920s.

kee-rect, 1930s, an old student pronunciation of "correct," its popularity was extended by its use in the *Abbie and Slats* comic strip.

yowzer, early 1930s, best known as the catchword of orchestra leader and entertainer Ben Bernie (from "Yes, Sir").

natch, "naturally," "yes," late 1930s jive use.

You can say that again!, 1941.

Right on!, "I agree," primarily Black use, 1967.

The colonists also brought with them the old *no* and *nay,* still used to indicate a negative vote in the U.S. Congress, and the rather new *negative,* meaning "no" (which the astronauts were to popularize again in the 1960s). We then added other ways to say "no" or express negative feelings:

uh-uh, 1830s (see HUH? AND UH-UH).

not by a jugfull, 1833; *not by a damned sight,* 1834.

I don't think!, 1837.

N.G., an abbreviation for *no good,* since 1839.

Ask me no questions and I'll tell you no lies, 1846; *Ask me something easy,* 1884; *Ask me another,* 1931.

nix (German *nichts,* nothing), first to mean "nothing, none" around 1855 and slowly also coming to mean "no" by 1900.

Nix on that, 1911.

Not much! Not much, Mary Ann!, 1866.

I'm afraid not, 1879. *I'm afraid—* came to mean "I'm sorry, but—" in the 1870s.

in a pig's eye/ass/ear, 1880s.

nope, 1890s, to match *yup.* Like *yep* it had some late 1880s use. The final *p* is added merely as a closing of the lips after saying *no.*

are you kidding?, 1890s.

not on your tintype, 1899 (*tintype* and *ferrotype* were first used in the early 1860s, being the thin iron plate on which a photographic positive was made).

nothing doing, 1902.

not a bit of it, 1910.

like hell!, 1918; *hell no!,* *the hell,* both 1921.

no can do, 1923.

Says you, sez you, says who? early 1920s.

Oh yeah?, 1920s.

no soap, 1924; *no dice,* 1932; *no sale,* 1934.

ixnay (Pig Latin for *nix*), late 1920s.

nah, 1931.

I should say not!, 1934.

No way!, never, impossible, I won't, mid 1960s.

Picture Credits

frontis, Culver Pictures. *page 1*, N. Y. Public Library. *page 2 (top)*, N. Y. Public Library. *page 2 (bottom)*, N. Y. Public Library. *page 3 (top)*, N. Y. Public Library. *page 3 (bottom)*, N. Y. Public Library. *page 4 (top)*, N. Y. Public Library. *page 4 (bottom)*, N. Y. Public Library. *page 5*, Chas. Scribner's Sons. *page 6 (top)*, N. Y. Public Library. *page 7*, N. Y. Public Library. *page 9*, N. Y. Public Library. *page 10*, N. Y. Public Library. *page 11*, Culver Pictures. *page 12*, U.S. Air Force. *page 13 (top)*, U. S. Navy. *page 13 (bottom)*, The National Archives. *page 14 (top)*, *page 14 (bottom)*, *page 15*, Culver Pictures. *page 16 (top)*, The National Archives. *page 16 (bottom)*, The National Archives. *page 17 (top)*, Culver Pictures. *page 17 (bottom)*, N. Y. Public Library. *page 18*, Frederic Lewis. *page 19*, N. Y. Public Library. *page 20*, Culver Pictures. *page 21*, Louisiana Tourist Development Commission. *page 22*, N. Y. Public Library. *page 23 (middle)*, *N. Y. Public Library*. *page 23 (bottom)*, Frederic Lewis. *page 24 (top)*, N. Y. Public Library. *page 24 (middle)*, *N. Y. Public Library*. *page 24 (bottom)*, N. Y. Public Library. *page 25 (top)*, N. Y. Public Library. *page 25 (middle)*, Museum of the City of New York. *page 25 (bottom)*, N. Y. Public Library. *page 26*, N. Y. Public Library. *page 27*, Frederic Lewis. *page 28*, Culver Pictures. *page 29 (top)*, N. Y. Public Library. *page 29 (bottom)*, N. Y. Public Library. *page 30 (top)*, N. Y. Public Library. *page 30 (middle)*, *N. Y. Public Library*. *page 30 (bottom)*, The National Archives. *page 34*, Library of Congress. *page 37*, N. Y. Public Library. *page 38*, N. Y. Public Library. *page 39*, N. Y. Public Library. *page 40*, Library of Congress. *page 41 (top)*, Culver Pictures. *page 41 (bottom)*, The National Archives. *page 42 (top)*, Library of Congress. *page 42 (bottom)*, Museum of the City of New York. *page 43 (top)*, N. Y. Public Library. *page 43 (middle)*, N. Y. Public Library. *page 43 (bottom)*, Library of Congress. *page 44 (top)*, Frederic Lewis. *page 44 (bottom)*, UPI. *page 45*, Museum of the City of New York. *page 46*, Museum of the City of New York. *page 48*, Library of Congress. *page 50*, Wide World Photos. *page 52*, Frederic Lewis. *page 53*, Frederic Lewis. *page 58 (top)*, Library of Congress. *page 58 (bottom)*, N. Y. Public Library. *page 59 (top, left to right)*, UPI, UPI, Atlantic Records. *page 59 (bottom, left to right)*, Frederic Lewis, UPI, N. Y. Public Library. *page 60*, Culver Pictures. *page 61 (top)*, Frederic Lewis. *page 61 (bottom)*, Frederic Lewis. *page 62*, N. Y. Public Library. *page 63 (top)*, Falls River Public Library. *page 63 (bottom)*, N. Y. Public Library. *page 64 (top)*, Library of Congress. *page 64 (middle)*, General Mills. *page 64 (bottom)*, General Mills. *page 65*, Culver Pictures. *page 66*, American Museum of Natural History. *page 67*, Library of Congress. *page 68*, N. Y. Public Library. *page 69*, N. Y. Public Library. *page 70*, N. Y. Public Library. *page 71 (top)*, Dunkin Donuts, Inc. *page 71 (bottom)*, Library of Congress. *page 72 (top)*, N. Y. Public Library. *page 72 (bottom)*, N. Y. Public Library. *page 73 (top)*, N. Y. Public Library. *page 73 (bottom)*, Frederic Lewis. *page 74 (top)*, Frederic Lewis. *page 74 (bottom)*, Ford Motor Co.. *page 75 (top)*, General Motors. *page 75 (bottom)*, N. Y. Public Library. *page 76 (top)*, N. Y. Public Library. *page 76 (top right)*, Library of Congress. *page 76 (middle)*, *page 76 (bottom)*, Detroit Public Library. *page 77 (top)*, Library of Congress. *page 77 (middle)*, Frederic Lewis. *page 77 (bottom)*, N. Y. Public Library. *page 78 (top to bottom)*, Automobile Manufacturers Assoc., Library of Congress, Ford Motor Co., Automobile Manufacturers Assoc.. *page 79* Library of Congress. *page 80*, N. Y. Public Library. *page 81 (top)*, Museum of the City of New York. *page 81 (bottom)*, Museum of the City of New York, Theater and Music Collection. *page 82 (top)*, N. Y. Public Library. *page 82 (bottom)*, Museum of the City of New York, Theater and Music Collection. *page 83 (top)*, Museum of the City of New York. *page 83 (middle)*, N. Y. Public Library. *page 83 (bottom)*, Museum of the City of New York, Theater and Music Collection. *page 84*, N. Y. Public Library. *page 85 (top)*, The Metropolitan Museum of Art, Gift of Mr. and Mrs. Carl Stoeckel, 1897. *page 85 (bottom)*, Library of Congress. *page 86*, Library of Congress. *page 87 (top)*, Library of Congress. *page 87 (bottom)*, Library of Congress. *page 88 (top)*, N. Y. Public Library. *page 88 (bottom)*, Library of Congress. *page 89*, N. Y. Public Library. *page 90 (bottom)*, N. Y. Public Library. *page 92*, Library of Congress. *page 93*, Library of Congress. *page 94*, Library of Congress. *page 97*, Library of Congress. *page 98*, Culver Pictures. *page 99*, N. Y. Public Library. *page 100 (top)*, N. Y. Public Library. *page 100 (bottom)*, N. Y. Public Library. *page 101*, N. Y. Public Library. *page 103*, Frederic Lewis. *page 105*, Frederic Lewis. *page 107*, Library of Congress. *page 109*, N. Y. Public Library. *page*

138, The Metropolitan Museum of Art, Gift of Miss A. Colgate, 1952. *page 139 (top)*, Museum of the City of New York. *page 139 (bottom)*, Mqseum of the City of New York. *page 140 (top)*, New York State Department of Commerce. *page 141*, Little Brown & Co. *page 142*, Museum of the City of New York, The Byron Collection. *page 143 (top)*, N. Y. Public Library. *page 143 (bottom)*, Randall Arthur. *page 145*, Library of Congress. *page 146 (top left)*, Library of Congress. *(top right)*, United Air Lines. *(middle left)*, Library of Congress. *(middle right)*, Pan American World Airways. *(bottom left)*, Eastern Air Lines. *(bottom right)*, Library of Congress. *page 147 (top left)*, United Air Lines. *page 147 (top right)*, United Air Lines. *page 147 (bottom)*, Library of Congress. *page 148*, Library of Congress. *page 149*, United Air Lines. *page 151 (top)*, N. Y. Public Library. *page 151 (bottom)*, N. Y. Public Library. *page 152*, Du Midi. *page 153*, N. Y. Public Library. *page 154*, Culver Pictures. *page 156*, Library of Congress. *page 160*, N. Y. Public Library. *page 161*, Wide World Photos. *page 110*, N. Y. Public Library. *page 111 (top)*, The National Archives. *page 111 (bottom)*, N. Y. Public Library. *page 112*, N. Y. Public Library. *page 113*, Courtesy of the American Museum of Natural History. *page 114 (top)*, N. Y. Public Library. *page 114 (bottom)*, N. Y. Public Library. *page 115 (top)*, N. Y. Public Library. *page 115 (bottom)*, N. Y. Public Library. *page 116*, Culver Pictures. *page 117 (top)*, Library of Congress. *page 117 (bottom)*, Library of Congress. *page 118*, Library of Congress. *page 119*, Randall Arthur. *page 125*, Museum of the City of New York. *page 128 (top)*, Frederick Lewis. *page 128 (bottom)*, UPI. *page 129 (top)*, Library of Congress. *page 129 (bottom)*, U. S. Department of Agriculture. *page 130*, Library of Congress. *page 131*, N. Y. Public Library. *page 132*, N. Y. Public Library. *page 133 (top)*, N. Y. Public Library. *page 133 (bottom)*, N. Y. Public Library. *page 134 (top)*, The Metropolitan Museum of Art, Harris Brisbane Dick Fund, 1941. *page 134 (bottom)*, N. Y. Public Library. *page 136*, N. Y. Public Library. *page 137*, Library of Congress. *page 162 (top)*, Library of Congress. *page 162 (bottom)*, N. Y. Public Library. *page 164*, Library of Congress. *page 166*, N. Y. Public Library. *page 168*, Culver. *page 170 (all)*, N. Y. Public Library. *page 175*, N. Y. Public Library. *page 176 (both)*, N. Y. Public Library. *page 177*, N. Y. Public Library. *page 178 (top)*, Culver Pictures. *page 178 (bottom)*, Culver Pictures. *page 179*, Culver Pictures. *page 180 (top)*, N. Y. Public Library. *page 180 (bottom)*, N. Y. Public Library. *page 181 (top)*, Courtesy of the American Museum of Natural History. *page 181 (bottom)*, Library of Congress. *page 182*, Courtesy of the American Museum of Natural History. *page 183*, Frederic Lewis. *page 184*, King Features Syndicate, Inc. *page 185*, National Archives. *page 186*, Neal Yedlin. *page 187*, The J. Clarence Davies Collection, Museum of the City of New York. *page 188 (top)*, Culver Pictures. *page 188 (bottom)*, *page 189*, Campbells Soup Co. *page 191 (top)*, N. Y. Public Library. *page 191 (bottom)*, Frederic Lewis. *page 192 (top)*, Wide World Photos. *page 192 (bottom)*, Museum of the City of New York. *page 193*, Wide World Photos. *page 194*, N. Y. Public Library. *page 195*, N. Y. Public Library. *page 198 (top)*, N. Y. Public Library. *page 198 (middle)*, Library of Congress. *page 198 (bottom)*, N. Y. Public Library. *page 200*, N. Y. Public Library. *page 201*, Library of Congress. *page 202 (top)*, The National Archives. *page 202 (bottom)*, Library of Congress. *page 203 (top)*, Library of Congress. *page 203 (bottom)*, N. Y. Public Library. *page 204*, United Press International. *page 205 (top)*, N. Y. Public Library. *page 205 (bottom)*, N. Y. Public Library. *page 206*, N. Y. Public Library. *page 207*, Culver Pictures. *page 209*, Library of Congress. *page 210 (top left)*, Frederic Lewis. *page 210 (top right)*, N. Y. Public Library. *page 210 (bottom)*, United Press International. *page 211*, N. Y. Public Library. *page 213*, Colt Archives. *page 214*, Frederic Lewis. *page 215*, N. Y. Public Library. *page 216 (top, left to right)*, N. Y. Public Library, Museum of the City of New York, N. Y. Public Library. *(bottom, left to right)*, N. Y. Public Library, Frederic Lewis, N. Y. Public Library. *page 218*, N. Y. Public Library. *page 219 (bottom)*, N. Y. Public Library. *page 219 (bottom)*, Library of Congress. *page 220 (top, both)*, National Archives. *page 220 (bottom)*, N. Y. Public Library. *page 221*, Culver Pictures. *page 222*, Culver Pictures. *page 224*, The Byron Collection, Museum of the City of New York. *page 225*, © 1948 United Features Syndicate, Inc. *page 226 (top)*, N. Y. Public Library. *page 226 (bottom)*, Culver Pictures. *page 227*, Library of Congress. *page 228 (top)*, Library of Congress. *(middle)*, Library of Congress *(bottom, top, left to right)*, N. Y. Public Library, N. Y. Public Library, Frederic Lewis. *(bottom)*, Frederic Lewis. *page*

230, U.S. Army Photograph.   *page 231 (top)*, U.S. Army Photograph.   *page 231 (bottom)*, U.S. Air Force Photo.   *page 232*, U.S. Army Photograph.   *page 233*, U.S. Army Photograph.   *page 234*, U.S. Army Photograph.   *page 235 (top)*, U.S. Army Photograph.   *page 235 (bottom)*, U.S. Army Photograph..   *page 236 (top)*, Rose Collection, Western History Collections, University of Oklahoma Library.   *page 236 (bottom)*, United Press International Photo.   *page 238 (top)*, © St. Louis Globe-Democrat, 1932.   *page 238 (bottom)*, The National Archives.   *page 241*, Colt Archives.   *page 242*, Library of Congress.   *page 243*, N. Y. Public Library.   *page 244 (top)*, N. Y. Public Library.   *page 244 (bottom)*, N. Y. Public Library.   *page 245 (top)*, Randall Arthur.   *page 245 (bottom)*, Library of Congress.   *page 248 (top)*, Gerard Cochepin.   *page 248 (bottom)*, Gerard Cochepin.   *page 249 (top)*, Gerard Cochepin.   *page 249 (bottom)*, Harold M. Lambert from Frederic Lewis.   *page 250*, Library of Congress.   *page 251*, Gerard Cochepin.   *page 252 (top)*, Gerard Cochepin.   *page 252 (bottom)*, Kit & Max Hunn from Frederic Lewis.   *page 253*, Culver Pictures.   *page 254 (top)*, The National Archives.   *page 254 (bottom)*, Library of Congress.   *page 255*, The National Archives.   *page 256*, Frederic Lewis.   *page 257 (all)*, N. Y. Public Library.   *page 263*, N. Y. Public Library.   *page 264*, Library of Congress.   *page 265*, Culver Pictures.   *page 266 (top)*, N. Y. Public Library.   *page 266 (bottom)*, N. Y. Public Library.   *page 267 (top)*, N. Y. Public Library.   *page 267 (bottom)*, Library of Congress.   *page 268*, Library of Congress.   *page 272 (bottom)*, N. Y. Public Library.   *page 274*, Library of Congress.   *page 275 (top)*, Culver Pictures.   *page 275 (bottom)*, Culver Pictures.   *page 276*, Frederic Lewis.   *page 277 (top)*, N. Y. Public Library.   *page 277 (bottom)*, N. Y. Public Library.   *page 278 (top)*, Wide World Photos.   *page 278 (bottom)*, N. Y. Public Library.   *page 279 (top)*, Culver Pictures.   *page 279 (bottom)*, N. Y. Public Library.   *page 280*, N. Y. Public Library.   *page 281 (top)*, N. Y. Public Library.   *page 281 (middle)*, N. Y. Public Library.   *page 281 (bottom)*, N. Y. Public Library.   *page 282*, N. Y. Public Library.   *page 283*, N. Y. Public Library.   *page 284*, N. Y. Public Library.   *page 285*, N. Y. Public Library.   *page 287*, Library of Congress.   *page 288 (top)*, Culver Pictures.   *page 288 (bottom)*, Culver Pictures.   *page 289*, Culver Pictures.   *page 290*, The National Archives.   *page 292*, Library of Congress.   *page 294*, N. Y. Public Library.   *page 295 (top)*, N. Y. Public Library.   *page 295 (bottom)*, N. Y. Public Library.   *page 297 (top)*, N. Y. Public Library.   *page 297 (bottom)*, Library of Congress.   *page 299*, Frederic Lewis.   *page 301*, Library of Congress.   *page 302 (top)*, Library of Congress.   *page 302 (bottom)*, The Metropolitan Museum of Art, Lazarus Fund, 1913.   *page 303*, N. Y. Public Library.   *page 304*, The Metropolitan Museum of Art, Gift of William H. Huntington, 1883.   *page 305*, Library of Congress.   *page 306 (top)*, N. Y. Public Library.   *page 306 (bottom)*, N. Y. Public Library.   *page 307 (top)*, Library of Congress.   *page 307 (bottom)*, N. Y. Public Library.   *page 308 (top)*, The National Archives.   *page 308 (bottom)*, Culver Pictures.   *page 309 (top)*, Library of Congress.   *page 309 (bottom)*, N. Y. Public Library.   *page 311*, Collection of Whitney Museum of American Art, New York.   *page 313 (top, left and right)*, Library of Congress.   *page 313 (bottom)*, N. Y. Public Library.   *page 316 (top)*, The Coca-Cola Company.   *page 316 (middle)* Library of Congress.   *page 316 (bottom)*, N. Y. Public Library.   *page 317 (top)*, N. Y. Public Library.   *page 317 (bottom, all)*, N. Y. Public Library.   *page 318*, The Coca-Cola Company.   *page 319*, The National Archives.   *page 320 (top)*, Library of Congress.   *page 320 (bottom)*, United Press International Photo.   *page 321 (top)*, N. Y. Public Library.   *page 321 (bottom)*, Frederic Lewis.   *page 322 (top)*, Wide World Photos.   *page 322 (bottom)*, Wide World Photos.   *page 323 (top)*, United Press International Photo.   *page 323 (bottom)*, N. Y. Public Library.   *page 325 (top)*, Library of Congress.   *page 325 (bottom)*, N. Y. Public Library.   *page 326*, Library of Congress.   *page 327*, Library of Congress.   *page 328*, N. Y. Public Library.   *page 332*, N. Y. Public Library.   *page 334 (all)*, The New York Historical Society.   *page 335 (top)*, N. Y. Public Library.   *page 335 (bottom)*, N. Y. Public Library.   *page 336 (top)*, N. Y. Public Library.   *page 336 (bottom)*, N. Y. Public Library.   *page 341*, Randall Arthur.   *page 344*, N. Y. Public Library.   *page 345*, The Harry T. Peters Collection, Museum of the City of New York.   *page 346*, N. Y. Public Library.   *page 347*, The Harry T. Peters Collection, Museum of the City of New York.   *page 351*, Library of Congress.   *page 352 (top)*, Library of Congress.   *page 352 (bottom)*, The Free Library of Philadelphia.   *page 353*, N. Y. Public Library.   *page 354*, Culver Pictures.   *page 355*, N. Y. Public Library.   *page 356*, N. Y. Public Library.   *page 357 (both)*, N. Y. Public Library.   *page 358*, N. Y. Public Library.   *page 359 (top)*, Culver Pictures.   *page 359 (bottom)*, Library of Congress.   *page 362*, Library of Congress.   *page 363*, N. Y. Public Library.   *page 366*, U.S. Army Photograph.   *page 367*, Frederic Lewis.   *page 370*, U.S. Army Photograph.   *page 371 (both)*, U.S. Army Photographs.   *page 372 (top)*, Frederic Lewis.   *page 372 (bottom)*, Frederic Lewis.   *page 373 (bottom)*, Frederic Lewis.   *page 374*, Frederic Lewis.   *page 377 (top)*, Culver Pictures.   *page 377 (bottom)*, N. Y. Public Library.   *page 378*, Public Archives of Canada.   *page 380*, N. Y. Public Library.   *page 382*, Library of Congress.   *page 383*, Frederic Lewis.   *page 387*, The National Archives.   *page 388 (top)*, N. Y. Public Library.   *page 388 (bottom)*, Library of Congress.   *page 391 (top)*, N. Y. Public Library.   *page 391 (bottom)*, N. Y. Public Library.   *page 392*, Museum of the City of New York.   *page 394 (top)*, N. Y. Public Library.   *page 394 (bottom)*, U.P.I.   *page 395 (top, left)*, N. Y. Public Library. *(top, right)*, N. Y. Public Library. *(bottom left)*, N. Y. Public Library. *(bottom right)*, Library of Congress.   *page 396*, Frederic Lewis.   *page 397 (top left)*, Frederic Lewis. *(top right)*, Frederic Lewis.   *page 399 (top)*, Culver Pictures.   *page 399 (bottom)*, U.P.I.   *page 401 (top)*, Library of Congress.   *page 401 (bottom)*, Library of Congress.   *page 402*, Library of Congress.   *page 403*, The National Archives.   *page 405*, The National Archives.   *page 407*, The National Archives.   *page 409 (top)*, N. Y. Public Library.   *page 409 (bottom)*, The National Archives.   *page 411 (top)*, The National Archives.   *page 411 (bottom)*, Frederic Lewis.   *page 412 (top)*, Frederic Lewis.   *page 412 (bottom)*, Frederic Lewis.   *page 413*, Culver Pictures.   *page 414*, The National Archives.   *page 418*, Wide World.   *page 420*, Library of Congress.   *page 421*, Collection of Paul Farrell. *(top)*   *page 421 (bottom)*, U.S. Marine Corps.   *page 423*, U.S. Marine Corps.   *page 425*, Wide World.   *page 426*, U.S. Navy Official Photo.   *page 427 (top)*, Frederic Lewis.   *page 427 (bottom)*, Wide World.   *page 429*, Wide World.   *page 430*, The National Archives.   *page 432*, U.S. Coast Guard.   *page 433*, U.S. Navy Official Photo.   *page 435*, © 1945 by United Feature Syndicate, Inc.   *page 436*, U.S. Army Photograph.   *page 437*, Wide World.   *page 443*, Frederic Lewis.   *page 445*, Wide World.   *page 447*, Frederic Lewis.   *page 448*, Wide World.   *page 451*, UPI.   *page 452*, Frederic Lewis.   *page 454*, Library of Congress.   *page 455*, U.S. Army Photograph.   *page 457*, Official U.S. Navy Photo.   *page 458*, N. Y. Public Library.   *page 459*, N. Y. Public Library.

462

Index

473

479

musical steam engine, 82
musk cat, 182
muskellunge, 200
muskrat, 182
Mussolini, Benito, 417–419, 433, 449
mustache, 152
mustang, 112
mustard gas, 407
mustered out, to be, 91
muster in, 91
muster out, 91
My ass!, 260
"My Country 'Tis of Thee," Samuel Francis
    Smith, 6
my eye!, 259
My eyes!, 172
My gracious!, 172
My Lai, 370
My Lai Massacre, the, 370
My lands!, 172
My stars!, 172
"Mystery of Life, The," 161

NAACP, the, 39
nab, 275
Nabokov, Vladimir, "Lolita," 282
Nagasaki, 11
nah, 419
nail polish, 279
Nam, 364
napalm, 370
Napoleon Bonaparte, 380, 397, 428, 440
Napoleon, the, 91
Napolean I, 21
Napoleon III, 91
Narragansett, 28
narrow, 22
Nash, 77
Nash, Charles, 77
Nassau, 133
Nast, Thomas, 292, 294, 363
natch, 419
natchez, 346–347
Nathan's Famous, 189
National American Woman's Suffrage Association,
    the, 393
National Birth Control League, 395
National Flag, the, 336
National Forest, 389
National League of Women Voters, the, 393
National Park, 250
National Radical Reformers, the, 393
National Woman's Suffrage Association, the, 393
Nation, David, 253
Nation, Mrs. Carry, 253
Nation of Islam, The, 46
National Urban League, the, 39
National Weather Bureau, 61
native born American, 194
Nat Turner's Insurrection, 37
Nat Turner's Rebellion, 38
Nat Turner's revolt, 37
Natural Bridge, 250
natural bridge, 250
naturalization acts, 194
naturalization laws, 194
naturalization papers, 194
natural selection, 137
Natural, the, 45
Nautilus, 413
Navy, 334
navy, 305
Navy colt, 305
Navy pistol, 305
Navy Plug, 334
Navy revolver, 305
Navy shark, 414
Navy six, 305
NAWSA, 393
nay, 419
Nazareth, 268
Nazi, 440
Nazis, the, 440

Neapolitan ice cream, 191
near, 287
near accident, 287
near beer, 27, 287
nebbish, 224
Nebraska, 339
necessary house, 18
necessary, the, 18
necker, 103
necker's knob, 103
necking, 103, 310
neck of land, 250
necktie parties, 239
neck, to, 103
needle beer, 27, 287
needled beer, 287
Negars, 57
negative, 419
neger, 57
negress, 56
Negri, Pola, 281
Negro, 45, 56
negro, 34–35, 53, 56
negro cabin, 36
negro catcher, 36
negro dog, 36
negroes, 34–35, 53
negro house, 36
negro hut, 36
Negro Loyalists, 304
negro overseer, 36
negro quarters, 36
negro race, 40
negro rights, 38
negro thief, 36
negro trader, 36
"negro world," 41
Nelson, "Baby Face" (Lester Gillis), 17
nerts!, 310
neurosis, 156
neurotic, 156
neutrality, 400
Neutrality Act of 1939, 438
Neutrality Acts, the, 419
Nevada, 339
new, 121
New Amsterdam, 130, 133
New Army, 410
New Bern, 170
"New Colossus, The," Emma Lazarus, 193
New Connecticut, 340
new deal, 254
New Deal
    agencies formed during, 256–257
    effects of, 258–259
    F.D.R., 258
    origin of phrase, 254
New Deal, The, 254–259
New Dunkers, 268
New England, 341, 342
New England dialect, 120
New Englander, 342
New England States, 342
New Era, 348
New France, 341
New Hampshire, 339
New Immigrants, 221
new immigrants, the, 193
New Jersey, 339
New Mexico, 113, 339
New Mexico Territory, 339
new Navy, 305
New Netherland, 130, 339, 340
New Orleans, 155, 344
New Orleans fever, 331
New Pledge, the, 355
New Rochelle, 153
news butcher, 205
New Sensation, 348
New Showboat, The, 348
New Spain, 319, 341
New Sweden, 338
Newton, Eddie and T. Lawrence Seiberg, "Casey

Jones," 206
Newton, Huey P., 46–47
New Utrecht, 133
new woman, the, 393
New Woman, The, 389–399
New World, 6
New York, 130, 339
New York Central Railroad, the, 209
New York, Chicago, and St. Louis Railroad, 209
"New York Crystal Palace," Nathaniel Currier,
    139
"New York Journal," 324
"New York Morning News," 144
New York State Barge Canal, 135
New York Times, the, 362, 376
"New York World," 324
New York Yankees, 419
nex(t), 121
Nez Percé, 379
N.G., 419
Niagara, 49
Niagara Falls, 249
Niagara Movement, the, 40
nice girls, 281
Nickel Plate, the, 209
Nicolau, General Valeriano Weyler Y, 324
nigger, 33, 57
nigger boy, 57
nigger breaker, 36
nigger dealer, 36
nigger English, 33
Nigger Head, 57
niggerhead, 57
nigger heaven, 55
nigger heaven, 57
nigger in the woodpile, 57
niggerish, 57
nigger killer, 57
nigger lover, 57
nigger luck, 57
nigger monger, 36
nigger shooter, 57
nigger show, 57
nigger thief, 36
niggertoe, 57
nightclubs, 288
night flying, 145
Night Hawks, 295
night raids, 427
night rider, 38
night riders, 296
-nik, 226, 374
Nile of America, the, 343
Nimitz, Adm. Chester W., 449
999, 209
19th Amendment, 392
90-day wonder, 440–441
NIRA, 258
Nissenhut, 444
Nissen, Lt. Col. Peter, 444
nitty-gritty, 49
nix, 167, 419
nix cum arous, 167
nixie, 167
Nixon, Richard M., 153, 258, 367, 369, 374, 376,
    382–386
Nixon tapes, the, 384
nix on that, 167
Nix on that, 419
nixy, 167
NLF, 371
NLRB, 258
no, 419
Noble, 169
Noble Experiment, 286
nobleman, 152
no-bra look, 396
no cake, 265
no can do, 419
no dice, 419
noggin, 360
no goodnik, 226
no-man's land, 411